FOR OUR CHILDREN:

Gina Bock
Samuel Bock
Carlos Gould-Porras
Gabriela Gould-Porras
Monica Gould-Porras
Philip Martin
Jennifer Patton
Andrew Riley
Anneke Riley
Damini Sayeed
Shaheen Sayeed

WITH OUR HOPE FOR A TWENTY-FIRST CENTURY
LESS VIOLENT AND MORE HUMANE THAN
THE ONE DISCUSSED IN THIS BOOK

Contents

Art List

Pictures and Illustrations

Maps

Tables

Figures

Preface and Acknowledgments

This book began in the classroom of a public university where teachers and students confronted the problem of deciding what to teach and what to learn about the twentieth-century world. Many modern world history textbooks focus on political history and use developments such as the Cold War as a unifying theme. Others chronicle main events in global history, especially political events. These are valuable approaches, especially because they point up the building blocks of history. They satisfy the teacher's sense that students need to be exposed to principal events and personalities, even if sometimes these books do not find as many main events or personalities outside the Western world as they do in the West.

This book arose from a search for something else. We wanted to supplement, or sometimes even to supplant, this master chronicle with writing that focuses on the principal themes of human experience in the twentieth century. That search poses its own problems because there are many possible themes, and because the themes, too, may favor some world regions over others. These are issues that the five authors of this book worked out from their own experience in teaching world history and in teaching the history of particular world regions: Choi Chatterjee is a specialist on Russia and Eastern Europe, Jeffrey L. Gould on Latin America, Phyllis M. Martin on Africa, James C. Riley on Western Europe, and Jeffrey N. Wasserstrom on Asia. Choi Chatterjee completed her Ph.D. at Indiana University and now teaches at California State University at Los Angeles; all four other coauthors teach at Indiana University.

We wanted to write thematic essays that would provoke students to think further about some of the leading problems of modern world history and of historical investigation. We also wanted to write chapters that could stand alone, so that a student might read one of them and understand its arguments and references. This approach, of course, means that some of the same developments are mentioned in more than one place.

The chapters that follow raise issues that people in the twentieth-century world tried to address. Some themes—crisis, revolution, and change—appear again and again. The text is often provocative. We have sometimes made claims that not everyone will accept, and sometimes refused to draw conclusions or to interpret evidence, thereby leaving a question open. Our aim is to help engage students in the most delightful parts of learning, enabling them to deal with making sense of the information that they have acquired.

We offer this book as a thematic history of the world in the twentieth century. In our judgment the "long" twentieth century extends from about 1880, when imperial expansion reached a new peak, to the year 2000, although we also find that certain themes spilled over into the twenty-first century.

We want to thank people who helped us prepare and revise this book. Those include the readers for Westview Press, who made extensive suggestions about how to improve earlier versions of the manuscript. The Graphics Department of Indiana University prepared the maps. Lynn Sargeant gave some research assistance with Chapter 5. And special thanks goes to Christine Nemcik, who helped gather and write captions for many of the illustrations.

Introduction

The modern period trumped the more distant past in several ways, all of which complicate the historian's task. In no century before the twentieth did so many people live and die, prosper and suffer. The world population in 1900 totaled 1.6 billion, and in 2000 more than 6 billion. In the century between those two dates, more than 50 million people died in famines and more than 100 million in warfare. By the century's end, annual economic activity surpassed the 1900 level by twenty times or more, holding prices constant. Telegraphs, radios, and steamships were joined and partly replaced by the Internet, television, airplanes, and rockets. Never before had so many inventions, books, or works of art been produced; never before had so many facts been accumulated, to be weighed and interpreted. The mass of humankind, which had been governed by monarchs, chiefs, and autocrats, increasingly shared in making decisions. Mere literacy and numeracy gave way, for most people, to mastery of complex literary and mathematical tasks and a degree of specialization not before attained.

Yet, at the century's end, nearly a billion people could not read, and many more could not read well enough to cope with the intricate literary and numerical tasks of daily life. More than a billion people remained poor, unable to claim so much as a dollar a day in resources, while a few people counted incomes of more than $150,000 a day. Surgeons could replace a human heart and scientists could clone a large mammal, but no one could deliver lifesaving vaccinations to all the world's children or explain how best to safeguard individual health to a public rabidly keen to know. In the twentieth century humankind learned how better to make war, efficiently killing millions of people and slaying tens of thousands with a single bomb or a single night's firebombing. People idealized peace but struggled with the problem of how to foster it. It was, in sum, a century of contrasts, of unprecedented achievements and of grotesque and gigantic failures. It was a century in which to take pride, and it was a century of shame.

Most of all, and for most of its course, it was a century of hope. The failures more than the achievements motivated people, propelling them into ever more hopeful attempts to better the human condition. Even so, as we shall argue in this book, confidence in this endeavor waxed in the early decades of the century but waned in the last decades, even though the conditions of life and health had improved so much in the interim. In 1900 most people believed that they could come to understand the operation of nature, that they could discover how to improve the institutions by which people were governed, and that they could advance human society, bringing about prosperity, longevity, and contentment. By 2000, ironically, more had been learned in each of these realms, but less seemed to be known. Confidence in human progress had given way to uncertainty. The belief in linear movement toward the goals of education, prosperity, happiness, and good government for all had been displaced by the sense that change might incorporate large elements of chaos, with no discernable trend—or perhaps circular movement, with peoples and cultures always reliving familiar hopes and disappointments.

The promise of a bright future is captured by the idea of the "modern," a term that the first cultures to achieve markedly greater wealth, more responsive government, broader education, and longer lives used to define themselves in contrast to the past and to those cultures and societies that lagged behind. The epicenters of modernity around 1900 were Germany and the United States, where cities bustled, manufacturing plants employed, engineers built, and people exuded unlimited confidence in themselves. Modernization defined the steps to be taken if another country wanted to join this pair of privileged nations. Later the word "modern" was used less often and with less confidence, but rather than give way to less hubris, it gave way to another term, "developed." Even in 2000 peoples usually wanted to be modern and developed rather than backward, poor, and traditional. Much of the most hopeful intellectual and scientific activity of the twentieth century centered on attempts to discover how the countries and societies that were not modern could be guided toward modernity and development. The complex story that unfolds in the chapters that follow will show that some features of development, such as literacy and longer survival, came to be shared by a much larger proportion of the world's people in 2000 than in 1900; that other features, such as high income and modern conveniences, were democratized much less; and that development and modernity as defined by the West itself came into question.

This book is divided into three parts. The first treats the period from about 1880 to 1945 in six chapters. The second part deals with the period 1945–2000, in four chapters. And the third part, composed of five chapters, engages issues and problems that cut across the entire century.

The first part begins with a chapter on things modern and their paradoxes. In the decades from the 1880s to the 1940s, the West defined its own image and, through imperialism, demonstrated its capacity to bring much of the rest of the world under its rule. The foundation of power consisted of the unprecedented material progress through which the West furnished itself with the military and political resources to take control of so much of the rest of the world and differentiated itself from other regions. Yet the engines of growth—capitalism and Marxist socialism—each contained major strengths and weaknesses, so that this period was both a contest between rival systems and a contest to keep growth going. It was also a period of struggle over who would benefit from material prosperity, and who would control the power that material wealth let its possessors exercise. Revolutions before and after the Russian Revolutions of 1917 represented an attempt to broaden the economic as well as the political franchise. In the aftermath of World War I this contest remained undecided. Capitalism faced crisis in the 1920s and 1930s. Socialism offered one alternative to capitalism in which power and material prosperity would be shared. Fascism offered another option whose goal was to let the masses vicariously share the power and wealth created more efficiently by an alliance between political dictators and business leaders. The two world wars, of 1914–1918 and 1939–1945, were part of this larger struggle about dominance within the West.

In 1900 capitalism appeared to have the advantage; by 1930 it seemed weak, even bankrupt, and either Marxism or fascism seemed likely to displace capitalism; by 1945 fascism had fallen to the side. In the aftermath of World War II capitalism seemed best at producing greater wealth, but Marxism seemed best at enabling a poor agrarian country to catch up rapidly.

In this part of the twentieth century, from 1880 to 1945, can be discerned many signs of hope and achievement, and a few harbingers of later disenchantment. Never before had armies or navies been so powerful. Never before had people built such huge and magnificent buildings and ships or devised such efficient means of communication and transportation. Never before had ordinary men and women been able to imagine not just sharing but even controlling wealth and power. Yet, in the killing fields of Flanders in World War I, never before had so many virile and promising youths died for so little. Some people turned on their former optimism out of despair with this war. Another source of despair lay in the disenchantment of colonized peoples with European rule. When they set out to conquer the rest of the world, in the 1880s, Europeans imagined the world would be a better place for their control of it. But the empires they built did not turn out as they had hoped, for colonized people resisted European control and the Europeans became increasingly cynical about their reasons for building colonial empires. Nevertheless, in this opening part of the twentieth century the most dramatic action was to be found in the achievements of the West and in the internal struggles for power within the West.

The second part of this book shifts the orientation of things to other parts of the world. In its initial chapter we examine disenchantment with European rule in Asia, Africa, and the Middle East, the construction of independence movements, and the victories of independence. The world swelled from an arena of 51 countries, the initial membership of the United Nations in 1945, to 127 countries in 1970 and 189 countries in 2000. In the structure of political power laid out by the UN Charter, which awarded each member a single vote in the General Assembly regardless of its size or wealth, every nation had an opportunity to be heard.

Some of the independence movements within European colonies, and some expressions of unrest in such countries as China, which had not been colonized, had already taken forms outside the Western framework. Independence movements in Vietnam and Kenya, for example, appeared first as agrarian and peasant movements, as did the attempt to make China a socialist country and the efforts to define nationhood in Nicaragua and Guatemala. Whereas the preeminent revolutionaries early in the century, Vladimir Lenin and Joseph Stalin, shared the Western vision of industrial progress, the preeminent revolutionaries of the century's second half—among them Mao Zedong and Fidel Castro—possessed a vision of human progress, which came to the fore in China's Cultural Revolution and in the year 1968, when students and workers across the world tried to find a way to collaborate in revolution. Still, no revolution had yet tried to discard Western ideas and values. The reassertion of Islam in the latter part of the century, especially in its conservative or fundamentalist form, did just that. It rejected the new values the West had devised while building wealth, material comfort, military power, and efficient political institutions.

The first part of the twentieth century reached a dividing line at the end of World War II, when attention shifted from war to peace, from colonization to independence and decolonization, from industrial progress to social development, and from the West to Africa, Asia, and Latin America. There was no such watershed in the last part of the twentieth century, for the orientation of things, the activities and the concerns of humankind evident in the period 1945–2000, spilled over into the twenty-first century. Just as the century began around 1880, in our sense of things it will end some time later than 2000.

Some of the leading themes of the twentieth century do not fit comfortably into this chronology. Part Three deals with five issues of considerable importance—feminism, war and peace, science, population growth, and the idea of nations at risk—that stretch across the entire century, evolving over time. They sustained their importance throughout the century and remained unresolved at its end.

How shall humankind cope with its power to destroy things and people, with the problem of soothing international and ethnic rivalries, and with the task of finding ways to make peace rather than war? What role shall women and men play in the household and in public life? Can science, that putatively objective treatment of reality, solve human problems? Will population growth, and the tendency people have to consume natural resources, surpass the earth's carrying capacity? And, finally, will technological progress, global trade, and regional or global markets create a more equitable world or a world permanently divided between favored and unfavored nations and classes? These are some of the most important questions that remained unanswered in 2000.

The 20ᵗʰ Century

A RETROSPECTIVE

TABLE 0.1 Time Line, 1900–1950

	Global Events & Issues	North America	Europe
Pre-1900	Germ Theory in Science, late 1850s The "new" imperialism from c. 1880	Monroe-Doctrine, 1823 Spanish-American War and U.S. annexation of Philippines, 1898	French Revolution, 1789 Karl Marx publishes *Communist Manifesto*, 1848 Paris Commune, 1871 Franco-Prussian War, 1870-1871 Berlin Conference, 1884-1885 Formation of Alliance System, 1879-1907 Modernism influential among intellectuals and artists
1900-1910	Decade of Arms Race Over 200 Worldwide Peace Organizations Women's International Congress, 1917	Roosevelt Corollary to Monroe Doctrine, 1904 Age of Consumerism entrenched	Trans-Siberian railway completed, 1905 First Russian Revolution, 1905 Austria-Hungary annexes Bosnia, 1908 Young Turk Rebellion, 1909 Women's suffragette movement gains momentum
1910-1920	World War I, 1914-1918 Paris Peace Conference, 1919 Founding of Communist International, 1919	U.S. Intervention in Nicaragua, 1912-1933 Intervention in Mexican Revolution, 1914 & 1916	Archduke Franz Ferdinand assassinated by Serbian nationalists, 1914 Bolshevik Revolution, Russia 1917 Establishment of Weimar Republic, Germany, 1919
1920-1930	Founding of League of Nations, 1920 Founding of War Resisters International, 1925 Alexander Fleming develops penicillin, 1929	Stock market crash, 1929	Italian Fascist Party founded, 1919 Factory occupations, Italy, 1920 Mussolini in power, Italy, 1922 Hitler's Munich putsch, 1923 Vladimir Lenin dies, 1928 Joseph Stalin rules U.S.S.R., 1928-1953
1930-1940	Great Depression, 1929-1935 World War II begins 1939 Era of the antibiotic begins, 1942	Presidency of Franklin D. Roosevelt, 1933-1945 New Deal, 1933-1939	British Union of Fascists, 1932 Nuremburg laws, Germany 1935 German rearmament begins, 1935 Rhineland remilitarized, 1936 Spanish Civil War, 1936-1939 Crystal Night, Germany, 1938 6 million Jews killed in the Holocaust, 1939-1945
1940-1950	Yalta Conference, 1943 End of World War II, 1945 United Nations formed, 1945 Nuclear era begins, 1945 Beginning of Cold War, 1947	Truman Doctrine, 1947	Soviet Union halts Nazi eastern expansion, 1943 D-Day landings, 1944 Establishment of East and West Germany, 1949 NATO formed, 1949

	Latin America	Middle East and Asia	Africa
Pre-1900	Presidency of Porfirio Díaz, Mexico, 1876-1911	Taiping Uprising, China, 1850-1864 Opening of Suez Canal, 1867 Meiji Restoration, Japan, 1868 Founding of Indian National Congress, 1885 Sino-Japanese War, 1894-1895 First World Zionist Congress, 1897	"Scramble for Africa," 1880-1910 Gandhi in South Africa, 1893-1914
1900-1910	Platt Amendment ratified by Cuba, 1904	Boxer Rebellion, China, 1900 Russo-Japanese War, 1904-1905 Founding of Indian Muslim League, 1906 Revolution ends Chinese Empire, 1911	Anglo-Boer War, South Africa, 1899-1902 South African Native National Congress (later African National Congree) established 1912
1910-1920	Opening of Panama Canal, 1914 Rise of trade unionism, 1910s Mexican Revolution, 1910-1920 Workers strikes and Semana Trágica, Argentina, 1919	Arab troops fight in WWI Balfour Declaration, 1917 May fourth movement, China, 1919	Land Act, South Africa, 1913 Creation of Union of South Africa, 1910 African troops fight in WWI
1920-1930	Civil War and U.S. interventions, Nicaragua, 1912-1933	Mandate system installed in Middle East, 1920s Founding of Communist Party in China, 1921 Turkish Republic founded, Kemal, 1922 Mustafa Pasha begins Turkish Reforms, 1923 Kuomintang gains control in China, 1928 Gandhi leads Salt March, India, 1930 Arab feminists expand struggle for women's rights	African nationalist movements gather momentum
1930-1940	Rise of dictatorships in Central America, 1930s Brazilian Integralist Party founded, 1932 "La Matanza," El Salvador, 1932 Fulgencio Batista, dictator of Cuba, 1933-1959 Lázaro Cárdenas presidency, Mexico, 1934-1940	Japan occupies Manchuria, 1931 Japan invades China, 1937 Rape of Nanking, 1938 Palestinian uprisings against Jewish settlers and British rule	Italy invades Ethiopia, 1935
1940-1950	Norman Borlaug works in Mexico, 1944 Democratic governments of Arévalo and Arbenz, Guatemala, 1944-1954 Juan Perón, president of Argentina, 1946-1955	Japanese alliance with Germany and Italy, 1940 Japanese bomb Pearl Harbor, 1941 Atomic bombs dropped on Nagasaki and Hiroshima, 1945 Chinese Civil War, 1945-1949 India and Pakistan gain independence, 1947 Israeli statehood, 1948 Mao Zedong and Communist Party in power, China, 1949	Apartheid Policy in South Africa, 1948 Nationalist leaders establish political parties thoughout the continent, late 1940s-1950s

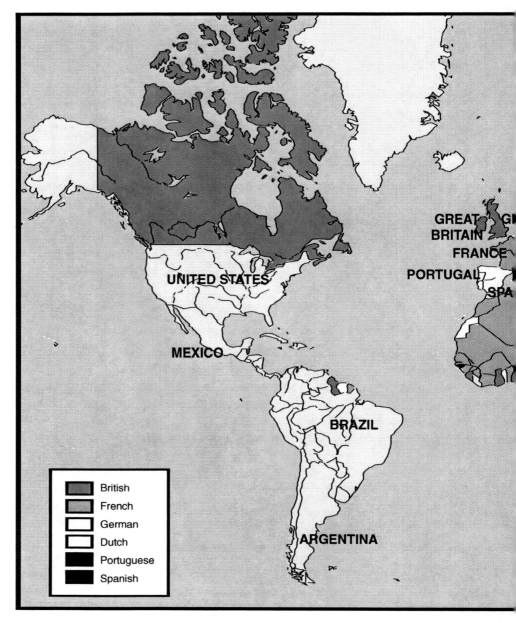

The World in 1900

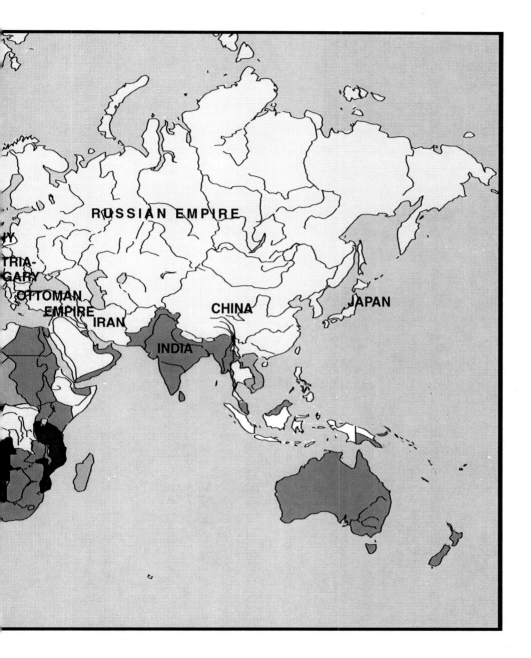

Part One

THE EARLY CENTURY

1

....

The Paradoxes of Modernization

One feature of the history of old Russia was the continual beatings she suffered because of her backwardness. She was beaten by the Mongol Khans. She was beaten by the Turkish beys. . . . She was beaten by the British and French capitalists. . . . All beat her—because of her backwardness, because of her military backwardness, cultural backwardness, political backwardness, industrial backwardness, agricultural backwardness. . . . We are fifty or one hundred years behind the advanced countries. We must make good this distance in ten years. Either we do it or we shall go under.

I. V. Stalin, *Works*
(1952–1955)

Consider the conveniences at the disposal of the fin de siècle [end of the century] housewife: a house with a good part of the old-fashioned portable furniture built into it, e.g., china cabinets, refrigerators, . . . electric lights, telephones and electric buttons in every room. . . . Thus has vanished the necessity for drawing water, hewing wood, keeping a cow, churning, laundering clothes, cleaning house, beating carpets, and very much the rest of the onerous duties of housekeeping, as our mothers knew it.

Adna Ferrin Weber,
The Growth of Cities in the Nineteenth Century
(1963)

H OW DOES A GENERATION DIFFERENTIATE ITSELF FROM ITS ANCESTORS? Is historical vision necessarily apocalyptic, cyclical, cumulative, or progressive? Why has the West labeled itself as *modern* when distinguishing the recent past from other ages of history? Finally, can the experience of millions of disparate and dispersed peoples fit under this adjectival umbrella? The English adjective "modern" came into usage at the end of the sixteenth century. Derived from the Latin word *modernus* ("just now"), the word referred to the present or recent past. "Modern" meant "new" but soon began to denote a qualitative judgment as well insofar as it suggested an improvement over the antiquated or obsolete past. European historians began to call their age modern to set it apart from the less advanced Middle Ages or the rude and barbarous kingdoms that lay beyond European boundaries. They used the slide rule of modern standards to judge the history of the European past and the non-European past and present.

The creation of this particular view of modernity as a revolutionary period of unprecedented and progressive change was the work of the Enlightenment, a period of unparalleled intellectual creativity in the Western world that substantially changed both popular and intellectual attitudes toward science, society, religion, and government. Faith in scientific reason and the empirical method lay at the center of the European definition of modernity. The small group of reformers who sparked the Enlightenment—the scientist Isaac Newton; the political philosophers John Locke and the Baron de Montesquieu; the writers Denis Diderot and Voltaire; and the philosopher David Hume, among others—decisively dethroned the primacy of religious knowledge, sometimes against their will, and established science and the scientific method of inquiry as the criterion for truth. They argued that the clerical monopoly and definition of knowledge was scandalous and that morality, politics, and history should be studied from an empirical and utilitarian standpoint. Saints and their miracles were displaced by a new pantheon of heroes that started with Copernicus and extended to Newton, truth-seekers who battled the censorship of church and state in their quest for knowledge. These thinkers visualized the world as an intricate mechanical construction and believed that the laws governing the universe could be deduced using empirical methods. In science, it was proclaimed, true knowledge about nature could occur only after replicable investigations yielded data that confirmed a hypothesis. Social science disciplines took their cue from science and tried, with significantly less success, to use variations of the scientific method to ascertain the truth in their fields of inquiry. Thus, historians tried to uncover universal laws governing human development, economists quantified the market, and psychologists delved into the workings of the human mind.

Borrowing from contemporary scientific models, thinkers in the eighteenth and nineteenth centuries such as the Marquis de Condorcet and Auguste Comte believed that human history was bound by laws. If these could be understood and the fruits of this research judiciously applied, time would bring progress. Instead of the Christian emphasis on the salvation of the individual, thinkers prophesied that all humankind could partake of this new prosperity and knowledge. This shift in historical imagination can also be traced to the eighteenth and nineteenth centuries, when the agricultural and industrial revolutions made prosperity possible for the multitude instead of the select few. Applied technology revolutionized old economic traditions wherein an elite minority thrived on the labor of serfs and slaves. The nineteenth-century industrial revolution proved the success of the happy union of science and applied technology that further fortified European optimism. Nature could be tamed, mastered, and manipulated to provide a harmonious and knowable world, and technology could be used to create wealth and exploit resources at an unprecedented rate. In this new age of optimism, a secular version of history highlighted the steady march of select nations toward progress, reason, and scientific knowledge. It replaced the Christian view of history, which traced humankind's sorrowful exile from the Garden of Eden.

The ideas of the Enlightenment also had a profound impact in the world of politics. Voltaire bitterly criticized the exercise of arbitrary power by absolutist governments and was an ardent proponent of individual civil liberties. Montesquieu, in his major work, *The Spirit of Laws*, praised the English political system as a guarantor of political liberty. Thomas Jefferson read Montesquieu and argued that the separation of powers among the executive, legislative, and judicial arms of the government prevented the concentration and misuse of power. This theory of "checks and balances" played a very important role in shaping the Constitution of the United States in 1787. Enlightenment political ideology discredited the exercise of unlimited and hereditary monarchical power as medieval or barbaric and helped popularize notions of the rights of the individual, especially as they pertained to their political freedom and control of their property.

Are We All Modern Yet?

By the late nineteenth century a typically modern country had experienced the industrial revolution and the bulk of its population was engaged in nonagricultural work. Secular and scientific knowledge formed the core of the educational curriculum in the newly expanding schools, vocational institutes, and universities. Millions of rural dwellers were drawn to the bright lights and employment opportunities that were to be found in the bustling cities, such as London and Chicago. By the 1890s electric streetcars, an American invention, carried workers, shoppers, and schoolchildren to their destinations in most of the European capitals. Governments grew apace, creating bureaucracies that engaged in rational planning to maximize the welfare of the citizenry as well as engaging in the more traditional duties of taxation, administration, and the maintenance of internal and external security. The newly emerging print media, especially national and international newspapers, helped define modernity and circulated its criteria for public consumption around the major economic and cultural centers of the world. Etiquette books, magazines, advertising, and popular fiction instructed readers in the intimate details of modern life, and on urban dress codes, appropriate leisure pursuits, civilized manners, and the new rules that governed the interaction of men and women on a more equal basis.

The word "modern" was mainly used in two ways: to valorize the history, culture, economics, and politics of those who considered themselves modern and, simultaneously, to castigate those who were "premodern," "underdeveloped," "backward," "antiquated," "reactionary," "benighted"—in short, those who had failed to match Western modernity. When the curtain lifted on the early part of the twentieth century, from Washington to Tokyo political leaders worried that their countries might not be sufficiently modern. Who constituted the charmed circle of

PICTURE 1.1
World's Fair, Paris, 1889. The Eiffel Tower and the exhibition on the Champ-de-Mars were highlights during the Paris World Exposition. Many of the buildings around the base of the tower were filled with representatives and artifacts of empire. (Photo from the Library of Congress)

modernization? How was this hierarchy created and maintained? Was modernization irreversible, and were all nations destined to experience it? Was there only one path to progress, or could the end be achieved in different ways? Some questioned the necessity of heedless modernization. These romantics yearned for a past before the enthronement of science and reason and looked for different endings to the historical story. Artists, poets, philosophers, and conservatives railed against the conditions of modern existence and through their critique highlighted the perils of modernization.

If we were to draw a mental map of the world in 1900, it would be possible to imagine a series of concentric circles narrowing down to a few countries at the center, such as Germany, France, and England. Of course, across the Atlantic lay the might of the emerging United States. It was becoming a major player in the international arena as American industrial and agricultural goods poured into the world market. By the late nineteenth century, the United States had set up German-style research universities and the work of U.S. scientists was beginning to gain the attention of the European world. At the periphery stood the vast majority in the colonized world, in particular the countries of Asia and Africa. The second series of circles comprised European nations that had failed to achieve the Enlightenment dream of a government limited by laws and franchise, education based on sciences rather than theology, and the replacement of an ossified feudal social structure by a society in which careers were open to talent and individuals could be compensated for the misfortune of humble birth through the acquisition of education and wealth.

The Grand Russian Empire, the Austro-Hungarian Empire, and to a lesser extent the Ottoman Empire, behemoths of another age, fell into this second ring. Culturally, the ruling classes looked to Western Europe, but they resisted the proliferation of Enlightenment ideas within their imperial boundaries and oscillated between fitful reform and an obstinate adherence to premodern methods of governance. In Russia the situation was particularly complex. While the Tsarist government realized that industrialization was vital if the empire was to retain its military authority on the continent, it feared the consequences of urbanization, unplanned population growth, and the rise of a professional middle class. Ultimately Tsar Nicholas II was convinced that the main function of the government was to retain the autocratic monopoly of power, and to that end he followed policies that both fostered and retarded modernization.

In a certain sense the situation of the countries of Latin America shared in this predicament. Mexico, Argentina, Brazil, and other lands had broken free from the colonial rule of Portugal and Spain during the course of the nineteenth century, and significant sections of the ruling classes believed in the Western ideas of progress, representational government, and the political and civil rights of the individual. But the colonial legacy of centralized and authoritarian governments frustrated the implementation of these ideas. At the same time, within the world economic order Latin American nations were primarily suppliers of agricultural goods and consumers of manufactured goods. This role worked to their economic disadvantage, as did the internal Creole elite monopoly on both political power and economic resources.

By the early 1900s the world looked to the West and had already internalized the West's evaluation of itself as scientifically literate, materially productive, and politically democratic. In this chapter we define the paradoxical nature of modernization. Several themes will be touched upon: industrialization; the philosophies of liberalism, socialism, feminism, and nationalism; the rise of the middle class and the working class; colonialism; and modernism. These ideas will be further elaborated in succeeding chapters.

Industry and Science

Western monopoly on what defined progress was of recent origin and rested on the material prosperity and technological superiority wrought by industrialization and capitalism. For example, fueled by new energies such as coal, steam, and water, the British cotton industry underwent a metamorphosis in the eighteenth century and proved to be the biggest source of British exports. By the late nineteenth century, the cotton textile industry was surpassed by a modern complex of heavy industry in which iron ore, petroleum, and electricity provided power for the production of iron and steel, machinery, chemicals, and textiles. Britain was able to effectively dominate the world economy because of a concurrent revolution in commercial transportation. The British merchant marine, flying under the protection of the Union Jack, had dominated commerce on the high seas since the seventeenth century. Initially, it brought the wealth of the world to England: spices from the East Indies, cotton from Egypt, tea and silks from China and India, sugar and coffee from the West Indies, and cotton and tobacco from America. But by 1900 Britain was exporting machinery, chemicals, and textiles. Great Britain, especially London, was also the financial capital of the world, setting the standards in investment, banking, and insurance.

The industrial revolution developed hand in hand with the scientific revolution, which, however, was not concentrated in Britain. For the first time in human history modern scientific discoveries became commercially viable through a process of applied technology. The telegraph had already been introduced in the nineteenth century, but now the telephone, an invention of Alexander Bell's in 1876, began to make its appearance in urban centers. By the late 1890s electric

PICTURE 1.2
Marie Curie in her laboratory. Marie Curie, Polish by birth, shared the 1903 Nobel Prize for Physics with her husband, Pierre, for their work on radioactivity. (Photo courtesy of the American Institute of Physics/Emilio Segre Visual Archives)

light not only made home illumination cleaner, safer, and more effective but also completely revolutionized the daily routine hitherto dictated by the sun. The adage "Early to bed and early to rise makes a man healthy, wealthy, and wise" was no longer a truism but a quaint echo of a premodern, agrarian lifestyle. Medical discoveries flowed apace, and the scientific work of Robert Koch and Louis Pasteur proved that many incurable diseases, such as diphtheria, typhoid, and scarlet fever, could be controlled by vaccination, medication, and good hygiene (see Chapter 13).

Other scientific discoveries followed. In 1895, William Roentgen discovered X rays, a form of radiation that can penetrate opaque objects. This technology was applied in many areas of physics and medicine. A more startling discovery was that of the French physicist Marie Curie, who found that atoms are composed of many small, fast-moving particles such as electrons and protons. She and her husband, Pierre Curie, found that the element radium does not maintain constant atomic weight but constantly emits subatomic particles. Building on their work, Max Planck, a German physicist, explained that subatomic energy is emitted in uneven little spurts. This finding led to the realization that matter and energy might be different forms of the same thing, a notion that shook the old view of atoms as stable building blocks of nature. Albert Einstein proved conclusively in his theory of relativity, published in 1905, that matter and energy are interchangeable and that all matter contains enormous amounts of energy. Yet, even though Einstein revolutionized physics by representing the subatomic universe as uncertain and undetermined, Newtonian physics of hard facts, controlled and replicable experimentation, and unchanging laws still regulated the way science was done in laboratories.

Liberalism and Democracy

The philosophy of liberalism, a central block of modernization, is built around two central concepts, liberty and equality. In the eighteenth century, when most monarchs believed that it was their divine right to interfere in private life, liberals, who were considered dangerous radicals, protested against the infringement of inalienable civil rights. Thus they demanded that governments abolish censorship and individuals be granted the right to express their beliefs freely in speech and print. Demands for basic personal freedoms were incorporated both into the U.S. Bill of Rights and the Declaration of the Rights of Man issued by the revolutionaries in France. Liberty also meant that sovereignty lay with the people and the people alone should have the power to legislate human affairs. In practice this principle meant that the people should choose their representatives, who would rule on their behalf and legislate for the common welfare. All citizens were to be considered equal in the eyes of the law and to enjoy the same civil liberties. Nobody could claim special legal privileges on account of their bloodline. Thus liberals were deeply opposed to the society of orders where the nobility and the clergy enjoyed special juridical and economic privileges. But when liberals spoke about equality, they did not mean to eradicate the differences between the rich and the poor; instead, they wanted to give everyone the same legal opportunity to pursue life, liberty, happiness, and property. In many ways political life in Britain was the pioneer of modern politics. The British had devised a unique political solution that combined aristocratic and monarchical privileges with popular representation. Although King Charles I lost his head in 1649, the monarchy had learned its lesson well and meekly submitted as generations of parliamentary leaders chipped away at its privileges. By 1900, the monarch was a figurehead and the royal family a comfortable source of gossip, pageantry, and entertainment. Within parliament, the aristocratic House of Lords was tamed by the House of Commons, and by 1911 the Commons had gained effective control of the budget. Lower down the political ladder, the Reform Bill of 1867 and the Franchise Bill of 1884 had virtually created universal adult male suffrage. Women, however, were not to get the vote until 1919.

The British congratulated themselves that they had thrown careers open to talent, ensured upward mobility, and broken the aristocratic and royal monopoly on power without spilling too much blood. Similar developments occurred first in America and then in France. At the end of their revolution against British rule, the Americans had established a system of government that was based on the rule of law, an elected legislature, an independent judiciary, and an executive unable to act without the consent of the other wings of the government. Of course, franchise was restricted to men of property exclusively and it would be many years before the African slaves would be freed and allowed to share in the political freedoms and rights that were considered the patrimony of Americans.

The French political system lacked the stability of the English and American systems but it, too, was dominated by a moderate and middle-class group of politicians. The French system offered a more radical vision of modernity than that of the British. The French Revolution of 1789 had not only ushered in republicanism as opposed to divinely ordained monarchy or even constitutional monarchy but also encapsulated a radical program of social reform. The revolution put forward a utopian vision of economic justice for the poor based on the redistribution of property and the welfare state. In the political realm, the French Revolution tried to replace a hereditary monarchy with a constitutional form of government in which people would be ruled by elected representatives. The heredity- and estate-based rights and privileges of the nobility and the clergy were severely abridged (see Chapter 4).

Apart from political democracy, there was also an alternate populist vision implicit in the French Revolution, one that haunted the terrified imaginations of conservative politicians in Europe in the nineteenth century. Although lawyers, merchants, and journalists could be accommodated in the postfeudal order, the country was not ready for the political awakening of the masses. The French Revolution created the nightmare of the urban revolt and through its strategies legitimized the principle of mass-based politics. The urban crowds—the fishwives, the hat makers, the butchers, the bakers, the prostitutes—had played a disproportionate role in revolutionary events between 1791 and 1793. To ensure economic justice for the poor, the government tried to guarantee wages, regulate prices, and provide work for the unemployed. In the countryside, marauding bands of peasants attacked manor houses and burned tax records in a symbolic repudiation of feudalism. The notions that the poor had certain rights and that the government should enforce a measure of economic justice and equality was to greatly energize French society and have a lasting impact on the development of popular politics in the modern world.

Yet, for all its successes, there was a dark side to the French Revolution. The state had employed terror against political enemies on an unprecedented scale. Thousands of people perished under the guillotine, including the king and the queen. The physical dismemberment of the king showed that the populace had neither fear nor respect left for the idea of monarchy. No longer could a king rule on account of his kingship; henceforth rulers would have to justify their leadership on standards that were different from that of divine right. Historians have claimed that the authoritarianism of the French Revolution and the state use of terror presaged the modern totalitarianism of Fascist Italy and Nazi Germany. This claim is debatable; nonetheless, the ideas spawned during the French Revolution developed into the modern ideologies of liberalism, socialism, and militarism.

Despite the sequence of revolutionary events, monarchy was restored to France in 1815 and it became a republic only in 1870. The political arena of the Third Republic was dominated by a group of moderate, middle-class politicians who held the center against the forces of a monarchical and clerical Right, on the one hand, and on the other, a socialist Left that sought to institute sweeping economic reforms to ameliorate the lot of the working class.

The Rise of the Middle Class

The nineteenth century marked the triumph of the middle class. What manner of beast was this middle class? How did it manage to leave its indelible mark on history? In 1900, most of the high civil and military posts in European countries were dominated by a small class of hereditary aristocrats. But for the most part they had lost control of the levers of political power. Claims to privilege and power based on birth were becoming increasingly meaningless in a time when the power of monarchy had been successfully replaced by the power of elected parliaments. The aristocracy was legally abolished in France in 1870 and survived in Britain only because the peers welcomed American heiresses, humble but rich ironmasters, and cotton textile manufacturers into its once exclusive ranks. Of the 159 peerages created in England between 1901 and 1920, 66 were given to businessmen and 34 to professionals.

PICTURE 1.3 "Even the Walls Have Ears." This French political cartoon, which depicts a Western European visitor at the mercy of Russian spies, poked fun at the autocratic government of the tsar. (Reprinted from *Histoire Pittoresque, Dramatique et Caricaturale de la Sainte Russie,* illustrated by Gustave Doré [Paris, 1854])

In Russia, the aristocracy failed to adapt to an increasingly modern world. It encouraged Tsar Nicholas II to pursue anti-liberal policies that led directly to the Russian Revolution of 1917. This elite class of proprietors failed to reorganize their landed estates on a footing of profitability rather than through maintenance of a feudal lifestyle. As a result they lost significant portions of their lands to more enterprising agriculturists. But in the political realm they clung to the monopoly of power and encouraged the tsar to dismiss and repress all attempts toward constitutional democracy and political enfranchisement. Like conservatives in Germany and the Austro-Hungarian Empire, the bulk of the Russian nobility defended institutions that embodied traditional practices and values, that is, the church, a monarchy based on divine right, and a powerful military.

In Russia the bulk of the nascent middle class looked to Western liberalism as a model, demanding freedom of speech, press, religion, and assembly. Its spokespeople also called for the extension of the franchise to men of property and for elected governments responsible to the electorate. But the middle class also feared Russian workers and peasants and their apocalyptic demands for the communalization of property. Russian peasants believed that as cultivators of the soil, they and not the nobility could rightfully claim the land as theirs. By choosing to collaborate with Tsarism in repressing the legitimate demands of the people, the Russian middle class unwittingly opened the floodgates to revolution (see Chapter 5).

Which segments of European society did the middle class encompass? Formidable men of business and capital defined themselves in unambiguous terms against a dissolute aristocracy and a drunken and lazy laboring class. Often the upper reaches of the rich bourgeoisie merged with the aristocracy. In the late nineteenth century the middle class was composed of men in business; those in professions such as medicine, law, or academia; the higher ranks of public service; and their families. The members of the managerial class, engineers and technical specialists, and clerical workers in the private sector also aspired to the middle-class lifestyle and were slowly amalgamated into it. The economic bonanza of the period allowed a substantial sector of society in Western Europe to aspire to a level of material comfort that included suburban homes with gardens, a few servants, and a certain idealized picture of domesticity that was copied by those below them. Above all, the middle class symbolized the principle of social mobility, a concept that lay at the heart of political modernity.

Social mobility was facilitated through formal education at select institutions. The French *lycée*, the English public school, the Prussian and Russian gymnasia, and U.S. private schools turned out gentlemen and women, members of the ruling class. With the requisite polish, the proper accent, and appropriate manners, one could forget one's social antecedents and confidently enter the ranks of an emergent class that deemed money as the main price of admission. From 1870, both secondary and university education grew apace in Europe and the United States while models of European universities were created to serve the colonized elites in such colonial cities as Calcutta and Cairo as well as in Nanking and Tokyo. Eschewing indigenous learning and education, these universities served to introduce the westernized "natives" to the mental constructs of what Europe considered as indispensable knowledge.

In manners, morals, politics, economic organization, and culture, the European middle class waged a relentless battle to establish what was "normal" and "decent." Thrift and property; the patriarchal family; the maintenance of public decency; hard work; the rewards of merit and talent; belief in social mobility; a reverence for God, empire, and national icons; and a mild suspicion of intellectuals, artists, and any others who were not like them—these were the virtues that the middle classes cherished and sought to impose on others both at home and abroad. In its mission of promoting civilization, the middle class was helped by the educational systems, especially the newly emerging disciplines of sociology, criminology, and psychology, which formalized structures of knowledge from a middle-class perspective. Psychologists such as Havelock Ellis in England, Sigmund Freud in Vienna, Richard von Kraft-Ebbing in Germany, Veniamin M. Tarnovskii in Russia, and Cesare Lombroso in Italy all tried to establish what was "normal" and, by definition, what was "abnormal." Socially abnormal people were either to be punished for deviance or socialized into accepting the normal codes of behavior. Various human pathologies were listed and characterized: the criminally insane, the hysterical woman, the neurotic, the lazy native, the sado-masochist, and others. Homosexuality, hitherto deemed acceptable in Britain, came to be labeled as deviant and in 1883 was made criminal by law.

Rebellion at Home

The rise of the middle class did not go uncontested. Few people denied the legitimacy of middle-class values, but disenfranchised minorities argued that the fruits of progress, political emancipation, and upward mobility should also be extended to them. Thus the movement for women's emancipation, which was greatly popular at the turn of the century, pinned the Enlightenment ideals of universal liberty and equality to its banner.

In Western Europe, as domestic and cottage industry began to decline and the workplace shifted from the home to the factory, it became more typical for the men to go to work in factories while the women stayed home taking care of the children and the household. In vast areas of rural Europe, though, especially in Central and Eastern Europe, the family farm still required women to labor in the fields. Even in urban centers, not all women could afford to stay home. Female workers were engaged in the food and textiles industries, in domestic service, and as clerks in shops and offices. Women were usually paid far less than their male coworkers and routinely suffered from sexual harassment, arbitrary dismissal from work when pregnant, and strict supervision of their manners, morals, and leisure activities by their employers.

In the middle class, where rising incomes allowed men to be the breadwinners, a certain ideology emerged that glorified women as innately domestic beings who were best suited to bearing children and caring for the family. Whereas bourgeois men worked in a public world of cutthroat competition and cash flow, the household was supposed to represent the precapitalistic values of unconditional love and support and to exude domestic peace and tranquility. Women were idealized as possessors of those virtues that men lacked: capacity for self-sacrifice, devotion to emotional interests over material concerns, collaboration rather than competition, civilization over the natural aggression of the marketplace. This sentimental ideal of Victorian womanhood was circulated through popular novels in which virtuous wives and mothers triumphed over selfish heroines and fallen women. Educated and career-minded women were lampooned as sexless bluestockings or lascivious lesbians.

Some women objected to the circumscribed roles expected of them. Most internalized the bourgeois creed of the woman as wife and mother but at the same time demanded that men live up to their part of the bargain. Thus social reformers in England such as Judith Butler exposed middle-class hypocrisy that castigated the prostitute but not her male patrons. This double standard that enjoined sexual control and monogamy on women was challenged by reformers of various hues. Dr. Maria Pokrovskaia in Russia actually talked of prosecuting the male clients of prostitutes. Similar proposals were raised in England. Female social workers in England such as Octavia Hill, although staunchly middle class and conservative in orientation, through their work on slum relief drew attention to what Victorian England wanted to hide: festering and vice-ridden slums, unhealthy children, cramped living conditions, and massive poverty in the richest country in the world. The evidence belied liberal claims that capitalism was both equitable and just and worked equally in the interests of the rich and the poor.

The period 1880–1920 witnessed a remarkable upsurge in political activism among women. Most of the leaders were members of the upper middle class and well connected with the governing male elites. Their efforts were centered in England, where they launched parallel efforts to gain the right to vote, reform the laws that governed women's property, and admit women to British universities and medical schools. Similar political movements were mobilized in the United States and other European countries. Oddly enough, Russian women became the first to obtain government-sponsored access to secondary schools and institutions of higher education. The spread of higher education among women, and the entry into professions such as medicine, law, and academia, gave these middle-class women economic independence and a stronger base from which to formulate their demands (see Chapter 11).

In the late nineteenth century, women figured prominently in parties on both extremes of the political spectrum. In France, as the Third Republic fought a rearguard battle to secularize the body politic, women served as the staunchest supporters of the clerical party, often to the disgust of their husbands and brothers. Although women made some political gains in France, namely over the control of their property, the suffragist movement was not a popular one. In Russia, in contrast, some women seemed irresistibly attracted to the most extreme of left-wing politics. Unlike women in Western Europe, Eastern European women were less hemmed in by the demands of domesticity, and aristocratic women had traditionally enjoyed more freedom than their middle-class counterparts. Rosa Luxembourg, from Poland, and Aleksandra Kollontai, from Russia, were perhaps the best known among the cohort of radical European activists.

In Russia, educated women from noble backgrounds forsook the comforts of large estates and long skirts and joined underground movements formed to violently overthrow Tsarism. Their political choices sent these women into Siberian exile, into solitary confinement in prisons, and often to the gallows. Similar signs of female dissatisfaction with the status quo could be detected in Japan and China. In Japan during the early years of the Meiji Restoration, which installed a modern-style government, female activists worked within the system for self-fulfillment and freedom, participating in the 1870s movement for "freedom and popular rights." But later, when they realized that the ruling elite wanted to build a strong and rich upper class at the expense of the people, many women joined the circle of budding socialists, communists, and anarchists to fight for social justice for the underprivileged masses. Legislation was implemented to forbid women from making political speeches or participating in political activities. Like the Russian martyrs, radical Japanese women endured imprisonment, humiliation, torture, sickness, and death. Yajima Kajiko and Yamamoro Gumpei, like their Victorian English counterparts, fought against prostitution and challenged official support for state-licensed brothels. The extremist Kanno Sagako even plotted to assassinate the emperor and was executed. Other socialist women tried to improve the terrible working and living conditions of women employed in silk and textile factories.

Conflict and Collaboration in the Workplace

While upward mobility, an essential characteristic of modernization, guaranteed assimilation of the bourgeoisie and the middle class into the ranks of the upper classes, few sons or daughters of workers or peasants were able to climb beyond the bottom rungs of the educational ladder. At the lower end of the scale, industrialization wrought a different story for workers as the mechanized loom replaced weavers and spinners. As the artisan lost control over both his tools and the production process, he was soon to be replaced by the blue-collar factory worker.

The number of people who earned their living from wage labor increased in all countries touched by Western capitalism. From the silver mines of Chile, to the gold mines of Siberia and South Africa, and to the oil fields of the Middle East, the proletariat was becoming conscious of itself as an exploited class. The working class grew as a result of a transfer of population from the handicraft and rapidly modernizing agrarian sectors, which needed fewer workers. With the influx of workers from the countryside, urbanization grew apace and cities swelled. What would happen if the workers mobilized politically?

Mass parties based on a socialist ideology grew quickly after 1870, first in countries with democratic and electoral politics, such as Britain, France, and Germany, and later in the Russian Empire, in colonies such as India, and in Argentina and China. In Europe, socialist and labor parties were serious electoral forces by 1914. In Russia, the government curbed labor disturbances with police violence and oppression. Worker-activists were sent to Siberia with monotonous regularity. In Western Europe, however, there was an attempt to co-opt the working class within the new nation-state and to make judicious use of repression. The case of labor politics emphasizes the dichotomy inherent in the debate on modernization. Labor politics could be either conservative or revolutionary, depending on the interpretation of the observers.

PICTURE 1.4   New York skyline. This view of the lower New York skyline in 1904 shows Manhattan Life, Standard Oil, Produce Exchange, Washington, Bowling Green, and other great buildings of the time. (Photo from the Library of Congress)

At a basic level, in Britain, for example, labor unions fought for better pay, improved working conditions, and the extension of the franchise—that is, the right to vote for all men regardless of property qualifications. In Germany, the socialist democratic parties fought for pension plans, health insurance, and unemployment benefits. In Russia, labor protests coalesced around shorter working days, higher wages, and the right to unionize. A close reading of these demands today reveals their moderate intent, and it seems that workers were merely asking for the right of inclusion within the body politic—the same thing the middle classes had demanded from the aristocrats. Laborers agitated for the right to vote and demanded a living wage, decent living and working conditions, and the right to be treated with dignity. Thus labor politics can be construed as modern. At the same time, they could also be read as revolutionary because they attacked what was at the heart of the new capitalist order, the freedom of the market.

Classical liberalism, in its economic implications, was based on the principle of the unregulated market, both domestic and international, and the unequal distribution of national resources. Liberalism advocated that political rights should be granted to men of property and not to the vast number of the uneducated and laboring poor, who were unqualified to exercise electoral rights. As a political philosophy, it helped the middle class gain political power through its acquisition of wealth, but trickle-down economics proved less advantageous for workers. Marxists argued that the market was not equitable and that state intervention was necessary in order to distribute resources fairly, prevent exploitation of one class by the other, and provide a minimum standard of living for the most indigent sector of society. The birth of the welfare state was a product of labor politics, and in places such as Germany, workers' economic demands were quickly adopted by the state and enforced on the capitalists in order to stave off something that was far more frightening than the more moderate labor demands—a workers uprising.

Like proponents of liberalism and the welfare state, Karl Marx, a German philosopher and political activist, derived his vision of a virtuous community based on the abolition of private property from the practices and precepts of the French Revolution. The attraction of Marxism as ideology lay in the fact that it articulated the daily experiences of injustice for workers in the workplace. In his writings Marx offered a systematic critique of capitalism and offered a new explanation for social and economic inequality. This philosophy explained poverty not in terms of religious dispensation or individual inadequacy but as a by-product of capitalism, a system that valued production and profits over human costs. Marx claimed that only the overthrow of the capitalist ruling class and the abolition of private property would end exploitation, and that the working class would be the inheritor of the postcapitalist future. Finally, Marxists believed that man was inherently good and that such evils as greed, drunkenness, gender inequality, and child abuse were social consequences of material inequality.

At the turn of the nineteenth century Marxism provided the organizational framework for labor parties. But it was not a monolithic ideology, and differences of opinion regarding tactics, organizational strategy, and the feasibility of revolution eventually splintered the workers movement. Some continued to advocate revolution as the only solution to the problem of the exploitation of the working class, but in Germany, Eduard Bernstein, a socialist intellectual, suggested that Marx's theory of the increasing impoverishment of the working class pertained to the middle of the nineteenth century exclusively and should be revised in the light of flourishing capitalism and the devolution of benefits to the working class. Instead of overthrowing capitalism, Bernstein argued, socialists should concern themselves with making the present living conditions for the working class more tolerable. This feat could be achieved by passing parliamentary legislation that would raise pay scales, improve workplace safety, and provide more comprehensive health and disability insurance.

Although Bernstein was initially derided for his conciliatory approach, social-democratic parties, with the sole exception of the Russian Party, heeded Bernstein's advice and grew more accommodating and bureaucratized, tending to accept their place within the parliamentary system. This tendency became more pronounced when capitalists in Germany and England, responding to the threat of socialism, raised salaries and marginally improved the working and living conditions of workers by instituting new laws governing work hazards, hours, and child labor. Meetings, strikes, and processions replaced riot and insurrection as the preferred choice of strategy. Left-wing politicians fought to gain power within the parliamentary system.

In the Russian Empire, the revolutionary commitment of Marxist leaders such as Lenin and Trotsky, and the absence of parliamentary politics, created a situation wherein revolution was seen as the only means of effecting equity and change. Even after the Revolution of 1905, which convulsed the Russian Empire for more than three years, the tsar remained obdurate in his unwillingness to countenance democratic reforms. A kind of parliament was created, but it had little control over the executive function or the budget. Furthermore, its composition was frequently changed by Tsarist fiat whenever the representatives became too critical of government policy. The Russian Marxists were appalled by the reformist tendency sweeping the social-democratic parties of the West and felt that only a proletarian revolution would create a more equal society and at the same time allow Russia to industrialize rapidly enough to catch up with the Western countries. Henceforth, the course of revolution moved eastward, from Russia to Asia.

While liberalism and Marxism seemed fundamentally incompatible, partisans of both creeds believed in the basic values of modernization and looked forward confidently to the future. Reason was valorized over superstition, and progress and science over tradition, and both sides advocated the secular trinity of liberty, equality, and fraternity. Marxists claimed that political democracy was meaningless without economic equality, whereas liberals believed that the right to vote guaranteed a sufficient measure of equality.

Nationalism and Popular Culture

Nationalism was another powerful force at work that seems linked with the project of modernization. The capacity to think beyond the local, the tribal, and the regional was an Enlightenment idea that fashioned a concept of national essence that transcended the feudal particularities. Nationalism, embodied in the notion of everyone being a citizen of the republic, was molded in the crucible of the French Revolution. Serving in the Napoleonic army, soldiers were taught a new emotional loyalty to the state. Nationalism was an irresistible force that swept Europe and beyond in the nineteenth century. Nationalist tendencies challenged the integrity of the Austro-Hungarian, the Ottoman, and the Russian empires. Germany and Italy freed themselves from Hapsburg overlordship, emerging as strong nation-states. The new Germany, under the tutelage of its "iron chancellor," Otto von Bismarck, played a particularly conspicuous role in European politics. Greece declared its freedom from the Ottoman Empire, and the Balkan Slavs, Arabs, and Kurds tried to follow suit. Poland tried repeatedly to break free of the Russian Empire, and national sentiment grew in the Baltic states, Ukraine, Trans-Caucasus, and Central Asia. In the course of the twentieth century, the colonized countries of Asia and Africa would also seek freedom in the name of nationalism (see Chapter 7).

Sometime in the nineteenth century it became fashionable to want to die for one's country. Love for the nation and duty to the state were inculcated as supreme virtues through the new national systems of education, through service in the armed forces, and in popular culture. Nationalism was represented as a male fraternity of brave soldiers and virile men and became inextricably linked with patriotism and serving one's country. Women, for their part, were enjoined to have children and instill in them a deep love for the nation. The new nation-state was imagined as a set of symbols consecrating the territory. Monuments, flags, literature, music, history, and art were all co-opted in the name of nationalism and were easily identifiable markers of national sovereignty and exclusivity. History especially was rewritten for public consumption in a heroic vein, depicting nations fulfilling their God-given destiny. The Germans sought to overcome religious, political, and regional differences by emphasizing military triumphs in the Middle Ages. Nationalistic Indians rediscovered the Emperor Asoka of the third century B.C.E., who had given the Indian subcontinent a temporary political unity. In France, the Third Republic saw itself as heir to the French Revolution. Nationalism focused on the so-called unique cultural characteristics of citizens of a particular country, and national traditions were commemorated by quasi-militaristic parades, marches, consecrations, and celebrations of national victories and heroes.

The proletariat was firmly drawn into the new imagined community, the nation. Standardized education, the birth of the penny press and mass production of literature, creation of a democratized leisure industry—which included football, bicycling, Boy Scouts, cafes and pubs, and the popular culture of theater and music—all bound the working class to the culture of the nation-state. If the notorious slums of the London East End were seen in the middle nineteenth century as dens of sin and vice, by the latter part of the century an army of middle-class reformers, mostly female, had invaded the homes of the poor. They attacked the evils of prostitution and wife beating, teaching working-class women how to be good wives and mothers—in short, how to remake themselves into their bourgeois betters.

Mass migration into growing cities produced a lucrative market for popular spectacle and entertainment. Traditional forms of popular entertainment were professionalized and transformed while new forms were simultaneously created. The roughness and violence associated with agrarian leisure pursuits were replaced by more "civilized" styles of entertainment. Music halls, cafes, taverns, and dance halls spread across frontiers and oceans. The practice of social dancing in public introduced a note of cosmopolitanism into various capitals. Thus the tango, a product of the brothels of Buenos Aires, reached European high society. The mass press boasted a circulation of a million or more in the 1890s. A powerful force for manipulating popular attitudes, it also created a conversational space in which to discuss government policy and shape public morality.

The content of popular culture tied the new citizen in the Western world to the nation-state as it was glorified and celebrated in various forms. But sometimes, national mythmaking was not a sufficient guarantee for social cohesion, as the tsar learned in Russia. There, the attempt to unify a fractious empire around the themes of autocracy, the Orthodox Church, and Slavic destiny found few adherents. But nationalism could also be configured in negative terms, and in Russian literature writers celebrated the Russian capacity for spirituality and contrasted it with the crass materialism that was to be found in the West. Slavic Christians under Ottoman rule were claimed as fellow crusaders against a fanatical Islam. Russian Pan-Slavists dreamed of uniting the Orthodox Slavs who chafed under Ottoman rule, but their desire to formalize this policy was frustrated by Austria. In the Ottoman Empire, ruthless attempts at Turkification alienated the fellow-religionists, the Kurds and the Arabs who constructed a local version of national consciousness.

The reverse side of nationalism was hatred toward the enemies of the state. Generations of young Frenchmen were nourished on ideas of revenge for France's inglorious defeat at the hands of the Germans in the Battle of Sedan in 1870. Political demagogues of various stripes called for the recovery of the lost provinces of Alsace-Lorraine from the Germans, even if it meant going to war. Concepts of national honor and French ideas of manhood had a distinctly anti-German cast. Denouncing Germany, England's military rival, became a common theme in English music halls as well as in English novels at the turn of the century. Hailed earlier as the country of Goethe and Beethoven by English intellectuals, Germany was soon turned into the country of the uncouth German burgher who slurped his soup and ate his peas with a knife as Anglo-German rivalry intensified in the first decade of the twentieth century.

The Enemy Within

National stereotypes coexisted with ethnic stereotypes, and even while nationalism strove to make nations more cohesive, there were always those who escaped proper categorization. The

"Mickey," or the Irishman, was the perennial butt of music-hall humor in England, but it was the Jews who faced the most severe consequences of a rabid nationalist consciousness in Europe. Although the nineteenth century had witnessed the lifting of restrictions on Jews, following the Enlightenment insistence on the universal application of laws to all men, the Jewish rise to prominence in cultural and financial circles unleashed a latent anti-Semitism that pervaded European politics by the latter part of the century. Anti-Semitism was not new to European civilization. Since the early Middle Ages, Jews had been portrayed as the murderers of Christ, and they periodically were subject to mob violence. In Russia, for example, they were physically separated from Christians and confined to ghettos. In the nineteenth century, in certain countries of Western Europe, Jews were given legal rights, but restrictions remained, and even the most assimilated Jews were never completely accepted as citizens.

As a result of limited liberalization, Jews left the ghettos and became successful in the arts, in professional careers, and in government. This development resulted in a conservative backlash. Many overtly anti-Semitic parties formed in Germany, Austria, and France. These political parties formed an important background to the rise of fascism in Europe. It should be remembered that Hitler was exposed to anti-Semitism in Vienna, one of the most cultured but at the same time most rabidly anti-Semitic capitals of Europe. By the nineteenth century, many Jews had assimilated into Western European culture, but the famous Dreyfus case in France showed their continuing precarious position.

The Dreyfus case, which dragged on from 1894 to 1906, became an international cause célèbre that polarized public opinion across Europe. In 1894 Alfred Dreyfus, a wealthy French Jew and a junior army officer, was convicted of selling military secrets to Germany. Tried in a hasty court-martial, he was sentenced to life imprisonment on Devil's Island. In fact, the case was a cover-up for a treacherous French officer, and Dreyfus had been selected as the scapegoat. Although the army tried to control the scandal, the case soon acquired wide notoriety as many famous Frenchmen intervened and demanded justice for Dreyfus. Radical republicans, socialists, liberals, and prominent literary figures rallied to the side of Dreyfus, whereas those opposed to reopening the case included monarchists, clerics, anti-Semites, militarists, and some conservative working people. The case was reopened, however, and ultimately Dreyfus was exonerated. The Dreyfus affair polarized French society and raised disturbing questions as to the nature of French justice. It caused a lot of heart-searching among French Jews, most of whom had hitherto seen themselves as Frenchmen and had little attachment to a Jewish identity. Assimilated French Jews started to look at their ethnic history and identity with more interest and concern.

Unlike France, where anti-Semitism was practiced covertly, the Russian Empire made anti-Semitism a basic policy of governance. The authorities routinely subsidized gangs of hooligans to launch indiscriminate pogroms against the Jewish quarter. The Jewish question was demagogically used to deflect the dissatisfaction of the starved and oppressed. Jews were made scapegoats for national calamities and disasters. Elsewhere in Europe, pseudo-scientific theories of racial exclusivity were developed to legitimize anti-Semitism. The Frenchman Arthur de Gobineau and the Englishman Houston Chamberlain used positivism and social Darwinism to claim the superiority of the Aryan-Nordic races. Crude anti-Semitic propaganda in Europe warned that Jewish blood was tainting that of the superior races, and racial exclusion was encouraged in the name of patriotism.

Imperialism

In the age of modernization, science and technology became lethal weapons not only because they enabled nations to attain their geopolitical goals but also because they could be twisted to justify and rationalize morally dubious projects. In the eyes of colonized peoples, advances in military and industrial technology buttressed the truth of the invincible West as it slowly drew technologically backward societies such as India, China, and Japan into its colonial ambit. Some areas, such as Africa and parts of Southeast Asia, were brought under the direct control of Western European powers; others, such as the Middle East, Japan, and China, were subject to indirect control when Western countries forced them to open their markets to Western goods and to export raw materials at unfairly low prices. In the middle of the nineteenth century, England fought two wars with China, winning the right to sell opium there legally.

The means of colonialism were primarily economic and military (see Chapter 2). Industrialization demanded raw materials and new markets at an ever-increasing rate. Modern banking, finance capital management, and the growth of multinational companies allowed the West for the first time to avail itself of a disproportionate share of the world's resources. This achievement was facilitated by superior military technology that allowed the West to put down abortive rebellions around the world—for example, the Indian Mutiny in 1857, the Mahdi uprising in Sudan in the 1880s and 1890s, and the Boxer Rebellion in China in 1900. Western powers forced open Japanese ports in 1858, claimed special rights in Chinese ports in 1898, and everywhere exploited mineral rights to their own advantage. Colonization was also possible because awestruck colonial elites acted as surrogates for Western rule and collaborated in the exploitation of laborers. To them, the westerner seemed immeasurably superior to any other invader. Western ideas swept the colonized world with the force of a tidal wave. Intellectuals in Peking, writing in such widely read magazines such as *New Youth* and *New Tide* in the 1920s, denounced traditional Confucian culture and thought. They advocated the modern virtues of individualism, democratic equality, and the critical scientific method. Marxism proved another fruitful Western import. Like liberalism, Marxism was modern, but unlike liberalism it could be used to critique Western imperialism. Ultimately, Mao Zedong, the leader of the Communist Party in China, was to reinterpret communism to suit Chinese conditions and forge a brand new path to modernization (see Chapter 8).

As the imperial reach widened, the colonized people came under the relentless scrutiny of the Western gaze. Local culture, literature, social values, religion, and political structures were measured against Western prototypes for invidious comparison, to be justified or rejected. Suddenly, centuries of tradition and history were seen as perishable, and the very identity of the colonized was in flux. Were the colonized abnormal Europeans, or non-Europeans, or as they themselves liked to put it, in a developmental phase that preceded European industrialization? Henceforth, if the West could ignore Asia, Africa, and the Middle East—and it did—the residents of these spheres ignored the West at their own peril.

Educated elites in Asia and Africa internalized the Western critique and swung between two courses of action. One was to accept Western domination and their own inferiority and engage in westernizing their countries. A certain pathology of self-hatred became the standard mental equipment of the colonized peoples. The Indian National Congress was formed in 1885 solely to convince the British authorities that their rule had created a class of westernized natives to whom

PICTURE 1.5   Queen Victoria presents a Bible to a colonial subject. Entitled "The Secret of England's Greatness," this painting by Thomas Jones Barker in 1863 shows Queen Victoria dispensing Christian civilization to a visiting colonial dignitary in the Audience Chamber of Windsor Castle. (Courtesy of the National Portrait Gallery, London)

the nation could be safely entrusted. This class of lawyers, doctors, merchants, and landlords engaged in British forms of political debate. They wrote editorials in the pages of the indigenous and the liberal English press, presented petitions to the British authorities in India and England, and worked to convince their overlords of the rightness of their cause through the use of reasoned discourse. The enlightened elites, however, refused to support repeated uprisings of Indian peasants against a ruinous British taxation policy that created conditions of near starvation. Like their colonial masters, they dismissed peasant insurgency as reactionary and premodern. The dismantling of feudalism also threatened the economic base of upper-class Indians.

Other members of the Indian elite responded differently to the lessons of the West. Their reaction was extreme xenophobia, defense of cultural traditions and values simply because they were homegrown and not imported. Indian patriots in the late nineteenth century were entranced with the newly introduced notions of nationalism and patriotism. In their romantic imaginings, the hundreds of tribes, languages, ethnic groups, and cultures coexisting within Indian borders were transmogrified into images of India as the holy Hindu motherland that demanded unquestioning love and sacrifice from her sons. The creators of this discourse were far more effective in galvanizing anti-British feelings in India than the earlier generation of parliamentarians had been, but their vision was essentially homogeneous, divisive, and exclusionary. In their notions of a Hindu past there was little room for women, members of the lower castes, or even Muslims, who had lived in the same geographical space for nearly a thousand years. As in Europe, nationalism in Asia provided the bedrock of proto-fascism. Nationalism in India often meant revival of a fictionalized Hindu past, reverence for the Indo-European legacy of antiquity, creation of a national history, and select suppression of alternative versions of the past.

Even the more liberal-minded members of the elite viewed the family and women as sacred elements of national culture that were to be guarded from the onslaught of the imperialists. Irrational defense of retrograde and ruinous aspects of culture was a hallmark of the response to colonialism. In India, for example, social reformers in the early part of the nineteenth century tried to deal with horrible social practices such as the prevention of widow remarriage, widow burning, child marriage, and polygamy. Once the nationalist movement got under way, these issues were subsumed under the anti-imperialist rubric. Women's liberation was dealt a serious blow by the new xenophobia, which sought to protect an imaginary national culture at any cost. Attempts to reform Indian social practices—for example, abolishing child marriage or universalizing female education—were often criticized as capitulation to the senseless demands of westernization.

Modernism

Modernism, primarily an aesthetic movement specific to art and literature, was deeply implicated with the project of modernization. This artistic movement critiqued the relentless drive to modernize and pointed to the dark side of rapid social change. To many observers, the experience of industrialization did not mean simply profit and progress; it represented alienation, the breakdown of family and community, and dehumanization. Similarly, contact with the "backward" countries did not produce unqualified derision. Some in the West found answers in the religions of the East: Hinduism, especially in its more esoteric variants, Buddhism, and Islam became fashionable in certain cosmopolitan circles. The work of anthropologists such as James Frazer was used by thinkers to romanticize premodern societies as repositories of archetypal myths, values, and traditions that the Western world had lost in its heedless rush toward modernization. In his well-known work *The Golden Bough*, Frazer showed that rather than being unique, the rituals of Christianity corresponded to the primitive practices and magical rites of other societies. Others, such as the French painter Paul Gauguin, went to the South Sea Islands in an attempt to escape the "modern" and "artificial" life of civilized society. In this quest, Gauguin depicted the premodern lives of the people in a highly romantic light.

To counter the scientific certainty of modernization, there arose an artistic revolt against it called modernism. These artists believed that there was an essence, a reality that underlay the unreliability of perception, but they questioned the positive value of the scientific method in apprehending it. Writers such as Franz Kafka, James Joyce, and T. S. Eliot and philosophers such as Henri Bergson, Friedrich Nietzsche, and Martin Heidegger argued that bureaucratic rationality and modernization came at a cost. They believed that human beings were alienated and disoriented by the experience of industrialization and that science could not regulate the contingency and irrationality inherent in the human condition. They also believed that a resourceful artist could cope with the predicament of modernity, the spiritual wasteland created by technology through creativity and antirationalism.

Cultural critics and innovators left a profound mark on every field of artistic endeavor. With impressionism and postimpressionism the artist rethought individual artistic strategies. Begin-

PICTURE 1.6   "The Seine at Argenteuil" (1874). Claude Monet was an early leader of the Impressionist style of painting. He was one of the first to concentrate on painting the outdoors, and through color and light he aimed to convey the physical experience of the moment. (Courtesy of the Indiana University Art Museum)

ning in the 1870s, rather than depicting nature as closely as possible, artists abandoned the photographic model of realism and experimented with ways of representing the reality underlying surface appearances. Artists such as Claude Monet and Auguste Renoir sought to translate on canvas the immediate sensory perceptions left by the object of study and let the viewer fill in additional details. Rather than viewing art as social commentary, modern artists saw it as the personal expression of the particular intellect of the artist. Thus Vincent van Gogh, the Dutch painter, communicated his passionate sympathy for human suffering through the dramatic use of color in his canvases. In literature, Aleksandr Blok, Andrei Bely, and Stéphane Mallarmé, and later the Bloomsbury group in England, which included writers such as Virginia Woolf, suggested a more mysterious and complex reality dependent on sensory perception. In their novels, such as Bely's *St. Petersburg*, these writers abandoned the realism of the nineteenth century.

Sigmund Freud, the renowned Austrian psychologist, perhaps best encapsulated the dilemma of being modern. In his methodology, Freud tried to be rigorous and precise. He took copious notes, made case studies, and followed the scientific method of hypothesis, observation, and conclusions based on data. Freud was a scientist par excellence and thought that it was possible to construct a comprehensive theory of the mind. But in his study of the human psyche, Freud did not find a coherent machine; rather, he found a seething cauldron of nonrational motivation

PICTURE 1.7   Sigmund Freud (1856–1939). Freud is pictured here with colleagues at Clark University in Worcester, Massachusetts. (Photo from the Library of Congress)

powered by the sexual libido. In his classic text, *Civilization and Its Discontents*, Freud advanced a stunning analysis of the reasons for religious belief and argued that religious feelings were a manifestation of infantile longings for security and protection. Freud also thought that God was a mental construct and that submission to divine will was a delusional state of mind. Having demolished religion with reason, Freud had more difficulty in explaining why the subconscious was irrational. He argued that civilization grew in direct proportion to the suppression of human libidinal instincts and attributed unhappiness to the innate conflict between biological human nature and the demands of society. He also tried to prove that the subconscious was torn between the desire to form community and the destructive instincts fueled by innate aggression. Although his insights were interesting as well as elegant, Freud's model was too general to sufficiently explain human behavior. His legacy sums up the ambiguity and paradox of modernity. Freud's findings opened up the school of psychoanalysis and research in mapping and understanding the unconscious through the application of scientific methods, but the less academic reading public used a gross simplification of Freudian thought as an excuse for sexual liberation and the overthrow of bourgeois morality between the two world wars (1919–1939).

As powerful as the modernist challenge was, it never fundamentally threatened the central ideas of the Enlightenment. The methodology of science and social science continued to be positivist. Freud saw himself as a rigorous scientist. Although modernist art produced some soul-searching and articulated a common theme of the dehumanizing nature of industrialization, the political disengagement of the modernists, and their insistence on art for art's sake, kept their critique fairly superficial and robbed it of didactic purpose. Modernists took refuge in exploding conventional assumptions about what constituted good art. Their antics shocked and titillated society, and their literature was profound and innovative, but in focusing on the general theme of alienation they overlooked the oppression inherent in their own society—that of women, workers, and colonists. Also, if modernists claimed that knowledge was more fragmentary and harder to obtain than the positivists had supposed, it did not necessarily follow that efforts at organizing culture were useless. They challenged the logic of capitalism but did not rock its foundations. Rather, in the celebration of individualism and the premodern world, some modernists contributed substantially to the rise of fascism. The poet Ezra Pound and the philosopher Martin Heidegger were actually co-opted by Fascist regimes.

Friedrich Nietzsche is usually credited as the first to systematically criticize the Enlightenment insistence on progress and reason, although in his condemnation of Christianity he stood in the succession of Enlightenment deists such as Voltaire. A particularly influential philosopher, Nietzsche believed that human beings in the West had sacrificed passion and emotion to rational thinking. He viewed reason, democracy, progress, and bourgeois morality as sociopsychological constructs constituting the major impediments to creativity. Nietzsche theorized that fin-de-siècle decadence, pessimism, and nihilism was not mere fashion but, instead, the end product of the Enlightenment values and ideals. Natural science produced anti-science, democracy led to socialism, genius was swamped by mediocrity, and strength by weakness. Nietzsche believed, in a bizarre twist to the Christian and Enlightenment myth, that the hope of the future lay with a few superior creative individuals, supermen who would free themselves of social conventions and the intellectual constraints of positivism.

Nietzsche and his gospel of moral relativism and celebration of irrationality was welcomed by a small section of the intellectual public in the prewar years, but for the most part thinkers remained bound to positivism and liberalism. In the years between the world wars Nietzsche was selectively appropriated by both right- and left-wing parties. In Soviet Russia, the *Stakhanovite* worker came to embody the Nietzschean prototype of the superman with the beautiful body and the creative soul. In Fascist Italy and Nazi Germany the influence of Nietzsche was writ large in their condemnation of democracy and contempt for the masses.

Conclusion

If the seeds of fascism were already being sown in Europe, its elaboration belonged to a future chapter of history. In the early twentieth century the threats of fascism and anti-Semitism paled in comparison to the abyss that yawned at the feet of Europe. Of all the wars in history, including the Peloponnesian War, World War I (1914–1918) has to count as one of the most senseless confrontations in history. Historians have drawn long lists of explanations that cover social, economic, political, diplomatic, and cultural causes, but the reasons animating the arguments, for the most part, ring hollow. Ideologically, Europe in the early twentieth century was united as never before. Unlike World War II (1939–1945) or the Cold War that followed in the later century, there were no competing ideologies or economic systems that battled for world dominance. National enmity was and is a standing feature of international relationships, and its existence, by itself, does not lead to war. England's naval rivalry with Germany could have been contained to saber rattling. Germany's desire for colonies could have been satisfied without a cataclysmic global battle. The systems of secret treaties and alliances that bound Austria and Germany, on one side, and England, France, and Russia, on the other, did not of itself guarantee war. Moreover, why did Russia, itself in the throes of developmental chaos and acute social frictions, mobilize the Grand Army on behalf of the insignificant province of Serbia? Surely Austria's depredations on Ottoman territory could have been resolved through international mediation, just as Russia's own pretensions in the Balkans had been decisively thwarted in the previous decades.

From the late 1890s, diplomatic tensions escalated considerably in Europe as two rival alliances formed pitting Germany and Austria-Hungary against England, France, and Russia. Germany believed that its colonial possessions were insufficient to satisfy its Great Power aspirations and challenged French rule in Morocco. Britain did not care to be France's ally in the international arena, but the rapidly escalating naval and military arms race with Germany in the first decade of the twentieth century pushed the country into a military alliance with France. Fear of Germany also led England to settle imperial disputes over Tibet, Afghanistan, and Persia with Russia.

Moreover, Russia, because of its kinship with the Slavic peoples, encouraged Serbian nationalism in the Balkans, but Austria-Hungary feared that these movements among the southern Slavs would lead to the collapse of its empire. Although the Balkans did provide the spark for the war, it is important to remember that intense national passions and rivalry, encouraged by competing modernization, had created the setting for conflict in the first place. In July 1914, a Serbian nationalist assassinated the Austrian heir to the throne, the Archduke Franz Ferdinand, in retaliation for the fact that Serbian territories were controlled by Austria. Austria decided that only a military attack would persuade Serbia to refrain from sponsoring terrorist attacks. Germany supported Austria, partly owing to the widespread belief that a world war was inevitable. Russia chose to defend Serbia in order to secure its prestige in the Balkans and retain its position as defender of the Slavs. But as the tsar called for a general mobilization of the Grand Army, Germany was frightened into declaring war on both Russia and its alliance partner, France. Britain was drawn into the fray as German forces rolled into Belgium, and World War I began in earnest (see Map 1.1).

World War I was terrible, with casualties in the millions (see Chapter 12). Civilians died from bombing, starvation, cholera, and influenza. For those who survived, four years of being bombed and gassed in trench warfare would leave permanent scars. Erich Remarque, in his classic novel, *All Quiet on the Western Front*, captured the experiences of a generation of German boys who were forced to participate in the senseless slaughter. World War I also led to economic devastation and global disruption of empires and nations. The Ottoman, Russian, and Austro-Hungarian empires were dismembered. Germany lay prostrate, Russia was convulsed by revolution, and the British and French economies needed massive doses of U.S. capital to remain solvent. The war, much more so than modernism, or Nietzsche, or Freud, proved the enormous irrationality that governed international relations and global politics. As the European nations sleepwalked toward the conflict, the Enlightenment dream of universal laws, reason, and fraternity came crashing down. The war proved that local culture, the idiosyncrasies of regional speech, suspicions about unfamiliar faces, the pathologies of nationalism, and unequal modernization divided people so devastatingly that unifying meta-narratives of Enlightenment philosophy and science were incapable of papering over the cracks.

MAP 1.1   World War I in Europe

2

Imperialism and Colonial Rule

I contend that we are the finest race in the world and that the more of the world we inhabit the better it is for the human race. . . . Africa is still lying ready for us. It is our duty to take it. It is our duty to seize every opportunity of acquiring more territory and we should keep this one idea steadily before our eyes that more territory simply means more of the Anglo-Saxon race more of the best the most human, most honourable race the world possesses.

Cecil Rhodes, "Confession of Faith" (1877)

I have listened to your words but I can find no reason why I should obey you; I would rather die. I have no relations with you and cannot bring it to my mind that you have given me a pesa *[unit of currency] or a quarter of a* pesa *or a needle or a thread. I look for some reason why I should obey you and find not the smallest. If it were only a question of friendship, I would not be unwilling, today and always; but to be your subject, that I cannot be. If it should be war you desire, then I am ready, but never to be your subject. . . . I do not fall at your feet, for you are God's creature, as I also am. . . . I am sultan in my land. You are sultan in your land. Look, I do not say to you that you should obey me; for I know that you are a free man. Since I was born I have not crossed the coast; should I now cross it because you summon me? I will not come, and if you are strong enough, then come and fetch me.*

Macembo, a Yao chief, in a letter written in
Swahili to Hermann von Wissmann, commander of
the German imperial forces in East Africa (1890)

THE WORLD OF 1900 WAS A WORLD OF EMPIRES. THE MAJORITY OF THE world's populations lived under imperial rule, subject to authoritarian and foreign governments in faraway capitals. The word "empire" derives from the Latin word for "power" (*imperium*), and, in a general sense, the subjects of twentieth-century empires were little better off than those who had lived under Roman rule. As colonial subjects, imperial subjects were often liable to pay taxes with little or no say in government; moreover, they lost their lands without compensation, provided labor or military service with little or no payment, and lived under discriminatory legal systems. In churches and schools, and through contacts in daily life, they were exposed to the values, history, culture, and language of imperial rulers who assumed that local beliefs and practices were hardly worth taking seriously. At the center of each empire was a Great Power whose wealth, technology, political stability, and commitment to the ideas of "modernization" propelled it into neighboring territories and distant corners of the world. The words of Cecil Rhodes (quoted above), only twenty-three years old at the time and a student at Oxford University, but well on his way to a private fortune through success in diamond-mining in South Africa, may sound absurd today, but he seriously believed them. Furthermore, this viewpoint was not a case of British idiosyncrasy. Administrators, settlers, traders, soldiers, teachers, and missionaries from other countries—all to some extent agents of imperial power—also believed in the superiority of their particular civilization and the inferiority of subject populations, whom they labeled "primitive," "backward," or "traditional," implying unchanging, even static, societies.

Two aspects of modern imperial rule are particularly noteworthy for their impact on the twentieth century. They seem obvious in retrospect, although a hundred years ago they were probably evident to only a few. First, within empires lay the seeds of their destruction, for empires were authoritarian, heterogeneous, and based on gross economic inequalities. Resistance to colonial rule, stated so eloquently by Macembo, the Yao ruler, as he faced the threat of conquest, existed from the earliest days of invasion and continued overtly or surreptitiously throughout colonial occupation. Opposition took many forms but coalesced around independence movements by midcentury. Following World War II, the struggle to end colonial rule reached a peak, and colonies finally gained their independence and took their seats with other nation-states at the United Nations (see Chapter 7). In some cases, territories occupied in the course of imperial expansion (such as Hawaii) were incorporated as provinces of the dominant power.

If political ascendancy came to an end, a second lasting impact of imperialism—continued dominance of world affairs by the capitalist and technologically advanced countries of North America, Europe, and Japan—was more persistent. Imperial power often involves conquest and formal colonial rule but can also be exerted informally through economic domination. This type of influence was demonstrated in U.S. relations with Central and South America, the Caribbean, and the Pacific, a situation that still persists. France, four decades after the end of formal colonial rule, continued to exert a large influence over francophone regions of Africa through cultural ties, economic power, and military assistance. In South Africa, a former British colony, the largest foreign investments are still those of British companies, and Russia at century's end was still locked in conflict with areas of its former inner Asian empire. Inequalities summed up in phrases such as "developed and developing" countries or "rich and poor" nations continue to pattern world relations. They are often a legacy of imperial rule. Although twentieth-century international alignments, such as the alliance systems of the two world wars and the Cold War, have not endured, the marks of imperialism and colonial rule are still deeply seared in global relations—economically, culturally, and socially.

All this is not to suggest that the imperial powers of the twentieth century completely dictated the course of their relations with the populations they colonized or dominated economically. To take this approach would be to oversimplify a complex situation. Nor is it to suggest that within new imperial structures, indigenous populations completely lost out. On the contrary, the more scholars have delved into world history, the more the role of subject populations in shaping colonial relations has become clear. Imperial power might look impressive when painted on a map, but on the ground it was often thinly spread, patchy, and dependent on indigenous auxiliaries for enforcement. Colonized peoples, whatever their class, ethnicity, gender, age, or occupation, actively responded to foreign occupation and forced governments both locally and in distant capitals to reassess and modify their policies.

There were many spaces for imperial subjects to fill with their own agendas. Those who lived under colonial rule might experience high levels of violence and coercion, but efforts at colonial hegemony were seldom successful without some kind of consent from colonial subjects who appropriated the institutions, values, symbols, and knowledge of the colonizers. In turn, new groups often emerged among the colonized to contest relations within their own societies as well as with colonial powers. Foreign occupation provided opportunities for social mobility, for example, so that a new upper class might emerge to contest the power and influence of traditional elites. Young people with cash from wage labor might undermine the power of their elders. Opportunities for boys and men, especially to pursue Western schooling and wage employment, might undermine the power that women had enjoyed in precolonial societies. All—young and old, women and men, rich and poor—had the potential to find "nooks and crannies" within colonial structures to exploit for their own ends.

Imperial Decline and Imperial Expansion

Some empires were long past the zenith of their power and influence by 1900, while others were expanding and continuing to incorporate subject populations. Among the "crumbling giants" were the Chinese, Russian, Austro-Hungarian, and Ottoman empires, which were to fall apart in the first two decades of the century. The collapse of these "old" empires was due to domestic conditions, ambivalence about "modernization," and competition from the dynamic new imperialism of Western Europe, the United States, and Japan.

In China, a fifth of the world's people lived under the Qing, or Manchu, Dynasty (1644–1912), which by the mid-nineteenth century had proved itself unable to resolve internal problems relating to the rising population, a land shortage, natural disasters, rising prices of staple foods, and corrupt and inefficient local governments. Large areas had fallen under the control of warlords and bandits and had become embroiled in civil war. Western traders, having encouraged drug addiction among coastal Chinese, then used it as a pretext to incite the Opium Wars and further

PICTURE 2.1   Imperial Palace, Peking. The imperial compounds of the dynastic era typically consisted of Outer Courts and an Inner Court that served as the private residence of the emperor. Pictured here is the Hall of Preserving Harmony, the innermost of the Outer Court structures, where the Qing emperors met with their ministers. (Photo courtesy of Lynn Struve)

undermine imperial power. Then, between about 1850 and 1864, about 20 million people died in the Taiping Uprising; others fought in Muslim wars of independence in the region of Turkestan (c.1860–1870). Although the collapse of the Manchu empire might have come about anyway, it was also fatally undermined by expanding Western imperialism, which found local allies as well as resistance. Merchants, for example, chafing against Manchu monopolies and tariffs and in search of ways to undercut such oppressive imperialist policies, welcomed foreign trading companies that sought to establish themselves in such coastal and river ports as Shanghai and Nanking. In 1860 a combined Western military expedition entered Peking, burned the emperor's summer palace, and imposed demands that included the right of westerners to live in autonomous enclaves subject to their own laws, the opening of ports to external trade, and the right of Christian missionaries to evangelize and establish schools. Although few Chinese converted to Christianity, mission stations became relay points for potentially revolutionary ideas of individual worth, egalitarian social relations, and democracy. Young men who graduated from mission schools were among the leaders of the nationalist movement that overthrew the last emperor in the revolution of 1911. Other more conservative elements resisted foreign attempts to undermine their beliefs, economy, and society and rallied in support of the Manchus. The Boxer Rebellion of 1900 resulted from an upsurge of popular protest that drew its inspiration from loyalty to the dynasty, fear of foreigners, and religious belief. So intense was this uprising in the capital that it took a combined force of British, Russian, U.S., and Japanese troops to suppress it. By the beginning of the century, not only had the old imperialism of the Manchus collapsed, but parts of China had become "spheres of influence" or colonies of foreign powers such as Britain (Hong Kong), France (Indochina), Portugal (Macao), and Japan (Formosa). Germany and Russia also had footholds on the Chinese mainland.

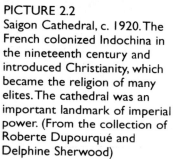

PICTURE 2.2
Saigon Cathedral, c. 1920. The French colonized Indochina in the nineteenth century and introduced Christianity, which became the religion of many elites. The cathedral was an important landmark of imperial power. (From the collection of Roberte Dupourqué and Delphine Sherwood)

A sixth of the world's population lived in another empire in decline, the multiethnic Russian Empire, which encompassed a vast area from the Arctic Circle to the arid lands of inner Asia, and from Poland in the west to the Pacific coast in the east. Although perceived by contemporaries as the Great Power with the largest land army in the world, the Russian imperial structures had developed severe cracks by the early twentieth century. Large numbers of peasants were in open revolt against landowners who kept them in debt and hung on to control of land. Soldiers and sailors in imperial forces mutinied because they went unpaid and suffered military defeats through poor logistics and incompetent generals. In towns such as Moscow and Saint Petersburg, factory workers labored long hours for little pay while living in sordid slums. At the same time, a small middle class—which benefited from foreign investment, education, and trade—called for reform and prepared to lead a revolution against the Tsarist regime, even in the face of imprisonment in Siberian labor camps. After the Russian Revolution of 1905 failed to produce results, other than an anemic parliament that served as little more than a rubber stamp on the policies of Tsar Nicholas II, the opportunity to end the imperial government came in World War I. The suffering on the war front and on the home front provided the conditions for the successful Bolshevik Revolution of 1917, the abdication of the tsar, and the end of the Russian Empire—although its contours and multiethnic composition were to be recreated in the new Union of Soviet Socialist Republics. The influence of Western imperialism was not as apparent in Russia as in China, but foreign capital did help to finance Russia's industrial revolution, and socialist and liberal ideas imported from Western Europe provided the basis for its revolutions. Furthermore, as far as many revolutionaries and socialists were concerned, World War I was a capitalists' war brought about by Western imperialism and the competition of Great Powers for control of world markets, commodities, and investments.

In Central Europe, the decline of the sprawling Austro-Hungarian Empire provided the immediate cause for the outbreak of World War I when the heir to the imperial throne, the Archduke Franz Ferdinand, and his wife fell victim to assassination by Serbian nationalists. Austria-Hungary's boundaries had been set through centuries of expansion under the German branch of the Hapsburg ruling house, which through conquest, marriage, and negotiated settlements had extended imperial rule to include a volatile mix of subject populations: German-speakers in Austria, Magyars in Hungary, and a range of Slavs (for example, Poles, Czechs, Slovaks, Serbs, and Croats) in the eastern and southern parts of the empire. These far-flung groups suffered from economic exploitation, political deprivation, and social frustration. Struggles for independence had played themselves out in the array of ways in which nationalists could "imagine" their common past. They used publications in indigenous languages, folk festivals, and athletic clubs as well as labor unrest, peasant uprisings, and political activism to achieve their ends. The nationalist attack against the archduke and his wife was one of many that might have occurred by 1914 against symbols of imperial rule in various parts of the empire, but this was the one that, by setting off a chain of events, ended in the epic disasters of a world war.

A fourth empire in decline was that of the Muslim Ottoman Turks, who had expanded their rule over the lands of the eastern Mediterranean following their capture of the capital city of Constantinople (Istanbul) in 1453 (see Map 2.1). At its height in the early seventeenth century, this empire had sprawled over three continents, including Christian and Muslim populations in the Balkans, the Turkish heartland in Asia Minor, and Muslim Arabs in the Middle East and North Africa. Subject populations were allowed some degree of autonomy as long as they paid their taxes, performed military service, and acknowledged the ultimate authority of the Sultan at Istanbul. As with the Russian and Chinese empires, the modernizing forces of Western Europe were important in undermining the old imperial regime. A prosperous merchant class in the Balkans exported food across the Adriatic and Mediterranean seas, traveled in Europe, and absorbed the ideas and culture of postrevolutionary France. Young military officers sent to academies in Germany read not only manuals of war but also books on democracy. In a belated effort to modernize the economy, the Ottomans borrowed from Western bankers and, when they could not repay their loans, had to accept financial advisers imposed to put their affairs in order. A series of rebellions in the nineteenth century, inspired by a myriad of problems but focused on nationalist uprisings against imperial rule, culminated in independence for several Balkan states. At the same time, Ottoman possessions in North Africa were being occupied by France and Britain, just as China had lost parts of its empire in the Far East. Finally, in 1909, the Young Turk revolt, led by junior army officers, deposed the despotic Abdul Hamid II and established a Turkish nationalist government in Istanbul. World War I brought the final collapse of Ottoman power, because the Istanbul government had allied itself to Germany. The empire lost its Middle Eastern possessions at the peace settlement in 1919. Turkey, however, emerged as a modern nation-state.

The decline of the old empires dissolved long-standing relationships, but meanwhile, the countries of Western Europe, the United States, and Japan were creating a different set of global relations. A search for markets, resources, and land for settlement had already been propelling Europeans overseas since the fifteenth century as part of what has been called the "old" imperialism. Their ships had crossed the Atlantic, rounded the coasts of Africa, and reached the Indian

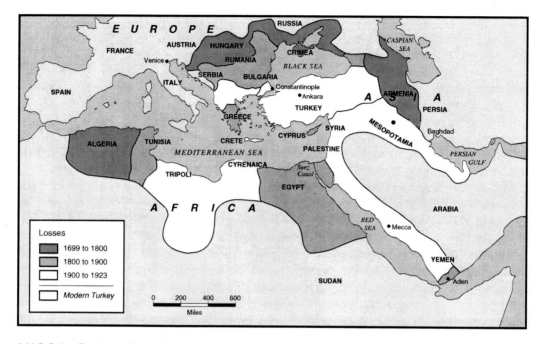

MAP 2.1   Decline of the Ottoman Empire

Ocean and the Far East. These ventures had resulted in British, French, Dutch, Spanish, and Portuguese colonies in the Americas and European footholds on the African and Asian coasts. The "new" imperialism was remarkable, however, for its extent and speed. One estimate notes that in a thirty-year period from about 1880 to 1910, Europeans extended their formal colonial empires by over 10 million square miles and 150 million people.

Nowhere was this process of imperial expansion more dramatically worked out at the turn of the century than on the continent of Africa. In spite of more than four centuries of contact, Europeans had made little headway in taking possession of land. By the mid-nineteenth century, with the exception of white settlement in South Africa, Europeans controlled only coastal footholds. Sustained local resistance, disease, geography, and well-organized trans-African trade networks that brought goods to the coast, were responsible for this situation. Yet, between about 1880 and 1914, the whole continent, with the exception of Ethiopia and Liberia, was divided up and occupied by European colonial powers in what historians have called the "Scramble for Africa." As conflicts escalated among British, French, Portuguese, and Belgian agents in the Congo, and between Britain and France in the Niger region, German chancellor Otto von Bismarck called representatives of the colonial powers to a conference at Berlin in 1884–1885. The hope was to inject some kind of international order into the process of land grabbing and thus avoid a European war over African territories. As was often the case in the "settlement" of colonial disputes at international conferences, none of the men gathered around the table had set foot in the regions involved, indigenous populations were not consulted, and the preexisting political, social, and economic realities were ignored when boundaries were drawn on maps. It is hardly surprising that decisions made during the European carve-up of Africa still cause problems today. Some guidelines on what constituted "effective occupation" (military occupation,

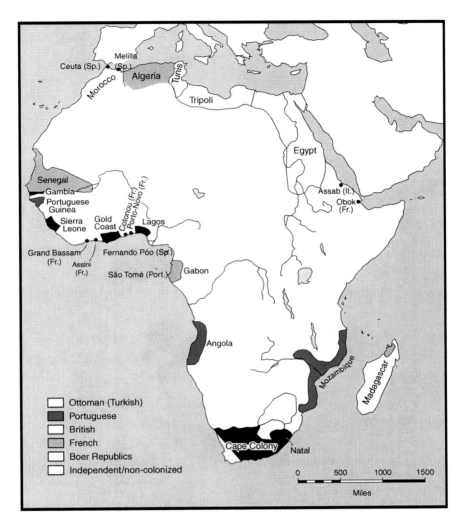

MAP 2.2   Europeans in Africa, c. 1870

treaties with local rulers) were negotiated for coastal regions of West Africa. Governments and individuals then went on to use and extend such spurious arguments to justify claims and counterclaims elsewhere as the scramble intensified (see Maps 2.2 and 2.3).

European expansion in Africa and Asia ran parallel to the spread of U.S. imperialism, which sometimes involved occupation, as it did in Alaska, Puerto Rico, the Philippines, and a string of islands across the Pacific. Throughout Latin America, however, U.S. policy was aimed at economic domination without formal colonial rule—a system constituting one form of "neocolonialism." Following its remarkable growth after the Civil War, the United States had emerged as the world's leading industrial power. By 1900, there was a surplus of capital, and business interests were pressuring the government to provide protection to companies engaged in overseas investment. By 1914, two-thirds of all U.S. foreign investment was in Canada and Latin America.

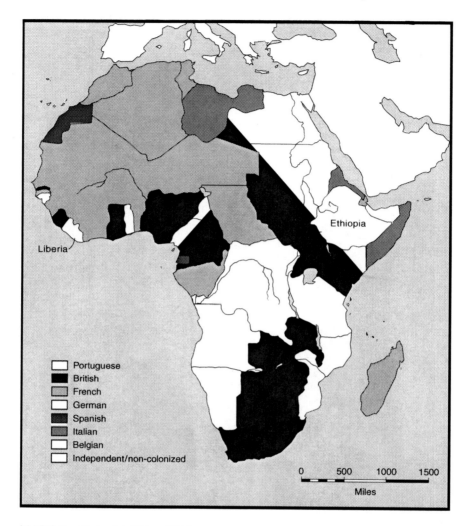

MAP 2.3   Colonial Africa, 1914

It was the Caribbean and Central America, however, which experienced the most intervention. In the Panama isthmus, U.S. capital, supported by Theodore Roosevelt's administration, intervened first in support of a Panamanian revolt against Colombia, then to negotiate the permanent lease of a strip of land across the isthmus, and then to complete the construction of the Panama Canal in 1914. Mostly, however, the policy of early-twentieth-century administrations was to safeguard economic expansion by marrying the presence of large U.S. companies with the positioning of marines at strategic bases. This strategy was used in the Panama zone and at Cuba's Guantanamo Bay. From there, troops could rapidly be deployed to quell opponents and could guard access to the Gulf of Mexico. By 1900, the Caribbean had become an "American Lake" and the United States had launched its "big stick" and "dollar diplomacy" policies. These concepts remained the cornerstones of its policy before World War II. Furthermore, in search of security and an optimum environment for U.S. business, the government turned a blind eye to dictators

TABLE 2.1   The Platt Amendment (extracts)

In 1898, Cuba, with the aid of the United States, became the last Latin American country to gain its independence from Spain. The cost to Cuba of this U.S. aid would be the subjugation of its independence to U.S. economic and military interests. Many of the aspects of this U.S. control over Cuba were spelled out in the Platt Amendment. Written by a U.S. senator, this amendment was signed by the two nations in Havana in 1903 and ratified to the Cuban Constitution in 1904.

ARTICLE I.

The government of Cuba shall never enter into any treaty or other compact with any foreign power or powers which will impair or tend to impair the independence of Cuba, nor in any manner authorize or permit any foreign power or powers to obtain by colonization or for military or naval purposes, or otherwise, lodgement in or control over any portion of said island.

ARTICLE III.

The government of Cuba consents that the United States may exercise the right to intervene for the preservation of Cuban independence, the maintenance of a government adequate for the protection of life, property, and individual liberty, and for discharging the obligations with respect to Cuba imposed by the treaty of Paris on the United States, now to be assumed and undertaken by the government of Cuba.

ARTICLE IV.

All acts of the United States in Cuba during its military occupancy thereof are ratified and validated, and all lawful rights acquired thereunder shall be maintained and protected.

ARTICLE V.

The Government of Cuba will execute, and as far as necessary, extend the plans already devised, or other plans to be mutually agreed upon, for the sanitation of the cities of the island, to the end that a recurrence of epidemic and infectious diseases may be prevented, thereby assuring protection to the people and commerce of Cuba, as well as to the commerce of the Southern ports of the United States and the people residing therein.

ARTICLE VII.

To enable the United States to maintain the independence of Cuba, and to protect the people thereof, as well as for its own defense, the Government of Cuba will sell or lease to the United States lands necessary for coaling or naval stations, at certain specified points, to be agreed upon with the President of the United States.

and oligarchies and trained national guards to suppress opponents, who after the 1917 Russian Revolutions could be labeled communists.

Thus, the United States, which had been born out of revolution, became the status quo power in the Americas. In Honduras, where a million acres of the most fertile land was owned and operated by U.S. fruit companies, U.S. troops had intervened six times by 1925 to ensure favorable and compliant governments. In Nicaragua, where about half the country's exports and nearly 40 percent of its imports involved the United States, U.S. troops occupied the country for twenty years, 1909–1929. Cuba, Mexico, Honduras, Haiti, Guatemala, and the Dominican Republic all experienced the landing of U.S. forces at some point in the early decades of the century. Even though it never became a formal colony of the United States, Cuba, through the Platt Amendment in 1903, was forced to accept U.S. domination of its affairs (see Table 2.1).

Finally, in the world of empires in the early twentieth century, another country that provided a particularly remarkable example of accommodation to Western imperialism, together with rapid development at home and expansion abroad, was Japan. Like China, this small island nation had to deal with the arrival of Western naval power and merchant capitalism, a contact initiated by four U.S. gunboats in 1853. Having observed the fate of China, and without the capacity to resist Western encroachment, the Japanese government adopted a defensive strategy. It agreed to open ports to foreign trade and allow foreigners extraterritorial rights—that is, the right to live under their own laws—and instituted an open-door policy in trade. In the Meiji Restoration in 1868, however, a group of reform-minded military officers and merchants overthrew the old government and put in power a young emperor who supported their program of selective modernization. Following this event, Japan embarked on a remarkable transformation. The government's collaboration with foreigners (the United States, Britain, France, the Netherlands, and Russia) turned out to be a good defensive strategy, buying time while the government implemented a conscious modernization policy. Business leaders, military officers, policymakers, and students who traveled overseas studied at foreign institutions and returned home to introduce models of modernization: for example, ideas from the German military, the British navy, the U.S. educational system, and parliamentary forms of government, which were modified to accommodate a strong role for the executive branch and the emperor. At the same time, the country embarked on a program of economic development through railroads, banking, and light industry. By the first decade of the century, Japan had signaled its emergence as an imperial power. It defeated China in the Sino-Japanese War (1894–1895) and forced it to hand over the island of Formosa (Taiwan). Even more stunning was Japan's defeat of Russia in 1904–1905, which led to the annexation of Korea as a Japanese colony (1910–1945). From this position of strength, Japan negotiated the end of the unequal treaties it had previously been forced to negotiate with the Great Powers and replaced them with new ones based on equality.

Imperialism clearly contributed not only to new patterns of subordination and dominance in global relations but to an intensification of rivalries between the Great Powers at the heart of empires. Imperialism, as it was contested between the Great Powers, was closely tied to another great international force of the twentieth century, nationalism. By the criteria of the time, a nation could hardly be considered a Great Power without imperial interests. Ultimately, tensions could not be resolved peacefully. They contributed to the outbreak of two major European wars, which became world wars as colonial populations were forcibly conscripted and drawn into the defense of empires. Such demands were fiercely contested by many colonial subjects who were to participate in decolonization struggles by mid-century.

Imperial Motives and Imperial Means

Reasons for the new imperialism have been the subject of hot debate among scholars ever since imperial expansion got underway. Some have emphasized conditions in Western countries that made overseas expansion a top government priority; others have focused on the agency of populations and conditions in overseas territories that "pulled" governments into imperial expansion, sometimes more than these governments originally intended. In this view, subject populations shaped the march of late-nineteenth-century imperialism as much as forces in Europe or the United States did. From the point of view of the imperial powers, several interrelated forces propelled them into the rest of the world at this point in time. These factors can be discussed separately, but in fact, when a specific incident, individual, or government is considered, they are almost impossible to compartmentalize.

PICTURE 2.3   "The Greedy Boy" (1885). This cartoon from *Punch* magazine (London) depicts the young "John Bull" of Great Britain and the elder statesman, Chancellor Bismarck of Germany, carving up the colonial "cake." (Reprinted from *Punch*, January 10, 1885)

Some historians have emphasized the importance of national prestige in the race for colonies. According to this line of argument, France, which had lost the province of Alsace-Lorraine to Germany following defeat in the Franco-Prussian War (1870–1871), saw colonial conquests as a means of reviving lost national pride. For Bismarck of Germany, promoting the colonization of South-West Africa, Togo, Kamerun, and East Africa was less related to their intrinsic value than to their potential as pawns in a diplomatic chess game in Europe. Portugal, a weak European power, in its conquest and occupation of Angola, Mozambique, and Guinea-Bissau, proved it was still a colonial power to be reckoned with in spite of the loss of the important colony of Brazil in the early nineteenth century. For Japan, imperial success meant recognition as an emerging power on the Pacific rim. Finally, the Monroe Doctrine, which asserted that the United States had particular rights and obligations in the Western hemisphere, was invoked as a patriotic rallying cry by the U.S. government against challenges from foreign powers.

A famous incident in the partition of Africa exemplifies the xenophobic emotions that imperial rivalries could provoke. The scene was an abandoned Anglo-Egyptian fort at Fashoda on the upper Nile in the region of modern Sudan. In 1898, a British expedition advancing from Egypt confronted a French expedition advancing from the Congo. When the incident was reported in Europe, national hysteria—from the level of the cabinet to the popular press—broke loose. It seemed as if Fashoda had become a test of national prestige and the power of London and Paris was on the line. In fact, Fashoda itself was a remote, largely depopulated, worthless territory. After frantic diplomatic negotiations, war was averted. The French backed off and agreed that Britain should keep the Sudan, and the British recognized French claims in the Sahara.

Other scholars have argued that in many regions "the flag followed trade." That is, economic interests were paramount, traders were often the first to arrive before soldiers or administrators, and lobbying groups in European capitals representing economic interests had the greatest influence in policymaking. This argument tends to emphasize the boom-and-bust cycles that gripped the industrial economies of Europe and North America in the late nineteenth century. In particular, a prolonged "Great Depression" plagued Europe between about 1873 and 1896 when overproduction and a glut of manufactured goods led to falling prices, unemployment, and economic instability. According to this view, capitalism's constant demand for new sources of raw materials for industry, ever-expanding markets for cheap manufactured goods, and new opportunities for investment provided the impetus for imperial expansion. Such an interpretation of the new imperialism seems to make good sense when one considers the vast potential markets of India and China; the mineral resources of Bolivia, Korea, and South Africa; the rubber in Sumatra, Malaysia, and Central Africa; and the array of cash crops around the world—from peanuts in Senegal to cotton in Mozambique, bananas in Honduras, coffee in Brazil, and, by the 1920s, petroleum in Mexico and the Middle East. Exploitation of such resources involved outlays of capital—for example, for the construction of railroads—that businesses wanted to protect through military intervention or colonization by their own governments. Furthermore, formal colonial rule, or informal rule through puppet dictators, was the best way to ensure profit in commercial transactions. Once a country had control of a region, markets could be protected by tariff barriers to keep others out. This arrangement was attractive to smaller imperial powers, such as Portugal, whose textiles could not compete on the open market with those of Britain, for example. As countries introduced such restrictions, even Britain, which from its position of imperial strength had supported free trade all through the nineteenth century, had to review its policy.

In the light of these specific examples of imperial expansion and conquest, such distinctions between economic and political motives easily become blurred. The race to Fashoda can be interpreted as a case of nationalism out of control, but the intensity of British reactions can also be related to broader British regional interests: the perceived strategic importance of the Nile in controlling Egypt; the Suez Canal as the gateway to India, the "Jewel in the Crown," which, with a market of 250 million people, accounted for 19 percent of British exports; British engagement in cotton production in the Nile Valley; and the significance of Egypt as a base in the eastern Mediterranean against Russian, German, and French competition for pieces of the crumbling Ottoman Empire. The case of Japan muddies the imperial waters even further. The Japanese defeat of first China and then Russia electrified the contemporary world, greatly enhancing the country's international reputation. Theodore Roosevelt pronounced Japan's triumph over Russia "the greatest phenomenon the world has ever seen." The Indian nationalist leader Jawaharlal Nehru wrote of the boost the victory gave to Asians faced with Western expansion—an opinion he may have reconsidered as Japanese imperial armies threatened the frontiers of India in World War II. And yet, the invasion of Korea was linked to economic imperatives. The peninsula provided new lands for Japanese settlers and coal and iron deposits that were lacking in Japan and necessary for its industrial revolution.

Unraveling motives for imperial expansion is even more difficult when ideology and religion are considered. Some have argued that traders and business interests pressured governments into colonial expansion; others have suggested that "the flag followed the cross." In some regions, Christian missionaries, sweeping into distant corners of the world on a wave of evangelical fervor, were the first whites whom indigenous people encountered. At home, missionary societies supported imperial expansion as a means of protecting their employees, forming an important lobbying group in favor of colonies. Home on leave, missionaries toured the country and related

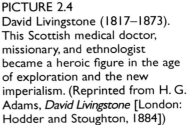

PICTURE 2.4
David Livingstone (1817–1873).
This Scottish medical doctor,
missionary, and ethnologist
became a heroic figure in the age
of exploration and the new
imperialism. (Reprinted from H. G.
Adams, *David Livingstone* [London:
Hodder and Stoughton, 1884])

their adventures and successes in converting the "heathen" in far-off lands. They could play a powerful role in persuading ordinary church members to support governments that would spend their taxes on noble colonial projects.

The potential influence that individuals could have, and the mix of motives that inspired them and their supporters, is exemplified by the career of David Livingstone. A Scottish medical missionary who worked for the London Missionary Society, Livingstone traveled widely in South and Central Africa between 1841 and 1873, just as conditions for the new imperialism were emerging. In between several expeditions to Africa, Livingstone returned to Britain to publicize his work. As he traveled around the country, he talked to local congregations that might donate pennies on Sunday to support foreign missions. He also lectured to more elite audiences, for example, at Oxford and Cambridge Universities, and at the Royal Geographical Society in London. Of course, such occasions were well written up in the press. Livingstone's own accounts of his travels, *Missionary Travels and Researches in South Africa* (1857) and *Narrative of an Expedition to the Zambezi and Its Tributaries* (1865), became bestsellers.

For Livingstone and others, the task of Christian missionaries was not just evangelism but also the transformation of the whole person and society; or, as he put it, the goal was "Christianity, Commerce, and Civilization." In the opinion of contemporary Europeans, being a good Christian involved not just religious belief but embracing the manners and values of contemporary Europe and practicing them in everyday life. It was part of leaving the "traditional" or "primitive" or "heathen" condition behind and becoming "modern." Thus, becoming a wage-earner who would consume material goods, such as cheap manufactured cloth or household possessions such as lamps, was an essential element in the process of becoming "civilized" and Christian. Missionary work went hand in hand with the expansion of Western capitalism. After one of Livingstone's visits home, the African Lakes Company was established by some Scottish businessmen to open up the Central African interior to trade. Inspired by Livingstone's lectures and sermons, new missionary societies were established in southern Africa. By the 1890s and the period of the Scramble for Africa, the presence of these British subjects and interests in an area where Portugal and Germany also had imperial ambitions influenced the government to annex the region of Nyasaland (present-day Malawi) as a British possession.

As for Livingstone, the ability of an individual to capture the imagination of the European public in the age of imperialism was demonstrated in the pomp and circumstance of his funeral at Westminster Abbey in central London in April 1874. It was attended by many of the great men and women of Victorian society. The coffin was borne by some of Livingstone's closest associates, including the U.S. journalist Henry Morton Stanley, whose "discovery" of Livingstone in Central Africa two years earlier had astonished the geographical establishment and the general population. Such stories of distant feats beyond known horizons were inscribed and reinvented in the stories and myths of empire. They became part of a national consciousness through museums, paintings, statues, inscriptions, place-names, children's storybooks and comics, stamps, and films. Livingstone's prominence in the annals of empire was assured through a memorial tablet placed in the central nave of Westminster Abbey, the last resting place of many members of the British royalty.

Support for imperial expansion was transmitted through different ideologies. For Americans, the notion of Manifest Destiny powerfully expressed the belief that they were a Chosen People peculiarly suited to spread their version of a model society from the Atlantic to the Pacific. In the twentieth century this notion spilled over into the Caribbean, Central America, and the Pacific, and by the 1920s it became a policy for justifying U.S. economic and security interests, and keeping European competitors out. Many Europeans also believed in their "civilizing mission," a concept that had both religious and secular connotations. In a famous poem, Rudyard Kipling wrote of "the white man's burden." Couched in heroic terms, it expressed the duty of whites to serve their country and humanity in distant corners of the world, whatever the personal cost, for the glory of spreading civilization to those the poet called "Your new-caught sullen peoples, Half devil and half child."

In fact, those who spread imperial power generally believed in their own superiority, whatever the time and place. China thought of itself as the "Central Kingdom" in a world where others were vassals and foreigners were barbarians. According to Bernard Lewis, the celebrated historian of the Ottoman Empire, at the height of its power Muslims "regarded western Europe as an outer darkness of barbarianism from which the sunlit world of Islam had little to fear and less to learn." Moreover, the Russian expansion eastward into Siberia was the work of missionaries, traders, and settlers who saw the tsar (derived from the Latin, *caesar*) as a ruler by divine right.

In late nineteenth-century Europe, theories of evolution powerfully affected the way people thought about themselves and others and justified their domination of the rest of the world. Biological theories of evolution and the survival of the fittest could be applied to human societies, which could be placed on a hierarchy of development. Thus, according to such pseudo-scientific theories, racial types could be correlated with levels of civilization, with the Christian, capitalist nation-states of North America and Europe at the top. Imperial domination and colonial rule was part of the natural order of things. As with missionary reports of "heathen" populations, such ideologies could grab the imagination of ordinary folk when transmitted through popular magazines, photographs, comic strips, songs, theater, radio shows, and films. Such representations often stereotyped and ridiculed peoples of whom the writers were, in fact, ignorant. Loot taken during violent attacks on old civilizations by Western forces was carted home by soldiers as trophies of war and sold to private collectors or museums. Thus, treasures from the imperial summer palace in Peking or from royal palaces in Kumasi and Benin in West Africa turned up as curios in the showcases of the Museum of Natural History in New York, the British Museum in London, the Musée de l'Homme (Museum of Mankind) in Paris, and the Berlin Museum für Völkerkunde (Berlin Folklore Museum). Curators cataloged and labeled such pieces according to the new science of anthropology, which often interpreted their meaning through Western eyes rather than local understandings. Fixed "tribal" categories emerged for regions and peoples even though social organization on the ground was much more fluid. The racism of the late nineteenth century continued in many forms in the twentieth, most potently in the fascist "master race" ideology of Hitler's Third Reich, which justified eastern expansion by the need to destroy lesser populations such as Jews, Gypsies, and Slavs (see Chapter 6).

Although historians have emphasized the motives for imperial expansion, they have also noted the significance of the means of conquest and colonial rule. According to this perspective, without the "tools of empire," the motives would not have carried whites very far. With the spread of industrialization in Europe and the United States, the ability of colonial representatives to impose their rule through superior technology improved dramatically. Repeater rifles and artillery in the hands of a few experienced soldiers could defeat opponents armed with traditional weapons or outdated guns bought on the second-hand market.

High mortality rates among whites due to exposure to new and lethal disease environments could be substantially lowered through new medications and vaccinations. In the 1840s, quinine, an anti-malaria drug, was used with some success by a British expedition to the Niger River in West Africa. Gradually scientists figured out how to regulate the dosage, greatly reducing mortality rates. The French Pasteur Institute in Paris and Brazzaville, the capital of French Equatorial Africa, also experimented successfully in the early twentieth century with a vaccination against sleeping sickness, another killer disease, which was actually spread by the mobility of migrant workers under colonial rule. With new drugs and vaccinations, most European and U.S. officials felt sufficiently secure to take their families to tropical zones by the 1920s, but the benefits of Western medicine took much longer to reach subject populations. Even then, they were usually available only through a few missionary hospitals or in occasional government campaigns against some disease threatening the supply of labor.

Improved communications also made imperial expansion possible and profitable. Submarine cables put military commanders and commercial company representatives more easily in touch with their headquarters in Europe. The first transatlantic telegraph cable was completed in 1865, and by 1870 an efficient telegraph line linked Britain to India so that a message could be relayed in five hours. Ironclad steamships, which were faster and had a greater carrying capacity than previous ships, made business more profitable, as did technological feats such as the construction of the Suez (1869) and Panama (1914) Canals.

Advanced shipping and railroad construction also sped up the final conquest of some areas, improving the ability to transfer troops and open up areas for trade. By 1875 the British had completed 5,000 miles of railroads in India. The Russians completed the trans-Siberian railway, from Saint Petersburg on the Baltic to Vladivostock on the Pacific, in 1905. The human costs of such engineering feats could be high: The Matadi-Léopoldville line that bypassed the rapids of the Congo River and joined the Atlantic coast to the Central African interior was only 241 miles, but it took eight years to build and cost 1,800 African and 132 European lives. The Chinese navy was no match for the latest gunboats that U.S. and European authorities used to patrol their interests along the coast or in the Yangtze River. And in Africa, river and lake steamers were central to the profitability of European commercial enterprises. In the heart of the continent, by 1902, more than a hundred steamers belonging to several commercial companies plied the navigable waterways of the Congo and its tributaries.

The balance sheet of these technological achievements for local populations is difficult to draw up. Although it can be argued that imperial intervention and colonial rule meant the introduction of Western public-health knowledge and the eradication of some diseases, it also meant the introduction of new diseases and the spread of preexisting illnesses through the migration of workers. In the case of imperial railroad systems, it can be claimed, on the one hand, that in many countries today they are the lifeline of the economy. On the other hand, it can also be persuasively argued that they were built primarily to facilitate the export of specific cash crops grown for the benefits of imperial rather than domestic economies. Such infrastructures have encouraged continued dependence on one or two export crops, which largely benefits foreign companies, retards the diversification of local economies, and stunts economic growth. A look at the map of railroads in West Africa or Central America shows how systems inherited from the colonial period usefully link the interior to the coast. They do little, however, to facilitate communication within individual countries or promote much-needed regional cooperation between neighbors (see Maps 2.4 and 2.5).

Imperialism and Colonial Rule on the Ground

Scattered throughout this discussion of imperial expansion have been references to local conditions and their role in shaping the course of conquest and consolidation of colonial rule. The history of imperialism was once written only from a Western, ethnocentric perspective, but as historians of other parts of the world have looked at the responses of people "on the ground," the significance of their initiatives and responses has become clearer. Statesmen in European or North American capitals might draw lines on maps of the world, develop blueprints for administering colonies according to policies of direct or indirect rule, engage in propaganda campaigns for public support, and otherwise promote imperialism on paper, but their ability to impose their rule was tempered by local conditions. These were nuanced and changing. Populations initiated a full range of responses to foreign intruders even within individual lifetimes.

Armed opposition of the type threatened by Chief Macembo could be persistent and sustained. In Angola, local forces mounted a fierce military resistance that involved pitched battles and guerrilla warfare when the Portuguese moved in to drive villagers from their land and take over a preexisting African trade in ivory, rubber, and beeswax. In the southern part of the colony, Ovambo leaders played one colonial power against another by selling commodities to the Germans in neighboring South-West Africa and buying modern repeater rifles from them to hold back the Portuguese invaders. Between 1879 and 1926, 30,000 Portuguese colonial troops were engaged in military operations throughout Angola. In the heaviest fighting, in 1902 and 1920, the colonial army spent 83 percent of its time putting down African resistance, at first to

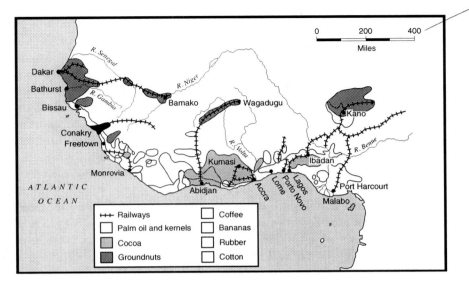

MAP 2.4   Railways and Cash Crops, West Africa

MAP 2.5   Railways and Cash Crops, Central America

European military invasion and then against forced recruitment for plantation work and road-building.

Local responses also forced action by the colonial troops, which were trying to delineate a stable frontier. These actions carried governments in Europe further into the interior than they had originally intended, leading to the deaths of white soldiers and draining imperial budgets. Trouble on the frontier could be "infectious" and encourage others to rebel within the colony. In northern India the situation was further complicated by British officers, who sometimes took matters into their own hands because of the long chain of command that separated them from London, on the one hand, and the threatening imperial expansion of Russia in Afghanistan and Persia, on the other. Actions that were too costly could bring down unpopular governments in European elections.

In South Africa, settlement of the interior by whites involved a continual reassessment of how far the frontier should be extended in an area where vulnerable settlers were ringed by powerful African states. In this poor colony, Britain had dragged its feet throughout much of the nineteenth century in what John Galbraith (*Reluctant Empire,* 1963) has described as a "reluctant empire," but the situation changed dramatically when diamonds and gold were found in the interior in 1867 and 1886. Disputes among the white population over control of this wealth were largely settled in the Anglo-Boer War (1899–1902) and the negotiations that followed. This resolution led to the formation of the Union of South Africa (1910) under white minority rule within the British Empire.

Sustained African resistance to incorporation into the expanding white settlement and into the mining economy also had to be resolved. Following the opening of the mines, some chiefs sent off groups of young men to find wage employment, since they were the most dispensable in terms of their labor contribution to local economies. They then used these wages to buy trade goods and guns to resist white encroachment in the 1890s. Even after conquest, many peasant households continued to resist incorporation into wage labor. They emerged instead as prosperous peasant farmers, growing food for mining towns, for imperial troops, and for administrative and commercial centers. They used cash incomes to pay taxes, update their farm equipment, increase production, go into the transportation business, and send their children to missionary schools. They thus adapted to white conquest and even prospered from it. A witness, George Warren, before the Cape Labour Commission, which was charged with investigating the labor shortage for the mining industry in 1893, when asked the question, "Is there any reason you can give for this want of labour with such a potential labor supply as we have in this colony?" answered, "The natives are independent. They have land and grow what they choose, and their wants are small."

For South Africa and for other settler colonies, such as Algeria or Kenya, where land and labor were in demand by whites, the ultimate solution from the government's point of view was to seize the land through military occupation, official decree, or legislation in white-dominated parliaments. This agenda had the effect of separating workers from their means of production and forcing men, and sometimes young women as well, into the colonial labor force so that they could pay their taxes. In 1913 in South Africa, the white government passed a draconian Land Act that left 7.3 percent of the land as reserves where Africans could legally own land and cattle. The remaining land was given over to white farmers, who constituted about 20 percent of the population. In 1936, the government reviewed the situation and increased African lands, but only to 13.7 percent of the total area of their country. Of course, such sweeping measures could only be gradually implemented, not only because of ongoing resistance and the lack of an adequate force to police such measures, but also because many white South Africans knew less about local farming conditions than the Africans they displaced. They thus had to allow Africans to farm illegally and live on their property in return for labor services. At the same time other forms of resistance were being launched. It was not coincidental that the first African political party, the South African Native National Congress (renamed the African National Congress in 1923), was formed in 1912, and a women's branch, the Bantu Women's League, six years later.

Such examples, repeated in many variations around the colonial world, demonstrate that colonial rule was shaped by local initiatives as well as imperial goals. Resistance could be sustained through what the historian James Scott has called the "weapons of the weak." During the conquest period, ordinary people did what they could to put obstacles in the way of invading armies. In Central Africa, the expeditions that moved into the interior might be written up in heroic terms for readers in Belgium and France, but reports and diaries give other insights. One reads of long delays as local chiefs refused to supply porters; villagers dragging their canoes away from the river so they could not be commandeered; people hiding in the forests; caravans attacked and robbed of trade goods that were intended for bargaining for supplies further in the interior; and white men squabbling among themselves as they faced endless frustrations and sickness from dysentery, malaria, and a myriad of fevers.

Workers on the job also resisted forced labor and poor wages. Plantation workers might boil cotton seeds so that they would not grow; laborers might disappear once they were paid, forcing employers to recruit new and inexperienced workers; machinery and railroad tracks were sabotaged; and work slowdowns might be explained by white employers as "laziness," confirmation of the low moral character of the natives.

Another type of response to imperial oppression involved nonconfrontational tactics such as withdrawal and flight. This happened on an individual basis and on a large scale. In northern Mozambique, where the Portuguese had handed over administration to a concessionary company, the Nyasa Company, which had a monopoly to exploit the area for cotton and sugar production, peasants experienced a particularly oppressive brand of colonialism. One European observer reported in 1914, "So far as the natives are concerned, this is a land of blood and tears, where the most brutal ill-treatment is no crime and murder merely a slight indiscretion" (from a letter in the British Colonial Archives in London). By 1919, 100,000 had fled into the neighboring British colony of Nyasaland, where they sought but did not always find improved conditions. Such everyday resistance, or "avoidance protests," were not intended to alter the political system radically, nor could the perpetrators hope to bring colonialism to an end. They were intended to protect individuals and families against excessive demands from those in power. Yet, incrementally, they could contribute to a consciousness of oppression and resistance that flowed into the broad-based movements of protest and liberation that eventually brought an end to colonial rule.

Colonial subjects had the ability to keep imperial authorities on a state of alert, but they also had the option of allying themselves with the foreigners. Preexisting rivalries among indigenous populations gave Europeans the ability to coax some groups to their side and, once imperial representatives were established, pursue strategies of "divide and rule."

If some impeded progress into the interiors of Asia and Africa, others were willing to provide logistical support. Local chiefs might be willing to enter into alliances with foreigners if it gave them advantage over long-standing enemies, forestalled invasion by a force armed with superior

PICTURE 2.5
Colonial District Officer from an African
perspective. Thomas Ona Odulata, a Nigerian
sculptor, was known for his depictions of European
themes. He was fascinated by the dress and
accoutrements of power. Here, he depicts a British
District Officer (D.O.) reading. The sculpture is in
wood, about 9 inches tall, and likely carved in Lagos
in the 1940s. (Photo courtesy of Matthew Sieber,
from the collection of Roy Sieber)

weapons, or brought potentially profitable commercial alliances. Individuals might also gain by signing on for service with white men, at least for a limited period of time. For young men, even a small cash income might provide a new measure of independence. In many African societies, it could, for example, give them the means to arrange their own marriage and bypass the elders, whose help in the form of cattle, goods, and land was previously essential in arranging the marriage contract.

Economic opportunities were an important incentive for those who worked in some colonial or neocolonial economies. Conditions varied widely under different forms of colonial rule and imperial exploitation. Although many lost land either to settlers or to concessionary companies and lived and worked in misery, others could profit from new opportunities within the world economy. In Ghana, Nigeria, and Senegal, where whites did not settle but rather stayed only for short tours of duty, peasant farmers mobilized family and migrant wage labor in the production of such cash crops as cocoa and peanuts. They set up their own credit associations and used their income to send their children to schools so that they could bring new expertise into the family business and become part of the emerging middle class. Although they had to sell their crops at prices fixed by colonial marketing boards, they nevertheless could prosper in new ways.

Within empires, colonial officials attempted to solve labor problems by contracting labor in one area and transferring it for use elsewhere. These foreign laborers with no ties to local people were often the backbone of colonial economies. Such strategies were common in the large British and French Empires. For the French, the most useful indigenous soldiers in their African campaigns were the Senegalese *tirailleurs* (riflemen), who had a long tradition of service in colonial armies. En route to other regions of West or Central Africa, it was common for an advance party to stop at the Senegalese capital, Dakar, to enlist young men as soldiers for a two- or three-year contract. These "outsiders" might then return home, or they might stay in the region of service, where employers were eager to hire them as foremen of work gangs, agents of trading companies, or workers in skilled trades such as carpentry or railroad construction. Emigrant workers might send for wives or marry local women and settle in local communities. Tens of thousands of Senegalese tirailleurs and other conscripted African soldiers were to die fighting for the French in the trenches of World War I.

In the lower levels of the colonial administration in Africa, the French also made use of trained personnel from their older Caribbean colonies of Martinique, Guadeloupe, and Guiana. Here, elite families sent their sons to church schools and sometimes for higher education in France. As black men who were the descendants of slaves, these individuals, together with female family members, found their way back to Africa in the colonial service. In the new society they had considerable status. They symbolized success and were models for a new way of life, especially in towns. They earned wages; had an array of material possessions; spoke a European language; often were Catholics; and wore uniforms, clothes, and accessories that expressed their place in society. Such individuals were trendsetters and purveyors of new ideas on leisure, fashion, sports, and music.

The British also depended heavily on divide-and-rule strategies, bringing in outsiders to control local populations and provide essential labor. Zulu policemen from South Africa were commonly used in British Central Africa, and coastal Swahili worked as imperial agents in the interior regions of East Africa. The most important source of imperial labor, however, was India, where the British East India Company had first arrived in the seventeenth century. Like the French, who used Senegalese soldiers in different parts of their empire, the British enlisted Indians in colonial regiments that served in different parts of the subcontinent, in South Africa, in the Pacific, and in Europe in World War I. Without Indian labor, both skilled and unskilled, economic projects in various parts of the empire would have been seriously retarded. A large population living in poverty provided a pool of cheap indentured labor that was especially important in the development of plantation agriculture. Workers usually contracted for a five-year period, with the possibility of renewing their contract and having their home passage paid, but many stayed in their new surroundings, although retaining their ties with their home areas. In total, some 1.3 million Indian contract laborers joined in a diaspora that took them to work in places as diverse as Mauritius, Fiji, Jamaica, British Guiana, Trinidad, St. Lucia, Granada, and Natal. Many stayed, and their descendants constitute sizable populations in these areas today.

Finally, India is an excellent place for considering how imperialism worked in practice. In particular, how did so few whites manage to rule millions of colonial subjects? Answers have already been suggested. Military power, technological superiority, surplus capital, and political stability were all important springboards for action that powered imperial advance even in the face of sustained resistance. Divide-and-rule strategies and the ability to exploit divisions within populations were also critical factors in any colonial situation. As local people acquired education and skills, they could fill crucial support roles. In 1900, the colonial administration of India consisted of 4,000 British civilians and 69,000 army personnel, supported by 250,000 Indian civil servants and 130,000 soldiers. At a local level, India was a patchwork of administrative units with some areas ruled directly by colonial officers and others under Indian control in about 550 native states. Such colonial arrangements were essentially haphazard and had evolved over time. Queen Victo-

PICTURE 2.6   Indian durbar. The superbly decorated state elephants of H. H. the Maharaja of Gwalior take part in a durbar at Delhi in 1903. (Photo from the Library of Congress)

ria had been given the title of Empress of India in an act of the British Parliament, but the allegiance of rulers to the British monarchy also suited local princes because it enhanced their status in local politics.

Just as national celebrations today confirm the hierarchies, shared interests, values, and loyalties to nation-states, so in India and other colonial possessions imperial populations were drawn together on great occasions. Empire Day in Britain and Bastille Day in France were recreated in a foreign context, incorporating old and new traditions for colonial ends. For local chiefs, educated elites, and those who served in lower positions in the hierarchy, such as soldiers or war veterans, these events were opportunities to display status; for colonial rulers, great festivals were extravaganzas demonstrating their imperial power and largesse; and for ordinary people, there were a myriad of ways to join in, boycott, or adapt the proceedings for their own ends.

In India, the grandeur of such occasions could be breathtaking, as descriptions of gatherings called durbars show. These assemblies of princes and subjects dated from the period of the old Moghul Empire, but under British imperialism the occasion was reinvented and amplified through the addition of British royal traditions. Under the viceroys (principal representatives of the British monarchy) of the late nineteenth and early twentieth centuries, elaborate festivals and rituals emphasized the British monarchy at the head of a hierarchy that included all subjects, Indian and British. Durbars were also occasions for rewarding loyalty with medals, awards, titles, and gifts. A particularly famous and elaborate durbar staged in 1877, when Queen Victoria was proclaimed Empress of India, became the model for others in the early twentieth century. Eyewitness accounts give a sense of the grandeur of the occasion and the incentives for local princes to participate in such imperial occasions. Indian princes and their entourages were given a place to set up their encampments around the viceroy's tents; march-pasts included both imperial troops and contingents from the armies of Indian princes. Wealthy Indians entered horses in races, and representatives of princes took part in competitions such as rifle shooting. The most important princes were invited to dinners and receptions, where their spokesmen gave loyal addresses. At the same time, the viceroy rewarded such shows of fidelity by "enhancing" the number of gunshots that could be fired to salute some princes, while conferring on others the title of "Counsellor of the Empress."

Conclusion

What can be drawn from experiences of imperialism and colonial rule in the early century? The immediate and long-lasting impact of these powerful forces are complex. But five related themes clearly emerge to influence the course of the later twentieth century. There was, first, a patterning of global economic relations—for example, between the "developed" and the "developing" world—that resulted from the spread of Western capitalist forces to other world areas. Imperialism and the power of capitalism also contributed to gross inequalities within states. Second, the creation of colonies cut across preexisting lines and included various ethnic groups within the boundaries of what later became independent states. These places were what J. Gus Liebenow, the political scientist of Africa, has called "nations in search of nationhood," a quest still not completed at century's end. Third, the world had become smaller, a process that greatly intensified in the later twentieth century. In a technological sense this was possible because of rapid developments in applied science, but it was also meaningful in human terms through the mobility of workers and the exchange of cultural values and ideas. The new technology was both dangerous and advantageous. Fourth, class structures developed that derived from traditional divisions enhanced by access to economic opportunities and education under colonial rule. Yet, new educational and employment opportunities also allowed previously marginalized populations to achieve status. In some areas, new socialist ideologies provided both the inspiration and the organization for bringing colonial rule to an end. And last, as noted at the outset, a distinction can be made between imperialism and formal colonial rule. Although the forces of economic imperialism or neocolonialism persisted in the second half of the century, mobilization of nationalist forces brought formal colonial rule to an end in most regions of the world and enabled the growth of international organizations. All of these concepts will be discussed further in future chapters.

3

Materialism and the Crisis of Capitalism

Modern bourgeois society, with its relations of production, of exchange and of property, a society that has conjured up such gigantic means of production and of exchange, is like the sorcerer who is no longer able to control the powers of the nether world whom he has called up by his spells.

Karl Marx,
The Communist Manifesto
(1848)

Less than seventy-five years after it officially began, the contest between capitalism and socialism is over: capitalism has won.

Robert L. Heilbroner
in the *New Yorker*
(January 23, 1989)

....

BY 1900 CAPITALISM HAD BECOME THE WORLD'S LEADING ECONOMIC system. It delivered vast new resources, and it held out the promise that everyone could be rich. In the capitalist countries of the West, rapid population growth in the nineteenth century was accompanied by even more rapid growth in income, which is an astonishing achievement. The number and variety of goods that people could buy grew as did the passion for possessions, making demand a motor of economic growth and of an outlook called materialism. (Materialism in this form differs appreciably from Marxian dialectical materialism, discussed in Chapter 4.)

Capitalism also delivered some troubling problems, however, and Karl Marx focused on these. In the nineteenth century, as the previous chapter explains, capitalism offered a new rationale for acquiring colonies: They could be exploited for minerals as well as crops. Applied in European colonies in Africa and Asia, capitalism made the colonizing nations richer but did not seem to offer a way to lift the colonized peoples up from poverty. Thus it fostered the rise of an uneven distribution of wealth and income, a world in which a few countries were rich but most remained poor.

Empowered by trade, capitalism rewarded entrepreneurs who found ways to move goods across national boundaries and by sea. In its earlier stage, trade was largely bilateral, linking colonial powers to their colonies, and regional, linking the industrial powers to one another. By the 1870s, however, the foundations of globalization had been laid; the largely bilateral and regional movement of goods was growing into a multilateral movement of goods and labor on an unprecedented scale. An interdependent global economy was abuilding. Capitalism gave rise to firms larger in their annual turnover, or even just their annual profits, than many countries. Such firms not only displaced small enterprises but also became rivals to countries in the power they exercised and the number of people dependent on them. They acted in the interest of their owners rather than that of their employees, compatriots, or human society. One of the great ironies of modern history consists of the simultaneous development of popular sovereignty in political life and corporate sovereignty in economic life. By 1900 it was difficult to say whether any leaders or institutions were in charge of the global economic system or it was instead controlled by market forces and the collective power of all that manufacturers could supply and all that consumers could demand.

Capitalist economies seemed, based on their performance in the nineteenth century, to be prey to boom-and-bust cycles rather than engines of continuous growth. Each boom carried production to new highs but after a few years was followed by a bust of unemployment and declining demand. Capitalism seemed to be a kind of manic economic system, alternating between highs and lows.

Those were the overt problems associated with capitalism. There was also a covert problem, one linked to materialism, which can be seen as the economic side of modernization. Economic modernization produced prosperity, at least for many people, and it helped to differentiate the modern from the traditional. Modern societies possessed great capitalist structures, such as big business, railroads, and steamships, which traditional societies lacked. But to many people, materialism—the attachment of value to material comforts and to their acquisition—seemed to conflict with spiritual and philosophic values. On the side of piety, materialism threatened the human soul with debasement. On the side of ideas, materialism elevated base values over the human spirit. What human qualities did people retain when they defined themselves by their possessions? These problems troubled observers, who subjected capitalism to ongoing scrutiny.

Whether capitalism would in the long run prove a satisfactory economic system, one able to overcome its problems, remained unclear up to World War II and beyond. Karl Marx described a socialist alternative, promising to make growth occur without capitalism's boom-bust cycles or its spiritual degradation. And, in the 1920s, another alternative, fascism, gained a following, promising efficiency and central direction rather than free markets guided by an invisible hand. The global Great Depression of the 1930s challenged capitalism and people's confidence in it as a system. Slowed by World War I, trade and globalization staggered under the weight of the depression. People began to think of their countries as best off when they were independent, rather than interdependent, economic actors. At the outbreak of World War II it was not apparent which of these three systems—capitalism, Marxism, or fascism—worked best, or whether one of them might ultimately dominate the others.

Economic Growth in Europe and North America

Adam Smith, after a comparative study of the wealth of nations, identified the division of labor as a key to economic growth. By specializing in the tasks they performed, pin makers could produce many more pins, for example. The productivity of labor increased, and its increase amounted to an earned income. Unlike a natural gas or oil discovery, productivity gains were not a gift. When countries specialized in certain economic tasks, selecting ones at which they had a comparative advantage, whole nations could add to their productivity by using existing resources. Smith exposed a way to augment the size of the economic pie, whereas the mercantilist thinkers before him had focused on ways to redistribute existing wealth. He also described a system under which the division of labor and the gains in productivity that it allowed could best be organized. That system came to be called capitalism.

The application of new technologies to the manufacture of cotton clothing in Britain and Belgium in the period 1780–1830 first tested Smith's ideas. Using labor-saving equipment and applying the division of labor in a factory system, manufacturers showed that new wealth could be created. The price of cotton clothing plunged, delivering more goods to consumers at cheaper prices and more profits to cloth makers.

In the mid-nineteenth century, heavy industry, which produced rails and rolling stock for railroads, ships, industrial engines, tools, metal parts, and other large and expensive equipment, displaced textiles as the centerpiece of manufacturing. Britain and Belgium made the transition from light to heavy industry; Germany, the United States, France, and a few other countries built heavy industry sectors. Throughout this period manufacturing drove economic growth; the nineteenth century was the great age of industrial capitalism.

The advent of ways to manufacture steel at prices competitive with the most widely used existing metal, iron, led the development of heavy industry after 1850. Harder, more durable, and less

PICTURE 3.1 Panama Canal. Opened in 1914, the canal made available a direct route between the Pacific and Atlantic Oceans. (Reprinted from Joseph Bucklin Bishop, *The Panama Gateway* [New York: Charles Scribner's, 1915])

brittle than iron, steel had been used chiefly for small but expensive items, such as watch springs. Henry Bessemer's 1856 introduction of a new process that allowed steel to be fabricated in large quantities directly from molten iron made steel into a commercial metal. Later innovations further improved its quality. Steel replaced wood in ships, it replaced iron in rails and steam engines, and in the form of girders it made possible the construction of tall buildings. Industrial capitalism took many forms, none more important than transportation improvements. Rail systems quickly reduced the time and cost involved in travel and the shipment of goods overland; steel ships powered by steam turbines accomplished the same thing at sea. Rail transport was much more efficient than horse-drawn carriages, the principal existing means of moving goods, and it was more flexible than canals, which many western countries had built in the eighteenth century to provide cheap inland water transport. Europe's rail system grew from not quite 4,000 kilometers in 1840 to 92,000 in 1870 and 285,000 in 1914. Britain led in the first phase; after 1870 every country in western and central Europe built new lines at a rapid pace. The new system also reduced travel time. In 1800 a fast ship required about thirty days, with good winds, to cross the Atlantic. By 1900 people and goods made that transit in a week, and information, carried by undersea telegraph cable, made it almost instantaneously. Travel between London and Calcutta took five months in the 1700s, but by 1914 only two weeks.

Technologically more sophisticated, industrial equipment demanded greater expertise in engineering and chemistry in place of the artisanal skills that stood behind earlier inventions and handicraft production. Thus the second half of the nineteenth century saw a closer alliance form between science and industry, an alliance that produced industrial chemicals, synthetic fibers, explosives, chemical fertilizers, rubber tires, and many other goods and services. The impact of technology on daily life expanded relentlessly.

Industrial modernization also drove down the price of consumer goods, letting people buy more. In the old artisanal system a single skilled person or a small team of people had made a carriage, a coat, a carafe, or a cabinet. Labor intensive, artisanal products were costly, and their cost limited the scale of goods that could be consumed. The rich owned far more of these products than did the poor, and there was not yet much of a class of middling consumers. The reorganization of production in factories, where workers specialized in performing a few tasks under the supervision of managers and used mechanical equipment, vastly augmented how much a worker could produce. Coal and, later, oil, rather than humans, animals, or running water, tirelessly powered the machinery. Manufacturers also learned how to extract investment capital from complete strangers, who lent money in return for bonds or who bought stocks. Thus arose a new market, not the ones where people bought goods or workers sold their labor, but one where people with savings to invest selected stocks and bonds to buy.

By the end of the nineteenth century most people living in the West owned wardrobes rather than a few items of apparel; they bought tableware, furnishings, decorative objects, and many other consumer goods on a rising scale. Bon Marché in Paris transformed itself into a department store in the 1860s, catering to the popular demand for light industrial goods. In the 1920s Henry Ford insisted that his factories make a car that his workers could buy. The agricultural revolution, led by artificial fertilizers and mechanized implements, drove down the share of a family's income spent on food. By the eve of World War I, westerners spent smaller sums and smaller shares of their income for more food, more industrial goods, and a greater variety of consumer goods than they or their ancestors had ever known. They could afford insurance, education, leisure and recreation, medical and dental services, and many other new things.

In some ways capitalism also empowered people, just as it empowered the new economic and political actors called firms. As consumers expressing individual tastes and demands, people could do more to influence economic systems than they had been able to do earlier, when they produced most of the goods they consumed but lacked the skills and resources to make richly varied goods. This new power resembled the kind of political influence that individuals gained when they could vote in democratic systems, compared to the monarchies and empires that these systems replaced. In the West the idea that the individual is an important actor who should be expected to express opinions or tastes dated to Renaissance humanism. Industrial capitalism and parliamentary or presidential systems added substance to this notion. By 1914 and the eve of the Great War an adult living in the West could define freedom not just as the right to help select political leaders or to express opinions about contentious issues, but also as the right to choose an occupation, to select from a variety of goods and services, and to enjoy the fruits of individual enterprise. Housing had not improved much as yet, nor was the West free from poverty, environmental degradation, or disease and early death. But capitalism had created both a middle class and a labor aristocracy, a prosperous group of well-paid, skilled workers. For those people housing had improved, the specter of poverty had receded, and material life was improving.

Adam Smith admired the eighteenth-century American colonies because they had evolved an economic system that benefited workers and owners alike, paying high wages and delivering high profits. The cotton textile factories of the early nineteenth century did not pay high wages. Making labor a commodity, they took advantage of population growth and urbanization, which augmented the supply of workers, to squeeze workers' wages. The result, partly an effect of the industrial revolution and partly an effect of cities growing more rapidly than housing or public services, was a threat to the standard of living of working people. By the 1840s the owners of manufacturing plants seemed to be making big profits, but their workers earned wages too modest to allow them even to maintain their standard of living. In those years industrial capitalism delivered greater productivity but it also encouraged an uneven distribution of the rewards of that productivity within the countries that industrialized.

From the mid-nineteenth century to World War I both capitalists and workers gained in Western countries. Marx's critique of capitalism, which had important weight in the mid-nineteenth century, lost authority. Rather than being impoverished, as Marx had predicted, many workers could afford better housing, a selection of foods more to their taste, clothing and household furnishings, even leisure. By the end of the nineteenth century, Marxist theorists, including Lenin, worried that workers earning higher wages were being co-opted, as indeed they were. Rather than being the vanguard of revolution, the labor aristocracy might be the vanguard of the petty bourgeoisie.

The Social Revolution of Capitalism

In Europe's old regime, which collapsed during the French Revolution, people had carried a legal identity; they were commoners, bourgeois, or nobles. Historians usually describe these stations as markers of status rather than of class. Whereas on average nobles were wealthier than bourgeois, and bourgeois than commoners, income and wealth did not define status. Status was inherited at birth, though it could also be purchased. Industrial capitalism and the rising importance of consumer goods in the spectrum of things that people valued made income more important than it had been and gave rise to people who possessed more wealth than status. Moreover, the institutions of capitalism and consumerism differentiated people by their occupations rather than by their status. Bourgeois rights—special rights in the city—ceased to have much importance even as a social class called the bourgeoisie arose. The nobility remained, but the French novelist who took the pen name Stendhal accurately captured its new position in the novel *The Red and the Black* (1831). Nobles still excelled in vanity and pomposity, but they were mere figureheads. In their place appeared an elite composed of people who made money from capitalism and consumerism, sometimes on such a vast scale that the wealth of nobles shrank into insignificance. Critics called these people plutocrats or nouveau riche, implying that they lacked refinement. Admirers called them capitalists or entrepreneurs, implying that they knew how to drive the engines of economic growth.

Some capitalists acquired fortunes on a scale that surpassed the wealth of princes or even kings, acting in the process with all the imperiousness of kings. Some of them mimicked kings also by endowing charitable foundations and founding universities. John D. Rockefeller and Henry Ford created foundations with resources greater than those available to governments in small and poor countries; Andrew Carnegie built libraries around the globe; James B. Duke endowed a university. Some capitalists built business firms of unprecedented size, so big and powerful that they easily swept small competitors aside. These families occupied the top of a new social hierarchy; they constituted a new aristocracy in which the inheritance of wealth conveyed status. Whereas the nobility had earned distinction by virtue of serving in the military or in administrative and judicial offices, the new elite earned distinction by virtue of its business acumen, the measures of which were profits and wealth.

Three other classes—the bourgeoisie, the working class, and the poor—filled out the other stations of nineteenth-century Western society. The bourgeoisie, defined now by trade or profession and income rather than by habitation in towns, occupied the middle ground. At the beginning of the nineteenth century this class made up only a small share of society; over the course of the century it grew irrepressibly. By 1900 the middle class was the largest of all the classes. In the discussion above, the working class was divided into labor aristocrats, skilled workers whose incomes matched those of the petty bourgeoisie, and others, who have not yet been characterized. They were semi- and unskilled workers, people who had jobs but whose earnings were meager. Then there were the poor. They, too, can be divided into two groups. The working poor held jobs that were irregular; for them periods of unemployment alternated with periods of employment. And the poor, with no modifier, were people who seldom worked. They included orphaned children, women out of luck, and older people, often in ill health, and they made up a sizable share of the populace in capitalist countries. These classes were more fluid than the categories of the old status system had been. People moved up and down the class hierarchy. Although many more moved up than down in the decades before the Great War, the poor, the working poor, and the poorly paid, unskilled workers all remained numerous.

In the old regime social philosophers took the view that people with high status deserved it; their ancestors or they themselves had earned it. In the class system emerging in the nineteenth century, however, there was much sharper criticism of one class by another. Poorer classes might submissively accept the higher status and income of plutocrats and bourgeois, but they denied these classes any claim to privilege, meaning the special legal rights that had added real value to status in old-regime Europe. Workers organized labor unions to define their interests against those of their employers, labor parties to advance their own political goals, and cooperatives to gain greater control over how goods and services were priced. Similarly, elite classes defined working people and the poor by their otherness: Poor because they lacked industriousness, they deserved their class standing. Elites, too, organized in the economic and political spheres; they formed chambers of commerce and associations of manufacturers and their own political parties. The class system aggravated social antagonism. For Marx, whose adult life was lived across the period from 1840 to 1883, class strife—its existence and his anticipation of it—seemed to be an overriding characteristic of the modern age.

Materialism as a Challenge to Traditional Values

Capitalism promoted an economy and society in which the popular demand for goods and services could keep pace with growing output and an expansive variety of products. Consider the kitchen as one locus of these changes. It evolved from an open fire or a fireplace, a few iron implements, a table, and some stools or chairs into the most elaborately appointed room in a bourgeois house. By 1900 the kitchen included a sink, an icebox, probably a machine for washing clothes, a wood or coal cooking stove, pots and pans specific to the varied tasks of frying, boiling, and roasting, and still the table and chairs. By 1950 or 1960 a refrigerator had replaced the icebox, an electric stove supplanted the old cooking stove, and a toaster and an electrical coffeemaker had been added. In the meantime the business of washing clothes had been relocated to a separate room, the hand-driven washer had been replaced by an electrical washing machine, and an electrical dryer had been added. Each new device, advertised aggressively in magazines and on

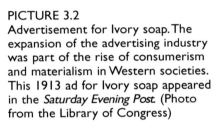

PICTURE 3.2
Advertisement for Ivory soap. The expansion of the advertising industry was part of the rise of consumerism and materialism in Western societies. This 1913 ad for Ivory soap appeared in the *Saturday Evening Post*. (Photo from the Library of Congress)

the radio, excited public interest and a desire to possess it. Much of this passion for new possessions was driven by the quickly growing ease of life assisted by these machines. Washing clothes, an all-day chore, had meant heating water in a large iron tub, washing by hand with the aid of a scrub board using harsh soaps, and hanging the clothes out to dry. Wealthy people engaged servants to perform such jobs. Each innovation in washing technology simplified and shortened the job, transforming it, by 1950, into a matter of collecting the clothes to be washed and tossing them into a machine that let its operator calibrate water level and temperature and vary the action of an electrically powered agitator according to how soiled the clothes were. Then the wet clothes could be transferred to an electrical dryer. In the meantime new fabrics reduced the requirement to press clothing to take out the wrinkles introduced by wearing, washing, and drying. Machines and implements that shortened ordinary tasks added leisure time and made life easier. How would people use the time and energy saved in this way?

Many observers feared that the rising importance of consumer goods threatened to create a new spiritual system, called consumerism or materialism, which might challenge religion or even ethics. Consumers were not just people who valued material possessions or understood the world in terms of its material elements, but also people who elevated the acquisition of possessions and conveniences to a rank that displaced the spiritual ideas and values that had been the centerpiece of traditional life. They were people who measured their worth by the inventory of their possessions. Thus consumerism threatened the things that had lent value to human existence. Capitalism and consumerism seemed capable of degrading life to the level of pointlessness. It was intellectuals, rather than the person in the street, who fretted over these matters. Sec-

TABLE 3.1   Estimates of World Population and GDP Per Capita

	1500	*1820*	*1992*
World Population	425 million	1,068 million	5,441 million
GDP per capita (1990 US $)	565	651	5,145

Source: Angus Maddison, *Monitoring the World Economy, 1820-1992* (Paris, Development Centre of the Organisation for Economic Co-operation and Development, 1995), p. 19.

ular thinkers, especially Jean Paul Sartre and Albert Camus, searched for alternative philosophies in the years immediately after World War II. John Kenneth Galbraith, an unconventional economist, made consumer society the object of witty scorn in *The Affluent Society* (1958), where he argued that the U.S. economy should provide better public services. But in everyday life, people accommodated to the secularism of capitalism and consumerism without profound misgivings. They left the spiritual implications of consumerism an unresolved question, for the time being.

The Scale of Growth

The singular characteristic of the nineteenth century differentiating it from earlier periods is economic growth. One way to measure economic activity is to assess the gross domestic product (GDP) per person, arrived at by summing the value of goods and services produced within a country and dividing that sum by the population. Historically, regional economies and the overall global economy had grown at minuscule rates or not at all: One estimate puts the range of growth between 1500 and 1820 at somewhere between 0 and 0.2 percent per year. That figure changed in the nineteenth century, and the change continued through the twentieth century. Table 3.1 shows the best available estimates of per capita GDP in three years representing different time periods.

If growth is the overriding characteristic of those seventy-five years, from 1870 to 1945, it was not evenly distributed among countries. Figures 3.1, 3.2, and 3.3 plot the level of GDP per capita in 1870, 1913, and 1950 in all countries for which reliable estimates are available: 30 countries in 1870, 47 in 1913, and 56 in 1950. The figures show that most of the growth occurred in only a few of the roughly 200 countries in existence by the end of the twentieth century. To an overwhelming degree the countries that do not appear in these figures were poor. A rough idea of how poor they were can be gotten by looking at the lowest points in the diagram at each date and enlarging the number of those points to represent the missing countries.

Australia was the richest land in 1870 and still in 1913, measured by GDP per capita. By 1950 the United States had taken the lead, a position it kept for most of the remainder of the century. Assuming that per capita GDP in the poorest country in 1870 was about $300 (1990 U.S. dollars) gives a rough idea of how much the disparity between rich and poor countries increased. In 1870 per capita GDP in Australia was about 13 times greater than what it was in the hypothetical poorest country, in constant values. By 1913 the poorest country still ranked around $300 and the richest country at 18 times more. By 1950 the disparity was nearly 32:1, and by 1992 nearly

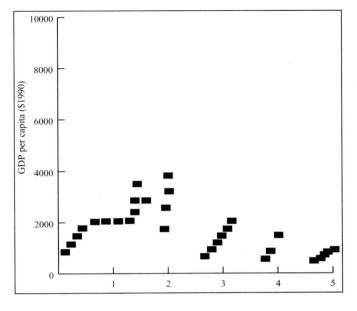

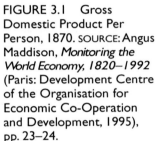

FIGURE 3.1   Gross Domestic Product Per Person, 1870. SOURCE: Angus Maddison, *Monitoring the World Economy, 1820–1992* (Paris: Development Centre of the Organisation for Economic Co-Operation and Development, 1995), pp. 23–24.

Key For Figures 3.1, 3.2, 3.3
Countries in:
1. Western Europe
2. Australia, New Zealand, the U.S., and Canada
3. Southern and Eastern Europe
4. Latin America
5. Asia
6. Africa

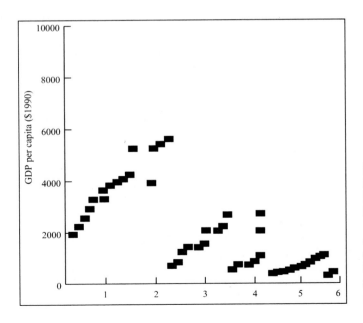

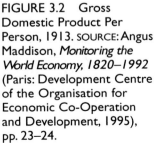

FIGURE 3.2   Gross Domestic Product Per Person, 1913. SOURCE: Angus Maddison, *Monitoring the World Economy, 1820–1992* (Paris: Development Centre of the Organisation for Economic Co-Operation and Development, 1995), pp. 23–24.

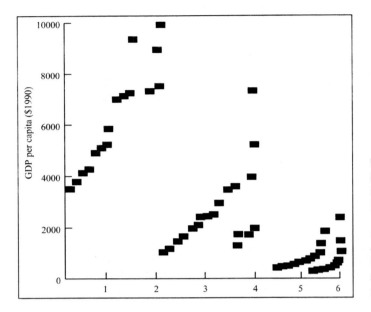

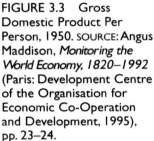

FIGURE 3.3   Gross Domestic Product Per Person, 1950. SOURCE: Angus Maddison, *Monitoring the World Economy, 1820–1992* (Paris: Development Centre of the Organisation for Economic Co-Operation and Development, 1995), pp. 23–24.

72:1. The rich countries had found a path not just to higher levels of income but to ongoing gains in income, a process called development.

The United States enjoyed nearly singular success at development in the period 1870–1945. In 1850 the U.S. economy was perhaps the sixth largest in the world, after China, India, Russia, Britain, and France. By 1870 it was the third largest, by 1890 the second, and before the end of the 1890s the largest in the world.

Trade and manufacturing drove economic growth and the differentiation of rich from poor countries. A symbolic innovation occurred in 1854, when ships of the U.S. Navy obliged Japan to open itself to trade. Within fifteen years Japan's foreign trade rose from nil to 7 percent of national income. Many countries had long participated in international trade, but the scale had remained modest. One estimate for 1820 puts the total value of global exports at $7 billion (in 1990 U.S. dollars), or around $6.50 per person in the world population. That amounted to less than 1 percent of the 1992 value of world exports per person. Trade resembled a snowball rolling downhill in the way it persistently gained size as time passed. Adam Smith had argued that countries should pursue their comparative advantage, meaning that countries should specialize in producing the goods and services for which their resources were best suited and from which they could earn the most. Trade on this growing scale made it plausible to adopt comparative advantage as a policy and a practice because it assured participating countries that they could afford to specialize. They could expect to sell the goods and services in which they held a comparative advantage, and they could expect to buy goods they did not produce from other countries. Trade therefore made economic activity more efficient and more productive. It also tied each individual country into a global network of trade relations, making the market a judge of which economic activities best suited a country. Thus a few countries—Canada, the United States, Argentina, and Australia—became the leading producers of wheat, which most countries had formerly tried to produce. Those four countries could grow and export wheat, corn, and other grains on favorable terms. The grain farmers of other countries had to find

PICTURE 3.3 View of Chicago. By 1900, the U.S. economy was the largest in the world. This photo looks west on South Water Street. (Photo from the National Archives)

new crops or give up farming. That story of adjustment to the effects of trade and of countries pursuing their comparative advantage lent drama to this era of economic growth because it demanded constant human adaptation. It also signaled one of the negative effects of trade's growth: Countries that entered the global trade network would not be able to withdraw without paying the penalty of having to give up goods and services they had become accustomed to getting through trade. Withdrawal from the network would mean an immediate and vast loss in income.

Marx and the Rise of Socialism

Karl Marx criticized capitalism on grounds that, even though it built wealth, it favored the people owning the means of production: factories, mines, land and farms, ships, railroads, and the like. Those people—capitalists in the sense of being plutocrats—would gain an ever larger share of wealth, Marx believed, because they were in a position to pay their workers low wages. Capitalism as a system therefore violated Marx's basic idea, which was that labor rather than ownership gives value to products and services. Hence labor should earn the decisive share of the sales price of the goods and services it produces. Whereas Smith, taking an optimistic view, insisted that free markets would guide owners and workers alike toward greater productivity, Marx, taking a less optimistic view, believed that free markets would tilt the outcome in favor of owners. To counter that outcome he proposed to control markets and prices in the service of social justice. Under such a system the state would take care that people had a minimum supply of life's necessities, education, and health care.

Operating on its own, capitalism would produce undesirable consequences. Socialism, said Marx, could cure these ills. Marx opted for public rather than private ownership of the means of production, giving the public sector—really the government—the power to set prices, wages, and production targets. Marx also argued that capitalism contained the seeds of its own destruction. More successful capitalists would drive less successful capitalists out of business and into the class of workers, the proletariat. Ultimately the class of workers would become so large that it could topple the capitalists and introduce socialism. Thus Marx's ideas included a reading of the past and the future, a concept called "metahistory." By understanding the past—Marx was a lifelong reader of history—one could deconstruct the present and anticipate the future. Marx expected socialism to emerge first in the most advanced capitalist states.

The first socialist state came instead in a backward economy, Russia. Seizing control of the political apparatus in October 1917 gave Lenin and his associates an opportunity to put their interpretation of Marx's ideas into practice. The most important modification they made was to apply Marx's ideas to what was predominantly an agrarian rather than an industrial country. Indeed Marxian socialism would repeatedly appear in agrarian rather than industrial countries: Russia, China, Vietnam, Cuba, Tanzania, Nicaragua, Ethiopia, and others. Lenin nevertheless agreed with Marx's reading of history, seeing capitalism as a stage in historical development leading toward socialism. In the Soviet Union, however, he opted to begin building socialism at once rather than trying first to complete the development of capitalism. Thus Lenin seized the means of production from the owners of Russia's factories, mines, lands, transportation facilities, and the like, put them under the direction of a command economy, and set out to compress the historical process.

How successful was socialism in building wealth and enhancing development? Like Smith, Marx, along with Lenin, Mao, and their counterparts, aimed to build the productive assets of the economy. Stalin, Lenin's successor in the USSR, decided to do that by squeezing the Soviet Union's vast agricultural resources to acquire the investment capital necessary to build heavy industry and transportation. Mao made the same decision, although he opted for limited rather than unbounded growth. Lenin expected the Soviet Union to match and eventually surpass capitalist countries in wealth and income. Mao, who valued a spiritual over a material transformation, was content with the idea of making China modestly rich.

In the years between the two world wars the Soviet economy experienced rapid development. The Soviet Union doubled its GDP between 1917 and 1950, from the prewar level of $1,500 to about $2,800 per person (in 1990 U.S. dollars). In a space of about a generation, the Soviets transformed an agrarian economy into an industrial powerhouse. They elevated literacy from 30 percent in 1919 to 87 percent in 1939. And they raised life expectancy to a level close to that of Western Europe. In the late 1940s and the 1950s, anyone casting about for a model economic system had to consider Soviet-style Marxism quite seriously.

Material Life in Latin America, Asia, and Africa

By any measure, Europe and the neo-Europes—the United States, Canada, Australia, and New Zealand—outpaced the rest of the world in economic growth in the period 1870–1945. Other countries mimicked Britain and Belgium, beginning with Germany and the United States. They showed that the puzzle of how to initiate national economic growth could be solved. In theory, every country could become rich. In practice, however, only a few countries outside Europe and North America did.

The difference between rich and poor countries is often overstated, because informal economic activity—growing your own food, trading goods and services via barter, and engaging in illegal endeavors—mostly escapes detection. In official values, the household in which a woman earns a wage seems to be much richer than the household in which women and children work for the household without earning wages, even though the possessions of the two households may be nearly identical. This phenomenon shows up on a grand scale in estimates of national income when wage-based economies are compared with economies where people do not earn wages, though their needs may be met in other ways. People in poor countries must have earned incomes that allowed them to live, since live they did. Thus poor countries are never quite as poor as the official values suggest.

Nevertheless, the development of market economies in Western countries made it possible for those countries to add to per capita income in impressive ways, not just to preserve the existing standard of living. Between 1850 and 1914 the economies of North America and Europe grew at a rate of about 2 percent per annum. Both the sustained nature of that growth and its scale departed from prior experience.

Economic growth has no fixed definition. Some scholars have taken it to mean chiefly a rise of industrial activity, such as characterized the industrial revolutions in Britain and Belgium. In that definition the concentration of people in urban markets and the rise of production outside the home are key elements. Others define growth more broadly, to mean a rise in output per capita, even if the additional output came from agriculture and trade. In both approaches the key evidence is rising income per capita. By the first definition, economic growth had not yet begun in many countries in Asia, Africa, and Latin America as of 1945. By the second definition, however, growth began in most countries of the world during the nineteenth century. Countries grew more food or mined more minerals per person, and they also exported more. The period 1870–1914 was the first era of globalization, not just an era of renewed colonialism. World trade grew by about 3.5 percent a year, which is a very swift pace of change for anything as vast in scale as trade. Regions that began the period with a chiefly internal trade, such as the Middle East, began to exchange goods on a rising scale with outsiders, especially Europe. Unfortunately, it is not clear that these types of growth benefited people living in poor countries. This thought leads to a description of colonialism and globalization as forms of exploitation by the dominant colonial and economic powers, especially Britain. Some scholars explain the economic growth of the West chiefly as a product of such exploitation.

Although there were many regional differences, there was a certain pattern to economic change in the period 1850–1914. The leading industrial powers, whose factories required enormous supplies of raw materials, pushed the development of mineral and agricultural commodities in Africa, Asia, the Middle East, and Latin America. They demanded copper, tin, rubber, cotton, indigo, palm oil, and many other goods. Popular demand for tropical foods, especially sugar,

PICTURE 3.4   Trading Company Building, Central Africa, c. 1930. European trading companies opened offices in African commercial centers to deal in the import-export business and promote a new consumer culture. The photo was taken in Brazzaville, the capital of French Equatorial Africa, in about 1930. (Photo courtesy of the Roger Frey collection)

tea, coffee, and cocoa, also grew. Much of the rest of the world began to produce primary goods—minerals and agricultural products—for the industries and households of Western Europe and North America. Cotton textiles give a telling example of the effect of Western industrial modernization. India, a British colony, exported cotton fabric to Britain in the eighteenth century. But in the nineteenth century, industrial Britain made India its leading market for cotton textile exports, even though Britain had to import all the raw cotton it used to produce those exports. Undercut by cheap fabrics made in Britain, many people working in the Indian cottage industry that had produced cotton textiles were forced into agriculture. The development of Indian manufacturing was temporarily stymied.

Meanwhile, transport costs plunged. The steam engine reduced shipping time and, together with other innovations, ultimately cut shipping costs by up to 95 percent. Between 1870 and 1910 oceanic freight rates dropped by about 50 percent. The introduction of refrigeration in the 1880s made it possible to add beef and other perishable food items to the list of goods regularly carried on ships engaged in transoceanic trade. Canals, railroads, and, after 1900, motor vehicles helped reduce transport costs still further. Tariffs on imports and exports remained low; it was, comparatively speaking, a period of free trade.

Western powers exported capital and technology to other regions of the world to promote the production of primary goods. They colonized Africa and parts of Asia, taking control of decisionmaking in those economies. As the earlier chapter on imperialism shows, Western capital built mines and railroads in developing countries, cleared land for plantation agriculture, and moved people from here to there to work in the new enterprises. It was in this period that British sugar growers brought Indian laborers to Fiji to grow and cut sugar cane and the United States imported Chinese workers to build railroads. The ways in which economies of developing regions began to grow in this period can be illustrated with three examples: Argentina, Sri Lanka, and South Korea.

Those years make up most of Argentina's golden age. The country exported wool, wheat, corn, and refrigerated beef to Europe. Even though millions of immigrants settled in Argentina, output per person rose at a yearly average of 1.5 percent or better. Indeed, it rose faster in those years than at any time since. After 1929 Argentina's growth decelerated gradually. Juan Perón and his Perónist successors, who gained power in 1946, controlled prices on food, which helped working people but undermined incentives for farmers. Agricultural output declined, and Argentina ceased to be a breadbasket of northwestern Europe. Since Argentina proclaimed its independence from Spain in 1815, it cannot be called a colony. But since most Argentine exports went to Britain, increasingly on terms set by the British, it also cannot be called an independent economy. Cheap imports from Argentina helped the British keep food prices low, which benefited the British economy and its working people. Brazil, Chile, Colombia, Cuba, Mexico, and Peru also showed signs of growth during the decades before World War I, although not as powerfully as Argentina.

Britain seized the colony of Ceylon, now Sri Lanka, from the Dutch in 1796. While it was still a colony Sri Lanka exported tea, rubber, and coconuts. By the 1880s, per capita incomes were rising, and they continued to do so up to World War II. Tamils, laborers brought in from India, worked the plantations. British colonizers owned most of the land producing these crops, exported most of what was produced, and took the profits for themselves. Some Sinhalese became estate owners and cultivated these export crops, but most remained subsistence rice farmers. Sri Lanka experienced economic growth, but the British seized much of the benefit of this growth.

Japan claimed a powerful influence in Korea after its defeat of rival Russia in 1905. Japanese control inaugurated the first of two periods of rapid growth in South Korea, the other beginning in the 1950s. Between 1910 and 1940 rice output doubled, Japanese manufacturing firms aggressively set up subsidiaries in Korea, and industrial output rose. Per capita income rose by 1.5 to 2 percent a year, but Japan expropriated most of the higher income.

Across much of Africa, Asia, Latin America, and the Middle East, the period 1870–1914 saw an initiation of sustained economic growth at impressive rates. Adam Smith's ideas suggest that a larger engagement in trade will help economies grow. By itself, however, trade could not do enough to stimulate growth. Even though they required vastly larger quantities of tropical goods, the industrial powers could not import enough to carry developing economies into sustained growth. Those economies needed to build their own capacity to produce finished goods and services. On the surface many countries in those regions seem to have been developing. But as the examples of Argentina, Ceylon, and Korea illustrate, globalization and colonialism benefited the powerhouses of Europe and North America more than the developing countries. In particular, it had little good effect on the well-being of ordinary people living in those regions. Some people in the local economies found ways to share in growth. Thus one can speak of economic growth not just in terms of the mines, fields, ports, and transport networks created in this period in developing regions, but also in terms of strong gains in national income. But the key fact is that domestic output did not expand very quickly. Most people remained poor even as they were drawn into a global system of production, trade, and consumption. At the end of the colonial era, between 1947 and 1965, these countries would be thrown into competition with one another because, too often, they produced the same goods. In the meantime they had developed exports but not their own shipping or other commercial services; they had grown more crops and extracted more minerals, but they had not usually processed those into final products. Their economic growth was one-dimensional.

The brief history of Peru's guano industry explains how this could happen. Bird droppings—guano—that had collected over the years could be mined on islands off the Peruvian coast by simple gathering methods. European farmers wanted guano to fertilize their fields. Guano exports began in the 1840s. The business required no processing, an unskilled labor force, and little capital. Most of the benefits from exporting guano went to shippers, who were mainly European, and to European farmers and consumers. Some gains went into the public purse as taxes, but they were not spent in ways that generated Peruvian development. By the 1870s the guano deposits had been exhausted. Peru's guano industry rose and fell without contributing to the economic development of the country.

There are other reasons, too, why trade failed to draw the economies of Africa, Asia, Latin America, and the Middle East into development. Countries in those regions entered the period with little or nothing in the way of a middle class, and they did not find a way to build one. Thus, the broad demand by consumers for local products, a factor that had played such a strong role in the economic development of Western Europe and North America, did not emerge. Poor countries eagerly borrowed European capital, spending much of it on building ports, railroads, and public buildings. But those investments did not earn enough to service and repay the loans, leaving these countries saddled with debts they could not repay. In colonies and in independent countries, most of the foreign capital had been spent on physical improvements rather than on training or education; most people found themselves in 1945 no more prepared as modern economic actors than their great grandparents had been in 1870.

Another factor that contributed to continuing poverty in Africa, Asia, Latin America, and the Middle East was the unequal division of wealth within those regions. The top 20 percent of the population often claimed more than half of the household income, but the bottom 20 percent less than 5 percent. In the rich countries, too, wealth was skewed, but the disproportion was not as great. Some historians also argue that the choices that wealthy people make about spending and investment matter a great deal. Specifically, some Latin American historians argue not just that exports failed to promote growth but that families that benefited from globalization preferred European to local products. Those families also invested less and consumed more than counterparts elsewhere. Thus the argument about inequality has two elements. In one, the key factor is the existence of a large enough middling group of consumers to stimulate production within the country through demand for goods and services. In the other, the key factor is the failure of elites to use their wealth in ways that stimulate national economic growth.

Developing countries also suffered even more than the industrial countries of Europe and North America did from capitalism's boom-bust cycle. Periods in which strong demand for primary products led to rising prices and profits alternated with periods in which demand weakened and prices collapsed. The first major crisis came with World War I, which enhanced demand for some primary products, such as oil from Venezuela and Mexico, but curtailed demand for others, such as Brazilian coffee. The war also severed trade to Germany and diverted European capital from foreign investments into the war effort. In the Middle East the collapse of the Ottoman Empire during the war ended regional free trade, replacing it with separate trade policies in each of the successor states. After the war, deflation made foreign debts grow to unsupportable levels.

PICTURE 3.5
Migrant worker in the Great Depression. The human costs are shown in this striking photo from 1936 of a destitute mother of seven children who had been a pea picker in California. (Photo courtesy of the Franklin D. Roosevelt Library, Great Depression and New Deal Digital Collection)

The demand for primary products rose more sluggishly in the 1920s as population growth in Europe lagged and synthetic substitutes competed with timber, rubber, and cotton. Also important, exporters of primary products found themselves caught in a trap called Engel's law (named after Ernst Engel, a German economist). As incomes rise, the share of household incomes spent on many primary products, especially food, declines. Thus demand for primary products did not keep pace with rising incomes in the world's rich countries.

The Great Depression struck export-led economies with force, to the point that the 1930s can be described as an era of deglobalization. On the eve of depression the same limited range of products still dominated exports from developing countries, and the same four countries—the United States, Great Britain, France, and Germany—still dominated the demand for these products. All prices fell as economies moved into depression, but the prices of primary products fell with particular force. By 1932 prices for Latin American exports had dropped to 36 percent of the 1928 level at the same time that the volume of exports declined. The dangers of participating in the world economy as an exporter of primary products had been demonstrated. But most of the countries and colonies of Africa, Asia, and Latin America participated in the world economy chiefly in this way and had little prospect of changing. They were poor, they were dependent in many ways on a few rich countries, and they had to that point followed economic strategies that kept them poor. It comes therefore as no surprise that after World War II they tried to find new strategies.

Refined sugar is a good example of a product that the West could produce for itself only with difficulty. But it could be grown in tropical colonies in the West Indies, the Pacific Islands, and South

Africa and processed in Europe at prices low enough to let sugar become a popular item in Western diets. It is a good example of the cheap goods that the rich countries enjoyed at the expense of people in poor countries in two ways. Westerners paid but little for sugar, so little that even the Western poor could eat it. And the producing countries paid dearly, drawing meager returns for their work, which in sugar cultivation is especially arduous. How far can we generalize from sugar and similar products?

Certainly the West monopolized the ways that capitalism adds value to minerals and crops. It controlled processing, that is, the various ways by which raw materials are turned into the goods that people actually use. In the case of sugar the cane was grown in European colonies, where some of the initial steps toward processing were also taken. But the major sugar refineries of the world were to be found in the West. Thus the value added to sugar by processing went mostly there. The West also controlled the marketing of colonial goods in the colonies and elsewhere. Colonial products were carried in ships owned and staffed by Western capitalists and insured by the same group. Westerners owned wholesale and retail outlets. Prices fluctuated with supply and demand, but westerners had much greater power to set prices than did people in the colonies.

Nevertheless, there are some important weaknesses in the argument that the West grew rich chiefly by exploiting its colonies. The United States in the nineteenth and early twentieth centuries rose to primacy in income but owned few colonies and exploited few resources outside its own borders. If a country's colonies mattered most, Britain, France, and Belgium should have led the world in rate of growth. This example suggests that the exploitation theory is incomplete. Moreover, even among poor countries, growth histories differed sharply. Some countries remained poor decade after decade. Some became middle-income countries. And a few became rich lands. Escape from the status of national poverty was not impossible.

World Wars and a Challenge to Capitalism

Only a few major wars were fought in the period 1870–1945, but those few were fought ferociously and at unprecedented cost. The wars of 1914–1918 and 1939–1945 shocked people by the large number of countries participating, the huge scale of the armies, the heavy demands they made on civilians, and the degree to which they disrupted material life.

World War I, sometimes called the Great War, of 1914–1918, cost millions of deaths from conflict, famine, and disease. Belgium, northern France, and battle areas along the eastern front suffered the most damage; all the belligerents shared the effects of wartime curtailment of trade and the reorientation of industry to war. The motors of economic growth in the years 1870–1914 were therefore curtailed. In that, Britain suffered most. By the war's end its industrial exports amounted to about half the 1914 level. World trade was reorganized to the benefit of the United States and Japan, which expanded their exports and their shipping services. Britain, Germany, and France lost much of the value of their prewar foreign investments; the Soviet regime's repudiation of Tsarist Russia's debt, owed mostly to France, made up the largest loss.

Europe and North America emerged from World War I still dominant across the globe in economic and political power. They still led the world in manufacturing, and Europe still controlled vast colonial empires in Asia and Africa and now also the Middle East, where former territories of the Ottoman Empire became British and French colonies. But they held that lead through the 1920s and 1930s less because of the dynamism of their own economies than because of the brutal effects of deglobalization on Latin America, Africa, Asia, and the Middle East.

PICTURE 3.6   German bank note. A 500 million mark German bank note printed in 1923. (Photo from the Library of Congress)

World War I ended with a settlement that had vast economic consequences. The victorious allies decided to make Germany acknowledge responsibility for causing the war and to impose reparations, hoping to recoup some of their losses. Germany, devastated by the war, could hardly afford to pay, and in any case resisted. The hyperinflation of the German mark—which was exchanged at 4.2 marks to the dollar in 1914 but, at the peak of hyperinflation, in November 1923, at 4.2 trillion to the dollar—persuaded the allies that they could not collect reparations. In the meantime they, too, had fallen into recession. French output did not surpass 1913 levels until 1923, German and British until 1925. The Great Depression, which began in 1929, followed after only a few years of prosperity.

World War I also brought an end to the gold standard. National currencies had been pegged to gold, and that scheme had served to stabilize currencies and exchange rates. Going off the gold standard, which most countries did during the war because they feared the loss of gold reserves, meant that the international community had to find another system to promote stable relationships among currencies. Years passed before a system was found, and in the meantime monetary turmoil threatened to prevent prosperity's return. The war also exacerbated economic nationalism; countries competed to gain an advantage rather than cooperating to promote mutual development. They raised barriers against imports and became less interdependent on one another. These problems—war destruction, monetary turmoil, curtailed trade, economic nationalism, and reparations—threatened capitalism as an economic system. When the Great Depression began, people already had doubts about capitalism. Part of the appeal of fascism and socialism lay in their promises, from quite different directions, to fix what capitalism had sent astray.

Capitalism's cycles had become familiar by the 1920s. During periods of expansion, employment, investment, and prices rose, only to be followed in unpredictable rhythms by periods of contraction, in which employment, investment, and prices fell. In 1876, 1896, and again in 1929 severe contractions began across Europe and North America, and in 1929 across the entire world. Triggered but not caused by the stock market crash in October 1929, the Great Depression posed the most serious challenge that capitalism had yet faced. Sharply lower stock prices undercut investors who had bought stock on margin, using credit. Their inability to repay loans in turn squeezed lenders, leading to a contraction in investment. Production languished, but demand fell faster still. By 1933 prices in the United States had dropped by more than 35 percent from 1929 levels; in the Netherlands East Indies (Indonesia), they had fallen by more than half. So many people lost their jobs that demand continued to contract and the global economy learned just how much damage a collapse of demand could wreak.

Bank failures shook the financial community, but the most poignant symbols of the depression for this sector were the suicides—by investors who could not cope with suddenly losing their paper wealth. For the ordinary person, the depression had its most severe effects in unemployment and the loss of savings when banks failed. The proportion of people out of work rose to 25 percent and more. This depression taught the adults and young adults of the 1930s a painful lesson about the need to save, to avoid being in debt any more than necessary, and to fear capitalism's ability to turn against its adherents and beneficiaries.

Three economic schemes offered an alternative to traditional capitalism. Fascism promised to bring economic turmoil under control by forming close cooperation between government and large-scale business enterprises. Socialism and communism promised to eradicate the boom-bust cycle, guarantee full employment, and provide social justice. And Keynesianism, a set of ideas promoted by British economic theorist John Maynard Keynes and implemented by Franklin Roosevelt, proposed to modify capitalism by showing how to overcome busts and moderate booms. The result would be a system in which fiscal and monetary authorities, appointed by government, would regulate interest rates and the money supply in the service of prosperity. Liberal capitalism, which counted on free markets to regulate themselves, would give way to Keynesianism, or managed capitalism.

Of these three schemes, fascism seemed in the 1930s to carry the greatest appeal. Italy, Spain, and Germany, turning to fascism and dictatorship, recovered more rapidly from depression as fascism invigorated their national spirit. Japan's economic growth, and certainly its military prowess, seemed to grow apace as the cooperation among government, business, and the military developed. Observers in other countries were drawn to fascism's orderliness, its promise of managed economic growth, and its system of clear priorities, but they were put off by its police-state tactics and its glorification of war and force. Communism in the Soviet Union had looked far more promising before it collectivized agriculture in the late 1920s. Stalin's purges further dampened its appeal. And Keynes's ideas had not yet proved themselves. On the eve of World War II, capitalism seemed to be in deep trouble. Each system therefore presented strengths and weaknesses.

Fought over a much larger portion of European territory than World War I, with forces that were at once more mobile and more destructive, World War II cost still more lives. Somewhere between 42 million and 50 million people were killed, more of them civilians than soldiers. An even larger number of people suffered injuries and severe deprivation. By the war's end, many Germans, Poles, Russians, Dutch, and other people had so little to eat that they faced starvation. Hundreds of thousands of people had lost their homes in the German bombing of London and Stalingrad and the Allied bombing of German and Japanese cities. In Germany, about 40 percent, and in Britain, about 30 percent of the stock of dwellings had been destroyed. Factories and transport systems—roads, railroads, and canals—had been turned into rubble. The war created refugees on an unprecedented scale. Their very lack of status denied them the opportunity of earning a living. The warring societies exhausted themselves, squandering resources in pursuit of the war, and fell deeply into debt. It was at once a staggering display of the violence and mind-

PICTURE 3.7   Bomb Destruction, England, 1940. In World War II, the development of air power meant that "total war" profoundly touched civilians. (Photo courtesy of the Franklin D. Roosevelt Library, World War II Digital Collection)

lessness of which humankind is capable and a heroic struggle between democracy and autocracy, between capitalism/communism and fascism.

There were two victors and one loser. The victors represented communism and capitalism, and the loser fascism. The Soviet Union, which added territory and economic resources, emerged from the war as unquestionably the strongest military power in Europe and Asia. Within the next twenty years it was able to engage the leading global power, the United States, in building atomic and then nuclear weapons and in putting machines and people into space. In 1960 at the United Nations, the Soviet leader, Nikita Khrushchev, boasted that the Soviet Union would bury capitalism. The United States added influence rather than territory as a result of World War II and the reconstruction programs that it funded after the war. The United States also emerged as the unequivocal economic leader of the world. In 1945 the average American enjoyed a level of income nearly twice that of the nearest competitor: Americans were the richest people on the globe. This war remade the economic inequality of nations, which had been fashioned between 1870 and 1939, into a scheme with three tiers, one occupied by the United States alone, a second by the other rich countries of Europe plus Australia and New Zealand, and a third by all the poor countries.

Even so, World War II played a beneficent economic role in some ways. So much of the stock of housing and factories, transport facilities, and other capital goods was destroyed that all the belligerents except the United States had to rebuild. Japan and Germany made a good thing of rebuilding, more so than Britain or the Soviet Union, in that they used the rebuilding process to catch up with and surpass their rivals. By the 1960s Germany had pulled ahead of other countries in Europe and closed most of the gap separating its income levels from those of the United States, and by the 1980s Japan had done the same thing. Modern structures, equipment, machinery, and transport facilities, replacing those destroyed by the war, enhanced productivity.

Conclusion

World War II defeated fascism, but it did not resolve two other contests. Which economic system, capitalism or communism, would prove superior at promoting economic development? Which spiritual system, materialism or social justice, would win the most adherents? By 1945 the United States and the USSR had become the leading rivals in an epic struggle. During the Cold War era in the second half of the century, they battled not just over the countries and regions each could incorporate into its system of dependent allies, but also over global economic and spiritual authority.

The United States had shown that a free-market economy could make a country and most of its population rich, by global standards. The USSR had shown that a command economy could produce rapid industrialization, even amidst near isolation from the global economy and in the face of the German invasion in World War II. Unquestionably the United States led the economic side of this struggle. Even though the economy of the USSR had grown faster than the U.S. economy during the 1930s and would do so again in the 1950s, the United States remained far ahead.

On the spiritual side, this contest was never so fierce or so apparent. The West accommodated to materialism. In the United States, private giving counteracted many of the ill effects of capitalism. It was not just a matter of capitalists endowing charitable foundations and universities; it was also the generosity of ordinary people that made a difference. And in the remainder of the West, full-blown social democracies, created just after the war ended, used the public sector to redress the effects of capitalism, providing national systems of higher education, health care, and social security. The Soviet Union, like the social democracies, enacted social justice by using public resources to underwrite education, health care, and pensions. It also controlled the price of many foods as well as heat and housing, ensuring that everyone's basic needs would be met. And it constrained, at least in official values, differences in compensation among workers. But Soviet authorities also perverted social justice by giving Communist party members special privileges and by denying citizens the right to express themselves freely. The economic and spiritual contests would continue in the latter part of the century.

4

··

Revolutions Before Bolshevism

Inferiors revolt in order that they may be equal and equals that they may be superior. Such is the state of mind which creates revolutions.

Aristotle, *Politics*
(4th century B.C.E.**)**

A revolution is not a bed of roses. A revolution is a struggle to the death between the future and the past.

Fidel Castro,
speech given in Havana
(1961)

....

THE PROBLEM OF REVOLUTION IS NOT A NEW ONE. AS THE EPIGRAPHS above suggest, for more than two millennia, theorists and activists living in very different parts of the world and in very different kinds of societies have struggled with questions such as the following: What kinds of factors trigger uprisings by people determined to alter the way power is exercised? Can anyone predict who will take part in and who will oppose revolutions once they begin? Why do some attempts to radically transform the status quo succeed while others fail? These questions, asked since ancient times, began to be asked with increasing urgency during the centuries following the American Revolution of 1776 and the French Revolution of 1789, which gave birth to an important new political form that has been closely associated with modernity— the self-governing nation-state. Moreover, even though the period since the Asian and European upheavals of 1989 has sometimes been referred to as a "postrevolutionary" one, questions such as those just described were still being asked when the twentieth century ended. Manifestations of unrest still appeared in many parts of the world, and many countries still had regimes that referred to themselves as "revolutionary." There was no sign that the modern age of revolutions had come to an end. *Calvo Sotelo assassinated by Republicans*

To come to terms with the revolutions of the twentieth century, it is worth looking first at earlier periods that also have been called "centuries of revolution." In this way, we can better appreciate the novelty of the upheavals of recent times. The phenomenon of revolutions and descriptions of their course can actually be traced back even further than Aristotle's day. Jack Goldstone, one of the best-known contemporary scholars of social upheaval, begins his edited collection *Revolutions: Theoretical, Comparative, and Historical Studies* (1986) with a quote from a text composed long before Aristotle was born. Written around 2100 B.C.E., this document describes the fall of an Egyptian Pharaoh and reads in part: "Men walk on the streets. . . . The king has been deposed by the rabble. . . . Every town saith: Let us drive the powerful from our midst."

Chinese texts from well before Aristotle's time also describe uprisings that overthrew and replaced the established political order. More than two millennia ago, in fact, a pair of political concepts was developed in China to explain the logic of such transfers of power. These are worth describing because Chinese revolutions figured prominently in the twentieth century. The first one concerned the idea of dynastic cycles. It was predicated on the notion that dynasties were morally pure when founded, but they tended to become increasingly corrupt over time as emperors lost touch with the needs of the common people. At this point, insurrections would take place to bring a just rebel leader to power, who in turn would found a new dynasty and begin the move from purity to degeneration all over again. Revolutions, or at least rebellions that replaced one ruler with another, were thus seen as good, even necessary things. They provided for a periodic cleansing of the body politic. *Nationalists: Church, landowners, Industrialists*

According to the basic premise of the second concept, all emperors ruled by the grace of Heaven (Tian), a deity that was not personified but viewed as a loosely defined supernatural force. The *ming* (or "mandate") of Heaven was, however, conditional. Heaven was free to revoke

Foreign Help: Germany, Italy - Planes, Men, Tanks

it if an emperor misbehaved, that is, showed himself to be insufficiently benevolent and mindful of the needs of his subjects. A right to rebellion, which legitimated a form of popular participation in government and provided for a form of accountability, was built into this concept. It was said that, although a ruler ruled under the protection of Tian, "Heaven saw with the eyes and heard with the ears" of the common people. These ideas concerning dynastic change and the contingent sacredness of Chinese rulers set China's political system apart from many others, including those of absolutist Europe and imperial Japan. In Europe before the era of nation-states, many monarchs were seen as semi-divine by virtue of the blood that ran in their veins, whereas each Chinese emperor was holy only to the extent that Heaven accepted him as a just ruler. In contrast to Japan, whose present-day emperor still claims to be part of the same lineage as the country's first ruler, China had already seen many different families seated upon the country's Dragon Throne even before the nation became a republic.

Prior to modern times, however, there was no mainstream acceptance, either in China or elsewhere, of the notion that full-fledged transformations of the political system as a whole—as opposed to just a change in the groups or individuals that held power—were beneficial. And the term "revolution" itself is now associated primarily with dramatic shifts that involve more than just the lineage of a country's ruler. If we are to single out any 100-year stretch as the century of revolutions, then, only the last several need to be considered. Here, however, it is difficult to pick among the possibilities, since the eighteenth and the nineteenth centuries each have taken on this label, and the 1600s had thoroughgoing upheavals as well.

We will argue, nevertheless, that the twentieth century has in many regards the best claim of all to the title. Thanks to the traumas of uneven industrialization, the concentration of wealth in the hands of certain countries and particular classes within them, and the modernist belief in totalistic solutions and grand plans, it is no surprise that the twentieth century was a time of radical upheavals that brought about more fundamental transformations of society than did the typical rebellions of old in China and elsewhere.

The revolutions of the twentieth century pose complex problems for the historian, in part because the struggles took a dazzlingly diverse array of forms. They were inspired by all kinds of ideologies and came in some cases from top-down initiatives (such as in Persia and Turkey, where elite groups led them), but in many more cases came from bottom-up movements, with the less privileged members of society taking active roles. Some were not carried out in the name of any ideology and garnered support from elite and nonelite groups alike, as was true in many struggles against imperialism that took revolutionary forms. In these events, what bound people together and spurred them to action was a desire to save their homeland from foreign oppressors, to protect an old nation, or to create a new one. How then, with all this diversity, can we hope to make sense of the modern revolutionary process and the twentieth century as an age of revolution?

One strategy for doing this, pursued in this chapter and the following one, is to divide revolutions into two kinds: those that occur when there is no clear model for what such an event should look like, and those that break out when one revolutionary vision predominates. The upheavals that took place during the period that preceded World War I, which are examined in this chapter, fit the former category. During this epoch, there was a proliferation of competing notions of what a revolution should be like. Many radical ideologies had adherents, including several different schools of socialism, which shared the common denominator of thinking that a dramatic redistribution of wealth within society was needed, but differed on exactly how a society with a less dramatic gap between "haves" and "have-nots" could be created.

A change in this thinking began in 1917. With the rise to power of the Bolsheviks, revolutionary activism came to be defined to an unprecedented degree by a single national model, the Russian one. The post-1917 period is thus a perfect example of the second sort of epoch. A particular pattern for action and a particular ideology—in this case a special version of socialism associated with the German theorist Karl Marx and the Russian political leader Vladimir Lenin—dominated debates within and between revolutionary groups.

It does not necessarily follow that distinctive visions of what a revolution should be like were unimportant to revolutionaries before the outbreak of World War I. In reality, several pre-Bolshevik visions proved particularly powerful between 1789 and 1917, serving as flash points that proponents and opponents of subsequent revolutions could and did refer to in defining their positions. In modern times, a handful of events stand out as constituting a category of inspirational revolutions, struggles that were influential on an international, sometimes continent-wide and even global scale. These events, which people in later times and in distant places sought to emulate, helped to define the revolutionary struggles of the early 1900s.

The point is, though, that it was only from 1917 on that a particular and clearly articulated ideology, which defined the goals and methods of revolutionary action, gained international adherents. This significant change happened first with Bolshevism and later with some other variants of Marxism. In this chapter we deal with four revolutionary visions that preceded the Russian model and are harder to pin down than Bolshevism. Each in its own way represents an important strand of the modern revolutionary experience. And each made a mark, directly or indirectly, on the tumultuous opening decades of the twentieth century, which saw successful or abortive revolutions break out in many parts of the world. To understand the varied forms that social unrest took immediately prior to World War I, as well as to make sense of events that took place in some countries later in the century, it is crucial to come to terms with these four pre-Bolshevik upheavals that proved inspirational. *Republicans: Liberals, Socialists, Communists*

More specifically, we look at the enduring power of two French revolutionary visions that predated the twentieth century, those associated with the dates 1789 and 1871, and at the radically different revolutionary visions provided by the Mexican insurrection of 1910 and the Chinese upheavals of 1911. The first two played a tremendous role in shaping the course of European radicalism and laying the groundwork for the rise of the Bolsheviks, who in turn would provide the most powerful global model for revolution for decades to come. Marx's version of socialist theory was derived in large part from his analysis of the dynamics of 1789; the events of 1871 led him to modify his revolutionary program. In addition, Lenin and other Bolsheviks often depicted their actions of 1917 as following in the footsteps of the French activists of earlier generations. The Mexican and Chinese events had comparably dramatic effects within the Latin American and East Asian worlds. The struggles of 1910 and 1911 would, through their legacies, define future political choices in Mexico and China throughout the 1920s–1940s. Up until the end of the twentieth century, in fact, powerful parties in each country would stake a claim to legitimacy on the idea that they were protecting the legacy of the struggles of the 1910s. In addition, early twentieth-century revolutionary struggles in Mexico and China would help lay the groundwork, indirectly, for such major late events as the revolutions that brought Communist parties to power in Cuba and Vietnam. *Known as popular front / lead to facism*

A Summary of Four Visions

The first of the two French visions is linked to the struggles of the 1780s and 1790s. It started with a financial crisis, caused in part by France's support for the American forces fighting for independence from Britain in the 1770s. Lack of funds forced Louis XVI to seek increased economic support from various social classes in order to shore up the royal treasury. The only way for him to do this was to convene a consultative assembly made up of members of the Three Estates—aristocrats, clergy, and a third, less easily defined group of well-to-do men. Such assemblies were a traditional part of the French political system but had not been called often, since bringing notables together made it possible for them to make demands on the king that he could otherwise ignore.

This was precisely what happened when Louis tried to solve his financial crisis: Once assembled, in 1789, the three groups, and particularly those belonging to the one least clearly defined, insisted that changes be made in the political order. Among other things, they demanded—and eventually got—more regular consultation between the monarch and representatives of the people. The Revolution ended a decade later with the rise to power of Napoleon Bonaparte, a military strongman who proclaimed himself emperor. In between 1789 and 1799 many important things took place: France was proclaimed a republic, an elected National Assembly was created to make laws and generally wield the power that had once belonged to the monarch, and the King and his wife, Marie Antoinette, were executed. So, too, were many others deemed enemies of the Revolution.

Highlights of the French Revolution included the issuance of "The Declaration of the Rights of Man and the Citizen," a document stipulating equal political status for all adult male residents of the republic deemed worthy of citizenship. The period from 1789–1799 also saw debates over how far the category of "citizen" should be extended, with women and members of other partially or fully excluded groups making claims that they, too, deserved basic rights. The upheaval affected not only the French heartland but also France's imperial domains. In an insurrection that broke out in the Caribbean colony of Haiti, slaves rallied to the same cry that was raised in Paris—"liberty, equality, fraternity." *Foreign help: USSR - Men, Planes, Tanks*

The second French revolutionary upheaval with lasting influence was the Paris Commune, the last of three nineteenth-century efforts by citizens of France to revive the spirit of 1789. The Commune, a short-lived struggle, began with insurrections in France's capital city in 1871. Like the French liberal revolts of 1830 and 1848, the Commune was led by activists inspired by the ideas embedded in the Declaration of the Rights of Man and the Citizen. The Commune had, however, a novel feature: socialist ideas. Advocates of revolution called for the principle of equality to be carried even further than it had been in the 1790s—into the realm of economics.

The immediate cause of the 1871 uprising was that the people of Paris believed the French government had become corrupt and had done too little to defend their city against foreign forces. The Communards, as activists came be to known, called for the transformation of Paris into a self-governing republic in which all residents would be treated equally and workers would have as much power in political life as their bosses. Responding to the widening gulf between rich and poor that accompanied industrialization, they thus combined calls for political equality with calls for minimizing economic inequalities. The Commune ended with bloody acts of repression in Paris in the same year that this utopian experiment began. The Communards, however, were defeated by well-armed outside armies and either killed in battle or shipped off to New Caledonia as criminals.

Despite its short life and unsuccessful conclusion, the Commune stands out as a turning point in the history of revolution, both because of the way it borrowed socialist ideas already in circu-

PICTURE 4.1
"The Storming of the Bastille, July 14, 1789." The fall of the Bastille, a symbol of the old regime, demonstrated the power of the Parisian crowd and the rapidly growing popular defiance to the government of Louis XIV. (Reprinted from John S. Abbott, *The French Revolution of 1789* [New York: Harper and Brothers Publishers, 1859])

lation from the early 1800s onwards and because of the way the upheaval itself inspired later socialists. It is by no means merely coincidental that the main anthem of the worldwide socialist movement that later developed, "The Internationale," was a hymn to the Paris Commune. Nor is it happenstance that a hundred years after 1871, Chinese Communist leader Mao Zedong, fearing that his country's revolution had become ossified, held up the Paris Commune as a symbol of socialism in its purest form. *Gold Reserve Exchange for Military equipment*

The French Revolution proper would for more than a century define for many people what a modern revolution was all about, and its basic features—the toppling of a monarch and creation of a republic—have remained a defining characteristic of revolutionary activism to this day. Terms and personalities linked to it would be invoked by revolutionaries rising up in times and places far removed from the Paris of 1789. The event's influence on the upheavals of late eighteenth-century Haiti and nineteenth-century France have already been noted, but consideration of them does not exhaust the issue. The ideas of 1789 were also invoked in early twentieth-century China, for example: Leaders of insurrection such as Sun Yat-sen insisted that they were only trying to do for their land what the heroic figures who stormed the Bastille had done for France. Sun went so far as to claim that his own "Three People's Principles," a unique combination of socialist and nationalist ideas, was nothing more than a variation on the call for "liberty, equality, and fraternity" first heard in France. And within Paris, arguments over 1789's meaning continue even now to shape the contours of political debate, with conservatives and radicals laying claim to different parts of that year's legacy. *Morocco Army lead by: General Franco*

The Paris Commune has had a less wide-ranging but still crucially important influence on French history and on world politics. In addition to providing the international socialist movement with its theme song, the Communards have long been the subject of intense debate within

PICTURE 4.2
Karl Marx (1818–1883). The German
political philosopher and his collaborator,
Friedrich Engels, critiqued the inhuman
nature of capitalism as witnessed in the
suffering of workers in industrial Germany,
England, and France. (Reprinted from John
Spargo, *Karl Marx: His Life and Times* [New
York: B. W. Huebsch, 1910])

radical circles interested in the meaning of socialism. When the Communards took to the streets, they were inspired by a host of competing versions of socialism, some of which emphasized the desirability of gradual transformation, others quick and radical change. In the aftermath of the events of 1871, both types of socialists saw the Commune as providing key lessons for the future. Among these was Karl Marx, who had written passionately about the lessons of 1789 and now began to celebrate 1871 as a more fully developed articulation of the revolutionary impulse that, he claimed, drove all history forward by advancing the struggle between socioeconomic classes.

Marx's most famous polemic, *The Communist Manifesto*, coauthored by Freidrich Engels, appeared more than two decades before the Paris Commune. One reason it had such little impact at first was that the claims the authors made about communism—the term Marx and Engels used to describe the ideal society that would emerge after socialist revolutions occurred, wealth was redistributed, and laborers gained control of the means of production and of government—seemed far-fetched. They spoke of it as "a spectre haunting Europe," but this phrase at first seemed hyperbole. True, workers had played radical roles in the revolutions that had swept through Europe in 1848, but those had ended with political systems altered but the social structure unchanged. Marx's claim that class struggle—a battle to the death between representatives of the haves and the have-nots—would transform the world still seemed a pipe dream at mid-century.

After 1871, however, though the *Communist Manifesto* would still only gradually gain influence, the prophetic visions of Marx and Engels began to acquire more substance. Both those who called for socialism and those who decried the violence that was likely to accompany the birth of a new order saw, in the Commune, tangible evidence of what the future might hold. Perhaps most important of all, when it comes to influence, both the Commune as an event and Marx's writings on it would have considerable impact on Lenin and other makers of the Russian Revolution of 1917. In an ironic twist, however, "The Internationale," a second national anthem in countries governed by Communist Party regimes, had even more influence than these regimes had bargained on. So open to competing interpretations are its lyrics—which speak of the need for mistreated people to rise up to fight to the death those who oppress them—that later in the century it was also sometimes sung by those protesting abuses committed by these very regimes. In the People's Republic of China, for example, it became a song that was almost always played at state ceremonies, yet it also served as a rallying cry for the demonstrators who gathered in Tiananmen Square in 1989 to call for an end to Communist Party corruption.

The Mexican Revolution of 1910, the third revolutionary event under consideration here, did not have the same kind of extended influence as the two French revolutionary struggles. Nor did it bequeath a slogan or song with the kind of impact that "liberty, equality, fraternity" or "The Internationale" had on the twentieth century. Nevertheless, it provided an important model for change throughout Latin America, and in one of its leaders, Emiliano Zapata, gave the world a potent symbol of revolutionary heroism. Zapata would live on in varied forms: in an inspiring Hollywood movie (*Viva Zapata!*), in which he was played by Marlon Brando and given dialogue by John Steinbeck; and in the name "Zapatistas", taken by rebels in the Mexican state of Chiapas in the 1990s. *Franco would be appointed head of Nationalist govern.*

The Mexican Revolution is important because, as essentially an agrarian movement, it foreshadowed many of the century's later developments. From the 1940s onward, peasant-based revolutions became an important element of the world political scene. In addition, the Mexican Revolution shared with the two French events already discussed a complex quality that is hard to pin down; it can be interpreted in contrasting ways by different sets of people, intellectuals and activists alike. There are famous names associated with it but, as in the case of the events of 1789 and 1871, there is no unified ideology. Nor is there just one name accepted as the key referent for the Mexican struggle of 1910. This fact sets it off from the Russian Revolution, which would become so closely tied to the ideology of Bolshevism, a very specific variety of socialism, and with one individual leader, V. I. Lenin—although other major figures, such as Joseph Stalin, Lenin's successor, were also prominent. In Mexico's revolution, the main legacy was institutional. The events of 1910 became a potent source of legitimacy for the Partido de la Revolución Institucional (PRI, Institutional Revolutionary Party), a political organization that would govern the country, in the name of defending the revolution, until it was finally defeated in national elections at the turn of the twenty-first century. *1939 - Nat. occupied Rep. Barcelona*

Like the French and Mexican upheavals that preceded it, the Chinese Revolution of 1911 sent shock waves through a continent, showing as it did that one of the great dynastic systems of Asia was not immune to the forces of republicanism. In contrast to the other three inspirational revolutions, however, this struggle came to be identified with a single individual, Sun Yat-sen. But once again we encounter in China a complex legacy and competing understandings of that legacy. Even though the revolution of 1911 was associated closely with Sun, there were wide divergences over just what he stood for and who could best be described as carrying on the struggle he began. *& Eventually captured Madrid / End of WAR*

These four inspirational events, particularly the Mexican and Chinese Revolutions of the early 1910s, reverberated throughout the century and were integrated into and transformed by various national revolutionary traditions. We trace these concepts in more detail before returning, in Chapter 5, to the questions about the nature of revolution posed at the beginning of this chapter, taking as our starting point the Russian upheaval of 1917. As will become clear, this upheaval was certainly influenced by earlier events but in the end changed forever the connotations and indeed the very meanings of terms such as "revolution" and "socialism" while also altering the debate on urban versus rural routes to social transformation. *Gt. B & France Stay Neutral*

1789 and Its Meanings

The French struggles of 1789–1799 bequeathed to the world many things, including a number of terms that have had enormous staying power. For example, those favoring extreme measures, including eventually the destruction of the whole system of kingship, sat on the left side of the National Assembly, while their opponents sat on the right. Thus, today we have the modern notion of "the Left" and "the Right" as designations for radicalism and conservatism, respectively. This etymology inflects the political vocabularies of Africa, Latin America, and Asia as well as of Europe and the United States. In addition, at a key moment in the French Revolution, the leading radicals were members of a group known as Jacobins, and those to their right were known as Girondists. Later twentieth-century revolutionaries would still refer to themselves as "Jacobins" or "Girondists," playing on the memory of these struggles.

The names of two major figures in the French Revolution, Robespierre (who ultimately favored a concentration of power within the hands of Jacobin Party leaders) and Danton (who was perceived as more populist and less authoritarian in his vision of revolution), would also prove lasting as touchstones for political divisions. More than two centuries after their deaths at the hands of other revolutionaries, the names of these two leaders are still being used by those pursuing radical change. In the 1990s, for example, student demonstrators in Serbia told foreign reporters of the tension within their movement between those whose approach was more like Robespierre's and those whose approach was more like Danton's.

The 1790s saw a series of developments that pushed the revolution in ever more radical directions. First, the revolutionaries experimented with creating a constitutional monarchy; then they founded a republic and tried and executed Louis XVI and Marie Antoinette; and finally they launched a Reign of Terror that put anyone suspected of being counterrevolutionary in great danger. Later in the decade, attempts were made to first check and then reverse the course of this radicalism. These efforts culminated first in a Thermidore period, in which many revolutionary policies were reversed, and then in the rise of Napoleon, who proclaimed himself emperor and effectively put a temporary end to all the revolutionary experiments.

The outbreak of the Reign of Terror, and Napoleon's assumption of control over the revolution, would prove to be two aspects of the French model open to the widest range of interpretations. Critics of radicalism are fond of pointing to these things as demonstrating the folly of revolutionary projects. In the eyes of conservatives, the Reign of Terror and Napoleon's rise show that radical revolutions tend to either devour their own children or merely replace one type of despot with another. And yet, radicals of later periods have sometimes defended the Reign of Terror, or at least the need for harsh measures against counterrevolutionaries, as a strategic necessity. And, to some, Napoleon remained heroic rather than villainous, in the sense that he carried through one part of the revolutionary program of 1789, namely, the transformation of France into a strong and modern country. For example, some of the same early twentieth-century Chinese revolutionaries who embraced the ideals of liberty, equality, and fraternity also said that China needed a Napoleon to save it from foreign domination.

The legacies of all these events, personalities, and terms were complex and multifaceted, and they remain so to this day. When taken as a whole they changed much about the way politics was envisioned and discussed, setting new standards for what was and was not a legitimate political goal to pursue. The term "revolution" came to mean something very different from its original meaning. The word is derived from the same root as ones such as "revolve," which suggest circularity, and it originally meant a return to an earlier point in time or the restoration of an earlier state of affairs. From 1789 on, however, it has tended to be associated with moves forward into uncharted waters that may or may not prove dangerous. Those struggling to make sense of revolutions in modern times have tended to see them as events that have the potential to usher in dark or glorious futures. They assume that revolutions make the world a different place than it was before they took place. The fact that they assume this is largely due to the French Revolution.

Yet, the most significant change in the political landscape had to do with the slogan naming liberty, equality, and fraternity as goals of government. The potency of these ideals proved so great that it became virtually impossible, first in Europe and later in other parts of the world, to present oneself as opposing them. Even an opponent of revolution had to argue that his or her goals were similar to or at least not radically different from those embodied in this slogan. Even a dedicated Marxist, who believed that the events of 1789 needed to be criticized for their bourgeois as opposed to proletarian class basis, needed to find a way to square this opposition with a positive assessment of liberty, equality, and fraternity as ideals.

Ruling groups typically tried to integrate a defense of liberty into a vision of politics that focused on the dangerous aspects of revolutionary upheavals. In this formulation, determined protection of economic freedoms and property rights was seen as the best way for a government to remain true to the spirit of 1789, even if this was done at the expense of including larger segments of the population in the democratic process. The argument here was that the price, in terms of social order, of pursuing the more radical political side of revolution was too high to pay, as it would involve giving up one form of liberty in order to further another.

At the same time, artisans and workers demanding inclusion in the new political orders taking shape in Europe in the nineteenth century utilized the same terminology inherited from 1789 to call for an expansion of democracy that would bring them into the fold. In their formulation, the price of upheaval was a small one to pay in order to achieve true liberty. This idea was behind some of the revolutions of 1848 in continental Europe. It was also an influential view in Britain, one part of Europe that did not undergo a revolution at this time, although radical movements of various sorts did break out there. A mid-nineteenth-century statement by labor activist Feargus O'Connor sums up the way this more radical form of the 1789 language played itself out in the decades immediately preceding the Paris Commune, an event that would again alter the terms of debate, though in somewhat subtler ways: "A great revolution . . . must be productive of hazard, vicissitudes, and perhaps calamity. But the question to you is, whether or not it is worthwhile to pass through the ordeal of temporary suffering to establish permanent liberty."

The Paris Commune as Inspirational Event

On March 18, 1871, shortly following France's capitulation to the Prussian army, the National Guard of Paris, angered by economic hardship and by the surrender, refused to turn over their artillery to the National Army commanded by Louis-Adolphe Thiers. That refusal announced the opening round of a two-month civil war that ended in defeat for the Parisians. The National Guard group had baptized their military and political organization "the Commune" in memory of the radical movement of 1793, during which that term was also used. Thus, a debt to the earlier French upheaval was acknowledged from the very beginning. The Commune also showed that it was a product of a later period: The roles that labor unions played in placing barricades on

PICTURE 4.3   "The Events of May 1870." Inspired by the French Revolution
almost a century earlier, republican and radical Parisians joined forces to
establish a Commune. Here cavalry charge the crowd gathered on the Place
du Chateau-d'Eau. (Reprinted from Jules Claretie, *Histoire de la Révolution de
1870–71* [Paris: Aux Bureaux de Journal d'Eclipse, 1872])

the streets to help the revolutionary cause were more reminiscent of 1848 than of 1789. In addition, the language of socialism employed by the Communards reflected the mixture of radical creeds that had begun to take shape in the mid-nineteenth century.

Crucial characteristics of the Paris Commune earned it a reputation as a revolutionary model both on the Left and the Right sides of the political spectrum. The Commune's practical critique of elite politics and hierarchy made a profound impact on all political tendencies. Communards practiced a form of direct democracy that included suppression of the standing army, election of all its authorities, and strict pay caps on the highest salaries. Moreover, they inscribed a new slogan on the banner of radical democracy: the principle of immediate recall of all elected officials. The Commune also enacted measures of a social nature, ranging from a rigid separation of church and state to a ban on nighttime work in bakeries to a plan for the establishment of large-scale cooperative industries.

The Communards engaged in more symbolic acts as well, including the dismantling of a statue of Napoleon, who was criticized for his autocratic behavior. Most significant, the Commune addressed the proletariat as the principal subject of its movement. Its first decree read: "The proletarians of Paris amidst the failures and treasons of the ruling classes, have understood that the hour has struck for them to save the situation by taking into their own hand the direction of public affairs." Finally, Communard forces, in addition to engaging in battles with government forces, executed some of their enemies, as did their adversaries.

Taken together, these acts gave ample reason for radical forces on the Left to view the Commune as an inspirational event and for conservatives on the Right to fear its potential influence. Conservative governments would, throughout the late 1800s and early 1900s, view the civil war in France as a consequence of the dangerous spread of socialist doctrines. They even referred to the need to avoid new events like the Paris Commune when defending the use of harsh, repressive measures against labor movements and socialist militants.

The impact of the Commune on the Left was complex. Karl Marx's reaction was both instructive and important. He hesitated briefly before embracing the Commune. His reluctance was due, in part, to the fact that his own party was barely represented in the Commune's ranks, dominated as they were by other types of socialists and by anarchists, who opposed all forms of organized government. But Marx soon supported the Commune with passion, concluding his 1872 essay, "The Civil War in France," with the following homage: "Workingmen's Paris, with its Commune, will be forever celebrated as the glorious harbinger of a new society. Its martyrs are enshrined in the great heart of the working class. Its exterminators, history has already nailed to that eternal pillory from which all the prayers of their priests will not avail to redeem them."

Marx sought to use its democratic and proletarian character against those who believed in elitist forms of revolutionary change. Yet, at the same time, Marx used the example of the Commune as an ideological weapon against Mikhail Bakunin and other anarchists (socialists who insisted that society could move quickly to a system in which there was no governing structure at all). Bakunin was one of those who believed that the Commune served as a model of a new society characterized by small village communes: "The City of Paris administering itself." Marx argued that the Communards did not oppose democratic forms of centralization of society and government but instead recognized the need for centralized government of some sort as a precondition for the emancipation of the working class.

Lenin also used the Paris Commune as a political model and as an ideological weapon. Basing himself entirely on "The Civil War in France," and later writings by Friedrich Engels, Lenin devoted an important part of his famous essay "State and Revolution" to summarizing their arguments and applying them to the contemporary political situation. His essay was paradoxical, because, on the one hand, his analysis of Marx and the Commune led him to extol an extremely democratic version of the new revolutionary government. Indeed, "State and Revolution" represents the most democratic example of all of Lenin's writings. On the other hand he made much of Engels's comment that if one wanted to understand the dictatorship of the proletariat, one should just look at the Commune. In his fights with both anarchists and democratic socialists he used this invocation of the dictatorship of the proletariat along with the peculiarly democratic inflection of the Commune.

The Mexican Revolution

The Mexican Revolution was one of the great agrarian revolutions of the twentieth century, inspiring peasants and intellectuals throughout Latin America. During the first part of the century, the Mexican Revolution continued to provide a model for proponents of agrarian reform (land distribution to the poor). It also supplied a new language of nationalism for intellectuals and politicians that ennobled their countries' Indian origins.

The Mexican Revolution had economic and political roots in the period of rapid modernization known as the Porfiriato, named after Porfirio Díaz, dictator for almost thirty years. Díaz came to power with strong popular backing. In fact, he was a national hero: He had been a brigadier-general in the Mexican victory against the French interventionist forces on May 5, 1862, immortalized ever since in annual Cinco de Mayo celebrations.

Díaz used his political legitimacy to mobilize resources on behalf of an ambitious program of economic growth and modernization. During the Porfiriato (he ruled from 1876 until 1911, except for a four-year period, 1880–1884, during which a close friend of his held power), the railroad network grew from 750 to 15,000 miles in order to transport a skyrocketing supply of manufacturing, mining, and agricultural products. Overall, exports increased from 25 million to 275 million pesos during this period. The value of gold production rose from 1.5 million pesos in 1877 to 40 million pesos in 1908, and silver production increased from 24.8 million to 85 million pesos during the same period. Similarly, coffee output jumped from 8,000 to 28,000 tons, and sisal exports (for use in rope manufacturing) went from 42,000 to 680,000 bales. Overall export agriculture increased at the rate of 6.29 percent annually during the Porfiriato. New manufacturing industries, such as breweries and textile mills, also became major pillars of the economy.

Yet this economic progress tended to favor a relatively small national elite and foreign investors, and it often came about at the cost of poor people. The exclusion of the poor from the Mexican road to progress, in the long run, undermined the legitimacy of the Porfiriato. First, this long bonanza for the elite did not lead to significant social investment in health and education. In 1900, 29 percent of children died before their first birthdays and 84 percent of the population remained illiterate. Second, the vast expansion of the railroad network usually involved the expropriation of peasant lands. The lands near the railroad increased substantially in value along with the jump in the value of export agriculture. Throughout Mexico, the guiding political philosophy of liberalism favored individual property ownership at the expense of communal holdings. This political bias against communal property, along with an authoritarian government that favored large landholders and the new role of banks, which were needed to finance export crops, were all factors that helped to push the poor off of the land. Nationwide, by the end of the Porfiriato agribusiness controlled over 70 percent of the land; in Central Mexico, 90 percent of the rural population was landless by the end of that period.

Third, the growth of export agriculture also dramatically affected corn and bean production. The high price of export commodities made it economically irrational to plant corn. As a result, the supply of corn dropped significantly and the price of corn rose by over 200 percent. Shortages of these basic food crops at times became acute, leading to food riots that played a part in destabilizing the regime.

Fourth, the development of both industries and mining concerns at the same time brought together large groups of workers who shared common conditions of exploitation; in the mining camps and on the railroads, this situation was exacerbated by discrimination against Mexican workers in favor of North American employees, who also participated in the discriminatory attitudes and practices. Moreover, numerous Mexican workers came into contact with U.S trade unionism, including the radical Western Federation of Miners and the Industrial Workers of the World (IWW). During the early 1900s, the Mexican government ruthlessly crushed several important strikes that erupted in the mining and textile sectors. That repression also chipped away at the legitimacy of the government.

Fifth, the Mexican army (known as the Federales) violently put down Indian resistance among the Yaquí of Sonora and exiled their warriors to the sisal plantations of the Yucatán, condemning them to virtual slavery. These actions enraged not only many Mexicans but also foreign observers. Finally, the Porfiriato engendered political antagonism. Liberalism was the dominant ideology in Mexico, shared by both Díaz and his antagonists, who believed that he had betrayed those political principles. Popular forms of liberalism included strong emphases on social justice, regional autonomy, and nationalism. Moreover, as the enormous gulf between the elite and the masses became ever more acute and visible, workers, artisans, peasants, and middle-class people began to look back fondly to the rule of Benito Juárez, the leader in the fight against the French intervention (1862–1867) and the subsequent ruler until 1872. In turn, they linked Juárez to the liberal constitution of 1857, which in fact had provided Díaz and his elite allies with a powerful legal precedent in favor of the privatization of communal lands. Thus, although Díaz and Juárez differed little in terms of ideological principles, growing numbers of people viewed Juárez (who was the child of Indian parents) as the father of the true Mexican nation and of liberalism, which they thought Díaz had betrayed.

Particularly among middle-class groups, these liberal currents surfaced in the early 1900s in the vanguard of resistance to the regime. In fact, the leaders of this movement pushed the boundaries of liberalism further and further to the Left. To cite an important example, Ricardo Flores Magón first joined liberal protests in 1892 against Díaz's reelection. Later, he founded the Partido Liberal Mexicano (PLM, Mexican Liberal Party). Yet he became disenchanted with a political program that aimed merely to oust Díaz and form a democratic government. By 1905 he came to see the necessity to end dictatorial rule and to stop the exploitation of workers and peasants, turning over the factories and mines to the workers and the lands to the peasants. In his vision of the revolution, the state would be superfluous because the workers and peasants could run society themselves. In short, Magón became identified with anarchists and pushed for an alliance with the radical IWW. Although his party, the PLM, participated in significant armed actions against the Díaz regime, Magón's radical politics led to repression and political marginalization on both sides of the U.S.-Mexican border. He spent many years in Leavenworth Federal Penitentiary, a victim of political repression, and died in jail in 1922.

Elite groups also viewed democracy as an important ingredient of modernity and therefore saw the Porfiriato as a reactionary obstacle to Mexico's development. Francisco Madero led this faction. In 1910, he participated in presidential elections that the Díaz regime rigged. In reaction he launched a rebellion in northern Mexico. Several agrarian movements added their weight to the democratic revolution. The most important of these movements were those of Emiliano Zapata in the southern state of Morelos and of Pancho Villa in the northern state of Chihuahua. In less than a year, Madero, in alliance with these movements, triumphed. He easily won the new elections and was inaugurated as president in November 1911.

Despite his great popularity, Madero's administration was plagued by indecisiveness. His largest organized base of support—the Zapatista peasantry of Morelos—remained adamant in its demand for land. And the remnants of the Porfiriato were poised to retake power. Soon Madero faced dissension and rebellion on both fronts. Amidst the ensuing conflicts, Venustiano Heurta, a general of the Porfirian army, deposed and then executed Madero in February 1913. Although Huerta expected to crush the Zapatistas and to beat the remaining democratic forces into submission, he sorely miscalculated the strength and determination of the revolutionary forces.

Two broad-based alliances emerged to fight Huerta and redeem the Mexican Revolution. Zapata and Pancho Villa joined forces around a program of land redistribution, local autonomy, and political democracy. Venustiano Carranza and Alvaro Obregón organized another armed force in Coahuila and Sonora. By mid-1914, the Constitutionalist Army (the name for the combined forces of the two alliances) defeated Huerta and the army.

The revolutionary alliance did not last long, however, and by early 1915 the forces of Carranza and Obregón were doing battle with those of Villa and Zapata. The roots of the competing al-

PICTURE 4.4
Emiliano Zapata (1879–1919). Zapata and
his peasant forces demanded the return
of land to the peasantry, adopting the
slogan "Land and Liberty." (Photo from
the Library of Congress)

liances were complex, having less to do with ideology than with regional, class, and cultural backgrounds. All of the leaders were ardently nationalistic. Similarly, both groups supported agrarian reform, although the Zapata/Villa commitment to it ran deeper. Both supported rights for labor, although Obregón was the only one of the four leaders with close ties to the workers movement. Indeed those ties allowed for the creation of the Red Brigades, forces made up of thousands of workers who fought against the peasant armies of Villa and Zapata. Cultural differences between the Zapatista peasants and the urban workers surely contributed to the split between these revolutionary groups. When, for example, the Zapatistas occupied Mexico City in 1914, the secular, urban population was shocked to see the peasants begging for alms under the banner of the Virgin of Guadalupe.

By 1916 the forces of Carranza and Obregón had defeated their antagonists. Nevertheless, the government could not dislodge Villa and Zapata from Chihuahua and Morelos, where they had overwhelming peasant support. As the new revolutionary regime attempted to consolidate itself, it had to make major concessions to the rural poor, who still largely supported Zapata and Villa, as well as to the urban workers, who had provided crucial support to the victors. Thus, the revolutionary Mexican Constitution of 1917 guaranteed land rights to peasants and union rights to workers. It also gave the government rights to the subsoil (because of the petroleum, to cite the most important concern). At the time, this constitution was the most radical legal statement of social rights in the world. The first Mexican revolutionary regime had learned a valuable lesson about how to incorporate the popular demands of the groups it vanquished.

There is no doubt that such a constitution could emerge only through a radical change in Mexico's political and social fabric. In this sense, the Mexican Revolution, despite its increasingly obvious flaws and betrayals, represented a particular kind of change that many groups throughout Latin America have tried to emulate: an agrarian revolution seeking to recover national dignity through control over its natural resources and its political destiny.

The legacy of the Mexican Revolution, however, has been complicated by several uncomfortable facts. The main hero of the revolution, Emiliano Zapata, was murdered in 1919 on orders from Carranza, one of its other heroes. Similarly, Carranza was killed fleeing from the forces of Obregón, and Villa was assassinated under Obregón's presidency (1923) in conditions that never were clarified. Notwithstanding, the official ideology of the Mexican Revolution has portrayed its founding fathers as part of a harmonious pantheon of revolutionary heroes. Yet, the official ideology of the Mexican Revolution also provoked a significant shift in intellectual and popular mentalities in that it exalted the Indian and mestizo (mixed blood) contribution to the country's history and social fabric. The greatest visual example of this *indigenismo*, as this ideological formulation is known, are the murals of the artist Diego Rivera, which have become synonymous with the revolution and with this revolutionary view of a society that previously had extolled only its European component.

The complexity of the legacy has served to a certain extent both the postrevolutionary state and the Mexican citizenry. The means of appropriating that legacy have in effect provided the state with a model for co-opting and integrating the social and economic demands of a wide range of social forces. This capacity reached great force during the 1930s under the presidency of Lázaro Cárdenas, when the revolutionary regime did support the demands of peasants, workers, and nationalists through the massive distribution of land, support for unions, and nationalization of the foreign-owned petroleum industry. Yet, during subsequent administrations, the Mexican government engaged in violent repression against workers and peasants and practiced notorious forms of corruption. The PRI did not rule primarily through repression, however, but rather via the legacy of the revolution, which obliged it, to some extent, to address the demands of peasants and workers. The elasticity of the Mexican revolutionary tradition also allowed the son of Cárdenas, an opposition leader, to nearly win the presidency in 1988 and to become the mayor of Mexico City in 1997, a major step toward breaking the PRI's monopoly of power.

The Chinese Revolution of 1911

The Chinese Revolution, like many others, began with a series of related crises and occurrences, none of which on its own would have toppled a dynasty. Through their accumulated impact, however, they did just this. Throughout the last years of the nineteenth century and the first years of the twentieth, the Qing Dynasty (1644–1911) was wracked by upheavals. The root causes of these crises can be traced to the onslaught of Western imperialism, which began with the Opium War of 1839–1842, and a population explosion that strained the government's resources. In fact, the dynasty's ability to maintain order had begun to crumble even before the first foreign gunboats arrived. Some of these late Qing-era upheavals had a loyalist slant, as was true of the anti-Christian Boxer Rebellion of 1898–1900, which was directed against foreign ideas and practices, not China's rulers. Other movements of the time were clearly oppositional in character, as was true of several abortive turn-of-the-century uprisings spearheaded by groups associated with Sun Yat-sen.

This period also saw prominent officials, as well as members of the imperial family itself, espouse and try to implement reform programs, some of them quite radical and wide ranging. The goal of these efforts was to make the Chinese governing system more flexible and open to international trends. Radical reformers in this category differed from revolutionaries on one main issue: whether China needed an emperor. Within each group were many individuals angered by certain actions of the Qing rulers: Whereas radical reformers insisted that the dynastic system should be maintained, but transformed into a constitutional monarchy, revolutionaries claimed that China must become a republic. The latter were also proponents of *geming* ("mandate-stripping"). Each group claimed that its strategy would help China regain its proper place in the world as a leader among "modern" nations, and each saw particular foreign lands as providing a blueprint for a new or renewed Chinese governmental system. The difference between the groups stemmed in part from which features of the outside world seemed most inspirational to them.

Those favoring constitutional monarchy saw Great Britain and Japan as potential models for China. The Japanese case was especially striking because, immediately after completing its transition from an imperial state to a constitutional monarchy and achieving success in educational and military reforms, Japan had begun to compete with Western countries on an equal footing. More than that, this small island country, which Chinese rulers had long considered a mere tributary state, had defeated China in a short war over control of Korea in the 1890s, and in 1905–1906 it had been the victor in the Russo-Japanese War.

Revolutionaries such as Sun Yat-sen were also influenced by Japan, since many of them had either studied or spent time there while in exile for radical activities, but they looked elsewhere to such republics as France and the United States for political models. Japan was important to them as an organizing site (Sun held the first meeting of his Revolutionary Alliance there) and as a conduit for new ideas. Indeed, many Western texts spelling out socialist and anarchist beliefs were encountered by Chinese radicals first via Japanese translations of these works. They did not, however, call for a Chinese equivalent to the Meiji Restoration, the 1868 event that had put Japan on the path toward becoming a constitutional monarchy. Instead, they called for China to produce equivalents to George Washington, the military leader of the American Revolution, and Jean-Jacques Rousseau, one of the intellectuals whose ideas had propelled the French Revolution. It was a counterpart to 1776 and 1789 that they sought to carry out. American imagery came particularly naturally to Sun, who had traveled extensively in the United States and had lived in Hawaii, but even revolutionaries who had never left China sometimes spoke of "Washingtons" and "Rousseaus."

Nationalist and republican imagery went hand in hand in the rhetoric of revolutionaries. They were fond of reminding their audiences that the Qing ruling house was a foreign one: Its founders had come from Manchuria to the north of China proper at the head of armies bent on conquest. Members of the ethnically and linguistically distinct Manchu group, Qing founders had displaced the ethnically Han Chinese Ming dynasty in 1644. Revolutionaries also castigated the Qing for being too weak in resisting a different type of foreign influence, that of Western imperialists and later of the Japanese. Figures such as Sun drew heavily on foreign ideas. These included not only the concept of a republic with an elected president at its head as an ideal form of government, but also socialism and land-reform policies that would narrow the gap between rich and poor in the countryside as ways of structuring the economy. Nonetheless, they presented these ideas as praiseworthy in part because they could be used so effectively to avenge the political and economic transgressions of foreigners. To overthrow the Manchus and establish a republic headed by Han Chinese would be one type of revenge. To establish a strong socialist state, capable of competing economically with the capitalist West and Japan, would be another. So, too,

PICTURE 4.5
Sun Yat-Sen (1867–1925). Sun Yat-Sen was the intellectual leader of the Chinese Revolution in 1911. (Reprinted from Arthur Judson Brown, *The Chinese Revolution* [New York: Student Volunteer Movement, 1912])

would redistributing wealth, since it would settle scores with officials seen as monopolizing too much of the nation's riches.

It was unclear as late as 1910 whether radical reformers or revolutionaries would carry the day, but in October of the following year a fluke occurrence in the city of Wuhan set off a chain reaction that toppled the dynasty. Explosives kept by a group of revolutionary activists with ties to Sun went off accidentally, destroying his organization's attempts to conceal its plans to carry out a new uprising. Instead of suppressing the group, however, military units that were formally linked to the state—but in reality beholden primarily to local generals—launched mutinies. Without any coherent plan, revolutionary insurrections swept the country.

In some of the provinces, local strongmen who had become disaffected with the central authorities had increasingly begun to go their own way in the decades preceding this event. Now, they declared themselves autonomous. Soon, the leaders of the dynasty, realizing that they no longer had control over much of the land or the empire's military forces, found their days numbered. When one of the most powerful generals in the Qing military system, Yuan Shikai, threw in his lot with the insurgents, the dynasty gave up without a fight. The year 1912 began with the last Manchu emperor abdicating, a new Republic of China being proclaimed, and Sun Yat-sen being installed as the first president of the nation.

When the Wuhan uprising broke out, Sun himself had been in the United States to raise money for his cause among overseas Chinese. His name nonetheless became that most closely associated with the events of 1911. One result was that up until the end of the twentieth century, most of the political groups that competed for power in mainland China based their claim to legitimacy on the idea that they were continuing in the revolutionary tradition of Sun and 1911. Both the Chinese Communist Party, which took power in the mainland in 1949, and the Nationalist Party, which moved its base of operations to the island of Taiwan that same year, continued to refer to Sun as a revolutionary saint, a founding father of the Chinese nation.

Styled at times as the Washington of his country, Sun has also been looked to as the creator of a new political creed. This he spelled out in a series of lectures (later published in book form) on the "Three People's Principles." One thing that makes these principles so powerful, although also problematic, is their vagueness. Sun's particular vision of nationalism, popular sovereignty, and social welfare—some of the terms that can be used to translate his principles into English—was an elastic one, capable of accommodating seemingly conflictual points of view. Thus, for example, his version of Chinese nationalism could be mobilized by Han chauvinists but also by people who wanted China to be a multiethnic state. Sun's principle of social welfare was attractive to some Marxists. To them, his stress on putting the welfare of the masses at the forefront in any crafting of economic policy was compatible with the idea of class struggle. Sun's principle of social welfare was also taken as a watchword, however, by some who saw class struggle as horrible, as was often the case with members of the Nationalist Party in its anti-Communist phases.

The one definitive element in Sun's vision of revolution, which can be criticized or praised for its flexibility and imprecision, is its eclectic and pragmatic nature. Sun was less interested in grand theory than in how to get certain things done for China. He was willing to combine foreign and indigenous ideas and symbols, so long as the result seemed to hold promise for solving the current national dilemma. He was committed to moving from rule by an emperor to some form of popular sovereignty, but beyond that he was open to many options. This pragmatism, and his popularization of the idea that tightly organized revolutionary parties were needed to guide young republics in the right direction, make him similar to some of the Mexican revolutionary leaders.

Even though Sun's influence extended far beyond his death in 1925 and his ideas would help shape important events in later Chinese history, his presidency was short-lived. Within months of taking office, he was forced to abdicate in favor of military strongman Yuan Shikai, who insisted that his troops would continue to support the republican cause only if he was given the presidency. Yuan's rise to power ushered in a period of disunity and warlordism that would plague China for the next decade and a half.

Patterns and Predicaments

These sketches of influential insurrections give a sense of the diversity of events carried out in the name of revolution before Bolshevism emerged and changed the political scene. Common to all of the events was an insistence that oppressed people have the right to take the law into their own hands and remake the political order. Common as well was a commitment to popular sovereignty and extending the role of ordinary people in the governance of the nation. So, too, was a belief in the need to reshuffle in some fashion the relationship between social groups, whether in the form of redistributing wealth or simply expanding the categories of people allowed to take part in official institutions. Finally, each of the four revolutions was carried out under the banner of an ideology that remained, through the unfolding of events, a work in progress.

Each of the revolutionary struggles surveyed was important within a given national context and had at least some international influence, but none of them produced a regime that made serious efforts to lead revolutions in other lands. The French revolutionaries of 1789 certainly hoped their upheaval would spark antimonarchical insurrections in other parts of Europe, and some moves toward establishing republics were made in neighboring lands. Nonetheless, even they did not actively pursue a global or even a continental revolutionary strategy. Ever since World War I, by contrast, the world has seen the rise and fall of revolutionary regimes with just such grand ambitions. The first, and in many ways the most significant of these in terms of shaping the twentieth century, was the Bolshevik regime, which took power in Russia in 1917. This turn in the history of revolutions represented not only an expansion of ambition but also a move from a time of flexible and eclectic ideologies to one of clearly defined and rigid blueprints for change. The turn had not taken place when the Russian upheaval broke out, but it had certainly crystallized by the time the Bolsheviks began to export their vision of revolution to other parts of Europe and beyond, including Latin America and China. A shift in thinking had occurred: Instead of thinking of revolutionary struggles as primarily events that affected individual countries, proponents began to see them as phenomena that were part of international movements. This shift was one of the most profound transformations of the twentieth century. The consequences deserve a chapter of their own.

5

Bolshevism Reshapes Revolution

Those who lose by a revolution are rarely inclined to call it by its real name. For that name, in spite of the efforts of spiteful reactionaries, is surrounded in the historic memory of mankind with a halo of liberation from all shackles and prejudices. The privileged classes of every age, as also their lackeys, have always tried to declare the revolution which overthrew them, in contrast to past revolutions, a mutiny, a riot, a revolt of the rabble.

Leon Trotsky,
History of the Russian Revolution
(1932)

Political revolutions transform state structures but not social structures, and they are not necessarily accomplished through class conflict. What is unique to social revolution is that basic changes in social structure and in political structure occur together in a mutually reinforcing fashion.

Theda Skocpol,
States and Social Revolutions
(1979)

TWO INEXTRICABLY ENTWINED EVENTS OF THE SECOND DECADE OF the century, World War I (1914–1918) and the Russian Revolution (1917), simplified and at the same time distorted the meaning of both "socialism" and "revolution" for decades to come. The events of these years also introduced into debates on socialism and revolution a variety of new specific terms. Some of these concepts were associated with radical leaders of the day, in particular, V. I. Lenin (1870–1924) and Joseph Stalin (1879–1953).

Lenin, who first came to prominence in the first years of the century as a journalist and editor of a radical newspaper, spent the years immediately preceding the 1917 Revolution in Switzerland. He was best known in his early years as the author of several pamphlets, such as a 1902 tract entitled "What Is to Be Done?" In that famous essay he stressed the role that a disciplined vanguard of activists committed to socialist ideas could play in leading a successful uprising: "Give us an organization of revolutionaries and we will overturn Russia!" he wrote.

He also later stressed the parallel between the way rich classes oppressed the poor, on the one hand, and the process by which wealthy nations exploited colonial possessions, on the other. "Leninism" thus became a common term for a particular vision of revolution that focused on the central leadership role of tightly organized vanguard parties, treated anti-imperialism as a powerful motivating force for struggle, and built on Marx's ideas relating to the tension between classes.

The name of Joseph Stalin, who succeeded Lenin to become the second leader of the new nation of the Soviet Union (or USSR, Union of Soviet Socialist Republics), eventually became linked to an "ism" and a particular vision of revolution. Stalinism would often be used outside of the USSR and, after his death, within it as well to refer to an authoritarian form of state socialism in which those at the top dealt harshly with all forms of opposition and relied heavily on surveillance, show trials, and secret police.

The first epigraph to this chapter is by yet a third leader of the Russian Revolution, Leon Trotsky, whose name also would become associated with a particular vision of the revolutionary process. When Lenin died and Stalin became supreme leader of the Soviet Union, Trotsky fled to Mexico (where he would eventually be assassinated), fearing quite rightly that to stay in Russia would be to court death at the hands of the new Stalinist regime. A longtime personal as well as ideological rival of Stalin's, Trotsky was less prone than other leaders of the Russian Revolution to insist that insurrectionists in other lands needed to bide their time and wait for approval from Moscow before taking to the streets. On the contrary, he thought that unless revolutions broke out in many parts of the world, with or without guidance from the Soviet Union, the Russian experiment would fail. Stalin came to defend a vision of "socialism in one country," predicated on the idea that the Soviet Union could make it on its own. But Trotsky insisted that, if capitalist countries were not forced to fight a "permanent revolution" on many fronts, they would band together to destroy Russia's new and still fragile socialist state.

Trotskyism, as a result, became linked to revolutionary movements that placed a high value on local autonomy. Another key Trotskyist belief was that Stalin was the arch betrayer of the legacy of Marx and Lenin. Trotskyists claimed that Stalin had recreated old forms of oppression in novel guise—a charge that others leveled as well. Finally, Trotsky's name became identified with the idea of "permanent revolution"; Trotskyists called for a continual battle against capitalism to be carried out by insurgents in developing countries as well as by the workers of industrialized nations, and they were more willing than most other socialists to welcome uprisings by nonsocialist groups, such as those linked to Third World independence movements.

Important commentaries on the Russian Revolution have been made not just by former participants but also by prominent social theorists, as the second epigraph indicates. Theda Skocpol is one of many influential social scientists who has treated the Bolsheviks' rise to power at the end of 1917 as one of the pivotal turning points of modern times. Skocpol included the Russian upheavals of that period in a select group of three Great Social Revolutions—a category that also includes the French events of 1789 and the Chinese transformations of 1911 through 1949.

If the role of the Russian upheavals in redefining understandings of socialism and revolution is easy enough to describe, what is the case to be made for saying, as we have above, that World War I contributed in very important ways to the same process? Perhaps the easiest way to answer this question is simply to underline the fact that, although it was a conflagration that ended up pitting workers of different lands against each other, it also nonetheless drew support from all Western European socialist parties except Italy's. This development had devastating consequences for radical organizations and socialist thought. One of the things that Marx and Engels had always stressed in works such as the *Communist Manifesto* was that the socialist struggle was an international one. Nonsocialist participants in nineteenth-century radical movements, including the revolutions of 1848, had often linked themselves to nationalist ideals. Socialists, by contrast, had tried not to do this, insisting on the primacy of class ties, which bound people of similar socioeconomic status, over those derived from common membership in a nation. Famous anarchists, such as Mikhail Bakunin (a contemporary of Marx and Engels) and Peter Kropotkin (a Russian aristocrat whose political views were heavily influenced by discussions in the 1870s with exiled participants in the Paris Commune), had also stressed internationalism as superior to nationalism.

The fact that various socialist parties—those linked to anarchist traditions, those linked to Marxist ones, and those linked to still other strains of radical thought—backed nationalist war efforts between 1914 and 1918 was significant. It compromised their legitimacy. After the war began and it weighed in on the side of the militarists, the German Social Democratic Party lost its credibility, at least within the international proletarian movement.

All this involvement played into the hands of Lenin and the other Bolsheviks, as the members of the group of Marxists who took power in Russia were known. They stood out in part because they had taken control of a major country by revolutionary means. They also stood out because they were among the small minority of Marxists anywhere in the world who had condemned the War to End All Wars—as World War I was optimistically called—from the moment it began. The fact that they had called it a "capitalist atrocity" throughout its course ultimately elevated the stature of the Bolsheviks within international socialist circles.

This process was partially accomplished before World War I had even ended. Radicals and nonradicals alike in many countries, including Russia, came to feel that the massive bloodshed taking place on European battlefields was too high a price to pay for whatever goals individual nations might claim to be pursuing. Anger at Russian involvement in the fighting was a key fac-

PICTURE 5.1
Vladimir Ilich Lenin (1870–1924). American Isaac McBride stayed in Russia for five weeks in 1917. He met several of the revolutionary leaders and reported sympathetically on the situation. This picture from his book shows Lenin in the Kremlin Courtyard in Moscow. (Reprinted from Isaac McBride, *Barborous Soviet Russia*, [New York: Thomas Seltzer, 1920])

tor in pushing that country toward revolution. It inspired many ordinary people to take part in marches for peace and in bread riots, which were economically motivated, shaped by a belief that the war expenditures had caused the food crisis. Outside of Russia, too, many people became convinced that whatever grievances particular national leaders might claim to have against each other, they could not justify the enormous death toll of fathers, sons, and brothers. The blood-drenched fields of the western front near the French-German border became a particularly powerful symbol for many Europeans of the senselessness of the war.

The idea that nationalistic wars were by definition wasteful and immoral enterprises, and the corresponding one that only those who opposed them deserved to be seen as true socialists, was hammered home by many radical groups committed to revolution around the time of the Armistice of 1918. Part of a manifesto by one such group, a German one that denounced the reformist approach taken by their country's Social Democratic Party and embraced the ideals and strategies of the Bolsheviks, illustrated this viewpoint:

PROLETARIANS! MEN AND WOMEN OF LABOR! COMRADES!

The revolution has made its entry into Germany. The masses of soldiers, who for four years were driven to the slaughterhouse for the sake of capitalistic profits, and the masses of workers, who for four years were exploited, crushed, and starved, have revolted. . . . Workers' and soldiers' councils have been formed everywhere. . . .

Proletarians of all countries! This must be the last war! We owe that to the twelve million murdered victims; we owe that to our children; we owe that to humanity. . . .

Proletarians of all countries! We call upon you to complete the work of socialist liberation, to give a human aspect to the disfigured world.

A Narrative of the Russian Revolution

The story of the rise to power of the Bolsheviks is the tale of a series of events that were to alter the course of twentieth-century revolutions. A good place to begin is March 1917, when, as war raged throughout Europe, the government of the Russian Empire collapsed in the face of mass protests and uprisings, primarily in the capital city, then called Petrograd (now St. Petersburg). The war had destabilized the Russian monarchy. Losses on the battlefield combined with food shortages to undermine the morale of both the upper and the lower classes. Scandals involving the imperial family, including the rumored relationship of the Empress Alexandra with the "mad monk" Rasputin, had undermined confidence in the government and popular faith in Tsar Nicholas II. Because the tsar had assumed personal command over the armed forces, he was blamed for setbacks in the military campaigns of the war, which further eroded public support for the regime. The stage was set for the collapse of the 300-year-old Romanov dynasty.

On International Women's Day (March 8), simmering discontent exploded on the streets of Petrograd as thousands of female textile workers, tired of standing in endless lines to buy bread and other essentials, went on strike. Male factory workers soon joined their demonstrations. Efforts to put down the striking workers proved ineffective, in part because the government failed to perceive the seriousness of the problem at first, in part because of poor leadership, and in part because of the unwillingness of police and military troops to fire on the strikers. The city was paralyzed. Communication and transportation systems were shut down. Unable to put the demonstrations down by force, members of the government looked for a political solution. In an effort to save the dynasty, they asked the tsar to abdicate the throne in favor of his son, Alexei, still just a boy. The tsar, however, decided after some hesitation to abdicate for both himself and his son in favor of his brother, Grand Duke Michael. When the grand duke refused the throne, the autocracy collapsed, only one week after the revolution had begun. As later events were to prove, however, Russia's revolutionary year had barely begun. Nine months later, in November 1917, Russia would experience a second traumatic upheaval, known to historians as the Bolshevik Revolution.

Why did revolution break out not once, but twice, in Russia in 1917? Even before World War I began, the Russian government had been at odds with its people. Tsar Nicholas II was an absolute ruler and an autocrat. Although massive public unrest in 1905 had led to some government concessions and the creation of a quasi-parliament or legislature known as the Duma, absolute authority remained in the hands of the tsar. Liberal public opinion resented the persistence of his autocratic authority. They wanted some form of representative and democratic government, perhaps a constitutional monarchy, instead. Ordinary people, mostly peasants but also an increasing number of factory workers, resented the difficulty of their lives and the government's seeming inability to cope effectively with crises that affected them. Even more ominously for the Tsarist regime, they had lost their faith in the tsar. Events such as Bloody Sunday, a massacre in January 1905 in which government troops fired on peaceful protesters, eroded popular trust in the government and faith in the tsar as a benevolent ruler.

World War I only made a bad situation worse. Before the war, there was hope that Russia would survive its growing pains and transform itself peacefully into a modern, industrialized nation with some form of democratic, representative government. The war placed enormous strains on the Russian economy and contributed to strikes and other protests by workers. Soldiers on the front lines, really peasants in uniform, were demoralized as the war bogged down.

Such conditions presented excellent opportunities to revolutionary organizations seeking support to undermine the Tsarist regime. Many historians have viewed World War I as the catalyst for the revolution.

Russia had a long history of revolutionary organizations. In 1917, the most important groups included the Bolsheviks and the Mensheviks. Both of these groups accepted socialist or Marxist ideas of political organization, but they preferred different revolutionary strategies. Both had dedicated, but limited, followings among factory workers. The revolutionary efforts of both groups were also constrained by the fact that many of their leaders, including Lenin for the Bolsheviks and Trotsky for the Mensheviks, were in hiding abroad or in exile or prison in Russia. They were able to return to Petrograd only after the fall of the Tsarist regime. Other revolutionary organizations also had an important following. The Socialist Revolutionary Party, in particular, was a serious competitor to the Bolsheviks and Mensheviks and was more popular than either of them among the peasantry (still the vast majority of the population). Still, it is important to remember that all of these revolutionary parties were relatively small. Most Russian subjects, even if they disliked the autocratic form of government, were not revolutionaries.

After the March Revolution, however, none of the revolutionary parties came to power. Those who had persuaded the tsar to abdicate had not expected the complete collapse of the monarchy. The protesters in the streets also had no clear conception of what kind of government they wanted to replace the autocracy. Members of the last Duma formed a provisional government to fill the gap. Because they were not elected and had no parliament or legislature to support their laws and decrees, the provisional government was weak and vulnerable, a situation that the revolutionary parties soon exploited. The position of the provisional government was made even weaker by two other factors. First, the members of the provisional government considered themselves to be only a temporary body administering the government until general elections for a Constituent Assembly could be held. Major decisions on pressing problems, such as the redistribution of land to the peasants, were deferred. Second, the provisional government felt it necessary to honor Russia's commitments to its foreign allies and refused to pull Russia out of World War I. As a result, it lost support among peasants and urban residents alike, especially factory workers.

At the same time, the revolutionary parties gained support among Russian citizens. The Bolsheviks, for example, gained many thousands of new members between March and November, transforming what had been a small, clandestine, revolutionary organization into something resembling a mass political party. The revolutionary parties played a key role after the March Revolution through their control of the Petrograd Soviet, or Council, of Workers' and Soldiers' Deputies. Although the provisional government was formally in control of the Russian state, it could do little without the consent of the soviet. The Petrograd soviet not only had a loyal following in the factories, it had effectively established control over the Russian military. This situation, known as "dual power," reduced the government's ability to make decisions and govern effectively.

Despite the weakness of the provisional government and the increasing popularity of the Bolshevik Party among workers and soldiers, the Bolsheviks did not yet feel confident of their ability to seize control of the Russian state. Several factors led to this delay. The first was a conflict within the party over whether or not they should even try to seize power. According to a traditional interpretation of Marxist doctrine, the March Revolution had been a bourgeois revolution to be followed by a capitalist society. Only when capitalism had run its course and proved itself to be corrupt, according to this doctrine, would a socialist revolution be possible. Lenin, however, newly re-turned from exile abroad, strongly opposed such hesitation and advocated, in his April Theses, the rapid overthrow of the bourgeois provisional government by the proletariat, led, of course, by the Bolshevik Party. Lenin's proposals caused consternation among his fellow Bolsheviks. Most had become accustomed to the idea of working with the other revolutionary parties in the soviet and maintaining a critical, but still supportive, attitude toward the provisional government.

Lenin's proposals would have done little to secure power for the Bolsheviks if the party had not begun to attract increasing grassroots support. As late as June, the Bolsheviks were still a mi-nority in the Petrograd soviet. Lenin's slogan, "All Power to the Soviets!" would not have resulted in the transfer of all power to the Bolsheviks at that point.

Popular sentiments, however, had remained explosive. The provisional government's failure to act on land reform alienated it from the peasants. Its failure to pull Russia out of World War I alienated it from almost everyone except the most educated and privileged layers of society. In June and early July, the provisional government embarked on a new offensive with disastrous con-sequences. Casualties were estimated at 200,000 or more. Military morale disintegrated, and de-sertion rates reached a new high. The government itself experienced a crisis as the man at its helm, Prince Lvov, and all of the liberal members of the committee resigned. The population of Petro-grad responded to this crisis with a wave of demonstrations, protests, and strikes during July 3–5.

The July Days protests and strikes proved to be a disaster for the Bolsheviks. The demonstra-tions proved Lenin's contention that popular sympathies were not with the provisional govern-ment and that the opportunity existed for the Bolshevik Party to seize control. The Bolsheviks, however, were not yet in a position to seize control and did not encourage the protesters. Never-theless, despite their lukewarm response to the demonstrations, the provisional government and other socialist parties blamed them for the disruption. The Bolsheviks lost popular credibility and were forced to retreat in the face of a government crackdown. Several key leaders were ar-rested and Lenin was forced to go into hiding.

The Bolsheviks, however, were not the only ones facing difficult times. The provisional gov-ernment was increasingly being challenged not only on the political Left—by the revolutionary socialist parties—but also on the Right—by conservative military officers, industrialists, and landowners. The shaky coalition on which it depended began to fall apart. In August, the Right attempted a military coup, under the leadership of General Kornilov, in an effort to stabilize the situation, prevent the socialists from taking control, and establish law and order. The coup failed, but the incident left the provisional government weaker than ever because people suspected it of encouraging General Kornilov in his ambitions. The Petrograd soviet, since the July Days con-trolled by non-Bolshevik socialists, also lost credibility, because its resistance to Kornilov had been organized by workers and factory committees, not by soviet leaders. All these things strengthened the Bolsheviks, however, and allowed them to assume leadership of the Petrograd soviet. Public opinion, moreover, was shifting in favor of the Bolsheviks.

By early September, the Bolsheviks were openly debating within the party the wisdom of an armed uprising against the provisional government. Despite the advance publicity, or perhaps in part because of it, the Bolshevik coup succeeded. The revolution, when it finally began, was something of an anticlimax. Few shots were fired; the Bolsheviks met little armed resistance. Events began on the evening of November 6 as the Bolsheviks began to seize control of key com-munication and transportation links. Despite our images of hand-to-hand fighting in the streets, the atmosphere was generally calm. By the afternoon of November 7, the revolution in Petrograd was all but over. All that remained was to take the Winter Palace, the seat of the provisional government. Even this event, celebrated in the Soviet era as *the* deciding factor of the Bolshevik Revolution, was much less heroic than it has been imagined by writers and filmmakers. The assault on the palace was more confused than heroic.

Although the Bolsheviks had seized power, they had yet to prove they could keep it. They enjoyed substantial popular support in St. Petersburg, Moscow, and other cities, but little support among the vast peasant majority in the countryside. Moreover, they soon faced challenges from the other socialist parties even though they had expected to work with them in a coalition government. The Bolsheviks, however, having attained power, had no intention of giving it up. The struggle for power pushed Russia into a disastrous civil war. One can argue that the revolution ended only with the Bolshevik victory in the civil war of 1921–1922, even though the party's influence on international revolutionary currents was strong from 1918 on.

The International Power of Bolshevism

Why was it that the Bolsheviks ended up in charge of the USSR, and how exactly did Leninism begin to make its mark beyond Russia? Perhaps the simplest answer to this question can be decided by noting that, even though the Bolsheviks had been just one of the groups that helped make the revolution, they had the clearest idea of how they wanted to run the country. This was through a dictatorship of the proletariat organized around a tightly disciplined party. They were, moreover, unusually effective at taking cues from the insurgent masses and linking their cause to rallying calls with broad popular appeal—not just "Bread, Peace, and Land" but also "All Power to the Soviets." In addition, they constituted one of the fastest growing revolutionary organizations in the land, going from having merely several thousand to more than 200,000 members in the course of a few months in 1917.

Anger at the suffering caused by war, disgust with hypocritical parties that claimed to be committed to an international working class but embraced nationalistic military efforts, and the success of the Bolsheviks—all of these things made the late 1910s and early 1920s seem ripe for worldwide revolution. Each element also placed Lenin and his followers in an advantageous position to assume leadership of this revolution once it began—and struck fear into all those who opposed the rising tide of socialism.

The events of 1917 sent shock waves through radical circles in many countries. Struggles ensued between those for whom the "red flag" was a beloved icon, on the one hand, and those for whom it was a feared symbol, on the other. These far-reaching results are the focus of the rest of this chapter. World War I and the Russian Revolution were events that, between them, created an unusual worldwide situation. In assessing their influence it is worth looking at three very different kinds of quotations from very different kinds of texts. These commentaries convey a good feel for the peculiar mixture of millenarian hope and red-scare paranoia that swept the world in the wake of the Bolshevik victory as people recoiled from the shock of an unusually bloody and widespread war. The first quotation is from the historical novel *1919,* the work of a radical American writer, John Dos Passos, that first appeared in print in 1930:

When the Russian Revolution came in February, Ben and the Steins bought every edition of the papers for weeks, read all the correspondents' reports with desperate intenseness; it was the

PICTURE 5.2
"Did You Join As Volunteers?" (c. 1920).
At a time when the revolution was
threatened by enemies from within and
without, propaganda, such as this
revolutionary poster, was essential in
persuading many people to work for the
success of the new Soviet state. (Photo
courtesy of the Funet Russian Archive)

dawning of The Day. There was a feeling of carnival. . . . The old people cried whenever they spoke of it. "Next Austria, then the Reich, then England . . . freed peoples everywhere," Pop would say. "And last Uncle Sam," Ben would add, grimly setting his jaw.

The second quotation is from a piece of congressional testimony given in 1918, at the height of the first major red scare in U.S. history. The author is A. Mitchell Palmer (1872–1936), then U.S. Attorney General. This former congressman's name has become associated with anti-Communist fervor thanks to the phrase "Palmer Raids," which was used to describe arrests of members of groups suspected of having Bolshevik leanings. It is worth noting that, to Palmer and other people of the time fearful of socialist parties, the term "Bolshevik" was often interpreted very loosely to include virtually any type of harsh criticism of the established order. The same was true of terms such as "agitator" and "revolutionist," each of which was, like "Bolshevik," treated by Palmer as an epithet, as the following quotation shows:

If there be any doubt of the character of the leaders and agitators amongst those avowed revolutionists, a visit to the Department of Justice and an examination of their photographs would dispel it. Out of the sly and crafty eyes of many of them leap cupidity, insanity, and crime; from their lopsided faces, sloping brows, and misshapen features may be recognized the unmistakable criminal type.

The third quotation is from a Chinese essay called "The Victory of Bolshevism," which was written in 1918 by Li Dazhao and published in a magazine called *Xin Qingnian* (New Youth). Li, who was at the time a professor and librarian at Beijing University, as well as a mentor to a young man by the name of Mao Zedong, would several years later help found the Chinese Communist Party.

Whenever a disturbance in the worldwide social force occurs among people, it will produce repercussions all over the earth, like storm clouds gathering before the wind and valleys echoing the mountains. In the course of such a world mass movement, all those dregs of history which can impede the progress of the new movement—such as emperors, nobles, warlords, bureau-

На току колхоза „Большевик" (Борисовский район Минской области)

PICTURE 5.3   Workers on a collective farm. In 1928 Joseph Stalin began to implement full collectivization of Soviet agriculture. This picture from 1944 shows workers on a collective farm near Minsk. (Photo from the Library of Congress)

crats, militarism, capitalism—will certainly be destroyed as though struck by a thunderbolt. . . . Henceforth, all that one sees around him will be the triumphant banner of Bolshevism, and all that one hears around him will be Bolshevism's song of victory. The bell is rung for humanitarianism! The dawn of freedom has arrived! See the world of tomorrow; it assuredly will belong to the red flag!

Revolution in the Wake of Bolshevism: Argentina

During the first decade of the twentieth century Argentina was one of many countries that experienced large-scale industrial protests, all of which over time developed complex relationships with the Bolshevik tide alluded to in the preceding quotations. In the remainder of this chapter we consider events in Latin America, Italy, and Spain, which were rocked by revolutionary movements in the late 1910s–1930s. In this way we may provide a clearer sense of how the Russian Revolution affected radical struggles around the world.

What exactly happened in Argentine cities in the first decades of the century? Let us begin with Buenos Aires, which was the scene of several anarchist-led general strikes involving hundreds of thousands of workers. By the time World War I broke out, anarchists had become the dominant force in the labor movement. The reason is that three-quarters of the Argentine capital's labor force (some 500,000 people) consisted of first- and second-generation Italian, Spanish, and Russian Jewish immigrants who were excluded from the political process. In those years the reformist Socialist Party, which called for working within a system that did not give these immigrants a voice, could have little appeal. Adding to the attraction of radical ideas was the fact that the ruling, landed elite, tied to meat, wool, and grain export interests, responded to social unrest with mass arrests and the deportation of anarchists. Unlike industrialists in other parts of the world, they showed little interest in making concessions to labor activists in the hope of eventually integrating the working class, via higher wages, into an expanding middle-class world of consumers. By 1910, the state, supporting elite goals, had deported or jailed most of the anarchist leaders, severely weakening the labor movement but simultaneously adding to the appeal of radical ideas within the working population. Universal suffrage in 1912 appealed to many second-generation immigrants. Such sentiments eroded support for the antiparliamentarian anarchists but left the disaffection of some laborers unchanged.

Although Argentina played no direct role in World War I, the working class there suffered its economic consequences. Unemployment climbed to 19 percent by 1917, and the cost of living jumped nearly 80 percent during the war. In 1916, thanks in part to workers' votes, the Radical Party (a centrist organization) was able to have its candidate elected president. President Hipólito Yrigoyen (1916–1922; 1928–1930), in turn, made overtures to the revolutionary syndicalist sectors of the skeletal labor movement. The leaders of the syndicalist movement, in response to the state overtures for union recognition, dropped socialist revolution from their agenda but in no way compromised their day-to-day militancy in defense of labor. During this same period the Argentine Socialist Party became the second strongest electoral force in Buenos Aires, electing several congressmen.

When the labor movement reignited following the war it did so at a time when nonrevolutionary ideologies had taken hold within the working class. Between 1915 and 1919 the number of strikers jumped from 12,000 participating in 65 strikes to 310,000 participating in 400 strikes. Organized labor increased its numbers from under 50,000 to probably 200,000 during the same period (the country's industrial working class numbered 400,000, with half in the capital).

One of these numerous strikes started in December 1918 at the Vasena metal works factory. Management had slashed workers' wages by 50 percent in 1918, and wartime inflation had exacerbated the problem. Hence the union demanded a substantial wage increase. For two months most workers at the plant were on strike while management attempted to continue production with strikebreakers. On numerous occasions police and hired guards protected the strikebreakers from the strikers' wrath. On January 7, 1919, a large crowd of strikers, women, and children marched near the plant and attempted to stop some trucks from passing the gates. When they threw rocks at the trucks, police fired back, killing four strikers.

The next day, both the syndicalist and anarchist labor federations called for a general strike, and an overwhelming majority of Buenos Aires workers responded to the call. On January 9, thousands of people attended a funeral procession in honor of the slain workers. At its head marched 150 armed workers. During the course of the march some youths looted gun shops and others burned automobiles. When the group arrived at the cemetery, the speeches commenced. As the leader of the printers union eulogized the slain strikers, the police opened fire on the crowd of mourners. Between twelve and fifty workers were killed by the gunfire.

The police action at the cemetery enraged the working class, and over the next twenty-four hours violence erupted throughout the poor neighborhoods of Buenos Aires. Armed workers attacked the Vasena management headquarters. About 30,000 army troops were mobilized to back up the police. Although the antilabor press claimed that youths attacked many police stations throughout the city, they could offer no proof. Indeed, rumors and expectations ran high on both sides. One antilabor account gives a sense of the fearful atmosphere:

> The news is serious: the strikers are armed to the teeth; they've built barricades throughout the city; they've burnt four churches, two orphanages and are preparing an attack against the rail-road stations. In San Isidro and other localities along the coast the inhabitants are organizing in their own defense as they fear that the anarchist bands . . . will attack their attractive country homes.

Although the bands of strikers and youths did not attack churches or even leave the working-class districts, they did some violence and did it with glee. One witness recalled:

> I could see that a group of rioters had stopped a bus and forced all the passengers off of it. . . . Then I saw how they poured some liquid all over it . . . and suddenly it was up in flames. . . . The spectacle enraged me not so much for the burning but because of the hysterical madness of the rioters, their leaps for joy and their passionate screams .

When police did open fire on demonstrators, they often received fire in return. But if indeed the rioters, whom the official reports dubbed "anarchists," had actually ambushed police, as was claimed, they were incredibly poor shots: No soldiers or police officers died in the battles. The anarchists, like the antilabor press, did contribute to the tension and violence of those hot summer days. On January 8, the anarchist paper incited the working class to seek revenge: "Dynamite is needed now more than ever. They can't die in silence. Burn and destroy! Revenge brothers! In response to this crime . . . the violence of the people is the only solution."

Although most workers and urban youths did not identify with the anarchists, their cries surely reflected the popular response to police violence. The general strike continued to shut down the capital through January 10, and it began to spread to other cities throughout the country. That afternoon, President Yrigoyen brought the managers of the Vasena factory to the Casa Rosada and compelled them to cede to the strikers' demands. The Vasena management, whose intransigence had helped to provoke the first acts of violence, offered the strikers an eight-hour day, raises from 20 to 50 percent, overtime pay, and the reinstatement of all of the striking workers. Moreover, the government promised to release all imprisoned demonstrators. In short, this event was a decisive victory for the Vasena workers, and the general strike was instrumental in their victory.

On the night of January 10, the syndicalist federation voted to end the general strike. Notwithstanding, and in part owing to poor communications, the general strike went on the next day. The syndicalists, along with the Socialist Party, immediately made it clear to their rank and file and to the government that they opposed this continuation. The syndicalist leaders publicly informed the minister of interior: "[We] only are in solidarity with the acts of the working class and we reject all actions like the assault on police stations and the Post Office, actions that were perpetrated by people who have nothing to do with our labor federation."

The same day, most of the press hammered home the point that anarchists and Bolsheviks (called Maximalists) were the cause of the violence and the continuation of the strike. But as the strike began to wind down later in the day, a new right-wing nationalist organization, the Patriotic League, burst onto the scene. This group was founded and armed at a naval base by an admiral who believed that the government was too weak to deal with the strikers and that "civilian support was necessary to counteract the action of the subversives." These groups of armed youths from the upper classes began to focus their own rage on two ethnic groups: the Catalans, accused of being anarchists, and Russian Jews, tarnished with the brush of Bolshevism. There were perhaps 30,000 Russian Jews in Buenos Aires and a substantially larger number of Catalans (but only very small minorities of those ethnic groups belonged to revolutionary organizations). Under the banner of "Patriotism and Order," and with the backing of the police and the military, the Patriotic League marched through a Jewish neighborhood. One league sympathizer recalled:

> I saw a pile of books and furniture burning in the street. I asked what was going on and was told that it was a Jewish merchant who was guilty of distributing communist propaganda. But then I saw that this cruel punishment was going on all over the Jewish neighborhood. The sound of boxes and furniture mixed with the shouts of "Death to the Jews! Death to the Maximalists!"

From January 12–15, the labor organizations, already committed to ending the strike (except the anarchist one, which had suffered the brunt of the repression), found themselves incapable of defending innocent victims of the Patriotic League and the increasingly aggressive police. By the end of the Semana Trágica (Tragic Week), between 100 and 700 people were dead, virtually all shot by government forces or by the Patriotic League; between 400 and 2,000 were wounded; and thousands of people were locked up in jail. The workers' victory of January 10 had turned into a nightmare for many families.

The legacy of the Semana Trágica of 1919 was a mixed one for Argentine workers and the larger society. First, it revealed a huge and ugly chasm between the working class and the upper classes and their institutions. That gulf would become world famous when Juan and Eva Perón came onto the scene during the 1940s, taking power via a populist movement that came to bear their name. Prior to the existence of the home-grown ideology of Peronism, however, labor activism proved capable in Argentina of challenging but not toppling existing power structures.

This observation leads to the second meaning of the tragedy of 1919: It revealed a less dramatic gulf, this time between organizations and the population they sought to represent rather than between classes. There was a chasm separating all organizations that claimed to represent the working class from the thousands of people who were on strike and in the street doing battle with the police. The first category included the government that had come to power via the votes of workers. Even the anarchists who tried to provoke revolutionary violence had absolutely no concrete advice to offer the masses. Their lack of strategy, combined with the fury of the repression directed at their ranks, would lead to their virtual eclipse by the 1930s. The syndicalists called off the strike just as the repression was getting severe, and the socialists limited themselves to parliamentary debate. Although the Radical government forced a solution on the Vasena management, it did nothing to stop the organized violence of the Patriotic League. The pro-Bolshevik socialists who had no organizational presence during the events would reap limited propaganda benefits by stressing the grievous errors of anarchists and reformists during the Semana Trágica.

The nonexistence of a viable pro-Bolshevik group underscores just how cynically the specter of the Russian Revolution was manipulated by the far Right. No doubt Argentine workers were inspired by the revolutionary spirit emanating from the Soviet Union, but the threat of a Bolshevik-style revolution was invented to justify the rage of right-wing nationalists against Jews and immigrant labor activists. Right-wing militarism tinged with anti-Semitism, which has emerged in Argentina with virulence at different times, notably from 1976 to 1983, had its origins in January 1919. Without preconditions for revolution such as those Skocpol and others have described—which include fissures within the ruling elites and fiscal crises—the existence of a model such as the Bolshevik one can end up being a mixed blessing or even a curse for radicals. In Argentina in 1919, it gave opponents of radicalism a scapegoat without simultaneously doing much to tangibly aid those struggling to bring about change. And this was not the only place where something like this took place in the aftermath of 1917, as the following section on Italy shows, though the patterns of radical action and government response were not always the same.

Revolution in the Wake of Bolshevism: Italy

In 1920 the Italian labor movement mobilized in a manner far more impressive than the general strike in Argentina had, but with even more tragic long-term consequences. The Italian Socialist Party, alone among leftist parties in Europe, maintained a position of neutrality during World War I, despite Italy's participation on the side of the Allies. That antiwar position found an important degree of support among industrial workers in northern Italy. Indeed, in 1917, workers went on strike and rioted against the war. The Italian Socialist Party emerged from the war as the country's strongest political party.

As in the rest of Europe, a severe economic crisis followed. In large part owing to the sudden lack of profitable outlets, industrial and agricultural production, which had soared during the war, dropped by 40 percent, and unemployment surged upward. The labor federation, allied with the Socialist Party, responded to the crisis by unleashing a wave of strikes in 1919. Most of the strikes in Turin and Milan were successful, including one that achieved an eight-hour work day. Labor's success on the picket lines derived from a massive rise in its numbers. The pro–Socialist Party labor federation entered a period of enormous growth, increasing from 250,000 members in 1918 to 2 million by 1920, roughly equally divided between industrial and agricultural workers (both groups located in the north). Revolutionary syndicalism also entered a phase of rapid growth: In 1920 the faction could claim 800,000 members. The Socialist Party, whose base was in the unions, also thrived. In the 1919 parliamentary elections it won 1.8 million votes, representing 33 percent of the national vote; a centrist party finished second with 20 percent.

In Turin, home to the Fiat automobile plants, the industrial workers, through their organization of workers councils in 1919, posed the issue of direct worker control over industry. Many Fiat workers believed that these democratic councils would become the germ of a new socialist society. The auto industry fought hard against the principle of worker control and managed to defeat a strike over their legal recognition.

The labor movement in 1920 appeared to be strong enough to take power, not only in manufacturing industries but throughout Italy. But the events that marked the high point of socialist activity started off as nothing more than a modest defensive move by the unions. In 1920, spiraling double-digit inflation pushed labor into action again. In May the steel and auto workers organization, the Metalworkers Union, demanded increases of 30–50 percent to match rises in the cost of living. The response of a management spokesman was blunt: "Since the end of the war the industrialists have done nothing but drop their pants. We've had enough, now we're going to start on you."

In mid-August, the union decided to press its demands through a slowdown; its members deliberately lowered production without abandoning their jobs. In one Fiat plant employing 15,000 workers, production dropped by 60 percent in one week. By the end of August, management in Milan responded to this successful tactic with a lockout, forbidding workers from entering the factories.

But workers responded immediately to the lockouts by storming into and then occupying the factories, not only in Milan but also throughout the industrial belt of northern Italy. One anti-union paper presented the following description from Milan:

> The factories yesterday evening presented a singular spectacle. One reached them through crowds of women and children, coming and going with dinners for the strikers, voluntary prisoners of the factories. Nearer to them, here and there, on the pavement or on the grass, were the debris of the day's bivouac. Entrances were strictly guarded by groups of workers. . . . The strikers were complete masters of the field. Whoever passed, in car or cab, was subjected to control as if he were crossing the frontier, control exercised by vigilance squads and their enthusiastic companions.

Another account elaborated on the festive atmosphere in a Milan factory:

> It is clear that for many participants this situation also offers some pleasures. Sometimes song and laughter are heard, and there is also a sense of fascination with the novelty of the movement. Red banners flying, guards at the door, . . . meals eaten almost communally, a sense of waiting for the unknown, and of joy brought on by hope.

Prime Minister Giolitti refused to send troops to remove the estimated half a million strikers from the 600 factories. He argued to his conservative critics that such a move would mean "civil war."

To many workers, the occupation represented an exhilarating inversion of the world but not necessarily the harbinger of a socialist revolution. It was a momentary turning of the tables on those in power, but true social revolutions—and socialist ones as well—have to find a means of institutionalizing temporary victories. Nevertheless, in Turin, the mood, if not the program, was definitely revolutionary. The revolutionary wing of the Socialist Party worked alongside the revolutionary syndicalists. The auto workers aimed to keep control of what they baptized "Soviet Fiat." They were intent on proving that they could operate the factories better without management. When the "red guards" captured three armed police spies who had claimed that they merely wanted to see what was going on, they put them to work at the blast furnace. When the agents complained bitterly about the intense heat, a worker responded, "For us it burns all our lives. For you it's burning only tonight so get on with it."

Antonio Gramsci, Marxist philosopher and leader of the Turin Socialist Party, explained what he saw emerging in the occupied Fiat plants: "Social hierarchies are broken, historic values overthrown. . . . [The workers] have taken possession of themselves, they have found within themselves men who will undertake all those tasks which will transform a primitive and mechanical human aggregate into an organic brotherhood, a living creation."

Despite the hope and militancy that emanated from the occupied factories, many realized that the workers' militant stride toward socialism was contingent on the belief that the army would not attack the factories and risk the destruction of machinery or perhaps even a civil war. But in order to push the movement toward a revolution, its advocates would have to leave the factory gates and take over the streets and the countryside.

Although the Fiat workers stated that they "intended to negotiate only in terms of the abolition of the ruling and exploiting class," Palmiro Togliatti, future chief of the Communist Party, argued that Turin was "ringed by a nonsocialist zone." For an insurrection to be successful, he claimed, it would have to be national in scope, or "Turin and Milan will be overwhelmed. Nothing is ready." Thus, the revolutionary leaders recognized that the movement, in such an early stage of development, was not capable of transforming itself into a broad-based, full-scale socialist revolution. This realization had lasting and far-reaching consequences. The Italian Socialist Party refused to offer strategic advice to the occupation movement. Rather, the party passed the buck back to labor. The national union confederation, at an emergency congress, debated two propositions. One position, although disavowing the possibility of immediate revolution, argued that the movement should be pushed "towards the maximum solution of the socialist program." Another, more moderate, position called for negotiations leading toward "the principle of union control over industry." The moderate proposition won, with 59 percent of the delegates at the emergency congress voting in favor of it.

Prime Minister Giolitti used the space provided by the nonrevolutionary union resolution to push the employers toward a solution, but management remained intransigent. A tense week ensued in which revolutionary workers became demoralized by the negotiating posture of the union federation. One radical worker recalled in his diary on September 16, 1920: "Great agitation among the workers . . . we saw defeat looming. In the factories practically nobody worked. . . . A sense of weariness everywhere now."

But the factories remained occupied, and under pressure from the Giolitti administration, management caved in and authorized increases of four lira per day (the union had demanded 7), paid holidays, cost-of-living bonuses, and overtime pay. On September 30 the occupations ended on a dramatic note. In Turin,

> between 8 and 9 the whole labor force gathered in the great workshops. . . . The comrades of the council explained the terms of the agreement. . . . The workers stayed for two more hours . . . waiting for the bosses who were to come to take over again. . . . A great shout greeted them, a cry which was all protest, all promise. *Eviva i Soviet!* The bosses passed livid between two ranks of red guards.

Measured in terms of material gain and class consciousness, the factory occupations of 1920 represented the apex of Italian labor history and indeed a high point in the history of working people around the world. Nevertheless, the immediate legacy of that movement was negative. Although management backed down, there were many Italians who saw in those occupied factories with red flags flying the threat of a Bolshevik revolution. Angelo Tasca, a participant in the occupations and a founder of the Communist Party, wrote:

> The occupation of the factories denoted the decline of the working class movement. . . . The former "victors" . . . were demoralized: they had attempted a superhuman effort, and had drunk at the intoxicating springs of free production only to find themselves at the end in an atmosphere of a wake—and more seriously, without prospect for the future.

In 1922, capitalizing on the workers' demoralization and the wealthy's fear and hatred of the Left, Benito Mussolini marched to power in Rome. His Fascist squads then systematically attacked the leftist parties, smashed the unions, and drove their militants to death and exile.

Placing the Argentine Semana Trágica of 1919 and the factory occupations in Italy of 1920 side by side reveals certain common characteristics. First, although the Russian Revolution did not directly provoke either movement, there is no doubt that it was a source of inspiration to both and a cause of fear and panic to their adversaries. Second, both movements resulted in immediate victories for labor that nonetheless turned into defeats at the hands of enraged and armed rightist counterrevolutionaries. In Italy that defeat at the hands of the Fascists lasted from 1922 until 1943; in Argentina the rightist violence was over in a few days. Third, the ultimate failure of the movements demonstrated the weaknesses of reformist socialism, revolutionary syndicalism, and anarchism. Thus the Communist International would use both the Semana Trágica and the Italian factory occupations to argue that only the Bolshevik model could lead workers toward a socialist revolution and avoid further catastrophes. Yet another battleground, on which this scenario would play itself out with tragic consequences for many workers, was Spain.

The Spanish Civil War and the Bolshevik Model

Spain would provide the setting for the last stage of this struggle for supremacy among competing revolutionary visions. As in Argentina and Italy, revolutionary failure would be a bonanza for right-wing authoritarianism. The Civil War in Spain (1936–1939) involved many competing political forces and ideologies. Primarily it was a conflict between the Republicans, loyal to the government that had been democratically elected in February 1936, and the Nationalists, who backed the military coup of July 1936. The war rapidly became internationalized: Nazi Germany and Fascist Italy militarily intervened on behalf of the Nationalists with arms, troops, and air support, while the Soviet Union (and to a lesser extent Mexico) sent arms and advisers to the Republicans. In addition, 60,000 volunteers from fifty countries, including 15,000 American, English, and French soldiers, fought on the side of the Republic (at most 1,000 fought for the Nationalists), although their governments refused any significant aid to the besieged democracy. The international array of forces tipped the military balance in favor of the Nationalists, whose 1939 victory was attained at the cost of several hundred thousand dead, an equal number in exile, and the profound demoralization of democratic forces around the world. The Nazi-Fascist alliance, in contrast, was infused with new strength.

The Left's slim victory in the parliamentary elections of February 1936 set in motion the events that led to the Civil War. The margin of victory was provided by the anarcho-syndicalist Confederación Nacional del Trabajo (CNT, National Labor Confederation), which for the first time counseled its members to vote for the Left rather than follow the organization's traditional policy of abstention. The triumph of a popular-front government committed to a nonrepressive policy against industrial and rural workers unleashed a wave of strikes and land occupations. The government-sponsored agrarian reform, which promised to redistribute unproductive latifundia (farms of more than 300 hectares), galvanized the poor and then legitimized what large numbers of organized, landless workers had done on their own. In one area south of Madrid, 60,000 peasants, organized by a socialist union, had occupied 3,000 latifundia. Similarly, the growth and power of industrial unions that had been organized by anarchists and socialists intimidated the upper classes and raised the very real specter of a proletarian revolution. The military coup responded to the fears of the landowners, industrialists, bankers, church leaders, and peasants of central and northern Spain.

In Barcelona, the CNT already had 2,000 people under arms when the military staged its rebellion at dawn on July 19. By the next morning some 100,000 people had joined in the defense of the Republic. Faced with such overwhelming resistance, soldiers began to desert, and within twenty-four hours the Nationalist officers capitulated. On July 20 the president of Catalonia, an autonomous province, called in the anarcho-syndicalist leaders and told them: "Today you are masters of the city and of Catalonia. . . . You have conquered and everything is in your power; if you do not need or want me as president of Catalonia, tell me now."

The ensuing debate among the anarchists and anarcho-syndicalists revolved around the issue of whether to impose their revolutionary vision on the majority of Catalonians (and even a greater majority of Spaniards) who did not share their goals. Their desire to stay true to their antiauthoritarian ethos led the majority of the CNT leaders to support the popular-front (anti-Fascist) governments in Barcelona and Madrid despite their opportunity to take power for themselves in Catalonia, a region with 3.5 million inhabitants. Within months, as a necessary means to defeat the Nationalists, CNT leaders would feel compelled to join those governments and thereby sacrifice a fundamental tenet of their philosophy.

In an important sense, the crucial involvement of Germany, Italy, and the USSR in the Spanish Civil War was a foreshadowing of World War II, which would pit the former two far-right powers and Japan against the Soviet Union allied with the democratic United States, the United Kingdom, and France. But the Civil War was something more than a prelude to the world conflagration. To the detriment of the Republican cause it pitted several competing visions of revolutionary change against each other. Between July 1936 and May 1937, the anarcho-syndicalist movement was the dominant political force in the Republican-held territory, and to a significant degree it pushed its agenda of equality, collectivization, and antimilitarism. Arrayed against the anarcho-syndicalists was the rapidly growing Communist Party, which benefited enormously by its control over Soviet military aid.

These ten months witnessed one of the most profound social revolutions in modern history, although it resulted in an imposition of an authoritarian, rightist dictatorship that isolated Spain from the forces of modernization for forty years. George Orwell, the English writer, best captured the appearance of a revolution in social relations when he described his arrival in Barcelona in December 1936. He provided this glimpse of a social revolution in process:

It was the first time that I had ever been in a town where the working class was in the saddle. Practically every building of any size had been seized by the workers and was draped with red flags or with the red and black flag of the Anarchists; . . . almost every church had been gutted and its images burnt. Churches here and there were being systematically demolished by gangs of workmen. Every shop and cafe had an inscription saying that it had been collectivised. . . . Waiters . . . looked you in the face and treated you as an equal. Servile and even ceremonial forms of speech had temporarily disappeared. . . . Everyone called everyone else "Comrade" and "Thou." . . . And it was the aspect of the crowds that was the queerest thing of all. In outward appearance it was a town in which the wealthy classes had practically ceased to exist.

PICTURE 5.4
Spanish battalion. Shock troops marching in
Madrid in about 1937, during the Spanish Civil
War. (Photo from the Library of Congress)

. . . Practically everyone wore rough working-class clothes, or blue overalls, or some variant of
the militia uniform. All this was queer and moving. There was much in it that I did not understand, in some ways I did not even like it, but I recognized it immediately as a state of affairs
worth fighting for.

If the CNT refused to take power and unleash a full-scale socialist revolution, large sections
of the Barcelona working class nonetheless interpreted the defeat of the military as the triumph of the social revolution. Orwell mentioned two dramatic instances of the ensuing spontaneous mobilization of industrial workers in Barcelona: the attack on churches and the collectivization of industry and enterprises. Spanish anarchists, like their brethren throughout
the world, were profoundly anticlerical. Not only did workers desecrate churches, they also assassinated an estimated 277 priests. Many of these actions took place despite the wishes of the
CNT leadership, which was unable to control the people who were doing these things. In fact,
the perpetrators were tagged the "uncontrollables." The deep-seated hatred of the Church was
largely political—the Church hierarchy had always opposed any rights for organized labor and
seemed only concerned with educating the children of the elite. One Catalan Catholic believed
that this mentality stemmed from "the idea that the church should be on the side of the poor
and isn't." In the words of an eminent English historian, the Spanish Catholic Church had "opposed all change since the Protestant Reformation." Hatred of the Church was not something
born of the revolution. An old Catalan street ballad went: "There were six bad bulls at the bull-
fight and so the people came out and burnt the churches." Of course, the antireligious violence
pushed many Spaniards into the rightist camp and intensified the Vatican's opposition to the
Republic.

Collectivization also became a reality in Republican Spain. The movement toward agrarian reform accelerated in the latter part of 1936. By the end of the year, hundreds of thousands of formerly landless workers had joined collectives occupying three-quarters of the land in Aragon and
one-half of the land in Catalonia and the Levante. The political and economic record of rural
collectivization was mixed. On the one hand, anarcho-syndicalist militias often expropriated
land and imposed their agenda on villages. In many instances, the CNT militia terrorized people
into joining collectives. On the other hand, thousands of previously landless laborers eagerly
worked to create this new egalitarian social order. According to one account: "In Maella today
there are no rich and no poor; there are only hard-working people. The only value for consumption is based on one's effort." Similarly, one farm worker recalled:

When we brought in the wheat crop—an excellent harvest because we had worked hard and it had rained at the right time—we knew we were right: all that grain which had been sown, reaped and threshed with our labor had previously gone to benefit the landowners who did nothing. How sad to think of what those landlords had been making out of us before; how happy we were now to see the fruit of our labor providing food for the collective, the whole village.

The experiences of rural collectivization ranged from terror, coercion, and inefficiency to liberation. Equally varied were the experiences of urban collective life. Many factory owners fled with the defeat of the military insurrection; workers seized the factories and began to run them collectively. They elected their own foremen and delegates to a factory council. The initiative of the unions was remarkable: An armaments industry to supply the Republican forces was literally invented overnight through conversion of the automobile and locomotive industries. By September 1936, these industries employed 50,000 workers in 500 plants and produced 3 million Mauser bullets and 4,000 artillery shells a month.

This achievement indeed marked a rare historic moment: Hundreds of thousands of relatively uneducated workers ran what were then considered technologically advanced factories. That unique experiment in worker self-management frightened capitalists and governments in the democratic countries just as it did the Communist leaders of the Soviet Union, who feared a genuine social revolution. Nevertheless, the relative success of industrial collectivization is difficult to measure in social and economic terms. Overall production dropped some 20 to 30 percent and unemployment increased significantly. However, the war contributed greatly to those problems: The Nationalist troops often cut off the coal supply to Barcelona, and the German and Italian navies curtailed maritime trade. Most significant, investors representing 75 percent of the total capital in the country fled, leaving the credit supply drastically reduced.

The CNT leaders, the main proponents of collectivization, recognized its severe limitations. They found that the collectives tended to reproduce significant inequities in society. As one text put it: "We refuse the idea that there should be rich and poor collectives. And that is the real problem of collectivization." A CNT leader complained in a similar vein that, "Only a minority [of workers] understood that collectivization meant the return to society of what, historically, had been appropriated by the capitalists." Many workers—despite their membership in revolutionary unions—simply lacked a strong spirit of class solidarity with workers outside their shop or on the front lines in the battle against the Nationalists. In many collectivized factories only 25 to 30 percent of the workers attended assemblies where basic production and distribution decisions were made. One CNT leader, citing the decline in both production and, more curiously, class solidarity wrote, "The immense majority of workers have sinned by their lack of discipline." He claimed that in "an infantile manner the workers have come to believe that everything was already won . . . when in reality the real social revolution begins precisely in the period of constructing the economy."

Confronted with an individualistic and even complacent working class, the revolutionary union leaders faced the prospect of growing social inequality combined with a continuing decline in productivity—trends that would aid the cause of the enemy. In response they would have to "socialize" the collectivized industries and businesses—that is, channel surpluses into less profitable but more militarily strategic enterprises and impose discipline over the labor force. Yet that strategy would involve imposing their vision on the majority, thereby violating their libertarian tenets. Similarly, such a revolutionary strategy would bitterly alienate the Communists and liberals within the Republican camp and, moreover, the Western democracies. With the benefit of hindsight, it is obvious that most of the Spanish middle class was already terrified of the collectivization process, as were the Western powers.

One anarchist leader laid out their dilemma: "We knew that it was not possible for the Revolution to triumph if we did not triumph in the war beforehand. We sacrificed the Revolution without understanding that this sacrifice also implied sacrificing the aims of the war." The fundamental tenet of anarchist philosophy—opposition to all forms of government—ran up against the grim reality of the Nationalist military advance. In early November, when the Nationalists attacked Madrid, the CNT sacrificed that sacred ideological tenet by accepting four cabinet posts in the Republican government. The willingness of these men to participate in the government did not, however, mean that they had sacrificed their belief in social revolution—the collectivization of land and factories—as a precondition for winning the war.

The Communist Party, in contrast, argued that the social revolution must be postponed—even reversed—until after the defeat of the Nationalists. A Communist lawyer summarized this bitter, fatal debate:

> It was the great theoretical and concrete problem of the war. . . . Could revolution coexist with anti-fascist struggle? . . . Were the people fighting to defend the republic of February 1936, a democratic, liberal, open republic, or were they fighting to transform that republic into a socialist, syndicalist, or some other type of republic? We communists maintained the former.

International and domestic factors conditioned the Communist view. First, the Soviet Union since 1935 had been pursuing an international policy of alliance with the Western democracies in opposition to Nazi Germany and Fascist Italy. The Communist International, the worldwide organization of Communist parties based in Moscow and controlled by the USSR, promulgated the strategy known as the Popular Front against fascism, that is, an alliance of all non-Fascist forces. The Communist International pursued this strategy until the Soviet Union signed a nonaggression pact with Nazi Germany in 1939. In Spain, the Communists translated the Popular Front strategy into an absolute subordination of revolutionary to military aims. Second, the nonrevolutionary policy dramatically aided the growth of the Communist Party. Its ranks had doubled during the first six months of war; over half of the new recruits belonged to the rural and urban middle classes.

George Orwell summarized the opposing view, shared by anarcho-syndicalists and anti-Stalinist socialists (social democrats and Marxists who were vaguely sympathetic to Trotsky but opposed to the Communists), when he stated in *Homage to Catalonia* (1938) that the Communists were working "not to postpone the Spanish Revolution till a more suitable time, but to make sure that it never happened." Retrospectively, many CNT survivors believe that their error resided in not standing firm enough against the Communist efforts to roll back the revolutionary advances of July 1936.

These two leftist positions came to a tragic head in May 1937. On May 3, the Catalonian government, under prodding from the now influential Communist Party, moved to take over the telephone exchange in Barcelona, which had been held by CNT workers since the previous July. The government charged that the CNT monitored its communications. The CNT and its allies viewed the takeover as a serious provocation. They responded with a massive general strike that quickly degenerated into armed conflict between the two Republican factions, with the Communist fighters supported by the provincial Civil Guards. Taking over the telephone exchange and occupying CNT headquarters were the two principal objectives of the Communist siege. This civil war within the Civil War raged for three days and resulted in a death count of more than 500. The CNT's participation in the central government severely curtailed its options, and its leaders refused to send the CNT militia from the nearby Aragon front into the fray, a tactic that would have ensured a CNT victory over the Communists and the Civil Guards. In a sign of deep frustration, recognizing that a truce would signal the beginning of the end for the revolution, when an anarchist minister broadcast an appeal for a cease-fire, embittered union militants shot the radio.

The premonition of the union militants proved to be correct. Following a truce on May 7, the Republican government sent in troops to ensure order—but a kind of order that involved violently repressing those leftists accused of Trotskyism by the Communists and increasingly marginalizing the CNT. On a national level, a new government came to power that was hostile and repressive toward any group that did not accept the popular front policy. This regime jailed thousands of CNT supporters; scores were assassinated. Moreover, the Communist-backed government began to reverse the collectivization process in the city and countryside by returning property to its original owners. There is ample evidence to suggest that following the events of May 1937, the will to fight the right-wing dictator Generalísimo Francisco Franco (1892–1975) was significantly diminished, perhaps destroyed, by the policy of authoritarian centralization undertaken by the Communists and moderates and carried through by force. "There was," observed one Italian militiaman, "no longer a war to build a new society and a new humanity."

Orwell had been moved by the appearance of a social transformation in revolutionary Barcelona. Following the May 1937 conflict, the English writer, now suspected of Trotskyism by the Communists, had to hide out from Republican authorities. From this new vantage point, he described the officers of the Popular Army, who arrived in the city "wearing elegant khaki uniforms. . . . All of them had automatic pistols strapped to their waists; we at the front, could not get pistols for love or money." He also observed the new social styles that surfaced following the defeat of the CNT. He depicted "fat, prosperous men, elegant women, sleek cars. . . . The normal division of society into rich and poor . . . was reasserting itself" (*Homage to Catalonia*, 1938).

Although the Spanish and Soviet Communists bore a great deal of responsibility for the May events and the thwarting of the revolutionary process, the anarcho-syndicalists were far from blameless. First, they were incapable of controlling the extremists in their own ranks. Political assassination of suspected Fascists and clergy had been standard anarchist fare, setting an ugly precedent. Moreover, the hundreds if not thousands of political and religious assassinations that they committed drove many middle-class people into the Nationalist camp, creating what Franco called his "fifth column" behind the Republican lines. Second, there was no solid evidence that a revolutionary, egalitarian strategy, involving militias on the front and autonomous collectives in the rear guard, could have defeated the Nationalists. Was decentralization—especially given the lack of a strong political commitment on the part of many collectives—a serious alternative to the unitary military and political will of the Nationalists? Indeed, the CNT leadership—constantly confronted by its own ideological contradictions—at key moments, such as in May 1937, was incapable of defending the revolution that it had done so much to promote.

The social revolution was defeated by the Communist-Liberal Republican forces in 1937, and in 1939 the Republic fell to the Nationalists. General Francisco Franco would rule until his death in 1975. Under his regime, democrats, liberals, socialists, Communists, and all types of anarchists were indeed treated as equals and were punished accordingly.

PICTURE 5.5   Striking workers, United States. Worker unrest in the Great
Depression and its aftermath was common worldwide. Here, police battle truck
drivers during a labor strike in Minneapolis in 1934. (Photo courtesy of the Franklin
D. Roosevelt Library, Great Depression and New Deal Digital Collection)

Conclusion

The seizure of power by Lenin and his Bolshevik Party after the overthrow of the tsar seemed to
represent the triumph of industrial workers and poor peasants over their capitalistic and aristocratic foes, and therefore people around the world saw hope for the future. The Russian Revolution was the first successful modern social revolution in that the landowning and industrial elites
were displaced from power, and workers and peasants received benefits—in the form of land, job
security, health care, and education—that were virtually unheard of in the rest of the world. Yet
those vast improvements came at the expense of individual liberties. The human costs of the Bolshevik project would only become gradually known, particularly under the brutal rule of Stalin.
Indeed, the remaining decades of the twentieth century can be read as a series of events illustrat-
ing disillusionment with the Russian Revolution and with those models of change that it inspired.

During the decades between the two world wars, though, there were still revolutionary socialist models that were distinct from the Marxist-Leninist version enshrined in the Soviet Union
and propagated by the Communist International. We have looked at labor movements in Argentina, Italy, and Spain that were led by people committed to social revolutionary change, but
that differed from the Marxist-Leninist model. In Italy, industrial workers occupied factories and

began to labor as if they owned them—in effect creating miniature socialist societies that operated internally on democratic principles. Despite the involvement of Marxists inspired by the Russian Revolution, the movement was characterized by the initiatives of the workers rather than by obedience to party directives. Notwithstanding its numerical and strategic strength, it was still limited largely to Turin and Milan, and its isolation left its leaders with little option but to negotiate the terms of their defeat. The end of this revolutionary surge prepared the terrain for the Fascist takeover of Italy. In Argentina and Spain, libertarian socialists, or anarchists, led movements committed to similar goals—worker control, ownership of factories, and peasant expropriation of large-scale landholdings without the participation of a political party. They believed that the vanguard party model would inevitably lead to the installation of a self-perpetuating bureaucracy that would rule again over the proletariat. Although the course of events in the Soviet Union, and later in other Communist countries, would prove the anarchists right, their own efforts at socialist revolution ended in abysmal failure. As in Italy, the fear of social revolution gave a great boost to the fortunes of the extreme Right.

Spain provided the most propitious field for libertarian socialistic experiments. Anarcho-syndicalists in the CNT dominated a large, expanding labor movement. Their efforts at creating an alternative socialist society in 1936 and 1937 fell apart for three reasons. First, the all-out war by the Franquist army created enormous burdens on the economy and on the people of Republican Spain. Second, the Communist International Popular Front strategy was bitterly opposed to social revolutionary experiments that would alienate middle- and upper-class anti-Fascists. Finally, the libertarian socialist project depended on a high degree of class solidarity because the better-off factory collectives would have to share with those workers in the poorer sectors of the economy. The majority of workers organized in the CNT, although eager to enjoy their immediate material gains wrought by the revolution, seemed to lose their formerly fierce notions of class solidarity as they came to control factories. These three factors doomed the Spanish Revolution and along with it any model of socialist revolution outside of Marxism-Leninism.

What we see then in the rise and fall of revolutions in the first decades of the twentieth century is a complex, tragic story. On the one hand, without a clearly articulated plan of action, revolutionaries all too often failed to achieve their goals or, even if successful, did not give people struggling for freedom in other lands anything more than vague slogans to work with. On the other hand, a grand model such as Bolshevism could bring with it tremendous costs—in human suffering, in an inability to adapt to local conditions, and in a tendency to reproduce in one way or another a situation in which a handful of people exert power over the great majority of the population. An exportable model for revolution it might be, but it was a deeply flawed vehicle to use in the pursuit of true liberation.

6

....

Fascism and the Holocaust

Peoples which are rising, or rising again after a period of decadence, are always imperialist: any renunciation is a sign of decay and death. Fascism is the doctrine best adapted to represent the tendencies and the aspirations of a people, like the people of Italy, who are rising again after many centuries of abasement and foreign servitude. . . . For if a doctrine must be a living thing, this is proved by the fact that Fascism has created a living faith; and that this faith is very powerful in the minds of men, is demonstrated by those who have suffered and died for it.

Benito Mussolini,
"The Political and Social Doctrine of Fascism"
(1935)

The cremation of about 2,000 people in five ovens took approximately twelve hours. In Auschwitz there were two installations with 5 double ovens each, and 2 installations with 4 larger ovens each. . . . All of the leftover clothing and effects were sorted by a group of prisoners who worked all the time and were quartered in the effects camp. Once a month valuables were sent to the Reichsbank in Berlin. After they had been cleaned, items of clothing were sent to armaments firms for the eastern labor working there or to repatriates. Gold from the teeth was melted down and likewise sent once a month to the sanitation office of the Waffen-SS. . . . The highest number of gassings in one day in Auschwitz was 10,000. That was the most that could be carried out on one day with the equipment available.

Rudolf Hoess,
camp commandant at Auschwitz, from his diary
(1939–1945)

IN EVERYDAY CONVERSATIONS WE TEND TO THROW AROUND THE adjective "fascist" rather incautiously, applying it to any form of authoritarian tendency manifest in the actions of a state, a group, or even an individual. Thus the media uses the term to describe military regimes in South America or Africa, or racist groups within the United States such as the Ku Klux Klan. Rush Limbaugh, the conservative commentator, even used the word to refer to certain feminist organizations. Fascism conjures up the negative image of a charismatic leader guiding jack-booted thugs in a quest for world domination, a perpetrator of indiscriminate force and brutality in an omnipotent state using ideological manipulation and propaganda to maintain control over the masses.

Fascism emerged as a political phenomenon when Benito Mussolini and his followers came to power in Italy in 1922. Adolf Hitler's abortive Munich putsch occurred in the following year. In the 1930s Fascist Parties sprang up in various countries in Europe, usually under the patronage of Hitler and Mussolini. Fascism became popular with the traditionalists on the Right, who were horrified at the prospect of a Bolshevik Europe and hoped to use new mass mobilization techniques pioneered by the Bolsheviks in order to co-opt the masses. But in several countries, such as Hungary, when traditional elites recaptured power they created a modern dictatorship without a populist Fascist Party that could mobilize popular consent. Thus, not every authoritarian state in interwar Europe can be labeled fascist. Fascism ended in 1945 with the defeat and death of the two dictators at the end of World War II and the collapse of their client states (see Map 6.1).

Fascism meant more than the control and authoritarian exercise of state power. It was a particular ideological mix of traditional and revolutionary values; ultimately the protean and nebulous nature of fascism was what made it so appealing to a cross-section of society. On the one hand, fascism can be labeled as conservative as it extolled the political authority of the patriarchal male, or the *Fuhrerprinzip*, while denouncing both parliamentary democracy and socialism. On the other, it was a radical phenomenon that held out the vision of a genuine national community, direct democracy, and technological mastery over the future. It was based on the power of the peasantry, of the urban and rural petty bourgeoisie, and of sections of the working class, but once in power, Fascists wooed both the business and agricultural elites. Finally, what made fascism unique was the blend of traditional goals and quintessentially modern methods used to achieve them. Thus, anti-Semitic attitudes and concepts of racial hygiene had been around in Europe for a while, but it was only the Nazis who actually implemented these bizarre ideas using advanced killing techniques perfected by scientists and medical technicians.

Although Fascist governments made liberal use of the repressive mechanisms of the modern state to control the people, fascism was ultimately made possible by the adherence of millions of people. Blue-collar workers and capitalists, doctors and lawyers, students and professors, petty bureaucrats and politicians, members of the Church, and even members of the artistic and literary intelligentsia found within the ideology and organization of fascism what seemed like meaningful answers to their questions in the bleakness that dominated post–World War I Europe. Indeed, many intellectuals

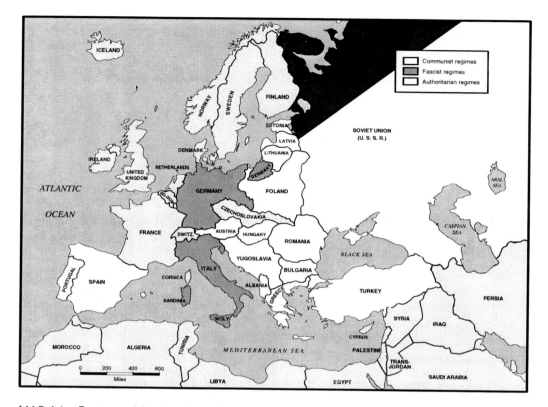

MAP 6.1   Fascist and Authoritarian States in Europe, 1920s and 1930s.

during this period believed that the bourgeois age, with its shallow and sentimental culture and hyperrationalization, was on the verge of collapse and that humans would rediscover the wellspring of an exuberant creativity in an authoritarian national state that would end all human isolation and class tensions. Thus, the German poet Gottfried Benn was convinced that the Aryan Germans would play a historic role on the world stage by battling modern decadence and imposing order and form on the chaos of the contemporary age. Although the mass popularity of fascism might be difficult for us to understand today, it is important to remember that German support for the Nazis was often leavened by overt and covert acts of resistance offered by youth groups, religious organizations, and left-wing parties, workers, and women. Also, support for Hitler was largely predicated on his ability to win military and diplomatic victories abroad. In the later years of World War II, the popularity of Hitler and the Nazis waned considerably among the Germans.

In this chapter we first give an overview of the development of Nazism in Germany, its ideological origins, the role of the leader, the nature of some of its economic policies, and its impact on world affairs. In the second part of the chapter we look at the reasons for its popularity in certain parts of Europe. Third, we discuss the nature and impact of the Holocaust as well as persecution of other minorities, such as gypsies and homosexuals. Finally, we briefly survey Nazi policies on the eastern front in Germany's war with the Soviet Union. The barbaric policies that the Nazis used toward both civilians and soldiers in this theater of war were comparable in certain instances to their treatment of Jews.

The Nazis Come to Power

Although fascism developed primarily between 1919 and 1945 in Europe under the direction of Benito Mussolini (1883–1945) and Adolf Hitler (1889–1945), its ideological roots can be traced to a profound crisis within the process of modernity. Fascism arose as a specifically open rejection of the modern parliamentary liberal form of government and of the central tenet of the French Revolution—the political equality of man. Although nineteenth-century Western European society was still marked by savage inequalities, proletarian movements in Germany, France, and England had increased the participation by working-class people in the political process. Moreover, an ascendant bourgeoisie had succeeded in destroying the corporate privileges of the nobility that had dominated Europe for centuries. *1923 - Hitler trys to overthrow local authorities*

Fascism, however, was powered primarily by a paradoxical tenet. Hitler was able to mobilize large numbers of people by offering them a vision of a corporate and harmonious society where everyone worked toward clearly defined national goals. According to Hitler, unlike representative democracy, a national socialist state would incorporate the people directly into the body politic through the party and adherence to the will of the leader, who embodied the nation. The Nazis (members of Hitler's National Socialist German Workers Party, or, in German, Nationalsozialistische Deutsche Arbeiterpartei [NSDAP]) used a range of activities, including paramilitary street displays, fighting, terror, and conventional associations of youth groups, women, and workers to control the citizens and give them a sense of direct participation in national goals and politics. Some people resented having their leisure time and private life invaded by the state, but the activities gave most citizens a sense of belonging to a distinctive race of people who were destined to play a historic role.

At the same time, Nazism was a deeply inegalitarian philosophy that valorized efficiency over humanity, racial purity over the right to live, and ultimately accepted or condemned individuals to death based on the their value to the Nazi state. Nazism therefore was both inclusionary and exclusionary, offering a distinct pantheon of good and evil prototypes and values. To those who fit the Aryan description, it offered an emotional experience of politics, a sense of deep wartime camaraderie, and a commitment to a glorious future that was widely at variance with the more sober political practices of either liberalism or socialism. *Thrown in jail for treason, writes Mein Kampf*

Although seeds of fascist ideology can be found in nineteenth-century intellectual thought, fascism emerged as a political force only in the aftermath of World War I. A highly destructive war, it discredited monarchies and broke up once mighty dynasties such as the Ottomans in Turkey, the Romanovs in Russia, and the Hapsburgs in Austria and Hungary. Meanwhile, it did little to usher in a new respect for either democracy or liberalism. Germany emerged from the war with a burning sense of humiliation and resentment. Not only had the "invincible" German army been defeated in battle, but in addition, the victors, France and England, forced Germany to sign the demoralizing Treaty of Versailles, which put responsibility for starting World War I squarely on Germany.

Under the terms of the treaty, Germany was forced to drastically reduce its armed forces, a measure that caused considerable discontent. Second, Germany was levied a bill for nearly $33 billion as part of war reparations. In the postwar economic context, this amount was an impossible sum for the country to pay. When Germany stopped making payments, French forces occupied the Ruhr in 1923 in a fruitless attempt to extract reparations. The Weimar Republic, a liberal democratic government that presided over Germany in this difficult time, was blamed for most of the disasters that beset Germany in the post–World War I period. Large-business owners and Prussian landlords, as well as the nationalistic middle class, blamed the socialists and Jews in the

PICTURE 6.1   Hitler and SA troops. SA troops parade past Hitler in Nuremburg, Germany, in November 1935. (Photo from the National Archives)

Weimar Republic for selling out to the Allies and accepting the harsh clauses of the Treaty of Versailles. Especially unpopular was the infamous war guilt clause, which held Germany solely responsible for World War I. Moreover, among the old and new middle classes, the unemployed, those who had lost social status, and a younger generation bereft of any hope for the future, Weimar democracy failed to find legitimacy. During the 1920s, as Germans struggled to cope with their loss of Great Power status, they were also plagued by terrible economic conditions: unemployment, spiraling inflation, low prices for agricultural products, and an economic slump.

The Weimar Republic was able to weather the storms and challenges to its rule, however, and by the late 1920s the economic situation had improved owing to the infusion of foreign credits and currency reform. But the Great Depression undercut all chances of social stability and economic prosperity in Germany and transformed the Nazi Party from a violent fringe movement into a dictatorial party that effortlessly dominated national politics. The success of the Nazis was predicated to a large extent on the charismatic authority of Adolf Hitler. Born into a lower middle-class Austrian family in 1889, Hitler was a failure at most occupations until he found his métier in politics. Both as an orator and as an organizer he proved extraordinarily successful. Under his leadership, the Nazis grew into a formidable organization. Drawing on the glory of his wartime experiences—for which he had received the Iron Cross First Class for valor—Hitler appealed to the military and the vast legions of veterans who responded to his message of ultranationalism and warmongering. At the same time, his low military rank of corporal and his humble origins made him appealing to the masses. He denounced the Weimar Republic, the Treaty of Versailles, liberals, socialists, and Communists. In fact, his critique of the Bolshevik menace helped endear him to the business elite and the middle class. Finally, Hitler added a unique racist ingredient to his message, one that was almost absent in Italian fascism, at least until much later.

Hitler extolled the Germans as a uniquely pure Aryan race responsible single-handedly for the development of Western civilization. In contrast, he held the Jews responsible for every evil of modern society, including capitalism and Bolshevism, feminism and the breakdown of the family, avant-garde art and decadence in literature, liberalism and democracy, prostitution and homosexuality. Jews were deemed to be an alien race bent on destroying the virile Aryan nation and culture by introducing effeminate, degenerate values. In the name of racial hygiene and the survival of the German peoples, he claimed, the Jews had to be eliminated, just as one would expunge an unwelcome pest or bacteria from one's home. The medicalization of the discourse on Jews was not merely coincidental. A vast number of doctors, medical technicians, biologists, and anthropologists cooperated with Hitler's agenda by conducting research to "prove" the existence of a racial hierarchy and enhance the racial purity of the Germans. Their participation bolstered Hitler's argument that society could benefit by eliminating and sterilizing all undesirables such as the Jews, gypsies, and the mentally deficient. *out of Jail tries to reform Nazi Party*

Surmounting the content of his message was the myth of Hitler himself as the Führer (leader). The larger-than-life cult of the Führer, the superman, provided the glue that held together the disparate acts, policies, and organizations that made up the NSDAP. Even Germans who were only marginally committed to Nazism adored the person of Hitler. Hitler himself paid the greatest attention to the construction of his public persona, creating a distinctive posture, manner, and rhetorical style. As the quintessential strongman of Teutonic myth and history, he refused to exhibit any human failings in public and to that end would neither wear glasses nor take part in any activity that might make him look ridiculous. Joseph Goebbels, his minister of propaganda, even portrayed his self-avowed celibacy as a sacrifice undertaken to ensure the happiness of the masses. The gesture was directed primarily at the women voters. *gain Support, not enough 2.6% in 27*

Hitler was an indefatigable public speaker who was in his element when addressing massive rallies, which he ran like revivalist meetings with the help of Goebbels. Loudspeakers, music, bands, poetry, films, theater, and relentless press campaigns helped to ground his popularity, though an atmosphere of intimidation and vigilance drastically reduced opportunities for onlookers to air negative comments or register disbelief. The manufacturers of the Hitler cult attributed to him every highly valued bourgeois quality, including a paternal concern for little children. He was represented as tough, severe, and virtuous, but at the same time caring, compassionate, and intensely lonely. City centers were decorated with busts and pictures of Hitler festooned with garlands and wreaths. Citizens used the phrase "Heil Hitler" to greet each other.

In retrospect it seems amazing that a nation and indeed a continent could be beguiled by the illogical ravings of a lunatic (and the notions of his ideologue, Alfred Rosenberg), but Hitler's ascendancy offers proof of the power of the irrational and the contingent in history. In 1923 Hitler attempted a putsch in Munich hoping to emulate Mussolini's success in Italy the year before by gaining power in Bavaria. But the coup was a failure and Hitler found himself in prison, where he wrote his autobiography, *Mein Kampf* (My Struggle), which was later to serve as a guide to Nazi policies. This rambling work hammered home two messages, the great and glorious mission of the German peoples in world history, which Hitler said demanded their territorial expansion, and its axiomatic corollary, the suppression of inferior peoples as the Aryans marched to fulfill their destiny. Released on parole in 1924, Hitler tried to revive the flagging fortunes of his Nazi Party, and with the help of Ernest Rohm, a captain in the German army, built up the party's paramilitary wing, the Sturmabteilung (SA), or Storm Troopers. Although Hitler would later persecute homosexuals mercilessly, he ignored Rohm's flagrantly homosexual lifestyle, presumably because he furnished followers, arms, and financial support for the struggling party. But as late as 1928 the Nazis could boast of only a dozen deputies in the Reichstag (the lower house of the German Parliament) and claim a mere 2.6 percent of the popular vote.

In 1929, however, as the Great Depression struck, unemployment figures reached frightening proportions. As more and more traditional industrial workers supported the Communists, the middle class and the lower middle class turned to the Nazis as a bulwark against social revolution. The Nazis also recruited heavily among young workers in the city—who, because of the depression, had to go straight from school to the dole—as well as from the lower ranks of the civil service and from the small-business sector of provincial Germany. After the 1930 Reichstag elections, the number of Nazi delegates jumped from 12 to 107. This success made the Nazi contingent the second largest after the Social Democrats. By 1932, when nearly 6.2 million Germans were unemployed, the Nazis claimed 230 seats out of the total 608 in the Reichstag. The aging president of the Weimar Republic, Paul von Hindenburg, was persuaded by nationalist and conservative politicians to appoint Hitler as chancellor. Hitler, presiding over a coalition government, proceeded to outmaneuver both the Left and the Right. In February 1933 he used a mysterious fire in the Reichstag to suspend civil liberties and arrest Communists and some Social Democrats. He prevailed upon the other parties to pass an Enabling Act, which gave him dictatorial powers for four years. Within weeks after its passage, he dissolved all other political parties. The suppression of the Communists greatly boosted the popularity of the Nazis among middle-class Germans and the rural population.

The SA, however, was getting restless, and Rohm aspired to subsume the traditional German army under its command. The army leadership, although supportive of Hitler, would not tolerate Rohm's ambitions. In June 1934 during the Night of the Long Knives, Rohm and his SA associates were killed in a bloody purge. Heinrich Himmler, the head of the Schutzstaffel (SS), or protective squads, used this bloodbath to consolidate his power within the party. The SS, an elite paramilitary formation, initially served as Hitler's bodyguards, but it eventually became an independent party organization that controlled the police forces, operated concentration camps, and had its own fighting units, the Waffen SS.

Strangely enough, Hitler was able to turn this civil war to his advantage by claiming that Rohm was liquidated on account of his homosexual practices, his luxurious life-style, and the violent excesses of his pro-Marxist followers. Thus political murder was justified in the name of social order and decency. Much of German society admired the fact that their leader was capable of bold and resolute actions against those who threatened public morality and bourgeois values.

The army, assured that it would remain in charge of the defense of the nation, agreed to Hitler's combining the posts of chancellor, president, and supreme commander of the armed forces. In 1938 Hitler was to restructure the German High Command to make it more responsive to his grandiose designs on Europe, but first on his agenda were the economic problems that beset Germany. Although the NSDAP called itself a workers party, in reality its program was deeply anti-labor. Within five months of coming to power the Nazis destroyed one of the most powerful labor movements in Western Europe and imprisoned thousands of Communists, Social Democrats, and union leaders. But terror was not the only instrument used to pacify the working class. Trade unions were dissolved and incorporated into the Nazi-run Deutschen Arbeitsfront (DAF, German Labor Front) in 1933. The DAF had no power to negotiate wage settlements and instead concentrated on improving worker productivity and conditions in the workplace. To this end, organizations such as the Beauty of Labor and Strength Through Joy brought culture to the workers by playing Wagner's music in tram depots or placing geraniums at the factory gates. The regime's efforts to organize working-class leisure practices were more popular. There were group excursions to the Black Forest and the North Sea Coast, and for the favored few, cruises to Norway and Madeira. Finally, the DAF institutionalized old age and disability pensions, expanded public housing, and improved medical care for workers. In a sense it anticipated many of the labor policies of the modern welfare state. *Hindenburg would continue running as President (@ 84, knowing Hitler would win, if not*

Although Hitler has been universally credited with instituting job creation schemes and wiping out unemployment in Germany, most of his agenda was a continuation of policies adopted under the Weimar Republic. In 1933 the government had begun allocating funds to public works projects in order to alleviate unemployment. A labor service that had begun under the Weimar Republic was expanded and then made compulsory after 1935. The German army, too, was greatly expanded after 1935, and military service became mandatory. The Nazis significantly increased funding for the rearmament effort and thereby stimulated the iron and steel industries, chemical plants, the automotive sector, engineering, and aerospace. The magnates of industry were especially impressed by the Nazi anti-labor policies that eliminating unionization and collective bargaining. Although wages for the average worker in agriculture or consumer goods did not rise significantly during this period, unemployment figures fell from more than 6 million in 1932 to less than half a million in 1937. And the regime, unlike the Soviet Union, took measures, despite shortages of foreign exchange and strict trade controls, to import materials for consumer goods. After 1939, once World War II broke out, Europe was plundered so that Germans could enjoy a relatively high standard of living.

In foreign affairs, too, Nazi policies enjoyed unilateral success. Hitler's aims were unambiguously militaristic and included a repudiation of the Treaty of Versailles, the conquest and colonization of Eastern Europe and the Soviet Union for German *lebensraum,* or "living space," and the exploitation and eradication of those deemed to be racially inferior. Within Germany, however, the Nazi propaganda machine, run very efficiently by Goebbels, propagated an image of Hitler as a man of peace. Unfortunately, European statesmen abroad consumed this version of the Hitler myth. In his public speeches, Hitler harped on the humiliation of Versailles but refrained from commenting extensively on *lebensraum.* That was wise, as the German population, though strongly desiring the restoration of national honor and greatness, was clearly unwilling to support another long, drawn-out international conflict. Hitler recognized this national feeling and worked on gaining quick and bloodless diplomatic coups. Later, because of the strategy of "blitzkrieg," or lightning military victories, in the initial two years of the war Germans believed that one could continue to score relatively painless victories over European nations.

Hitler managed to exude an air of reasonableness and caution that impressed the leaders of Western European nations as well. In 1935, when he announced German rearmament, and in

1936, when he began remilitarization of the Rhineland, most international statesmen agreed that these were legitimate demands. A major European power could not be expected to be relegated to third-rate status beyond a certain time frame. England and France protested against the annexation of Austria in 1938, and of German-speaking Sudetenland from Czechoslovakia the same year, but no one was prepared to go to war over these two international incidents. Neville Chamberlain, prime minister of England, Premier Edouard Daladier of France, and Mussolini of Italy met with Hitler in Munich in 1938 and sanctioned the loss of Czechoslovakian territory.

Germany's alliances with Italy, Japan, and later, through the Non-Aggression Pact, with the Soviet Union merely strengthened the German position on the continent. Hitler continued to gamble on Western pusillanimity when his army invaded Czechoslovakia in March 1939 and prepared for an invasion of Poland. This action finally convinced the British of the foolhardiness of appeasement, and they guaranteed the sovereignty of Romania and Poland. When German troops invaded Poland on September 1, 1939, France and England finally declared war on Germany.

At this time Hitler Received 37% of the Votes

Fascism in Italy

Benito Mussolini, like Hitler, rose from humble social origins to become a European dictator in the interwar period, but in his case the setting was Italy. Although he began his political career as a socialist, he founded the first Fascio di Combatimento (Combat Group), in Milan in March 1919. This group later became the core of the Italian Fascist Party. Like Hitler, Mussolini succeeded as a politician primarily because of the disastrous economic conditions engendered by World War I. Some 650,000 Italians had lost their lives in battle, yet Italy had not been adequately recompensed for joining the Allies in the war. Instead, the national debt swelled to astronomical proportions, depressing wages and increasing prices. Also, as in Germany, many Italian intellectuals in the prewar era had been critical of liberal democracy and glorified an ultranationalist and authoritarian state as the solution to Italy's political paralysis. Thus, to a certain extent, Mussolini was preaching to a crowd that had already been converted to his vision of a strong corporate state.

To the many who were discontented, disillusioned, and rootless, fascism offered the salvation of engaging in a national movement that was fired by the romance of nationalism and community. After the war large numbers of demobilized soldiers failed to find employment. The *fascio*, the basic cell of the party, tended to be organized by ex-servicemen seeking to revive the camaraderie of the trenches. The party also attracted idealists and prewar syndicalists who were hostile to capitalism, but unlike the socialists, they believed that the class conflict of capitalism could be transcended in a society where producers and workers worked in harmony for the greater national good. Fascists argued that whereas liberalism promoted the individual at the cost of the community, socialism exacerbated class conflict between workers and capitalists alike. Only fascism promised to bridge the cleavage of social interests and legislate in the interest of the national weal. The loose structure of the Italian Fascist Party facilitated autonomy at the grassroots level, and support for Mussolini grew dramatically. *1933 Hindburg appointed Hitler as chancellor*

But Mussolini, like Hitler, abandoned his flirtation with syndicalism and tried to ingratiate himself with the traditional Italian elites by attacking the socialist and Catholic labor organizations. In the Italian workers revolution of 1920 and later in that decade, Catholic and socialist parties threatened a genuine revolution from below in Italy. The occupation of factories and landed estates by organized groups of peasants and workers became fairly frequent occurrences. Mus-

PICTURE 6.2   Mussolini and Hitler. Fascist allies Adolf Hitler and Benito Mussolini are pictured in Munich, Germany, in 1940. (Photo from the Library of Congress)

solini's black-shirted paramilitary supporters terrorized the leftist organizers of such movements, disrupted rallies, and destroyed socialist property. Large-factory owners in the north and the landlords of the Po Valley rewarded these militant attacks on organized labor, trade unions, and cooperatives with generous financial assistance. The Fascist action units escalated their activities and threatened to march to Rome to destabilize the national government. King Victor Emmanuel III, who did not want a confrontation with the Blackshirts, named Mussolini prime minister of Italy in 1922. Although he presided over a fourteen-member coalition government, Mussolini quickly maneuvered himself into a position of supreme power as he took over the portfolios of both the minister of interior and the minister of foreign affairs. When elections were held in 1924, the Fascists won 66 percent of the national vote, testifying to the fact that they not only were the paramilitary wing of the business and agricultural elites but also had some support among the poorer sections of society. Meanwhile, in European ruling circles the Fascist seizure of power in Italy was looked upon quite benignly. In London and Paris the Fascists were regarded primarily as an anti-Bolshevik force that stood for law and order and strong government.

In 1926 Mussolini abolished all opposition parties, ended the freedom of the press, and started replacing elected officials with his henchmen. Compared to Nazi Germany, however, very few political opponents of the Fascists wound up in jail or in penal colonies. Also, Mussolini, unlike Hitler, did not directly engage with the powers of the monarchy, the military, or the Vatican. In fact he was quick to normalize relations with the Church by signing the Lateran accords of 1929. Finally, Italian fascism adopted anti-Semitic laws and policies only after Mussolini moved into closer relations with Germany in 1938. Fascism as a political ideology glorified war as the principal sphere of male activity and national statecraft, and to this end, it was desired that the state be as economically self-sufficient as possible in order to wage prolonged war. In reality, Fascists rarely interfered with the decisions of big corporations, and Italy, like Germany, continued to depend on imports of raw materials. In the arena of foreign politics, Mussolini was not as successful as Hitler. Italy lacked the economic and military resources to play an important role in European politics. Mussolini's boastful rhetoric about Italy's right to exploit the Balkan–Danubian area and to colonize Africa sounded impressive but lacked conviction. In 1923 Mussolini failed to seize the Greek islands of Corfu, but he was more successful in his 1935 invasion and occupation of Ethiopia. This event reversed the Ethiopian victory over Italian forces in 1898 and thus was symbolically very important. The League of Nations responded with anemic economic sanctions, but Mussolini chose to ally himself more closely with Hitler and collaborated in propping up General Franco's regime in the Spanish Civil War. Italy agreed to Hitler's annexation of Austria in 1938 and formally joined Germany as a partner in World War II.

Britain: A Fascist Minority

In the interwar period, Fascist Parties existed even in countries with long democratic traditions. Thus the case of fascism in Britain is an interesting one, as it offers an example of a wider European phenomenon. Fascism never became an organized political movement in Britain, but its existence showed the innate appeal of the ideology even in a land of liberalism and democracy. There were several small Fascist groups in operation in England in the 1920s, such as the British Fascists and the Imperial Fascist League, but they were very limited in size, organization, and reach. The British Union of Fascists (BUF), founded in 1932 by Sir Oswald Mosley, was in existence for nearly eight years, however, and had a membership of between 30,000 and 40,000. Although he came from a wealthy landowning family, Mosley had a career in labor politics before embracing fascism. He had been disappointed with the politics of compromise in Parliament and wanted to build a land fit for heroes. His experience in air combat during World War I instilled in him a fascination with war and martial action. And his upper-class English background made him uncomfortable with the politics of both liberalism and socialism.

An ardent admirer of John Maynard Keynes, Mosley proposed that the government should organize public works and invest in industrialization to deal with the crisis of unemployment engendered by the Great Depression. At the same time he was convinced that workers and industrialists could be united in a common party to their mutual benefit. Organized resistance from the Labor Party pushed his movement to the Right, and he was soon advocating a dictatorship by the British Union of Fascists and an end to all political parties and labor organizations. A trip to Italy in 1932 convinced him that only a dynamic dictatorship like Mussolini's could secure national unity and welfare. He tried to make alliances with select industrialists and owners of influential newspapers to further his cause, but the BUF appealed mainly to the petty bourgeoisie and the unorganized section of the working class, such as servants, rather than to conservatives. Certain sections of the self-employed middle class adhered to the BUF; so did women, who constituted 20 percent of the membership. Mosley traveled with his "private army," dressed in Fascist paraphernalia and looking for trouble, and few of his organized meetings were free of violence.

He even adopted anti-Semitic propaganda in order to justify his diatribes against international finance and communism and provide his supporters with something concrete to hate, but after 1937 when the BUF was brought under control by the British government, he toned down his

PICTURE 6.3
Fascist party leader in Brazil.
Authoritarian and fascist regimes came
to power not only in Europe but also in
some parts of Latin America. Pictured
here is Plínio Salgado, the young leader
of the Brazilian Integralist Party in 1932.
(Photo courtesy of the Embassy of Brazil
in Washington D.C.)

Would use the Enabling Act to his advantage to become Fuhrer

anti-Semitic rhetoric. By then, the organization was racked by both organizational and financial crises. He then tried to agitate for a negotiated international peace. BUF candidates fared miserably in a number of by-elections. With the onset of war, Mosley and 700 of his supporters were interned as a security risk, and the BUF was disbanded in May 1940. Despite the superficial appeal of fascism, the British government, unlike the Weimar Republic, had enough political legitimacy to defuse the challenges posed by such extremists. Moreover, unlike Italian and German Fascists, major radical British intellectuals tended to be attracted more to Marxism than to fascism. The adherence of a few eccentric writers, such as Ezra Pound and Wyndham Lewis, did not have a significant influence on public opinion. Finally, England, thanks to its superior economic strength and control of colonial markets, weathered the storm of the Great Depression far more easily than the continental powers and thus had fewer unemployed people to respond to Mosley's proposals.

The Roots of the Holocaust

Although there were a variety of Fascist movements in Europe in the interwar period, German Nazism was unique in its single-minded persecution of the Jews. There had been a long history of anti-Semitism in Germany predating Hitler's ascent to power. In the late eighteenth century, in response to colonialism, a very specific form of racist discourse developed that deemed Africans and Asians less beautiful and less intelligent than whites. This attitude was refined in the nineteenth century. Popular racial-anthropological theories sought to create a hierarchy of states among the European nations themselves. Often race and nation were intertwined. Johann Gottfried von Herder, a late-eighteenth-century German thinker, argued that among Europeans, Germans not only possessed great physical beauty and strength but also deserved credit as the creators of European civilization. In the vulgarization of this racial stereotype, Germans were held to be superior to the Latin races. Racial preeminence was also cited as adequate reason to justify German domination over the Slavs.

But racial theories had little scientific legitimacy before the advent of Charles Darwin and the publication of his biological findings in the *Evolution of the Species*. A liberal, reclusive, Victorian gentleman who supported the idea of human equality, Darwin's scientific findings were twisted out of context to provide justification for capitalism, colonialism, and racism. Darwin propounded the theory that, in the plant and animal kingdoms, there was constant struggle for existence, and the species that was most capable of adapting to the environment would reproduce the most successfully. Darwin's theories were adopted by those who were interested in improving the biological health of the human race, such as Francis Galton. The founder of the term "eugenics," Galton wanted to increase the reproduction of the educated middle classes and reduce it among people who had failed the test of hereditary health. By the early twentieth century some zoologists and doctors in Germany were advocating the sterilization and eventual extermination of the weak, the sick, the criminal, and the insane as a legitimate way to improve the health of the nation, especially the genetic stock of the Aryan or Germanic race.

After World War I the issue of the genetic health of the nation took on a fiscal aspect as the German government grappled with mass unemployment and the allocation of welfare resources to the "asocial and the handicapped." Sterilization for this section of the population was routinely advocated by various members of the educated bourgeoisie as a humane solution to the problem. Proposed eugenic measures predated Hitler's rise to power. It is interesting that the person most responsible for fusing racial-hygienic ideas with anti-Semitism was an Englishman, Houston Stewart Chamberlain (1855–1927). An obsessive Germanophile, Chamberlain extolled the supposed superiority of Germanic peoples and identified the Jewish race as the primary threat to their existence and domination. Many Protestant and Catholic theologians joined in the chorus of disapproval, blaming the evils of modernity, communism, liberalism, and secularism on the influence of the Jews. Powerful Jewish industrialists were blamed for the negative effects of industrialization. And though thousands of Jews had bravely fought in the war for the Fatherland, the community was held responsible for the defeat at Versailles. Finally, Jews were accused of encouraging white slavery and prostitution, spreading sexually transmitted diseases, and corrupting the German race by seducing its women.

Although it is unclear how well read Hitler was in this anti-Semitic literature, his autobiography contains a very comprehensive political program for maintaining the purity of the Nordic-Germanic peoples, the race that in his view was responsible for the creation of culture. In Hitler's hierarchy of races, the Chinese and the Japanese were capable of bearing culture, but the Africans and the Slavs were of infinitely lesser value. The Jewish race personified all evil and was engaged in a war to dominate and destroy the world. According to Hitler, the state should facilitate the reproduction of only healthy people through child allowances, public housing, and educational opportunities and at the same time obstruct the reproduction of those afflicted with hereditary or chronic diseases. Finally, the Jew, as a parasite, fungus, vermin, or bacillus that threatened the health of the nation, deserved nothing but total extermination.

Nazi racial policy was formulated and implemented with the enthusiastic participation of many anthropologists, biologists, historians, and sociologists who volunteered their services to the Nazi state in an ongoing effort to identify and categorize people according to racial origin and reproductive fitness. They were rewarded with funding and government posts and were convinced that their work was in the interests of science and progress. Thus they justified their killings in the name of cures. Most of these professionals escaped retribution and passed back into professional life after the end of World War II.

The fury of the Nazi state directed toward the Jews was quite disproportionate to the actual size and influence of the community. Jews constituted about 1 percent of the population and were largely found in cities such as Berlin and Frankfurt, where they were well represented in the banking and commerce centers, in the legal and medical professions, and in the arts and sciences. Nearly 18 percent of the German Jewish population had served in World War I, a fact that made a mockery of the Nazi claim that the Jews lacked nationalism and patriotism and were unfit for military service. In fact, Hitler received one of his two Iron Crosses for valor in battle on the recommendation of his Jewish regimental adjutant, Hugo Gutmann.

Anti-Jewish laws promulgated as early as April 1933 were aimed at dismissing Jewish employees from public service and restricting their access to professions such as education and medicine. Jewish businesses were boycotted, department stores ransacked, and the chambers of Jewish lawyers and doctors papered with posters carrying messages of hate. The SA tortured Jewish communists and socialists with impunity in temporary concentration camps set up in major German cities. In May 1933, the Nazi Party organized the public burning of books written by Jewish authors such as Marx, Einstein, and Freud. About one-third of the university teaching staff was forced to leave the country, including several Nobel Laureates. Museums containing the works of Jewish artists were targeted and "cleansed" of the offending artifacts. Even the works of Marc Chagall, the celebrated Russian painter, were removed.

The Nuremberg Laws passed in 1935 rendered Jews second-class citizens and dismissed them from all state service, both civil and military. These laws also forbade Jews to marry or have sexual relations with Aryan partners. *Mischlinge,* or those of mixed Jewish-German blood, could not marry Germans without official consent and were excluded from the ranks of the civil service and the Nazi Party. The list of proscriptions grew apace. Jews were driven out of practically all jobs; they were not allowed to be gun dealers, tourist guides, or marriage brokers. By 1938–1939 the majority of Jewish-owned businesses were expropriated without compensation by the Nazi state. Jews were also driven from public places such as theaters, concert halls, restaurants, and baths because their presence supposedly offended Aryan racial sensibilities.

A concerted propaganda effort led by Goebbels indoctrinated Germans in anti-Semitic sentiments. Newspapers and films represented Jews as decadent, depraved, diseased, and predatory, and Germans were taught to be revolted by their allegedly dehumanized visages and twisted bodies. Although the German government advocated the emigration of Jews, it refused to let them take their assets with them. At the same time European governments were unwilling to let in Jewish migrants, especially those pauperized by the Nazi regime. South Africa, Canada, Australia, and the United States raised barriers to Jewish immigration in the 1930s, and even liberal England forbade Jewish immigration once World War II broke out.

On November 9–10, 1938, Goebbels unleashed the infamous *Reichkristallnacht,* or Crystal Night. In this atrocity, 7,000 Jewish businesses were destroyed, every synagogue in Germany was burned down, and 26,000 Jews were sent to concentration camps. These actions were undertaken by party comrades and SA squads in full view of the public, and if there was little participation in the widespread arson and looting, very few Germans were willing to actively oppose the actions of the state or even voice their disapproval. Before the application of the Final Solution to the Jewish Question, Jews in Germany had lost all their rights as human beings. They were isolated from the non-Jewish population and eliminated from economic and professional life. By the time they were finally removed to concentration camps and exterminated en masse, many ordinary German citizens had become hardened to their plight and considered the terrible actions to be nothing more than fairly routine bureaucratic matters.

Once World War II broke out, the "Jewish question" became much more pressing because German military expansion began to bring the Jewish populations of Europe under Nazi control. Moreover, international opinion ceased to matter to the Nazis, as did moral considerations, especially on the eastern front where they acted barbarously. Soon after the occupation of Poland in 1939–1940, SS groups started shooting Jews. Under the leadership of Heinrich Himmler, the SS took upon itself the job of rendering the newly conquered areas free of Jews to prepare them for the resettlement of ethnic Germans. To this end, 3 million Polish Jews were rounded up and put in special ghettos in eastern Poland, where they worked as slave labor. And with the German attack on the Soviet Union in 1941, the fate of European Jewry was sealed. Einsatzgruppen, special commando units within the SS, were instructed to execute all Soviet functionaries, gypsies, Jews, and "less valuable Asiatics." These mobile killing units had been formed on the eve of the invasion of Poland to rid the country of the ruling class and subsequently played a crucial role in the genocide in the Soviet Union, where they murdered between 1 million and 1.5 million Jews. People were randomly shot, gassed, or beaten to death with heavy metal objects.

Members of the SS were deeply indoctrinated in anti-Semitism and had to prove their racial purity—and that of their spouses—as a condition of membership. Once in the organization, many exhibited few moral scruples at wholesale murder, and later they tried to explain their actions by claiming they were merely following orders. Adolf Eichmann, a member of the Gestapo later entrusted with the implementation of the Final Solution, claimed in his trial in Israel in 1961 that he was just a desk-bound bureaucrat trying to do his job. The rationalization and even denial of genocide was perhaps the most horrifying aspect of the Holocaust and persists to this day among certain sections of the German public.

To eliminate the Jews as a people, the Nazis created a highly efficient bureaucratic structure that was placed under the supervision of Reinhard Heydrich, head of the main office for the Security of the Reich, who in turn reported directly to Himmler. The first mass killings of Jews involving the use of toxic gas were conducted in Chelmno in Poland. The SS used mobile vans for this purpose, most of which were deployed on Soviet territory. The use of euthanasia to rid the state of undesirables had already been tried by Nazi doctors, medical aides, and members of the SS. In one program, nearly 100,000 incurably ill patients were gassed in rooms camouflaged as showers, but owing to outspoken public disapproval—in this case by clergymen and members of both the Protestant and Catholic churches—the program was ended in 1941.

The use of vans as mobile killing units was problematic. They were inefficient, and they tended to break down frequently on the poor roads in the Soviet Union. The Jewish problem was too big for Heydrich and Himmler to handle alone; the Nazis concluded that the Final Solution required the cooperation of other government agencies. The Wannsee Conference was convened in a suburb of Berlin on January 20, 1942. Heydrich had invited representatives of all the most important ministries of the German government. They discussed the fate of 11 million European Jews, trying to determine how many were to be used for slave labor, what percentage would perish in the process, what would happen to the "half Jews," and finally, how they ultimately were to be exterminated entirely. Eventually special camps were constructed in German-occupied Poland: in Belzec, Sobibor, Majdanek, Treblinka, Auschwitz, and Birkenau, to name only the most infamous of the killing centers. The last two also served as a source of slave labor for the factories of I. G. Farben, Krupp, and other German industrial concerns located nearby. Jews were often worked to the point of collapse and then gassed to satisfy the needs of both the factory owners and those who advocated Jewish extermination. In the Lodz and Warsaw ghettos, Jews perished in large numbers of starvation and disease long before they reached the camps.

Researchers who have studied the Holocaust have repeatedly raised two important questions. How did ordinary rank-and-file members of society in both Germany and the occupied territories react to the deportation of the Jews? And was there any resistance to Nazi policies aimed at Jews? The Holocaust was made possible by the cooperation of many in Germany: railway officials who facilitated the transport of European Jews to the designated killing centers, industries that used them for slave labor, members of the medical profession who used them for experiments in

PICTURE 6.4 Holocaust. As Allied liberation forces moved through Germany and Eastern Europe they uncovered the horrors of Nazi concentration camps. (Photo courtesy of the Franklin D. Roosevelt Library, World War II Digital Collection)

camps, and engineers and architects who installed these camps. Although the German masses seemed somewhat indifferent to the Jewish Question and actively evaded taking moral responsibility, a powerful minority sided with the Nazi policies and vocally approved of the deportations of German Jews.

With the war underway, the Nazis sought to export their anti-Semitic policies to the other nations of Europe. The process was a complicated one. Victims had to be identified, deprived of their assets, rounded up for deportation, and then transported to the camps. In France, the Vichy government, which collaborated with the German occupation, initiated anti-Jewish procedures voluntarily. Members of the legal profession helped in the identification and exclusion of Jews from civilian, military, and professional life, and in the confiscation of their property. Although the French authorities distinguished between native French Jews and foreign Jews, handing over the latter to the Germans while retaining control over the former in internment camps, nearly 90,000 members of the Jewish community in France perished. In the Netherlands, despite protests by churches and determined resistance from the general Dutch public, the occupying Nazis were able to destroy 75 percent of the Jewish population. In Bulgaria, the Orthodox Church, helped by outraged public opinion, prevented the Bulgarian government from complying with Nazi demands for the forced deportation of the Jews. Likewise, in Denmark members of the resistance, heads of the churches, and Danes in general defied the occupying Nazis, ferrying many Jews to safety in Sweden. In Italy, too, despite the enactment of anti-Jewish legislation, the Final Solution was never implemented. And even after the Germans occupied Italy in September 1943 and started deporting Jews, approximately four-fifths were saved because of the assistance rendered by ordinary Italians. In all, about 6 million Jews perished in the Holocaust.

The issue of resistance and compliance among the Jewish victims themselves is more difficult to address. It seems presumptuous to sit in judgment on a persecuted minority, but the issue has been raised by many, including a well-known Jewish moral philosopher, Hannah Arendt. In her book *Eichmann in Jerusalem,* Arendt accused the Jewish councils—who ran the ghettos for the Germans and supplied slave labor for factories—of playing an important role in the destruction of their own people. Indeed, Mordechai Chaim Rumkowski, head of the Lodz ghetto, did indeed behave like a Nazi functionary with his authoritarian ways. Many of these leaders reasoned that as long as the Jews provided necessary labor they would be spared extermination, and that it was better in the long run to comply with the German authorities than to resist them. But economic productivity did not save the Jews. Only a few thousand survived the ghettos in Russia and Poland. In the long run, neither armed uprisings in the ghettos of Warsaw, Lvov, and Bialystok nor the revolts by inmates at Auschwitz and Sobibor was going to save the Jewish prisoners from Nazi predation. At the same time it should be remembered that in both camps and ghettos Jews were underfed, overworked, emaciated, sick, debilitated, and routinely brutalized. This weak state made acts of resistance even harder. *WWII, Hitler invades Poland*

Resistance was no easier on the outside. There were a few armed bands of Jewish partisans who fought the Nazis in Eastern Europe and the Soviet Union. There were circles of Jewish resisters in cities such as Berlin who maintained an underground existence and tried to help those sought by the Gestapo. Some of these groups, such as the one that gathered around Herbert Baum, a skilled electrician at Siemens, tried to put out posters and even attempted arson against a propaganda exhibition in Lustgarten on May 18, 1942. But virtually all were caught and arrested. The ringleaders were shot, and many others were sent to concentration camps. Although there were individuals who attempted courageous acts, such as Maria Countess von Maltzan, who hid the Jewish writer Hans Hirschel and others in her apartment in Berlin, by and large the German people acquiesced or acted indifferent to the elimination of the Jews. Neither the Protestant Church in Germany nor the Vatican abroad openly condemned the Nazi policies. Although a few Catholic priests did attempt to help Jews, the fact is that the Vatican helped Adolf Eichmann and Dr. Josef Mengele, the butcher of Auschwitz, to escape to Latin America at the end of the war. This troubling information enormously complicates the question of moral responsibility. Likewise, the British and the Americans, despite being in possession of the facts regarding the Final Solution, went to extraordinary lengths to avoid devising a strategy to help or save the European Jews, short of defeating the Germans in the war. They even avoided bombing Auschwitz or the railway lines leading to it, pleading tactical difficulties. *G.B & France declare war*

Other Victims of Fascism

As mentioned earlier in this chapter, the voracious Nazi state also saw several other groups, including homosexuals, asocials, the mentally ill, and gypsies, as undesirable and targeted them for elimination. The Nazi goal was to create a unified national community of healthy, efficient, hardworking, and ideologically reliable Aryans, and to this end the authorities utilized a variety of murderous policies. Thus, between 1934 to 1945, between 320,000 and 350,000 men and women who were diagnosed with schizophrenia, hereditary simple-mindedness, manic depression, and even chronic alcoholism were forcibly sterilized against their wishes. In many cases the evidence used by the so-called hereditary courts was extremely scanty, often reflecting the prejudices of medical and welfare authorities.

Gypsies, who had long been treated as social outcasts in Germany, became another group of victims that engaged the interest of the Nazis. Originally from India, they had appeared in Germany in the late fifteenth century after having converted to Christianity. Gypsies had long been regarded as racially and culturally inferior to Germans and a source of crime and immorality. Their nomadic lifestyle was especially abhorred by the German population, as was their lack of hygiene. Since gypsies numbered a bare 30,000, initially they were not seen as a major threat, but the Nuremberg Laws banning sexual relations between Aryans and non-Aryans targeted gypsies as well as the Jews. The Research Center for Racial Hygiene and Biological Population Studies tried to identify pure and mixed gypsies based on the research of racial experts with dubious credentials. Ultimately, gypsies were rounded up and shipped to Poland where they were killed. Only 5,000 of the German gypsies survived the war. It is estimated that half a million gypsies perished throughout Europe under Nazi occupation.

The Nazi state also tried to target social deviants, lazy workers, tramps, prostitutes, alcoholics, beggars, and pimps, with varying degrees of success. Many were sent to concentration camps or to various enterprises run by the SS to work. Some were dispatched to the euthanasia program. Homosexuals were also marked for persecution. Although nearly 15,000 wound up in concentration camps, others were subjected to a variety of gruesome medical experiments intended to reverse their sexuality. It was claimed that the German race would sink into insignificance if the racially pure and sexually capable male population did not want to father children. Homosexuality was seen as a degenerate phenomenon, and Nazis deemed that it should be punishable by death.

German Blitzkrieg overwhelms France, operation Barbarossa = Invade U.SSR

Fascist Policies on the Eastern Front

Japs Bomb pearl harbor - U.S involved

In September 1939, Europe was drawn into another global war. Whereas World War I had been greeted with naive and universal enthusiasm, this time Europeans were more apprehensive. In particular, they were worried about the devastation that the Nazi war machine could wreak. The Polish armies were routed in three weeks after the initial attack on September 1, 1939. The Germans resumed hostilities in the spring of 1940. Using the strategies of blitzkrieg, or "lightning war," the Germans knocked out Norway, Denmark, Belgium, the Netherlands, and France. French and British forces were driven back against the English Channel at Dunkirk in Belgium. Despite continuous German air attacks, the British were able to evacuate 300,000 troops. Northern France was occupied by the Germans, and in the south, Marshal Henri-Philippe Petain established a French government loyal to the Nazis. From August 1940 to June 1941, the Germans kept up a relentless bombardment of British ports, air defenses, and industrial centers. More than 40,000 civilians were killed in this Battle of Britain, but the British held firm. The German army moved eastward into the Balkans, conquering the Romanians, Hungarians, Bulgarians, and Yugoslavs. Then, on June 22, 1941, Hitler authorized a massive invasion of the Soviet Union (see Map 6.2).

If Hitler's militaristic policies were primarily to blame for World War II, then part of the blame must also lie with mistaken policies followed by the German Communist Party under the direction of Moscow. Hitler had been very explicit in his autobiography that he intended to resettle ethnic Germans in Poland and Russia and that the local populations and lands would be ex-

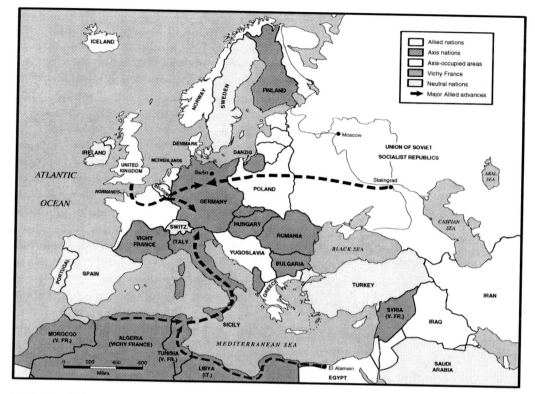

MAP 6.2   World War II in Europe

ploited in order to serve the master race. He believed that Bolshevism was a virus begotten by
Jews, and that once it was eliminated, the colossal Soviet Empire would collapse. But the Com-
intern, the Communist International, consistently underestimated the power of fascism and
merely saw it as an extreme form of bourgeois rule and advanced capitalism. During the Great
Depression, the Communists believed that the world economic crisis would create new revolutionary opportunities. To that end, Moscow instructed Communists both in Spain and elsewhere
not to build coalitions with other working-class parties or trade unions. As a result, the Communists grew isolated from the rank-and-file German working class and more dependent on
Moscow. Between 1933 and 1934 the Communists and socialists rejected attempts to come to
any electoral agreements, and Stalin, for his part, renewed the treaty of alliance with Germany in
May 1933. Mistakenly believing that fascism represented an extreme form of capitalism, the
USSR refused to defend the Weimar Republic from a Fascist takeover, instead concentrating their
ire on the only party capable of offering resistance to the Nazis, the Social Democratic Party. This
tragic misreading of German politics fatally divided the German Left when it required unity.
Hitler, through a policy of terror and repression, was to eliminate the Left as a political force.

It was only in 1934 that Stalin became aware of the ominous threat that Hitler represented
with his concept of *lebensraum*. Finally, he engaged in a quest for collective security through alliances with Western nations. In September 1934, the USSR joined the League of Nations, a powerless but not yet entirely discredited body that was established in the aftermath of World War I
in order to resolve international conflicts. But the Soviet faith was entirely misplaced. Despite

protests, the League failed to take action against the Italian attack on Ethiopia and against Hitler as he systematically violated the terms of the Treaty of Versailles. The Soviet Union appealed for the creation of a Popular Front, an international coalition of Nazi and anti-Nazi parties that would intervene decisively on the side of the democratic forces in the Spanish Civil War. While Hitler and Mussolini dispatched thousands of volunteers to fight alongside the authoritarian General Franco, Britain and France refused to take action. The Soviets dispatched ammunition, weapons, and military-political advisers, but ultimately Franco won as the Soviet Union became engulfed in an internal civil war and Stalin lost interest in Spain.

Thereafter, as Stalin observed, the West had little interest in containing the German threat and even less in forming a military alliance with the Soviet Union. Indeed, the West regarded the Nazis as the lesser evil compared to the Bolsheviks. Stalin therefore decided to negotiate directly with the Nazis, hoping to ward off an attack. On August 23, 1939, the Germans and the Soviets signed a Non-Aggression Pact promising that neither country would attack the other or lend its support to any invading third power. The two dictators had also secretly agreed to divide up a good part of Eastern Europe, primarily Poland. The Soviet Union sent raw materials and food to Germany and refused to shore up its own western defenses to avoid any kind of provocation to the Germans. Stalin refused to countenance any information from Western intelligence sources that an attack was imminent in June 1941. When Germany attacked the Soviet Union on June 22, 1941, it constituted the largest invasion in history. For the rest of World War II, the Soviet Army single-handedly held down nearly 70 to 75 percent of the German forces while the Allies together dealt with all the rest. *Allies victorious in Africa, Invades Italy / Italy Surrenders*

As Hitler saw it, the war in the East was to be a war of extermination, plunder, and enslavement. The Soviet Union was the major stumbling block to Nazi expansion and presented an ideal opportunity for colonial exploitation. Military commanders were exhorted to give up their humanitarian reservations and exploit the local populations ruthlessly. Slavs were represented alternately as subhuman beings or as wild beasts fit for annihilation. Communists, partisans, and guerilla leaders alike were to be killed outright without trial. German soldiers were not liable for crimes committed against civilians. It is telling that, although only 3.5 percent of the British and American prisoners of war died in Germany, nearly 3 million Soviets, or nearly 57 percent of the Soviet prisoners of war, perished. In the siege of Leningrad, a city that Hitler was determined to starve into submission in order to break the Soviet spirit, nearly 1.5 million people died of hunger or bombardment. However, the city itself was never taken by Nazi forces, and the example of its resistance helped Soviet morale considerably. Nearly 2.2 million Jews were killed by Germans in killing fields such as Babi Yar near the Ukrainian capital, Kiev, or in concentration camps. In Minsk, Riga, Vilnius, and dozens of other towns, Jews died in mass executions conducted in ghettoes. In Latvia, Lithuania, and the Ukraine, local anti-Semites helped the Nazis carry out their grim operations. *Germany continues to fight*

Overall the Soviets lost between 7 and 8 million soldiers and about 19 million civilians in the war against Germany. Of those, 20 million were men, which caused a huge population imbalance. Soviet postwar society was dominated by households composed of fatherless children and headed by women. The economic effects of the Nazi invasion were equally devastating. Some 1,700 towns, 70,000 villages, and 31,000 industrial enterprises were destroyed. Thousands of kilometers of railroad tracks were obliterated. Soviet industrial and agricultural production fell catastrophically. Vast sections of the population suffered from semi-starvation and, in many cases, only survived because of the U.S.-sponsored lend-lease operations.

PICTURE 6.5 Soviet poster from the World War II period. The words exhort people to rally to defeat the Nazis: "Led by Stalin's military commanders onward to the liberation of our Fatherland from German invaders." (Photo courtesy of the Funet Russian Archives)

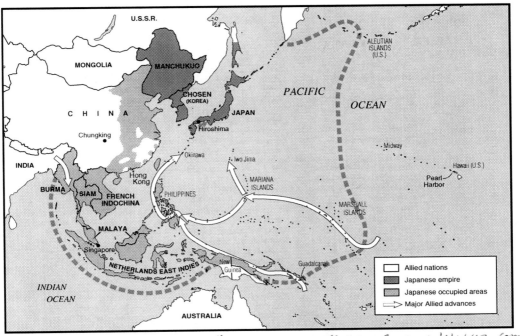

MAP 6.3   World War II in East Asia

[handwritten annotations: Russia Reaches Berlin / Hitler commits Suicide / Germans Surrenders May 7
U.S bombs the Shit out of Japan / Surrenders August, 14]

Stalin repeatedly asked the Allies to open a second front in the west in order to relieve Nazi pressure on the Soviet Union, but Allied troops invaded France only in June 1944 when the tide of war had already turned on the eastern front. Meanwhile, the Soviets had stopped the German advance at Stalingrad in 1943. After the loss of Stalingrad, German armies were compelled to retreat. Soviet troops captured Berlin, and on May 2, 1945, the Soviet red banner was hoisted on the Brandenburg Gate. A few hours earlier, Hitler had killed himself in the bombproof shelter of the Chancellery.

The cooperation of the Allies and the Soviet Union fragmented even before the German threat was neutralized. As World War II ended, the Cold War began to take on concrete shape, opening a new chapter in world history. As the importance of England and Germany ebbed in world politics, the United States and the Soviet Union emerged as the new leviathans of the modern age. Japan, whose imperialist expansion had been stopped in the Far East, found itself constrained in the peace settlements imposed by the Allies, but it nevertheless emerged as an Asian economic giant in the second half of the twentieth century. As colonized countries in Asia and Africa broke free of colonial constraints, they became the sites of competition and control for the new superpowers, which sought to impress their particular vision of modernization, whether through free-market capitalism or state-sponsored socialism, on the rest of the world. Neofascist parties and organizations of the extreme Right sprang into existence in most Western European countries following World War II and, after the collapse of communism, in the Soviet Union and the countries of Eastern Europe as well. Despite their rabid nationalism and belief in an authoritarian state and a pure people, they failed to create a sizable popular base. In spite of the fact that from time to time these organizations have secured electoral advances in France, Germany, or Russia, it seems unlikely that they will break the parliamentary framework of European politics.

[handwritten: Ans Axies — Germany, Italy, Japan, Bulgaria, Hungary
Allied. Britain, France, U.S.S.R, U.S, Poland]

TABLE 0.2 Time Line, 1950–2000

	Global Events & Issues	North America	Europe
1950-1960	Hydrogen bombs tested, 1952-1955 Bandung Conference of non-alignment of African-Asian nations, 1955 Green Revolution, 1950s-1970s Worldwide baby boom, 1950s	Korean War, 1950-1953 Dwight D. Eisenhower, president, 1953-1961 Eisenhower and John F. Dulles formulate "Domino Theory" on spread of communism Supreme Court rules against racial segregation in schools, 1953	U.S. nuclear weapons stationed in Western Europe, 1953 Formation of European Economic Community, 1958 Hungarian revolution put down by Soviet forces, 1956
1960-1970	Population growth becomes major Third World issue Founding of Organization of Petroleum Exporting Countries organization (OPEC) founded, 1960 Cuban Missile Crisis, 1962 Moon landing by U.S. astronauts, 1969	John F. Kennedy, president, 1961-1963 Martin Luther King, Jr., wins Nobel Peace Prize, 1964 Martin Luther King, Jr., assasinated, 1968 Woodstock Music Festival, 1968 Kent State and Jackson State students killed in anti-Vietnam War demonstrations, 1968 Feminist movement gains support	Prague Spring, Czechoslovakia, 1968 Paris student uprisings, 1968 Soviet troops roll into Czechoslovakia, 1968 Workers protests and strike wave in Italy, 1968-1969
1970-1980	Biological Weapons Convention, 1972 SALT I, Nuclear Arms Treaty, 1972 First UN International Women's Year, 1975; 1975-1985 UN Decade of Women SALT II, Nuclear Arms Agreement, 1979 Global immunization campaigns 1970s-1980s	Watergate scandal, 1972-1974 Roe v. Wade decision of Supreme Court, 1973	Berlin Treaty, 1972 Helinski Agreements, 1975 Soviet invasion of Afghanistan, 1978-1989 Antinuclear demonstrations gain support
1980-1990	Appearance of AIDS virus, 1980 Agreement between U.S. and Soviet Union to destroy inter-mediate-range missiles, 1987 Fall of Berlin Wall, 1989 Cold War abandoned, 1989	U.S. funds and supplies Contra War in Nicaragua, 1982-1990 Stock market crash, "Black Monday," 1987 Invasion of Panama, 1989	Founding of Green Party in Germany, 1980 Polish Solidarity movement, 1980 Chernobyl nuclear accident, Ukraine, 1986 Economic deterioration of Soviet Union, 1980s Gorbachev leadership of Soviet Union, 1985-1991 Collapse of Communist governments, Eastern Europe, 1989
1990-2000	Arms reduction agreements between U.S. and Soviet Union Collapse of Soviet Union, 1991 Global Conference on the Environment in Rio de Janeiro, 1992 Chemical Weapons Convention, 1993 International campaign to ban land mines, 1997 Summit on global warming, 1997 Comprehensive Nuclear Test Ban Treaty, signed 1999	Gulf War against Iraq, 1991 World Trade Center bombing, New York, 1993 North American Free Trade Agreement, signed 1994	East and West Germany reunified, 1990 Boris Yeltsin elected president of Russia, 1991 Independence of former Soviet Republics, 1991 European Economic Community becomes European Union, 1994

	Latin America	Middle East and Asia	Africa
1950-1960	CIA coup against Arbenz regime, Guatemala, 1954 Castro in power in Cuba, 1959	Korean War, 1950-1953 Abdel Nasser in power in Egypt, 1952-1970 Beginning of Japanese "economic miracle," 1956 China's Great Leap Forward, 1958-1962 Overthrow of monarchy, Iraq, 1958 Collectivization in China, 1959	French war in Algieria, 1955-1963 South African Freedom Charter, 1955 34 African countries gain independence, 1945-1968 Independence of Gold Coast (Ghana), 1957
1960-1970	Cuba aligns with Soviet Union, 1960-1990 Bay of Pigs invasion in Cuba, 1961 Military governments in Brazil, 1964-1985 Military control of Argentine political situation, 1966-1973 Emergence of rural protest movements in Nicaragua, Guatemala, and El Salvador, 1960s and 1970s Student protest and massacre in Mexico, 1968 Soccer War between El Salvador and Honduras, 1969	Vietnam War, 1963-1973 Shah in power in Iran, 1963-1979 Indira Gandhi, Prime Minister of India, 1966-1977 and 1980-1984 Cultural Revolution in China, 1966-mid-1970s Palestinian Liberation Organization created 1965 Six Day War between Israel and Egypt, 1967	Declaration of South African Republic, 1960 Independence of Zaire (Belgian Congo) and other francophone countries, 1960 Angola war against Portuguese, 1961-1975 Military oust Nigerian republic, 1966 Biafra War in Nigeria, 1967-1970 Nelson Mandela imprisoned by apartheid government, 1964-1990
1970-1980	Military dictatorship against Allende government, Chile, 1973 Juan Perón president in Argentina, 1973-1974 Military in power in Argentina, 1976-1985 Augusto Pinochet, dictator of Chile, 1973-1989 Triumph of Sandinista revolution in Nicaragua, 1979 Civil War in Guatemala and El Salvador, 1970s-1992	Anwar Sadat president of Egypt, 1970 Arab-Israeli War, 1973 Independence of Bangladesh, 1973 Death of Mao Zedong, 1975 Vietnam reunified, 1976 Soviet invasion of Afghanistan, 1978-1989 Hostage crisis in Iran, 1979 Revolution in Iran and coming to power of Ayatollah Khomeni, 1979 Treaty between Egypt and Israel, 1979 One-child policy in China, 1979	Drought, malnutrition, and famine in the Sahel, 1970s-1980s Revolution in Ethiopia, 1974 Soweto uprising in South a Africa, 1976 Angola and Mozambique independence, 1975
1980-1990	Return to civilian government in Argentina, 1985 Return to civilian government in Brazil, 1985 Election of civilian government in Chile, 1989 U.S. invasion of Panama, 1989	Sadat assassinated in Egypt, 1981 Deng Xiaoping in power in China, 1980-1997 War between Iran and Iraq, 1980-1988 Arab-Israeli War, 1982 Assassination of Indira Gandhi, 1984 Chinese repression of democratic movement, 1989	Severe droughts in Ethiopia International economic boycott of South Africa, 1984 Township insurrections in South Africa, 1984-1987
1990-2000	Sandinistas voted out of power in Nicaragua, 1990 Contra War ends, 1990 Civil War in Guatemala ends, 1996 Civil War in El Salvador ends, 1992 PRI loses presidency of Mexico, after seventy years in power, 2000	Kuwait invaded by Iraq, 1990 Gulf War, 1991 Tansu Çiller becomes first woman prime minister of Turkey, 1993 Israeli-PLO peace accords, 1993-1995 Hong Kong returned to China, 1997	U.S. and UN intervention in Somalian Civil War, 1992 End of Apartheid in South Africa, 1994 Nelson Mandela elected president of South Africa, 1994 Eight countries are drawn into war in Central Africa

Part Two

THE LATER CENTURY

7

Independence: Achievement and Continuing Struggle

The end of the struggle approaches and the British Empire will soon go the way of all the Empires of old. The strangling and degradation of India has gone on long enough. . . . It has been the greatest joy in my life to serve in this glorious struggle and to do my little bit for this cause. I pray that my countrymen and countrywomen will carry on the good fight unceasingly till success crowns their effort to realize the India of our dreams.

Jawaharlal Nehru,
Selected Works
(1972; written while in prison in 1930)

To develop friendly relations among nations based on respect for the principle of equal rights and self-determination of peoples and to take other appropriate measures to strengthen universal peace.

Article One,
UN Charter
(1945)

THESE TWO STATEMENTS, ONE BY A LEADER OF THE INDIAN NATIONALIST struggle who eventually would become prime minister in 1947, the other a foundational provision of the United Nations Charter, show that by mid-century the days of formal colonial rule were numbered. Nehru wrote down his thoughts in Niani Central Prison, where he was being detained for the fifth time following arrest for demonstrations against British rule. Some subject populations attained political independence when crumbling empires collapsed during World War I; most of those that came under colonial rule during the period of the new imperialism won the struggle for self-government in the two decades after World War II. In 1960, when the great majority of African countries were in the process of gaining independence, Harold Macmillan, the British prime minister, declared in a speech to the South African parliament in Cape Town, "A wind of change is blowing throughout Africa." Black South Africans themselves had to wait until 1994 for democratic elections to be held for the first time—and for Nelson Mandela, who had spent twenty-seven years as a political prisoner, to become president.

What did "independence" mean in the context of world history? Did it mean "flag independence," as J. Gus Liebenow called the transfer of political power in Africa, evoking those dramatic moments in colonial history when the flag of the imperial power was lowered for the last time and the flag of the new nation-state raised to the accompaniment of a new national anthem? Or was "independence" something bigger, and did the transfer of power from colonial rulers mark a beginning as much as an end? What had been achieved and what was yet to be achieved?

In Parts Two and Three of this book, we demonstrate that political independence did prove to be just one point in a continuous struggle by colonial *and* former colonial peoples to resist imperial forces and concomitant social inequities. The struggle had started with Western conquest and would continue in various forms throughout the twentieth century. This long view of political independence was certainly recognized by Nehru as he wrote out of the Indian experience. While celebrating the coming and inevitable end of British rule, he exhorted his "countrymen and countrywomen" to "carry on the good fight unceasingly . . . to realize the India of our dreams." But what were these "dreams"? For those inspired by Marxist-Leninist-Maoist visions, the achievement of independence was intimately tied to radical social revolution. Others supported the capitalist model of development and continuing partnership (albeit an unequal one) with the former colonial power as a means of furthering economic and social goals. For many, the rhetoric of liberation was focused and strident, but future postcolonial strategies were not clearly articulated. "Seek ye first the political kingdom" said Kwame Nkrumah, leader of the nationalist struggle in the Gold Coast, and the rest would follow.

The future path to social justice, economic opportunity, and international dignity was full of obstacles. In Central America, where political independence had been achieved more than a century before, imperialism had not faded away; on the contrary, it persisted in many neocolonial forms. Struggles against the powerful, who were perceived to have distorted the independence dream, were waged by peasants, workers, women, youth, and the urban poor. In the Middle East,

PICTURE 7.1
President Julius Nyerere (1922–1999). One
of the heroic figures of the African
nationalist struggle against British colonial
rule, Julius Nyerere, president of Tanzania, is
photographed here addressing the United
Nations General Assembly in 1985. (Photo
courtesy of the United Nations)

continuing imperial intervention crystallized feelings of discontent. People continued to organize against economic deprivation and social injustice in rural uprisings, trade unions, and urban neighborhoods. Aspirations and "dreams" were given expression in religious belief, revolutionary thought, gendered politics, and popular culture (see Chapters 8, 9, 10, and 11). "A Luta
Continua!" ("The Struggle Continues!") was the cry of fighters in the Frente da Libertaçao de
Mozambique (FRELIMO, Front for the Liberation of Mozambique) as they waged a fourteen-
year war of independence against the Portuguese dictatorship. And, after achieving political independence in 1975, the leaders of the new government continued to shout this slogan as they
exhorted the masses to resist outside intervention and rededicate themselves to the construction
of a new society.   *1932 - First Concentration Camp*

Yet, political independence in itself marked a huge accomplishment. It came at the end of
decades of struggle and sacrifice that became enshrined in national histories. In some places, it
had cost many lives. It was the essential prerequisite for achieving long-term social and economic
goals. Furthermore, the process of winning political independence often shaped the future of
newly independent states. To document the multiple paths to political independence is the main
purpose of this chapter.

The number of states that joined the United Nations, the new international organization of
the post–World War II period, demonstrated the centrality of the liberation process in the history of the late twentieth century. At its foundation in 1945, the world assembly had 51 members;
two decades later the number had doubled, and by 2000 membership totaled just under 200 nation-states (see Table 7.1). The formation of the world body was a landmark in the independence
struggle. When leading colonial powers such as Britain and France signed the UN Charter, they
were acknowledging the right to self-determination of all people. The two superpowers, the
United States and the Soviet Union, both members of the United Nations, did not have formal

[handwritten: Nazis Boycott Jewish Shops & Businesses, Burn Jewish Books,]

TABLE 7.1   United Nations Members and Years of Admission *[handwritten: Prohibited from owning land editors for newspaper]*

Afghanistan – 1946	Dominica – 1978
Albania – 1955	Dominican Republic – 1945
Algeria – 1962	Ecuador – 1945
Andorra – 1993	Egypt – 1945
Angola – 1976	El Salvador – 1945
Antigua and Barbuda – 1981	Equatorial Guinea – 1968
Argentina – 1945	Eritrea – 1993
Armenia – 1992	Estonia – 1991
Australia – 1945	Ethiopia – 1945
Austria – 1955	Fiji – 1970
Azerbaijan – 1992	Finland – 1955
Bahamas – 1973	France – 1945
Bahrain – 1971	Gabon – 1960
Bangladesh – 1974	Gambia – 1965
Barbados – 1966	Georgia – 1992
Belarus – 1945	Germany – 1973
Belgium – 1945	Ghana – 1957
Belize – 1981	Greece – 1945
Benin – 1960	Grenada – 1974
Bhutan – 1971	Guatemala – 1945
Bolivia – 1945	Guinea – 1958
Bosnia and Herzegovina – 1992	Guinea Bissau – 1974
Botswana – 1966	Guyana – 1966
Brazil – 1945	Haiti – 1945
Brunei Darussalam – 1984	Honduras – 1945
Bulgaria – 1955	Hungary – 1955
Burkina Faso – 1960	Iceland – 1946
Burundi – 1962	India – 1945
Cambodia – 1955	Indonesia – 1950
Cameroon – 1960	Iran (Islamic Republic of) – 1945
Canada – 1945	Iraq – 1945
Cape Verde – 1975	Ireland – 1945
Central African Republic – 1960	Israel – 1949
Chad – 1960	Italy – 1955
Chile – 1945	Jamaica – 1962
China – 1945	Japan – 1956
Colombia – 1945	Jordan – 1955
Comoros – 1975	Kazakhstan – 1992
Congo – 1960	Kenya – 1963
Costa Rica – 1945	Kiribati – 1999
Côte d'Ivoire – 1960	Kuwait – 1963
Croatia – 1992	Kyrgyzstan – 1992
Cuba – 1945	Lao People's Democratic Republic – 1955
Cyprus – 1960	Latvia – 1991
Czech Republic – 1993	Lebanon – 1945
Democratic People's Republic of Korea – 1991	Lesotho – 1966
Democratic Republic of the Congo – 1960	Liberia – 1945
Denmark – 1945	(continues)
Djibouti – 1977	

[handwritten: Passports Stamped with Red "J"]

[handwritten: Forbid Jews being outside past 8]

TABLE 7.1   (continued)

Libyan Arab Jamahiriya – 1955
Liechtenstein – 1990
Lithuania – 1991
Luxembourg – 1945
Madagascar – 1960
Malawi – 1964
Malaysia – 1957
Maldives – 1965
Mali – 1960
Malta – 1964
Marshall Islands – 1991
Mauritania – 1961
Mauritius – 1968
Mexico – 1945
Micronesia (Federated States of) – 1991
Monaco – 1993
Mongolia – 1961
Morocco – 1956
Mozambique – 1975
Myanmar – 1948
Namibia – 1990
Nauru – 1999
Nepal – 1955
Netherlands – 1945
New Zealand – 1945
Nicaragua – 1945
Niger – 1960
Nigeria – 1960
Norway – 1945
Oman – 1971
Pakistan – 1947
Palau – 1994
Panama – 1945
Papua New Guinea – 1975
Paraguay – 1945
Peru – 1945
Philippines – 1945
Poland – 1945
Portugal – 1955
Qatar – 1971
Republic of Korea – 1991
Republic of Moldova – 1992
Romania – 1955
Russian Federation – 1945
Rwanda – 1962
Saint Kitts and Nevis – 1983
Saint Lucia – 1979
Saint Vincent and the Grenadines – 1980

Samoa – 1976
San Marino – 1992
São Tomé and Principe – 1975
Saudi Arabia – 1945
Senegal – 1960
Seychelles – 1976
Sierra Leone – 1961
Singapore – 1965
Slovakia – 1993
Slovenia – 1992
Solomon Islands – 1978
Somalia – 1960
South Africa – 1945
Spain – 1955
Sri Lanka – 1955
Sudan – 1956
Suriname – 1975
Swaziland – 1968
Sweden – 1946
Syrian Arab Republic – 1945
Tajikistan – 1992
Thailand – 1946
The former Yugoslav Republic
    of Macedonia – 1993
Togo – 1960
Tonga – 1999
Trinidad and Tobago – 1962
Tunisia – 1956
Turkey – 1945
Turkmenistan – 1992
Tuvalu – 2000
Uganda – 1962
Ukraine – 1945
United Arab Emirates – 1971
United Kingdom of Great Britain
    and Northern Ireland – 1945
United Republic of Tanzania – 1961
United States of America – 1945
Uruguay – 1945
Uzbekistan – 1992
Vanuatu – 1981
Venezuela – 1945
Viet Nam – 1977
Yemen – 1947
Yugoslavia – 2000
Zambia – 1964
Zimbabwe – 1980

colonies in regions such as Africa, but they added their weight in the world body to the independence process. *1939. Jews rounded up in ghettos in Poland*

Newly independent states also joined in the movement to bring colonial rule to an end. Nkrumah, now the first prime minister and president of Ghana, acknowledged the need for a common front with colonized populations everywhere. As he celebrated the end of British rule in his country, the first black African nation to gain its independence, he noted in his autobiography, "The independence of Ghana is meaningless without the independence of the rest of the African continent." At the same time, countries following a socialist model of development continued to urge an end to imperialism on their terms. The broad-based nature of the struggle was emphasized by Mao Zedong in an interview with Hsinhua News Agency (September 29, 1958) when he said: *2/00,000 in Warsaw, Genocide of 6 mil Jews, Communists, Soviet prisoners, Polish and Homos*

Imperialism will not last long because it does evil things. It persists in grooming and supporting reactionaries in all countries who are against the people, it has forcibly seized many colonies and semi-colonies and many military bases, and it threatens the peace with atomic war. . . . Imperialism is still alive, still running amuck in Asia, Africa, and Latin America. In the West imperialism is still oppressing the people at home. This situation must change. It is the task of the people of the whole world to put an end to the aggression and oppression perpetrated.

Decolonization - Involving World Empires into independent countries

Nationalism, in some places infused by religious as well as secular ideologies, was an inspirational force in the independence struggles. In this context, it can be broadly defined as the shared aspirations of subject populations to end colonial rule. Unlike nineteenth-century European nationalism, which drew on a shared language, culture, and history to construct a sense of identity within an emerging nation-state, colonial subjects often had little in common. Indeed, they might live within political boundaries that were not much more than geographical spaces created arbitrarily by the Great Powers in the race for colonies. At the Berlin Conference, white men who had never been in Africa gathered in a European capital to draw boundaries on the map and to work out the rules of "effective occupation" of colonial territories. The colonies they created might randomly group together traditional enemies and competing ethnicities, divisions that were accentuated by imperial policies of divide and rule. Nationalists who sought an end to colonial rule were drawn together by a shared experience of discrimination and oppression at the hands of foreign governments and their local agents. Their unity, inspired by an intense desire for liberation, masked divisions that were to reemerge in the decades following independence.

The process of winning political independence is often called "decolonization." The term has been criticized because it sounds like a top-down process, one decided by the Great Powers and granted to their subjects. This is not what is meant here. As was noted in Chapter 2 on imperialism and colonial rule, local populations through their initiatives and responses actively shaped the nature of the European presence and forced foreign governments to reassess the nature of their rule. Like colonialism, decolonization was influenced by small-scale and personal aspirations and by regional and global forces. It was sometimes a gradual process but it could involve dramatic change. It usually developed in the context of individual colonies, but the struggle could escalate as other powers intervened. Negotiations leading to political independence might be relatively peaceful, but decolonization could also involve violence, war, and suffering on a tragic scale. At the end of the century, the decolonization process had left its mark on political institutions, on social formations, on individual lives, and on global relations. *3rd World countries Under-developed / less-developed*

The Early Years of Decolonization

The old empires of the Ottoman Turks and Austria-Hungary were already in disarray at the beginning of the century. World War I led to their complete demise when subject populations wrested their independence from weakened imperial forces. The Russian Empire, although still an imperial power in Central and Northeast Asia, had lost large territories on the Baltic Sea and in Eastern Europe. German imperial rule was also a casualty of the war. In the 1919 Treaty of Versailles, the victorious powers invoked the concepts of "war guilt" and reparations to dismantle the empires of their enemies. U.S. President Woodrow Wilson also promoted the concept of "self-determination." He came to the Paris Peace Conference armed with Fourteen Points as the basis for a new world order. These included the establishment of a League of Nations as a consultative and peacekeeping body, and recognition of the principle of "absolutely impartial adjustment of all colonial claims," that is, giving equal weight to the interests of the colonial populations and "the equitable claims" of imperial governments.

When the peace treaties were signed, the vast majority of colonial subjects had lost out, however. The idea of "self-determination" seemed to apply to the European subjects of imperial powers, so that Poland, Czechoslovakia, Yugoslavia, Finland, Estonia, Latvia, and Lithuania emerged as nation-states from the remnants of the Russian, German, and Austro-Hungarian Empires, but Arabs, Africans, and Asians continued under Great Power domination. Some imperial powers even extended their territories through the League of Nations mandate system in which former territories of Germany and Ottoman Turkey were given to victorious powers such as France, Britain, Australia, South Africa, and Japan to administer. In theory the League of Nations was to safeguard the interests of the subject populations, but in fact the Great Powers treated the mandated territories in much the same way that they treated their other colonial possessions. *Britain would lose all their territory (India, Burma)*

Such disregard of nationalist aspirations angered colonial subjects, especially veterans who had volunteered or been conscripted into imperial armies and expected some rewards for their loyalty to empire. Some 800,000 Indian soldiers had fought on the Allied side in Europe and the Middle East and half a million noncombatant laborers had worked in support roles. Africans had also contributed to the war effort in British, French, and German armies. The French had mobilized 200,000 West Africans, who fought on the western front with high casualty rates at the height of the war in 1916–1917. In the campaigns fought between Britain and Germany in East Africa, 60,000 Kenyans, who had been conscripted in noncombatant roles as porters, cooks, and laborers, had died, mostly from disease and malnutrition. For the fortunate who returned home, there were few rewards. "I wanted my land back," recalled a veteran in an interview for a film on the colonial experience in Kenya, "and they gave me a medal." He went on to tell how he and other former soldiers had to watch as a new wave of white settlers, escaping from the economic disarray of postwar Europe, arrived and took their land. Africans remained an underclass and continued to be treated as inferior beings. Yet, the mystique of the white "civilizing mission" was fatally damaged for those who had experienced the barbarous nature of modern warfare. Furthermore, soldiers who had previously experienced whites as distant authority figures had fought side by side with white men and found white girlfriends when they went on leave to large cities such as Paris. Common humanity with all its flaws was starkly experienced.

On their return home, some veterans joined with the educated elite in providing leadership for associations, religious groups, and trade unions, which drew together thousands disgruntled

Difficulty w/ Modernization issues (economic, cultural)

with white rule for a myriad of reasons. In the 1920s and the 1930s these groups were hardly radical in their demands; rather, they wanted better working conditions, the return of land, more respect, and participation in government. "If Africans were good enough to fight in the Empire's cause, they are good enough . . . to have a share in the government of their countries," a writer in the *Gold Coast Independent* claimed in 1921. Political parties were formed but they tended to enroll small groups of the educated elite. It was only after World War II that the nationalist struggle in Africa became politically organized on a mass basis.

Two events in the 1930s added force to the rising tide of anticolonial sentiment in Africa. The Great Depression, which cut demand for raw materials, threw tens of thousands of laborers in cash-crop agriculture and mining out of work. The unemployed migrated to towns but did not always find jobs. Such conditions contributed to social unrest, which found expression in growing criticisms of European administrators, employers, farmers, and teachers. The Italian invasion of Ethiopia (Abyssinia) under the Fascist dictator Mussolini also shocked Africans in the diaspora, adding to the anticolonial debate. In Nigeria, an Abyssinian Association and Ethiopian Fund was established to collect money for refugees and to aid resisters; 20,000 people demonstrated in New York; Rastafarians protested in Jamaica; and black expatriate groups discussed the situation in Paris, London, and Lisbon. Jomo Kenyatta, the future prime minister and president of Kenya, published an article entitled "Hands off Abyssinia." Kwame Nkrumah remembered in his autobiography how the invasion had heightened his sensitivity to the "wickedness of colonialism" and how he had prayed that "the day might come when I could play my part in bringing about the downfall of such a system." Britain, France, and the United States protested against Italian aggression, but their oil companies, which continued to fuel the Italian military machine, only increased the outrage. Clearly, the tide of opinion was running against colonial rule.

Before World War II, the nationalist struggle was most advanced in India. The process of decolonization followed there was similar to those commonly experienced elsewhere in the colonial world, especially in British-ruled territories. It was a gradualist approach to decolonization, punctuated by colonial crackdowns on those labeled "extremists" and by negotiations that inched forward. Early in the century, the contradictions inherent in a colonial policy that educated an indigenous middle class while denying it participation in the political process were already obvious. In 1900, there were 23,000 Indian university graduates and 600,000 attending secondary schools. In 1885, the educated elite established the Indian National Congress to lobby for political rights. Twenty years later it adopted the goal of self-government within the British Empire. It could not, however, accommodate deep-seated religious divisions, and in 1906 a comparable Muslim League was founded. This organization demanded and won separate electorates for Muslim candidates in elections.

Resistance by villagers and townspeople continued on many levels, but educated Indians such as Jawaharlal Nehru took their case to the British authorities. Nehru, like many other leaders, was well educated. He had gone to a private school in Britain and had graduated with a law degree from Cambridge University. He came from an aristocratic family in northern India; his father was a High Court judge and a founding member of the Indian National Congress. Back in India, Nehru spent years in colonial prisons for his political views, which were considered seditious by the British authorities. He and other nationalists adopted the platform of *swaraj,* or "self-rule." Also inspirational in the nationalist struggle was another British-trained lawyer, Mohandas (later called "Mahatma," or "Great Soul") Gandhi, who returned to India in 1915 from South Africa, where he had organized anti–pass law demonstrations and developed his ideas

PICTURE 7.2   Mohandas Gandhi (1869–1948) with three women.
Women contributed much to the Indian independence struggle. Many
joined with Gandhi in campaigns of civil disobedience against British rule.
(Photo from the Library of Congress)

and strategies on nonviolent resistance (*satyagraha,* or "soul-force"). In 1919, he launched his first large civil disobedience campaign to protest a law that allowed emergency powers of detention without trial. Leaders such as Nehru, who supported democratic socialist goals and more radical confrontation with the British, were often impatient with Gandhi, but they saw the importance of his mass appeal.

Gandhi touched millions with his ideas of self-reliance, his promotion of Indian culture (*swadeshi*), and swaraj based on village communalism. Women had been a part of the resistance movement for decades, but under Gandhi they were recruited in greater numbers. If the masses united to boycott British goods, Gandhi argued, export-dependent British industries would be crippled. Imported textiles became the focus of a boycott in favor of locally produced cloth, and the spinning wheel became the symbol of resistance to imperialism. In 1930, Gandhi expanded his campaign to challenge the British monopoly on salt. He and a crowd of followers undertook a 240-mile journey to the coast, where they collected and processed sea salt. This Salt March grabbed the imagination of many. Gandhi, like Nehru and many other men and women in Africa and Asia, was imprisoned by colonial authorities. Nationalist leaders joked, but not without good reason, that to be a prime minister or president of a newly independent state, one had first to earn the degree of "P.G.," or "Prison Graduate."

While cracking down on demonstrations, strikes, "seditious" writings by journalists, and other forms of resistance, Britain was also reviewing its imperial options and reluctantly entering into negotiations with nationalist leaders. In 1909, the British Parliament passed the Indian Councils Act, which introduced a limited male franchise and gave limited powers to councils at a local and national level. Following World War I, the Government of India Act introduced the principle of divided responsibility, handing some departments, such as education and health, over to Indian administration, and keeping others, such as security, defense, and foreign policy, under British control. The central government in New Delhi also remained in British hands, although the legislative assembly now had an elected majority. Indian women won the same voting rights as men in 1926. Then, in 1935, the electorate was enlarged and given the right to vote for representatives to the provincial and federal legislatures. More than 500 states administered by princes were also to send representatives. Each province became self-governing, with British governors limited to emergency powers. At the federal level, the viceroy, or British governor-general, was advised by an Executive Council chosen from elected members of the legislature. Muslims continued to elect their own representatives on a separate electorate.

In the Middle East, the anticolonial struggle was particularly complex. Arab nationalism collided with Jewish aspirations for a national homeland and Great Power interests in the region's rich oil reserves. Arab nationalism had first emerged in the cities of Damascus and Beirut under the leadership of both Christian and Muslim intellectuals. Prior to World War I, it remained mainly an elite urban movement in the cities. Still, the period after about 1870 was important in shaping the main tenets. Its adherents looked back to the Abbasid period (from the eighth to the thirteenth centuries), the "golden age" of Arab-Islamic history, to find the literature, laws, inventions (especially those involving scientific and mathematical principles), and victories that had made the Middle East the most powerful world region at that time. They formed secret societies, established nascent political parties, initiated a movement to make the Arabic language more accessible, and founded journals to debate and spread their ideas. Arab nationalism, as enunciated by its proponents, had a coherence—unlike African nationalism—since Arabs shared a common past. At the same time, Islamic modernists in Egypt worked to bring Islam into the twentieth century. They looked to basic texts and history and proclaimed that Islam, with its proven record of innovation and invention over the centuries, could serve as a vehicle for modernization in the Middle East. Arabs did not have to copy the West to be strong; they only had to utilize the inherent strengths of their history and culture. In the decades just before World War I, the Arabs developed a sense of a separate identity from that of their Ottoman rulers, a tendency enhanced by the aggressive turkification policy mounted by the members of the Young Turk movement that came to power at the same time.

World War I allowed Arab nationalists to develop plans about how to achieve their goal of independence from Ottoman Turkish rule. In a secret correspondence written at the height of the war in 1915, British agents promised the influential ruler of the holy city of Mecca, Sharif Husayn, a new pan-Arab state stretching from Turkey to the Arabian peninsula in return for Arab military help against the Ottomans, who had entered the war on the side of Germany and Austria-Hungary. Also in 1916, however, British and French ministers had reached a secret and contradictory understanding: Their two countries, they decided, would divide the regions of the defunct Ottoman Empire in the Middle East into their own spheres of influence at the end of the war.

Jewish aspirations for a national homeland further complicated the situation. In 1896 these hopes had found concrete expression in a book by Theodore Herzl entitled *The Jewish State*. The meeting of the First World Zionist Congress in the following year confirmed the same view. From the Jewish perspective, the claim to a homeland was legitimized on religious grounds, through covenants with God recounted in the Old Testament, and by the centuries-old oppression of Jews in the diaspora. Their legal status had improved in Western Europe, but continuing anti-Semitism was expressed in discrimination. In Eastern Europe and in Russia, pogroms continued in the late nineteenth century. With funding from Jews worldwide, the first modern settlers arrived in Palestine to join Jewish communities that had lived side by side with Arab populations under Ottoman rule for centuries. In 1909 the city of Tel Aviv was established, and the next year the first communal farm came into being. By 1914, there were about 85,000 Jewish settlers in Palestine. The permanence of their presence in the region seemed assured in 1917 when British Foreign Secretary Alfred Balfour wrote to Lord Rothschild, an influential leader of the British Jewish community, "His Majesty's Government views with favour the establishment in Palestine of a national home for the Jewish people." The note did not specifically mention the Palestinian Arabs, but it did hold out a caveat that it should be "clearly understood that nothing shall be done which may prejudice the civil and religious rights of existing non-Jewish communities in Palestine." Thus, these three agreements—one with the Arabs, one with France, and one with the Jewish community—made to garner support for the British war effort, promised similar pieces of land to different groups. They were a recipe for broken promises, a resentful Arab population, and struggles for land, resources, and power that still embroiled the Middle East in conflict at century's end.

Arabs felt betrayed when their nationalist aspirations were not realized in the settlements at the end of the war. It seemed that they had merely exchanged Ottoman imperial rule for that of Britain and France. Under the League of Nations mandate system, Syria and Lebanon were put into the French sphere of influence, while Britain was given responsibility for Iraq, Palestine, and some regions in the Persian Gulf (see Map 7.1). Only Turkey wrested its independence from the imperial grasp. There, a massive nationalist movement adopted a modernization campaign (not unlike that of late nineteenth-century Japan); it emerged as a modern secular nation-state in 1922.

Arab hatred of Western imperialism and Jewish settlement was at the center of Middle East developments in the interwar years. This was not only a struggle over political independence intensified by religious and cultural differences, but over land and resources. In 1914, Jewish settlers constituted about 10 percent of the population, and access to good land was not yet a problem, but in the 1930s and especially with the persecution of the Jews in Nazi Germany, the number seeking refuge in the region increased dramatically. The Balfour Declaration and the increase in Jewish settlement heightened nationalist sentiments among the Palestinians. Threatened by land shortages and wanting more power in local government, they began organizing political parties, social welfare organizations, schools, and militias to resist British forces. Sporadic uprisings culminated in a major revolt in 1936–1939 and the imprisonment of leaders by the British authorities. Elsewhere in the Middle East, France and Britain struggled to develop policies in the face of sustained Arab hostility. Some countries were granted independence—for example, Iraq in 1930 and Egypt in 1936, although in both cases Britain retained the right to maintain a military presence.

The discovery and exploitation of oil further complicated relations in the already volatile Middle East region. It was discovered early in the century, but exploitation was intensified in the 1920s and 1930s in response to growing demand in the industrial world. A consortium of seven companies, called the "Seven Sisters" (Exxon, Shell, BP, Gulf, Texaco, Mobil, and Standard of California), negotiated highly favorable terms with Arab leaders, whose countries had low energy needs and lacked capital and technology. By late century, Middle East oil had not only become

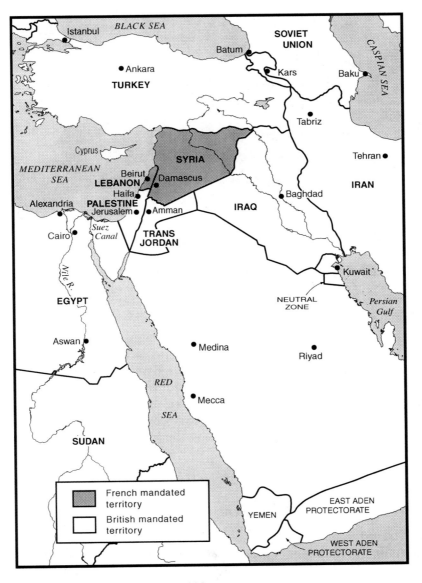

MAP 7.1   The Middle East, c. 1922.

essential to the economies of the industrialized Western world, it had become pivotal in the struggle of the West to stabilize the region in their terms. The oil issue had thus become critical, not only in Arab economies but also in their relations with the West.

By the eve of World War II, the forces of Asian, African, and Arab nationalism were becoming increasingly articulate and organized. These forces were not developing in isolation. As was evident in the reaction to the Italian invasion of Ethiopia, transcontinental connections between colonial populations were extensive, especially among future leaders, who often met as students while studying abroad, where they compared experiences and shared ideas. Africans who traveled to the United States were appalled at the levels of racial discrimination there and felt in-

PICTURE 7.3   Jewish Settlers. As Jewish settlement in Palestine increased, new areas were brought under cultivation through arid-land technology. This photo was taken at a Jewish settlement in the Negev Desert, Gouloth, in 1946. (Photo from the Library of Congress)

spired by the struggle of African Americans. European cities such as Paris, Lisbon, and London were gathering points for students and intellectuals from the West Indies, Africa, the Middle East, and Asia. Within regions such as the Middle East and southern Africa, networks of contacts developed as migrant workers searched for employment, refugees fled over colonial borders, traders crossed frontiers, performing artists traveled to give concerts, and students sought out the best schools. The groundswell and the organizational models for a second wave of decolonization were already in place.

Decolonization in the Postwar World

World War II created economic and social conditions that nationalist leaders could exploit. At the same time, the increasing costs of maintaining a colonial presence caused Europeans to review their options and in many cases hasten decolonization. In a few colonies, intransigent white settlers refused to give up land or grant indigenous populations democratic rights. In these cases, nationalist guerrillas took up arms in the liberation struggle.

Neither of the two superpowers dominating the postwar world had significant colonial interests in Asia or Africa. In 1935 the United States had begun a ten-year transitional period leading to Philippine independence; in spite of Japanese occupation during the war, the process was complete by 1945. Although attentive to its neocolonial interests in the Pacific, Central America, and the Caribbean, the United States was only likely to get drawn into decolonization struggles elsewhere when its strategic and economic interests were at stake. Increasingly, these concerns became equated with the competing interests of the Soviet Union and fear of communism. The Soviet Union, which by the end of the war had extended its control into Eastern Europe to occupy much the same territory as the old Russian Empire, was deeply embroiled in the affairs of its satellite states. It was also concerned about its borders with China and with supporting socialist revolutions wherever it could. Both superpowers were founding members of the United Nations and had supported its commitment to "self-determination." They were prepared to support decolonization efforts as well if these were compatible with their strategic interests.

In Europe, the two most important colonial powers, Britain and France, were weakened by the war. Their economies were in ruins, and official policy focused on the role of the colonies in helping postwar recovery. Left-wing governments also favored a changing relationship with the colonies, not so much a lowering of the imperial flag as a reform and revitalization of the colonial relationship, which they envisaged as a "partnership"—with the colonial power as the senior partner. The emphasis of colonial policy shifted to what the British called "welfare colonialism." Proponents of this concept encouraged public and private investment in new infrastructures, education, social services, health care, and technical development. The goal was to develop European commerce, industry, and investments and a "stable" indigenous workforce. Politically, the European powers, which saw their international influence slipping with the rise of the two superpowers, hoped to maintain their influence through collaboration with rising elite groups. By the late 1950s, this policy shift was clearly a case of too little too late. Social and economic benefits only increased the aspirations of an indigenous middle class for a more equitable share of resources. The colonial policy of controlled participation in the political process by indigenous peoples also backfired because political reforms increased nationalist expectations of full independence.

In the colonial world, World War II—even more than the war of 1914–1918—had been waged at great costs to local populations. The indigenous peoples had been conscripted into imperial armies and forced to grow strategic crops at the expense of household production; moreover, in towns they had suffered from miserable conditions and inflation. After the war they were often confronted with unemployment and low wages. Veterans who had served in North Africa, Europe, the Middle East, and Burma returned home radicalized, as had happened after World War I. Ndabaningi Sithole, a leader of the Zimbabwean nationalist struggle, wrote in his book *African Nationalism* (1959) that World War II "had a great deal to do with the awakening of the people of Africa." They began to see through "European pretensions." The war "had a revolutionizing psychological impact on the African." In these conditions, mass political parties were established by nationalist leaders in the late 1940s and 1950s.

Countries in the Middle East and Asia that won their independence soon after the war served as examples for movements elsewhere. In the Middle East, the British withdrew from Palestine, and Jewish leaders announced the creation of the state of Israel in 1948. This decision led to the first Arab-Israeli war: Israel expanded its territory and forced tens of thousands of Palestinians to flee to refugee camps in Lebanon, Jordan, and Gaza. Over a million Palestinians were left homeless and landless. A problem of international proportions, still unresolved at the end of the century, was created.

Elsewhere in the Middle East, young army officers with a vision of modernizing and industrializing their country took control in a 1952 coup in Egypt. The young president, Gamal Abdel Nasser, became a heroic figure for Arab and African nationalists when he embarked on a nonalignment policy. He adopted this approach after attending a 1955 conference in Indonesia, where he had met India's Nehru and other leaders promoting nonalignment for newly independent states in the Cold War era. In accordance with the policy he bought arms from Czechoslovakia rather than his usual suppliers, the United States, Britain, and France. When the United States and Britain retaliated by withdrawing an offer to help finance the high dam at Aswan, Nasser nationalized the Suez Canal. In an old-fashioned imperialist move, Britain, France, and Israel launched an invasion of Egypt to recover the canal by military means. Lacking support from the United States and unwilling to sustain a war in the region, the two European powers soon abandoned the enterprise, however, and opened negotiations with the nationalists. Nasser became an African hero and an inspiration in the decolonization struggle worldwide. Colonial subjects listened to Egyptian radio broadcasts and learned how the two imperial powers had been forced into a humiliating retreat.

In Asia, Japanese imperial expansion came to an abrupt end in 1945, but Japan's wartime occupation of areas such as Indochina and Indonesia weakened European control and encouraged local nationalists. After a fierce war of liberation, the Vietnamese won independence from the French, although they had to accept the partitioning of their land in 1954. The Dutch, who had ruled the East Indies as a commercial empire for more than two centuries, had granted Indonesia independence in 1949. The nationalist struggle in the Indian subcontinent also came to a head during and after the war. The National Congress Party had declared as early as 1927 that India should not be dragged into a foreign war without the consent of the people. Nationalists reacted angrily when the viceroy declared India to be at war without consulting Congress party leaders. In 1942, as the Japanese advance through Indochina and Burma threatened the Indian frontiers, the All-India Congress Committee passed a "Quit India" resolution demanding an immediate end to British rule. Britain responded by imprisoning Congress leaders. Thousands reacted by joining the India National Army to fight on the side of the Japanese. Most Indians, however, had little desire to exchange British rule for Japanese rule, and they once again rallied to the British cause. In 1947, India and Muslim Pakistan were granted independence.

In Africa, the process of decolonization lagged behind that of most Asian countries, but once underway it moved quickly—indeed, more rapidly than the colonial powers had envisaged. Between 1945 and 1968, thirty-four African states became independent, seventeen of them in the "miracle year" of 1960. The end of colonial rule came about through a complex mix of local initiatives and changing colonial interests, along with a global climate in which other former colonies were taking their seats as independent states at the United Nations.

A major issue for colonial governments was the cost of colonial rule. The difficult conditions during the war have already been mentioned and these continued in the postwar period. Many African cities doubled in population between 1940 and 1950, and some even quadrupled in size. Poor living conditions and unemployment raised levels of criticism of imperial rule that were expressed in worker action, political pamphlets, public and secret meetings, demonstrations, and even songs, drama, novels, and paintings that ridiculed the colonizers. Peasants with grievances relating to land shortages, preferential prices for white farmers, and lack of credit opportunities also gathered at political meetings in regional centers.

Worker protests helped shape imperial responses. The Great Powers were forced to look at the balance sheet of colonialism, and European ministries debated whether formal colonial rule was viable and affordable. During the war, many Europeans had left the colonies to fight in campaigns, opening up jobs for Africans. The indigenous people moved up the employment ladder and became a more important part of the skilled labor force. The policy of "welfare colonialism" in British and French colonies had also increased the numbers of Africans moving into towns. Creating a skilled labor force proved to be counterproductive for the colonizers, however, as workers seized the initiative and demanded the same kind of benefits enjoyed by workers in Eu-

PICTURE 7.4
Governor-General's Palace, Brazzaville, Congo. The governor-general's residence in the capital of French Equatorial Africa symbolized power and permanence in a region where local people lived in simple dwellings, c. 1935. (Photo courtesy of the Roger Frey collection)

rope. In close contact with European unions, African labor leaders set about forming trade unions to demand pensions, decent wages, vacations, and other benefits. The postwar years saw many strikes, from the mines on the Central African Copperbelt to the docks of East African ports, and from the factories of South Africa to the railroads of West Africa. Virtually no African colony went unscathed by major strikes in the late 1940s. These protests proved to be a potent force in nationalist politics. Employers and colonial governments failed to accommodate workers' demands; however, the strikes did force colonial governments to reconsider their goals. From their point of view, the costs of maintaining a formal colonial presence were mounting. It was not just a matter of policing mutinous town populations or maintaining a commitment to social reform; it had become a question of how to respond to the demands of militant workers. These were the conditions that caused Britain and France, in particular, to abandon formal colonial rule in favor of negotiating with nationalist leaders.

Most British colonies followed the Indian model. Nationalist parties first won the right to representation on legislative and executive councils, then the right to hold democratic elections; these steps led to local self-government and finally full independence. The same states of emergency, suspension of human rights, and jailing of nationalist leaders prevailed as colonial governments tried to control the pace of decolonization. In the Gold Coast, for example, Kwame Nkrumah founded his Convention People's Party in 1949 with the motto "Self-Government Now." He and other leaders were jailed as political agitators, but the British were not prepared to invest the resources needed to contain the nationalist tide. In 1951, when the governor-general agreed to general elections for internal self-government for the Gold Coast, Nkrumah's party won by a large margin. Nkrumah was released from prison to be the leader of the government. Further concessions by the British led to national independence for Ghana in 1957. Other British colonies where no settlers were present also followed this model of gradual concessions. Newly independent states now joined the liberation lobby at the United Nations and in European capitals.

Reeling from the effects of the war and economically weakened, France had most to lose from the winning of independence among African colonies. France had always depended on its colonies for prestige. The process of decolonization in its African colonies thus followed a pattern different from the British one. The goal was to transform colonial possessions into *France d'Outre-Mer,* or "Overseas France." It was hoped that this formula would perpetuate a reformed colonial relationship within a French Union. In 1944, General Charles de Gaulle met with the governors of France's African colonies and a few African observers at Brazzaville, the capital of French Equatorial Africa and of "Free France," to discuss the future of the colonial relationship. The worst colonial abuses, such as the harsh "native" legal code and forced labor, were abolished. Independence was ruled out, but a small number of the elite and some traditional chiefs were allowed to vote in a special electoral college that sent representatives to the French National Assembly in Paris. The rest of the population remained effectively barred from political participation. Politicized elites set up study groups in a number of colonies and were formative in establishing black Africa's largest radical party, the Rassemblement Démocratique Africaine (RDA, African Democratic Alliance), founded in Bamako in 1946. Although influenced by Nkrumah's political struggle, the main goal of the RDA was to mobilize workers in the effort to improve living and working conditions. In Ivory Coast in 1949, 50 demonstrators were killed and 3,000 jailed. In 1955, France introduced sweeping reforms that allowed local assemblies to be elected by universal suffrage. Powers of local government were also transferred to Africans.

Finally, by the late 1950s, chronic difficulties in the French economy, political instability at home, defeat in Indochina, high death rates among soldiers fighting colonial wars in Algeria, and the growing costs of colonial rule brought Charles de Gaulle to power in France. He was given special powers to devise a new association with the African colonies. In 1958, he offered them independence. Only Guinea voted in favor of complete independence; other colonies voted to stay in a French-dominated union. Guinea's independence acted as a catalyst for change elsewhere, however, and in 1960 all of France's African colonies were granted political independence, although they continued to maintain close economic, military, and cultural ties with their former colonial ruler. This new situation was to be a "qualified independence," as powerful neocolonial relations remained entrenched from Senegal to Niger and from Cameroon to Congo, and African elites continued to beat a path to and from the Elysée Palace.

Not all Africans experienced this gradual approach to decolonization. In Belgian Congo, the largest and strategically most important colony in Central Africa, independence, when it came, was abrupt and unexpected. As late as 1955, King Baudouin, in a speech summing up his country's policy toward Belgian Congo, completely misread the wave of decolonization when he said: "Belgium is one and indivisible, the Belgium of Europe and the Belgium of Africa." In 1958, a Belgian minister predicted that Congo might be ready for independence in thirty years. Yet, two years later the government was forced to grant its colony independence in the face of a growing debt, a mutinous army, and riots in Léopoldville, the Congolese capital. Although Belgium, like Britain and France, had increased educational opportunities in its colonies after World War II, it was at the primary-school level only because Africans were to be restricted to low-level jobs. The year before independence, there were no Africans in the officer ranks of the army, and only 3 among the top 4,500 civil servants. At independence there were less than 20 university graduates in this huge colony, and Africans had little experience in national government. Furthermore, they were deeply divided, in part due to the colonial divide-and-rule strategy. Caught in the web of the Cold War in the 1960s, the circumstances of Congo's independence were a recipe for future disaster.

The presence of white settlers in several African countries made the path to independence particularly treacherous. Settlers had no desire to return to Europe; nor did they wish to return land they had occupied or live under black majority rule. Almost without exception, in settler colonies sub-

PICTURE 7.5
Big Three at Yalta.
The Allied leaders,
Franklin D. Roosevelt,
Winston Churchill,
and Joseph Stalin, met
at Yalta in the Crimea
in February 1945 to
discuss peace
arrangements. (Photo
courtesy of the
Franklin D. Roosevelt
Library, Franklin and
Eleanor Roosevelt
Digital Collection)

ject populations had to wage wars of liberation in order to win independence. The African settler colonies included the important French colony of Algeria; the Portuguese colonies of Guinea, Angola, and Mozambique; and the British colonies of Kenya and Southern Rhodesia (Zimbabwe).

Independence Struggles in the Cold War Decades: Vietnam and Angola

In some areas, the insertion of Cold War rivalries into local situations greatly distorted the decolonization process, escalating the scale and intensity of conflicts. The use of modern weaponry, from blanket bombing to rocket attacks and from napalm to land mines, wrought havoc in the lives of ordinary people. By the time the United States and the Soviet Union abandoned the Cold War around 1989, their intervention in independence and postcolonial struggles had resulted in wrecked economies, deep divisions, dislocated families, and a great deal of human suffering. Only a study of particular examples can fully make the point. Here, two case studies are discussed: the French Indochina colony of Vietnam and the Portuguese Central African colony of Angola. In both cases, nationalist liberation fighters were inspired by Lenin's teachings on the connection between imperialism and capitalism, by neo-Marxist and Maoist ideologies, and by successful socialist revolutionary struggles elsewhere in Latin America and Asia. Their adherence to socialist models was both complicated and strengthened in the Cold War that overtook global geopolitics in the years that followed World War II.

As World War II was ending in Europe, the "big three"—Franklin D. Roosevelt of the United States, Joseph Stalin of the Soviet Union, and Winston Churchill of Great Britain—met at the Yalta conference to work out the postwar distribution of power. World War II had accelerated U.S. involvement in world affairs compared to the 1930s, when policy had focused on reconstruction in domestic matters and nonintervention in foreign affairs, except as necessitated by imperial interests in Latin America. After 1945, U.S. international policy was based on fear—of expanding Soviet power and the threat of communism to overseas markets, resources, and in-

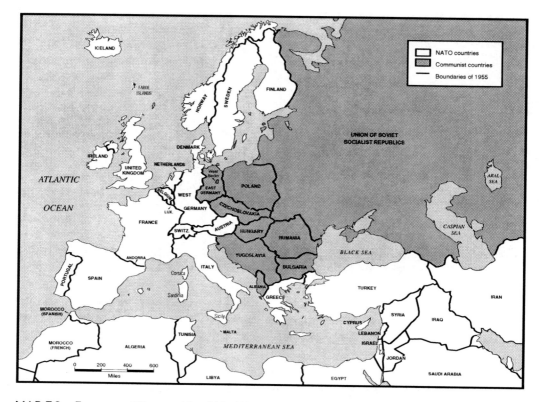

MAP 7.2   European Alliances After World War II

vestment. At Yalta and after, the Soviet government showed it had no intention of giving up the Eastern European territory that it occupied at the end of the war. Protecting its southern borders and preserving long-standing spheres of influence in regions such as Iran and Afghanistan were other Soviet priorities. In 1946, Winston Churchill, no longer in power in Britain but still much admired in the United States, visited America and declared that an "iron curtain" had descended over Europe. By that year negotiations to end military stockpiling and to establish international control of atomic weaponry had ceased. The development of competing military alliances in the North Atlantic Treaty Organization (NATO) and the Warsaw Pact in Communist Eastern Europe further solidified the divisions (see Map 7.2).

By 1947, the Cold War was the paramount issue in U.S. foreign policy; for its part, the Soviet Union was concerned about U.S. attempts at "encirclement." The Truman Doctrine, articulated in that year, suggested the willingness of the United States to intervene worldwide. It said, "It must be the policy of the United States to support free people who are resisting subjugation by armed minorities or outside pressures. . . . We must assist free peoples to work out their own destinies in their own way."

Several historians have come to the conclusion that in spite of crises involving Berlin, Hungary, and Czechoslovakia, there was little real danger of armed conflict in Europe. Although there was a great deal of brinkmanship on both sides, postwar agreements and zones of influence were generally recognized. In the United States, the fears expressed in anti-Communist rhetoric and apocalyptic references to nuclear war were due as much to domestic exigencies as to foreign policy: Domestic worries included not only fear about communism as a popular ideology to rival that of capitalism and democracy but also concern about voter reaction if the government appeared "soft" in foreign affairs. The rhetoric was also influenced by the military-industrial complex, which had greatly expanded during and after World War II.

If the situation in Europe was relatively predictable, it was much less certain in other regions of the world. Independence from colonial rule meant that new governments were emerging, and it was difficult to discern their future. U.S. fears of the spread of communism, economic loss, and threats to democracy seemed confirmed by the successful Chinese revolution and Mao Zedong's coming to power in 1949. The next year, North Korean Communist forces invaded the southern part of the Korean peninsula. The United States and Communist China intervened, initiating a war that dragged on from 1950 to 1953 before an armistice, but not a permanent peace, was reached.

In 1952, the administration of General Dwight D. Eisenhower (1952–1960), a Republican, moved the rhetoric of U.S. policy beyond the "containment" of communism to the "liberation" of Soviet-occupied territories. John Foster Dulles, an ardent and outspoken anti-Communist, was appointed U.S. secretary of state. Newly independent states, and those where decolonization was still in process, were potential zones of friction as the superpowers competed for influence in Asia, Africa, the Middle East, and Latin America. Even when it became clear that most postcolonial states were not "turning Communist" but rather wanted nonalignment in foreign policy and a mix of capitalism and socialism in economic planning, tensions remained high.

Southeast Asia, where decolonization was rapidly unfolding in the 1940s and 1950s, was an important testing ground, from the U.S. perspective, for demonstrating that the "free world" could defend against Communist expansion. It was in this context that Dulles and Eisenhower saw evidence for their "domino theory." According to this theory, the spread of communism was infectious: If one state fell to Communist influence, others would follow. The intersection of decolonization with Cold War rivalries was especially marked in Vietnam.

By 1945, Vietnam had experienced Chinese, French, and Japanese imperial occupation. Thus, the arrival of U.S. soldiers was for local people just another strand in a long line of foreign intervention. Vietnam had once been the southernmost province of China, and it continued to pay tribute to its powerful neighbor in the early nineteenth century, as did neighboring Laos and Cambodia. With the coming of traders, missionaries, soldiers, and administrators in the age of European imperialism, Indochina became part of the French colonial world. In the 1920s, French Minister of Colonies Albert Saurrat described Vietnam as "the most prosperous of our colonies." Rice, rubber, sugarcane, cotton, and coffee were produced for export, often on plantations owned by foreigners and worked by the Vietnamese under miserable conditions. The French displaced the ruling class of mandarins and installed their local clients, who converted to Catholicism, spoke French (the teaching of Chinese was prohibited), and adopted Western clothes and lifestyles.

Vietnamese nationalism paralleled the rise of Indian nationalism and was influenced by it. In 1904 a group of young Vietnamese intellectuals, inspired by the rise of Japan as a modern state, the imminent end of empire in China, and nationalist parties in India, founded the Reform Association. Since it supported peasant demands against high taxation and forced labor, this group was predictably persecuted by the French authorities. Many had to go into exile or go underground. In 1917 a nationalist party was formed in Saigon. It demanded representation in government, but unlike the British, who recognized the legitimacy of the Indian National Congress, the French would not recognize the organization. Overseas, young nationalists were traveling and learning from developments in Europe and elsewhere. Among them was Ho Chi Minh (meaning "he who enlightens"; his real name was Nguyen That Thanh), the future leader of North Vietnam, who left Indochina in 1912 and returned thirty years later after visiting and working in Africa, France, the United States, the Soviet Union, and China. While in Paris, in 1919, he organized a group of Vietnamese living in that city and together they presented an eight-point petition to the representatives of the Great Powers at the Versailles Peace Conference.

This document demanded that the French colonial power grant its Indochina subjects the same rights as the French. Like other nationalists at the time, Ho Chi Minh and his friends aimed not at independence but at equal treatment within the French Empire. The radicalization of the independence struggle was to come later. Having read Lenin's writings, which made sense given the oppression of townspeople and peasants in his own country, Ho Chi Minh became a convinced Communist and helped found the French Communist Party in 1920. He further developed his ideology and strategies during stays in Russia and China, where a Communist Party was established in 1921, and he became an Indochina representative at the Communist International, the international body of world communism. Thus, for Ho Chi Minh and other Vietnamese revolutionaries the decolonization struggle was as much inspired by social revolution as it was by nationalism. The struggle was against both French colonialism and wealthy Vietnamese, who formed an indigenous upper class of landlords, businessmen, and administrators and benefited from French colonial rule. In 1929, he helped establish the Indochina Communist Party. During World War II, he returned to Vietnam together with other exiles, and in August 1945, after the Japanese surrender, nationalists seized control of Hanoi and declared the independence of the Democratic Republic of Vietnam.

After World War II, Cold War politics intervened in the decolonization struggle. The French, unlike the British in India, were not persuaded that a colonial retreat was necessary, and they returned to Vietnam. They were supported in the United States by the Truman administration, which now saw Ho Chi Minh as suspect because of his Communist leanings. For eight years, the French tried to reestablish their rule in Vietnam. They restored as a puppet ruler the emperor who was known more as a playboy in the casinos of the French Riviera than for his knowledge of Vietnam. In the anticolonial war, the broad-based coalition forged by Ho Chi Minh received reinforcements from Communist China and the Soviet Union. In 1954, the nationalist forces cut off 16,000 French troops at Dien Bien Phu. It was the climax of the war of independence and a landmark victory in the history of decolonization. The French decided to cut their losses in Indochina and retreated; Laos had already become independent in 1949, as did Cambodia in 1953.

Thus, the victory of anticolonial forces in Indochina was achieved at a time when Cold War rivalries were at a boiling point. In 1955, John F. Kennedy, a U.S. senator at the time, said, "Vietnam represents the cornerstone of the Free World." The Chinese also had their own "domino theory," surrounded as they were by U.S. allies in Taiwan, South Korea, and Japan. At the Geneva conference, which tried to settle the Vietnamese situation in 1954, the United States refused to consent to a united Vietnam, instead agreeing to the division of North and South Vietnam with the promise of future elections. The elections were not held, however, and two states emerged. The French handed over power in the south to Ngo Dinh Diem, an anti-Communist who had spent time in the United States. He ruled through an extensive and corrupt family, and his persecution

PICTURE 7.6   Vietnamese refugees, 1968. M-113 armored personnel carriers stand by as Vietnamese refugees evacuate the village of My Tho, Dinh Toung Province, during the American Tet offensive. (Photo from the National Archives)

of opponents helped to turn peasants into guerrilla fighters who looked to the north for support. North Vietnam was administered from Hanoi by a government headed by Ho Chi Minh, who became convinced that his forces must join in the struggle in the south. The United States funneled advisers and arms to the south, while China channeled arms to the Communist forces. Under the Johnson administration in 1964 the war escalated, and in 1965, the United States began bombing North Vietnam. In eight years of war, 57,000 Americans were killed and well over half a million Vietnamese died.

The ill-judged aspects of U.S. military and diplomatic policy in Vietnam are beyond the scope of this discussion; however, the ability of the North Vietnamese and their southern allies to defeat U.S. and allied forces can be well understood in the context of imperialism, colonialism, and decolonization. The struggle was not only about communism and capitalism. From the point of view of U.S. opponents, it was also an anti-imperialist struggle rooted in the colonial past, in the exploitation of land and labor by foreigners, and in opposition to the Vietnamese upper-class elites who had long collaborated to their material advantage with colonial and neocolonial forces. Mao Zedong's words relating the class struggle to the anti-imperialist struggle were full of meaning for the Vietnamese peasants who joined the guerrilla forces. In comparison, the Cold War conflicts of the two Great Powers were distant for the villagers who proved so resilient in the face of heavy bombing by the world's greatest military power. With the withdrawal of U.S. forces in 1973, the Republic of South Vietnam only lasted two years, and in 1976 the formal reunification of Vietnam took place.

Perhaps less well known but also caught in the snare of Cold War politics was the decolonization struggle and its aftermath in Angola. Unlike neighboring French, British, and Belgian territories, the Portuguese colony seemed far from liberation in 1960. There were several reasons for colonial intransigence. First, since 1933, Portugal itself had been under the authoritarian rule of António Salazar. His government not only survived longer than the better-known Fascist dictatorships in Spain, Italy, and Germany; it also showed its commitment to authoritarian government after World War II by establishing a secret police in Portugal and the colonies. This force was notorious for cracking down on dissident groups with torture and imprisonment. Democratic government was hardly likely in Africa when it was denied at home. Second, unlike Britain or France, which could hope to maintain their dominance through economic muscle and neocolonial strategies, Portugal, a small and poor state on the fringes of Europe, could not hope to keep out strong competitors once colonial trade barriers were lifted. Thus, political rule was necessary to maintain economic dominance. Third, after World War II, a wave of state-sponsored settlers arrived in Portugal's African colonies. Their prosperity depended on preferential treatment from the colonial government. Whereas the door to independence was ajar in the colonies of Britain and France by the late 1950s, it was firmly locked as far as Portugal was concerned. Transition to independence in Angola (and Mozambique and Guinea-Bissau) could only be won through armed struggle.

The "winds of change" sweeping through Africa could not be held back indefinitely, however. Anger and resentment were commonplace among people who suffered under Portuguese colonialism and who watched as their neighbors celebrated independence. Forced labor, which had been outlawed by the International Labor Organization, was still practiced in Angola, Mozambique, and Guinea-Bissau. In Angola in the 1950s, less than 1 percent of the colonial population had rights of citizenship. The vast majority were subject to a harsh penal code that included forced labor for women and children as well as men. Just as bad was the arbitrary treatment meted out by white settlers to local people, who had little recourse to justice. Economic and social benefits granted to whites were denied to Africans. Education, which was mostly in missionary hands, touched only a small fraction of the population. Religious persecution was common and racism was endemic. All this was a potent combination of grievances.

Resistance to Portuguese rule simmered in underground organizations and broke forth in sporadic rebellions. Younger generations found inspiration in the history of all this activism and joined in the liberation struggle. The few who found missionary scholarships for overseas studies engaged in nationalist activities abroad, planning rebellions within the country. Three separate uprisings in 1961 sparked off a fourteen-year liberation war. In January, in the cotton-growing regions of Central Angola, small producers, frustrated by low prices and delayed payments, attacked European stores and river barges and blocked roads with barricades. Troops were sent to quell the rebels, and villages were strafed by the Portuguese air force. A few weeks later, in the capital, Luanda, an angry crowd stormed the prison where political prisoners were being held. White vigilante groups retaliated by rampaging through black slums. Not long after, workers on northern coffee plantations, where white immigrants had recently taken over land, gave vent to their anger. Several hundred Europeans and thousands of Africans died in the violence.

Independence wars in Angola intensified in the 1960s as Cold War adversaries, supporting three different African political parties, intervened. Each of these factions had its own ideology, region of support within the country, foreign base, and source of international aid. One group drew its inspiration from Marxism and its internal support from the capital and the central regions of the country; it was based in Zambia and received weapons from the Warsaw Pact countries of Eastern Europe. A second, based in neighboring Congo-Léopoldville (formerly Belgian Congo, later Zaire, and then the Democratic Republic of Congo), was oriented to capitalism and fought with arms provided by Western countries, especially the United States. A third drew its strength from the eastern and southern regions of the country and had no particular ideological orientation but received weapons from China through the neighboring country of Zambia. Each group had a charismatic leader who traveled to foreign capitals to make his case and receive funding.

Portugal sent thousands of young conscripts to fight in the African campaign with a full range of modern arms. As in Vietnam, the nationalist forces largely waged guerrilla warfare, obtaining arms from a range of sources, often from the Communist world. The sudden end to colonialism came in 1974 when a coup in Portugal swept away the dictator and brought to power a democratic government bent on granting independence to the colonies. The colonial wars played a role in the overthrow of the dictatorship, for 50 percent of the national budget had been swallowed up in Portugal's Africa wars. In 1974, Guinea-Bissau became independent, and in 1975, it was the turn of Angola and Mozambique.

As in Vietnam, in Angola (and Mozambique) decolonization did not end the conflict. Cold War politics now intervened to escalate the struggle. In the case of Angola, geographical considerations and natural resources, the strategic position of Angola's harbors on the Atlantic coast of Central Africa, the mineral and agricultural wealth of one of Africa's richest countries, and huge off-shore oil deposits were also at stake for the Soviet Union and the United States. The United States was also concerned that Angola might become an African domino, bringing communism to the borders of Zaire and South Africa, two countries with important U.S. investments. As the war dragged on, the conflict gained its own momentum, like other Cold War struggles.

After one of the sides in the decolonization war dropped out, the lines were drawn between the Marxist party, Movimento para a Libertacão de Angola (MPLA, Popular Movement for the Liberation of Angola), which controlled the government—in part because it controlled Luanda—and the more opportunist and Western-oriented União Nacional para a Independência Total de Angola (UNITA, National Union for the Total Independence of Angola). Neither the Soviet Union nor the United States sent their own troops to support the opposing parties; rather, they provided arms to their surrogates to try and win the war for the party they favored. East European technical experts advised the MPLA government; Czechoslovakia, Yugoslavia, and East Germany supplied arms; and Cuban troops spearheaded military assaults, flew government planes, drove the tanks, taught Angolans how to use rocket-launchers, built and destroyed roads and bridges, and provided medical aid. At the height of the mission there were 30,000 Cuban troops and advisers in Angola. At the same time, the U.S. Central Intelligence Agency channeled arms and military advisers to UNITA through Zaire and South Africa. South African troops also supported UNITA forces and at one point menaced the capital with their tanks before being turned back by Cuban reinforcements. Their advisers gave UNITA technical help, and their planes provided an air-shield for ground forces. For the South African government, holding the line in Angola was holding back the forces of black nationalism that threatened white minority rule.

As the war dragged on into the 1990s, the losers were Angolan farmers and townspeople caught in the terror of war. Many sought refuge in the capital, which mushroomed to a population of almost 2 million, although it did not have the infrastructure to sustain this many people. Tens of thousands fled as refugees to neighboring territories; others were conscripted into rival armies; and tens of thousands died or were maimed by land mines. At century's end, Angola had achieved the horrifying record of having the greatest percentage of amputees

PICTURE 7.7   Celebrating democracy, Windhoek, Namibia, 1990. Namibia was the last African country to achieve independence. The billboard ad reminds people to turn out to vote in their country's first democratic election. (Photo courtesy of the United Nations/John Isaac)

of any country in the world. Most of them were civilians—children, women, and men—whose limbs had been blown off as they walked along roads to their farms or worked in the fields. Decolonized Angola lay in ruins. Even after the end of the Cold War, the withdrawal of foreign troops, and the coming of democracy to South Africa, the war dragged on into the twenty-first century.

Conclusion

In this chapter we have considered a struggle for independence that was far from incomplete in the eyes of many people worldwide at the close of the twentieth century. Certainly, the transfer of power to indigenous populations from the West Indies to the Philippines and from Iraq to South Africa was a watershed in world and national history and recognized with huge celebrations. Independence days were widely reported on newsreels and in the international press. In scenes of pageantry, new flags were raised and new leaders sworn in. People marched in parades, dressed in new clothes, watched fireworks, and danced in street parties. Bands played music especially composed for these events—music like the "independence cha-cha," which was performed not only in Léopoldville and Brazzaville but for cheering crowds in Brussels and Paris. Euphoria was high, and for good reason, for independence brought an end to the day-to-day humiliation of life under colonial rule and the hope of a more equitable distribution of resources. Beyond independence, however, new governments faced a complex mix of problems.

First, although the Great Powers relinquished political control, they nonetheless retained influence over their former colonies. In newly independent states, fragile governments and ambitious politicians were often eager to sustain neocolonial relations through formal linkages and personal friendships with civil servants, business leaders, and politicians in Europe. This connection was especially important in the economic, military, and cultural relations between France and its former possessions in Africa. In some cases, the governments of former colonial territories actively sought out new but dependent relations with wealthy countries such as the United States and Japan.

Second, and related, was the economic weakness of most newly independent states. The celebrated historian of Africa, Walter Rodney, in a famous book entitled *How Europe Underdeveloped Africa* (1972), noted, "The vast majority of Africans went into colonialism with a hoe and came out with a hoe." Conflicts and mismanagement exacerbated economic problems in some areas. By the end of the century, world economic institutions such as the World Bank were dictating terms for economic reconstruction, or "structural adjustment." A favorite remedy for national indebtedness was to cut back on the number of civil servants, but in the short term such belt-tightening measures only exacerbated misery. They created unemployment and a fall in the standard of living of the middle class and had accompanying spin-off repercussions for the rest of the population.

Third, although some of the new states were based on a common culture and a common past, many others were artificial, created by European powers. The "nation" was the category that politicians recognized in the dismantling of empires after World War I, and the "nation" remained the unit that they recognized in the decolonizing process later in the century. In popular experience, however, other loyalties were at least as powerful as national ones. Old and new ethnic identities became powerful rallying points around which factions mobilized. The importance of ethnic loyalty was dramatically shown in the 1990s when Yugoslavia, created some seventy years earlier from the remnants of the Austro-Hungarian and Ottoman Empires, fell apart in genocidal fighting.

Fourth, at independence, colonial rulers left in place fragile political institutions that had been transplanted from Europe and had no time to take root. As we have demonstrated throughout this chapter and the previous one on imperialism, colonial rule was no school for democracy. On the contrary, it was largely maintained by authoritarian governments and widespread corruption. In the early years of independence, democracy proved to be an unworkable model for many independent states. They were taken over by strongmen (often brought to power by military coups) who accentuated their country's multiple economic and social problems through inexperience, mismanagement, and corruption.

Thus, at century's end, the optimism of independence was tempered with reality. If political independence had been achieved, the dominance of the Great Powers continued in a different guise. Furthermore, all kinds of class, ethnic, and religious divisions within the newly independent states ensured that the struggle to construct new societies would continue to be fraught with complex problems. We discuss these problems in more detail in the rest of Part Two and in Part Three.

Postscript

As the twentieth century drew to a close, the era of formal colonial rule had come to an end. Apart from the upsurge in the number of members of the United Nations, nothing illustrated this change more than the history of the British Empire, which at the beginning of the century encompassed about a quarter of the world's population. In June 1897, when Queen Victoria celebrated her Diamond Jubilee, tens of millions on all continents celebrated her sixty years on the throne of an expanding British Empire. A hundred years later, in June 1997, Prince Charles, the heir to the British throne and the representative of Queen Elizabeth II, traveled to Hong Kong to be present as that important colonial territory was handed back to China, from which it had been wrested by British imperial power in the nineteenth century. All the pomp and ceremony of such independence moments was observed. With the end of colonial rule in Hong Kong, the subjects in Britain's dependent territories numbered only 180,000, little more than the inhabitants of a medium-sized U.S. city. The most populous of these territories was the island of Bermuda in the Atlantic, with a population of 60,000, a place principally known for its beaches, for giving its name to a style of shorts, and for providing a tax haven for the wealthy. The sun had set on the British Empire, as it had on other great empires.

8

Peasants and Peasant Revolts

The [French peasantry acted in ways that were] clumsily cunning, knavishly naïve, . . . [it bore] the unmistakable physiognomy of the class that represents barbarism within civilization.

Karl Marx,
"The Class Struggles in France, 1848–1850"
(1850)

Peasants are the majority of mankind. . . . Yet one has to be reminded of this [because] in the growing flood of social science publications [one finds very few] rural studies. . . . But reality seems to confute this solipsism of the "civilized" mind. Day by day, the peasants make the economists sigh, the politicians sweat and the strategists swear, defeating their plans and prophecies all over the world—Moscow and Washington, Peking and Delhi, Cuba and Algeria, the Congo and Vietnam.

Teodor Shanin,
"The Peasantry as a Political Factor,"
in *Sociological Review* 14
(1966)

THE RADICAL THEORIST KARL MARX AND HIS MAIN EARLY INTERPRETERS, including Vladimir Lenin, placed little faith in the revolutionary potential of peasants. And yet Communist revolutions of the mid-to-late twentieth century carried out under the banner of Marxism-Leninism tended to prove most successful in countries where the vast majority of people still lived in villages. This paradox is one of several associated with the history of peasants in the modern world. Another is that it was only after waves of urbanization had drastically reduced the size of the peasantry in many nations that peasants, as political actors, finally began to get the kind of scholarly attention that Shanin, quoted in the epigraph above, called for.

A third conundrum relating to peasants requires some more explanation. Despite all the scrutiny of peasant revolutions that theorists and activists have recently engaged in, many aspects of these events remain enigmatic. It is now widely acknowledged that between the 1920s and the 1980s rurally based revolutionary movements transformed whole multinational regions (such as Latin America, Africa, and Southeast Asia) as well as some of the world's largest countries (most notably China). It is also generally accepted that even peasant rebellions that did not aspire to be or succeed in becoming part of full-fledged revolutions played major roles in the political transformations of other regions and countries that took nonrevolutionary routes to their modern forms. The case of India is an obvious one here: Although its vast rural population did not contribute to a "peasant revolution" per se, it was often far from quiescent. And upheavals in the countryside shaped India's postcolonial transformation in many important ways.

Yet, in spite of all this, there is no consensus or clear understanding among scholars on why peasants rebel, why those who rise up do so when they do, and why the actions of some peasant rebels end up furthering, others frustrating, the goals of particular revolutionary movements. The extent to which peasants are drawn into radical movements because of pragmatic calculations—for example, a belief that they will benefit from land reform programs promised by revolutionary parties—or less rational factors—for example, the charisma of particular leaders or the appeal of particular symbols—also remains subject to debate.

Thanks largely to research done after Shanin warned of the tendency of social scientists to ignore the peasantry, however, a great deal is now known about the lives and twentieth-century political actions of peasants in various parts of the world. As a result, many old, misleading notions and stereotypes, such as the idea that villagers are capable only of passivity or bouts of irrational collective violence, have been swept away by scholarly investigation, the course of events, or a combination of the two.

Perhaps most important, scholars now have a better appreciation of how dangerous it is to think of all peasants as being alike. Even within a single country, their lifestyles can vary greatly, and so, too, can their political inclinations. To take but one example, where it was once common to speak of "the" Chinese peasant or "the" family structure of Chinese peasants, Sinologists (specialists in Chinese studies) are now very much aware of the differences between northern and southern China, as well as the variation within these two geographical zones. The contrast between north and south manifests itself in many things. For example, in the types of crops on which peasants relied: Wheat was the staple in the north, rice in the south. This simple fact influenced not just what kinds of foods farmers ate but how they organized intra-familial divisions of labor and decisions, by those who could afford to make them, about hiring or not hiring non-family labor. The contrast between north and south also showed up in the internal cohesion of villages. This was much higher in southern provinces like Guangdong (where many communities were made up exclusively of members of the same lineage) than in northern ones like Shanxi (where this was much less often the case and households were more autonomous, self-contained units).

Most significant, when it comes to the history of insurrection, these kinds of variations could and did greatly affect patterns of peasant rebellion, as well as the strategies urban-based revolutionaries needed to mobilize support in the countryside. For example, the key to revolutionary success in southern China often lay in the ability of activists to make use of familial ties that would bring entire villages into a movement. In the north, by contrast, capitalizing on intra-village tensions between better-off peasants (who owned some land that they worked themselves but also rented out other plots) and the poorer members of the community (who did not own any land at all) often proved a more effective strategy. Adding to this mix were the contrasting rebellious traditions of northern and southern Chinese peasantries. Those in the south had a stronger tradition of "secret society" activism, in which male-to-male links established through ties of fictive kinship, as in sworn brotherhoods, were the key and mutual aid was a central source of solidarity. In the north, by contrast, millenarian religious beliefs associated with folk Buddhism were a more important part of the rebel tradition, and female religious figures often played a more important role in heterodox movements, both as symbolic figures and as transmitters of teachings.

Such specific differences between the peasantries of various lands and those within each individual country demonstrate the significance of local situations in understanding why some villagers turn to radicalism and others do not. The specific factors that differentiate groups of rural dwellers from one another are not constant. In some settings, such as Central America, ethnicity may prove in many cases a more important variable than kinship structure. In others, such as Algeria, the religious boundaries separating Muslims from members of other groups may be more significant than ethnicity. And so forth. In all cases, however, there is a need to think in terms of many different sorts of peasants who can and often are inspired to rebel or resist rebel forces for complex reasons.

There are many ways that Marxism can be and has been modified to make room for visions of the peasant. Some Marxist-Leninist theorists have arrived at positions very different from those of Marx himself, as stated in his 1850 treatise, and also very different from those of Lenin and other Bolsheviks. Mao Zedong and Fidel Castro, leaders of the Chinese and Cuban revolutions, respectively, are among those best known for their efforts to rework Marx's assessment of villagers as passive without abandoning Marxist concepts of class struggle as the driving force of history or of communism as revolution's ultimate goal. Their revisions of not just the ideas of Marx but also Vladimir Lenin's concept of the role of vanguard parties and the nature of imperialism have proved controversial, both inside and outside of socialist circles. There is no question, however, about their influence, especially after Mao succeeded in transforming China into a Communist Party–led country in 1949 and then Castro did the same for Cuba a decade later. There are other modifiers of Marx as well, such as the radical West Indian psychologist and

PICTURE 8.1 Chinese Cultural Revolution poster. During the Cultural Revolution (1966–1976), posters were displayed on walls or distributed in handbooks of propaganda materials. The slogans tell people that by following the ideas of Chairman Mao, they will build a more productive country and free themselves from the pernicious influence of "revisionists" and "demons" (terms used for those dubbed counterrevolutionaries). (Courtesy of the collection of Jeffrey Wasserstrom)

champion of African anticolonial movements Franz Fanon, who never ran a regime yet still had an impact on visions of socialism.

Finally, as twentieth-century history demonstrated over and over again, when peasants are living in countries that have been subjected to imperialist domination, they are much more likely to revolt on their own and to make alliances with insurgents from other classes. When the protection, creation, or reclaiming of a nation is at stake, we now know, the peasantry is always a force to be reckoned with. The proliferation of such struggles between the 1920s and the 1980s meant that, as Fanon noted in his particular modification of classical socialist visions of revolution, peasants became part of "the revolutionary proletariat of our times." He wrote, in his best-known tract, a classic study entitled *The Wretched of the Earth* (1961), that nationalist parties often "disregarded" the "peasantry" in their propaganda, yet "it is clear that in the colonial countries the peasants alone are revolutionary, for they have nothing to lose and everything to gain."

At century's end it was clear, in other words, that villagers can and often do play the sort of vanguard role in struggles against oppression that Marx insisted, in the mid–nineteenth century, could only be performed by factory workers and other urban laborers. This notion is acknowledged directly by Chinese Communists in their translation into their own language of Marxist terms. In most Western languages, the word "proletariat" has been understood to mean "urban worker." The Chinese equivalent for that word, however, is *wuchan jieji*, which literally means anyone who does not own property. The term is regularly used in China to stand for landless farmers as well as urban wage laborers. The rising importance of rural activism in worldwide revolutions of the past century is also acknowledged, albeit less directly, in the tendency of many radical organizers, from the 1940s onward in particular, to speak of the need to arouse "the people" or "the masses" as opposed to just "the workers" and to assume that peasants constitute a significant segment of these general categories.

The potential revolutionary role of peasants has also been acknowledged recently in scholarship that modifies Marxist categories still further. Radical scholars—drawing on a term made famous by the well-known Italian Marxist theorist Antonio Gramsci—now often avoid class-specific labels and refer instead to "subalterns" (literally, the "powerless" or "dominated") when alluding to the most oppressed members of any society. Here, in analytic terms, there is as much room for peasants as for workers, depending on the context.

In this chapter our goal is not to resolve the conundrums alluded to above and explain away the disjuncture between the crucial but often underestimated or unacknowledged revolutionary potential of peasants. Nor do we try to provide a simple answer to the common question of why peasants, who are almost always oppressed in some fashion and often impoverished, rise up at some moments and remain passive at others. Nor do we even try to sort out which activist-theorists have come closest to getting the peasant question right. Our central argument is, in fact, that simple answers to virtually all of the questions that can and should be asked about peasant insurrections will be off base. We provide a context for thinking through the variability of peasant revolutions, as well as simply describe some events that demonstrate this variability, all the while trying to move beyond the stereotypes of peasants as passive or merely reactive.

The focus, more specifically, is on two sets of key struggles in which peasants played undeniably important roles, often as actors in their own rights as well as reactors to external phenomena. The upheavals singled out for scrutiny are those that occurred in the multinational region of Latin America, where successful uprisings involving peasants led to the creation of many new regimes and failed insurrections often ended in waves of violent oppression, and those that occurred in China. The attraction of these two sets of struggles is that they are both different from one another and internally varied. In the Chinese case, no less than in the Latin American one, there was not just one upheaval and one outcome, but many interlocking events, many victories, many defeats, many fleeting moments of liberation interspersed with long stretches of violence and oppression. After tracing the roles that peasants played in the events that brought Castro to power in Cuba, Mao to power in China, and so forth, we conclude the chapter with some comments on the nature of peasant unrest in the twentieth century overall. Before turning to the case studies, however, we need to define the term "peasant" as it is used here. A bit more also needs to be said about the place of rural unrest in the main streams of radical thought that existed before theorists such as Mao and Fanon revised Marxism to make more room for a revolutionary peasantry.

Pre-1920s Theories of Revolution

A good working definition of peasants—a term understood by some to refer to people who live in a particular manner, by others as people who have a particular place in the economy, and by still others as people exhibiting a combination of these factors—needs to be both simple and multifaceted. Following Shanin, a leading student of the subject, it makes sense to assume that what makes a peasant a peasant is some combination of the following four things. First, he or she contributes labor to the operation of a "family farm," a farm on which most or all of those working the land are related to one another by blood or marriage. Second, he or she consumes largely, but not necessarily exclusively, food and goods produced on this essentially autonomous family farm—that is, there may be some but not much dependence on market transactions. Third, he or she participates in an enduring form of communal culture, which is rural in basis and thought of by insiders and outsiders alike as in some meaningful sense traditional. Fourth, he or she occupies an "underdog position" within the larger society. That is, such people are more likely to be viewed as part of the have-nots than the haves; they are subordinated to others instead of holding dominant social positions. The term "villagers" will be used at times as a synonym for "peasants," with the understanding that this word does not include unusually rich members of rural communities or those who make most of their livelihood from market transactions.

Most revolutionary theorists of the nineteenth century tended, like Marx—one of the very first to try to define in systematic terms the nature of peasants—to dismiss the potential of villagers to bring about radical change. People who lived off the land and were tied directly to the land were thought of as being inherently conservative and apathetic, in large part owing to the precariousness of their economic position, their cultural conservatism, and their subordination to members of other social groups. They were typically seen as being capable at best of only three sorts of political action, none of which were ultimately of much use to revolutionaries, or so, at least, the common wisdom had it.

It was thought, for example, that they could be mobilized to support members of dominant classes or demagogues attempting to stem the tide of radicalism. It is true that in the French Revolution of 1848–1850, as commented on by Marx, support for Napoleon III came from rural small holders. Thus there was a valid basis for this idea. It was also thought that they could lash out against change on their own accord. Riots occasioned by the imposition of new taxes or the introduction of other new kinds of economic systems were viewed as typical of this mode of peasant activism. Finally, it was assumed that they could rise up in rebellion against a particular hated lord or group of power-holders, demanding that these unjust rulers be replaced.

This last type of peasant action, which might seem at first glance to have a good deal of revolutionary potential, was still dismissed by most radical theorists as ultimately unhelpful to those seeking to bring about a complete change of the social order. In most cases, peasant rebellions of this sort could be found to have a restorationist aspect. That is, peasants rose up not in the name of creating a new kind of regime but rather to resurrect an old one or purify the current one. They might demand the removal from power of a current lord, but usually they saw the individual ruler as the main problem because he had failed to behave in the benevolent fashion of the famous "good kings" (or tsars or emperors) of the past. The problem, in the eyes of the peasants, it was assumed, lay in individuals, not in the social or political system as a whole.

In short, the peasantry was, in the eyes of most nineteenth-century radicals, a generally passive entity that was all too ready to do the bidding of the ruling classes. Its members might occasionally be roused to advance their own interests or resist a threat, but they would typically go no further than demanding a preexisting status quo, in which their oppression and misery seemed less onerous and somehow fairer than it had recently become. Like Marx, most nineteenth-century advocates of revolution accepted modernist assumptions relating to social evolution, so it was easy for them to see in peasants a semi-bestial remnant of the past instead of a group of people who might help create a utopian future. There were, it is true, some anarchists and populists who romanticized village life and saw a kind of basic democracy and egalitarianism worthy of emulation existing within rural communities. Even they, however, rarely argued that the peasants were capable of playing key roles in genuinely revolutionary struggles for change.

Curiously, at least in retrospect, this vision of peasants as a drag upon revolution as opposed to the potential motor behind it remained dominant within radical circles even after villagers had played central roles in the Russian Revolution of 1917. Even within Russia itself, the dominant interpretation of the revolution, though praising the bravery of peasants who had risen up against the tsar, gave the lion's share of the credit for the victories of 1917 to members of other groups. Workers, soldiers, and intelligentsia as members of revolutionary parties were all portrayed as playing more central roles in bringing the Bolsheviks to power than were ordinary villagers. Lenin was more willing than Marx had been to see revolutions as the work of pan-class alliances that included peasants, but he insisted that villagers ultimately played subordinate roles in these alliances and always needed to be kept on track, managed by members of vanguard groups. Without proper guidance, he said, the "natural" conservatism of the peasant would reassert itself.

Some literati supporters of the revolutionary cause were particularly dismissive of the potential of villagers to help bring about genuine social change. Consider, for example, the following 1922 assessment of the Russian peasant put forth by Maxim Gorky, a leading radical writer living within the then newly formed Union of Soviet Socialist Republics. Gorky argued, in a book entitled *On the Russian Peasantry* (1922), that those who work the land are unable, without the help of outsiders, to appreciate and feel part of the accomplishments of civilization. Their very conditions of life, he claimed, are such that they never produce anything of lasting value, and the "boundless plains on which the wooden, thatched-roofed villages crowd together have the poisonous effect of emptying a man, of sucking dry his desires." The Russian peasant, according to Gorky, lacked an "ability to think, to remember his past, to work out his ideas," and in the place of all this had only "superstitions" to rely on. He quoted the claim of a leading historian of Russia's peasant rebellions that revolts by villagers of the centuries preceding 1917 "changed nothing, brought nothing new into the mechanism of the state, into the structure of understanding." The revolution, to him, was not something that peasants carried through. It was rather the culmination of an ongoing struggle by members of the intelligentsia to "courageously . . . lift on to its feet the heavy Russian people, lazily, carelessly, incapably slumped on its land." It was, in short, an event that "awakened" the Russian peasants to the possibility of a new sort of existence. The Soviet order would be one in which the "half-savage" villagers of old, to Gorky an "almost frightening" sort of people, would be replaced by a "new breed" of "reasonable" folk.

Comparable expressions of the notion that revolutions were needed to change peasants, as opposed to being movements that villagers could help to create as equal partners in a radical alliance, can be found in the writings of many other militants of the day working in other lands. From the 1920s on, however, a growing tendency to rethink the potential of the peasantry as a radical force began to take hold. The idea that revolutionary ideas and classes could come from villages as well as cities became more common. Shifts in Marxist thought, the experiences of vanguard parties in the field, and the rising importance of Third World countries as major centers of revolutionary change all played roles in changing the climate of opinion. To see some of the ways that these factors could and did intertwine, we consider three Latin American case studies—El Salvador, Guatemala, and Cuba—and then end with a discussion of the Chinese experience.

Rural Revolts in Latin America

During the first part of the twentieth century, Latin American peasant movements played crucial roles in each nation's history. Recall the most famous and successful example: The Mexican Revolution involved hundreds of thousands of rural workers and peasants, and agrarian reform was one of its major achievements (see Chapter 4). By 1940 most of the country's large estates had been expropriated, and many formerly landless peasants had received land. Other rural movements of importance occurred in Colombia and Costa Rica involving banana workers. In Cuba, sugar workers played the principal role in the 1933 revolutionary movement. From 1927–1933, Augusto César Sandino led peasants in battle against the United States, which in many parts of the region, via military intervention or economic imperialism carried out by major corporations, was a major colonialist presence. In the Dominican Republic and Haiti, peasants played a similar role in resisting the early stages of U.S. interventions during the late teens and early twenties (see Map 8.1). With the exception of the Mexican Revolution, none of these movements could be considered successes. The United States withdrew its military forces from Nicaragua, the Dominican Republic, and Haiti but left authoritarian, pro-elite governments behind. The labor movements gained partial victories in Costa Rica and Cuba, but the unions were dealt harsh blows in subsequent repression. The Colombian banana workers movement ended in a massacre at the hands of the army.

The most notable failure was "La Matanza" (The Massacre) in El Salvador in January 1932. The repression of an increasingly powerful, Communist-led labor movement played a major role in creating the conditions for the rebellion. The global economic crisis, combined with a wave of land dispossession that had taken place over the previous decade, helped to spark an impressive labor-organizing drive. By 1931, 50 percent wage cuts drove the increasingly landless rural folk in the coffee zone below subsistence levels. Labor organizers mobilized around the wage cuts and increased their membership from a tiny minority of the workforce to an estimated 75,000 mem-

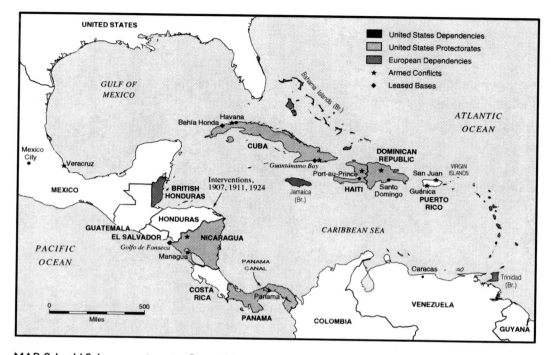

MAP 8.1   U.S. Interventions in Central America and the Caribbean, Early Twentieth Century

bers (concentrated in the coffee zone of Western Salvador) out of a total national population of 1.5 million.

Since 1927, the authoritarian regime had allowed a democratic opening that permitted the growth of social democratic and Communist parties, in the latter case directly tied to the unions. In 1931, in the first free elections in Salvadoran history (and the last until the 1980s), Arturo Araujo, a reformist inspired by the British Labour Party, was elected president. Significantly, the Araujo administration raised hopes of land reform among the rural poor, and the failure to meet that promise provoked further discontent.

In addition to economic and political factors, there was a cultural dimension to the mobilization. The majority of the inhabitants of the coffee-producing departments of Ahuachapán and Sonsonate were self-identified Indians, most of whom spoke Nahuatl and dressed in a distinctive style. Indigenous *cofradías,* lay confraternities, combined religious and political functions. In the years preceding the rebellion, and especially since the political opening of 1927, Indians had battled *ladinos* (non-Indians) for control over municipal governments in the region. Previously, indigenous political control had often been assured through an alliance with the elite governing party. With the election of Araujo, that alliance crumbled, and some indigenous *caciques* (chieftains), undoubtedly responding to pressure from their unionized rank and file, pushed the cofradías into an alliance with the Communist Party. The combination of this political alliance, sharp ethnic polarization in the municipalities, and the union activism of many Indians gave a strongly indigenous cast to the rebellion.

On December 2, 1931, a military coup overthrew Araujo and installed his vice president, General Maximiliano Hernández Martínez, as president. One of the first actions of the military gov-

PICTURE 8.2
Banana plantation, Costa Rica. This photograph at a Delmonte Company plantation from February 1997 shows the railroad that facilitated movements of export crops—primarily bananas and coffee—from plantations to the coast. (Photo courtesy of Todd Richardson)

ernment was to postpone the municipal and congressional elections until early January. It is open to debate whether or not the regime consciously used the elections to provoke an uprising and then repression. Surely, the authorities were aware that Communist slates would triumph in Ahuachapán and Sonsonate and perhaps in the capital, San Salvador, and that, particularly in Western Salvador, given the bitter labor conflicts, peasants and workers would violently respond to any attempt to tamper with the votes. Similarly, there is little doubt that they would have been willing to use the public voting and the party lists for repressive purposes. Whether in conscious provocation or not, the Martínez government did steal the elections from the Communists in Western Salvador, in so doing sparking several spontaneous revolts. The Communist Party leaders, in part following the broad revolutionary guidelines of the Communist International—a Moscow-dominated consortium of Marxist organizations—and in part fearing a significant loss of legitimacy if they did not respond to the government provocation, reluctantly opted for an insurrectionary adventure. The insurrection failed before it began. The government arrested the Communist leadership and some key supporters in the military several days before the scheduled insurrection on January 22. Poor communication, exacerbated by the military alert, however, thwarted attempts to call it off.

Thousands of rebels, armed mostly with machetes, assaulted local government buildings and looted stores in a half dozen municipalities on January 22 and 23. A handful of people were executed, and rebels killed some sixty people in combat. Although the rebels were mostly Indians, in some places ladino peasants and workers played a major role. Within in three days the military crushed the insurrection. The rebels could only hold out a few days longer in the isolated village of Tacuba, where a group of 5,000 proclaimed a soviet. Then the killing began in earnest: Government troops and civil guards executed more than 10,000 people, mostly indigenous males.

The Matanza ushered in rigid military rule that endured for more than six decades. Any efforts at peaceful social change during this era were beaten down by the regime.

Until 1944, in neighboring Guatemala the situation was similar to that of El Salvador. In that year, a democratic revolution overthrew a landed oligarchy that for decades had coerced hundreds of thousands of Indians to labor seasonally on their coffee plantations. In 1952, the democratically elected president, Jacobo Arbenz, promulgated an agrarian reform law that expropriated uncultivated land over 223 acres and distributed it to landless peasants. By 1954, the government had distributed more than 1 million acres to some 100,000 rural families.

Much of the land reform was carried out in response to the growth of a peasant movement. Indigenous and ladino peasants and rural laborers organized to pressure the government to expropriate and distribute the land. Often rural activists organized land takeovers in order to present the reformist government with a fait accompli. Some 100,000 people joined the National Confederation of Peasants, and thousands of rural laborers, particularly those on the banana plantations owned by the United Fruit Company, joined labor unions. Combined, these movements provided a significant base of support for the government and threatened the economic and political power of the landed oligarchy. In short, the elite viewed them as a revolutionary movement intent on destroying the existing system of land tenancy.

As the Cold War intensified, the U.S. government viewed the Arbenz government as Communist dominated and thus entered into alliance with conservative forces in the country. In fact, Arbenz did have some Communist advisers who played an important role in the agrarian reform, but the party only had 5 representatives out of 57 in the Guatemalan congress. Nevertheless, the CIA sponsored an invasion by exiles and provided planes to bomb Guatemala City. The U.S. government, in effect, provoked a coup d'état that overthrew Arbenz's democratically elected government in 1954.

The crushing of the peasant movement accompanied the fall of Arbenz. Thousands of peasant activists were jailed. Most significant, the agrarian reform was reversed: 90 percent of the distributed land reverted back to its original owners. By the 1970s, 25 percent of the rural population was landless and another 57 percent had insufficient land for family subsistence. Meanwhile, 2 percent of the population owned over 70 percent of the land. The U.S. intervention, and the failure of the peasant and rural laborers movement to resist it, effectively blocked any possibility of democratic reforms in Guatemala and set the stage for bloody confrontation in the ensuing decades.

The Cuban Revolution: A New Role for Latin American Peasants

A twenty-five-year-old Argentine physician named Ernesto "Ché" Guevara witnessed the overthrow of Arbenz in 1954. The successful U.S. intervention convinced him of the futility of peaceful efforts for social and political change. In 1956, in Mexico City, he met Raul and Fidel Castro, who were plotting to overthrow the Cuban dictator Fulgencio Batista. In 1953, Fidel had led an unsuccessful attack on the Moncada Army barracks in Santiago. His courtroom speech, "History will absolve me," earned him admiration throughout the island. In 1955, in a gesture of moderation, the Batista regime had freed Castro.

The Castro brothers, Ché Guevara, and 79 others set sail on the *Granma,* an old boat, from the Yucatán to Cuba. Only a dozen survived the first combat with Batista's troops upon landing on the island. This tiny band sought refuge in the mountains of southwestern Cuba known as the Sierra Maestra. There they encountered a unique group of people who would add a peasant dimension to their political movement.

The inhabitants of the Sierra Maestra were in large part squatters on the land, pushed off of the lowlands by the phenomenal growth of sugar mills and plantations. Twenty-eight mills owned one-fifth of the island. Those mills and plantations employed more than 500,000 workers (out of a total island population of 6 million people) on a seasonal basis. Yet, the Rebel Army only had mediocre success in mobilizing this rural proletariat. Rather, the inhabitants of its own zone of refuge provided the key to victory. In the words of Ché Guevara in a 1961 essay on Cuba:

> The first area where the Rebel Army operated was an area inhabited by peasants whose social and cultural roots were different from those of the peasants found in the area of large-scale semi-mechanized agriculture. In fact, the Sierra Maestra, the locale of the first revolutionary beehive, is a place where peasants struggling barehanded against latifundism took refuge.

By accident, the guerrillas had stumbled into an area where the legitimacy of the political regime and the power of the *latifundistas* (large-scale landowners) were at their weakest. The rebels gained the support of this peasantry by carrying out a rudimentary agrarian reform, by trading with them on favorable terms, and by promising to ensure their property rights after the triumph of the revolution. With the support of this squatter peasantry, the Rebel Army could resist Batista's army and indeed consolidated itself over the next two years.

On January 1, 1959, Fidel Castro's guerrilla army entered triumphantly into Havana. Within several months, the new regime followed through on its promise of agrarian reform. The new law expropriated estates of more than 1,000 acres and distributed the lands to some 100,000 peasant families who had previously been renters, sharecroppers, or squatters. Most of these families received more than fifty acres of land.

Thus, the Cuban Revolution created a class of peasants where before there only existed large landholders, tenant farmers, squatters, and seasonal laborers. This reform had two immediate repercussions. First, it created hostility in Washington because U.S. companies had owned half of the expropriated land. Second, the reform inadvertently stimulated the mobilization of the vast sugar proletariat, whose main demand had not been met: an end to the suffering of the *tiempo muerto*, those six to eight months of seasonal unemployment. Through petitions and land occupations, the sugar workers demanded "land or work." This agrarian insurgency pushed the Cuban regime toward more radical measures, including the nationalization of industries and the expropriation of all land holdings of more than 140 acres. Much of the newly expropriated land was converted into collective farms that employed their workers throughout the year. This internal pressure from the countryside, combined with the external pressure of the United States, which, as in Guatemala, backed an armed counterrevolution, pushed Castro into an alliance with the Communist Party of Cuba and eventually into an alliance with the Soviet Union.

The Cuban Revolution signified a fundamental change for the Latin American rural poor. From U.S. State Department officials to student activists, from millionaire dictators to humble peasants, the Cuban Revolution radically changed the way people thought about social and political change in Latin America. For the first time, the rural masses of Latin America were acknowl-

PICTURE 8.3
Fidel Castro (1926–). On January 1,
1959, Cuban revolutionary forces led
by Fidel Castro and Ernesto Ché
Guevara overthrew the dictatorship of
Fulgencio Batista. While other
Communist regimes fell from power
after the collapse of the Soviet Union,
Castro's government survived into the
twenty-first century. (Photo from the
Library of Congress)

edged as the principal subject of the continent's revolutionary movements. Until the Cuban Revolution, both Marxists and U.S. policymakers relegated the peasantry to at best a secondary role. In most of the failures discussed in the beginning of the chapter, neither side had planned on incorporating the rural poor into its struggles. Now pro-Cuban revolutionaries—in opposition to the Latin American Communist parties—would look to the peasantry as the key to success. Second, the lesson of Arbenz in Guatemala was confirmed by Castro's triumph. There was no alternative to armed struggle in order to achieve social and political change.

The two lessons from the Cuban Revolution were to be put into practice through the *foco* (guerrilla band) strategy, which would generate a revolutionary movement in the countryside. As expounded by Ché Guevara and the French philosopher Régis Debray, a political-military vanguard would initiate a guerrilla war in a geographically propitious zone. As in the Sierra Maestra, the peasantry would come to support the movement. This strategy of copying the Cuban experience was deeply flawed, principally because Latin American rural society is tremendously diverse. Ethnic and economic relations vary from region to region; the notion that one set of conditions could be replicated betrayed the revolutionaries' profound ignorance of the countryside.

Armed revolutionary groups sprouted up throughout the Latin American countryside. Argentina, Bolivia, Colombia, Guatemala, Mexico, Nicaragua, Peru, and Venezuela all experienced armed conflict in the countryside during the 1960s. By the end of the decade, the national armies, supported by the United States, had either crushed or crippled these revolutionary groups. Ché Guevara was murdered at the hands of the Bolivian army in 1967. His death symbolized the end of a series of revolutionary adventures that sought to reproduce the Cuban experience. What the revolutionaries lacked in these countries was the active support of the rural poor. Without that support, to paraphrase Mao, the foco died like fish washed up and stranded on the beach.

PICTURE 8.4   Indian peasant family, Monimbó, Nicaragua, 1992. In the 1950s and 1960s, Nicaraguan peasants fought elite encroachment on their land caused by the cotton boom. In the 1970s, peasants joined with the Sandinistas to help bring about the success of the Nicaraguan Revolution in 1979. (Photo courtesy of Jeffrey Gould)

A New Tide of Rural Insurgency

Ironically, the success of the capitalist system, as evidenced by the phenomenal growth and modernization of agriculture, created the conditions for revolutionary change, in particular in Central America. In all the Central American countries, the countryside underwent a major structural transformation during the 1950s and 1960s. Export booms of cotton, sugar, and beef were meant to diversify the economy—as opposed to its previous reliance on coffee and bananas—and to create a healthy hedge against world price fluctuations. Still, the export boom had two negative effects. First, the expansion of cotton and cattle lands led to peasant dispossession. In El Salvador, for example, the percentage of rural people with no land rose from 15 to 41 percent between 1963 and 1975. Most of the new landless peasants had been cultivating food crops and were evicted to make way for export crops or cattle. Thus, this transformation in the countryside also meant a smaller domestic food crop. Second, this export boom offered no stimulus to the domestic market. Despite the huge increase in beef exports—in Nicaragua they rose from zero in 1957, to $10 million in 1966, and to $40 million in 1972—the consumption of beef dropped in every Central American country. The failure to stimulate domestic consumption meant, in part, that industry could not grow enough to absorb the surplus rural population into the workforce.

In El Salvador, Guatemala, and Nicaragua, rural protest movements emerged in the 1960s and 1970s in response to these profound structural changes. Yet all peaceful efforts at improving the lot of the poor in the countryside were met with jailings and assassinations. In Guatemala, peasant organizing began through the efforts of Catholic Action, a group that originally intended to combat communism and to transform indigenous religious practices along more orthodox Catholic lines. Yet any organizing was met with terror. Between 1970 and 1974, during a period when there was virtually no guerrilla presence in the country, 15,000 people were "disappeared," mainly by army-backed death squads. In a bittersweet irony, while the United States was pumping $2 million into the Guatemalan military, the U.S. Agency for International Development (AID) was supporting the cooperative movement of Catholic Action. Catholic Action successfully organized more than 100,000 Indians (the total population of Guatemala was 5 million, with 50 percent Indians). Those cooperatives became the target of army violence, particularly in the department of Quiché, where authorities claimed that the Catholic activists were backing guerrillas.

Rigoberta Menchú, the Nobel Peace Prize laureate and a member of Catholic Action, related how she came to understand the Bible:

> Throughout his life, Christ was humble. History tells us he was born in a little hut. He was persecuted and had to form a band of men so that his seed would not disappear. They were his disciples, his apostles. In those days, there was no other way of defending himself or Christ would have used it against his oppressors, . . . but Christ did not die, because generations and generations have followed him. And that's exactly what we understood when our first catechists fell. They're dead but our people keep their memory alive through our struggle against the government, against an enemy who oppresses us.

Between 1975 and 1977, forty-seven cooperative project leaders were assassinated or disappeared. A survivor related how he witnessed the murder of thirty members of his community. Government repression of Catholic Action had pushed priests and peasants into more radical postures along the lines of Liberation Theology, a doctrine that emerged in the Latin American Bishops Conference in Medellín, Colombia, in 1968. Yet they remained committed to nonviolent action.

The combination of structural dislocation, Catholic activism, and indiscriminate government repression pushed Guatemalan peasants, Indians, and rural workers into action. On May 29, 1978, to cite one important example, some 700 unarmed Kekchí Indians gathered in the town square of Panzós in the department of Alta Verapaz to present a petition to the mayor in protest over their land loss. A large army battalion encircled them and then, in response to the speech of a machete-wielding leader, the troops opened fire, killing 114 of the demonstrators. Dubbed the "My Lai" of Guatemala, the event stands out only for its daytime drama. Usually the death squads picked off Indian and peasant activists one by one at night.

Ladino encroachment on land formerly controlled by indigenous groups, and the natural effects of soil erosion, pushed some 300,000 Indians along the road to migration mainly to pick cotton and cut cane. One migrant explained the situation succinctly: "My family doesn't have enough land. There is much pain. . . . Sometimes it makes me mad but I have no choice but to go." Although migrant labor is notoriously difficult to organize under the best of conditions, the Comité de Unidad Campesina (CUC, Committee of Peasant Unity) began to organize Indian and ladino migrant workers from the cotton fields and sugar plantations of the Pacific Coast. By 1980, the CUC was capable of launching a strike involving 70,000 cane cutters and 40,000 cotton pickers from sixty plantations. This strike was perhaps the largest one ever in the Latin American countryside. The rural workers won increases in the minimum wage from $1.12 to $3.20 a day. Although the military-run government and the plantation owners ceded to union demands, soon after the settlement the army began to kidnap and kill the strike leaders. It then began a campaign of terror that aimed to eliminate all those involved in rural organizing, community development, or education.

The level of death squad terror was already high before the strike. According to official estimates, during one year in the late 1970s, death squads murdered more than 5,000 people. Many of the targets were moderate politicians and university professors. Two hundred and fifty centrist Christian Democrats were killed. One exile remarked, "To be a Christian Democrat was to have your cemetery plot picked out."

In this context of violence, many Indians began to support the leftist guerrilla groups because they offered the only guarantee against army repression. By the early 1980s, probably hundreds of thousands of Indians provided logistical support for some 5,000 ladino and Indian guerrillas. A *New York Times* correspondent, Alan Riding, wrote at the time:

> Throughout the highlands the Indians are beginning to stir. . . . Entire villages now sympathize with and feed and shelter the guerrillas. And when the army arrives after rebel occupation it can find no one who has seen a thing. "There are places where the guerrillas have executed all government informers," a priest said, "there they feel entirely safe." Although conservatives and the State Department by and large believed that the guerrillas were controlled and financed from Havana, the Indians may be fighting more against repression and the theft of communal lands than for the socialism espoused by the guerrillas. But they are nonetheless beginning to fight.

The army clearly did not care much about the Indians' level of ideological commitment to the guerrillas. Rather, they simply sought to crush the base of the guerrillas into submission, to simply annihilate the lake in which the guerrillas swam. As one army general commented to a conservative politician:

> Look, I'm going to give it straight. We did kill a lot of people in this area [department of Quiché]. We would get orders from the Army Chief of Staff to go in and eliminate two or three peasants. We would arrive at the village and if the suspects weren't there or if the people wouldn't talk, we'd just raze the entire place.

In fact, the army razed some 400 villages, killing more than 50,000 Indians, driving 150,000 into Mexico and another half a million into the cities. By 1984, the army had effectively crushed the guerrillas, and with them, the rural protest movements from which they had drawn their sustenance.

El Salvador suffered the most extreme structural disruption of all the Central American countries. Its situation was compounded by the "soccer war" with Honduras. In 1969, a fight at a soccer game erupted into a border war. The principal result involved the deportation of 100,000 Salvadoran peasants, who joined the ranks of that country's dispossessed.

The legacy of the 1932 La Matanza rebellion continued for decades to weigh on the minds of the Salvadoran rural folk. Very few people dared to protest against the harsh living and working conditions. But beginning in the 1970s, as in Guatemala, Christian activists played a crucial role in this organizing drive. Once again, priests and lay activists gave a social context to Christianity. In 1974, one Salvadoran peasant spoke for many when he commented, "Most of the people talk about social sin, that is when some people dominate others, take advantage of others. Before people didn't think like that, now they do." From this changing understanding of social morality, Salvadoran rural folk began to struggle for a decent livelihood.

Throughout the 1970s peasants and rural workers organized in unions and peasant leagues to struggle for decent wages and for land. Despite the military rule, peasants and rural workers organized peaceful land takeovers and strikes. Many of these movements had, at least, an initial success, but as in Guatemala, the army responded with brutality. As one large landowner commented, "We have always bought the military guns and paid them to pull the trigger." The military government also established a powerful network of civilian supporters through largely clientelist means—lands and credit. Some 100,000 peasants organized in ORDEN often informed on their neighbors and sometimes carried out death squad activity.

Thousands of civilians were gunned down by the military and faced death squads in their homes and at demonstrations from 1977 until 1979. During this period, priests in rural parishes were special targets of the death squads. One rightist urged: "Be a patriot. Kill a priest!" In October 1979, a coup d'état replaced the hard-line government with one made up of moderate civilians and military officers who promised to end the violence. But the landed oligarchy and its military allies had no intention of ceding ground to the organized peasants and workers. At the same time, an important sector of the revolutionary Left had no trust in the new government and continued to defy it.

The moderates within the government resigned by January 1980 and the repression intensified. On January 22, in memory of the victims of La Matanza, more than 100,000 people shouting revolutionary slogans marched through the capital, San Salvador. The army opened fire on the demonstration, killing more than 100 people. As the military violence increased, the archbishop of San Salvador, Monseñor Oscar Arnulfo Romero, actively opposed the regime and beseeched the U.S. government to stop aiding the government that was killing the Salvadoran people. On March 23, he addressed the Salvadoran armed forces with the following words: "In the name of God and in the name of this suffering people whose sorrows rise up to the daily more turbulent skies, I beg you, I order you in the name of God: Stop the repression!" The next day Monseñor Romero was murdered while he delivered his Sunday sermon. Two months later, the army gunned down 600 peasants as they tried to cross the Sumpul River to seek refuge in Honduras.

The country folk who had been fighting for social justice over the previous decade saw little option but to flee or to support the various revolutionary forces. That same year, these forces joined together to form the Frente Farabundo Martí de la Liberación Nacional (FMLN, Farabundo Martí National Liberation Front, named for the Communist leader assassinated in 1932). From 1980 to 1992, the FMLN battled the Salvadoran military backed by a billion dollars in aid from the United States. Fifty thousand people, mostly peasant civilians, died in the conflict. As in Guatemala, military and oligarchic efforts to block peaceful change initiated by peasants and rural workers ended in bloody tragedies.

Nicaraguan Peasants and the Revolution

The triumph of the Nicaraguan Revolution in 1979 embodied the aspirations of millions of people throughout the hemisphere. The electoral defeat of the leftist Frente Sandinista de Liberación Nacional (FSLN, Sandinista National Liberation Front) in February 1990 symbolized not only

PICTURE 8.5
"Viva Sandino." The Sandinistas who came to power in the 1979 Nicaraguan Revolution took their inspiration from the legacy of Augusto César Sandino, who fought U.S. occupation forces earlier in the century. This 1983 photo shows "Viva Sandino" ("Sandino lives") written on the side of a building. (Photo courtesy of Jeffrey Gould)

the failure of the revolution but the end of an era that had promised profound social change in the Americas. Some observers attributed the Sandinista loss to the machinations of U.S. foreign policy; others read it as proof that the revolution had been condemned to failure in its inception and flawed in its adherence to a Marxist myth of state-sponsored social change.

The historical roots of the revolution can be traced to U.S. military and political intervention in Nicaraguan politics from 1912 to 1933. The U.S. government originally intervened primarily to ensure a friendly conservative regime in a country of strategic importance owing to its proximity to the Panama Canal. When the United States attempted to extricate itself in the mid-1920s, the partisan conflict it had stymied flared up again in civil war. In an attempt to end the armed conflict, the U.S. government sent thousands of troops to pressure the Liberal Party insurrectionist army into signing a peace treaty. One Liberal Party general, Augusto César Sandino, refused to go along with the treaty, and in 1927 he launched a war of resistance against the U.S. Marines in Nicaragua and their allies in the Nicaraguan National Guard. In 1933, after six years of guerrilla warfare, the Marines withdrew; shortly thereafter, Sandino's troops laid down their weapons. In 1934, Anastasio Somoza, appointed by the United States as the chief of the National Guard, arranged to assassinate Sandino. Within two years, he seized power in a military coup, and he ruled the country until his own assassination in 1956. His sons, Luis and Anastasio, would rule until 1979, when the Sandinistas (FSLN), a group of leftist guerrillas inspired by Sandino's resistance, toppled the regime.

The success of the revolution had much to do with the tremendous social dislocations wrought by the agricultural export booms of the 1950s and 1960s, which, as in El Salvador and Nicaragua, displaced large sectors of the rural population. In 1978, the children of the displaced in the villages and cities to which they had migrated would form the nucleus of the insurrectionary movement.

From 1950 to 1979, while Nicaragua's annual population growth increased by 3 percent, its domestic production, fueled by cotton, beef, and sugar, increased by 5.2 percent annually. These figures were indicative of a very healthy economy. However, the benefits of that growth were not shared equally by the population. In 1970, the lowest 50 percent of the population earned only 13 percent of the total national income. Moreover, the increased government revenues resulting from that growth were not spent on housing, education, or health: 52 percent of the population before 1979 was illiterate, and 120 out of every 1,000 children died before the age of five. These figures declined dramatically during the first years of the revolution.

The quality of life, especially in the western Nicaraguan countryside, entered a rapid decline during the 1950s with the growth of the cotton industry. First, thousands of people were kicked off haciendas (large estates). Landlords who previously had allowed their workers to plant corn on hacienda land in return for labor services decided that they needed all available space for planting. They required only four or five months' labor from their workers, who thus not only lost their homes and land but also lost full-time employment. Cotton plantings increased from 2,000 to 100,000 acres in the space of five years.

The view from the northwestern Nicaraguan village changed from verdant, lush forests and hilltop pastures into brown, barren hills and white fields of cotton. Where a decade earlier, men would hunt birds to provide extra protein for the family diet, from the 1950s on small propeller planes sprayed insecticide, poisoning men, women, children, and animals, destroying water supplies, and contaminating the maternal milk of many women who worked in the fields. The landed elite prospered in ways their forefathers had only dreamed about, while 50 percent of the population suffered from malnutrition. Many of the evicted peasants built huts near the haciendas, so as to be on hand for seasonal labor. Others went to the city, but few ever found stable employment or decent housing there. Many of those who stayed in the countryside engaged in a twenty-year battle with the landed elite for decent wages and land to cultivate.

The story of one group of peasants is illustrative of the birth of the agrarian protest movement. In 1957 thirty families in the village of San José del Obraje protested against the usurpation of 800 *manzanas* (about 1,600 acres) of common land. This event signaled the beginning of the Chinandegan peasant movement, which by 1964 involved some 10,000 participants (perhaps one-half of the region's rural population). At the dawn of the movement, elite cultural forms dominated the peasants' lives so powerfully that some literally bowed down to the lords of the land. Moreover, the agrarian elite did not automatically lose legitimacy among the peasantry during the cotton boom; it had not directly expropriated the peasants' land or physically forced them off of the haciendas. Many landlords managed for several years to continue to project the image of the "benevolent patron." Peasants struggling for cultural autonomy therefore could not appeal to images of some simpler and purer past. Before the arrival of capitalism, after all, they had often been isolated from one another and trapped in relations of dependency with one or another patron. To improve their lot, peasant activists realized, they had to develop a new language of protest capable of comprehending and changing the social order.

The interrelationship between dependency and autonomy in peasant consciousness can be seen at crucial junctures in the evolution of the peasant movement. Throughout 1958, the San José peasants legally and extra-legally battled the 50,000-acre Campuzano hacienda, the largest in Chinandega, over their land claim. The peasants looked for and received the support of some figures of the Somoza regime, including the National Guard commander of León, while other military officials, tied to the local elite, hauled them off to jail. The owners of Campuzano, tired

PICTURE 8.6
Sandinista peasant demonstration, 1984.
When the Sandinistas came to power
they were supported by a broad-based,
multiclass coalition, including peasants who
had been struggling against the elite class
and the Somoza government since the
1950s. (Photo courtesy of Jeffrey Gould)

of the peasant harassment, offered to sell the land at a bargain price. Recognizing that the price was indeed cheaper than their legal fees, most members of the village organization were eager to accept the hacienda's offer. Their leader, a peasant named Regino Escobar, however, argued that the peasants should not buy back the land because it had always been used by the people. After a year of struggle, learning about the differences and similarities of good and bad authorities and big landholders, the peasant leader came to see that the problem of land went beyond a question of immediate need and involved issues of rights and dignity. The leader then shamed the rank and file into accepting his position because, although they did not like it, they had shared in the outlines of his learning experiences and recognized the correctness of his position.

The peasants thus gained a new understanding of their necessity for land. This change was an essential precondition for the growth of peasant solidarity. Indeed, by February 1961 the peasants had voluntarily set aside their own immediate objectives to lead a regional movement. In 1977 and 1978, these veteran peasant militants and their children actively supported the Sandinista Revolution against the same dictatorial Somoza regime backed by the National Guard.

The San José movement and others like it throughout Nicaragua played important roles in the Sandinista Revolution. Their history serves as a corrective to the common view of the Sandinista Revolution as a primarily political struggle against oppression—a view that at once gives the Sandinistas too much and not enough credit. Too much because the peasants struggled on their own for many years and developed their own notions of social change. Too little because the Sandinistas were able during the 1970s to weld together a broad-based, multi-class coalition despite intense class conflict within it.

The Sandinista victory also had to do with the nature of the Somoza dictatorship; it was quite unique in that it formed both a regime and a key sector of the economic elite. The Somoza regime, as pointed out earlier, was a product of U.S. involvement in Nicaragua from 1912 to 1933. The U.S. Marine legacy included the founding of the National Guard, and of the Somoza dynasty itself. It seemed to many Nicaraguans just historical retribution that the Sandinistas laid effective claim to Augusto Sandino's legacy in battle against the same national guard that had murdered him. By the late 1970s, the National Guard had earned the bitter hatred of most Nicaraguans owing to its indiscriminate killing of civilians. Those civilians accounted for most of the 50,000 deaths during the war (out of a total population of 3 million in Nicaragua at the time).

The Somoza regime was unique because of its economic dominance. By the end of their reign the Somozas owned 25 percent of the country's industries and 25 percent of its land. This enormous concentration of wealth in the hands of the ruling family caused strains with other sectors of the elite. Nevertheless, the non-Somoza elites, despite their antipathy for the Somozas, did not actively oppose the regime until the workers and peasants began to back the Sandinista alternative.

These elites joined the anti-Somoza battle too late to come out winners. The reason for their reluctance, in part, was that they owed their prosperity to the Somoza regime. When peasants attempted to occupy land or go on strike for a subsistence wage, elites would just call to the National Guard to haul away the troublemakers. This piece of the puzzle helps to explain why the Sandinistas and not the elites led the revolution of 1979, and why the elites in general despised the Sandinistas. Notwithstanding this characterization, there were also many people from varying social backgrounds who simply despised the Somoza regime but in no way sympathized with the political agenda of the Sandinista leadership.

Despite the prospects for social change in the countryside, the Sandinista Revolution did not live up to its promise of social justice and national liberation. In trying to evaluate the decade of revolution it is absolutely essential to understand the context in which the Sandinistas tried to carry out their policies. That context can be summarized by one word—war. In 1982, the United States began to back a group of former National Guardsmen, then exiled in Honduras, who became the "Contras," short for counterrevolutionaries. Eventually, the Contras, trained and supported by the U.S. army, gained significant popular support and came to represent a serious threat to the Sandinista regime. The Contra war after 1983 cost the Nicaraguans another 50,000 lives, displaced hundreds of thousands of civilians, absorbed close to 50 percent of the government's budget, and damaged the Nicaraguan economy to the tune of $12 billion, when the country's annual income from exports was under $500 million a year during the 1980s. That amount translated into economic disaster and effectively undermined all government attempts to improve the lot of the poor.

But the Contra war does not explain all of the failures of the revolution. Rather, the disaffection of peasants and workers who had been Sandinista supporters stemmed from one important ideological source: the FSLN's failure to recognize that autonomous forms of class and ethnic consciousness can aid rather than impede the development of the revolutionary process. This ideological rigidity, rooted in an adherence to certain Marxist-Leninist tenets, led directly to the grave errors committed by the Sandinistas that provoked the armed rebellion of the Miskito Indians on the Atlantic Coast in the early 1980s.

The Sandinista Revolution did put into practice an agrarian reform that virtually eliminated latifundismo and distributed land to some 100,000 families, a substantial majority of the landless peasantry. Yet, the reform also created political problems for the revolution in two respects. First, the Sandinistas politicized the reform by pushing people into forming cooperatives that owed some degree of political loyalty to the government. Second, they tried to pursue the same kind of reform in areas that for specific historical reasons needed different policies, for example, in the highlands where land distribution was more equitable than in the coastal areas. And it was in the highlands that the Contras gained support.

We have seen how in Guatemala, El Salvador, and Nicaragua hundreds of thousands of peasants supported revolutionary movements that promised radical change in rural society. Were they foolish? Was the concomitant suffering worth it? What did they gain from it? Such questions are difficult to answer in a strictly material sense. The Nicaraguan peasants who, like those of San José de Obraje, had been pushed off the land by the cotton boom did make some significant gains during the Sandinista Revolution. Yet, since the electoral defeat of the Sandinistas in 1990, many have lost their land to bank mortgages (and, of course, many lost it—or their lives—to the mudslides and floods of 1998). Salvadorans gained some similar advantages through an agrarian reform legislated in the early 1980s to steal the thunder of the revolutionary movement. But in 1987, 1 percent of the population still controlled the use of 70 percent of the land. Guatemalan peasants won nothing from their sacrifice.

But perhaps the real question is, Did those Central American peasants have a choice? Faced with intolerable levels of degradation, they began to organize to demand the most elemental of rights. By the 1970s, priests often accompanied them in their struggles. The military regimes countered with unspeakable brutality. Most of the peasants either fled or opted to support the revolutionary Left, which began to organize guerrilla warfare. The revolutionary Left certainly had a different agenda from that of its peasant supporters. And when it achieved power, as in Nicaragua, the results were mixed for the rural poor. But the military regimes' repression pushed them into such alliances. Therefore, unlike those insurgencies in the 1960s that tried to copy the Cuban Revolution, these groups could count on the support of the rural poor. The regimes did not consider negotiated settlements until the guerrilla movement was virtually defeated (Guatemala in 1997) or it was obvious that it could not be defeated (El Salvador in 1992). Those authoritarian governments, in particular, were emboldened by the huge amounts of money poured into them by the United States, which viewed the guerrilla movements as proxies of Havana or Moscow. Thus the wars dragged on and tens of thousands of peasant lives were lost. Were they lost in vain? Perhaps. But it is also possible that the survivors, however miserable their current circumstances, have learned something fundamental about their rights and that the new, more democratic governments—the end result of the civil wars—will learn to respect them.

Chinese Peasants: From Rebellions to Revolution

The Chinese peasants pose one of the greatest challenges to analysts of revolution, in part because of the complex legacy of accomplishment and suffering associated with Mao Zedong, a man who relied heavily on armies of rural insurgents in leading the Communist Party to victory four years after the end of World War II. Scholars continue to debate how best to make sense of this complex figure, who was born into a fairly well-to-do but by no means especially wealthy village family in the hinterland province of Hunan and went on to serve as the first paramount leader of the People's Republic of China (PRC) after this most populous of contemporary nations was founded in 1949. Mao continues to be revered by many within China for the crucial role he played in reunifying and pacifying the nation. His 1949 victory put an end to a period of almost half a century during which civil wars and foreign invasions had ravaged the land. Inside the PRC, however, he is also held responsible for committing mistakes in his later years that led to catastrophes such as the great famine of the late 1950s and early 1960s and the chaos of the Cultural Revolution (1966–1976). Internationally, his reputation has long been and remains ambiguous as well. He has been hailed as a positive alternative, or merely a Chinese equivalent, to Stalin. The model of peasant-led guerrilla revolution that he championed, meanwhile, has been dismissed by some as a fluke that only succeeded because of nefarious conspiracies and luck; yet it has also inspired insurgents everywhere, from Vietnam to Tanzania to Peru, where would-be Maos have tried to follow in the footsteps of the man known for decades in the PRC as the "Great Helmsman" of the revolution. Since Mao himself insisted that he spoke above all for China's peasants and could not have achieved anything without their support, to come to terms with him requires that we address a series of issues associated with villagers and revolt.

The central issues to be grappled with here include the following. Did China's long tradition of peasant rebellions, which had helped to topple dynasties but had never created a sustained alternative political order, play a key or only a peripheral part in the rise to power of the Communist Party? Mao was fond of presenting himself as merely the latest in a long line of insurrectionary leaders who had managed to harness the anger that Chinese villagers felt when repressed by corrupt officials and grasping landlords. And yet, he also claimed at times that the Communist Revolution was something radically different from any mass movement that China had seen before, inspired as it was by Lenin's critique of imperialism and ideas concerning the importance of disciplined vanguard groups and by Marx's ideas concerning class struggle. Which Mao gets us closer to the truth?

How much difference did international interference on behalf of or against Mao and his followers make in deciding the outcome of the Civil War (1945–1949) that followed Japan's surrender to the Allies? Surviving members of the Nationalist Party of Chiang Kai-shek, who lost the war, have long claimed that if only more foreign aid had come to them from the West, and less support from Moscow gone to the Communists, the PRC might never have come into being. There is reason to doubt this speculative theory, however—not least because the Soviets were often ambivalent at best about Mao, seeing him as a renegade Marxist too ready to alter official orthodox positions when it suited him. Moreover, it is questionable just how much foreign aid to either side had to do with determining the actions of those peasants who helped decide their own fate by supporting the Communists.

Another set of questions relates directly to those peasant supporters. Why did they find Mao's cause worthy? Was it the appeal of his social programs (for example, calls for land reform, policies that granted women more equality within villages, and an insistence that power be shared more equally between members of different generations within lineage groups) that secured his base in the countryside and ultimately laid the groundwork for his victory? Or was it instead his appeal to nationalism that was the primary factor? (That is, the fact that when Japan invaded China in the 1930s–1940s the Communists seemed more genuinely committed to defeating this foreign aggressor than the Nationalist Party did.) Or was it, finally, the special organizational qualities and propaganda skills of Mao's party as opposed to Chiang's that swung the balance in favor of the Communists? Were they simply better at establishing effective groups of cadres in the countryside and communicating their message in terms peasants could understand?

Leaving aside these questions for a minute, we give a quick run-down of what is generally agreed to have taken place in the decades leading up to 1949. As noted in Chapter 3, a political transformation had taken place in 1911, when the last dynasty was overthrown. Between 1924 and 1927, the Nationalist Party and the Communist Party worked together in a United Front designed to defeat the warlords who had seized power after the 1911 Revolution. This alliance was made possible by the fact that the two groups had several things in common: admiration for Sun Yat-sen, the great hero of 1911; an interest in working with the Soviet Union, which was the only foreign power of the time that had renounced all claims to colonial privileges within China; and hatred of the warlords. The alliance became endangered in 1925 with the death of Sun, which among other things precipitated a battle for succession within the Nationalist Party. Still, the Nationalists and Communists continued to work together until the spring of 1927, when three things happened. First, thanks to a combination of Communist-led strikes within the city and the arrival of Nationalist-led troops from outside, the United Front forces took control of the Chinese-run sections of Shanghai, China's largest city and one that also included two foreign-run enclaves. Second, though proclaiming that their goal was to free China from imperialist domination as well as to defeat the warlords, the Nationalists quickly made it clear that they would not follow up this victory with an effort to take back control of Shanghai's foreign concessions. Third, and most important for our purposes here, Chiang Kai-shek, who had won the battle within the Nationalist Party to succeed Sun, launched a "white terror" purge of all Communists and suspected Communists within the United Front.

These actions had many long- and short-term effects on Chinese politics, setting the stage, among other things, for Chiang Kai-shek's assumption of national power a year later, when the warlords were defeated. What is of most significance here, though, is that it shook up the Chinese Communist Party (CCP). Until then, in orthodox fashion, the CCP had focused most of its attention on organizing workers, assuming that China's socialist revolution would be carried out in its cities. Some members of the party had been arguing that more attention should be paid to organizing peasants, but these voices had not commanded much attention. In the aftermath of the purges of 1927, however, CCP activists fled to the countryside for cover, and those calling for a strategy that privileged rural revolt over urban upheaval began to be taken more seriously.

Mao was the most eloquent proponent of the new rural strategy. He dared to suggest that Communist organizers should not just pay attention to the countryside but should take their cues from peasant insurgents. In his most famous early tract, "Report on the Hunan Peasant Movement" (1927), he wrote of the peasantry as an elemental and potentially invincible progressive force. "In a very short time," he predicted, "in China's central, southern, and northern provinces, several hundred million peasants will rise like a tornado or tempest, a force so extraordinarily swift and violent that no power, however great, will be able to suppress it." The peasants, he said, would "rush forward along the road to liberation" and "send all imperialists, warlords, corrupt officials, local bullies, and bad gentry to their graves." The only question, he felt, was whether the CCP would try to "march at their head and lead them" or prefer to "follow at their rear gesticulating and criticizing them," and Mao left no room for doubt about where he wanted the party to be.

The next decades were momentous ones for China. The Nationalist Party made extermination of the remnants of the CCP one of its primary tasks, and the Communists evolved from a ragtag group of guerrillas to a major political force. By the Civil War era, the Communists, after their epic Long March across much of the length and breadth of China to escape the Nationalist armies, had established several base areas under their control in northern China. Here, efforts were made to put socialist ideas into practice and elevate peasants to positions of equality with other members of society. Yan'an, the most famous of these sites, eventually assumed mythic fame in CCP histories as a utopian achievement. In these base areas, mass literacy drives were carried out, for example, to ensure that more peasants learned to read, something virtually unheard of in earlier times. The Communists also carried out efforts to equalize land distribution. Here, as scholarship conducted outside of China has convincingly shown, many residents were also exposed to the harsher side of Chinese communism. There were purges within the CCP's ranks in an effort to cultivate and ensure orthodoxy; Mao's cult of personality began to take shape; and a complex and often cruel system of surveillance and control was developed.

The relative importance of the utopian and dystopian aspects of base-area society continues to be debated by scholars. Some stress the relatively high degree of equality that prevailed between members of different social groups, different generations, and both sexes, at least in comparison with other Chinese settings, which were structured in a very hierarchical fashion. Others emphasize that, even at this point, many of the problems that would later resurface in the PRC and cause suffering could be found in embryonic form: thought-control policies and purges, special perks for well-connected cadres, and efforts to transform Mao into not just a leader among equals but a god-like figure. Most analysts, nonetheless, agree on a few things. First, that the base areas were thought of positively by increasingly large numbers of Chinese, who heard about them via personal reports from visitors, published accounts by sympathetic Chinese journalists, and articles by Western writers such as Edgar Snow. The Communists began to be seen by many as providing a less corrupt alternative to the Nationalist Party, which by the 1940s had a very bad reputation indeed in much of the country. China's poor economic state, combined with reports of nepotism and other moral failings within official circles, had badly tarnished the Nationalists' image.

Most commentators agree, however, that the CCP's appeal cannot be reduced in the end to either its nationalism or its social programs. Rather, its popularity must be seen as some kind of combination of the two. Many also accept the idea that above and beyond the appeal of the CCP was the simple fact that it had, by the 1940s, developed such a sophisticated organizational, propagandistic, and military apparatus. It was better positioned than the Nationalist Party to get its message across to people in an effective manner and take full advantage of any support from ordinary people, particularly peasants. Thanks to all of these factors, by 1949 Mao was leading a massive peasant army that succeeded, against what had seemed insurmountable odds, in defeating the Nationalist Party. That victory was soon being extolled in CCP textbooks as a combination of brilliant leadership by Mao and other Communist heroes, such as General Zhu De, and spontaneous enthusiasm for the radical cause by China's oppressed peasant masses. Mao and Zhu, it was stressed, took their cues from the peasantry, and hence the CCP was merely the natural voice for the aspirations of villagers.

One possible criticism of this interpretation is that external factors definitely played some role in this victory. Soviet support for the CCP, even if grudgingly given at times, did contribute to its ultimate success. But later efforts to portray the CCP's victory as the result of Soviet interference and guidance or manipulation are fundamentally flawed. First, the Soviets at various points aided not just the Communists but also the Nationalists, hedging their bets, as it were. Second, as noted above, there was already tension at this point (and this tension would increase after the PRC was founded) between the Soviets and the CCP over matters of doctrinal orthodoxy—or rather Mao's lack thereof. This tension limited the extent of Soviet Communists' support for and influence over their Chinese proteges. Third, the United States, though never giving as much support to the Nationalist Party as Chiang Kai-shek would have liked during the mid-to-late

PICTURE 8.7   Rice-growing commune in China, 1979. High-yield, wet-field rice cultivation, in the past confined largely to South China, has been extended into drier regions by modern developments such as the use of electric pumps, scientific seed hybridization, and new forms of labor organization. This commune lies near the foothills that mark the northernmost limit of the North China Plain. (Photo courtesy of Lynn Struve)

1940s, and though it often sought to encourage the two warring groups to form a coalition government, did give aid throughout this period to the opponents of the Communist Party.

For obvious reasons, the Nationalists were particularly fond of stressing references to outside interference after their defeat in 1949, when Chiang Kai-shek's and other Nationalists fled to Taiwan. If these references do not seriously invalidate official CCP accounts of Mao's rise to national power, however, some other factors do. One of these is simply that the Communists did not merely give voice to peasant aspirations but put their own distinctive stamp on them. They even, at times, did things that were directly contrary to the beliefs of many peasants. These actions reflected instead the ideas that Mao and other CCP leaders had embraced during their time as student radicals (in the 1910s and 1920s), when they came under the influence of liberal Western ideas as well as Marxist theories. Efforts to institute new marriage policies, for example, were not bottom-up initiatives. Such moves to restructure family relations—such as allowing young villagers to choose their own mates (as opposed to having them selected by familial elders) and allowing women to seek divorces, were actively resisted, in fact, at various points by older villagers (particularly males) who saw them as threats to traditional values and their own positions of power. Nevertheless, such policies were instituted locally in base areas before 1949 and nationally in the PRC in 1950.

Another problem with the official Communist version of the story of Mao and the peasants is that, even though the revolution was ultimately won in the countryside, urban mass movements by students and workers were also of vital importance. They called attention to the corruption of the Nationalist Party and weakened its symbolic and economic hold on the country. In official histories of the period, the significance of this urban activism was consistently downplayed. This version of history minimized the glory of some of Mao's competitors for power within the CCP who had spent the Civil War years in the cities instead of the base areas. It also added greater luster to the cult of personality of the great leader. The end result was distortion: A largely peasant revolution with an important worker (and intelligentsia) component was made to seem as though it was a purely rural upheaval.

Conclusion

In this chapter we have raised more questions than we have answered about why and how peasants rebel and the mark peasant revolutions left on the twentieth century. One key lesson to be drawn from it is that it may be helpful to think in terms of peasantries as opposed to an unchanging peasant who is the same across time and across space. Another is that peasant movements have long followed and continue to follow complex trajectories—ones shaped not just by the aspirations of villagers themselves but also by the ideas of those who seek to mobilize them.

A good note to conclude on is to stress a paradoxical contrast between the nineteenth and twentieth centuries. In the 1890s, the vast majority of the world's people lived in villages and worked the land. The possibility that rural dwellers could be at the heart of revolutionary struggle for change was not taken seriously by most radical theorists or agitators—populist anarchists being among the only exceptions. By the 1990s, in contrast, many countries had undergone processes of urbanization that had drastically reduced the number of residents living off the land. Rural-urban calculations are always imprecise, since the line between a village and a small town in the orbit of a city is often a blurry one at best. Still, it is commonly claimed that China went from being roughly 80 percent rural and 20 percent urban around the year 1900 to being more like 60 percent rural and 40 percent urban around 2000. Many other countries in Asia went through similar transitions, and elsewhere nations that formerly had largely peasant economies now have more than half their populations living in cities and doing things other than working the land. Ironically, however, though the twentieth century saw a dramatic decline in the size of peasantries, it also saw a dramatic rise in assessments of the revolutionary potential of villagers. How could it fail to do so when, as of the 1990s, some of the only Communist Party regimes still in power were ones, such as those of China and Vietnam, that had gained control of their countries via revolutions that were largely the work of peasants? And when one surveys the writings of the major revolutionary theorists, activists and scholars alike, one also finds that the twentieth century was one in which the peasantry gained a central place in analyses of struggles for change. The cases of Mao and Fanon have been discussed above. It is also worth noting that many of the major recent contributors to scholarship on revolutions have been people, such as Barrington Moore and Theda Skocpol, who are best known for their discussions of relationships between peasantries and other social groups. Just as peasants began to dwindle in numbers, in short, they began to get their due.

9

1968 and New Radical Visions

History does not usually suit the convenience of people who like to divide it into neat periods, but there are times when it seems to have pity on them. The year 1968 almost looks as though it had been designed as some sort of signpost. There is hardly any region in the world in which it is not marked by spectacular and dramatic events which were to have profound repercussions on the history of the country in which they occurred and, as often as not, globally.

Eric Hobsbawm,
1968: Magnum Throughout the World
(1998)

The principal objective of our action . . . is the total and real liberation of humans, the abolition of all forms of human slavery (economic, political, cultural, etc.) . . . that prevent progress.

Polish Student Activists,
"Theses of the Program of the Young Generation"
(1968)

T HE YEAR 1968 WAS A TIME FOR A NEW KIND OF REVOLUTION— or rather a series of overlapping yet distinctively novel sorts of revolutionary movements—to break out. It was not a revolution centered in any one major city, though most of the social struggles associated with that momentous year were urban ones. It was not carried out in the name of any single, clearly defined ideology, though there were many places in which variations on Marxism were important inspirational forces. It was not something that was easy to associate with the anger of any particular type of social or economic group. In fact, though the most vocal participants in the upheavals were often workers and students, they often claimed an affinity of purpose with oppressed rural groups in general and with participants in Third World peasant revolts in particular, which increases the difficulty of characterizing the events.

What exactly were the common denominators, if any, among the disparate movements that broke out in 1968, or broke out somewhat earlier but reached apogees of some sort around the time of that pivotal year? What gave the upheavals of the year enough coherence to have it make sense to think of them—as many participants and observers did—as interconnected? Why does it make sense to speak of a "1968 generation"? These questions are taken up in the following pages. In our analysis of the 1968 revolutionary tide, we move back and forth between events in different parts of the world, continually returning to the theme of diversity as a key factor.

Common Threads in the 1968 Story

We can change the world,
Rearrange the world.

Stephen Stills,
"Chicago" (1968)

Speak, for your two lips are free;
Speak, your tongue is still your own;
This straight body still is yours . . .
Speak, your life is still your own.

Faiz Ahmed Faiz,
Urdu poet (1968)

All power to the imagination!
Paris demonstrators
(1968)

One of the main factors linking the different local and national events of 1968 was a tendency for youthful activists to play leading roles. And these young people, moreover, had some beliefs and concerns in common as well. There indeed is a logic to describing urban participants in the protests described below as members of a "1968 generation," a general term for activists born between the mid-1940s and the early 1950s. Even though they spoke different languages and called the cities of very different lands home, they shared a desire to overturn all forms of oppression and a conviction that militancy in and of itself was a good thing. They also, in most cases, had a shared sense that totalistic change was something that the younger generation would, could, and should bring about.

There was a feeling in the air as well—sensed by those who feared as well as those who welcomed radical movements—that the kind of change that would come about if the revolutions of

211

1968 succeeded would involve sweeping cultural as well as political transformations. Finally, there was a feeling that the struggles were part of a common tide. This sense in part reflected the growing prominence of the mass media, especially television. The images of events crossed national borders, allowing activists in one land to see what those in other lands were doing. It also reflected in part the fact that certain international events, in particular the Vietnam War, were points of reference and sources of anger for many different sorts of youths in many different sorts of lands.

Third World Inspirations and Patterns

The conflict in Southeast Asia provided one kind of connecting thread linking many movements, and an upheaval in another part of that continent, China, also provided the 1968 generation with powerful images of mass activism and totalistic change. Here, two years before 1968 itself arrived, Chairman Mao Zedong called for a Great Proletarian Cultural Revolution to revitalize the Communist Party and by extension the nation as a whole. Even though he had used the term "proletarian" (meaning, in this case, workers and peasants), Mao initially turned to young student militants to serve as the main activists in this campaign. Soon known as "Red Guards," these radical youths were encouraged by Mao to attack the Communist Party bureaucracy in order to cleanse it of impure elements and hide-bound practices. Their own experiences with bureaucratism, combined with their devotion to Mao, made many of them eager to follow this directive. They desired to contribute to the sacred revolutionary cause the way earlier generations of young Chinese patriots had. They took their own initiative in doing things related to Mao's instructions. They held "struggle sessions" against despised teachers, for example, that were modeled on the ritualized attacks on landlords that peasants had carried out during the land reform campaigns of the 1940s and 1950s.

Soon, the Red Guards were taking part in massive rallies at Beijing's Tiananmen Square, where Mao sometimes greeted them in person. They also traveled around the country to "share revolutionary experiences" with their counterparts in other regions. They seized control of campuses and turned university hierarchies upside down by putting top administrators on trial for alleged crimes against the people, asserting that their educational policies subverted the true goals of Maoism. Images of Red Guard militancy, and especially of massive numbers of impassioned youths waving Mao's little red book (of collected sayings), became one of the enduring symbols of 1968 fervor in the global imagination. And Mao's writings were widely quoted. Particularly attractive to many 1968 activists were his denunciations of imperialist powers such as the United States as "paper tigers"—in other words, less dangerous and powerful than they appeared. They were also drawn in by his insistence that the most important revolutionaries of the day were the young people of the world.

The Cultural Revolution was a very complex event that ended up being many things, and arguments over its meaning and even its duration (some claim it ended in 1969, others much later) continue to this day. Certainly, it had run its course by the middle of the 1970s, however. It was, in some stages, characterized by seemingly random purges of anyone deemed insufficiently loyal to Mao. At other points it degenerated still further into a combination of witch-hunt and chaotic civil war. Universities at times became battlegrounds, and there were periods when Mao and those close to him tried, at first unsuccessfully, to rein in the energy of youthful activism, even

PICTURE 9.1   Cover of a children's propaganda magazine published in Beijing in the 1960s. Individuals of various nationalities and ages hold up copies of the collected sayings of Chairman Mao Zedong (his famed *Little Red Book*). The placard at far left says, "Long Live the Thoughts of Chairman Mao!" The multinational and multiracial crowd shows that Mao's ideas had adherents worldwide. (From the collection of Jeffrey Wasserstrom)

going so far as to call in troops to restore order to campuses. There were also stages of the Cultural Revolution when campuses were not the main centers of activism at all, when the focus was on the countryside or the factories of Shanghai, the city whose "rebel workers" (labor militants) took center stage at some points in the 1970s. There were also periods in what is now called the Ten Years of Chaos when things spun madly out of control. It was sometimes hard to tell whether the settling of scores taking place between rival groups had any ideological grounding at all.

Mao's Cultural Revolution began, however, as something quite different and there was, at least initially, at its heart a concern with rooting out corruption and furthering or reinvigorating egalitarian impulses that had formerly been at the heart of the Communist ideology. The program was intended all along simply as a plan to help Mao reassert his own power vis-à-vis competitors within the Chinese Communist Party. These rivals had allowed him to keep his title of chairman but had taken much of the daily decisionmaking into their own hands. It was also, though, at the beginning, an effort to breathe new life into a revolutionary struggle that many were convinced had begun to ossify and lose its bearings—just as Mao claimed had occurred in the Soviet Union after Lenin's time. The Cultural Revolution's proponents claimed that this degeneration showed through in everything from the kinds of plays being produced and performed on Chinese stages to the way university classes were taught.

The Red Guards and their allies argued that, to get the revolution back on track and prevent further regression into patterns associated with the ancient regime that had preceded the Communist takeover, the people who needed to be mobilized were youths. Young people were, after all, the only Chinese who had not been shaped in their formative years by the outmoded ideas of Confucianism, which had, it was claimed, crippled the nation up until 1949. This idealistic kernel within what ultimately became the social and political catastrophe of the Cultural Revolution is often forgotten now when, within China and elsewhere, the darkest moments of the period are the main focus of attention. It is worth bringing to the forefront here, however, since it is that idealistic and youth-oriented part of the struggle that resonates so powerfully with the experiences of youths elsewhere in 1968.

There are, in other words, links between China's Cultural Revolution—with its ritualized personality cult rallies and its struggle sessions—and calls for change that were echoing almost simultaneously in other countries with state socialist regimes, such as Poland and Czechoslovakia. These movements took seemingly very different forms and lacked the sort of top-level support that Mao gave the Red Guards. Still, in many of them, young people argued, as the Red Guards did, that the bureaucrats calling themselves "Communists" were in fact no different from their capitalist counterparts in other lands or their feudal predecessors in now socialist countries. A total recreation of the cultural as well as political and economic order was needed, they claimed, again like the Red Guards. If it did not occur, this pattern would continue indefinitely, they said—with new oppressive classes taking shape as soon as old ones were overthrown. Variations on this kind of argument were heard in university circles in many of the main countries of the Soviet bloc, such as Hungary and the German Democratic Republic (East Germany), as well as in outlying parts of the European state-socialist world that were less directly tied with Moscow, such as Yugoslavia and other Balkan countries.

In the end, the fate of youthful protesters outside of China calling for changes in state socialism was very different than that which befell the Red Guards. For example, the brave young Czech protesters of Prague Spring, who supported the development of "socialism with a human face" in their country, were silenced by Soviet tanks sent from Moscow to suppress this "heresy." There were arrests and purges in Poland as well. Nevertheless, the link between even these groups and the Red Guards was there in a shared concern over the ease with which those who were once revolutionaries could evolve into tyrants. Young people throughout the state-socialist world were concerned that those who had once been opponents of the capitalist ruling classes were developing into a new class of bureaucrats who stood above ordinary members of society and above the law. Variations on the new class theory were developed most fully by Yugoslavian intellectuals operating in a state socialist setting that was more tolerant of open discussion than countries closer to the core of the Soviet Empire. Their ideas were articulated in many other lands, including China.

The desire to change the whole culture—everything from basic public rituals to the structure of family life—and not just rules relating to governance and economic life, was a major force in youth movements in many countries ruled by Communist Party regimes. This same desire was also important elsewhere. In the West, too, young people of the 1968 generation complained that something was deeply wrong with the way their societies were being run. Affluence was not enough, those in these developed countries argued, and a culture could be rotten to the core even if it provided increasingly comfortable lives for those who belonged to it. This critique was based in part on a feeling that the increasing wealth of the industrialized countries of North America and Western Europe, as well as Japan, was made possible by unjust exploitation of Third World workers. It went deeper, though, to include a complaint that even within the world of the "haves," the quality of individual lives was being degraded. The forces of mass production, mass culture, and mass violence—in the form of wars fought on foreign shores to suppress national liberation movements—were blamed for this process. People were being reduced to numbers, their individuality was being squashed, and their capacity for joy diminished. Revolution was embraced as something that would, if successful, change the affective as well as material aspects of life. One sense in which 1968 was a watershed moment, therefore, was that it was a turning point in a shift from a tendency toward thinking of revolutionary struggle primarily in socioeconomic terms to thinking of it as involving, centrally, changes in the way people thought and acted, individually as well as collectively. It was no accident that "All power to the imagination" was a rallying cry in not just Prague but also Paris.

There were other rallying cries and linking symbols as well, and these, too, deserve to be remembered. There were also important contrasts between different "1968s." Some rallying cries drew attention very sharply to the extent to which people of the time genuinely believed that whole continents were at the cusp of a momentous change—and that perhaps even the entire world would be involved in this transformation. This hope was evoked in the many slogans of the day that called for or described the spread of a particular kind of revolutionary activism. For example, frequently quoted and repeated then was the 1966 call of the Latin American guerrilla fighter Ché Guevera, who died just before the epochal year began, for Third World activists to follow the lead of the Vietcong and challenge imperialist authority wherever it could be found. The world needed, he said, "two, three, many Vietnams" to neutralize and eventually destroy capitalist world domination. And Mao made similar statements, saying that multiple challenges to capitalism would be required to prove that the imperialists were actually the paper tigers he had dubbed them.

European and U.S. Variations

Third World activism was not the only kind prominent in 1968. The developed countries of the West were being challenged as well. This fact can be attested to in numerous ways. The front cover of the first issue of a famous radical London newspaper, *The Black Dwarf,* which was started that same year, provides a good example. It read as follows, in a kind of rough poetic form:

> WE SHALL FIGHT
> WE SHALL WIN
> PARIS
> LONDON
> ROME
> BERLIN

A sense that 1968 was something special, though in this case because it marked the beginning of worrisome as opposed to glorious times, was conjured up not so much by slogans as by keywords and phrases. The fascination many commentators had that year with the need to prevent "crises" from destroying forever the political fabric is a case in point. References to "crises" filled the U.S. press—the crisis of urban violence, of racial tension, of youthful contempt for authority—all were decried and analyzed endlessly.

PICTURE 9.2
Page from a Chinese art magazine published in Beijing in the early 1960s. A Vietnamese guerrilla holds aloft a revolutionary flag. The words in Spanish demonstrate the unity of oppressed people worldwide in a single battle against capitalism and imperialism. The main slogan reads, "Vietnam, we are with you. . . " It was said to be the watchword of a Cuban committee for solidarity with Vietnamese activists. (From the collection of Jeffrey Wasserstrom)

Another catchphrase of 1968, among those who feared either revolution in general or simply particular types of revolutionary activism going too far, was that a return to "order" was needed. It was, as we have already noted, the year when Soviet tanks rolled into Czechoslovakia to put an end to the reformist experiments known as Prague Spring. And it was even the year when Mao himself, who prided himself on thinking that "more revolution" was always better than less and that no form of militancy was too extreme, expressed concern that society had become too chaotic. In 1968, in short, visions of utopian and more disturbing sorts of fundamental change seemed to be everywhere, and interest in chaos as a liberating or debilitating force was on everyone's mind. There is good reason, therefore, why people look back to it as a time when upheavals in every part of the world were, for a brief time and for better or worse, closely connected in some fashion with each other.

And there is good reason why, even today, to refer to the year 1968 in almost any country is to conjure up a series of dramatic images of struggles for change—some peaceful, others violent, some localized, others national or international in scope. In both the realm of events and that of memory, it was and remains a year of genuine world historical importance and global dimensions.

Location does matter, though, regardless of the realm being considered. There is a great deal of overlap, but there is also a great deal of divergence and variation in the responses provoked by the name of this year—depending on where exactly it is spoken. To paraphrase Guevara's famous comment about multiple Vietnams, we need to think not of one but of many interconnected 1968s of history and of popular memory. To show how these different 1968s have always been and continue to be inflected with national meanings, we look below at a couple of specific cases: a massacre in Mexico and worker strikes in Italy, chosen particularly because of how they diverge and because of the different issues they raise. For now, however, to further a sense of just how varied a year it was, despite the common threads running through it, we provide a montage of other sorts of images. Some of these pictures fit in with those associated with the case studies to come, but others are quite different.

One logical place to start is Paris. That city's 1968 is remembered very vividly by most of the men and women who were born before, during, or just after World War II. Many of them recall the year as a time of barricades, of the sort protesters erected in the streets, as they had in radical struggles of the eighteenth and nineteenth centuries as well. It was a period that saw a revival, or perversion—depending on one's perspective—of a national revolutionary tradition that stretches back to 1871 and the Paris Commune and even further back to 1789. The site of the most intense and dramatic struggles of this particular 1968 was the Sorbonne, France's most exalted place of learning and a place that, for a time, was transformed into a student-run counter-university where only radical ideas were taught. It was here that references to the power of the imagination were taken up with the greatest gusto, in a student movement that was supported by many French laborers (and not-so-young radical philosophers, such as Jean Paul Sartre) and looked upon with admiration by angry educated youths of other lands.

Connected to but following ultimately a radically different trajectory from this French 1968 was that of Poland. One link between the Parisian and Polish cases was provided by texts. According to some memoirs, the most widely read publications at the Sorbonne in May 1968 included writings by Polish dissidents. These texts tried to carve out a political position that was critical of all forms of bureaucratic authoritarian rule, Communist and non-Communist alike. They had been translated into French—in some cases by a young radical named Adam Michnik, who had already drawn the attention of Poland's Communist Party authorities because of his unorthodox political views, and who would spend much of his youth serving prison sentences for his activities. A quintessential "1968er" in his contempt for all forms of authority, he would go on to become, in the 1980s, one of the leaders of the Solidarity Movement that competed for power with (and eventually helped to topple) Poland's Communist Party in 1989.

In Poland, however, the word "1968" does not just conjure up memories of these early steps in the transition away from the state socialism of the 1980s and 1990s but also much darker things. To counteract the radical stirrings on campuses and in the arts—Michnik and others gained fame initially for protesting the censoring of a play—the Polish state launched a virulent anti-Semitic campaign in 1968. And to say the name of that year in Poland to this day, in some quarters, is to remind people not of struggles for change but of the government's efforts to convince the populace that a vast Jewish conspiracy was underway to destroy all that Poles held sacred.

To speak of 1968 in the United States, meanwhile, is to conjure up a range of varied but interconnected images. Some of these pictures have to do with discrimination of a different sort—racism against African Americans. One enduring symbol of the year for some Americans is the "black power" salute that several African-American athletes gave upon winning medals at the Olympic Games in Mexico City. The U.S. images of 1968, like the French ones, also have to do with student activism. Although they do not involve visions of workers and students coming together in common cause on the streets, à la the Parisian case, as tensions between educated youths and laborers were common at the time in the United States, there is still a strong link between the French 1968 and the American one. Student activism was a major part of the American story, with universities such as UC Berkeley being transformed, much as the Sorbonne was for a time, into counter-institutions. What links all of the American images of 1968 to one another—

PICTURE 9.3 Summer Olympic Games in Mexico City, October 19, 1968. U.S. track and field athletes Tommie Smith and John Carlos, first- and third-place winners in the 200-meter race, protest racial discrimination in the United States with the "black power" salute as they stand on the winner's podium. (Photo courtesy of Archive Photos)

and ties them to some extent to Polish and French ones as well—is a core set of themes. One theme is upheaval; another is that of people speaking out in daring and novel ways. A third is a belief in the cleansing or destructive power of fiery forms of radicalism to purify or destroy the world—but in one way or another make it different from what it was before.

Some of the images from the United States, admittedly, are actually tied most closely to events that took place a few years earlier or later than that year. They are all, nevertheless, part of the 1968 of historical memory. The year's name serves as a metonym for the whole period lasting from the mid-1960s to the beginning of the 1970s. The era stands out as a watershed in the history of radicalism, separating the era of the "Old Left" from that of the "New Left." Some of the main images that come to mind when 1968 is mentioned in the United States are linked to the quintessential New Left struggle, the fight to end U.S. involvement in Vietnam. The term 1968 is thus linked in historical memory with all antiwar demonstrations, including the massive ones that came a couple of years later following incidents at Kent State and Jackson State universities

PICTURE 9.4
Jimi Hendrix (1942–1970). One of the greatest and most publicized events staged by the counterculture in the United States in the tumultuous 1960s was the Woodstock Music Festival of 1968. Prominent rock-and-roll bands of the time, including Jimi Hendrix, performed for the hippie crowds. (Photo courtesy of Archive Photos)

in which several students were killed by National Guardsmen (four and two, respectively). The carpet bombing raids on Cambodia about the same time also caused renewed protests. The year is also linked to the crowd actions that took place in Chicago during the 1968 Democratic Convention, which were again inspired largely by opposition to the war. Finally, images of marches associated with the Civil Rights Movement also come quickly to mind.

Other images of 1968 prevalent in American minds have to do not with formal political protest but rather with counterculture events such as hippie happenings, from be-ins to love-ins. Here, too, should be placed images of the Woodstock festival. That famous gathering featured performances by some of the era's leading folk singers and rock-and-roll musicians, including Jimi Hendrix, whose version of the "Star Spangled Banner" on a distorted electric guitar became a counter-anthem for a generation that had grown suspicious of official patriotism. The year 1968 evokes, more generally, images of an entire world that was suddenly gloriously or frighteningly cast free of its moorings as young people took to the streets to demand a change in the political systems of many countries. These struggles were each unique, differing from one another in terms of tactics and specific goals, but all seemed somehow connected. Americans saw U.S. events as the center of the storm, not a peaceful eye of a hurricane but the giant thunderhead in the midst of the clash of the elements in the skies and on the ground.

Continuities and Convergences in Leftist Thought and Action

Conjuring up memories of 1968 inadvertently raises three big issues that any attempt to come to terms with that watershed year must address. One has to do with continuity. Just how different were New Left ideas and patterns of radicalism from Old Left ones? It certainly meant something that young people inspired by the idea of revolution began to find more to admire in Third

World figures such as China's Mao, Cuba's Castro, and Vietnam's Ho Chi Minh than in such earlier models as Lenin and Stalin, It also clearly meant something that New Left theorists were more ready than their predecessors had been to think that divisions other than those based on class—from the tensions between generations to those between members of different ethnic groups and eventually also genders—could be crucial to political equations. And it was definitely important that there was an increasing willingness to think that the tactics one chose could be of crucial symbolic and not just purely strategic importance. Still, there were continuities as well as ruptures between the Old Left and the New Left. It is only by looking carefully at how the movements unfolded in specific countries that we can chart more accurately the extent to which the two kinds of Lefts converged and diverged.

The second issue has to do with a different sort of convergence, that between radical politics and counterculture trends. There was definitely a connection between the rise of the hippie lifestyle and the rise of the New Left, and slogans such as "All power to the imagination" appealed as much to those who identified primarily with political radicalism as to those who identified primarily with counterculture trends. The difference lay in whether "imagination" was to be used mainly introspectively, to explore new inner worlds of spirituality, or externally, as a tool through which to transform political and social relations. Each group also celebrated the notion that new kinds of community, among like-minded individuals, could and should emerge.

There was also some link between frequent use of marijuana and experiments with psychedelic drugs such as LSD and various forms of activism. Similarly, there was considerable overlap between the participants in be-ins and the participants in antiwar marches, often the same individuals, people who admired revolutionaries such as Ché Guevara and despised figures representing the establishment, such as Presidents Lyndon Johnson and Richard Nixon. But it is possible to overstate just how closely linked the two strands of 1968 really were. It was possible to be an apolitical fan of psychedelic rock music or to be a straight-laced protester who never smoked a joint. Here, again, it is only by looking more closely at individual events and how 1968 played out in particular settings that we can get a clearer sense of actual degrees of convergence and divergence.

The third issue that needs to be examined has to do with internationalism. There was a sense at the time that upheavals occurring nearly simultaneously in different parts of the world were closely related. But were they really as interconnected as they were imagined to be? At the time, there seemed good reason for both proponents and opponents of revolution to think that protests happening in places as different from one another as Paris and Prague, Beijing and Berkeley, Milan and Mexico City were closely interconnected. The common valence in disparate settings of certain symbols—the Little Red Books of Mao, posters with the Christ-like image of Ché—and antiauthoritarian slogans gave a sense of coherence and relatedness to demonstrations by people who spoke different languages and lived under very different political systems. So, too, did the common concern with certain key international struggles, particularly the Vietnam War, which united youths who otherwise had little in common. Cognizant of these things, it was easy to imagine that revolution was sweeping the globe and to concentrate on figuring out how exactly to help or hinder its triumph.

Intense debates were held, among those who welcomed the idea of revolution, as to what exactly the New Society to come should be like. Some argued about whether it should be organized around Marxist-Leninist or libertarian socialist principles. There were debates as well about what the most important forms of oppression to uproot really were—in addition to class-based inequities and race-based ones, many stressed the need to take into account generational hierar-

PICTURE 9.5   Student demonstration, Prague, 1968. Alexander Dubcek began a policy of liberalization in Czechoslovakia in 1968. On August 21, Soviet troops and tanks responded by invading Prague. Students shared in popular resistance by participating in a general strike and by helping to publish underground newspapers, which they are holding here. (Photo courtesy of Hulton/Archive Photos)

chies, and a smaller group emphasized the links between all these forms of domination and sexism. Arguments were held as well over tactical issues. There were those who insisted that supporting guerrilla movements was the key to bringing the revolution to completion, whereas others saw mobilizing the new middle class in developed countries as crucial.

On the other side of the political fence, among those who feared that revolution would destroy much that was good about their societies, there was also debate about the hows and whys of the 1968 revolution in the making. It was criticized by some as part of a grand Communist conspiracy, emanating from Moscow and spread through secret agents on college campuses. Others argued that Dr. Spock's popular parenting books were responsible for the breakdown of systems of authority. After all, Dr. Spock was a prominent critic of U.S. involvement in Vietnam. Or perhaps it was the unresolved Oedipal complexes of youth around the globe (that is, based on the Freudian concept, the notion that youths subconsciously hated their fathers and were directing this rage at authority figures in general).

Less rarely debated then, but needing analysis now if we want to rescue the historical 1968 from that of myth, is whether the very notion of a global revolutionary tide was overstated. Local variations could be so great that the very idea of a single 1968 must be called into question. Once again, only a series of considerations of individual countries can help clarify the issue. Even so, we do not expect to provide answers to either/or questions—Did the Old and New Lefts have things in common? Were the political and countercultural movements linked? Was 1968's revolution a global one?—but rather to assess degrees of connectedness.

Keeping these three general sorts of questions in mind, it is time to look at some specific cases in detail. One dramatic place to begin is Mexico. In addition, though no one site is representative of 1968, this country did see everything from a social movement among workers and students resembling those of Italy and France to a massacre reminiscent in some ways of the one at the end of the Prague Spring. Issues of internationalism also come together in interesting ways in Mexico, since the unusually politicized Summer Olympics were held there in 1968.

Case Study One: Mexico in 1968

Late on the afternoon of October 2, 1968, between 5,000 and 10,000 people gathered in the Plaza of Three Cultures in Tlatelolco, Mexico City, built amongst pre-Hispanic ruins. The demonstrators, mostly students, but many families as well, had come together to protest the military occupation of the National University and police brutality against students and other dissidents. Residents of a thirteen-story building, the Chihuahua, observed the demonstration from their windows overlooking the plaza. One of the apartment dwellers remembers looking at his watch at 5:50 P.M. just as flares were shot into the middle of the plaza. At that same moment, he heard gunshots. The group around the speakers platform shouted through the microphones for the people not to panic because the police were trying to provoke them. But at the same time, rounds of machine-gun fire were coming from the top of the apartment building. He described the scene: "In the plaza, it looked like someone threw a drop of oil on water; the drop began to expand. The kids, the women, all of them started running to the edges forming a large circle. I saw someone drop, I suppose wounded, who then rolled towards the ruins." From the fourth floor of the Chihuahua, large numbers of people saw that plainclothesmen, wearing white gloves, were shooting both at the demonstrators and at the soldiers below. The soldiers then returned the fire and general chaos broke out. One demonstrator recalled:

There was a general stampede then, because just after the first shot, all hell broke loose and a hail of bullets started raining down on us from all directions. I saw several comrades fall to the ground, and I tried to make my way over to help them, but the gunfire got heavier and heavier and there was nothing I could do but run for cover. The soldiers had already blocked off (exits) and I saw that people were leaping down into the pre-Hispanic ruins; it was utter madness, because they were all landing one on top of the other; everyone was screaming and moaning—women with little babies in their arms, workers, students, railway men and little kids. The soldiers were advancing toward us with fixed bayonets like in the movies.

But it was no movie. Conservative estimates placed the figure of dead at more than 300. All were gunned down by fire from the soldiers and the plainclothesmen. The government of President Gustavo Díaz Ordaz initially claimed that there were only eight deaths and that the soldiers were responding to shots from student terrorists. After more than thirty years, some of the crucial facts are only now coming to light. It is now clear that the shooters with the white gloves were members of the elite Presidential Guard. They shot at both demonstrators and soldiers with the intention of provoking a massacre. But why would the government go to such incredible extremes to stop a demonstration? The answer to this question is twofold: The regime perceived the protest movement as a dangerous threat and was alarmed by the depth of its support, and authorities also feared that the protesters would disrupt the upcoming Olympic Games of October 1968.

To understand how the student movement could have seemed so threatening to the regime, we should know something about its origins and development. The student movement in Mexico resembled that of the United States in that, in large part, it derived from a profound generational rift in Mexican society. The parents of the generation of high school and college students in Mexico at that time looked similarly askance at their daughters in mini-skirts and their sons with long hair. Communication between the generations became exceedingly difficult as youths challenged the status quo in their homes and schools.

The student movement also resembled the Italian and French movements in that it attempted to support the workers movement. Indeed, its principal demands called for the release of union leaders who had been arrested in 1959. Those labor leaders had led the railroad workers' strikes of 1958–1959, the most important social movement in Mexico since the 1930s. The strike movement, heavily repressed by the government, had broken with and frontally challenged the regime-controlled labor movement, a key pillar of the one-party state. Since the regime had repressed the rank-and-file labor movement, only workers as individuals or in small groups were able to support the student movement. Indeed, many Mexicans of all walks of life sympathized with the main student demands that aimed to democratize the political system.

During the 1930s, the government of Lázaro Cárdenas, through an audacious program of land reform, workers' rights, and nationalization of the oil industry, earned a great deal of legitimacy for the Mexican state and for his political party, the Partido de la Revolución Institucional (PRI, Institutional Revolutionary Party), which became the dominant political force in the country. Over the next several decades, the PRI became increasingly conservative and undemocratic, and Mexico became, in effect, a one-party state. Those right-wing tendencies reached their apex under the six-year presidential term of Gustavo Díaz Ordaz (1964–1970).

The student movement's single-minded focus on the democratization of the regime—the abolition of its repressive laws and police-state apparatus—make it more similar to the Eastern European than to the Western European movements. Although the student activists had been mobilizing support for several years, real enthusiasm caught fire after an unexpected incident. When a street fight broke out between students from two rival schools, the police intervened with unexpected brutality. University and secondary-school students marched in protest against the repression, and then the police—in particular the *granaderos*, the riot police—violently attacked the demonstration, killing seven, injuring hundreds, and imprisoning hundreds more protesters. In response, 150,000 students—with support from many schoolteachers and college instructors—went on strike. Their list of demands included the disbandment of the granaderos; the release of all political prisoners, including the late-1950s railroad strike leaders and the recently arrested student activists; and the abrogation of undemocratic antisubversive laws.

The strike movement grew rapidly for two main reasons. First, the fundamental demand, summed up in the slogan *"Mexico, Libertad"* ("Mexico, Freedom") struck a deep chord in the populace and gained active adherents to the cause. Second, the university students dedicated much of their energy to direct organizing. Consider this testimony from a rank-and-file organizer:

You know what? The brigades were the very core of the movement. People went to the demonstrations because of the brigades. Why did everyone follow the students' lead? Because of the brigades. Before the demonstrations we handed out leaflets on the buses and trolleys, in the markets, in the big department stores, the workshops, on the corners where we held "lightning meetings" scattering to the four winds when we smelled a *granadero* coming.

By mid-August, the strike organizers were capable of bringing together some 250,000 people in a demonstration in the Zócalo, the main plaza in Mexico City. That enormous demonstration energized the student activists even more:

Groups of two to four hundred students were formed soon after. Teachers joined us and supported us . . . and this made us feel more confident and more responsible. This is how we organized in the schools: when the meetings ended, we gathered together in three classrooms and planned where each brigade would meet; we passed out boxes to collect money and the handbills the brigades needed. . . . At this point we were passing out six hundred thousand handbills a day and taking in one to two thousand pesos a day.

The student tactics worked effectively and the movement continued to grow. The national strike council, democratically elected, represented 128 schools on strike. The regime, which rarely had entered public dialogue with opposition sectors, proved unwilling to negotiate publicly with the movement leaders, and thus the strike carried on throughout September. The state was threatened by the prospect of having to respond to citizen voices and pressures and engage in dialogue with civil society.

With the Olympics looming, on September 18 the regime sent in tanks and troops to occupy the Universidad Nacional Autónoma, Mexico's most important university. The rector (president) of the university resigned in protest against the violation of university autonomy, and students and others vowed to continue to fight for their democratic demands. The massacre at the Plaza of Three Cultures (usually referred to by the district name, Tlatelolco) thus occurred in the context of three pressing factors: A military occupation in progress at the university; the governmental refusal to negotiate in good faith with the powerful strike movement; and the Olympic Games, with all the attendant international attention, which were scheduled to begin in just a few days. The government decided to stop the embarrassing and threatening strike movement in its tracks, whatever the cost.

The massacre did stop the movement, and the Olympic Games proceeded with little interruption. But the political cost to the regime was significant. First, the repression drove many activists underground. From 1968 until 1974, the regime had to battle various guerrilla groups made up of veterans from the 1968 movement. The regime eliminated (mostly assassinated) some 1,500 people suspected of supporting the guerrillas during that period. Yet the cycle of repression and armed resistance did produce some significant changes. On the one hand, the state realized that there were crucial limits to its power. The Mexican government recognized the need to respond to demands for social reforms and to begin, however slowly, with the democratic reforms of the state and party structure. Following the defeat of the guerrilla groups, the Left came to recognize that the armed overthrow of the regime was an illusion and that it had to win power by democratic means, by continuing to push citizens into participatory activities.

Twenty years later, in 1988, the crisis of the regime provoked by the 1968 movement and massacre became highly visible in the presidential elections. Cuauhtemhoc Cárdenas, the son of the popular president from the 1930s, broke with the PRI and ran as the head of a center-leftist coalition. By most accounts, he won the three-way race with over 40 percent of the vote. Although the regime engaged in fraud to win the elections for the official candidate, it showed just how delegitimized the party-state had become. The elections also showed that the democratic Left that in many Latin American countries was born in 1968 had come of age. In 1997, the democratic Left scored major gains in the congressional and municipal elections, by all accounts the first completely free and uncorrupted ones in Mexico's history.

Latin American Variations on the Mexican Pattern

The Mexican student movement was by no means the only important one in Latin America during the late 1960s. During that period, the continent was dominated by right-wing authoritarian regimes. Here, too, students were in the forefront of the struggles against such regimes. And as in Mexico, the educational system and the job market had some difficulty responding to the vast increases in the number of students seeking university training and entering the workforce. In Central America, for example, the number of university students leapt from fewer than 2,000 during the 1940s to roughly half a million in the 1970s.

In Guatemala, Nicaragua, and El Salvador there was little opportunity to engage in nonviolent campus protests. In Nicaragua, for example, the 1967 protests against the electoral fraud perpetrated by the Somoza regime (1936–1979) ended in violent repression, with the National Guard killing an estimated 200 protesters. By the 1970s, most Nicaraguan students who wanted an end to the Somoza regime opted to join the guerrilla movement, the Frente Sandinista de Liberación Nacional (FSLN, Sandinista National Liberation Front). Secondary-school and university students made up a substantial minority of Sandinista forces during the insurrections of 1978–1979 (an estimated one-third).

Similarly, students were in the forefront of social and political struggles against the military regime of El Salvador. When peaceful protest became impossible by the late 1970s, many students joined the guerrilla movement. A similar process took place in Guatemala, too, where university students and professors became targets of death squads during the 1960s and 1970s. Many then formed the leadership of the various guerrilla movements that emerged in the latter part of the 1970s.

In South America, as well, student protest was rampant. In 1966, the Venezuelan government sent in thousands of paratroopers to the Central University of Caracas to put down a strike. Ecuadoran students led a general strike that drove out the military regime that same year. Students also participated actively in protests and actions against the authoritarian regimes that came to rule Argentina, Brazil, and after 1973 Chile and Uruguay. In 1968, the Brazilian student movement became a violent opponent of the military regime. Most notably, students engaged in two weeks of rioting following the death of a protester in a demonstration. After that outburst, they combined political and university reform goals, fighting against government repression, against the military regime, and for greater federal aid to the universities. Following the arrest of 1,240 student activists later that year, the movement died down. Many students then opted to join or support an ill-fated urban guerrilla movement. Eventually, the generation of the 1960s came to play a major role in the democratization of Brazilian society. And students played a similar role in opposition to military rule in Argentina, with the notable difference that many more engaged in guerrilla activities that eventually brought about a brutal military response: "the dirty war" that involved the disappearance of some 30,000 leftists.

In summary, although students participated in many armed activities that led to disastrous consequences, they must also be credited with playing a major role in democratizing Latin American political and social structures. What factors pushed students into action on the Left? In many respects, the same issues that prompted student unrest around the world were prominent in Latin America. Massive urbanization was accompanied by a huge increase in the demand for higher education. Yet neither the economy nor the universities were prepared to absorb the new influx of students. Thus, there were many educated youth being exposed to critical thought who confronted societies that seemed thoroughly unjust politically, socially, and economically. At the same time, these societies offered them little prospect of personal economic success. The Vietnam War also outraged Latin American youth. But in Latin America, rather than merely protest the war, students and youth were more likely to follow Ché Guevara's cry, "Create two, three, many Vietnams." That willingness to engage in armed opposition to what they considered to be U.S. imperialism stemmed from the tendency of the U.S. government to actively support the ruling military regimes in the region. Those regimes in turn typically blocked peaceful avenues of protest. The combination of nationalist fervor and military repression proved too explosive, driving hundreds of thousands if not millions of students to the barricades and to the battlefields. Although armed struggle proved largely fruitless, the democratic impulse nurtured during the 1960s is quite alive in the early twenty-first century as veterans of those protests occupy important posts in governments—including the presidency of Brazil—and cultural establishments throughout the region.

Having surveyed the Latin American scene, it may be useful to look in similar detail at a European setting. Although the importance of France is unmistakable because of the famous takeover of the Sorbonne by student radicals, Italy is in some ways an even more interesting country to examine. There, the actions of workers and students came together in unusually close ways, making for an urban movement that was genuinely a cross-class upheaval.

Case Study Two: Italy in 1968

As in France, the merging of a student protest movement with an explosive workers movement made the Italian radical movement of the late 1960s extremely threatening to the ruling order. The Hot Autumn, as the labor protests of 1969 were called, involved the third largest strike wave in the history of Europe, and it seemed capable of significantly transforming Italian politics and society.

Italy also shared with France a political landscape that featured strong, but antagonistic, socialist and Communist parties. In France, the Communist Party had a powerful presence in a robust labor movement, but the Left had little representation in the presidential system dominated by conservative Charles de Gaulle. On the contrary, Italy, since 1963, had been governed by a center-leftist coalition (Christian Democrats and Socialists). The coalition attempted to isolate the Communist Party but, at the same time, created the framework for progressive political and social activity by both making it more difficult to repress labor on the Left and by placing structural reforms on the agenda. Yet, the labor movement, dominated by the Left, was relatively weak and incapable of organizing unskilled workers.

The student movement first emerged during the mid-1960s, provoked, as elsewhere, through a sense of outrage against the Vietnam War, but more specifically in protest against an extremely outmoded university system. The postwar economic boom had created a substantially larger middle class whose children attended universities in the 1960s. Without any significant expansion of the facilities or the faculty, roughly twice as many students attended college in 1968 as in 1951. One engineering student recalled:

> The courses were rigidly determined from above. . . . Books were rare, and when we could lay our hands on them they were disgusting, full of mistakes. Rich students could buy other books, but for us the only way was to take a tape-recorder into the classes. We recorded hours upon hours of lectures every day and then had to transcribe them at night.

Moreover, the university system had very limited offerings. In fact, it was in response to the lack of degree offerings in sociology that one of the first student protests erupted in 1966. Students also deeply resented the authoritarian extremes of the faculty. Typically, students were expected to digest lectures and repeat even the examples on the exams with no room at all for class discussion. Indeed, free speech became a key student demand.

Free speech and student control over the democratization of the university became main issues in student occupations throughout Italy in 1967. To cite one important example, in November 1967, students occupied the Humanities Faculty of the University of Turin in protest over the administration's decision to move the science faculty to a location removed from the other facilities. Yet the movement immediately questioned broader aspects of the university and society. One of the first manifestos explained to the larger community the students' resolve to "throw completely open to debate the didactic structure and the scientific and cultural content of university teaching."

Another leaflet argued: "What sense is there in a university based on terror, where we don't learn anything except to obey? It's easy to seize freedom for ourselves: just disobey!" A leader later reflected upon the movement's major achievement: "The real discovery of the occupation, which had started for rather banal reasons was that students *found* a *voice*, spoke out for the first time about authoritarianism and cultural emptiness at the university, began to live daily life differently" (italics in original). At Turin, as in other European universities, the movement organized a counter-university offering many courses that had not been taught before, ranging from the history of Vietnam to psychoanalysis. Notwithstanding the democratic procedures of the movement, including a university-wide vote in favor of the occupation, a large majority of the student body chose not to participate.

During the first months of 1968, the government sent in police to end the occupations in Turin and elsewhere. In Rome, street fights broke out between police and protesters, resulting in some 300 injured from both groups. In Turin, police arrested nearly 500 students. This repression broke the back of the student movement, and throughout the rest of 1968, it entered into decline—even though student movements in the rest of Europe and the United States were still expanding.

During this decline, however, the Italian movement unexpectedly entered into alliance with a burgeoning workers movement. Strike activity increased dramatically, from 2 million workers in 1967, to 5 million in 1968, to 7 million in 1969. Just as the postwar economic boom had increased educational opportunities for the middle class, through migration it had vastly increased economic possibilities, especially for workers from southern Italy, the most impoverished sector of the population. Northern cities doubled in size between 1950 and 1970, almost entirely through migration from the south. In 1967 alone, attracted by assembly-line jobs at the huge Fiat Mirafiori works (which had more than 50,000 workers), 60,000 southerners arrived in Turin. It was those new migrants who became allies of the student radicals. The first symptoms of that alliance developed in May 1968, when students supported the Turinese Fiat workers when they went on strike to demand a forty-hour week. In the fall of 1968, that alliance began to blossom when <u>students invited workers to an assembly</u>. One student activist recalled:

> And they came in hundreds! The hall was full, packed—it was amazing! Most of them were migrants. And they didn't only pack the hall, they took the microphone and spoke out about their living conditions. "We've had enough" they said. "We live in miserable conditions in the slums and the pensions, sometimes able only to rent a bed for the night, half a dozen in a room. And during the day our beds are rented to workers on the night shift. . . . We support what you're doing, you students are right." What could one say after that?

Students and migrant workers from the south were <u>divided by class and even by language</u>. Yet they were <u>united by a pervasive sense of powerlessness in society and a lack of representation.</u> Students felt that the university administration and faculty did not represent their interests, and the new workers who manned the assembly lines of northern industry felt that the unions and political parties did not represent theirs.

Throughout 1969, student radicals met with workers in a bar near the Mirafiori plant. Soon the bar couldn't hold the crowds, and the informal organization, now known as Lotta Continua (Continuous Struggle), began to meet in hospital space donated by sympathetic doctors. A flavor of that encounter is captured in the reminiscence of the student leader, Guido Viale:

> Here were those who had been silenced discovering themselves as themselves, as the protagonists of their own lives, expressing their needs in a new language. Their descriptions of the assembly line or their emigrant pasts—the language of shepherds mixed with an industrial idiom—were a thousand times more expressive than anything one could imagine.

Students who themselves were just emerging from their own kind of silence were particularly empathic listeners. This interaction produced, however briefly, a movement that threatened to resurrect the Marxist and libertarian dream of a revolutionary working class.

This new worker movement made several demands on the Fiat management, which in turn inspired other industrial workers throughout northern Italy. First, echoing the student influence and migrant needs, the workers demanded equal pay raises, rather than percentage increases. In a similar attempt to break down hierarchies favoring management, they demanded the reclassification of assembly-line workers as semi-skilled rather than unskilled. Finally, as the students did in the universities, they pushed for direct democracy on the shop floor.

Workers pursued these radical goals with a new repertoire of protests. Two particularly innovative forms involved the internal march and the "hiccup strike." Their marches, sometimes involving thousands of workers, moved from one section to another of the vast Mirafiori complex. The carefully orchestrated "hiccup" strikes meant stopping work for an hour in one shop, then in another. These stoppages blocked production effectively with a minimum of loss of pay to the workers. These new forms of protest not only placed pressure on management, they also escaped union control.

After two months of these new forms of labor protests, on July 3, 1969, the workers and their student supporters staged a public demonstration in support of their demands. The unions had called for a one-day strike to protest high rents, which enabled more workers to participate in the demonstration than would have been possible without union participation. Thousands of workers and students assembled at the plant gates. One student radical recalls that the chief of the *carabinieri* (the federal police force) started screaming at the gathering demonstrators:

"Sons of bitches go home and see who your sister is screwing." Immediately after that the carabinieri charged. The people fought back. Inhabitants threw flower pots and other objects from the roof tops. . . . A truck was used to make a barricade. . . . I felt like I was in the midst of a mass insurrection.

For one day, Turin did seem to be *"in mano ai proletari"* ("in proletarian hands"), as the slogan went, and pitched battles with the carabinieri spread throughout the neighborhoods near Mirafiori. Yet the uprising did not receive support elsewhere in Italy and remained an isolated incident.

The movement, however, continued to grow throughout the rest of the year. Although the Hot Autumn was one of the greatest strike movements in history, involving a large majority of Italy's industrial working class, it did not lead to the revolutionary outcome envisioned by student and worker radicals. Several factors influenced the reformist—rather than revolutionary—path taken by the movement. First, the reformist unions ended up gaining ground while the radical Left stagnated. The workers involved in the movement were never against the unions per se and thus worked with them. The unions, by coordinating on a national level, were able to achieve significant victories, including vast improvements in pension plans, salaries, and worker representation in production decisions through workers councils, a concept first developed in the 1919–1920 movement in Turin. Locally, unions were able to improve housing conditions for the migrants. These victories helped recruit workers to the unions, often ideologically committed to the reformist Communist and Socialist Parties. At the same time, the unions and not the radical Left were far more capable of protecting militant workers against management and state reprisals.

Second, the radical Left was weakened because it could only mobilize according to terms dictated by union contract negotiations (for example, in the fall of 1969). It did not have the independent strength to maintain an active movement on its own. Third, the radical Left suffered from severe factionalism, a common problem for leftist groups throughout the twentieth century. In this case, the main result was to alienate its base of support among the workers who had migrated from the south. Finally, the real locus for a revolutionary workers movement was only in the industrial north. The central and southern parts of the country remained largely under the control of the Church and the Christian Democratic Parties or the reformist Communist Party, which had no interest in pursuing revolutionary goals.

Conclusion

Having looked in an impressionistic fashion at many parts of the world and in detail at a couple of sites, we are now in a good position to return to the general questions raised above about 1968. Should the revolutionary struggles linked to that year be seen as part of a single process, and if so, should that process be treated as rupturing or merely adding new wrinkles to past patterns of radicalism?

Like so many historical questions, these are best answered by both yes and no. There were important similarities between many different urban upheavals, with youthful outrage, desire for liberation from structures of authority, and radical dogmas and orthodoxies alike providing a common denominator in many places. There were also, however, important differences that often added up to make one country's 1968 so unlike another's as to make the idea of a single movement seem misguided. When taken together, all the contrasts between the various groups—for example, the Red Guards in China calling out their loyalty to Mao in officially sanctioned rallies and the youths who died in Mexico City at the hands of the Mexican state—make it foolish to treat them as common participants in a single struggle. One thing that even these two disparate movements did have in common, though, was that each simultaneously built upon and broke with patterns of radicalism. So, here again, we find a yes and no answer to the second part of a major question.

One less ambiguous conclusion we can come to is that the late 1960s were a formative period for modern political cultures throughout the world. We can clearly see the indirect influence of that era in the United States, where recent presidential elections have seemed to be referendums on the cultural conflicts generated then. Many politicians on the Right rail constantly against the "excesses" and putative lack of patriotism of the 1960s generation, and those who were influenced by the counterculture and the New Left seem to bend over backwards to distance themselves from their former politics and lifestyles.

However, the political cauldron of radical politics in the 1960s also produced more direct influences on contemporary political culture, especially in three specific areas. The feminist movement emerged in 1968 as a protest against male behaviors within the radical Left. To cite one important example: the occupation of Columbia University by students protesting university involvement in the war machine and perceived racist practices toward Harlem residents. Female students organized within the occupation to demand an end to the division of labor whereby women had to do the cleaning and cooking and were denied meaningful participation in decisionmaking. Since then, the feminist movement has grown from what the media originally presented as a fringe group of "bra burners" into one of the most important forces in reshaping U.S. society, pushing it toward more egalitarian economic and social relations between men and women. The gay rights movement, similarly born during the late 1960s, has also grown significantly since then, becoming an important force in society.

Earth Day, April 22, 1969, marked the dawn of yet another social movement, environmentalism. As with the women's and gay rights movements, a relatively small effort portrayed as "fringe" and unimportant continued to grow steadily throughout the 1970s. By the 1990s, these movements had become mainstream political forces occupying central positions within the Democratic Party (though present, in diverse forms, in the Republican Party as well). The Seattle protests of 1999 reveal the power of the environmental movement and its connection to the legacy of antiauthoritarianism.

The New Left also had a lasting influence on progressive politics around the world in two major respects. First, leftist parties absorbed 1960s politics. For example, the democratization of the Italian Communist Party during the 1970s was attributable directly to its incorporation of workers who had participated in the rank-and-file labor movement of the late 1960s. In Latin America, the 1960s generation, as we saw, directly shaped the development of radical and guerrilla

PICTURE 9.6   Fall of the Berlin Wall, 1989. Activism among young people continued into the 1970s and 1980s over a wide range of issues. In 1989, the collapse of communism in the Soviet Union led to the fall of the Berlin Wall, which had divided the two Germanys for some thirty years. (Photo courtesy of Reuters/David Brauchli/Archive Photos)

movements in the late 1970s and 1980s. The forging of a revolutionary politics that struggled for independence from Soviet influence was the most clear ideological legacy of the 1960s in Latin America.

The antiauthoritarian, participatory democratic style of politics that emerged forcefully throughout the world during the 1960s also left varied legacies. In Eastern Europe, many of the leaders of the anti-Soviet revolutions of 1989 began as student activists inspired by the waves of antiauthoritarianism that swept over the 1960s generation. In Western Europe, the green parties that have become such powerful political forces, especially in Germany, owe their inspiration to the antiauthoritarian movements of the 1960s as well as to the environmentalist movement. In Latin America, in those countries where the Left is important, the New Left generation has been instrumental in democratizing the parties and organizations. Of course, the fall of communism and the end of the guerrilla movements also played an important role in this transformation. And the most important left-wing party in the hemisphere, the Partido dos Trabalhadores (Workers Party) of Brazil, which made its greatest political strides during the 1980s, developing an antihierarchical and anti-elitist style, was also very much influenced by the 1960s origins of many of its political activists.

The 1960s witnessed the emergence of a generation of young activists who believed that they could create a significantly better world, guided by an abhorrence of the Vietnam War and an ethos of egalitarianism and direct democracy. Yet despite the idealism, and often because of it, the generation of activists was guilty of political and cultural excesses. Those excesses ironically created the conditions for powerful right-wing movements and governments that embodied the antitheses of all the political values of the 1960s generation. Politically, the leftist excesses often led to right-wing regimes or administrations. Culturally, the counterculture had two contradictory and unintended results. On the one hand, the tremendous growth of consumerism can be traced to the glorification of individual (anti–mass society) tastes that emerged in that decade. On the other, particularly in the United States, the Christian Right developed, in large part out of revulsion against the cultural and social practices that characterized the counterculture. Despite those dramatic reverses, the 1960s generation also produced a political legacy that lives on today.

10

Islamic Fundamentalism in Critical Perspective

There are a good many people who think that the war between communism and the West is about to be replaced by a war between the West and Muslims.

William Pfaff,
"Help Algeria's Fundamentalists,"
The New Yorker
(January 28, 1991)

Whether it was the Ottoman attempt to thwart Christian nationalists or the Muslim attempt to gain independence from the West, Islam was fanatical because it ran counter to imperial interests. But it was the converse formulation that became the standard explanation of Muslim conduct: Islam was hostile to the West because it was fanatical. . . . Consequently, Muslims came to be seen as a uniformly emotional and sometimes illogical race that moved as one body and spoke with one voice.

James P. Piscatori,
Islam in a World of Nation States
(1986)

THE HOSTAGE CRISIS IN IRAN IN 1979, WHEN RADICAL ISLAMIC STUDENTS seized the U.S. embassy in Tehran, the continual U.S. engagement in Iraq since 1992, the World Trade Center bombing in New York in 1993, the attacks on U.S. embassies in Kenya and Tanzania in 1998, and the attacks of September 11, 2001, on the World Trade Center and the Pentagon have created a permanent place for Islamic fundamentalism in the American popular imagination. The term "Islamic fundamentalism" itself is a critical one as it carries an awesome burden of responsibility. As a catchphrase it has the entire emotional connotation that communism carried in the United States at the height of the Cold War. It is a blanket definition of the enemy so comprehensive that it seems to adequately explain such disparate things as the actions of the Saudi monarchy, Iranian student support for the clerical regime, and modest dress customs among Turkish women. In the United States of the 1990s, Islamic fundamentalism was overwhelmingly characterized in negative terms, as an antimodern phenomenon that sought to subvert liberty, equality, and freedom of expression through the use of violence and terror. The actions of fundamentalists were rarely explained in rational terms. Instead there is a tacit understanding that if one is an Islamic fundamentalist, one necessarily wants to bomb, kill, or maim. Violence appeared to be a legitimate instrument of Islam and often seemed inseparable from it.

These fears about a monolithic Islamic world bloodying the edges of Christian civilization are not new. In fact, they go back long before the Crusades to the Battle of Tours in 732, when Islam seemed poised to strike at the heart of Christendom. Charles Martel, the celebrated Frankish leader and the victor over the Arab Muslim armies at Tours and Poitiers, saved Europe from the peril of conversion to an alien faith. The Muslim armies withdrew to the south of the Pyrenees, but Spain remained under Muslim rule until 1492, when the emirate of Granada was defeated and destroyed. In the eleventh century, Islam girded itself for another conflict with Christian Europe, but this time under the leadership of the Ottoman Turks. The conflict was a protracted one, and it was not until 1683 that the Turkish armies were defeated at the walls of Vienna. As late as the seventeenth century, Algerian corsairs under Ottoman suzerainty were raiding the southern coasts of England and Ireland.

In addition to the Moors and the Turks, the Khanate of the Golden Horde, who converted to Islam in the thirteenth century, attacked Europe from the East. Although the Russians freed themselves from the Tartar yoke in 1480, the Tartars under Ottoman command continued to raid the villages of Russia, Ukraine, Lithuania, and Poland until the eighteenth century. For almost a thousand years Europe was under the constant threat not only of invasion but also of conversion and assimilation. After all, North Africa, Egypt, Syria, and even Iraq had been Christian longer than the Europeans yet had been incorporated into the Islamic empire. Clerics in medieval European universities learned Arabic and translated the Qur'an and other Islamic texts in an attempt to forestall the enemy in his triumphal march.

The images of Islam changed in the West as the power equation between the two civilizations was reconfigured. With the advent of mercantilism and then industrialization in Europe, the

Turkish threat was contained. Europeans themselves embarked on their process of world conquest and domination. In the intellectually sophisticated milieu of a Renaissance and post-Renaissance Europe, Islam was no longer feared as a rival religion. Instead, the Turk was seen as a barbaric invader, a conqueror, and often a trading partner as the Ottomans voraciously consumed weapons and slaves sold by Europeans. The Turkish sultan was also quite unjustly accused of being a capricious and autocratic ruler whose power was untrammeled by laws or interest groups. From the eighteenth century on, as European powers counterattacked, the lustful barbarian and menacing Turk was replaced by images that bespoke weakness and decadence.

In fact, to the post-Enlightenment European mind Islam no longer seemed a central category explaining the curiosities of Turkish or Middle Eastern societies. Indeed in the aftermath of World War I many Islamic societies embraced policies of modernization that were designed to displace the central role of religion, and Western scholars devoted their attention to the politics of secularism and to political and economic change. Although there have been numerous religious revival movements in Islamic societies throughout the twentieth century, these were considered unfortunate remnants of backwardness that Islamic states would outgrow in their march to modernity. In the last three decades, however, Islamic fundamentalist politics, culminating in the Iranian Revolution of 1979 under the leadership of the charismatic clerical leader of Iran, Ayatollah Khomeini, have again claimed the attention of the West. And following the international power vacuum that emerged in the aftermath of the collapse of the Soviet Union in 1991, Islamic political discourse in the 1990s offered a real alternative to the resounding international success of liberalism as a political philosophy. So much so that U.S. foreign policy expert Samuel Huntington predicted that the next significant world conflict would be between Western and Islamic civilizations.

Huntington's thesis was politically persuasive, even though nationalism, especially ethno-nationalism, provided a very powerful ideological rationale in world politics. It was the primary animating force in the wars in Bosnia, Chechnya, and Sri Lanka, and nationalist ideologies are responsible for the popularity of various political movements around the globe. Also fundamentalism is not the preserve of Islam alone. Christian fundamentalist movements were extremely powerful in the United States in the 1990s, and the same decade also witnessed the emergence of a paramilitary Hindu fundamentalist movement in India that appealed to the Indian diaspora in Europe and America.

In the Western media around 2000, Islam was often presented as monolithic and impregnable, its followers fanatical and deaf to reason, bent on world domination. George Kennan had argued in 1947 that the Soviet Union was an aggressively expansionist power that could only be stopped by the use of force; it appeared that the West had reached similar conclusions about the Islamic threat. The barbarism of Islam apparently justified policies of equal ferocity. In general, the Western press accorded favorable coverage to the U.S. bombings of supposed terrorist camps in Afghanistan, the imposition of harsh economic sanctions on Iraq, which have resulted in the deaths of thousands of children, and the continued oppression of Palestinians who were driven out of their homeland in 1948.

Often Western stereotypes of Islam have been reinforced by contemporary events in the Islamic world. Thus, after the Taliban came to power in Afghanistan following the collapse of the Soviet-backed regime, this party, composed of mountain villagers, banned women from public places and forbade them from attending educational institutions. Whereas events like this tend to form the staple of reporting on Islamic countries, positive developments are often ignored. For

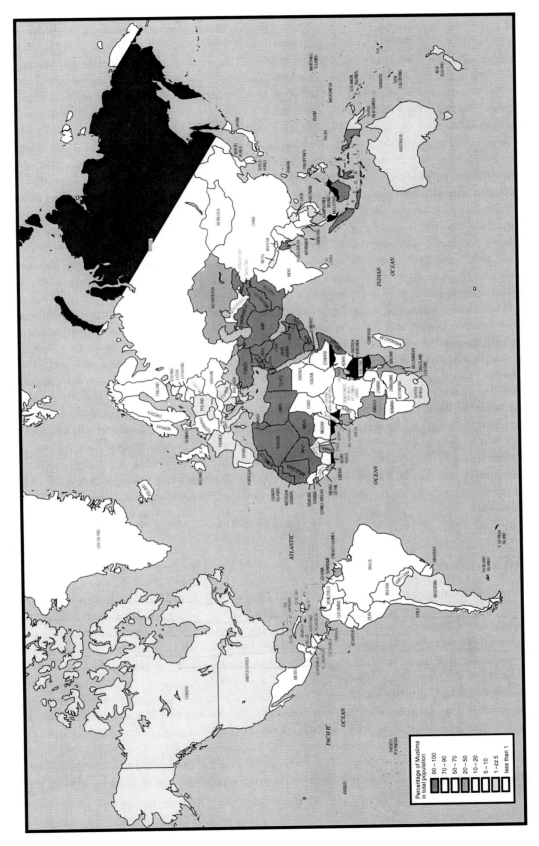

MAP 10.1   The Islamic World, 1990s

Percentage of Muslims
in total population

90-100
70-90
50-70
20-50
10-20
5-10
1-zz.5
less than 1

example, after the conservative clerical revolution in Iran in 1979, female literacy rates rose significantly, as did female participation in politics and public life. This fact was barely mentioned by the Western media. Islamic fundamentalists in different parts of the globe espouse radically different agendas and policies, and it is a mistake to see fundamentalism as an undifferentiated phenomenon.

In this chapter we do three things. First we look briefly at the various strands of thought that are embedded within modern Islamic fundamentalism, emphasizing how it offers a vision of a good life and a just society to millions around the world. Then we consider how Islam offered emerging nations a ready-made ideology of protest against the legacy of imperialism and colonial dependency. The virulent anti-Americanism that most fundamentalists exhibit is understandable only in this context of prolonged foreign rule. Finally, we examine the successes and failures of Islamic fundamentalist attempts to attain state power in Iran, Egypt, and Turkey. These three case studies have been especially chosen because they demonstrate that fundamentalism emerged as a specific response to Western processes and ideas such as colonialism and modernization and as a result cannot be understood without reference to them.

Whereas Iran was home to the first successful modern fundamentalist revolution in the twentieth century, in Egypt and Turkey fundamentalists have paid a terrible price for their criticism of the existing governments. Activists have suffered torture, imprisonment, and death. Of all the Islamic nations, Turkey is both geographically and culturally the closest to Europe, and under Ottoman rule Turkey had prolonged contact with Europe. In the beginning of the twentieth century, the Turkish state adopted a crash course in westernization that included attempts to secularize the society and remove the influence of Islam from public life. As a result, Turkish fundamentalists fought a rearguard action to preserve their indigenous culture and religion. Similarly, when Egypt was brought under the direct colonial rule of the British in the last quarter of the nineteenth century, Islamic fundamentalists structured their movement primarily as an anticolonial struggle. Finally, Khomeini's popularity in Iran was due in part to the fact that the people felt he was a strong leader who would end the continual Western interference in internal Iranian politics.

Fundamentalism as Ideology

There can be no fundamentalism without belief in God: The idea of God as an omnipotent abstract identity is at the core of the three major world religions—Judaism, Christianity, and Islam. Each has at its center the notion of God as the creator of the universe, a Supreme Being who has expressed His will through prophets such as Moses, Jesus, and Muhammad, and the codification of revelations in a book, be it the Torah, the Gospels, or the Qur'an. Adherence to the scripture both defines the community of believers and excludes outsiders. Scripture functions as the standard against which all other knowledge is to be tested. Adherence to biblical principles, for example, explains why certain evangelical Christians reject the theory of evolution and insist that creationism should form a part of the core curriculum in the public schools. It should be remembered that our modern separation of divinely revealed versus empirically verifiable knowledge is of fairly recent origin. It was only during the Enlightenment that certain Western philosophers tried to establish the primacy of science as the only true form of knowledge, dis-

PICTURE 10.1
The Great Mosque, Mecca.
The holy city of Mecca
draws hundreds of
thousands of pilgrims from
around the world each year.
Extended five-fold under
the Saudi dynasty, the Great
Mosque includes the Ka'aba
and other holy shrines.
(Photo courtesy of the
Information Service of the
Royal Embassy of Saudi
Arabia, Washington, D.C.)

counting religion as a prerational belief system that, instead of explaining the totality of human existence, itself required analysis as a social phenomenon.

The religious community, whether Christian, Muslim, or Jewish, is constituted through participation in mandated rituals and members who advocate that public behavior should be regulated by religious values and norms. But, despite the deep theological similarities among Judaism, Christianity, and Islam, believers have not only emphasized differences from each other but have sought to carve out exclusive groups within their own original traditions. The word "fundamentalism" itself is of Christian origin. It originated in the United States in the early part of the twentieth century when ultraconservative Protestant Christians drew up a list of fundamentals, that is, beliefs separating true believers from the rest of the Christians. Christian fundamentalists tend to take the Bible literally and believe in its inerrancy.

In the case of Islam, the Qur'an is the Holy Scripture. All Muslims believe that it is the revealed word of Allah (God) to the Prophet Muhammad (570–632 A.D.). The Qur'an states that God had previously communicated His word through other prophets sacred to Jews and Christians, but over time, their messages had been distorted. So Muhammad was sent to warn humankind of their wrong ways and provide them with the definitive version of God's word. For Muslims the first sign of identity is the shared importance of the Qur'an in the community. But if Muslims agree on the authenticity of the Qur'an, they differ with regard to its meaning. Learned jurists, the clergy, and even the *umma,* the community of living Muslims, may variously interpret the Qur'an, and over time the exegetical literature has grown enormously with different schools of interpretation.

All Muslims believe in the five pillars of Islam, which include the belief in one God, Allah, and the Prophet Muhammad. Muslims are also supposed to pray five times a day, fast during the holy month of Ramadan, donate a fixed percentage of their income to the poor, and during their lifetime make the pilgrimage to Mecca. According to Islam these communal rituals emphasize the individual's equality before God as well as submission to His will. Also important are the six arti-

PICTURE 10.2
The Ahmadiyya Mosque in Wa, Ghana, 1997. The Ahmadiyya movement is not fundamentalist but reformist. Such movements are transnational and communicate through the latest technology. The leader of this movement is in Pakistan but the headquarters of the Ahmadiyya are located in London. From there, messages and information are broadcast to quite remote areas, such as the town of Wa in northwestern Ghana. (Photo courtesy of John Hanson)

PICTURE 10.3
Satellite dish at the Ahmadiyya Mosque in Wa. Ghana receives the educational and religious programs of Muslim Tele-Vision, the broadcast service of the Ahmadiyya movement. (Photo courtesy of John Hanson)

cles of faith specifying belief in Allah, His messengers, Holy books, angels, a Day of Judgment, and destiny. Since adherence to all these is an integral part of the faith it is impossible to distinguish between Islamic groups on this basis.

As with all major religions, however, Islam has had a rich and varied expression since its development 1,400 years ago. The dominant order within the Muslim community is the Sunni Muslim sect. Influenced primarily by literate teachers, Sunnis emphasize the divine transcendence of God; Sufis, in contrast, stress the importance of mystical closeness with the divine presence. The Sunnis underscore the importance of the *hadith,* or the collected sayings and traditions of the Prophet, as well as the Qur'an as the basis of a just legal society. However, even within the Sunnis there are four major schools of legal thought. The Sunnis believe that the *umma,* or the Islamic community, should choose its leaders; the Shia, the other main branch of Islam, contends that Muhammad designated Ali, his son-in-law, as successor, and moreover, that God has designated an *imam,* or sinless leader, for each period of history. In addition to the major division in Islam, the one between the Shia and the Sunni sects, there are many other groups that claim to be Muslim, such as the Aga Khanis, or the Bahai, but these are shunned by the dominant orders because they recognize the sanctity of prophets other than Muhammad.

Islamic Fundamentalism and State Power

Islamic fundamentalists have rarely played an important role in state politics, and the bulk of them are distinctive in that they have little access to centers of political power. Their lack of state privilege, however, has allowed them to employ a critical stance against the state and has garnered them popular support. Thus, for instance, in Saudi Arabia a hereditary monarchy is outwardly devout in its guardianship of the holy places in Mecca and Medina and imposes a certain Islamic pattern on daily life. Yet the ruling family is interested in maintaining the status quo and is deeply opposed to fundamentalists who use religion to challenge their royal hold on power. On November 20, 1979, when a group of religious militants seized the Grand Mosque at Mecca, the government felt little compunction in sending in the troops to restore order and executing the ringleaders, Juhaymna ibn Muhammad al-Utayba and Muhammad ibn Abdullah al-Qahtami. This group repudiated the House of Saud for its impiety and chastised the Saudi *ulama* (clergy) for participating in government-sponsored modernization. Thus, in Pakistan, a country that was created especially for Muslims by the Indian-based Muslim League led by Muhammad Ali Jinnah, the military leadership completely marginalized the Jamat-e-islami, the fundamentalist group that advocated the transformation of Pakistan from a nation-state to the vanguard of an international Islamic revolution. Syria and Iraq fell under socialist dictatorships during the 1960s and 1970s. And in Egypt, Gemal Abdel Nasser, the military hero who sponsored an Arab coalition against Israel in the name of his Islamic coreligionists, persecuted Muslim fundamentalists at home with terrifying zeal.

What distinguishes Islamic fundamentalists from their Christian counterparts is the fact that they are not theologians but social thinkers and activists who are less interested in interpreting the Qur'an than in attaining political power and creating an Islamic state on the basis of the *Shari'a*. The Shari'a is a corpus of juridical decisions based on the Qur'an, the hadith, and the judgments of Muslim jurists. Islamic fundamentalists across the globe, despite their disagreements on goals and means, share this commitment to activism. The rise of contemporary Islamic fundamentalism is usually dated from the 1967 war between the Palestinians and the Israelis. In that war, a coalition of Arab states, led by Egyptian President Gemal Abdel Nasser, failed to recapture Palestine and wound up losing more territory to Israel. This disaster shook faith in the nationalist Arab regimes and the policies espoused by them. The death of Nasser a few years later reversed the faith in Western liberalism, and Islamic fundamentalism emerged as an ideological response to the failure of both modernization and socialism as a means to solve the problems of the Muslim world. In fact, modernization had created new problems: urbanization, overcrowding, and the breakdown of the social infrastructure in cities such as Cairo under the impact of rising populations. Even the spread of formal education, the central tenet of modernization, had created expectations of good jobs that the governments were unable to meet.

It was a phenomenon that grew in the 1960s and 1970s, when rising expectations among the petite bourgeoisie in the cities of Cairo, Karachi, and Tehran went unfulfilled because of slow economic development. Moreover, the so-called nationalist-liberal regimes, composed primarily of corrupt parties of propertied classes, did little to address the basic concerns of the people such as access to clean water, food, housing, and employment. In this context, Islam furnished a ready-made ideology of social justice based on the redistribution of wealth, immediate action to redress moral degeneration, and a virulent condemnation of the ruling class. Moreover, Islamic fundamentalism had the advantage that, unlike imported Western solutions, it was homegrown and seemed authentic to peoples who had long been colonized by foreign powers and felt that they were losing their cultural identity and sense of self under rampant westernization.

In the 1970s, some leaders of Muslim countries, such as Anwar Sadat in Egypt and Zia ul-Haq in Pakistan, tried to harness the fundamentalist movements to shore up their legitimacy in a frantic bid to stave off democratic reforms. Finally, the United States and its Western allies, caught in the escalating Cold War, encouraged the growth of Islamic groups in order to counter the proliferation of Communist influences in the Middle East. The defection of Egypt to the Soviet camp under Nasser had been a severe blow to U.S. influence in the region. In order to deal with the Soviet invasion of Afghanistan, U.S. policymakers encouraged the formation of militant Islamic guerrilla bands such as the Mujahideen and lavishly provided them with funds and weapons.

According to Mahmud A. Faksh, a contemporary Western scholar, unlike Christianity, which has given the West its concept of the separation of church and state (dating from Christ's injunction to render unto Caesar what is Caesar's and unto God what is God's), Islam was initially conceived in terms of fusion with state power. Under successive caliphates, theocratic governments ruled by the successors of Muhammad (632–1258), however, the religious character of the original Islamic state was eroded. By the eleventh century most Middle Eastern societies were built around separate political and religious institutions. The experience of colonialism further weakened Islamic influence, as it had to compete with modern ideologies such as nationalism, secularism, modernization, and socialism, all of which were innately antireligious. The ulama, the Shari'a, and the *madrasa,* or parochial schools, were eclipsed by state bureaucracies, civil servants, European law codes, and Western educational establishments that emphasized the primacy of science. Under the flamboyant rule of the Shah of Iran, there was little room for religion in national political life; Islam was relegated to a set of ossified rituals presided over by state clerics. It was this marginalization of Islam from mainstream politics and daily life that the fundamentalists resented. They believed that a decadent West acting through the collaboration of local elites who had abandoned their native heritage was arbitrarily imposing the modern secular order on them with its values of materialism, secularism, and cultural degeneration.

Islamic fundamentalism in the late twentieth century thus emerged as an ideology of the marginalized and the dispossessed. Fundamentalists are rarely at the center of power, and they are reviled and oppressed by Muslim and non-Muslim governments alike (although there are a few notable exceptions, such as Sudan and Iran). It is important to remember that in most fundamentalist thought, the individual is subordinate both to God and to the godly community, and Islam is no different in mandating this than any other monotheistic religion. Islamic ideals privilege the collective over the individual and locate sovereignty in the Shari'a rather than in the people. The pursuit of life, liberty, and happiness of the individual is secondary to the establishment of an Islamic state, and it is only within the contours of an Islamic society that Muslims can lead a meaningful life. Moreover, as noted earlier, there is no place for the separation of church and state in Islamic political thought. Thus state and religion are indelibly fused, as the purpose of the state is the fulfillment of divine imperatives. Unlike the Western contract, which proposes a theory of state framed in terms of the fundamental separation of civil society and the state, the Islamic fundamentalist goal is to institutionalize a state that would live up to the mandates of religion.

The challenges that fundamentalists pose to the governments of the Middle East are threefold. First, they insist that the Islamic state should embody the kingdom of God on earth and therefore should be ruled by a pious male Muslim well-versed in the Qur'an and the hadith. In Islamic

PICTURE 10.4
Member of the Saudi Arabian royal family. The royal family of Saudi Arabia continues to occupy the principal offices of state. Crown Prince Abdullah Iban Abdul Aziz is deputy prime minister and commander of the National Guard. (Photo courtesy of the Information Service of the Royal Embassy of Saudi Arabia, Washington, D.C.)

thought, sovereignty is located not in the people or in the person of the ruler; rather, sovereignty is divine and rests only in God. Indeed, according to Abul Ala Maududi, an important Pakistani ideologue who formulated many of the categories of contemporary Islamic fundamentalism, all legitimate forms of authority stem from God alone, and human control of one by another negates God's commands. Therefore, for a member of the ruling family of al-Saud in Saudi Arabia to claim hereditary monarchical power is anti-Islamic.

The second issue concerns who should then rule as God's legitimate representative. According to the Ayatollah Khomeini, the ruler of fundamentalist Iran, only the clerics who are jurist-theologians can rule. Khomeini based his opposition to the Shah's regime on the support of the Muslim clergy and urged them to take control of the state. Under his guidance, the Shiite clerics of Iran were turned into revolutionary soldiers, and Shiism evolved from a religion of quietism and resignation into an activist ideology that fused religion with power and politics. But this clerical monopoly of power was very unusual in the Islamic context as theocracy in Islam means the rule of God, not of a priestly class.

According to Maududi, leadership should rest in the hands of a tightly knit group of believers who are dedicated to realizing the Islamic transformation of society. He believed that the Muslims in the twentieth century were living through the epoch of *jahiliyya* (godlessness and confusion) and that it was the duty of true Muslims to withdraw from this society and establish a righteous one. But Maududi emphasized persuasion and propaganda rather than the use of militant tactics to create a Muslim order. The Egyptian thinker and activist Sayyid Qutb, like Maududi, emphasized the radical equality of all true believers. Finally, all Muslim fundamentalists agree that human beings should not be guided by independent choices and private codes of conduct; instead, legislation deriving from the Shari'a should regulate both public and private behavior.

Across the political spectrum, fundamentalists are unanimous in their condemnation of westernization or any modernization that entails secularism, consumerism, and loss of morality. They denounce the decadence brought about by the Western-dominated media. Part of their antipathy to Western culture stems from the legacy of colonial domination and the continued interference of Western countries in the internal politics of the region. Western interest in the Middle East began in the early part of the century when oil was discovered in the region. In the 1930s, Texaco and Standard Oil Company, operating through Aramco, were granted concessions to exploit the petroleum deposits of Saudi Arabia. In the latter half of the twentieth century, the United States depended on Saudi Arabia for about 20 percent of its oil imports, and in return the Middle East invested a bulk of its petrodollars in the U.S. economy. The West had also been a source of military equipment. The Shah of Iran spent $36 billion on military purchases between 1959 and 1978. Finally, during the Cold War, as the United States and the USSR competed for world domination they established extensive patron-client relations throughout the region. Thus, Syria and Nasserite Egypt were pro-USSR, but Saudi Arabia and Iraq in the 1980s were primarily Western client states.

But if fundamentalists are critical of the West, they are even more critical of Muslim reformers and rulers bent on a disguised course of secularization by coupling modernity with Islam. Such rulers, such as the Shah of Iran or Nasser in Egypt, are seen as most threatening to the Muslim order because they have sought to import foreign ideologies of socialism, liberalism, and nationalism instead of stressing Islamic ideals of communal solidarity (umma) and social welfare.

Muslim fundamentalists reject the secular nation-state, arguing that Islam is inherently antinational. At its inception in Asia in the seventh century, Islam sought to eradicate the preexisting ideas of the particularities of race, ethnicity, language, tribe, and nation and create a universal Muslim community based on religious identification. The first Muslim commonwealth—in Medina under Muhammad in 622–632 A.D.—tried to unite separate tribes under the umbrella of faith. These goals have inspired Islam over the centuries, and today fundamentalists advocate that one's national identity should not subsume the individual's primary religious identity. A true Muslim state ought to deny race and nationality as a means of social organization. Maududi thus opposed the creation of Pakistan in the 1940s as he felt that national self-determination for India's Muslims meant a negation of Islam. He wrote that Islamic nationalism was a contradiction in terms, as the religion had no geographical boundaries. He enjoined his followers to start an Islamic transformation of the world rather than focus on the national aspirations of Pakistan. Following the partition of the Indian subcontinent in 1947, Maududi moved from India to Pakistan and continued to propagate his conception of an Islamic order, but he failed to achieve any electoral success under successive military and civilian governments. And Khomeini tried to present himself as an Islamic leader to Muslims throughout the world, not just to Iranians.

Fundamentalists have tried to solve the problems of the Muslim world by reactivating the concept of *jihad,* the duty to wage holy war against the internal and external enemies of Islam. Political struggle, rebellion, and direct action are the favored means of struggle to revitalize a passive Muslim people. Faith is tied to action, and there is no separation between doctrine and practice in Islam. Power has to be wrested from the governments of the wicked and transferred to the believers. Indeed, it is the obligation of all Muslims to struggle against tyranny and unlawful governments and establish the kingdom of God on earth. Unlike Western revolutionaries, who focused on building the utopia of the future, Islamic fundamentalists look to the past, desiring to revive the community of the Prophet and his caliphs in the seventh century. They see Islamic history as a degeneration from the ideal, not a triumphal march of progress and reason. Fundamentalists believe that only an Islamic government can maintain a virtuous and civilized life and that Islam is self-sufficient, autarkic, and offers a message for all humankind. There are numerous voices within the fundamentalist community, including the Hizbullah in Lebanon, the National Islamic Front in Sudan, the Islamic Salvation Front in Algeria, Hamas in Gaza and the West Bank, and the Wahhabi fundamentalists in Saudi Arabia. Since these organizations are bent on acquiring state power as the basis of founding a just society, they have come into conflict with government authorities.

Islamic fundamentalism in its general outlines has thus far been the subject of this chapter. In the rest of the chapter, we trace the evolution of Islamic politics in three societies: Turkey, Egypt, and Iran. In Turkey, the most Europeanized of the countries in the Middle East, despite the attempts of the ruling military elite to separate religion and politics Islam has resurfaced in recent decades. In Egypt, the state tried to harness fundamentalism for its own ends, failed, and wound up following a path of intense repression. Iran is one of the very few countries where the fundamentalists actually came to power, but their hold seemed tenuous at the century's end.

Turkey and Modernization

Turkey today is a small, truncated shadow of the glorious Ottoman Empire that terrorized Europe for centuries. Medieval Christians were convinced that the sultan-caliph and his armed hoards were the instruments of the devil, and the failure of the Crusades and the fall of Constantinople seemed to confirm their worst foreboding about this highly organized empire. In the seventeenth century the Turks were finally expelled from Hungary, but the Ottoman Empire continued to make its presence felt in international politics until the late nineteenth century because it ruled not only over what we call the modern Middle East but over North Africa and parts of southeastern Europe as well (see Map 2.1). The majority of the subjects were Muslims, but Jews and Armenian Christians could practice their religion and be exempt from military service by paying a special tax. The Ottoman sultan dispensed legitimate justice through the Shari'a, and the judges were paid and appointed by him. He organized the annual pilgrimages to the holy places in Mecca, and the Ottoman army and navy protected the empire after a certain fashion.

During this time the empire could neither hold its own against the modern military power of Europe nor prevent its growing commercial penetration. Russia had established itself on the Black Sea, and England had become the paramount naval power in the Mediterranean. Whereas Russia wanted to absorb the Balkan territories of the Ottoman Empire and gain access to the Mediterranean, the British wanted to shore it up as a bulwark against Russia and protect their own imperial interests in the Mediterranean, the Middle East, and India. For the rest of the century the empire was the site of struggle among various European powers, and its complete partition was prevented only by European rivalries.

As could be expected, there were loud and protracted internal debates within the empire on how to restore political integrity and effectiveness to the regime. Some advocated a return to the ways of Suleiman the Magnificent of the 1500s; others, more prosaically, called for the thorough modernization of state and society along European lines. In the nineteenth century the tradition-alists were crippled by certain key reforms carried out by those in favor of modernization. The absorption of many *waqf* endowments (charitable institutions), courts, and schools into the new state-controlled ministries weakened the ulama, the mouthpiece of conservatism. The abolition of the janissary corps (the Sultan's personal army) and the partial dismantling of feudal tenures helped propel Turkey on the path of modernization.

After 1908 the concept of Ottoman reform was overtaken by the promotion of a specifically Turkish nationalism. For the Muslim it had been historically difficult to disentangle nationalism from Islam, but now a Turkish cultural consciousness began to take shape, aided by European students of Turkish language and culture and local literary clubs. New, Western-style law codes and law courts were introduced, and finally, the new family law of 1917. By adopting a European system of personal law, Turkey made a complete break with the Muslim past.

World War I greatly assisted the progress of Turkish nationalism by stripping the empire of all its non-Muslim and non-Turkish populations. Having entered the war on the side of Germany and Austria-Hungary, the Ottoman Empire suffered the retribution of total dismember-ment. As a result of military campaigns, by 1918 the French and British militaries controlled Istanbul, the central government, and the Arab provinces of the Ottoman Empire. Britain and France agreed to divide the Middle East into a number of new states (see Map 7.1). Lebanon and Syria fell into the French sphere of influence, but Britain was allotted Transjordan, Pales-tine, and Iraq and charged with the special obligation of facilitating the creation of a "Jewish national home" in Palestine. In addition, Armenia was given independence, Kurdistan achieved the status of an autonomous province, and the former empire in the Balkans was divided into independent states.

After the war, under the leadership of Kemal Mustafa Pasha, an Ottoman army officer, the Ot-toman Empire evolved into a national, secular state. Alone in the Muslim Middle East, it emerged as an independent country led by an elite composed of army officers, bureaucrats, politicians, lawyers, and intellectuals. Pasha believed that Islam was unable to provide a basis for national co-hesion in Turkey or raise the social consciousness of the people. He wanted the Turks to find in science and Western civilization the source of all true knowledge and behavior and strove to lib-erate individuals from the traditions of a community-based life.

In 1923 Pasha was named president of the republic for life. Head of the government and of the Republican People's Party, he was called the Ataturk, or the father of the Turks. His regime was highly intolerant of opposition. The clergy were excluded from political power, as the regime was committed to modernization of society and the economy. The state reduced taxes on agricultural products and invested heavily in transport and communications. Key sectors of the economy were nationalized and factories built. At the same time as peasants were being turned into work-ers, Kemal Pasha's government sought to wean them from Islam and reform daily life along per-ceived Western and secular ways. The Caliphate was abolished in 1924. The clergy and religious endowments were put under state control. In 1925 mystical Sufi orders were declared illegal and disbanded. All education was put on a secular footing. The Shari'a court system was abolished and replaced by civil law borrowing heavily from the French and Swiss legal systems. Moreover, the practice of polygamy sanctioned by the Qur'an was abolished. A husband's right to unilater-ally divorce his wife was radically restricted as divorce proceedings came under the purview of the courts. Women now had the right to vote and be elected to public office and were given greater access to education and the professions.

PICTURE 10.5   Turkish girls marching in formation, 1949. With the proclamation of a modern republic and the coming to power of Mustafa Kemal (Ataturk), the Turkish government embarked on a modernization campaign that included the emancipation of women. Turkish girls participated in education programs. (Photo from the Library of Congress)

With the secularization of law and education, the ulama lost all their power and authority. All religious seminaries were closed down, and the use of religious titles prohibited. The state forbade the wearing of ecclesiastical clothing outside the mosque. Part of the reason for the all-out assault on the religious establishment was that Sufi brotherhoods, such as the Naqshbandi and the Tijanniyyah, had joined the opposition movement in an attempt to curtail the program of secularization. Arabic pan-Islamism was replaced by a Turkish Islam. To this end the Qur'an was translated into Turkish, and even the muezzin now called the faithful to prayer in Turkish.

The radical replacement of the Arabic script with the Latin alphabet meant that the younger generation of Turks lost access to the religious and literary heritage of Islam. Even the Ottoman fez and turban, traditional headgear, were replaced by Western hats; any opposition to this symbol of modernity was ruthlessly crushed. Islam did not disappear, however; it merely went underground. Many educated Turks who embraced the values of nationalism and modernization remained practicing Muslims, and Islam remained the basis for morality and culture.

In the post–World War II era, when the Democratic Party came to power, restrictions on religious practice were loosened and there was a public resurgence of faith and observance. Thus religious instruction in schools was reintroduced. New mosques were built and old ones restored, and mosque attendance soared. The pent-up religious feelings of the Turkish people were manifested in pilgrimages to Mecca and attendance at Qur'an courses and Sufi gatherings. The government did not intend that Islamic organizations be used to advance a political critique of the regime, however, so despite the liberalization, religious practices continued to be strictly monitored by the state. Thus, when in 1948 the newly created Nation Party began advocating a greater role for Islam in the political arena, the government became alarmed. The party was outlawed in 1953 for attempting to subvert the republic. Similarly, the Sunni National Order Party, founded under the auspices of Professor Necmeddin Erbakan in 1970, was outlawed for antisecular activities. But it reappeared as the National Salvation Party in 1972 and was critical of Turkey's relentless Europeanization, calling for a return to a more authentic Islamic past.

The decade of the 1970s was a violent one in Turkey; the state was headed toward anarchy owing to the battles between Sunni and Shiite groups and terrorist acts by both radical secularists and religious fundamentalists. In 1980 the army took control, hoping to revive Kemal Pasha's brand of secularism. Erbakan was arrested and imprisoned for using Islam for political purposes. Civilian rule was restored in 1983, and parliamentary democracy was reintroduced in a restricted form. The military retained its preeminent position and supported Islamic measures in an attempt to counterbalance the power of the Left, which was seen as the major threat—so much so that compulsory religious education was reintroduced at the primary schools. At the same time, the ban on Islamic parties continued. Erbakan resurfaced in 1994–1995 as head of the Welfare Party, which took on the character of a nationwide mass political movement. Since 80 percent of the Turkish population favored secular parties, whether on the Right or Left, the Welfare Party had a way to go before capturing political power. Nevertheless, its resilience and popularity in the face of continual political persecution was impressive. The ideology of the Welfare Party, and of Erbakan himself, is worth examining briefly. The party advocated an unabashed synthesis of Islam and Turkish nationalism. It stressed that the Turks had lost their cultural heritage in a mad bid to westernize, resulting in a loss of power and influence in world politics. The party was opposed to pornography, prostitution, alcohol, and birth control and advocated more modest dress for women. It mainly emphasized a larger role for religious instruction in schools to counteract lawlessness and violence among the youth. The party also called for a closer unity between Turkey and other Islamic nations rather than integration into the European community.

On the economic side its program was surprisingly secular. Although wanting to abolish the lending of money for interest, the party advocated rapid industrialization. It promoted the interests of the poor through the abolition of taxation on minimum wages, through the creation of an unemployment insurance program, and through workers' participation in management and profit-sharing. It did not support nationalization of private enterprise or land reform, but instead it advocated measures that were favored by merchants, artisans, and small businessmen. With the decline of social democratic politics on the Left and the emphasis on state-sponsored welfare policies for the poor, Islam seemed to be the only ideology that spoke in the voice of the rural and urban poor. Morally, Islam favored social equity, and the Welfare Party sponsored certain highly visible antipoverty measures. At the same time Islam also appealed to the newly emerging educated businessmen and professionals who were not integrated into the traditional elite and used Islam to fashion a cultural identity. Therefore, Islam as an ideology transcended class barriers and challenged the viability of both left- and right-wing parties.

In Western terms, Turkey was considered a success story and served as an alternative model to Islamic republics such as Iran. Because of its commitment to a secular nationhood and integration into global capitalism, Turkish politics seemed modern in the context of the Middle East. In the 1980s and 1990s, however, there was an erosion of commitment to Western secular values and a rise in Islamic activism among the most modern sectors of the population, such as university students and upwardly mobile professionals. Among sections of the merchants and craftsmen in provincial towns and countryside there had always been considerable opposition to the modernizing policies of the elites and their attempts to destroy the Islamic identity of the citizens, but this new opposition among modern sectors was surprising.

Some scholars, such as Ziya Onis, have advanced economic reasons for the rise of Islamic activism in Turkey. Formerly, Turkey followed a path of development that favored domestic industry and instituted welfare policies that tried to redistribute wealth and aimed at egalitarianism. However, in the 1980s the military regime moved to encourage Turkish participation in the international market. The benefits of global capitalism accrued to a limited sector of the population only. Those who were disaffected were the Muslim petite bourgeoisie and owners of small independent businesses threatened with extinction. They had long espoused Islam and rejected the ideology of Turkish nationalism and modernization as an alien imposition engineered by the West. In addition to sectors of the marginalized and dispossessed in provincial towns and metropolitan centers, there were now not only university students and upwardly mobile young professionals but also many disillusioned ex-Marxist intellectuals converting to Islam. Thus, rather than being a conservative movement, the Islamic movement in Turkey had a fairly radical orientation and growing support from those who yearned for a return to a more authentic culture.

Iran: The Failure of Fundamentalism

Iran is the only country in the world where the Shiite Muslims constitute a majority. Iran's population is roughly 55 percent Shiite. In speaking of Shia Islam in Iran the reference is specifically to the Twelver or Imami sect to which all but a small minority of Shiites belong. The adherents of Twelver Shiism believe in a line of twelve pure and sinless imams, or spiritual leaders, the first of whom was Muhammad's cousin and son in-law, Ali. The last imam has been hidden from view since the ninth century and is expected to return as a messiah near the end of time. After Muhammad died in 632, the question of succession became a problematic one. Some Muslims, known as Shia, or the faction of Ali, proposed that Ali should become the imam of the Islamic community because Muhammad had designated him as his successor. But the Sunnis believed that the elders of the Islamic community should choose the successor from among the men of the Prophet's tribe, Quraysh.

The majority of the elders of the Islamic community in Medina chose three other men as caliphs, or successors of the Prophet, before finally selecting Ali in 656. The Shia view the ten years of the Prophet's rule, and the four and a half years of Ali's rule, as the Golden Age of Islam. Everything else is seen as a long process of corruption and decay. The Shia believe that the imams of Islam have to be pure and sinless; therefore the idea that the Islamic community should elect its leaders is emphatically rejected in traditional Shia doctrine. Apart from Ali, his two sons Hasan and Husayn, both of whom were killed by Ali's political rivals, are important figures in Shiite history. Ayatollah Khomeini used the example of their martyrdom and resistance to oppression and tyranny to stir the Iranian people against the Shah. Furthermore, there is a belief in Shiism that the *al-mahdi,* or messiah, will return before the end of time to end inequity and oppression and usher in justice and happiness. Finally, the ulama play a much greater role among the Shia than among the Sunni.

In the past 200 years the struggle between the state and the clergy was one of the principal features of Iranian politics. In the late eighteenth century, a powerful tribal coalition, the Qajars, extended their rule over the whole of Iran without ever consolidating their power. Owing to a weak political center, not only were local tribal chiefs virtually autonomous but the power of the religious establishment was greatly enhanced. As interpreters of the religious law, the Shiite clergy claimed that they had the right to exercise independent judgment and to make new interpretations in religious matters. They also claimed that the pious and spiritual leaders, in the absence of the imam, were the true leaders of the Muslim community. The ulama were constantly in touch with the common people as they administered justice, charities, and trust funds. The rites of birth, death, and marriage all required the presence of the ulama. Furthermore, they actively solicited donations from the artisan and merchant class thus furthering their penetration of society. They also guarded the Shia shrines and held passion plays that mourned the martyrdom of Husayn. As a result, the ulama formed a national and fairly autonomous body capable of mobilizing the masses.

During the nineteenth and twentieth centuries, the Iranian Empire lost considerable territory to the expanding imperialism of Britain and Russia. In 1907 an Anglo-Russian agreement formally divided the country into two spheres of influence, the Russians in the north and the British in the south with a buffer zone in between. Although the Qajar rulers were nominally independent, in reality they assumed the status of a colony. Qajar attempts to strengthen and modernize the state failed as they lacked the revenues, the will, and the support of more than a minority portion of the population such as westernized court officials and journalists. The tribal leaders resented military centralization in the Qajar quest for modernity, and the ulama prevented attempts at secularization. The ulama became the leading opponents of foreign influence. By the late nineteenth century, the clergy, along with the merchants, liberal intellectuals, and officers, opposed granting lucrative commercial deals to imperial Western powers. Some of the liberal ulama also opposed Qajar despotism on political grounds and advocated constitutionalism, not anticipating the possible conflicts that could arise between Muslim and secular law in a constitutional monarchy.

From 1911 to 1925 Iran experienced near anarchy as the experiments with constitutionalism led to further foreign penetration. Iran became a virtual protectorate of the British, but following the Bolshevik Revolution, the Soviet Union concluded a treaty very favorable to the Iranians, forgave debts, and withdrew from occupied territory. This change gave Iran the confidence to renounce British control. In 1925, an officer named Reza Khan Pahlavi made himself the Shah, or ruler, of Iran. For the first time in history, Iran was ruled by a strong, centralized state committed to an ambitious program of economic modernization and cultural westernization.

Bolstered by the army, the new regime overcame the opposition of religious, merchant, and tribal groups. The Pahlavi dynasty created a secular system of education and extended government supervision of religious schools. The Ministry of Education also founded a new curriculum for theological schools. In 1928 new law codes were promulgated that replaced the Shari'a, and the ulama were effectively barred from presiding over the new civil courts. In the post–World War II phase of Iranian history, the United States replaced the British and the Soviets as the major patron. Part of the Western interest in the Middle East was due to the growing importance of its oil resources to the world economy. In the 1930s the oil industry in Iraq and Iran was run by international companies with the help of British, French, Dutch, and American investors and engineers. After 1945, as the exploration of oil began in earnest in Kuwait and Saudi Arabia, Western influence and interest in the region became even stronger.

PICTURE 10.6
Tankers loading crude oil at Ras Tanura on the Arabian Gulf. The existence of vast oil reserves has ensured continuing intervention in the region by the United States and other industrialized nations, thus perpetuating the imperial presence as far as many Arab radicals are concerned. (Photo courtesy of the Information Service of the Royal Embassy of Saudi Arabia, Washington D.C.)

There were many in Iran who resented Western control of their economy and society. When in 1953 Muhammad Mossadeq, the prime minister of Iran, called for the nationalization of the Anglo-Iranian Oil Company, he was supported by a powerful coalition that included small merchants, clerics, and members of the Iranian middle class. His policies constituted a major challenge to Western interests and he was soon ousted as the U.S. Central Intelligence Agency orchestrated the Shah's return to power. As British power waned, it was the Americans who reorganized the Iranian army and the dreaded secret police, the Savak. In 1963 the Shah contracted a $200 million loan with the United States for military equipment. With U.S. help, Muhammad Reza Shah ruled as a virtual dictator helped by a small elite of officers, administrators, landowners, wealthy merchants, and religious leaders. There was widespread opposition to these dictatorial policies; they created much hardship among the peasantry and lower middle classes. Slowly the opposition began to coalesce around the ulama, merchants, artisans, and leftist intellectuals, but repression intensified as well. The ulama opposed the extension of suffrage to women and resented Iran's close ties with the United States and Israel. As wealthy landowners, the ulama also resented purported land reforms that the Shah wanted to institute.

In the political disturbances of the 1960s Ayatollah Ruhollah Khomeini of Qum, a Shiite leader, emerged as a prominent critic of the Shah's regime. In his sermons he criticized the Shah for his autocratic and corrupt politics and his subservience to the West. The Shah cracked down on the growing antigovernment demonstrations, and Khomeini was arrested several times and finally exiled. Khomeini, in exile first in Iraq and then in France, waged a relentless campaign against westernization, Western imperialism, and the state of Israel—all things the Shah's government supported. In his book, *The Islamic Government* (1979), he called upon the clergy to rebel against the regime. He declared the monarchy an un-Islamic institution and called for the creation of a new society in which the ulama would take a direct and active role.

The Pahlavi regime responded by intimidating, arresting, torturing, and assassinating key members of the opposition. A narrow elite surrounding the Shah spent the profits from sales of oil; meanwhile, inflation was undermining the standard of living for merchants, artisans, and industrial workers. Millions of Iranian peasants invaded the cities, creating a permanent class of underemployed and unemployed workers. In 1979, the Shah, unable to quell the rising disturbances and protests of workers, peasants, students, professionals, and women, fled the country. A new regime came to power, led by the Ayatollah Khomeini. He prevailed at the head of the ulama, supported strongly by student activists and town and village militias. With this base, the Islamic leaders quickly eliminated their liberal, nationalist, and radical Marxist allies in the name of Islam.

The ease with which the ulama prevailed was also due to the fragmentation and confusion of the left-liberal forces. Part of it was due to the anti-Western feeling that the Shah's modernizing policies had evoked. Moreover, after the revolution, there was no national organization to manage the affairs of the state. Once the Iranian army announced its neutrality, Khomeini encouraged raids on its barracks and headquarters. The summary trial and execution of the Shah's generals and the appointment of clerics as military prosecutors were designed to bring about the disintegration of the armed forces. Khomeini also disarmed the Islamic guerrilla groups and rejected proposals from them to form a People's Revolutionary Army.

There was no national organization capable of managing the revolution, but the fundamentalists took the lead in forming hundreds of local committees across the nation that performed tasks such as caring for the wounded and aiding striking workers. By the end of 1987 every neighborhood mosque had become a revolutionary headquarters as well as a place of worship. The centralization of this network under Khomeini's leadership was a significant aspect in the fundamentalists' ability to establish a theocratic state. From the very beginning Khomeini reserved for himself the right to appoint the imams who led the Friday prayers, religious judges, and revolutionary prosecutors. These clerics, along with the religious guards, became the wielders of real power in the provinces after he came to power. The Islamic Republican Party of Ayatollah Khomeini was able to become a national mass organization because it could rely on the network of imams to represent its interests and policies throughout the nation during Friday prayers. By 1981 the ulama-controlled Islamic Republican Party dominated the executive, judicial, and legislative arms of the government as well as the media and the educational institutions.

The Iranian Revolution had tremendous impact on the Muslim world and the Third World in general. It was seen as a blow at Western imperialism, especially because the Shah, with his CIA-trained army and intelligence services, had failed to stem the tide of popular rebellion. It also showed the durability of indigenous traditions and the failure of modernizing policies. Finally, it meant a victory in the name of Islam for non-Western countries. Within revolutionary Iran, members of the Left underestimated the power of Khomeini and his forces. They believed that while Khomeini was necessary to win the war against the Shah, his forces could be made redundant in the aftermath. But since Khomeini was able to neutralize them pretty effectively, after 1983 most of the left-wing parties became disillusioned with the Iranian Revolution.

Although Western observers were afraid that Khomeini's brand of militant Islam would spread, Saddam Hussein of Iraq, with the support of moderate Arab states, the United States, and Europe, invaded Iran in 1980. During the protracted Iran-Iraq War (1980–1988), the Shiite population in Iraq never rallied to the side of their coreligionists across the border. Although in Lebanon and Pakistan, countries with Shiite minorities, there was a growing adherence to Iranian interpretations of religious and hierarchical aspects of Shiism, the governments of these countries cracked down very successfully on pockets of Shiite militancy. Moreover, the Shia population in Pakistan did not want an Islamic state as this would mean a society dominated by that country's Sunni majority, further marginalizing the Shia. Similarly, in Turkey, the local branch of the Shia, called the Alawi, backed Ataturk's secularism because it granted them freedoms they had never enjoyed under the Sunni Caliphate. Among the Sunni Muslim countries, the radical students in Malaysia,

Tunisia, Nigeria, and Indonesia wholeheartedly endorsed Khomeini and incorporated his message into their program. Still, there is no unified Islamic world movement that includes Iran. And the Iran-Iraq War increased solidarity with Iraq among the Arabs rather than inspiring any sympathy for the Persian-speaking Iranians. At the end of the century, it was becoming apparent that Khomeini's brand of Islamic politics was losing its popularity as Iranian students, the mainstay of the revolution, began protesting poor economic conditions and the lack of freedom of expression. There is a growing demand for liberal reform within the country, and it will be an interesting phenomenon to see whether Iranian fundamentalists can adapt themselves to the demands of global economic integration as the Welfare Party seems to have done in Turkey.

Egypt: Reform and Repression

Egypt in the nineteenth century was a province of the Ottoman Empire. But during the second half of that century, Turkish rule was replaced by that of the British, and indeed, imperialism furnished the context in which fundamentalism emerged as a major force in Egyptian politics. British troops occupied Egypt in 1882 to suppress a nationalist revolt and stayed in control until the 1950s when they were forced to leave by Gamal Abdel Nasser. Although some leading scholars, such as Jamal al-Din al-Afghani, Muhammad Abduh, and Rashid Rida, had advocated militant anti-imperialism and resistance to Western domination by returning to a purely Islamic state and society, it was under Hasan al-Banna (1906–1949) that Islamic fundamentalism emerged as a cohesive political movement in Egpyt. Al-Banna, a schoolteacher, founded al-Ikhwan al-Muslimun (the Muslim Brotherhood) in 1928. The organization had two basic goals: the liberation of the fatherland from foreign domination and the creation of an Islamic state that would function according to the rules of Islam.

A charismatic leader, al-Banna personally supervised the organization and kept power in his own hands. He was guided to adopt his work by an impending sense of crisis that he felt was menacing the Islamic world. Part of this was the crisis of colonialism, but he was also very critical of the Islamic clergy and felt that they had allied themselves with the colonialists to further their worldly ambitions. Al-Banna founded the Ikhwan with a view to propagating true Islam, establishing a just Islamic society, and spreading Islamic knowledge throughout the world. In his view there were five reasons for the disintegration of the Islamic state. These were religious and political differences among Muslims, self-indulgence and luxury, the transfer of authority to non-Arabs, indifference to the applied sciences, and the Muslim infatuation with authority. Unlike other Muslim reformers, al-Banna, as a result of his Sufi training, could speak in the idiom of the people. His organization took on the character of a mass movement that appealed to the poor and emerging middle class of Egypt. Its following was drawn mainly from students, teachers, civil servants, shopkeepers, small businessmen, and laborers, who felt lost in the secular urban environment and found the Ikhwan's message comforting and appealing.

Al-Banna called for a life of faith and piety and urged his followers to familiarize themselves with the Islamic message and build an Islamic society. He advocated that, after a period of preparation, the Ikhwan would overthrow the state, but he was suitably vague about the timing and tried to restrain his more radical followers. By the late 1940s, the Brotherhood had become the most powerful Islamic movement in the world, with half a million members and a complex network of schools, businesses, and clinics in Egypt alone, plus an important branch in Syria. Its re-

PICTURE 10.7
Gamal Abdel Nasser
(1918–1970). A hero of
Arab nationalism, Colonel
Nasser is seen in 1965 on
a visit to Belgrade, where
he was welcomed by
President Tito of
Yugoslavia, a fellow
member of the Non-
Aligned Movement.
(Photo from the Library
of Congress)

lentless anti-imperialism, expressed in many ways including large anti-British demonstrations, brought its followers into conflict with the monarchy.

After Israel declared itself an independent state in 1948, the Ikhwan blamed the government for the loss of Palestine and led the way in acts of sabotage and destabilization of Egypt. It also sent members to fight in Palestine. It was disbanded in 1948 because of its growing strength and the terrorist activities of its secret apparatus. A Muslim Brother acting without al-Banna's consent assassinated Prime Minister Nuqrashi, who had presided over the dissolution of the organization. Although al-Banna worked furiously to ease the tension and head off the impending collision between the government and the Brotherhood, a government agent killed him in revenge. By 1949 there were about 4,000 Brothers in Egyptian prison camps.

When Nasser and his group of supporters, the Free Officers, overthrew the Egyptian monarchy in 1952, the Brothers were delighted. Nasser shared their goal of ending the foreign domination of Egypt. But Nasser was also committed to the gradual secularization of Egypt through the promotion of a pan-Arab nationalism and Arab socialism. In 1956 Nasser nationalized the Suez Canal and defeated the combined colonial forces of the French and British who had hitherto controlled the profits accruing from it. This made him an Arab hero abroad, but at home he had to cope with the challenge of the Muslim Brotherhood, which was opposed to his policies of secularism. Although Nasser could not ignore the Islamic aspects of Egypt's heritage, it was never his intention to create a strictly Islamic state. In response to the Brothers' attempts to assassinate him, he had several members hanged and over a thousand arrested.

The Brotherhood was a crippled organization at this point. In 1966, Sayyid Qutb, the leader of the Brotherhood who had advocated the forceful overthrow of corrupt rulers, was hanged, and many others were imprisoned. Nasser proceeded with a course of secularization to eliminate the influence of the ulama. The Shari'a courts were incorporated into the civil legal system, and the network of Friday preachers at the mosque came under the centralized control of the state. Nasser retained his luster in Arab eyes despite the failure of his quasi-socialist economy and his ruthless suppression of all opposition. He formed alliances with Jordan and Syria with the goal of eliminating Israel from the map. In 1967, when he closed Aqaba, Israel's only access to the Red Sea, Israel responded with a surprise attack on Egypt and its allies. The Arab forces were routed in six days, and Israel proceeded to occupy the Gaza Strip, the Sinai Peninsula, and the West Bank of the Jordan River. In the wake of the humiliating defeat at the hands of the Israelis in the Six-Day War in 1967, a wave of religious fervor gripped Arab society. When Anwar Sadat became president after Nasser's death in 1970, he decided to free the Brothers and use Islam to counteract Nasserite socialism and the popularity of the Marxists on the university campuses. The alliance between the Brotherhood and the government was strained, however, after the signing of the Egypt-Israeli Treaty of 1979 that restored the Sinai Peninsula to Egypt. The Brothers, along with other leftists, felt that Sadat had betrayed the Palestinians by entering into negotiations with the Israelis without exacting a promise of autonomy for the Palestinians from them.

The Islamic revolution in Iran under Khomeini only emboldened the radicals in Egypt. Opposition to Sadat grew even as he tried to depict himself as a believer. On October 6, 1981, soldiers who were members of the Munazzamat al-Jihad (The Holy War Organization) assassinated Sadat. Serious fighting ensued in certain localities, and Hosni Mubarak, the successor, responded with a wave of arrests and tightened security. At the end of the 1990s there were two currents within the Islamic fundamentalist movement in Egypt. The first represents a continuation of the Brotherhood and emphasizes the gradual islamization of society through education, demonstration, electioneering, and lobbying. The other comprises radical branches of the Brotherhood that want to overthrow the secular state and advocate the use of violence as a means to achieve that end. These radical groups are especially popular among the young and the newly urbanized members of the lower middle class. Led by the Islamic Jama'a and the Jihad organizations, militants have killed or attempted to assassinate government officials, members of the Coptic Christian minority, secular writers, and foreign tourists. The attacks on foreigners were motivated by the desire to aggravate the economic crisis in Egypt by cutting off tourist dollars and stifling foreign investment. The fundamentalists assumed that the greater the economic hardships, the more people would be attracted to their cause. At the same time, to their credit, Islamic fundamentalists in neighborhoods under their control have set up social welfare services and economic support services that contrast richly with the near absence or terrible inefficiency of government institutions.

The tale of Islamic fundamentalism ends on a frightening note of repression. Since 1992 the Jihad movement has been systematically destroyed by intense police action. Entire neighborhoods were placed under surveillance, and random and arbitrary arrests helped deplete the ranks of activists. Military courts were set up to execute a swift death penalty on the accused. Protests by human rights organizations both in Egypt and abroad were dismissed, and Egypt led a campaign against both Sudan and Iran, accusing them of fomenting Islamic radicalism worldwide. The Egyptian state even co-opted the clergy to denounce militants as ignorant or even un-Islamic and heretical. At the same time, the government has followed a policy of gradual islamization of society. This program included an amendment of the Personal Status Law of 1979 that gave women more liberal rights in matters of divorce, child custody, and alimony. It is harder today for Egyptian women to initiate divorce or gain custody. Moreover, the activities of liberal secularists came under scrutiny, and literature, scholarship, and the arts were increasingly censored for espousing liberal values. Some books of the Nobel Laureate Naguib Mahfouz were even banned for their anti-Islamic content. Liberals have no choice but to cooperate with the state against Islamic militants, as they fear their ascendancy even more than a repressive state.

PICTURE 10.8
Intifada youth, 1989. In the 1980s and 1990s popular resistance *(intifada)* among Palestinians to Israeli occupation reached new heights. Rock-throwing youth who engaged Israeli police and soldiers in the streets were filmed by international media, thus drawing attention to the plight of Palestinians. (Reprinted from *Human Rights for the Palestinians* [New York: UN Special Commission to Investigate Israeli Practices, 1989], courtesy of the United Nations/Neal Cassidy)

Toward a Conclusion

Although Islamic fundamentalism has fostered the growth of an Islamic cultural consciousness worldwide, especially among the young and the poor, it has been less successful in initiating political change or even attaining political power. The rhetoric remains and the regimes that have survived the fundamentalist challenge seem better entrenched than ever. After the Gulf War against Iraq in 1990, the United States is even more powerful in the Gulf region than it was formerly. Today Sudan is the only Arab country that has a fundamentalist regime, the National Islamic Front, but it is clearly dictatorial—the product of an army coup, not a popular Islamic revolution—despite staged elections. The regime has waged a genocidal war against the black African Christian Sudanese population in the south. Its dismal human rights record and the impoverishment of the people hardly make it appealing as a prototype. As the first Sunni Muslim fundamentalist state, it is an aberration, not the norm.

As both Iran and Sudan have demonstrated, the fundamentalist premise of Islamic self-sufficiency and intolerance of ethnic and religious minorities runs completely contrary to the modern conditions of economic interdependence, diffusion of an international popular culture, and growing multiculturalism. Islamic movements have not been able to transcend the bounds of the modern nation-state in their quest for the universal Muslim community. The Shari'a restrictions on usury and the fundamentalist scorn for materialism and wealth are rarely upheld in Muslim countries, and very few of them have secluded women from all public activities. In Palestine the culture of militancy and martyrdom is gradually giving way to an emphasis on nation building as Yasser Arafat, the leader, despite challenges by the Hamas militants, continues his process of peace-building with Israel.

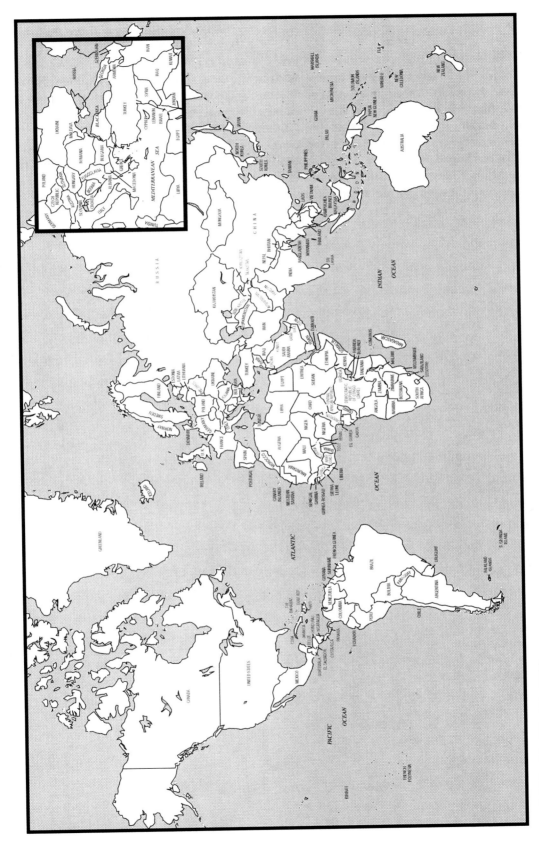

MAP 10.2   The World in 2000

While Middle Eastern states seemed to have contained the phenomenon of fundamentalism, they face the larger challenges of promoting economic development, ensuring a certain level of material comfort to their burgeoning populations, and advancing political democratization of their highly autocratic regimes. Most fundamentalist movements have a pronounced socialist bent and aim at the creation of a more equitable society that provides equal opportunities for all their members rather than privileges for a small elite. This striving for equality and democracy often gets buried in the media rhetoric about a violent and war-mongering Islam, but the fundamentalists' ability to articulate universal and modern aspirations explains their appeal as well as legitimizes their critique of state and international policies.

Part Three

CENTURY-LONG THEMES

11

Feminism in the Modern World

I wonder why there should be any distinction between males and females in a fight for the cause of the country's freedom? If our brothers can join a fight for the cause of the motherland why can't the sisters? Instances are not rare that the Rajput ladies of hallowed memory fought bravely in the battlefields and did not hesitate to kill their country's enemies. The pages of history are replete with high admiration for the historic exploits of these distinguished ladies. Then why should we, the modern Indian women, be deprived of joining this noble fight to redeem our country from foreign domination? If sisters can stand side by side with their brothers in a Satyagraha movement, why are they not so entitled in a revolutionary movement?

Pritalata Wadedar, Indian nationalist revolutionary,
cited in Tirtha Mandel, *Women Revolutionaries of Bengal,*
1915–1939 (1991)

We are economically oppressed: in jobs we do full work for half pay, in the home we do unpaid work full time. We are commercially exploited by advertisements, television and the press; legally we often have only the status of children. We are brought up to feel inadequate, educated to narrower horizons than men. This is our specific oppression as women. It is as women that we are, therefore, organizing.

Marsha Rowe (ed.),
Spare Rib Reader
(1982)

DESPITE THE IMPRESSIVE AMOUNT OF RESEARCH DONE IN THE PAST three decades on women's history, professional historians have had a difficult time integrating the results into the master narrative found in textbooks. Several questions arise: Should women's history be studied as a separate subject? Do women live their lives outside the ambit of revolutions and counterrevolutions? Have women's lives, in different parts of the world, been fundamentally the same, or did, say, Russian women experience modernity in the twentieth century in a different way from Arab women? Historians have grappled with such questions in various ways. In this chapter, we look at women's roles in historical perspective and attempt to provide a foundation for answering them.

Societies have purveyed the obvious biological differences between men and women into sex-specific codes of social behavior. Historical and anthropological research has shown that gendered behavior is less a product of biology and much more a result of imposed social norms and values. Thus female identities and idealizations about women are differently constructed in separate parts of the globe and are greatly influenced by the economy, religion, politics, and culture. Gendered agendas, both progressive and reactionary, have been present in political movements that seek change, regardless of their political orientation. This agenda may be explicitly stated, as in the legal reforms of the Russian Revolution of 1917, which proclaimed the equality of men and women, or coded, as in the Bill of Rights of the French Revolution, which only defended the inalienable civil liberties of men while failing to mention women at all. From Khomeini's Iran to Nazi Germany to Maoist China, revolutionary manifestos have encoded strong notions about sexual relations and mores, the form and size of the ideal family, and the appropriate sociopolitical roles that men and women should play.

In this chapter we analyze how the ideologies of liberalism, socialism, and anticolonial nationalism decisively shaped women's movements around the globe. To that end we have selected five case studies to trace the history of feminism in the modern world: the impact of the French Revolution in giving voice to the movement, its development during the Industrial Revolution, its modification by the theories and practices of communism in the twentieth century, and its permutations in the non-European contexts of Asia and Islam. Most historians would agree that modern politics began with the French Revolution. Liberalism ushered in radical ideas about the rights and freedoms of the individual, and feminists used these philosophical arguments to claim equality for themselves. During that time the status of women became explicitly politicized. Liberalism, however, only postulated political equality; it was socialism that offered a material critique of social inequality. Marxists believed that women's oppression could be traced to the creation of private property and hoped that its abolition would lead to a change in the status of women. After the Russian Revolution of 1917, the Communists had a chance to institute their program for women. But as it turned out, the program itself was revised several times and the results were quite different from what its originators had intended. Building on the chapters on colonialism and the independence struggle, we move to a discussion of women in the colonial context, showing how the British invasion of India led to dramatic changes in the way Indians perceived women. Women used this confrontation as well as Western ideologies to carve out new identities and roles. Finally, the discussion of feminism in the colonial context continues with an analysis of the roots and impact of Arab feminism, perhaps one of the least understood phenomena in the Western world.

The French Revolution and the Birth of Modern Western Feminism

The uprising in the American colonies in the late eighteenth century ushered in the modern age of revolutions. Across the Atlantic, an equally exciting time of experimentation in politics was in progress. The revolutionary era discredited absolute monarchy and brought in new forms of constitutional government and parliamentary rule. Although France was the center of activity, the revolutionary principles found their way to the rest of Europe. The salons of aristocratic French women as well as street-side assemblies of market women rang with passionate discussions on the inequities governing women's lives.

Women played a dynamic role in the events on both sides of the Atlantic. In America, as the demand for consensual government erupted into a full-fledged war of independence against the British, women were important in extending the scope of the struggle. Some, like Mercy Otis Warren, wrote propaganda pamphlets intended to deflate the pretensions of monarchy; others, like Abigail Adams, wife of John Adams, argued that the rights to liberty and freedom should be extended to women as well as men. Women boycotted British goods, appeared in anti-British demonstrations, and competently managed the home front while the men were away. There was a dramatic upsurge in popular revolutionary consciousness among both men and women that helped in the easy transition from monarchism to republicanism.

In France the revolutionary events affected all classes. As the economic situation deteriorated, between 8,000 and 10,000 market women marched to Versailles in October 1789 to bring the king back to Paris to solve the grain crisis. The sight of surging crowds of militant women was enough to scare many an honest male liberal, and events such as these were later cited in order to justify the exclusion of women from the political sphere. Middle-class women, meanwhile, were much impressed by the ideals of liberty, equality, and fraternity and believed that they too would be beneficiaries under the new political order. They took it for granted that henceforth they would be accorded political and civil equality and would be allowed rights to property and education. Women made it a point to attend political assemblies and meetings, and they vociferously participated in the discussions on the affairs of the state. Some even formed their own clubs and advocated reforms that would broaden the role of women in politics. Other women petitioned for reform of the institution of marriage. They argued against patriarchal authority, under which women were coerced into marriages that served to promote the fortunes of the family. Instead, a new sensibility arose in Europe, one that promoted the ideas of a companionate marriage based on love and freedom. As civil marriages were instituted, the Catholic Church lost control over a significant social institution. Divorce, too, became easier to obtain and socially more acceptable.

In 1791, Olympe de Gouges, the daughter of a French butcher, produced a remarkable document called the *Declaration of the Rights of Women*. In this treatise, de Gouges, a moderately successful playwright, argued that since in the natural world animals did not subjugate the females,

PICTURE 11.1
Mary Wollstonecraft (1759–1797). A writer and feminist, Mary Wollstonecraft participated fully in the English Enlightenment and published several radical works. This portrait was painted just before she died in 1797 after giving birth to her daughter. (Courtesy of the National Portrait Gallery, London)

human society had no reason to perpetuate the inferior status by enslaving women. She demanded that society award women and men equal rights to property and taxation, allow women to participate in public administration, and ensure that they receive equal treatment under the law. In 1793 she was unjustly accused of being a royalist and condemned to death. As revolutionary ideas spread across the continent, women's associations were formed in Germany and Italy. Across the Channel, Mary Wollstonecraft published her famous tract, *A Vindication of the Rights of Woman,* in 1792. In it she argued that women should be trained and educated so that they could be exemplary mothers, citizens, and professionals.

Not all agreed with the tenets of the revolution. Women employed in the luxury trades of silk making and millinery were hit particularly hard by the decline of the aristocracy. Others were appalled by the atheism of the revolutionaries and the attacks on the Church. Peasant women protected priests who refused to take the oath to the new French Republic. As the revolution wore on, women's roles and voices became increasingly conspicuous and contentious. Members of the leftist Society of Revolutionary Republican Women called for government control on prices of essential items, but women traders were passionately opposed to price controls. Clad in the Phrygian cap, these revolutionary women forced people on the street to prominently display the revolutionary colors of red, white, and blue. Soon the activities of these clubs were deemed injurious to public order and safety, and the French Parliament argued that women's political role should be limited to educating good citizens in the spirit and virtues of republicanism. Women's clubs were banned and women were prevented from attending public meetings and assembling in groups.

This growing conservatism reached a crescendo under Napoleon. Under the terms of the Napoleonic Code of 1804, the patriarchal family was seen as the cornerstone of a healthy and disciplined nation. According to the new laws, a woman had to reside with her husband and acquire his nationality. Women could not participate in lawsuits or serve as witnesses in courts. Female adultery was punishable by imprisonment and fines. Women had no control over property, a woman's wages were to be collected by the husband, and women could not engage in business without the permission of their husbands. Women's inherent weakness and inferiority were invoked as the chief reasons for these institutionalized inequalities. Legislators argued that women needed protection, which was best afforded by the home. Henceforth, women were enjoined to divide their time equally between reproduction and the family.

Although the Napoleonic code sought to instill the patriarchal order of ancient Rome, the ideas spawned by the French Revolution were not to disappear so easily. Throughout the nineteenth century, feminists used the arguments about the natural rights of human beings to win acceptance and equality. Meanwhile, the Industrial Revolution did much to undermine the cohesion of European society. The intrusions of the economy created new patterns in women's lives. Whereas lower-class women exchanged fields for the factory and mines, middle-class women saw themselves bound by the trappings of Victorian femininity and domesticity. The result was modern feminism.

The Industrial Revolution and Modernization

By the beginning of the nineteenth century, the textile factory had become a feature of life in certain areas of Western Europe. Many families could no longer survive on cottage industry and farm work, and men and women alike migrated to urban areas to work in factories. In most cases women were engaged in low-skilled jobs that paid considerably less than those held by their male counterparts—often only 60 percent as much. Although factory work took a toll on workers' diets, health, and general standards of living, it also allowed for new forms of working-class activism. Workers formed mutual aid or friendly societies. Each worker paid weekly into a common pool, the sum of which was used for emergencies such as death, sickness, or incapacitation. Unionization was to usher in considerable improvements in the working class of the European proletariat in the late nineteenth century, but these were overwhelmingly male dominated. Male workers tended to regard working women with hostility. Women not only worked for lower wages, they were also docile and resistant to political organization. In return, the Social Democrats, the chief spokesmen for organized labor, expended little effort in attracting women to their ranks or elaborating a special program addressing the immediate concerns of women workers.

The Industrial Revolution ushered in the system of sexual division of labor. In preindustrial England, families had worked as a unit. Of course, within the farm economy, men and women did engage in different tasks. While women did the milking and spinning, the men plowed the fields and wove the cloth. But the tasks were interchangeable as families battled for survival. The importance of women's contribution to the family economy was undermined by the Industrial Revolution. Initially, factories hired entire families, including children, but with the passage of time men became the primary wage earners and women were expected to concentrate on unpaid housework, child care, and craft work at home. Married women with children were the least likely to work full-time, and those that did generally came from the poorest homes where the husband was either missing or disabled. Most women were confined to dead-end jobs that paid very little. By 1850 urban England was in the grips of the pernicious ideology of separate spheres.

Undoubtedly factory work and work in the mines were especially hard on women, who also had to take care of the children and run the family economy on a meager budget. This situation, coupled with a lack of well-paying jobs, may have provided the reason for many women to stay at

PICTURE 11.2
American Suffragettes. Middle-class women gather at the suffragette headquarters in New York City in 1912. (Photo from the Library of Congress)

home if they could afford it. E. R. Pike, in *Hard Times: Human Documents of the Industrial Revolution* (1966), quoted an Englishwoman who expressed satisfaction with her new role as a housewife in 1844:

> While I was working in the pit I was worth to my [miner] husband seven shillings a week, out of which we had to pay 2 1/2 shillings to a woman for looking after the younger children. . . . Then there was one shilling a week for washing; besides there was mending to pay for, and other things. The house was not guided. The other children broke things; they did not go to school when they were sent; they would be playing about, and get ill-used by other children, and their clothes torn. Then when I came home in the evening, everything was to do after the day's labor, and I was so tired that I had no heart for it; no fire lit, nothing cooked, no water fetched, the house dirty, and nothing comfortable for my husband. It is all better now and I wouldn't go down again.

A new middle-class ideology of separate spheres for men and women continued to influence gender relations in the nineteenth century. This arrangement was reinforced by women's lack of legal rights. In England a wife had no legal identity and could not own property in her own name. Domesticity was elevated to the status of an art, and the Victorian wife was supposed to preserve the virtue of the hearth and home. Queen Victoria set the royal precedent in Britain. Her reign put an end to centuries of royal misconduct. She and her consort, Prince Albert, served as the archetype of domestic felicity and conjugal bliss. The home was idealized as an oasis, removed from the cutthroat competition of capitalistic relations that governed the male business world. Women were expected to run the household, supervise the servants, instill morality in children, and engage in charitable works. At the same time, journalistic tracts and literature idealized Victorian women as delicate, ultrafeminine, and prone to fainting spells and nervous headaches.

Given these limiting constructions of womanhood, it was not surprising that women rebelled in an organized manner. Gone were the debates over womanhood and women's roles. In the middle of the nineteenth century, women formed organizations that would serve as the institutional basis of the modern feminist movement. Feminists in England worked for various reforms, including the right to work, the right to own property, the right to enjoy equal access to education, and the right to vote. Other goals included easier divorce laws and the right to gain custody of children. The Women's Property Act of 1870 allowed a woman to keep her earnings after marriage even though her property and her savings went to her husband. Women also waged a bitter struggle to enter universities and gain degrees. But British feminism was the exception rather than the rule, and in both Germany and France the women's movements were cautious and subdued. In the last decade of the nineteenth century, Western European governments enacted legislation that was aimed at ameliorating some of the legal disabilities of women. By 1910 married women in France were allowed to control their property and wages. The system of higher education finally opened up to women, and in France and Switzerland medical schools allowed women to enter.

For the underprivileged, too, the end of the century saw an increase in job opportunities for women. For unmarried country girls, domestic service was the most common occupation. It has been calculated that in Britain in 1911, one out of every seven employed persons was a domestic servant. This kind of job meant hard work with low pay and few benefits. Domestic servants lacked personal independence, and the lady of the house strictly monitored her servants' movements. In spite of these onerous conditions, large numbers of country girls flocked to domestic service in the city, lured by the attraction of urban life and its amusements, the theater, the music halls, and the shops. Some girls in domestic service became prosperous working-class wives. Still others ended up laboring in sweatshops or did piecework for a pittance at home—that is, in attics and garrets. With the advent of the sewing machine, women's labor accounted for the bulk of ready-made clothes available in stores. By the late nineteenth century, as the fields of health, education, and family life came under increasing supervision of the state, women found employment in government bureaucracies. Banks, businesses, and libraries started hiring women in the service sector. Teaching, especially, brought a large number of women into the workplace. Teachers, though underpaid and closely supervised, were at least often assured upward mobility. But it seemed that as soon as women entered a profession, both the status and the salary declined.

World War I temporarily interrupted the growing success of women's movements because some feminists suspended their activities in deference to the war effort. But as the war dragged on, governments drafted women to work in industry, transportation, and agriculture. For many women the loss of a breadwinner and the transition to laboring outside the home was difficult, especially as gender relations were tense at workplaces. These problems were compounded by inflation and soaring prices. When the war ended in November 1918, women won the right to vote in many European countries, including Denmark, the Netherlands, Czechoslovakia, Austria, Poland, and Hungary. In England, female suffrage was limited to women who were thirty years old and who either had an established residence or were married to a man who did.

At the same time, Europe was awash in a sea of conservatism. In France, in an effort to raise the birthrate, the government banned the sale of all contraceptive devices and literature on birth control in 1920. This mindset was especially apparent in countries such as Germany where there was a violent backlash against feminists and socialists. When German men came home from war, they found the world had changed considerably in their absence. Instead of prosperity, they found unemployment, soaring inflation, and the specter of communism and feminism. The National Socialists, or the Nazi Party, claimed to have a solution for all these problems and by paramilitary behavior managed to convince a defeated citizenry of its competence. Fascist parties in Europe proposed a variety of measures to restore the patriarchal family and society.

From the podium, Hitler ranted that Bolshevists, feminists, and Jewish intellectuals had betrayed the German race. According to the Nazis, the best way to solve the problem of unemployment was to remove women from men's jobs. Under the 1933 Law to Reduce Unemployment, couples were given subsidies if the wife gave up her job and had babies. Similar policies governing marriage loans were also introduced in Italy, Sweden, France, and Spain in the 1930s and 1940s. Attempts were made to channel women into low-paying jobs in domestic service and farm work that were supposedly commensurate with their capabilities. Women were purged from the universities, civil services, and professions in record numbers; not surprisingly, a disproportionate share of them were Jewish. However, when Germany started rearming after the mid-1930s and labor became scarce, the regime reversed its policies on the employment of women. But an effort was made to employ women at low wages in jobs that required little skill. Although working women had few options, German middle-class women, having internalized Nazi ideology of separate spheres, refused to work at all.

According to the Nazis, women's primary function was to reproduce and raise large families for the Fatherland. Women were awarded the Mother Cross in recognition of their reproductive capabilities, and a massive propaganda campaign was unleashed to encourage women to fulfill their patriotic duties. But the Nazis wanted to control the breeding process by ensuring the reproduction of superior Aryans only. To this end, they advocated and initiated the sterilization of mothers deemed as degenerate, such as prostitutes, alcoholics, agitators, gypsies, and of course, Jews. Beginning in 1941, sterilization was replaced by policies of mass extermination.

The Nazi Party attracted a large female following. From the early days of Hitler's struggle for power, talented women such as Guida Diehl and Elsbeth Zander vied for control of Nazi women's organizations. Women served the party by raising money, cooking, and sewing. These women were highly vocal in their criticisms of feminists and suffragists and believed that they would find an important niche within a party that openly subscribed to theories about the inferiority of women. Gertrude Scholtz-Klink became the National Women's Leader and was responsible for destroying many independent women's groups. Scholtz-Klink insisted that the "woman question" took second place behind the struggle against ethnic degeneration. She also stressed the responsibilities of German women, rather than their rights, and argued that marriage and motherhood should adapt to the new laws on race and sterilization. She deplored women's general lack of sympathy for the policies of sterilization, especially among Catholic women. Fortunately, Nazi women's organizations had less success than their male counterparts in mobilizing women for their propaganda courses on race politics. Most women preferred less esoteric courses on housewifery, nursing, and social welfare, and until the end of the war, Nazi authorities continued to lament German women's lack of racial consciousness!

Marxism and Feminism

Marxist theoretical works on the "woman question," though sparse, marked an important step forward in feminist thinking. Engels, in his *Origin of the Family, Private Property and the State* (1884), asserted that the form of the family was tied to the structure of the economy and that the origin of patriarchy as a social system could be dated to the creation of private property. Engels argued that men, in order to ensure the transmission of property, had to ensure monogamy for women. Herein lay the origin of bourgeois morality and sexual ethics that mandated strict control of female sexuality and relative freedom for the male. Marxists argued that since women's subordinate status was directly related to the existence of private property, the elimination of the latter would perforce lead to the disappearance of the former. Thus women's complete liberation would only be possible with the completion of a successful proletarian revolution.

August Bebel, a German Marxist, in *Women Under Socialism* (1883), painted a picture of a postcapitalist socialist society in which human beings engaged in productive work without compulsion or fear. With the dawn of socialism, he argued, the bourgeois nuclear family would be redefined. No longer would the family act as a unit of consumption and reproduction. Domestic duties that tied women ineluctably to the hearth and the home would be socialized. Communal organizations would take on the tasks of cooking, cleaning, and washing. Churches, kindergartens, and schools would care for children in a hygienic and scientific manner.

There was an essential contradiction in Marxism, however. On the one hand, it saw the bourgeois state as a repressive mechanism enabling property owners to effectively protect their privileged class status and perpetuate the exploitation of the masses. On the other, it arrogated an incredible array of functions to the socialist state. Who would organize the laundries, dining halls, and childcare facilities? Until the dawn of true communism, when the state would disappear, the Marxists felt that the state had to protect the rights of women and children, ensure that women had access to education, relieve women from the burdens of domesticity, and promote women to positions of power and authority. The modern vision of the welfare state derived both from Marxist thinking and subsequent Soviet practice.

Although Marxism was intended to be instituted in an industrial society, Russia was the first country that claimed to constitute a proletarian government. Here, in this semi-feudal land, the Russian Communist Party, or Bolsheviks, set out to create a workers paradise. Whatever the shortcomings of the revolution, Bolsheviks were the first set of politicians in the twentieth century who had an explicit agenda for women and set about instituting it in a systematic manner. In Russia, the word "woman" carried a heavy burden of meaning. Centuries of misogynistic pronouncements by the Orthodox Church had taken deep root in the popular culture. Peasants believed that beating a woman was tantamount to beating the devil. A favorite peasant saying opined that a hen was not a bird and a woman was not a human being. Apart from being the objects of physical abuse, peasant women labored long and hard both in the fields and in the home, tending the cattle and poultry, spinning cloth, and marketing the produce of their garden. Large numbers of peasant women fled to cities in the late nineteenth century where they worked in domestic service or factories, and often as prostitutes.

Although violence against women was endemic in peasant Russia, upper-class women in Russia, unlike their Western European counterparts, enjoyed a rather dignified past. Among the Russian gentry, married women had far more freedom than in the West. Women owned property, which they administered themselves. They were competent businesswomen, and it was fairly common for landowners to leave their estates in the hands of their wives while they were serving in the imperial army or bureaucracies. The constricting prototypes of languishing Victorian womanhood never took root in this harsh soil. Women invented and fulfilled a variety of roles. Moreover, when Tsar Alexander II abolished feudalism in Russia in 1861 and a large number of noble families declined economically, women's work was often integral to the maintenance of the family economy. Women's overwhelming demand for educational opportunities led to the creation of secondary schools, teacher training institutes, and even university courses for women.

Upper-class Russian women also played an important role in politics—oppositional, that is. While other countries in Western Europe were moving toward some form of parliamentary rule, Russia was governed by an autocrat, an absolute monarch. Educated Russian society blamed the

PICTURE 11.3
Aleksandra Kollontai (1872–1952).
Although the daughter of a Tsarist
general from an ancient noble family,
Aleksandra Kollontai joined a Marxist
workers movement and was forced to
flee to Germany, where she became
active in the international socialist
women's movement. Under the
influence of Lenin, she joined the
Bolshevik Party, and upon returning to
Russia after the 1917 Revolution she
was appointed head of the women's
section of the Communist Party.
(Reprinted from *Album of Revolutionary
Russia* [Petrograd: Russian Socialist
Federation, 1919])

intransigence of the tsar for their backwardness vis-à-vis Europe and agonized about the wretched state of the peasantry, who constituted nearly 90 percent of the population. Generations of Russians were consumed by the notion of instigating revolution in their country. Women students joined these conspiratorial circles, distributed revolutionary literature, and worked in fields and factories trying to propagandize the people. Several women carried out daring assassination attempts: Sofia Perovskaya was at the head of the group that killed Tsar Alexander II in 1881. Women revolutionaries suffered exile, beatings, imprisonment, and solitary confinement with exemplary fortitude and were careful to subsume their own goals as women to the larger cause of revolution.

It was the quest for a radical and communitarian politics that attracted Russians to communism. World War I proved to be the final test for the durability of autocracy. The economy was unable to produce the material necessary to successfully prosecute the war or keep the civilian population housed and fed. German military defeats took a tremendous toll of Russian lives abroad and at home; in the nation's capital, Petrograd, a lack of bread and coal produced a revolutionary situation in February 1917. The tsar resigned and after a series of ineffectual coalition governments, the Russian Communist Party (Bolsheviks) took power in November 1917.

The Bolsheviks, who had inherited a definite agenda for women, tried to institute it as soon as they came to power. The Soviet government passed a series of laws designed to benefit women. Marriage was declared a civil rather than a religious act. Divorce became easy to obtain—too easy, according to many Russian women, who were abandoned in droves by itinerant husbands. Abortion was legalized, and the state made some effort to provide prenatal education and medical care for pregnant women. Finally, educational institutions opened their doors to women. A lot of the legislation remained on paper as the Soviet government concentrated its energies and limited resources on winning the civil war against a coalition of Tsarist and foreign forces. The long years of war took a dreadful toll on Russian women. Abandoned or widowed women tried to keep body and soul together and raise children in the middle of terrible privations. When peace was achieved in 1921, the situation scarcely improved. Female unemployment remained dangerously high, and often prostitution was the only means to avoid starvation.

During this time, the Bolsheviks spent lavishly in promoting the "New Soviet Woman." They argued that in order to achieve true equality, women would have to shed certain characteristics that perpetuated their backwardness. Accordingly, the Bolsheviks launched antireligious campaigns in order to free women from what they saw as religious superstition. Through an imaginative use of plays, limericks, songs, verses, and posters, the Bolsheviks promoted new revolutionary values for women. Women were exhorted to eschew the domestic sphere and participate in community affairs as well as national politics. Wife beating was soundly criticized, and women were encouraged to stand up against domestic abuse. Literacy circles in the countryside worked through reading centers to eliminate illiteracy. Peasants were urged to send their daughters to school.

These efforts bore limited fruit. Propaganda, however well intentioned, was a poor substitute for economic modernization. Moreover, women felt that the Bolshevik legislation on marriage and divorce worked against them. Women demanded that the state reintroduce restrictions on divorce and force errant husbands to provide alimony. When Joseph Stalin assumed power in 1928 and instituted the First Five-Year Plan, aimed at rapid modernization and growth of all sectors of the economy, the state began addressing many of these issues. The inception of the First Five-Year Plan created a huge labor shortage in the country, and women were recruited into industry in significant numbers even though factory conditions were appalling. Women were encouraged to join technical schools and colleges, and the state reserved a certain proportion of seats in various educational institutions exclusively for women students. Also, the state started spending precious resources on the construction of day care centers, kindergartens, and medical facilities. During this period the state enacted a spate of conservative legislation undoing much of what had been achieved in the 1920s. Some of these acts were widely popular, such as restrictions on divorce and penalization of men who defaulted on alimony and child support payments. The decision to criminalize abortion, however, met with widespread resistance, and despite the state's best efforts, the birthrate continued to be stubbornly low.

It is hard to draw up an objective balance sheet on Soviet achievements in the area of women's rights. State propaganda on the subject was riddled with contradictions. Even though the quality of service and care tendered by institutions such as childcare centers, laundries, and medical clinics left much to be desired, over the years Soviet women became accustomed to these free services provided by the welfare state. In the post–World War II period, women never reached the inner circle of Soviet decisionmakers, but they were widely represented in the various fields of the economy, bureaucracy, and modern professions such as law, medicine, and engineering. Although women were discouraged from experimenting with Western feminist thought, the Soviet state publicly adhered to the ideals of gender parity. Women were exhorted to participate in the workforce, politics, and social organizations yet to also raise large families. Amenities that Western women take for granted, such as household appliances, contraceptive devices, and well-stocked grocery stores, continued to be an abstract dream in the Soviet Union. Women spent long hours standing in line in an attempt to provide their families with the basic necessities.

When the Soviet Union collapsed in 1991 and the Communist Party fell from power, women were the primary victims in the transition to a market economy. By the late 1990s in Russia, fe-

PICTURE 11.4
Soviet revolutionary poster. The words exhort women, whatever their backgrounds, to participate fully in the construction of the new socialist society: "Worker women and country women. Fight the rudiments of the past. Build a new socialist existence." (Photo courtesy of the Funet Russian Archives)

male unemployment figures were significantly higher than those of males. The end of state-sponsored child care forced many women out of the labor market. Pornography and prostitution flourished, and one could hear new antifeminist ideologies proclaiming the inferiority of women and their fitness for domesticity and reproduction only. Many criticized the Soviet efforts to create gender equality as a pernicious Marxist attempt to emasculate the Russian male and destroy Russian culture and traditions. Feminist organizations struggled to establish networks and garner support for their programs.

On the other side of the Iron Curtain, in the post–World War II era in the West, the 1960s proved a fertile decade for the revitalization of feminist movements. Despite widespread prosperity, it was a decade that was marked by massive social protest against the Vietnam War, governmental authority, and bourgeois values that legitimated the patriarchal family, the accumulation of wealth, and savage social inequalities. Undoubtedly, women's control of their reproduction through the availability of the pill and abortions facilitated the awakening of women's consciousness to new possibilities. In contrast to earlier feminist movements, the new women's liberation movement was founded on a new attitude of opposition to men. Feminists critiqued the gap between the lofty ideals of equality inherent in liberalism and socialism and the reality of differential access of men and women to education, wages, promotions, government services, and representation in media, art, and circles of power. Philosophers such as the famous French intellectual Simone de Beauvoir, author of the influential *The Second Sex* (1953), argued that women's basic freedoms had been limited by men, who had judged women and their achievements by male values and from a male perspective. Thus women were made and not born inferior and deficient.

In Europe and the United States, feminist organizations sprang up overnight. Some of them were involved in consciousness raising; others created journals, newspapers, and magazines; and still others formed political organizations. Women established their own bookstores, coffee houses, women's centers, shelters, courses, and seminars. The issues of rape, domestic abuse, and violence against women, hitherto taboo, were raised publicly as both social and political topics for discussion and denunciation. In literature and academia, feminist scholars explored the reasons for the suppression of women's voices in literary canons, texts, and sources. Women also became active in ecological movements, protested the escalation of nuclear weapons and the use of nuclear power, and sought to reverse the destructive consequences of science and technology. Feminist groups also reached across national boundaries to form links with women's groups in Asia, Latin America, the Middle East, and Africa.

Colonization and Women: The Example of India

As we have seen in preceding chapters, colonization was not restricted to the exploitation of natural resources and the economy. As the colonizers tried to change the unfamiliar societies they encountered, the indigenous populations reacted variously to what they recognized as illegitimate assaults on their culture. In Bengal, a province in India, the British colonizers used the status of women to explain the backward character of the "native" civilization. This analysis of the status of women became a justification for continued colonial domination. In a defensive reaction, the upper-class Bengali males advocated reactionary policies toward women in an attempt to guard their families from the disruptive effects of Western culture. The treatment of women therefore became a locus of repressive colonial policies and anticolonial struggles.

In Bengal, as in most of India, the strictures of caste governed everyday behavior. Although according to the classic Vedic texts Indian society was supposedly divided into four occupational orders (the Brahmin, or priestly, class; the Kshatriya, or warrior, class; the Vaishya, or trader and agriculturalist, class; and the Shudra, or menial, class), in reality there were thousands of subcastes, or *jatis,* that evolved according to local practices and needs. It was fairly common for jatis to move up and down the social ladder and more often than not, caste distinctions were maintained through policies toward women. Just as the middle-class woman in nineteenth-century England functioned as a social marker of domesticity and purity as against the imagined sexual licentiousness of the upper and lower classes, in India caste practices and rituals governing Bengali women were particularly severe and constraining.

Bengali women were not entirely bereft of power, however. Literary sources show that within the family, older married women often wielded considerable authority. In the public sphere Brahmin women played an important role in religious ceremonies and social events such as marriages. Moreover, women from the Vaishnavite tradition, a reform movement within Hinduism, were well known as poets and composers. Men who ran traditional schools in the rural areas often educated their daughters. Ancient texts referred to phenomenally learned women, such as Kshana, who bested their male opponents in philosophical and logical disputations. The names of Gargi, Lilalvati, and Matreyi were routinely invoked by Hindu nationalists who wished to prove in the face of overwhelmingly contrary evidence that women had always enjoyed extraordinary freedom within the Indian tradition.

The upper-caste status of Brahmins was maintained by enforcing a strict control of female sexuality that was in contrast to the relative freedom allowed to women from the lower classes. Thus, although widows from the lower castes were permitted to remarry or initiate divorce, an extraordinary degree of fidelity was demanded from upper-caste women. Not only was remarriage or divorce strictly forbidden, but also the dreaded practice of *sati,* whereby the widow immolated herself on the funeral pyre in complete identification with her dead spouse, was fairly common. Control of female sexuality included exclusive seclusion in the women's quarters and early marriage, but on the lower end of the caste spectrum, women worked outside the home. Available sources suggest that upwardly mobile subcastes often adopted the practice of sati in order to cement their social status, and one saw a rapid increase of such occurrences in the early part of the nineteenth century. Though ostensibly widows who killed themselves did so voluntarily, it appears that property considerations often led to undue pressure being applied to these women.

The British were shocked and appalled at customs such as sati, and the status of women in India seemed to justify their tutelage over these barbaric people. As James Mill wrote in his highly influential *History of British India,* published in 1840, "The condition of women is one of the most remarkable circumstances in the manner of nations. Among rude people, the women are generally degraded; among civilized people they are exalted. . . . A state of dependence more humiliating than that which is ordained for the weaker sex among Hindus cannot easily be conceived."

Although some Indian nationalists tried to defend Hindu treatment of women, attributing their degraded status to the deleterious impact of prolonged Muslim rule in the subcontinent, British scorn and condemnation roused the ire of a handful of Western-educated Indians. Iswar Chandra Vidyasagar, perhaps one of the best-known social reformers of the nineteenth century, was particularly passionate on the subject of widow remarriage. He also denounced the practice of polygamy and became an ardent advocate of female education. Social reform proceeded very slowly or in some cases not at all. Sati was abolished in 1829 under the Widow Remarriage Bill, which passed only with immense opposition from the upper-caste Hindus. But it had little impact on the lives of most Indian women.

Indian women found it equally difficult to carve out their independent niche in the political sphere. Although the Indian nationalist movement represented the nascent Indian nation as the "motherland" and the "goddess" in political and literary writings, every act of social reform that was aimed at alleviating the condition of women was represented as a frontal attack on Hindu civilization. Reformers from within Hindu society were denounced as having sold out to decadent Western ways, and safeguarding the purity of the Hindu woman became an integral part of the nationalist discourse. Prominent nationalist men were unhappy when organizations such as the All-India Women's Conference, or the National Council of Women in India, raised sensitive issues such as child marriage or the elimination of veiling, and they accused feminist leaders of being disloyal to their culture.

Women found a place within the nationalist struggle and were welcomed as long as they accepted the goals of the political parties and eschewed all attempts at meaningful social reform. The Indian National Congress founded in 1895, the largest anti-imperialist coalition in India, refused for years to endorse women's right to vote. Gandhi encouraged women's participation in the nationalist movement, but initially he, too, believed that the suffrage movement was both ill advised and ill timed and served to divert attention from the struggle against British rule. The Congress endorsed women's right to vote only in 1926.

Jawaharlal Nehru, the first prime minister of independent India, made forceful public pronouncements on the debased status of Indian women. In 1928 he said, "The future of India cannot consist of dolls and playthings and if you make half the population of a country the mere

PICTURE 11.5
Women in the Salt March,
1930. Women participated
fully in the civil
disobedience organized
by Gandhi and other
nationalist leaders against
British colonialism in
India. Here, women carry
ovens, fuel, and earthen
pots to the Madras beach
to prepare salt from the
water, in defiance of the
salt monopoly imposed
by the government.
(Photo from the Library
of Congress)

plaything of the other half, an encumbrance on others, how will you ever make progress?" Yet when the All India Women's Conference initiated the Hindu Code Bill suggesting legislation that would ban polygamy, legalize divorce, and give women the same inheritance rights as men, it was derailed both in 1934 and again in 1943.

Despite the slow progress on the front of social reform, women were strongly encouraged to participate in the anticolonial struggle from within the domestic front. In Bengal, in the early part of the twentieth century women hid weapons and sheltered anti-British terrorists. They also were in the forefront of the boycott movements of British-made goods and used their power as consumers to buy Indian-made products exclusively. But it was only after Gandhi's ascendance to leadership in the 1920s that women were recruited in meaningful numbers. With the approval of their menfolk (partly due to Gandhi's moral stature), upper- and middle-class women left the seclusion of their homes and started attending political meetings.

Gandhi first used women as political activists in his noncooperation movement in 1920. Women joined rallies, spoke at public meetings, picketed stores selling British cloth, and in defiance of a British ban, sold homespun cloth on the streets. Many were sent to jail, and Gandhi realized that the arrest of respectable women was an excellent way to galvanize the nation into action. He soon acquired a formidable array of talented women in his coterie. Gandhi also appealed to marginalized women, such as prostitutes and temple dancers. These women donated jewelry and raised funds for the Congress. In 1930, when Gandhi launched his civil disobedience campaign with a 240-mile march to the sea to make salt in defiance of the British monopoly, women turned out in thousands. During this campaign, women were arrested in large numbers, but the presence of women at nationalist demonstrations often precluded police violence, as officers feared the wrath of the crowds.

In the 1930s, women students joined underground revolutionary cells where they acted as housekeepers, messengers, and custodians of arms. Some women even formed paramilitary organizations. Others became terrorists. Santi and Suniti, two schoolgirls from Comilla, a district in Bengal, killed the district magistrate of the region in 1931. They presented him with a petition to allow a swimming competition, and when he went to sign it, they both pulled out revolvers and shot him. Both admitted their guilt and were mortified to hear that they would be imprisoned rather than hung. The next year, Bina Das attempted to shoot the governor of Bengal at a university convocation in protest against the ill treatment her colleagues were receiving in British prisons. A well-educated woman from a middle-class home, she had seemed an unlikely recruit to revolutionary operations.

Prison was not always glamorous. Although women from prominent families were treated solicitously in prison, other women prisoners and demonstrators were often raped, starved, and beaten unconscious. Though the British authorities in India denied these charges and sought to malign the character of these politically active women, the Indian League of London found substantial evidence of police brutality in their investigation conducted in 1932. The British acknowledged the fact that the involvement of women in the nationalist struggle gave it a moral urgency and helped in the recruitment of activists.

In the late colonial period, women moved into the modern professions of law, education, medicine, civil service, and journalism in record numbers but had to guard their reputations with redoubled vigor. It was common for the few female students attending coeducational institutions to be seated separately from the males, and there was no question of them attending any of the extracurricular activities. Often female students were harassed on the streets as they traveled to and from classes. Once employed, Indian professionals earned a fraction of what their British counterparts did, and, if unmarried, often faced sexual harassment in the workplace. Nonetheless, women persevered on the professional front with increasing success.

However, the gains of feminist activity were disproportionately distributed. Although professing to represent all Indian women, in reality the bulk of the political activists came from the middle and upper classes. At the turn of the twentieth century, most of the Indian female population was employed in agriculture, and a smaller percentage worked in mines, textile and jute mills, tea gardens, and domestic service. The lives of these working women deteriorated considerably under colonial rule. The terms and conditions of employment, whether in British-owned plantations or Indian-owned factories, were ghastly, but there was little acknowledgement of the fate of this vast and silent majority in the feminist literature from the nationalist period. Nor was there any push from the Indian National Congress to institute factory legislation aimed at ameliorating work conditions. It was the British who introduced factory legislation, in the face of local opposition regulating working hours for women and limiting night work. Indian feminism focused on traditional issues such as legal rights, franchise, and educational opportunities. Few leaders envisioned women as productive salaried workers, and the interest in women workers from their upper-class counterparts was often fitful and desultory.

Some women employed a Marxist framework of analysis. These women, often attracted to the Communist Party of India, tried to understand the economic bases of prostitution and the degraded status of women. Lakshmi Menon, a teacher and later India's representative to the UN, was a great admirer of the Soviet code, which she believed struck at the root of inequality for women. She argued that guaranteed employment, training programs, protective legislation, and a new sex code that abolished double standards was the answer to women's problems. However, Menon was not taken seriously, and the governmental neglect of women's issues is one of the most persistent problems facing modern India even today.

PICTURE 11.6
Prime Minister Indira Gandhi (1917–1984) with President Richard Nixon (1913–1994). Indira Gandhi was one of the most popular and longest-serving prime ministers of India. The daughter of India's first prime minister, Jawaharlal Nehru, she was originally voted into office in 1966 on the strength of her family name and connections, but she soon broke free from the tutelage of senior members of the Congress Party. Although an influential politician and world leader, at home she evinced little interest in feminist issues. Here she hosts President Richard Nixon on his visit to India in August 1969. (Photo from the National Archives)

Women and Islam

Islamic feminism is one of the least understood phenomena in modern times. Although in the West, Islamic practices toward women are seen as monolithic and repressive across the spectrum of Arab and non-Arab states alike, in reality the Qur'anic injunctions on women are invariably influenced by local customs and cultures. Thus, female genital mutilation in Egypt and Sudan, the Semitic practice of veiling in the Middle East, and the Hindu tradition of caste and dowry in India and Sri Lanka all are purveyed as Islamic. There is little unanimity even among the so-called Muslim states on the correct policies to adopt regarding such vital issues as contraception and abortion. Both are legal in Tunisia. Both are enforced on women in Bangladesh along with state-sponsored sterilization programs. In Pakistan contraception is allowed, but abortion is forbidden, although doctors routinely perform abortions in urban centers such as Karachi and Lahore. Algeria initially forbade abortions and contraception after gaining independence from the French but retracted its prohibitions when population growth took on explosive dimensions. The governments of all these nations, however, claim that their policies are inspired by Islam.

There is little consensus on what Islam has to say about gender and the relations between the sexes. The Qur'an, the central text of the religion, offers little more than general guidance and vague pronouncements on the subject. The *hadith*, collections of the sayings, life, and times of the Prophet Muhammad, allow such a wide variety of interpretations that it is difficult to distill an essentialist position from them. The body of Islamic law, the Shari'a, contains more specific rules governing gender relations. These include the right to practice polygamy, the right of men to initiate divorce unilaterally, and the male right to child custody. Surprisingly, Islam, unlike many other religions, grants women complete control over their property.

Granted this diversity in the actual application of Islam, some scholars argue that it does contain a certain set of fundamental assumptions about women and their appropriate roles that governs attitudes toward women in Islamic societies. Islamic jurists, influenced by Greek philosophers, have opined that women are physically and intellectually inferior to men and that these handicaps are compounded by their emotional instability. According to the Shari'a, Allah created men and women differently and assigned different roles and responsibilities to each. This biological determinism underlies policies that seek to confine women to domesticity and reproduction while prohibiting them from playing an active role in the public sphere. Islamic texts also warn of women's sexual power, which constitutes a threat to the integrity of the Muslim community. In order to save men from the consequences of their primordial lust, women should be confined, and when they appear in public their dress and behavior should obscure their sexual identity. But again Islam shares this traditional view of women as dangerously sexual beings with both Hinduism and Christianity.

There are basically two schools of interpretation on the position of women in the Islamic tradition, one modernist and the other conservative, or fundamentalist. The modernists view Islam as dynamic and open to modern interpretation; the conservatives seek to resist modernity and what they see as Western cultural pollution. A prominent contemporary modernist, Dr. Muhammad Ahmad Khalaf Allah, claims that the Qur'an gave women political rights during the time of the Prophet but that these were later disregarded under the caliphs. According to him, the Qur'an gives women the right to work outside the home; as for the contentious issue of veiling, the Qur'an merely enjoins modesty in behavior and dress for both sexes. A woman has the right to choose her husband, and an Islamic society has the right to decide whether the practice of polygamy is in the public interest. Dr. Khalaf Allah represents the school of thought that sees Islam as a dynamic religion that is well suited to modern times.

The conservatives, on the contrary, oppose the prospect of a mutating and evolving Islam and believe that the social and legal inequality of women mandated by the scriptures should be implemented to secure a truly Islamic society. They view the free woman as a source of social anarchy and moral corruption and see marriage, domesticity, and subordination to male rule as the only way to preserve the integrity of Islamic societies. Fundamentalists seek to create a society based on justice, equality, social order, and the appropriate seclusion of women; in reality they are struggling with rapid socioeconomic change and declining patriarchal authority. It should be remembered that conservatives and fundamentalists in the Arab world, like those in the West, often do not speak from a position of unassailable power. Although their ideal may be that of patriarchal authority, they are confronted with the sight of women making rapid gains in education, employment, and political power. These conservatives, given the fact that most of the Arab world was under colonial rule in the early twentieth century, naturally interpret this new phenomenon in terms of an unwanted modernity thrust upon them by the West.

The status of Muslim women is not only determined by state policies but to a large extent also stems from colonial policies dating from the nineteenth century. Although the British exerted nominal control on the indigenous culture in Egypt, French acculturation was so pervasive in Algeria that modern feminists still write in French. The Arabian Peninsula, in contrast, was never under colonial rule and entered the European-dominated market system only after Western exploitation of oil resources started in earnest in the 1930s. Accordingly, Islamic authorities there retained fuller control over women's lives. At the beginning of the twenty-first century, feminism had a more visible face in Egypt than in Saudi Arabia, where the government created completely segregated workplaces for women. And although Egyptian women have their own publications and a prestigious literary tradition, in Saudi Arabia female journalists have to submit to the dictates of male editors, few of whom allow a feminist perspective to appear in their pages.

Egypt was the first country to establish de facto independence from the Ottoman Empire, only to fall under British control in 1882. In the nineteenth century, upper- and middle-class Arab women lived within the harem system. This system mandated the seclusion of women to a certain quarter of the house and veiling in the presence of all males except the father, brother, uncle, or grandfather—that is, men with whom marriage was not a possibility. Many lower-class urban women veiled, but peasant women who worked in the fields, or Bedouin women who took care of livestock, could not afford to do so. In Egypt and the Arab lands of West Asia, such as Lebanon, the Arab elite and the state authorities embraced policies of modernization and secularization that clashed with the existing patriarchal ideology. Upper- and middle-class women in Cairo were exposed to conflicting ideas, and whatever choices they made in their private lives were bound to infuriate one side or the other.

In the last decades of the nineteenth century, male tutors had been brought into upper-class Egyptian homes to instruct women in Arabic, Persian, and Turkish. In 1925 the Egyptian government opened the first institution offering a secondary education for girls. As early as 1929, Egyptian women could avail themselves of a university education, whereas women on the Arabian Peninsula had to wait until the 1960s for similar rights. These new educational opportunities challenged traditional gender relations and led to the articulation of a new consciousness. Women began to publish articles in national journals, and soon a feminist press emerged that took up issues of feminism, religion, and nationalism. Gradually, the harem system and the usage of the face veil began to disappear among upper- and middle-class Egyptian women.

Perhaps one of the most famous Egyptian women of this pre–World War II era was Huda Shaarawi. Born in the household of a wealthy landowner and provincial administrator, she was raised within the harem system. At an early age she was married to an elderly cousin who already had a wife and three daughters, all older than her. In her memoirs, Shaarawi wrote poignantly about how she was coerced into this highly distasteful marriage. She overcame the limitations imposed by her social surroundings, however, and became a well-known feminist and nationalist leader. She founded several organizations for Egyptian women, edited highly influential journals, and gave numerous speeches in Egypt, the Arab East, Europe, and Turkey. The Egyptian Feminist Union, founded by Shaarawi, called for political rights for women, the right to work, the right to receive an education, and controls on divorce and polygamy. Shaarawi was also involved in delineating feminism with a social conscience. She and other upper-class women engaged in acts of public philanthropy that involved bringing medical assistance, child care, and vocational education to poor women.

Initially, Egyptian women sought liberation within the context of Islam. But soon, as the anti-British struggle gained momentum, feminism became intertwined with the nationalist discourse. This shift was not limited merely to Egypt; women played an active role in the liberation movements in Algeria, Sudan, and Palestine as well. Soon it became a fairly common sight to see women participating in highly public anticolonial demonstrations. Egyptian feminism continued to find new adherents and spokespersons among the expanding middle class. Some feminists allied quite prominently with members of left-wing parties. New leaders such as Inji Aflatun went directly to women workers in textile factories and drew attention to both class and gender oppression.

In 1952, Gamal Abdel Nasser consolidated his power as president of the new Egyptian republic. Under the modern laws of the regime, women were given the right to vote. Moreover, women's participation in education and employment was encouraged. During Nasser's rule, women made huge gains insofar as they were employed in every aspect of the economy. Countries such as Egypt gained a large coterie of professional women, university professors, journalists, and others who sought to preserve their feminist identities in increasingly conservative social surroundings. But the onerous personal laws governing marriage and divorce remained intact, and Nasser's government clamped down severely on militant feminist organizations, preventing them from organizing politically. Aflatun was jailed for four years; others were placed under house arrest. Other forms of feminist activism included the publication of women's journals, organization of public forums, and practical outreach work among low-income women. But often, these feminist organizations were harassed by governments and their publications shut down.

In the 1970s, Anwar Sadat, Nasser's successor, reversed the trend of socialism and reintroduced capitalism. These changes coincided with a resurgence of Islamic fundamentalism. Among university students and lower middle-class women, veiling became increasingly common. Contemporary Egyptian women expressed reservations about using the title of "feminist" to describe themselves. Partly they viewed this label as limiting, but also feminism was often interpreted as stridently anti-male and in violation of reigning moral norms regarding sexual behavior. In the postcolonial context the label "Western" was often perceived as extremely derogatory, and too often feminism was seen as an alien Western import, a viewpoint that conservatives have exploited endlessly. And socialist women saw feminism as politics primarily having implications for privileged women, that is, something a Third World country like Egypt simply could not afford.

Finally, there were women fundamentalists who insisted that women should return to the harem system. This phenomenon emerged in countries such as Pakistan when in the 1980s the ruling military regime of Zia-ul-Haq sought legitimacy by espousing a radical Islamic position. These fundamentalist women, primarily from the lower and newly emerging middle classes, were relentlessly opposed to upper-class feminists and denounced their activism as modern and therefore un-Islamic. Part of this conflict was class based and reflected the tension between the old colonized urban elite and its traditionally pro-Western orientation and an emerging middle class of traders and entrepreneurs in Pakistan's expanding cities. These fundamentalists rejected the concept of gender equality and believed that women should primarily be mothers and wives with restricted rights and limited mobility.

Interestingly enough, a large number of women on the religious Right have been educated at universities and professional institutions, although they represent the first generation of women to study and work outside the home. According to a Pakistani scholar, the political positions that they espouse are often contradictory. Thus, on the one hand they preach that a woman's place is at home, but on the other they demand that the government set up universities and workplaces exclusively for women. It has apparently escaped the attention of these activists that through their vocal public appearances and prominent political involvement, which includes representation in the National Assembly, they are negating many of the values of the ideal docile wife that they seek to impose on others. Fundamentalist women are bitterly opposed to polygamy and easy divorce, both sanctioned by Islam, but believe that complete sexual segregation and the veiling of women will end the evils of corruption, adultery, and polygamy.

The classic example of women's activism emanating from within the context of radical Islam is of course Iran. It should be remembered that the *hijab,* or Islamic dress, was donned by Iranian women, especially college and high-school students in Tehran, to protest the profligacy and corruption of the Pahlavi regime in the early 1970s. Despite the regime's policy of banning the *hijab* in the

PICTURE 11.7
Afghanistan woman under
the Taliban regime. Under
the ultra-fundamentalist
rule of the Taliban in
Afghanistan women were
subjected to severe
repression. This photo,
taken in Kabul, shows a
woman wearing the full
burqa required in public.
The woman holds a
picture of her dead
husband. (Photo courtesy
of the Revolutionary
Association of the Women
of Afghanistan [RAWA])

workplace, women wore it as a sign of solidarity. Few of them realized that it would become mandatory in 1979 and that women would be severely harassed under the Ayatollah's regime for lack of appropriate veiling. Shortly after the revolution, the new regime abrogated the Family Protection Law enacted by the previous regime and gave men custody of children and the unilateral right to divorce. The new regime also made a concerted effort to return working women to their homes. These policies primarily targeted middle-class women who had benefited from the Shah's policies of modernization and were present in business and government offices in the urban centers. Harassment, purges, monetary incentives, mass retirements—these were some of the policies that the government pursued in order to create an Islamic society. However, it soon became impossible to remove all women from the civil service—in part because of the lack of qualified personnel. Some women chose to brave the harassment and retain their jobs in resistance to the regime.

For every woman who resisted, there were twice the number who supported the regime's policies by increasing their adherence to Islamic principles in their daily lives and calling for a segregated society. In 1989, a survey was conducted among middle-class women in Tehran in order to gauge the impact of a decade of fundamentalist rule on women's expectations. According to the survey, women recognized mothering and housework as their primary functions but did not believe that women should stay out of the formal job market or that women's education should be limited to training for motherhood. Nor did they believe that they should play a subservient role in the family. The majority of the respondents bitterly disapproved of men's unilateral right to divorce and the law that allows men to have custody of the children.

It is understandable that conservative Islamic movements wish to reverse and erase the results of Western-style feminism from their societies, but it is more difficult to fathom why some women have been actively complicit in efforts to ensure their own subordination. Some scholars have argued that the rejection of feminism is part of a rejection of continuing patterns of cultural colonialism. At the end of the century women in Muslim countries were trying to find an authentic feminist identity that incorporated their religious beliefs rather than be branded as dupes of Western imperialism. Finally, one cannot rule out the fact that conservatism carries immense appeal in the face of severe social and economic dislocation. Countries such as Egypt and Pakistan are struggling against problems of underdevelopment that include rising population, high

PICTURE 11.8
Taliban women demonstrating in Peshawar. The Revolutionary Association of the Women of Afghanistan (RAWA) was formed in 1977 to fight for human rights and social justice. After the end of Soviet occupation (1989) and the overthrow of the Soviet-supported government (1992), the focus of the RAWA's political struggle was the Taliban and its repressive regime, especially their treatment of women. Here RAWA demonstrates on the Pakistan border protesting the sixth anniversary of Taliban rule. (Photo courtesy of the RAWA)

unemployment rates, illiteracy, and lack of health care. In uncertain economic contexts women's dependence on men becomes amplified. This phenomenon was present in Nazi Germany, where women widely supported the regime's efforts to destroy liberal and social feminism and replace it with conservative policies that emphasized womanly duties of motherhood and domesticity.

Conclusion

Intellectually, the battle for gender equality may be won, but the struggle still continues on the ground. In the twentieth century, women gained more rights than in all the years of previously recorded history, but the saga was replete with zigzags and reversals. Although few publicly question the legitimacy of universal franchise or education, world opinion has yet to reach a true consensus on the issue of gender equality. In times of crisis or war, the relative fragility of the gains of feminism become painfully apparent. At the century's end, in the civil war in Sarajevo the organized raping of Muslim women was an acceptable part of the Serbian battle offensive. In times of peace, many are still afraid of strong women. Both Hillary Clinton and Eleanor Roosevelt were severely criticized for playing an active role in politics, whereas Pat Nixon was praised for silently countenancing the nefarious activities of her husband, Richard Nixon. Other challenges lie ahead. The feminization of poverty today is a universal phenomenon, and even in the West, where women have made the most gains, a disproportionate share of families headed by women fall under the poverty line. Women have yet to break through the glass ceiling in corporations or achieve parity in pay in either the United States or Western Europe. In many countries, such as India and Bangladesh, domestic abuse and violence against women are just beginning to be recognized as social problems by the governments. But the dismantling of the welfare state and the repudiation of the role of big government, both in the United States and in parts of Europe, provide organized feminism with new challenges. Historically, disadvantaged minorities have relied on state support to gain equality. Now, women will have to find new avenues of support and sustenance.

12

War and Peace

1 million 500,000 morts. Est-ce que les mots et les chiffres peuvent encore signifier quelque chose dans une société d'indifférence et de repli sur soi? (Trans.—1 million 500,000 dead. Can the words and the numbers still signify something for a society that is indifferent and self-absorbed?)

Municipal poster,
L'Haye les Roses, France
(November 1998)

Under these circumstances [rapid development of war technology] the search for peace takes on an urgency and intensity which it has never before had. . . . The problem of the abolition of war is essentially a problem in social learning. . . . It is important to notice that it is the management of conflict and not the elimination of conflict which is the essential problem.

Kenneth Boulding,
The Meaning of the Twentieth Century
(1964)

⋯⋯⋯⋯⋯⋯⋯⋯⋯⋯⋯⋯⋯⋯⋯⋯⋯⋯⋯⋯⋯⋯⋯⋯⋯⋯⋯⋯⋯

THE FIRST HALF OF THE TWENTIETH CENTURY WITNESSED TWO WORLD wars that were the most destructive in human history. In the second half of the century, in the period called the Cold War, humanity seemed to teeter on the brink of nuclear annihilation. In the last decade of the century, the Great Powers, although no longer overtly hostile, continued to invest large resources into military programs in the cause of national security. In 1998, India and Pakistan carried out underground tests of nuclear weapons and joined the ranks of the nuclear club. In the mid-1990s some thirty "small wars" spread human suffering from Central America to southern Europe and from central Africa to Asia and the Pacific. The "secret wars" of terrorists targeted sworn enemies but killed innocent victims, and millions of unexploded land mines from past conflicts threatened civilians.

The concept of a "just war" has long been accepted in human history. As Charles Chatfield noted in *The American Peace Movement* (1992), war is Janus-faced. It is destructive, sometimes devastatingly so, and yet it is rationalized through high ideals, even that of peace itself. In the Western world, the early Christian church condemned warfare, but once Christianity became the official church of the Roman Empire leaders such as Saint Augustine developed the view that war might be justified under certain conditions. The "just war" theory has thus been invoked by governments as they call upon their citizens to send their sons—and sometimes daughters—to lay their lives on the line. Since the rise of nation-states, war has frequently been invoked as a necessary tool of "national security," and military power has been elevated in ministries of war and defense. Even if nations "stagger and stumble" into war, as seemed to happen in 1914, national propaganda quickly demonizes the enemy and rallies people to the patriotic cause. President Woodrow Wilson, in justifying the entry of the United States into World War I, argued that it would "make the world safe for democracy." World War II—only two decades later—was considered by U.S. citizens and their European Allies to be a "Good War," fought against fascist evil and boundless Japanese military aggression. Fascists, bent on demonstrating national virility and the power of a master race, took the glorification of war to new heights, or as Mussolini proclaimed: "War alone brings up to their highest tensions human energies and puts the stamp of nobility upon peoples who have the courage to take up the challenge." Many twentieth-century nationalist fighters argued that the powerful imperialist forces ranged against them could only be defeated through armed struggle, including terrorist attacks, and in the cause of socialist revolution, Mao Zedong wrote: "War is the highest form of struggle for resolving contradictions of property and classes," and "History shows that wars are divided into two kinds, just and unjust. All wars that are progressive are just, and all wars that impeded progress are unjust."

Yet, if the twentieth century was the most violent of centuries—according to one estimate more than 100 million people lost their lives in war—it also witnessed the spread of ideas, practices, and institutions of nonviolence. The media made known worldwide the words and actions of individuals such as Mohandas Gandhi and Martin Luther King, Jr. The one implemented nonviolence in the movement to end British imperial rule in India; the other used it in the African-

PICTURE 12.1
Martin Luther King, Jr.
(1929–1968). The U.S. civil
rights leader addresses the
crowd on the occasion of
the Civil Rights March on
Washington, D.C., August
1963. (Photo from the
National Archives)

American struggle for civil rights. Both became heroic symbols in trying to end oppression by peaceful means. Their great contribution to the nonviolent struggle was to link peace with an end to broader forces of social injustice and to put into practice methods of civil disobedience. While Gandhi was a product of Eastern thought, his reasoning was in tune with King's Christian gospel-inspired message. Both saw violence and nonviolence as part of a moral and spiritual problem inextricably intertwined with basic human rights. At the ceremony in Oslo where he received the Nobel Peace Prize in 1964, King linked an end to war with social justice:

> Sooner or later, all the people of the world will have to discover a way to live together in peace and thereby transform this pending cosmic elegy into a creative psalm of brotherhood. If this is to be achieved, we must evolve, for all human conflict, a method that rejects revenge, aggression, and retaliation. The foundation of such a method is love. The most pressing problem confronting humanity is the poverty of the human spirit, which stands in glaring contrast to our scientific and technological abundance. This is apparent in the three terrible evils that have grown out of our ethical infantilism: racial injustice, poverty, and war, which are all intertwined.

In the twentieth century, more effort than ever before was put into the peaceful resolution of conflict through lobbying efforts, demonstrations, and countless other means. If the two world wars were tragic and costly in terms of lives and resources, they helped to bring about international organizations such as the League of Nations and the United Nations, which sought to manage conflict and create conditions that make wars less likely. Efforts focused not only on arms control but on a reduction of poverty, protection of the environment, and a more equitable distribution of social resources such as housing, education, jobs, and health care. Public and private national and international agencies rushed in food and medical supplies to refugees caught in conflicts. The concern was not only for humanitarian aid but also for world peace as these agencies set about to diffuse the conditions that would retard a return to peaceful conditions. The development of weapons of mass destruction made the task of conflict resolution all the more urgent.

How much progress was made in the twentieth century toward the social learning that Kenneth Boulding wrote about at the height of the Cold War? And in the twenty-first century, what will it take for the world to achieve what Boulding called a "stable peace," rather than an unstable one? How does one define "just wars," and are they necessary? The relevance of historical experience for contemporary generations was questioned in the poster displayed in a small French town to commemorate the eightieth anniversary of the armistice that ended World War I. Can these deadly statistics be meaningful to those who live at the dawn of a new century, whether in comfort or under oppression? Does the future of world peace lie with nation-states pursuing their own security or with international organizations and agreements that can only be effective if member states give up some autonomy? In this chapter we trace experiences with war and peace in the twentieth century but come to no easy conclusions.

The Experience of War

The early twentieth century was dominated by two wars that engulfed most of the world. Many of the circumstances surrounding these two world wars have already been discussed in previous chapters, where frequent allusions to war have been necessary in order to put other significant historical themes into context. The later century avoided such cataclysmic events, but war continued on a smaller yet still devastating scale from Central America to Indonesia and from Chechnya to Mozambique. These last wars were often fought by guerrilla forces, an important feature of warfare in the twentieth century. It is not the purpose of this chapter to dwell in detail on the reasons for the outbreak of specific wars or on the course of events in these wars. Rather, it is the experience of war, particularly the two world wars, which seared the consciousness of those who lived through them, that is the subject here.

As World War I threatened to erupt, emperors, ministers, and generals might have used their influence to draw back from the abyss. Indeed, some historians point to the role of individuals in history, thus putting "flesh and blood" on the abstractions of short- and long-term causes of war. In 1914 there were no hotlines between Great Power governments to diffuse tensions, no shuttle diplomacy by jet planes, and no global organizations to mediate disputes. Of the major combatants, few could have foreseen the horror that their decisions unleashed. Western Europe had not experienced a major war since the 1870 Franco-Prussian War, and Britain had not known a major war close to home since the Napoleonic Wars a hundred years before. Yet, the European Great Powers, with the exception of Britain (which had the largest and best-equipped navy), maintained large armies and reserve forces. No one knew what a war in the modern, industrial age would be like. The weapons developed in the arms race at the turn of the century were largely untried.

Indeed, many wanted to go to war and thought it would be over in a few months—"back in time for Christmas," they said, as they marched off to the battlefront in August. Sir Edward Grey, the British foreign secretary, was one of the few who understood the situation. He noted with foresight: "The lamps are going out all over Europe; we shall not see them lit again in our lifetime." Posters and cartoons depicting the "rights" and "wrongs" and the "guilty" and "innocent" filled the popular press and festooned public sites from Australia to the United States and Europe; national propaganda machines and popular media moved into high gear to mobilize public opinion, volunteers, and resources in the war effort. Those who hesitated were portrayed as traitors. The war started in Europe and the major confrontations took place there, but imperial rivalries quickly spread the fighting to China, the Pacific, the Atlantic, Africa, and the Middle East.

PICTURE 12.2
Trench Warfare. A U.S. Marine receives first aid before being sent to a hospital behind the lines in the Toulon Sector, France, in 1918. (Photo from the National Archives)

Imperial troops were also conscripted and deployed far from their homeland in the defense of empires, with subsequent repercussions in the decolonization process.

The character of the war was a lasting legacy for future generations to sort out, and other wars of the century were built on its foundation. Throughout the century, the means of human destruction in the various wars were powerful and many. The enemy was dehumanized and even unseen. War involved gas, aircraft, bombs, submarines, shells, and tanks. The military historian John Keegan, in his book *The Face of Battle* (1974), estimated that about 30 percent of new wounds at the Battle of the Somme were bullet wounds and 70 percent were caused by shells and bombs. Wounds from "edged-weapons" were rare.

On the western front, the contours of battle were set within a few weeks. The German drive to Paris, where the generals hoped to knock out the French quickly so as to concentrate their might on the eastern front against Russia (thus avoiding a war on two fronts), was stopped by the Allies at the Marne River at a cost of half a million lives on each side. Both sides dug in along a 450-mile front of trenches weaving from the French-Belgian coastline to Switzerland (See Map 1.1). In October 1914 and only two months into the war, a British captain wrote home: "It's absolutely certainly a war of 'attrition', as somebody said here the other day, and we have got to stick it out longer than the other side . . . until they cry quits, and that's all, as far as I can see." On the eastern front, the fighting was less static, and vast distances from the Baltic to the Balkans had to be covered. Germany was initially successful and advanced along a 200-mile front into Russian territory. By 1916 Russia had lost 2.5 million men, 20 percent of its civilian population, 15 percent of its territory, and 30 percent of its industries. But by 1916, Germany was without sufficient troops to launch a further decisive attack and a stalemate had been reached. In the south, Italy was lured by promises of territory onto the Allied side and became bogged down in a war against the Austrians. In the southeast, the Arabs were enticed into the war on the Allied side by promises of independence. They rose up in revolt against the Ottoman Turks, who had joined with the Central Powers (Germany and Austria-Hungary).

In 1916, as each side tried and failed to make a decisive dent in enemy lines, reporters and writers on the western front struggled for words to describe the "indescribable horror" of trench warfare. Two million soldiers were killed and wounded in battles at the Somme and at Verdun with little land changing hands. At the Somme, the British High Command underestimated the ability of the Germans to protect their artillery and men in deep, reinforced bunkers. After a week of bombarding the German lines with 1.5 million heavy shells, the High Command sent wave after wave of Allied troops forward in broad daylight to be mowed down by enemy guns. It was the biggest tactical blunder in British military history. Some 60,000 were killed, wounded, or missing on the first day of action. Between July and November, Allied troops gained a strip of land about 7 miles deep and 25 miles wide and lost 600,000 soldiers in the process. German losses brought the total killed to more than 1 million. To the south, at Verdun, the Germans tried to break through the French lines. For 10 months and along a front of about 15 miles, it was the same story of indescribable horror. The same story of stalemate ensued, with a loss of 700,000 lives. Prince Max of Baden wrote of Verdun in his memoirs: "The campaign of 1916 ended in bitter disillusionment all round. We and our enemies had shed our best blood in streams, and neither we nor they had come one step closer to victory."

World War I set a precedent for the "total wars" of the twentieth century. Civilian populations were deeply affected and governments heavily engaged in orchestrating the war effort. It involved controlling the news, tending to refugees, raising money in war bonds, or rationing food, clothing, and other essential resources. Such patterns of central planning continued at war's end. The extraordinarily high casualty rate among soldiers meant that few civilians were left untouched by deaths of family members or friends. At the Somme, the British sent into battle "pals" battalions—soldiers from the same village or club who enlisted together and were wiped out together. The war memorials of small villages in remote corners of Europe bear witness to a whole generation of young men dead—a "lost generation"—and a generation of young women who did not marry. The Great War left about 3 million widows; some 6 million children lost their fathers. In the 1920s, numerous disabled veterans had to be supported—in France alone 1 million received pensions as invalids—while others suffered without compensation from "shell shock" and psychological traumas that were not recognized and addressed as they were in later wars.

Although many women suffered in their personal lives, war also brought opportunities for them in the realm of work and responsibility in the public sphere. Wage-earning jobs left vacant by enlisted men had to be filled. Women took over strategic positions in the civil service, in factories, in hospitals, and on farms. Their efforts were essential on the home front and they expected rewards when the war was won. But rewards were not always forthcoming; postwar economies plunged into depression with high unemployment. In the United States and many European countries, women were able at least to win the vote in the postwar years, and young women became part of a new youth culture that sought freedom from the social controls of the older generation.

The end of the war was mainly due to exhaustion. In March 1918, after the Bolshevik Revolution in Russia, the new Communist government concluded the Treaty of Brest-Litovsk with Germany and pulled out of the war. The peace involved far-reaching concessions, with the Russians handing over territories in the Baltics, Poland, and the Ukraine. The Germans were able to then focus more forces on the western front. The possibility that they could achieve a breakthrough was removed, however, with the U.S. entry into the war on the Allied side in April 1917. The U.S. action was largely provoked by Germany's unrestricted submarine warfare, which had sunk several U.S. ships. By the spring of 1918, the United States had raised, trained, and transported to

Europe a large conscripted army. By August, German forces were falling back under relentless pressure. By November, Germany's allies had already surrendered, and although the Allies had not yet crossed into German territory, the government saw the need to conclude an armistice. The challenge then was to craft a peace settlement that would prevent a world war from ever happening again. This must be "the war to end all wars," said President Wilson.

Yet, twenty years later World War II was to cost about 50 million lives—about half of them civilian. Intense fighting took place on a much larger scale than in World War I. The extermination of Jews in Europe, the firebombing of whole cities, and the dropping of atomic bombs on Hiroshima and Nagasaki in Japan introduced violence on a scale previously unknown. As already suggested, many would argue that World War II was a "just war" fought to defeat the fascist dictators led by Nazi Germany. In this view it was Hitler's war: He caused it, planned it, and started it. The line of responsibility stretched from Hitler's book, *Mein Kampf* (1925), where he sketched out his ideas of expansion, to the invasion of Poland, which provoked the Allies to declare war in September 1939. On one hand, viewed in those terms the explanation for the outbreak of World War II was not in doubt; it had to do with the specific goals of fascist dictators. On the other hand, the conditions that allowed the rise of the Nazis were created by World War I and the Treaty of Versailles, which did not prove to be the basis of a stable peace. In this view, the seeds of World War II were planted almost as soon as World War I ended, and they flourished with the onset of the Great Depression. The Allies, by failing to conclude a stable peace—not only in the document itself but by creating broader economic, social, and political conditions for peace—encouraged the rise of extremism in Europe (see Map 6.1).

In 1939, therefore, after Germany overthrew the peace settlement through remilitarization and occupied the Rhineland (1936), Austria (1938), Czechoslovakia (1938), and Poland (1939), the Allies declared war. In 1941, following the Japanese bombing of the U.S. Pacific fleet at Pearl Harbor, the United States entered the war. The first three years of World War II were predominantly a success story for Germany and its major allies, Japan and Italy. In a rapid blitzkrieg, Nazi forces moved eastward across the flatlands of Eastern Europe to launch their invasion of the Soviet Union (overthrowing the Non-Aggression Pact). They also tore through French defenses to occupy Paris, a feat that had eluded them in the trench warfare of World War I. By the end of 1941, Hitler's Germany dominated Europe from the Pyrenees to the gates of Leningrad and Moscow, although the effort to knock out Britain had failed in the Battle of Britain, when the British air-defense system repulsed Nazi planes. In North Africa, German troops went to the help of Italy, and German submarines threatened Allied supply lines in the Atlantic. In the Far East, the Japanese advance through China had started in 1931 with the invasion of Manchuria, and eleven years later, the Japanese empire occupied a vast land and sea domain from the borders of British India and Australia to the central Pacific (see Map 6.3).

Yet, by drawing the United States and the Soviet Union into the war, the Axis powers had overreached themselves. By late 1942 the tide of war had turned against them. The unlikely alliance of the world's greatest capitalist and communist powers worked in the struggle against fascism. At a series of conferences, the "big three" (the United States, the Soviet Union, and Britain) coordinated their strategies to achieve victory and end the war. Within occupied countries, resistance forces kept hopes of liberation alive. Britain provided a launching ground for the invasion of northern Europe, and the United States brought its huge industrial and agricultural resources to bear on the Allied side. Germany, in contrast, waged the war with little help. The Allies continued to chip away at German forces at vulnerable points in North Africa and the Middle East, which became the basis for

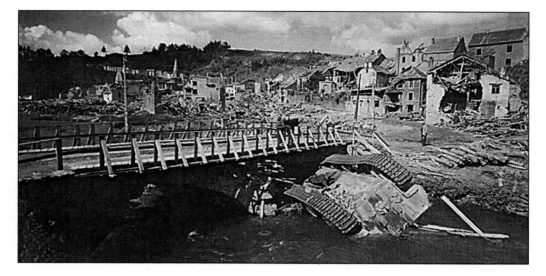

PICTURE 12.3   War-ravaged Belgium. An overturned German tank lies in a shallow stream alongside a rebuilt bridge in Houffalize, Belgium, in 1945. (Photo courtesy of the Franklin D. Roosevelt Library, World War II Digital Collection)

the liberation of southern Europe. By the middle of 1944, D-Day landings on Germany's western flank had allowed the Allies to establish a European foothold from which to advance on the German heartland. U.S. and British ships had asserted their dominance in the Atlantic; Rome had fallen to Allied troops advancing from North Africa and the Mediterranean; and U.S. forces had inflicted major defeats on Japan in the struggle to control strategic islands in the Pacific and Southeast Asia. As noted in Chapter 5, it was on the eastern front that Germany's leaders most miscalculated their strategy. Bogged down in the sieges of Leningrad and the Battle for Stalingrad for months at a time, struggling to survive the Russian winters, and suffering from overextended supply lines, the soldiers of the Third Reich were forced to start a retreat that only ended when Russian tanks arrived at Hitler's bunker in Berlin. May 1945 saw the unconditional surrender of Germany to the Allies. In August, U.S. President Harry S Truman authorized the dropping of atomic bombs on Hiroshima and Nagasaki. Within a few days, Japan had surrendered.

If World War I showed the human and economic costs of twentieth-century wars, World War II brought home even more the implications of "total war" as civilians became the specific target in military strategy. Whereas the casualties of World War I had been about 5 percent civilian, the figure was over 50 percent for World War II. The new technology unleashed on civilians ranged from "carpet-bombings" to atomic radiation and annihilation—and the "final solution" of gassing in concentration camps.

The brunt of the land war was borne by the Soviet Union. The most terrible battle—the savage four-month German-Soviet campaign for Stalingrad—resulted in combined deaths exceeding 1 million. Neither side tried to limit civilian casualties or spare the lives of troops: The final goal of victory for the nation-state justified the "sacrifice." Throughout the Soviet Union, which lost about 27 million people, few families were untouched by the war. The brutal and systematic killing of the civilian enemy reached new heights. The Japanese advance through China included the Rape of Nanking in 1938. Here, 300,000 noncombatants were killed in a few months and often in the most brutal manner. Victims were mutilated and shot; women were raped and coerced into providing sex for Japanese soldiers at special "facilities." In Europe, 7 million captives, or "undesirables," in areas occupied or under German influence were sent to Germany as slave labor. Yet, each country had its stories of courage and suffering, from Botswana forces in the Italian mountains, to Canadians on Normandy beaches, to Americans on Pacific Islands.

Air power was used especially to inflict mass destruction. In February 1942, a directive to the British Royal Air Force (RAF) Command ordered bombings of urban areas in Germany for its impact "on the morale of the civilian population." Thus, moral restraints on bombing civilians were abandoned. Night raids over Germany targeted whole towns for firebombing. In 1945, 796 RAF bombers attacked the German city of Dresden in two waves, followed by 300 U.S. bombers the next day. The town was flattened; estimates of the deaths reached 100,000. In the last months of the war, the United States followed a similar policy, firebombing Tokyo and other major cities so much that they were destroyed even before the ultimate attack on civilians was unleashed at Hiroshima and Nagasaki.

The dropping of atomic bombs in 1945 was a watershed for war and peace in the twentieth century, changing the course of international relations for the remaining decades. The development of weapons of mass destruction paralleled the rise of a new global order. Two centers of world power now existed, one dominated by the Soviet Union, the other by the United States. Some contemporaries and historians have argued that Japan was already defeated and in the process of negotiating a surrender when the bombs were detonated over Hiroshima and Nagasaki. In this view, the U.S. government was not only trying to bring World War II to a rapid end but also attempting to shape the postwar world. In this calculation, the power of the Soviet Union came into play. As Truman, Stalin, and Churchill met at the Potsdam Conference in July 1945 to negotiate postwar settlements, the alliance that had defeated fascism was giving way to competing ideologies and spheres of influence. By demonstrating its awesome military power, the United States would not only bring a quick end to the war against Japan but also strengthen the hand of the Western world against the Soviet Union, which now occupied Eastern Europe and a large part of Germany. In the Far East, the USSR was also poised to take advantage of the crumbling Japanese empire and threaten U.S. hegemony in the Pacific. Thus, it has been said that the atomic bombing of Hiroshima and Nagasaki was simultaneously the last act of World War II and the first act of the Cold War. Until 1989 and the collapse of communism, spheres of influence in Europe remained similar to those existing at the end of World War II. Previous arms races paled in comparison with what was to follow. The world had been brought closer to a nuclear holocaust, a risk that had diminished but had not disappeared by century's end.

Remembering War

While we can trace the course and results of wars in statistics, strategies, and settlements, the individual voices of ordinary people are a powerful testimony to everyday experience: stories of refugees, bombing victims, home-front heroics, and frontline heroes. They tell of hand-to-hand combat, triumph and fulfillment, loss and suffering. These are the stuff of memoirs, journals, letters, poetry, and novels, all of which can be used by the social historian who approaches the past from a "bottom-up" perspective. For those who lived through wars, coming to terms with these experiences can be a drawn-out process never fully resolved. As the British army was wiped out

in the trenches in the early years of World War I, new conscripts, many of them young, well-educated, middle-class civilians, enlisted. Their poetry is a haunting reminder of the horrendous
conditions and the waste of human life. One such writer was Wilfred Owen, who enlisted at age
twenty-two in 1915 for service on the western front. He was wounded, evacuated, and then returned to the front only to be killed in a German machine gun attack seven days before the
Armistice was signed. In a poem drafted in 1917, "Dulce et Decorum est," which he referred to as
"a gas poem," he wrote:

> Bent double, like old beggars under sacks,
> Knock-kneed, coughing like hags, we cursed through sludge,
> Till on the haunting flares we turned our backs
> And towards our distant rest began to trudge. . . .
> Gas! Gas! Quick boys!—an ecstasy of fumbling,
> Fitting the clumsy helmets just in time;
> But someone still was yelling and stumbling
> And flound'ring like a man in fire or lime. . . .
> Dim, through the misty panes and thick green light,
> As under my dreams, before my helpless sight,
> He plunges at me guttering, choking, drowning.

On the German side, so powerful a critique of war was the novel *All Quiet on the Western Front
(1928)* by the soldier and writer Erich Remarque that it was banned by Hitler's government as
unpatriotic and subversive. The shocking and grotesque images of trench warfare that appeared
in paintings by the German artist Otto Dix, who had spent three years at the front in Flanders,
France, and Russia, were also interpreted as unpatriotic by the Nazi government. German authorities stripped Dix of his academic affiliations, banned his exhibitions, and jailed him. In contrast, for many Americans who were distanced from the physical realities of the conflict, World
War II is remembered as a necessary war: The United States, from this perspective, led the free
world in defeating fascism, brought an end to the Great Depression, and emerged as the richest
nation in human history. Individual opportunity abounded, and popular culture reflected a kind
of optimism. Women on the production line, for example, were symbolized in images of "Rosie
the Riveter," a character depicted on posters used by the U.S. government to encourage women to
work to aid in the war effort.

Experiences of war are variously remembered and portrayed at different points in time. Memories are more like a script that is continually being revised than a definitive retelling of events.
Memorializing war involves both remembering and forgetting. Hollywood has produced war
films for all occasions and tastes. *Mrs. Miniver,* which won an Academy Award for Best Picture in
1942, emphasized the heroic efforts of English villagers who met the challenges of war with bravery and fortitude. Other films featured prominent stars such as John Wayne who were associated
with noble causes, adventure, and courage in the face of a villainous enemy. They omitted the
carnage of battle, however. Films that realistically portrayed trench warfare and the human frail-
ties of fighting men, such as *All Quiet on the Western Front* (1930) or *Paths of Glory* (1957), were
rare. In later decades of the century, films set aside a one-dimensional view of war and drama-
tized its random, brutal, and dubious nature. "Getting at the truth" became part of how war was
remembered. U.S. audiences saw films about Vietnam such as *Apocalypse Now* (1979), *Platoon*

PICTURE 12.4
Women factory
workers. Landing gear,
ready for assembly on a
B-25 bomber, is rolled
into place by a factory
woman on the final
assembly line of North
American's Inglewood,
California, plant in 1942.
(Photo courtesy of the
Franklin D. Roosevelt
Library, World War II
Digital Collection)

(1986), and *Born on the Fourth of July* (1989) that were realistic, even cynical. They attempted to portray the ambiguities of the war in the American consciousness. Made after the country had recovered from the divisiveness of the 1960s, they could be critical without betraying the troops. In the 1990s, Hollywood returned to World War II for its subject matter. *Saving Private Ryan* (1998) realistically portrayed the horrors of the Normandy beach landings but little dented the notion of war as glorious, patriotic, and right in defense of a just cause. In *The Thin Red Line* (1998), about the battle for Guadalcanal, individual dramas were highlighted rather than fused in a saga of patriotism and purpose. The enemy was more human and less demonic than in earlier films about the Pacific campaigns. Thus, the script of war and its meaning goes on being written in popular culture.

At century's end, although it was acceptable to flesh out the complexity of war in the popular media, national identities still relied in part on the essential necessity of war as an instrument of national security, the rightness of past wars as viewed from individual national perspectives, and the necessity of dying for one's country. Any tampering with public memory and with national symbols was the stuff of controversies. Two examples can illustrate this point.

The eightieth anniversary of the armistice that ended World War I, 1998, was a time of special celebration in countries such as France and Britain, and the United States, as usual, celebrated Veteran's Day. There were no grand events to mark the occasion in Germany. Queen Elizabeth II of Britain crossed the Channel to visit the cemeteries of Flanders, where tens of thousands of war dead were buried. She later joined the French president at the Arc de Triomphe in central Paris to lay wreaths at the Tomb of the Unknown Soldier, a memorial erected in 1920. A few surviving veterans, by then in their nineties or over a hundred years old, participated. Troops marched down the Champs-Elysées in the blue uniforms of the period, and the same bugle that had relayed news of the cease-fire at 11 A.M. on November 11, 1918, sounded again at the same moment eighty years later. It was a ceremony that passed off without a hitch. A deep respect for sacrifice for one's country was palpable, according to a reporter, although there was no false sentiment about a glorious cause. He was told by one veteran, "It was a useless war," and a teenage girl said, "It was silly."

Behind the public events lay another story, which was also featured in the press even as official arrangements were being made. It involved a difference of opinion between French President Jacques Chirac and Prime Minister Lionel Jospin over who should participate and who should be memorialized in the celebrations. In 1917, several French infantry divisions had mutinied. The previous year they had experienced the trauma of trench warfare at Verdun, where they had sustained heavy casualties. Exhausted by months on the frontlines, when ordered into what they perceived as another useless battle (a classic World War I confrontation, which left 200,000 dead and little to show for it), thousands of troops "plunged into bottomless despair" and "refused to be sacrificed," according to Prime Minister Jospin's statement. Thousands were punished and several hundred were sentenced to death as traitors before the mutiny was put down. Eighty years later, the prime minister suggested that the mutinous soldiers should finally "be reintegrated into our national collective memory" in recognition of the mitigating circumstances of their action and the sacrifices that they had made earlier to hold the line against enemy attacks. This sort of reconciliation was more than the national "honor" could bear, however. The office of the president received outraged complaints from the families of soldiers who had been killed in the war and from surviving veterans. The president issued a statement: "At the moment when the nation is commemorating the sacrifice of more than a million French soldiers who gave their lives . . . any public statement that could be interpreted as the rehabilitation of the mutineers is inopportune." At the heart of the controversy was a deeper cultural and political divide, which memories of war had aggravated. On the one hand were the supporters of the president's conservative and overtly patriotic party; on the other, the prime minister's socialist party, which had been accused by its adversaries of having pacifist leanings.

A similar controversy erupted in the United States when preparations to celebrate the fiftieth anniversary of the end of World War II were being made. At the Smithsonian Institution, the curators of the National Air and Space Museum decided to put the fuselage of the *Enola Gay,* the bomber that carried the atomic bomb to Hiroshima, on display. Their plan was not just to show the plane but to address the context in which the decision to use the bomb was made. In the script of the exhibition, for example, dissenting voices in the formulation of strategy, notably those of General Dwight D. Eisenhower, the Supreme Allied Commander, and Admiral William Leahy, the top-ranking military officer in the Pacific, were noted. Eisenhower had maintained that the bomb was not necessary to defeat Japan or to save American lives. Leahy also believed that Japan could be made to surrender without the use of the bomb. Other controversial issues, such as estimates of American lives saved through the dropping of the bomb, the amount of warning given to Hiroshima and Nagasaki populations, and the extent to which these towns harbored military operations as opposed to civilians, were also to be raised in the exhibition, as they had been in 1945. The curators had miscalculated the furor that would be raised if some of the complexities surrounding President Truman's decision were discussed. Powerful lobbying groups such as the American Legion and the Air Force Association opposed any effort to question the necessity of the bombing in ending the war and insisted on the removal from the exhibition of all documents critical of the bomb's use. Some members of Congress lashed out at the organizers. Pressure was brought to bear on the Smithsonian administration so that the director of the Air and Space Museum had to resign. For some critics, the whole project was the work of unpatriotic intellectuals. Indeed, some opponents blamed the same

PICTURE 12.5
Vietnam Wall. The Washington
Monument towers in the
background. (Photo courtesy
of Todd Richardson)

groups that had opposed the Vietnam War in the 1960s for supporting the proposed show. In the end, the Smithsonian put on a small exhibition. It featured the fuselage of the *Enola Gay,* but without any visual or textual reference to the devastation that had descended on Hiroshima and Nagasaki or to the long-term effects of radiation.

Such selective and contested public remembering of wartime actions have been common. Japan for decades refused to acknowledge its brutal treatment of civilians on the Korean and Chinese mainland; French Vichy collaboration with the Nazi occupation has only recently received attention; and Germans are still struggling with the Holocaust. Memories of war invariably become "tangled," not least when they seem a threat to individual and collective identity.

War memorials are also important symbols in the shaping of a nation's consciousness of its past. Their very design and location can be politically charged as memory and history overlap and different interests contest how a war should be commemorated for present and future generations. The construction of a national memorial to those who died in the Vietnam War was steeped in intense public debate, which was hardly surprising given that the war had deeply divided American society. Veterans were ignored and stigmatized when they returned home. Nevertheless, they initiated the rehabilitation of the war in the public memory by raising funds from private donors and negotiating a site in the Washington Mall at the heart of the nation's capital. They launched a competition for a memorial stipulating that it contain the names of all those who died or were missing in action, that the design not espouse a political stance in regards to the war, and that it be harmonious with the site. The design chosen was by Maya Lin, a twenty-one-year-old architectural student at Yale University, who submitted her plan anonymously. After the selection was made, the design immediately came under attack, not only from the aesthetic point of view, but because it seemed so different from other war memorials. It was black and seemed to symbolize mourning and defeat rather than honor and sacrifice; it did not glorify war and was seen by some as a political, pacifist statement. The long list of names—of 58,196 Americans (including eight women nurses)—seemed to emphasize individual deaths over the cause for which they had collectively died. The architect herself came under attack as not representing veteran interests well. She was a young woman and a Chinese American. Lin noted, however, that she grew up in Athens, Ohio, worked at McDonald's as a teenager, and had little sense of her ethnic background; rather, she considered herself an average midwesterner.

PICTURE 12.6
The Nurses' Memorial. The more traditional memorial to the women who served and died in Vietnam stands a short distance from The Wall. (Photo courtesy of Todd Richardson)

Others liked the starkness and simplicity of the design, its statement about the complexity of war, and its seeming acknowledgment of the need for healing. Rather than try to bring closure to an unresolved and divisive experience in the nation's history, as other war memorials did, it stood as a symbol of remembrance that individuals could relate to in their own way. Once "The Wall," as it became known, was finished, much of the debate disappeared; the experience of visiting it was so powerful that criticism became muted. In 1984, a more traditional figurative sculpture of three soldiers was placed in a group of trees to the south of The Wall, and in 1993 a statue, financed by funds raised by women veterans and commemorating the 11,500 women who served in Vietnam, was dedicated nearby.

The success of the Vietnam Veterans Memorial seemed to lie in its ability to speak to those who visited it, whatever their political persuasions. Indeed, individuals can see their reflections mixed in with the names on the burnished black surface. The memorial honors the dead, but it also evokes the mixed emotions that surround war as diverse populations try to come to terms not only with the Vietnam experience but with broader notions of war and peace.

Peace Movements

At a 1955 Congress of Scientists, Albert Einstein and Bertrand Russell introduced a manifesto that addressed the perils of the nuclear age. At the time, ballistic missiles and a hydrogen bomb 2,500 times as powerful as the one that had destroyed Hiroshima had been developed. Humanity had the potential to self-destruct or, as the distinguished scientist and philosopher wrote, the continued existence of human beings "is in doubt." They challenged the world community:

We have to learn to think in a new way. We have to learn to ask ourselves not what steps can be taken to give military victory to whatever group we prefer, for there no longer are such steps; the question we have to ask ourselves is: what steps can be taken to prevent a military contest of which the issue must be disastrous to all parties?

PICTURE 12.7
Chinese student poster. Peace movements were an international phenomenon in the twentieth century. This poster was created and displayed on a Shanghai university campus in May 1999 by students angered by NATO's bombing of the Chinese embassy during a raid on Belgrade. It shows a map of Yugoslavia and a slogan in English, "Pray for Peace." (Photo courtesy of Jeffrey Wasserstrom)

The emphasis on "learning" echoes the words of Kenneth Boulding noted at the beginning of this chapter. The development of nuclear weapons and the tensions of the Cold War gave new urgency to the quest for alternatives to war as an instrument in international relations: The search for peaceful resolutions of conflict went on throughout the century even as wars raged. If the twentieth century saw the most destructive wars in human history, it also saw sustained efforts to create conditions and structures that would make war less likely and the peaceful resolution of conflict more possible. At century's end, organizations for international cooperation were more in place than ever before, even if large military budgets and terrible regional wars showed that groups and nations continued to see war as an essential and viable means of securing their interests.

Advocates of peace espoused a large spectrum of beliefs and ideologies, both religious and secular. How to ensure peace was the subject of intense debate, encompassing deep-seated differences in values, morality, and strategies. Some, indeed many, would support the position that a strong military is essential in the preservation of peace. That the Cold War between the Communist and Western bloc countries did not become "hot" because of the resources poured into a strong Western deterrent was just such an argument. In this view, the developing and stockpiling of military weapons was regrettable but necessary and justifiable since a nation could only bargain for peace from a position of armed strength.

Peace itself became an ideological tool in Cold War conflicts. In the former one-party socialist states of the Communist bloc, peace activities were defined, organized, and managed by the single political party on behalf of the state. In the former German Democratic Republic (GDR, also East Germany), the "fight of peace" was a term applied to activities that contributed to the GDR's economic strength, advanced socialism, and raised citizens' standards of living. When on World Peace Day workers committed to long shifts to maximize output, they were contributing to peace. After the division of Germany at the end of World War II and the establishment of the

GDR, the party organized "peace committees," and in 1953 the German Peace Council was set up by the government. From the Western viewpoint such efforts were only the propaganda tool of a one-party state that did not tolerate autonomous peace groups. Socialist states, for their part, pointed to the fact that peace activists in democratic countries were often hauled off by the police and detained for demonstrating their opposition to social violence and war, portraying them as the victims of imperialist, capitalist, and war-mongering governments.

Peace activists reject any position that equates peace with military power. In their view, the old "balance of power" theory, which had not prevented wars between Great Powers early in the century, had been replaced by a "balance of terror" in the nuclear age. Furthermore, many would agree with Boulding that a "stable peace" is not just the avoidance of war; rather, it is about creating conditions that lessen conflict, even when wars are not on the immediate horizon. National budgets cannot sustain the development of expensive arms *and* finance more equitable social conditions. One stealth bomber equals "x" number of hospital beds or schoolteachers, and nations cannot afford both, in other words.

In the twentieth century, and historically, a small minority maintained that violence was morally wrong and refused to go to war under any circumstances. In the past, such a position usually had a religious basis. Whereas most Christians supported the idea that a "just war" against tyrants was morally defensible, a few denominations (Quakers, Brethren, and Mennonites, for example) were convinced pacifists. They supported the view that war was not an isolated phenomenon but a symptom of deeper problems relating to social ills and chaotic international relations. When wars break out, they believe, people have failed in their goals since it is the management of conflict that is the long-term problem. In war, pacifists are left with options. They may go to prison for their beliefs or perform some alternative service such as driving an ambulance, or aiding refugees.

Activists searching for nonviolent resolutions of conflict and participating in war resistance efforts have formed many streams within the peace movement. They have targeted different subjects as being critical to their cause (for example, disarmament, international arbitration, draft resistance), and they have chosen different conflicts as being worthy of opposition. Even as militarism, the arms race, imperial expansion, and nationalist propaganda gathered steam, peace activists promoted disarmament and peaceful resolution of international conflict. By 1900, there were well over 400 peace organizations around the world, many of them in Scandinavia—79 in Sweden alone at the turn of the century, but also 70 in Germany and 40 in Britain. From the 1840s onward, Peace Societies in Europe and North America convened international conferences to discuss the spiraling violence in international politics.

Transnational organizations that coordinated activities on certain issues (draft resistance or disarmament), focused on certain population groups (women or workers), or concentrated their efforts against war in any form existed throughout the twentieth century. After World War I, for example, the War Resisters International was founded by men and women who had been harshly treated and jailed for refusing military service. In 1925, the organization issued its first statement of principle, which declared, "War is a crime against humanity." The organization, based in London, still existed at century's end with the broad goal of working "for the removal of all causes of war." To this end it engaged in peace education based on the philosophies of Gandhi and King. Members of the U.S. branch, the War Resisters League, worked in the civil rights campaign of the 1950s and the women's movement of the 1980s.

Women were at the forefront of the earliest peace movements. They and their children experienced twentieth-century conflicts firsthand as "total war" became the norm and civilian populations became the target of warring forces. Women frequently combined the struggle against armed conflict with broader issues such as equal rights, winning the vote, health, education, the environment, and domestic violence. As mothers, women have a particular interest in peace, although once a war breaks out the desire for peace may be subsumed by the need to support male family members who are conscripted and sent to the battlefront. In the midst of World War I, 1,136 delegates from twelve countries traveled to the Netherlands (a neutral country) for a Women's International Congress organized by a Dutch physician and a Scottish lawyer. Some governments prevented delegates from attending since they viewed the congress as an act of disloyalty in wartime. In November 1918, as the war ended, the same group organized another congress in Zurich. Observing the suffering of civilian populations, they urged the Allied governments to lift the naval blockade of German ports. Their resolutions were more farsighted than those of the framers of the Treaty of Versailles: They protested blaming Germany for the war and warned that resentment would lead to more war. They also approved a League of Nations but said that it must be open to all. The congress changed the name of the organization to the Women's International League of Peace and Freedom, established its headquarters in Geneva, and elected the American Jane Addams as League president. The League proved to be another transnational peace organization that weathered the storms of the later twentieth century, continuing its lobbying efforts for peace, for the United Nations, and for civil rights. It still existed at century's end.

While tens of thousands of peace activists joined national and transnational organizations, others worked in small, uncoordinated groups to pursue the cause from different angles. Peace groups tended to spring into action at particular moments in time when a specific issue grabbed public attention. Among prominent issues that provoked challenges to governments and mainstream opinion were conscription and campaigns to reduce and eliminate arms—especially weapons of mass destruction (chemical, biological, and nuclear).

In countries where conscientious objection was allowed, public debate centered on motivations for refusing to serve in the armed forces. Generally, a distinction was made between those who declared that they would not take up arms under any circumstances—"absolute pacifists"—and those who refused to fight in a particular war on circumstantial grounds. Up until about 1940, most conscientious objectors (COs) were members of pacifist churches and opposed war on religious grounds, but the second half of the century saw the secularization of draft resistance. COs had to prepare their case and present it to local courts or draft boards, which were more likely to exempt those who resisted on religious grounds as members of pacifist churches than those who opposed participation in a particular war.

Conscription laws and punishments for offenders evolved over time. In the United States, the 1917 Draft Law provided for exemptions of members of "any well recognized religious sect or organization whose creed or principles forbid its members to participate in war in any form." President Wilson authorized a Board of Inquiry to decide who could legally be granted CO status. Those who qualified had to perform alternative service or face imprisonment. Those who resisted military service were vilified by mainstream society, especially in wartime, and even denounced as enemies. A few might have agreed with the Quaker peace activist Mildred Scott Olmstead, who wrote: "I have often wondered why it is that a family which would make a great protest if the government took away their automobile or even their dog, says nothing when the government takes away their sons."

During World War II, the Selective Training and Service Act was more flexible in its treatment of war resisters and provided for alternative service in Civilian Public Service Camps, a government-sponsored program that put men to work doing things "of national importance" such as forestry, soil conservation, and mental health care. Under this program, 6,000 men refused to cooperate in any manner and were sent to prison, a tiny minority compared to the hundreds of thousands who served in the armed forces.

Many Western European countries had similar arrangements for dealing with war resisters by mid-century, but in some countries there were no such provisions. Men who refused to serve in the Russian campaigns in Afghanistan in the 1970s were harshly treated. In South Africa during the apartheid era, some young, white males were forced into exile or sentenced to years in jail for refusing to serve in an army that they said was not primarily for national defense but used by the government to enforce racist laws and oppress resisters in black townships.

Disarmament has also been a principal focus of peace movements throughout the century. Government representatives met at international disarmament conferences, for example, in 1900, 1907, 1921, and 1932. Participants were little prepared to make concessions, however. Peace activists continued to exert pressure. Women's organizations collected 8 million signatures on a peace petition that was presented to the 1932 League of Nations–sponsored Disarmament Conference. In the nuclear age after World War II, "ordinary" people who had not been peace activists previously became participants. Groups mobilized around specific aspects of the nuclear problem. Women were particularly active in opposing nuclear weapons testing because of the inherent danger of radiation, contamination of the earth, and genetic birth defects.

Protesters searched for and found new and imaginative ways of demonstrating grassroots resistance. Among these were peace camps where activists lived in tent cities near military bases and nuclear power plants. They demonstrated outside the gates, blocked roads, and climbed over barbed-wire fences, thus courting arrest. As Petra Kelly, a member of the Greens Party in West Germany, said, "Non-violent opposition has nothing to do with passivity" (contrary to the term "pacifist," which may invoke an image of doing nothing). Thousands were charged with "breaking the peace" or threatening national security and jailed. In 1979, protests in Europe reached a new crescendo when Western governments announced the development of the neutron bomb, a "smart" bomb that killed people but brought minimal damage to buildings. A new campaign to "rid the world of nuclear weapons" was launched in the Netherlands and Denmark. In the following year, another popular campaign got underway when the North Atlantic Treaty Organization (NATO) announced that American cruise and Pershing II missiles carrying nuclear warheads were to be stationed in five European countries.

Among the most dramatic and confrontational of the antimissile demonstrations was the peace camp established by women around the U.S. air base at Greenham Common outside of London where ninety-six cruise missiles were to be based. This protest became a model for peace activists in other countries as far away as Australia and Canada. In August 1981, thirty-six women set out from Cardiff in Wales on a 120-mile march, a "Walk for Life on Earth," to the Greenham base. Ten days later, they arrived at their destination and demanded a televised debate with the government on the nuclear issue. Four women chained themselves to the fence to underline their demands. The government ignored them, but other women did not. The camp—which included children—grew and the women became a focus of media attention. In December 1982, 30,000 women joined hands to encircle the base or to "embrace the base," as they said. Some scaled the fence and danced on cruise silos. Strategies became controversial when the women decided to exclude men. The camp had become a statement for feminist causes, linking gender and global power politics. It was embraced by popular culture, which produced Greenham badges, postcards, cassettes, videos, shirts, and books. The women stayed on through icy winters, rain and mud, thousands of arrests, and repeated evictions and confrontations with the police. In 1983, in spite of their protests, the missiles arrived at Greenham. But the year was a high point in the European peace movement. Five million women had participated in the protest rallies. News of such activities often made the headlines. In 1987, U.S. President Ronald Reagan and Soviet leader Mikhail Gorbachev signed an Intermediate-Range Nuclear Forces Treaty in which NATO agreed to remove cruise and Pershing missiles in return for the Soviet Union scrapping its SS-20s and other short-range missiles based in Eastern Europe. At the time, a few women were still left at the Greenham camp, but most had been forced to leave to get on with their lives and tend to their family responsibilities. It is difficult in the complexities of international relations to make any direct connection between treaties and pressure from public actions. Indeed, it could be argued that even the removal of the Greenham missiles was but a small accomplishment, since the missiles could still be launched from land and sea. Furthermore, nuclear warheads that could destroy humanity were still stockpiled by the thousands. Yet, women had demonstrated their concerns at considerable personal cost, they could point to results, and they remained an inspiration for others. Peace activists know that their project is for the long haul and that peaks and troughs are intrinsic to their movement.

Finally, on a national level, the development of one of the most dynamic peace movements in the post–World War II world must be mentioned. Not surprisingly, this effort evolved in Japan and was led by the *hibakusha*, those who had survived the atomic bomb attacks at Hiroshima and Nagasaki. At the time, a news blackout had suppressed access to information about the impact of the bomb for several years after the end of the war. But in 1954, when the crew of a Japanese tuna boat, the misnamed *Lucky Dragon,* was smothered with radioactive ash from a U.S. nuclear test off the Bikini Atoll in the Pacific, panic ensued. The incident became a catalyst for the growth of the Japanese peace movement. A women's reading circle in Tokyo initiated a signature campaign for a petition to prohibit atomic and hydrogen bombs; for this effort, a national council was formed and more than 30 million signatures were collected. A World Conference held in Hiroshima in 1955 provided hibakusha with an opportunity to speak out for the first time about their experiences during and after the blast; in addition, they demanded health care and disability benefits from the government. Since then the hibakusha and their supporters have been at the core of a Japanese peace movement that has graphically publicized the terrible, long-lasting, and lethal effects of radiation. They insisted that the government disseminate information on the impact of the bombing and demanded that the United States apologize for dropping the bomb and acknowledge the action as an act against humanity and a violation of international law. At the same time, they have worked to create a nuclear-free zone in Asia and the Pacific—small wonder, therefore, that crowds took to the streets when word was received that India and Pakistan were testing nuclear weapons in 1998.

If memorials to war dot all corners of the world, memorials to peace are much harder to find. Here, the cities of Hiroshima and Nagasaki have taken a lead as strong proponents of a worldwide ban on nuclear weapons. In 1955, in another response to the *Lucky Dragon* tragedy, a memorial Peace Museum and Peace Park were opened in Hiroshima. The park includes the Atomic Dome, one of the few buildings at the hypocenter of the blast not totally flattened. It stands as a moving symbol for world peace. The museum displays all manner of artifacts recov-

PICTURE 12.8   Atomic Bomb Dome, Hiroshima. The building, preserved as a symbol of peace, is all that remains of the Hiroshima Industrial Promotion Hall, which was almost directly under the atomic bomb blast of August 6, 1945. (Photo courtesy of James Madison)

ered from the hibakusha and the atomic bomb site. Yet, like the *Enola Gay* exhibit at the National Air and Space Museum, the Hiroshima Peace Park has also had its share of controversy. The original Japanese display memorialized the victims of the blast, but it had nothing to say about the Chinese, Koreans, and others victimized in the course of Japanese imperial expansion in Southeast Asia. It is an interesting commentary on what we choose to remember in official and public views of the past that the Smithsonian exhibition ended with the dropping of the atomic bomb and the Hiroshima exhibit started with the same event. These are examples of what M. R. Trouillot has called "silencing the past" and the "power of the story," but which story?

International Peace Organizations

While a multitude of groups pressured and lobbied national governments on peace issues, the twentieth century also witnessed the proliferation of international organizations that aided global contacts and worked to create conditions that diffused conflict. The scientific advances that threatened humanity also turned the world into a global village. Many nongovernmental agencies (Doctors Without Borders, Oxfam, Red Cross, Amnesty International, and the like) developed out of individual initiatives and were supported by the private donations of millions. Such private agencies also cooperated with national and international organizations to work on problems such as refugees, health, famine, shelter, and conflict resolution.

The United Nations was the most important and ambitious institution founded in the twentieth century to promote world peace. It was established after World War II in New York from the ashes of the doomed League of Nations. The fifty-one original members who signed the UN Charter in 1945 in San Francisco agreed that the United Nations existed "to save succeeding generations from the scourge of war, which twice in our lifetime has brought untold sorrows to mankind, . . . to reaffirm faith in fundamental rights . . . and to establish conditions under which justice and respect for . . . international law can be maintained." Another key document of the twentieth century was the Universal Declaration of Human Rights (1948), commissioned by the UN General Assembly and signed by member states (see Table 12.1). This document contains thirty articles that the signatories claimed set "a common standard of achievement for all people and nations."

The United Nations membership expanded as colonial territories became independent and took their seats in the General Assembly. An inner council, the Security Council, has fifteen members but is dominated by the five permanent members who were the victorious powers in World War II—the United States, the Soviet Union, Britain, France, and China. In 1971, the People's Republic of China took the seat previously held by Taiwan; and following the collapse of the Soviet Union, that seat was taken by Russia. A full-time bureaucracy (Secretariat) carries out the day-to-day business of the UN. It is headed by the secretary-general, whose power grew as the Cold War increasingly impeded positive interaction between the United States and the Soviet Union. An Economic and Social Council oversees action on social and economic problems through such agencies as the Food and Agricultural Organization (FAO) and the World Health Organization (WHO). The International Court of Justice, consisting of fifteen judges who are elected by the General Assembly and the Security Council, is located in The Hague and deals with problems of international law and international treaties. A number of other agencies, such as the United Nations Educational Scientific and Cultural Organization (UNESCO), the United Nations International Children's Emergency Fund (UNICEF), and the United Nations High Commission for Refugees (UNHCR), carry out the humanitarian aspects of UN activities.

The UN, since its inception, has been a perpetual punching bag for the individual and collective problems of its member states. It is accused of being hobbled by an unwieldy bureaucracy, of being too expensive, and of being cumbersome and slow to act. Yet, there have been many important achievements, especially in the realm of social and humanitarian aid: The UN has helped ensure the smooth working of the decolonization process in many countries; it has monitored elections in places such as South Africa, Haiti, and Cambodia; it has worked toward global standards on such problems as children's welfare and environmental management; it has rushed emergency relief to countries faced with natural and human-made emergencies; and it has promoted world trade, population, and disarmament conferences.

The most controversial area of activity in the last decade of the century was the UN's role as a peacekeeping body. Here, the secretary-general has a variety of aids, such as sending special ambassadors to mediate disputes (as in the Middle East) and bring hostile parties to the conference table. Unlike the League of Nations, the United Nations also has "teeth": It can send peacekeeping troops into a region to stabilize a fragile and hostile situation. Such peacekeepers were sent to Cyprus, Somalia, Bosnia, Mozambique, El Salvador, and Cambodia, for example. During the Cold War, many activities requiring Security Council compliance were stymied due to the conflicting, vested interests of the Communist and Western blocs. For example, the UN could not intervene in wars in Vietnam, Iran-Iraq, and Afghanistan. After the end of the Cold War in the

TABLE 12.1 Universal Declaration of Human Rights (extracts)

In 1948 the General Assembly of the United Nations adopted the Universal Declaration of Human Rights, in "recognition of the inherent dignity and of the equal and inalienable rights" of all humans. The United Nations asked that all member nations publicize the document, making it available in government offices, schools, and other educational institutions. Over the past half-century this declaration has served as the foundation of numerous human rights organizations, as the basis of struggles against dictatorships and other forms of oppression, and as the underlying support for the international struggle to achieve basic human rights for all people.

Article 1.

All human beings are born free and equal in dignity and rights. They are endowed with reason and conscience and should act towards one another in a spirit of brotherhood.

Article 3.

Everyone has the right to life, liberty and security of person.

Article 4.

No one shall be held in slavery or servitude; slavery and the slave trade shall be prohibited in all their forms.

Article 5.

No one shall be subjected to torture or to cruel, inhuman or degrading treatment or punishment.

Article 6.

Everyone has the right to recognition everywhere as a person before the law.

Article 9.

No one shall be subjected to arbitrary arrest, detention or exile.

Article 10.

Everyone is entitled in full equality to a fair and public hearing by an independent and impartial tribunal, in the determination of his rights and obligations and of any criminal charge against him.

Article 19.

Everyone has the right to freedom of opinion and expression; this right includes freedom to hold opinions without interference and to seek, receive and impart information and ideas through any media and regardless of frontiers.

Article 23.

(1) Everyone has the right to work, to free choice of employment, to just and favourable conditions of work and to protection against unemployment.
(2) Everyone, without any discrimination, has the right to equal pay for equal work. . . .

Article 25.

(1) Everyone has the right to a standard of living adequate for the health and well-being of himself and of his family, including food, clothing, housing and medical care and necessary social services. . . .
(2) Motherhood and childhood are entitled to special care and assistance. All children, whether born in or out of wedlock, shall enjoy the same social protection.

Article 26.

(1) Everyone has the right to education. Education shall be free, at least in the elementary and fundamental stages. Elementary education shall be compulsory. . . .
(2) Education shall be directed to the full development of the human personality and to the strengthening of respect for human rights and fundamental freedoms. . . .

1990s, a whole new situation emerged in which there was an explosion of demands for UN intervention in war zones and in regions where tensions were mounting. In 1994, peacekeeping operations peaked, with 18 operations involving 80,000 peacekeepers from 82 countries at a cost to UN members of $3.3 billion.

Thus, the world organization ended the century in crisis. It had come into existence to deal with international peace and security, but it was being called on to intervene in bitter civil wars where historic, economic, religious, and class enmities were mobilized along ethnic lines. Ironically, through force of arms, it had some success as a peacekeeper—in Cyprus, for example, where UN "blue helmets" patrolled the border between the Greek and Turkish sections of the island—but it was less successful as a peacemaker. UN resources were stretched to the limit. It was not only a problem of determining the conditions for intervention by peacekeeping forces in violent conflicts, but of whether member countries were even willing to volunteer their troops (many refused), and who would pay. The organization did not have the means to intervene in many instances, especially since important member states such as the United States and Russia had fallen behind in paying dues. One important development at century's end was the increasing intervention of regional bodies in the management of conflict. Thus, in 1999, NATO intervened to try and resolve the crisis in Kosovo in Yugoslavia, and the Organization of African Unity attempted to bring an end to war in Central Africa.

Conclusion

Considering war and peace as a balance sheet, one could chalk up successes and failures for the twentieth century. On the plus side, Europe, the battleground for two world wars, was united as never before at century's end. There was a European parliament, an increasingly integrated economy, and a security organization (NATO) that was expanding to include the states of Eastern Europe that had been under Communist rule during the Cold War. A war between traditional enemies such as France and Germany seemed very unlikely. Following the fall of the Berlin Wall, the divided territory of Germany was reunited without an outbreak of major violence. In the 1990s, the collapse of the former Yugoslavia and the turmoil in Bosnia and Kosovo were contained even if the crisis was far from over and the Balkans as much a trouble spot as it was in 1914.

On the positive side, too, several treaties to limit nuclear weapons and to outlaw land mines and chemical and biological warfare had been concluded. A Biological Weapons Convention, in which parties undertook never to develop, produce, stockpile, or otherwise acquire biological agents or toxins, opened for signatures in 1972. In 1997, the International Campaign to Ban Land Mines, which was the culmination of a campaign started by concerned individuals and NGOs, won the Nobel Peace Prize. In the same year, 132 nations gathered in Ottawa to sign an international treaty banning the production, use, export, and stockpiling of anti-personnel land mines, a type designed to wound and kill people. The treaty was ratified by the required number of states (although not by the United States) and came into force early in 1999. Strategic Arms Limitation Talks between the major powers had resulted in cuts in nuclear weapons stockpiles, and a Comprehensive Nuclear Test Ban Treaty had 152 signatures by mid–1999, although only 41 ratifications.

The work of the United Nations and its agencies might also be seen as a positive step in an interdependent world, even if peacekeeping operations were fraught with problems and the institution was badly in need of strengthening and organizational reform. There were also a multitude of international, national, and local organizations dedicated to promoting peace, not only through disarmament but also through a more equitable distribution of the world's resources. In Germany, founded in 1980 to promote peace issues, the Greens Party gained sufficient support among voters to gain parliamentary seats three years later, and it had representatives in the national government in 1999.

Yet, was the planet any safer, and could there be talk of a stable peace? Nuclear submarines still prowled the Atlantic and Pacific at century's end, a decade after the Cold War had ended. Even if all the existing treaties to destroy and limit nuclear weapons were signed and ratified, the Soviet Union and the United States alone would still hold 3,000 each. The Nuclear Non-Proliferation Treaty had not been ratified by many states, and the same was true for the treaties against land mines and biological and chemical weapons. In the post–Cold War era, there was always the danger that weapons of mass destruction would "fall into the wrong hands" (defined according to individual and national perspectives). Conventional weapons were easily available on the world market. Secondhand arms flooded markets where customers could not afford sophisticated new weapons. In Rwanda in the mid–1990s, opposing sides imported arms from more than ten different countries. Even if wars between Great Powers were less likely at century's end, bitter civil wars could spill into neighboring areas and become larger conflagrations that threatened regional security, as happened in Central Africa. At the same time, terrorists, fighting from their position of weakness, planted bombs in urban areas and intentionally killed themselves and bystanders to make a statement for their cause.

Searching for a stable peace will take more than considering balance sheets, even if acknowledging past successes and failures in global conflict resolution is part of the "social learning" that Kenneth Boulding wrote about. The same author wrote, in *Stable Peace* (1978):

> If we had a policy of a stable peace, what would it look like? Up to now peace has been regarded either as a utopian ideal or as something like the weather, over which we have no control. . . . The problem of peace policy is seen not as how to achieve immediate and certain success but as how to introduce a bias into the system that moves it toward stable peace at a more rapid rate.

Are there lessons to be learned from twentieth-century experience? Are there connections between grassroots peace movements and governmental policy? Are war and peace gendered issues? Is peace a luxury for the "haves" but not for the "have-nots"? It seems appropriate to end this chapter not with well-rounded conclusions but with the words of Javier Pérez de Cuéllar, who said in 1988, in an acceptance speech for the Nobel Peace Prize on behalf of the UN peacekeeping forces:

> Peace is an easy word to say in any language. As Secretary-General of the United Nations, I hear it so frequently, from so many different mouths and different sources, that it sometimes seems to me to be a general incantation more or less deprived of practical meaning. What do we really mean by peace?

13

Science: Giant Leaps for Humankind, with Misgivings

The first essential component of social justice is adequate food for all mankind.

Norman Borlaug,
Nobel Peace Prize acceptance speech
(1970)

It may become possible [in the immediate future] to set up a nuclear chain reaction in a large mass of uranium, by which vast amounts of power and large quantities of new radium-like elements would be generated.

Albert Einstein,
letter to Franklin Roosevelt
(August 2, 1939)

DURING THE TWENTIETH CENTURY THE OUTLOOK TOWARD SCIENCE turned topsy-turvy. At the century's opening many scientists and laypeople believed that the material problems humankind faced, and perhaps some of its spiritual problems as well, could be solved by science. Science explained Nature, allowed a better human adaptation to Nature, and could modify Nature to suit humankind. Science offered breakthrough discoveries. Science delivered the goods, and the goods were good. By the close of the century, however, confidence in science had turned to skepticism. Many breakthrough discoveries had occurred in the meantime, and many problems had been resolved. Each breakthrough created new problems, too. What is more, the pace at which problems presented themselves and the gravity of those problems had increased.

Along the way something curious happened. The solutions that science offered to material problems, and there were many, came to be taken for granted. Attention focused instead on the unresolved problems, on the new problems created by science, and on the gap between expectations and achievements. In the 1990s, many intellectuals argued, in a series of debates called the science wars, that science is no more able to produce secure knowledge than is art or philosophy.

Three breakthroughs draw close scrutiny in this chapter: antibiotics, the Green Revolution, and nuclear energy. Many breakthroughs might be discussed, among them flight, rocketry, computers, the transistor, and genetic engineering. We have chosen these three because they illustrate an important theme, that is, that each scientific solution created new problems. These three also demonstrate well the fact that solutions, even when lasting and beneficial, received less attention than either the new problems that had appeared in the meantime or the problems created by the solutions themselves.

Antibiotics and Biomedicine

In September 1928 Alexander Fleming, a microbiologist working in a laboratory at St. Mary's Hospital in London, looked and, after some time had passed, looked again at a petri dish with a curious appearance. Fleming had used the dish to grow cultures of a staphylococcal strain of bacteria. He had left it at room temperature, rather than in equipment able to maintain the higher temperature at which the staphylococcal strain had initially multiplied. What Fleming noticed was that mold had accidentally contaminated the dish, and that the staphylococcus colonies had disappeared in the area where the mold grew. For Fleming, the mold contaminant, which he named penicillin, was interesting because it showed that a particular fungus possessed antibacterial properties. It did not occur to Fleming to consider penicillin's therapeutic potential. He published a paper about his findings. He and others tried but failed to replicate the mold contamination, not understanding the essential role that room temperature had played in the original accident. And he laid the matter to rest.

PICTURE 13.1   Alexander Fleming (1881–1955). The bacteriologist whose
discovery of penicillin prepared the way for antibiotic therapy is
photographed here in the early 1940s in his laboratory holding a petri dish.
(Photo from the Portrait of America Collection, Library of Congress)

Fleming's actions that September day exhibited the carefully plotted work of a scientist trying
to employ the rigid procedures of the scientific method while building on predecessors' findings.
They also contain elements of serendipity. On the side of serendipity, one might emphasize the
second look, which led Fleming to photograph the petri dish and write a paper about its contamination with mold. Or one might emphasize Fleming's concentration on this example of bacterial antagonism rather than on the implications of the mold's having suppressed the staphylococcal bacteria. One might celebrate this well-documented discovery of a particular antibacterial
substance. Or one might lament the passage of another decade before Fleming's work was replicated so that another scientist could draw appropriate conclusions about its implications for use
in combating disease.

Both plotting and serendipity played their roles in the development of the biological sciences
in the modern era, and in their application to improving the quality of life. The romantic version
of the story, the one sometimes favored by scientists who want to call more attention to their genius than to the plodding nature of laboratory work, favors serendipity. But science builds on science. How much weight each factor deserves can be seen in the history of biology and medicine
between 1857, a date worth noticing because a pathbreaking scientific paper was published that
year, and the present. This history concerns the things Fleming may have had in mind when he
took a second glance at that petri dish, and the things that he overlooked. It is also a history of
how science and scientists learned to draw public attention to their findings, and to claim more
intellectual and financial resources for their projects. And, finally, it is a history of the public's
mixed feelings about science. On one hand, biomedical discoveries promised to prevent many
diseases and to cure others, saving lives, helping people to avoid discomfort, and sharply raising

the quality of life. On the other hand, the public remained ever ready to criticize a scientist or a particular result that failed. To put the story of biomedicine and antibiotics together requires a survey of scientific work on three topics: germ theory, immunology, and bacterial antagonism and antibiotics.

Antony van Leeuwenhoek, a seventeenth-century Dutch draper, assembled microscopes that allowed him to detect single-celled organisms including protozoa, spermatozoa, and bacteria. He called the protozoa "animalcules." They were living organisms, albeit so small their existence had not previously been suspected. A number of scientists in Leeuwenhoek's day and afterward thought that diseases might be transmitted by unseen, or barely seen, substances, probably carried in the air. They did not expect those disease agents to be living organisms, and they did not think that the life forms Leeuwenhoek had seen caused disease. Environmental medicine, the most widely accepted explanation for epidemic diseases in Western countries in the eighteenth and early nineteenth centuries, attributed disease to filth communicated through the air and water. Filth theory provided a rationale for ventilating a house, collecting refuse for disposal, purifying water, and treating sewage.

Between 1857 and 1879, a period bounded by two important scientific papers, a new theory emerged. It held that decomposition itself, fermentation, and many diseases, too, are caused by living microorganisms. This is germ theory. It was worked out chiefly by three scientists: Louis Pasteur, Robert Koch, and Joseph Lister. Germ theory laid the foundations of modern medicine, which carefully differentiates diseases, assigns to pathogens the capacity to cause disease, and urges that disease can be cured or prevented by attacking these pathogens.

Louis Pasteur, a chemist, argued in a brilliant 1857 scientific paper that microorganisms do not arise spontaneously, as most scientists believed, but are generated by other microorganisms and, furthermore, that microbes cause fermentation. In the process Pasteur lent animation to yeast, explaining its actions as bacterial and therefore biological rather than chemical. In fermentation, where living cells degrade glucose, he provided an analogy for his idea that microorganisms cause disease. He also showed how microorganisms cause food and drink to go bad, and explained how that natural course of events can be prevented by a process that came almost immediately to be called pasteurization.

Robert Koch, a biologist, worked out the etiology of anthrax in sheep, giving a nearly conclusive demonstration that living organisms of a particular type cause a particular disease. In 1879 he published a paper showing that bacteria, rather than being products of disease, cause disease. A few years later he identified the bacillus responsible for tuberculosis, the leading cause of death in Europe in his day, and not long after that the bacillus that causes cholera. Koch also articulated the postulates upon which to decide whether a given bacteria found in the blood of a diseased person should be accounted responsible for the disease. In the last two decades of the nineteenth century biologists and other scientists identified the pathogens causing some twenty diseases. Ultimately it was discovered that slightly more than a hundred bacteria cause disease in humans and animals, and additional numbers cause plant disease.

A few years earlier, in 1865, the British surgeon Joseph Lister demonstrated the same point in a different way by showing that substances that killed bacteria could protect people with wounds or people undergoing surgery from infection. He called surgery accompanied by periodic spraying of diluted phenol "antiseptic surgery." Lister dressed surgical wounds with carbolic acid dressings.

Pasteur, who had a knack for seeing the practical implications of his scientific experiments, suspected that he could develop substances from living pathogens that would prevent disease.

Pasteur and his assistants developed vaccines against anthrax, fowl cholera, swine erysipelas, and rabies. All illustrated the principle of using living disease cultures to induce immunity artificially.

Originally "germ theory" referred to the processes of fermentation as well as disease development. Gradually this meaning evolved until the term referred to the idea that diseases in general, not just infectious diseases, are caused by microorganisms, and to the further idea that the human frailty apparent in disease can best be treated by attacking the germs themselves. Environmental medicine, which the germ theory displaced, pointed to underlying causes of disease, which people in Pasteur's day identified as filth, crowded housing, and poverty. Pasteur's demonstration that vaccines could be found in the laboratory raised the possibility that disease could be treated and even prevented by means more direct and less expensive than redressing the social ills of humankind.

Two controversies, both still ongoing at the end of the twentieth century, emerged in debates about germ theory. One deals with the nature of sickness, and it has two facets. First, many diseases are caused by germs, but many more do not appear to be. Germ theory drew attention and resources to diseases caused by pathogens at the expense of the larger group of maladies. Second, germs may be necessary for many diseases to occur, but are they a sufficient cause of disease? Is it good for health to leave the underlying causes of sickness untreated? Is it this narrow concentration on germs that allows the rich in nearly every country to live, on average, several years longer than the poor?

The other controversy in debates about germ theory concerns the treatment of animals. Pasteur sacrificed countless numbers of laboratory animals—sheep, dogs, rabbits, and mice—in experiments. In the process he helped show the efficacy of animal models for solving problems in human health: What he learned in animal experiments could often be transferred to humans. He also sacrificed animals in order to produce vaccines against animal diseases. Antivivisectionists objected. Lister felt unable to experiment as widely as did Koch and Pasteur because antivivisectionists were much stronger in Britain than in Germany or France. Germ theory seemed to require the use and sacrifice of experimental animals.

Important by itself, germ theory also played a major role in the development of science as heroic and the scientist as hero of the modern world. Pasteur's father, Jean-Joseph, fought with Napoleon and always counted his service in the Peninsula campaign the high point of his life. His hero was Napoleon, the military leader who might have conquered Europe. Louis Pasteur helped fashion for himself the mythical status of a scientific hero. Pasteur's first contribution to his own myth consisted of the story of his scientific life, which he dictated to his nephew in 1878 to be used as a school report. The man he described made important discoveries and defended his work successfully against critics. He also stood above the fray in the objectivity of his outlook and the consistency of his devotion to experimentation. The patient brilliance of a man who worked seven days a week in his laboratory surpassed the aggressive brilliance of the military hero. Twentieth-century French schoolchildren ranked Pasteur and Napoleon as the two greatest French heroes, but they were much likelier to identify Pasteur as the greater hero, as someone better to admire and emulate.

The heroic image that Pasteur cultivated brought rewards in money and status. He won an annuity from the French government that allowed him to concentrate entirely on research, leaving the classroom. He also raised enough in public and private donations to endow the Institut Pasteur, which became a model for the scientific laboratory of the twentieth century. By demanding it for himself and by showing the effectiveness of money spent on science, Pasteur helped inaugurate a century of major spending on science and helped elevate science to a special status among academic disciplines in its claim on public resources. Pasteur became the leading model for the twentieth-century biomedical scientist and science across the Western world.

Pasteur and his assistant, the physician Emile Roux, managed in 1879 to cultivate an attenuated form of fowl cholera that, injected into healthy chickens, protected them against the disease. Thus Pasteur and Roux showed the possibility of manufacturing vaccines in laboratories by modifying cultures of the very organisms that caused a particular disease. On the same principle they showed that it should be possible to devise any number of vaccines by discovering how to attenuate living disease matter. Pasteur used heat. Other scientists employed chemical agents, including ultraviolet light. Still others worked on finding doses of disease matter small enough to provide protection without having to be attenuated. Nevertheless, the mechanism of protection remained obscure. Especially in the case of rabies, Pasteur and Roux were both lucky and well informed. Since rabies is a viral disease, Pasteur could neither see the pathogen nor culture it. The electron microscope, the first instrument powerful enough to pick out viruses, which are much smaller than bacteria, was introduced in 1932. After determining that the pathogen multiplied in the brain and spinal cord as well as in saliva, Pasteur was able to extract disease matter without having to know its composition. He discovered that passing infected tissue through animals' brains increased its virulence for rabbits but decreased it for dogs. Pasteur further attenuated this material by drying it in sterile air. Varying the period of drying allowed him to vary the degree of virulence. By 1884 he was able to vaccinate dogs against rabies, taking advantage of the lengthy incubation period of this disease to begin treatment after exposure. The next year, presented with a desperate human case, a nine-year-old child who had been bitten repeatedly by a rabid dog, Pasteur collaborated with a physician in using his canine procedure on the child, who lived and recovered.

Pasteur promoted the idea that vaccines might be made only from live pathogens. Scientists working in Koch's lab experimented with other approaches. In Berlin Emil Adolph von Behring and Shibasaburo Kitasato repeatedly injected animals with nonlethal doses of toxins produced by two diseases, diphtheria and tetanus. The animals' serum neutralized these toxins, allowing extraction of a diphtheria antitoxin introduced in 1890. Around that time two theories were ventured about natural immunity. I. I. Mechnikov, a Russian zoologist, suggested a cellular theory: White blood cells defend against bacterial invaders. Another explanation, which attributed immunization to blood serum, emerged from Koch's lab in Berlin. Franco-German military rivalry echoed in science throughout the last decades of the nineteenth century, and nowhere more fiercely than in the competition between Pasteur and Koch.

The proponents of cellular and of humoral immunity alike could point to strong supporting evidence. Mechnikov watched as pathogens he could see in a transparent water flea were surrounded and killed by white blood cells. He believed that the cells played an active role in mounting a defense against pathogen invaders. But Koch described Mechnikov's white cells as mere disposers of refuse. Behring and Kitasato, working in Koch's lab on the particular case of diphtheria, showed that injections of immune blood serum protected animals against disease. Their success with diphtheria immunization meant that attention focused on humoral theory. Serum research also identified the blood groups, opening the way for the use of blood transfusion as a medical therapy. Nevertheless, transfusions were used only sparingly until the late 1930s.

Hoping to devise an immunization against tuberculosis, probably the leading cause of death in the nineteenth-century West, Koch identified a substance that arrested the development of tuberculosis in guinea pigs. He hoped that it was another antitoxin, on the model of diphtheria antitoxin, and in 1890 started testing this material, which he called tuberculin, on people. Pressed by a public avid for results, Koch moved faster than caution warranted. When some patients died after injections, the public turned angry. Koch's tuberculin not only failed as an agent of immunization, it also caused harm. In the public eye it was allowable for an agent of immunization to cause some harm, but the harm had to be outweighed by the number of people helped by that agent. Thus from the first people made an explicit cost-benefit analysis of new immunizations.

Two Frenchmen, Albert Calmette and Camille Guérin, found that they could protect cows from bovine tuberculosis by inoculating uninfected animals with an attenuated form of live bacteria produced in the lab, a material called BCG (bacille Calmette-Guérin). The first human subject was vaccinated in 1921, with good results, and human trials continued. In 1929, however, Calmette sent some BCG to Lübeck where it was prepared and put to use. This time 72 of 251 children vaccinated with the material died of tuberculosis, and an additional 135 developed the disease against which they were meant to have been protected. As with Koch, scientists defended Calmette, but the public scorned him.

These two stories show that people were both credulous and skeptical toward the emerging biomedicine. On the credulous side, people accepted claims about the miraculous efficacy of vaccines, even to the point of allowing themselves to be experimented on when evidence in favor of a particular treatment only consisted of success with laboratory animals. People also remained skeptical, ready to withdraw their endorsement of particular scientists, such as Koch, and of particular procedures.

Even so, immunization quickly claimed a place of honor in biomedicine. Vaccines effective against smallpox, diphtheria, tetanus, tuberculosis, typhoid, whooping cough, influenza, poliomyelitis, and other usually less often fatal diseases were devised. It was learned that vaccines could be administered in combinations. And in the 1970s and 1980s global immunization campaigns were launched, aiming to protect the world's children against immunizable diseases and to catch up the vaccinations of children in poor countries with those of children in rich countries.

Since vaccinations pose risks, both in the preparation of the material and in its administration, interest has focused also on finding alternatives. For some diseases, such as scarlet fever, the development of antibiotics made treatment superior to prevention in risk and cost. A major step toward safer vaccination seems to have emerged in the 1980s and 1990s from genetic engineering. By extracting segments of DNA containing the genes of disease pathogens rather than the pathogens themselves, genetically engineered vaccines promise fewer accidents and lower risks. They also promise polyvaccines that could protect people against as many as a dozen diseases in one dose.

Public interest in germs turned rapidly in the late nineteenth century to bacteriomania, a fascination with these commonplace organisms suddenly seen as dangerous. H. G. Wells's 1898 *War of the Worlds* illustrates this attitude. In that science-fiction novel, invading Martians, seemingly impregnable against Earth's weapons, are defeated by exposure to pathogens against which they have no resistance.

Pasteur also worked on the antagonistic effects of some microorganisms upon other microorganisms, using the term "antiseptic" to describe such effects. He suggested the therapeutic potential of bacterial antagonism: It should be possible, he recognized, to use this principle not just to vaccinate people against disease but also to treat sick people. Other scientists explored such antagonisms and tried to find chemical and microbial substances that would control infectious diseases. Most of the materials experimented with were themselves toxic, with the result that the idea of finding antibiotic substances remained unresolved.

Fleming's 1929 discovery of the bacterial antagonism of mold constituted a breakthrough in a fifty-year-old problem. Ten years later, using some of Fleming's mold, which had been preserved, the Oxford microbiologist Ernst Chain isolated penicillin anew and, with Howard Florey, began a series of experiments on its toxicity in mice. Chain found, also by accident, that penicillin had pronounced therapeutic properties, and he began to use the fungus in deliberate experiments on mice injected with bacteria. He published his results in 1940 in *Lancet*, and then he went on to assist in experiments on ten patients. The results were mixed but promising. Chain showed that Fleming's mold had the capacity to reverse certain bacterial diseases that had previously resisted chemical therapy.

Although it was initially difficult to produce large quantities of penicillin, British and U.S. scientists managed to make ample supplies by the 1943 Sicilian campaign of World War II. Japanese scientists also experimented with penicillin during the war, by November 1944 arriving at significant results obtained with very little information about research by British and American counterparts. Soviet researchers worked instead on gramicidin, an antibacterial substance derived from bacteria in 1940 by the bacteriologist René Dubos, and introduced a related agent, gramicidin S. Clinically tested in 1943 and applied to battlefield use in 1944, gramicidin S proved most useful in the treatment of wounds and burns.

During the war researchers also discovered the antibacterial properties of some soil-dwelling actinomycetes, an insight that led to the development in 1943 of streptomycin. Thus was launched the era of the antibiotic, a term coined in 1942. Released for civilian use in 1945, antibiotics proved effective against many bacterial maladies. Each tended to have the most marked effects against specific diseases, thus streptomycin worked against tuberculosis, and penicillin fought scarlet fever, tonsillitis, and wound infections. Medical researchers, journalists, and physicians themselves were astonished at the power of these new drugs to the degree that they labeled them "miracle drugs." By the end of the 1940s doctors were using antibiotics to treat bacterial diseases, prescribing them in anticipation of bacterial diseases that might develop, and often also employing them in cases where no benefit could be expected.

Antibiotics confirmed the public's belief in the utility of medicine, the efficacy of doctors, and the healing powers of the personal physician. But it is important to notice that these drugs became available at a time when the role of bacterial disease in human sickness and death was already receding. Dubos, who in 1939 initially showed the power of antibacterial agents and stimulated interest in using them for therapeutic purposes, later pointed out this paradox. Antibiotics seemed to have quickened the pace of death rate declines, but in developed countries mortality from diseases not treatable with antibiotics also declined more rapidly after the mid-1940s. The effects of the new drugs, taken in terms of human survival, were most noticeable in the fatality rates from bacterial diseases, which plunged.

Antibiotics also confirmed the importance of the germ theory of disease. Here, after all, were specific diseases that could be treated with specific chemical compounds, initially using material extracted from nature but soon enough employing synthetic substitutes. Germs retreated and patients recovered. Before the introduction of sulfa drugs in the 1930s, medical practitioners possessed only a few drugs of unequivocal effectiveness, such as quinine, digitalis, and opium. Those produced results that obviously surpassed what doctors could do by showing their interest, recommending rest, and perhaps also playing on their patients' emotions, which were standard devices of treatment. But quinine, digitalis, opium, and the other effective drugs helped in only a few ailments. On the eve of the antibiotic era, doctors could not effectively treat most diseases, though they could often do useful things to slow a disease's progress. Antibiotics greatly augmented the number of diseases that doctors could treat; doctors and patients alike counted antibiotics as pathbreaking cures. What is more, antibiotics sped up the pace of cure so that no one could confuse their action with Nature's own cures.

Antibiotics had their disadvantages, too. Fleming reported penicillin as nontoxic because it seemed so in animal models. Later experience showed that penicillin produced allergic reactions in more than 5 percent of people treated, some so serious that they resulted in death. The later antibiotics also had toxic effects in some people, although less often than penicillin. Thus both the appropriate use of antibiotics, which led to side effects in some people, and the widespread use of diluted and adulterated antibiotics in the mid-1940s, when these drugs were scarce, led to iatrogenic, or doctor-induced, illness. On one hand, the miracle drugs seemed to promise a quick resolution to the problem of human and not just bacterial disease. Early experimentation suggested that some antibiotics also acted against tumors, and many scientists hoped that antibiotics could be found to counter all kinds of infectious diseases. On the other hand, a smaller group of scientists and physicians warned against side effects as well as drug-resistant strains of bacteria, a development reported already in the mid-1940s. Penicillin continued to prove itself effective against most bacteria sensitive to it, but bacteria showed a capacity to develop resistance against the other antibiotics in common use. Each new antibiotic seemed to promise a possibility of disease eradication. But none could be brought to bear widely enough against a global pool of disease to conquer a particular pathogen before it began to show resistance.

Tuberculosis once more provides an illustration. Streptomycin, introduced in 1943, proved by 1944 to be a powerful weapon against tuberculosis. But drug-resistant strains of the disease also developed. Microbiologists countered by deriving new antibiotics, and physicians sought the most powerful combinations of drugs and regimens of drug use. Successful drug therapy meant that tuberculosis caused fewer and fewer deaths. At the same time, more fiercely resistant strains appeared, making some cases intractable and raising fears of a resurgence of drug-resistant strains of the disease. In 1944 it was predicted that tuberculosis would eventually be completely under control; however, in the 1990s it remained a significant medical problem. Nevertheless, mortality from the disease had dropped sharply in the rich countries of the globe.

Immunizations, antibiotics, and germ theory, plus noteworthy advances in surgery and the use of chemical tests to aid in the diagnosis of disease, provided a solid foundation for biomedicine, a field distinctive for its efficacy in preventing and curing disease. Although it was created in the West, biomedicine was from the start more cosmopolitan than Western. The scientists themselves moved about freely. The Frenchman Dubos immigrated to the United States, where he studied with a Russian Jewish émigré, Selman Waksman, who devised streptomycin. Mechnikov, the Russian, did his best work in Paris, though he also conducted important experiments in St. Petersburg, Sicily, and Odessa. Kitasato, who worked on diphtheria in Koch's lab, returned to Japan where he organized a lab for the manufacture of vaccine and trained new bacteriologists, including Kiyoshi Shiga, who did pioneering work on bacterial dysentery. Koch traveled to Egypt and India in the 1880s to study cholera. What distinguished the people who made leading contributions to biomedicine was not so much that they were mostly westerners; rather, it was their shared confidence in the scientific method, in the use of technology in science, and in a form of scientific capitalism. Like Pasteur, all these people believed in the efficacy of investments in scientific education, well-equipped laboratories, and time free for research.

PICTURE 13.2
Nurse administering vaccination. This young patient is taking part in a government-sponsored program in Papua New Guinea. (Reprinted from UN Economic and Social Commission for Asia and the Pacific, *Population Headlines,* October 1994)

Most immunizations and antibiotics merely hastened the struggle against childhood disease and death in the developed countries. These innovations were introduced later in developing countries, where such diseases remained major killers. Thus biomedicine had a pronounced effect in Africa, Asia, and Latin America. Nigerians, for example, added fourteen years to life expectancy at birth in the initial twenty years after the country gained independence from Britain in 1960. The leading tactic lay in using oil revenues to expand the number of biomedical practitioners and to widen access to antibiotics and immunizations. Even so, biomedicine failed, by itself, to protect people from disease and premature death to the degree to which their counterparts were protected in the developed countries. It made rapid gains possible, but not a closure of the gap between life expectancy in Nigeria and that in Europe or North America.

On balance, biomedicine reassured people about science's potential far more than it undermined confidence. The new problems it created, such as drug-resistant strains of disease, seemed small when compared to the premature deaths avoided and the discomfort relieved. The most striking shortcoming of biomedicine lay instead in what it failed to be able to do, which was to address such underlying causes of sickness as poverty, poor housing, and poor nutrition. It was a palliative.

The Green Revolution

Growth in the world population, which went from fewer than 1 billion people in 1800 to more than 6 billion in 2000, increased the demand for food. So, too, did urbanization, which transformed people who had grown some or all of their own food into people dependent on others. The demand for animal protein also increased, making food output less efficient. Feeding cattle, pigs, and other livestock requires as much as six times more land than it takes to grow grains and vegetables for direct human use. The rising demand for food was felt keenly in the period 1940–1960, when developing countries began to share in rapid population growth, urbanization, and changes in diet.

PICTURE 13.3
Norman Borlaug (1914–)
Scientist Dr. Norman Borlaug
stands with a fellow researcher
in a wheat field in the Sonora
region of Mexico. Borlaug won
the Nobel Prize for developing a
hybrid wheat that saved many
from starvation. (Photo courtesy
of Ted Streshinsky/Corbis)

Three types of grain—wheat, corn or maize, and rice—constitute the dietary staples of most people. Each plant derives certain nutrients from the soil. The historic problem of agriculture has been to extract yields from these plants greater in volume than the seed planted while also sustaining the soil's capacity to bear future crops. The historic solutions have been to compensate for the plants' demand for soil nutrients by sowing crops thinly, leaving land fallow periodically, and adding animal and human excrement as fertilizer. Thin sowing also protects plants because insects and diseases cannot spread as rapidly.

Experiments undertaken in Mexico in 1944 and thereafter, directed by Norman Borlaug, a parasitologist specializing in plant rusts, and funded by the Rockefeller Foundation, showed new ways to augment wheat and corn yields while maintaining soil quality. The key knowledge was gained in experiments that identified the characteristics of specific varieties of wheat and corn, considered in terms of yield, demand for nutrients, resistance to pathogens, and need for water. Those experiments showed the possibility of crossbreeding different varieties in order to select for certain traits. The key breakthrough in plant engineering came in the understanding that these plants expend much of their energy, and many of the nutrients they take from the soil, in producing a tall stem. Selecting for shorter stems would channel more soil nutrients into eatable grains, thereby increasing yields. Japanese agronomists pioneered the dwarfing of wheat and rice in the late nineteenth century, searching for ways to add to the effectiveness of fertilizer, but dwarf varieties were not widely used until the Mexican experiments.

But the experimenters were bolder still. The things they learned working in Mexican soil, with an enormous number of native varieties of wheat and corn, showed that many other elements of the complex business of agriculture could be manipulated in favor of higher yields. In Mexico and at a growing number of experimental stations across the globe, agronomists experimented with different quantities of fertilizer to determine how to produce maximum yields in particular plant varieties. They selected and engineered varieties for the length of time required for the plant to mature and bear. They tested strains for resistance to rusts, fungi, plant bacteria, insects, and other pathogens. And they studied each variety's need for moisture. As a result scientists working in these stations were able to produce seeds whose characteristics were known before they were planted. In place of the knowledge patiently won by farmers using traditional varieties with limited yields, the plant engineers were able to identify modern varieties (MVs) that promised high yields and came with instructions.

Moreover, they foresaw some of the problems created by the new style of agriculture they recommended. Heavier fertilizing made it possible to plant thick crops, but thick crops, which make it easier for pathogens to move from one plant to another, increase the risk that pests will eat or destroy the grains before they can be harvested. Plant scientists expected most varieties to have a short useful life before pathogens adapted to them. Thus they anticipated a future of continuing work on new varieties, selected and reselected for the characteristics required in given circumstances.

By 1950 most of the land that could be put under tillage in Asia, Europe, and the Americas was already being cropped. The Green Revolution promised to show how to extract a great deal more food from the same amount of land. For many areas it promised also to shorten the growing season enough that farmers could plant two or three crops in the same year, in place of one or two.

Recent discoveries in plant biology promised an easy solution for an apparently intractable problem. Under the threat of a population catastrophe in the classic form—something Thomas Malthus had warned about in a 1798 essay—the Green Revolution promised a painless solution. Malthus had warned, in "An Essay on the Principle of Population," that population tends always to grow at a faster rate than does the food supply. That warning had proved wrongheaded in the face of two agricultural revolutions in the period 1840–1950, one emphasizing artificial fertilizers and the other the mechanization of farm equipment. Both innovations augmented farm productivity. By 1950 the number of people working in agriculture in the developed countries had declined dramatically, the use of fertilizers and mechanization had significantly increased, and the price of farm products had fallen. Whereas working people in Malthus's day spent half or more of their income on food, as much as 80 percent in some places, that proportion had dropped to one-third or less by 1950 in the world's rich countries.

The Green Revolution promised the biggest rewards exactly in areas where population growth had recently blossomed, and where the fewest gains in agriculture had yet been achieved, such as Asia and Latin America. Moreover, it promised to do as much for small as for large enterprises because no farmer could escape using its key input, seeds. Most people in developing countries still, around 1950, earned their livelihoods by farming, either as farm laborers or by working small plots of their own, often no more than two or three acres. Mechanization offered little to people in such circumstances because they could not afford such equipment and they did not need it. Moreover, if they saved labor on the scale that Western farmers had done, how would the workers—no longer required to till, plant, and harvest—find livelihoods? What seemed to be needed was something that would stimulate output without costing jobs. The Green Revolution seemed to provide an answer. Because at the heart of things it required only two innovations, new seeds and more fertilizer, it seemed as likely to benefit small as large farmers, as likely to help poor countries as rich ones. It promised a revolution in the cost of staple foods because it promised to augment output even faster than populations were growing.

No group was more enthusiastic than the Roman Catholic Church, which resisted any form of birth control, whether traditional or modern. The Church recognized the problems of rising fertility and rapid population growth, however, and realized that its own image had been damaged by doctrine that resisted what most other religious and cultural groups across the globe regarded as perfectly acceptable means of limiting population growth. Pope Paul VI greeted the Green Revolution with a euphoric welcome: "The new name for peace," he said, "is development."

Even before farmers planted the new seed varieties, however, many observers began to question whether euphoria was warranted. Since these seeds required heavier investments in fertilizers and often also in irrigation, would not farmers owning large enterprises plant them first, before farmers of small tracts could afford them? And would not those same farmers sell their larger crops for bigger profits and then buy out the smaller farms before those people could begin to plant MVs? If these things happened, then the Green Revolution would have negative effects as vast as the positive effects initially forecast for it. Skepticism about the Green Revolution set in during the early 1970s.

This skepticism was warranted. The agronomists who pioneered the Green Revolution, and the foundations that supported their work, had failed to grasp that the problem of producing more food had two aspects. On one hand, it was a problem of bulk—and this part they understood. More people would require more food, but the area of land available to be cultivated would not increase much. On the other hand, any innovation would upset the balance of power within communities across the globe, since some farmers would plant new varieties and others would not. The researchers had missed this aspect. Amartya Sen, who developed a theory that the key food problem is not so much its supply as its distribution, was hopeful about the Green Revolution, believing that it promised food and jobs for all. Many other observers saw that any innovation would distribute its benefits inequitably. They worried especially that people with little or no land would suffer, either absolutely or relatively.

This skepticism led to an important intensification of social science research, which in the 1970s turned attention to evaluating the effects of the Green Revolution. Where were the new seeds being used, and with what effects on income and its distribution, the social system, and the environment? Never before had so many social scientists studied problems of economic development at the local level so closely. Initial skepticism about the effects of the Green Revolution asked, in effect, that the implications of innovations be anticipated. And if they were undesirable, the scrutinizers of the Green Revolution suggested, the innovations might be foregone.

After prolonged study most social scientists concluded that the Green Revolution had achieved neither what had been forecast by its euphoric proponents nor what had been dreaded by its severest critics. Much of the closest scrutiny fell upon India, Bangladesh, and Pakistan, lands where population growth was rapid, landholdings were fragmented, and initial agricultural output low. South Asia was a critical test case of whether the Green Revolution would actually mean higher yields, and whether it could solve more problems than it created.

Initially the skeptics seemed to have the better argument. Productivity rose, but not nearly as rapidly as the Green Revolution's proponents had predicted. The first to plant MVs in India were the wealthier farmers with large landholdings. Because of population growth, the demand for wheat and rice, the two crops where MVs were used most in India, rose. Thus, initially, prices continued to increase, meaning that the earliest farmers to introduce high-yield varieties gained huge rewards. Some studies suggested that access to food among the vast poor segment of the Indian population had actually deteriorated. India was growing more food but was building up its reserves and exporting grain rather than providing better diets for the poor. Farmers with small plots and landless farm laborers had not gained, but their capacity to buy food had shrunk and many were hungry. What is more, the irrigation of MVs had aggravated a shortage of drinking water, and the wider use of pesticides had contributed to environmental degradation.

More prolonged planting of MVs and more follow-up studies showed another picture, however. By the mid-1980s, the owners of the smaller farms had also adopted MVs. Even though they were using less fertilizer, irrigation, and pesticides than their counterparts on large farms, they, too, were profiting. Indeed, in the second stage of the Green Revolution in India, owners of small farms and landless laborers gained more than did farmers owning large enterprises, while households not engaged in agriculture gained the least. Throughout India people ate better diets, in terms of caloric intake.

That second stage had not been anticipated by critics. Nor had observers foreseen that the Green Revolution would have some desirable side effects. As the skeptics had predicted, the MVs demanded more pesticides and more chemical fertilizers and put more stress on water supplies. None of those developments proved critical, however. What had not been foreseen was that the higher incomes that owners of both large and small farms enjoyed from MVs would lead them to invest more heavily in agriculture. For example, they bought electrical pumps to irrigate their fields. Their larger yields meant more jobs in processing and marketing rice and wheat and, more positive still in its effects, even owners of small farms and landless laborers became consumers, using their higher incomes to buy new goods and services. In the intermediate run at least, from the 1960s through the 1980s, MVs meant more jobs because there was so much more to be harvested and processed.

The anthropologist Murray Leaf did fieldwork in a Panjab village he called Shahidpur on the eve of the Green Revolution, in 1965, and again in 1978, once the new system was well underway. In 1965 the villagers were subsistence farmers who could not imagine being able to afford even small purchases. Output grew by more than 300 percent in those thirteen years, faster than the Indian average. By 1978 the village had a paved road to the nearest market, regular bus service, and electricity, all lacking in 1965, and its residents raised goats and ate meat, broadcast prayers over a loudspeaker, regularly dealt in credit, lived in better and more spacious houses, and in many other ways enjoyed a higher quality of life. Leaf's study gives a human face to scientific achievements.

Not every part of South Asia prospered. Bangladesh adopted MVs later and benefited less. From the 1970s to the 1980s Bangladesh's food output kept pace with population growth, or nearly so. Meanwhile, MVs became more difficult to afford because the fertilizers crucial to their most successful use had to be imported. Mohammed Alauddin, a writer on the Green Revolution, worried that Bangladesh might have to choose between importing the foodstuffs its people needed and importing the inputs its agriculture required to be highly productive.

Asia gained more from the Green Revolution than did Latin America or Africa. India, Indonesia, and the Philippines, all traditionally food importers, became self-sufficient, and India not only built up large grain reserves but also began to export wheat. Even so, it was the richest countries, especially the United States, Canada, and Australia, that gained the most. In the aggregate, world food output outpaced population growth between 1960 and 2000, although some areas, chiefly the former Soviet Union and Sub-Saharan Africa, grew more dependent on food imports. At the end of the 1980s only about three percent of Africa's arable land was irrigated, compared to an average of 40 percent of the cultivated area in South Asia, Indonesia, and the Philippines. Large areas of Asia, especially highland regions, likewise lacked the water resources needed to grow MVs. In addition, the staple foods of many people, more often in Africa than on other continents, came still from plants (such as yams, cassava, and sorghum) where little progress had yet been made in finding more productive varieties.

The Green Revolution did not solve all the problems of feeding a growing population. Its most enthusiastic proponents had argued in the 1960s that the new agronomy would give the world breathing space, during which population growth might be slowed. Agronomy put off the moment of reckoning and moderated famines, but it did not conquer Nature. Population growth did not begin to slow down until the 1990s. By that point the overriding question was this: Could future improvements in agronomy keep ahead of future growth in population? To this question the Green Revolution offered two answers. First, the new plant varieties and techniques could be adopted more widely, and they might be adapted to the foods preferred by people living in Africa and the South Pacific. Second, genetic engineering promised to open up a new and more flexible way of modifying plants to augment their food output even further.

Nuclear Energy

On the morning of August 6, 1945, three B-29 aircraft approached the Japanese city of Hiroshima. At 8:15 one of them, nicknamed the *Enola Gay,* released a uranium bomb, which exploded at 1,900 feet. The bomb produced a flash of light, a high fireball resembling a jellyfish registering 300,000 degrees centigrade at its center, and a rolling cloud of flames and smoke that swept across the city and the delta on which it is situated. The second plane carried equipment to photograph the explosion, and the third instrumentation to measure effects. The bomb exploded with a force of 12.5 kilotons (a kiloton is equivalent to 1,000 tons of TNT, and a megaton to a million tons of TNT). The nuclear age had begun, meaning that the era of warfare based on chemical explosions, which dated from the advent of gunpowder, gave way in 1945 to a new source of energy. Whereas chemical explosions use energy released by only the outermost electrons of the atom, this atomic explosion used the atom's nucleus.

Some 70,000 to 80,000 people were killed in the blast and its aftermath, and a roughly equal number wounded. Another 177,000 people lost their homes, either from the blast itself or from fires that occurred when the blast overturned coal stoves. About 60 percent of the city was destroyed, including most of its facilities to fight fires, tend to the wounded, or even count the dead.

Having built a weapon of such force in an effort to beat Hitler's Germany to the bomb, the United States elected to use it against Japan, the remaining belligerent in World War II after Germany's surrender in May. The moral implications of using this weapon drew far less attention before August 6, 1945, than did the scientific, logistic, and financial problems of building it. The Japanese, it was hoped, would surrender quickly following the bomb attack, making an invasion by troops on the ground unnecessary and thus saving American lives. But the decision to drop the bomb, and to drop a second one on Nagasaki three days later, was made casually rather than as part of a careful strategy plotted to secure Japan's surrender. U.S. President Harry S Truman took no specific step to authorize use of the bomb, although he did deliberate and decide not to overrule its use. The bomb was meant to be a demonstration of the power of a new weapon; as a demonstration, it succeeded. Japan asked for peace terms on August 10 and agreed to Allied demands on August 14.

A mere half-century passed between the discovery of radiation, which is usually counted the first step leading to nuclear fission and fusion, and the Hiroshima bomb. Initially unsure of the implications of discovering radiation, science came to the view that it had uncovered a limitless supply of cheap energy. In 1939, well before any bombs had been built, Albert Einstein alerted

PICTURE 13.4
Atomic bomb. A dense column of smoke rises more than 60,000 feet into the air over the Japanese port of Nagasaki. The mushroom cloud was the result of the dropping of the atomic bomb on the industrial center on August 9, 1945, from a U.S. B-29 Superfortress. (Photo from the National Archives)

U.S. President Franklin D. Roosevelt to his belief that uranium could be turned into a source of energy, that a nuclear chain reaction might be possible, and that the result would be a powerful bomb. Harnessing the atom promised to solve the problem of energy but posed the problem that humans might use it to destroy their species. Einstein, later a pacifist, came to regret his letter because it helped spark the Manhattan Project, a code name for the U.S. program to build an atomic bomb. Even so, neither prospect—unlimited cheap energy or mass destruction—was fulfilled in the twentieth century. Nuclear energy thereby illustrates the complexity of the issues that science and technology raised. Not even the best-informed scientists could foretell the implications of the science in which they engaged.

Henri Becquerel, a French physicist conducting research into fluorescence in 1896, accidentally discovered radioactivity while working with minerals containing uranium. That curiosity drew attention because a German physicist, William Roentgen, had just the previous year reported his discovery of short-wave radiation, which he called X rays. Research on radioactive elements was carried forward by the Polish-born physicist Marja Sklodowska, who took the name Marie, and her husband Pierre Curie. Marie Curie measured radiation in pitchblende, an ore containing uranium, discovering that the uranium in the ore was not enough to account for its radiation. That finding led to the discovery of two unknown and radioactive elements, polonium and radium. She died in 1934 from a disease brought on by overexposure to radiation.

The New Zealander Ernest Rutherford, working in Canada and Britain, began the process of breaking radiation down into its components and formulated a picture of the atomic structure as a dense nucleus surrounded by electrons moving in orbits. Rutherford found a world where Newtonian physics does not apply. Some years later, in 1919, he also created the first nuclear reaction by bombarding nitrogen gas with helium nuclei, transmuting nitrogen into oxygen.

These findings, which showed that energy lies embedded in mass, stimulated interest in nuclear transformations and in uncovering the properties of radioactive substances. The context for this work was provided by Albert Einstein, a German-born refugee from Nazism working in the United States, and Niels Bohr, a Danish physicist. Einstein's famous formula, $E = mc^2$ (energy = mass times the speed of light squared), proposed in 1905, expresses the rate at which mass is converted into energy. The awesome scale of energy that might be released is evident in the last term, since the speed of light amounts to 186,000 miles per second. Even tiny quantities of mass could unleash huge quantities of energy. (At Hiroshima about one gram of mass was expended to produce the August 6, 1945, explosion.) Einstein's quantum theory and theory of relativity set forth the principles upon which nuclear weapons might be constructed. Bohr devised a theory of atomic structure between 1913 and 1915 and, many years later, showed that the isotope uranium-235, which constitutes only a tiny part of uranium, is fissionable. In 1938 Lise Meitner and Otto Frisch added the key finding that if uranium atoms are bombarded with neutrons they will split into nearly equal parts, releasing some of their mass as energy.

Two types of problems stood in the path of using this knowledge to build an atomic bomb. Matters of organization and finance were solved by the Manhattan Project. Gradually the Americans built a vast, well-financed, secret project in which work took place at half a dozen sites across the country. More than $2 billion was spent on the bomb during World War II, nearly all of it from the president's discretionary funds and thus without congressional oversight. Ironically, the secrets of the project were kept better from the U.S. public than from curious Soviet allies. At Potsdam in 1945 President Truman told Stalin that the United States possessed a powerful bomb. Truman was surprised that Stalin barely reacted; he suspected that Stalin had not understood his point. But Stalin knew immediately what Truman meant, and knew that the U.S. effort to build nuclear weapons had advanced ahead of the Soviet effort.

Three problems in physics also had to be solved: extracting enough U-235 to build a bomb, testing the theory of a chain reaction, and designing a bomb. The first was solved by building a complex apparatus capable of extracting the rare element U-235 from uranium ore. Enrico Fermi solved the second problem in December 1942 by creating a chain reaction in his laboratory built under the stands of the football stadium at the University of Chicago. And the third was solved by July 1945. In that month, a test device was successfully exploded near Alamogordo, New Mexico.

Although the awesome power that nuclear energy could unleash had been anticipated among scientists, political and cultural leaders, and the general public, few people fretted about this issue before the Hiroshima explosion. After the explosion, immediately and in the longer term, many people reflected more carefully. In an address at the Massachusetts Institute of Technology in 1947, J. Robert Oppenheimer, the U.S. scientist who directed the atomic bomb project at Los Alamos, New Mexico, told the audience: "Physicists have known sin; and this is a knowledge which they cannot lose." Physicists working on radiation had understood within the first decade after 1896 that they were working with forces that might be capable of producing an unprecedented release of energy. Hearing such discussions, H. G. Wells wrote *The World Set Free* (1914), a novel imagining atomic bombs. Others likened the power that had been discovered in atomic and hydrogen bombs to a force able to cause among humans a catastrophe similar to what had eliminated the dinosaurs. Yet the physicists worked on, pausing only occasionally to ponder where this research might lead and whether the things they feared might actually become possible. Asked later to justify themselves, most pointed to their scientific curiosity as the thing that had kept them going. They concentrated on solving each of the problems that the enterprise posed and did not worry about the moral issues. In the 1950s, however, when the decision had to be made whether to build a hydrogen bomb, and when the means had to be found to maintain the balance of terror between two superpowers armed with hydrogen weapons, many physicists promoted arms control.

The public's appraisal of the bomb is more difficult to discover, except insofar as it is represented in statements by opinion leaders. Secrecy before the Hiroshima explosion meant that the public neither knew what was in prospect nor played any role in deciding whether it would be a good thing to use the new weapon. After Hiroshima many editorialists condemned the bomb as shameful and barbaric. John Hersey, an American novelist, visited Hiroshima soon after August 6 and wrote a memoir about six people who had survived the bomb. In photographic images the destruction at Hiroshima seemed little different from what had happened in Dresden and Tokyo during firebombing. Hersey's prose brought home the human dimensions of the bomb. Other commentators feared that use of the bomb at two Japanese cities had opened a path to humankind's self-destruction. Edward R. Murrow, a radio journalist famous for his broadcasts from London during the blitz, warned that, with this bomb, "survival is not assured." Most observers, however, accepted the bomb as a necessary, or even desirable, step in defeating Japan. In opinion polls the U.S. public approved retrospectively of the bomb's use and hoped the United States would construct more powerful weapons. Gradually, however, they came to fear that such weapons would be used against the United States. Only a few commentators lamented the effects of secrecy on democracy.

Military leaders disagreed after the fact about the desirability of using the bomb and the need for it. An impressive group, including Dwight Eisenhower, Douglas MacArthur, George Marshall, and William Leahy, expressed reservations or opposition. U.S. political leaders believed otherwise. Impressed by what they perceived as the public's demand for unconditional but also speedy surrender, they rejected proposals to blockade Japan, or to wait for Japanese authorities to resolve their own conflicts between a party of peace and those who wanted to fight on.

Many scientists who had worked on making the bomb hoped that sharing the physics they had learned with other countries would lead to an agreement about how to control nuclear energy. But U.S. and Soviet authorities opted instead to keep as many secrets as possible, each to promote its own nuclear weapons program. The Soviets succeeded in making an atomic bomb by 1949. Already in the 1930s it had become apparent that the most powerful devices would implode rather than explode. Work along that avenue had been deferred because it was also apparent that implosions must be initiated by temperatures imaginable only in atomic explosions. After World War II, U.S. scientists returned to the problems involved in making a hydrogen weapon, and they exploded one in 1952. The Soviet Union tested its own hydrogen bomb only nine months later, in 1953.

By 1981 the acknowledged nuclear powers, the United States, the USSR, Britain, France, and China, possessed some 50,000 nuclear warheads with an explosive yield of some 20 billion tons of TNT. The United States and the Soviet Union alone had enough weapons to destroy each other several times over, but no number seemed sufficient. Nor was any delivery system safe against the real and imagined defensive systems of the enemy. Thus the two countries engaged in a race for arms and the technology to deliver those arms across the oceans. It was the most expensive endeavor in which humankind has ever engaged. Cumulative U.S. spending by 1997 surpassed $4 trillion, an amount nearly equal to the national debt. Soviet spending totals remain unclear. By 1997 eleven countries possessed nuclear weapons: the five of 1981 plus Belarus, Ukraine, Kazakhstan, India, Pakistan, and Israel.

If the Soviet Union could discover how to make a bomb, resulting in the bilateral arms race of the Cold War, what would prevent other societies from acquiring the same knowledge, resulting perhaps in a multilateral arms race? During World War II, U.S. political leaders believed that the Soviet Union would not be able to build its own bomb for twenty years or more, although the physicists working at Los Alamos predicted much quicker Soviet success. When the Soviets tested an atomic weapon in 1949, suspicions were quickly roused that they had acquired the know-how through espionage, perhaps with the collaboration of U.S. scientists. The release of documents after the collapse of the Soviet Union in 1991 showed that they had learned some things through spying on the Manhattan Project. Most of their quick success depended, however, on the work of their own physicists. Even on the eve of the war too much information about nuclear energy was already available to people with the training to understand it; there was no possibility of halting the spread of such weapons.

British and French scientists contributed much to the development of knowledge about nuclear energy, and both countries built their own nuclear weapons during the 1950s. The international community, which sought to control the spread of weapons while allowing the development of nuclear energy, organized a series of agreements. Some countries declined to sign, and others refused to live up to their earlier agreement not to develop weapons. The most powerful weapons, hydrogen bombs, remained outside the reach of most countries, but plutonium, a byproduct of nuclear reactors and the substance used to make the Nagasaki bomb, became more and more difficult to control as its supply increased. If a third bomb were to be exploded in anger, it seemed likely that it would be a plutonium device, which any number of countries—and perhaps nothing more than a band of determined terrorists—could command.

Becquerel and the Curies had shown that certain elements emit radiation. Atomic explosions release radiation in large quantities, and hydrogen explosions in still larger quantities. Although some scientists had speculated about dangers associated with exposure to radiation, there was little initial concern. U.S. sailors watched test explosions at Bikini atoll in the Marshall Islands in 1946 at distances close enough to receive high doses of radiation, and civilian populations across the country, from the Rocky Mountains to the East Coast, were exposed to fallout from bombs tested in Nevada in the 1950s and 1960s.

Serious concern about the effects of radioactive fallout dates from the March 1954 test of a 15-megaton hydrogen device at Bikini atoll. The device was designed to generate fallout. People on two nearby islands and the men on a Japanese tuna boat received large doses of radiation, enough to cause sickness, hair and fingernail loss, and damage to the immune system. A Japanese fisherman died in September from liver and blood damage, and islanders suffered high rates of thyroid cancer and leukemia. The harmful effects of radiation had been proved.

Twelve days after a cinematic account of a nuclear accident, *The China Syndrome,* opened in theaters across the United States on March 16, 1979, an actual disaster began at Three Mile Island, Pennsylvania. Faults in a nuclear reactor, inadequately tracked by instruments, led to a release of radioactive gas. The fictional account related a threatened catastrophe due to poor design

PICTURE 13.5
Chernobyl nuclear disaster.
In 1986 the Soviet Republic
of Ukraine experienced the
worst nuclear power
disaster in history. Tons of
nuclear reactive particles
were released into the
atmosphere and distributed
by the wind across Europe.
(Photo courtesy of the U.S.
Department of Energy)

and management that nearly resulted in the meltdown of the reactor core. The actual event resulted in release of unmeasured amounts of radiation, which spread unevenly over a wide area.

The most serious reactor accident of the second half of the twentieth century began with a fire in the Unit 4 reactor at Chernobyl, in the Soviet Ukraine, on April 26, 1986. Some of the reactor fuel disintegrated, evaporating the water used for cooling. This error led to a steam explosion and a second explosion of hydrogen gas, throwing radioactive debris to the height of a mile. Meanwhile, the graphite core pumped out more radioactivity. Soviet authorities built a giant tomb to house the damaged reactor and abandoned the site and the city. Fallout spread across twenty countries.

In the 1970s and early 1980s many authorities predicted that the impending exhaustion of petroleum and cheaply available coal would be made up by nuclear energy. At the end of 1996, 442 nuclear reactors generated electricity in 32 countries, and an additional 36 units were under construction. The leading industrial powers of the world—Canada, France, Germany, Japan, Russia, the United Kingdom, and the United States—were heavily dependent on nuclear power. Between 1975 and 1985, in the aftermath of the 1973 oil price shock, new reactors were built at a particularly rapid pace, nearly twenty a year. Then, in Chernobyl's aftermath, new construction slowed as many people concluded that the side effects of nuclear energy were too costly.

In the 1950s a proponent of nuclear energy had predicted that the cost of generating electricity in nuclear reactors would be too low to make it worthwhile to send out bills. Such claims played a role in the growth of public interest in nuclear-generated electricity. They proved to be false. Once powered up, nuclear plants did produce electricity at very cheap rates. The costs lay in design and construction, in the length of construction time, often ten years, and in the short useful life of many plants. By the end of 1996, 71 reactors had already been shut down.

The physicists who worked out the implications of the discovery of radiation showed the awesome power of modern science in its capacity to discover knowledge ahead of the human ability to assimilate and cope with that knowledge. Nuclear power promised some good. At the end of the twentieth century it seemed possible that the cyclotrons that had been built to obtain U-235 and to conduct experiments in atomic theory might prove useful for treating certain human diseases. Yet no realm of discovery showed science's two faces more clearly than nuclear energy. Against meager amounts of good could be counted tens of thousands of deaths—at Hiroshima and Nagasaki, at Bikini atoll, and in the areas surrounding other nuclear tests and accidents. Vast tracts of land had been contaminated and would remain so for centuries. Uncounted numbers of people had their health compromised by exposure to radiation. Public confidence in the credibility of science and scientists had been tested and, in many ways, compromised. In the 1964 film *Dr. Strangelove,* Peter Sellers played the part of a deranged scientist mad to use the weapons he had helped to create. Such caricatures were commonplace in film and fiction. Sadder still, the physicists who had made the bomb were not, in reality, mad. Shrouding the development of nuclear weapons in secrecy introduced a new element that no one understood or controlled. Secret projects meant that in democratic societies, too, the people did not always get to participate in important policymaking decisions.

Of the three areas of scientific breakthrough discussed here, nuclear power most clearly shows science as a sword with a two-edged blade. It can produce good things, such as safe nuclear energy, but it can also produce evil things, such as the bomb. It can insidiously undermine democracy; it can even threaten the survival of humankind.

Conclusion

Science proved unable to meet the high expectations that the late nineteenth-century public held for it. Two problems proved insurmountable. First, science could not deliver the life of complete ease and security that had been imagined. At best, it could deliver increments toward such a life. But human misery remained. Second, science could not restrict its innovations to things that people deemed good. It also created evil. In the twentieth century science showed that knowledge is not neutral. It may work to human benefit, but its effects may also be malign, even when there are no mad scientists or evil dictators directing the process.

Thus the path of science helps explain why, during the twentieth century, optimism and faith gave so much ground to pessimism and doubt. Even as mastery over such phenomena as the pathogens causing disease, plant use of soil nutrients, and the composition of the atom produced concrete results, the results were mixed in both practical and moral terms. Few would dispute the efficacy of antibiotics, new plant varieties, or nuclear energy. But each thing has created its opposite, too, or at least such a strong prospect of an opposite that pessimism has as much claim to the territory of appraisal as does optimism. This result is obvious in the case of nuclear energy. More surprising examples come from antibiotics and the Green Revolution. In our suspicions, if not quite in reality, antibiotics are able to cancel themselves out by inducing the microbes they are meant to kill to adapt in order to survive, and many strains of microbes have adapted. In the case of the Green Revolution, each gain in productivity is suspected of producing unwanted social effects that outweigh its value in the added output of foodstuffs. Twentieth-century science helped teach humankind the need to appraise things critically.

This great struggle between optimism and pessimism, faith and doubt, draws attention away from some other features of science that deserve notice. All three of the examples of scientific discovery discussed in this chapter show the role that international collaboration played in scientific discoveries in the twentieth century. Although France and Britain took a particularly large part in scientific discoveries up to about 1930, and the United States and the USSR since then, no one country can claim more than a tiny share of credit for working out the implications of any particular innovation. Western countries invested more in training scientists and funding research, and most of the discoveries occurred in Western laboratories. Nevertheless, the Green Revolution projects in Mexico and the Philippines, staffed by an international cadre of agronomists, point up the cosmopolitan nature of science in the modern and postmodern eras. In the twentieth century scientific information crossed national boundaries even more readily than did people or trade goods.

Finally, there was a gap between rhetoric and reality in the way science was appraised in the twentieth century. On the side of rhetoric, science was scrutinized and often condemned. On the side of reality, however, people accepted Pasteur's advice that it is useful to invest in science and science education. In that sense the hopes held out for science in 1900 remained strong in 2000. Rich universities and rich countries competed with one another to modernize research and development, and poor countries competed to build scientific and technological infrastructures. And people, even while they had acquired some skepticism about science's capacity to bring their hopes to realization, still turned to science as the most promising road to a better life.

14

··

Population Growth

Human numbers and human behavior must be brought into line with . . . the limits of [the] Earth.

Paul R. Ehrlich and Anne H. Ehrlich,
The Population Explosion
(1990)

The standard of living has risen along with the size of the world's population since the beginning of recorded time.

Julian L. Simon,
The Ultimate Resource
(1981)

PEOPLE MAKE REVOLUTIONS IN MORE WAYS THAN ONE. THE INTIMATE decisions of everyday life—marriage, sex and reproduction, exercise, diet, residence—make up much of each person's identity. For individuals these are personal matters and their resolution is a personal decision. People also do these things collectively, and the sum of all those personal decisions constitutes the dynamics of population change. People can make a revolution, one largely outside the orbit of influence from higher authorities, by changing the decisions they make about these intimate matters. Although people living in the same country share many common characteristics, the decisions they make about such matters often transcend national or even continental boundaries.

In the twentieth century the people of the world made three capital revolutions by changing their personal decisions and personal behavior. The first, taking these revolutions in sequence, took the form of a sharp rise in the proportion of people living into old age. In 1800 the average expectation of life at birth across the globe certainly did not surpass 30 years and may not even have reached 25 years. By 2000 the average totaled 67 years, rising toward an optimistic forecast, for 2050, of 76 years. In this revolution, called the health transition, the most common age for dying jumped from infancy to old age.

The second revolution occurred in reproduction. Partly in response to the fact that more of their children were surviving, people across the globe decided to have fewer children. These decisions became apparent first in the 1880s, when European fertility began to decline; by the 1990s, virtually every world region had joined the fertility transition. There were other reasons for this change, too. In the 1960s new chemical and mechanical devices of family planning let people reduce fertility without forgoing the full pleasure of sexual activity. These innovations sparked a sexual revolution, a lesser element within the fertility transition.

The result of this combination of rising survivorship and, after a lag, declining fertility was unprecedentedly rapid growth in world population. In 1800 fewer than 1 billion people made up the world population. By 2000 the number of people had grown to 6 billion. Rising survivorship and declining fertility constituted good news: People lived longer, and they invested more resources in fewer children. Such rapid population growth alarmed many people, leading to recurrent questions about how so many people could be employed, fed, and housed. This third revolution is sometimes called the population explosion and sometimes the demographic revolution.

These three revolutions posed problems outside prior human experience. How could so many more people be accommodated? Who would take care of the old people, whose numbers expanded as survivorship rose? Would these revolutions lead to famine, violence among people too closely packed together, or other crises?

From Population Increase to Alarm

One convenient scheme furnishes a succinct description of how these changes in survivorship and fertility could result in such startling population growth. In the eighteenth century birth and

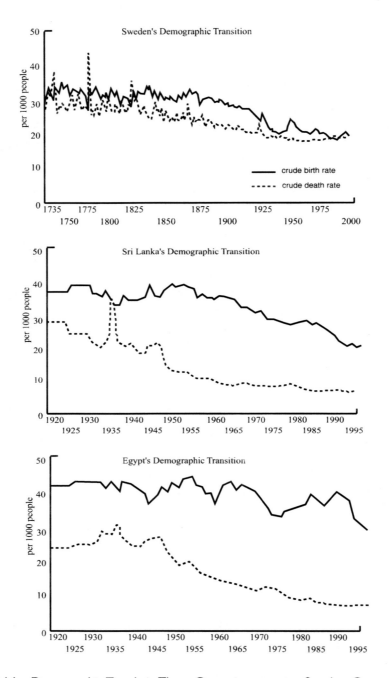

FIGURE 14.1   Demographic Trends in Three Countries. SOURCES: Sweden: Gustav Sundbärg, *Bevölkerungsstatistik Schwedens, 1750–1900* (Stockholm: National Central Bureau of Statistics, 1970), pp. 77–79; *Statistisk Årsbok för Sverige* (Stockholm: National Central Bureau of Statistics, various years). Sri Lanka and Egypt: *United Nations Demographic Yearbook* (New York: UN Statistical Office, various years).

death rates seem to have been high and close to one another—though not at the same particular level—in every part of the globe. Then both declined, but with different timing. Figure 14.1 sketches the demographic transition over time in three countries in quite different world areas. Sweden moved through a gradual transition lasting some 175 years from the beginning of mortality decline around 1795 to about 1970. Sri Lanka's mortality decline began in the 1920s, or perhaps earlier; its fertility decline began in the 1950s, and the transition is still in progress. In Egypt the mortality decline began in the 1940s and the fertility decline began in the late 1960s. Notice the telescoping process, whereby latecomers seem likely to complete the transition faster than Sweden did. Notice also the lag between the onset of mortality decline and the onset of fertility decline. In Sweden's case that lag amounted to some 75 years, in Sri Lanka's case to about 40 years, and in Egypt's case to about 20 years. In the later transitions people seem to have responded more quickly to the implications of lower mortality.

The difference between mortality and fertility accounts for population growth. The long history of high death and birth rates accompanied by slow population growth shows that humans have usually kept population close to equilibrium. The demographic revolution is an exception. It occurred both because death rates declined earlier than birth rates did and because of the extra years that people lived as death rates fell. The baby boom, the name given the temporarily larger families that Western parents preferred in the years 1945–1965, and the larger families that people living in former colonies wanted upon gaining independence in the years 1945–1970, added to rapid population growth but did not alter fundamental demographic characteristics.

In countries that entered demographic transition early, such as Sweden, the process of transition was comparatively mild. Mortality declined slowly, leading to moderate rather than rapid population growth. Latecomers—countries that began the transition in the twentieth century, which includes most of the globe—faced a different situation. Mortality declined rapidly, leading to rapid growth and making the issue of finding ways to reduce fertility more urgent.

One of the best-known population diagrams, reproduced in Figure 14.2, shows just how rapidly world population has increased in the past 200 years. After some 100,000 years of very slow growth, at a rate rarely as high as 0.3 percent a year, population growth took off, peaking at a growth rate of 2 percent a year. At its height, in the late 1980s, population growth added more than 90 million people a year. But consider also the second part of the figure, which shortens the perspective using United Nations projections. In the first part of the figure what seems to be underway is a frightening, unprecedented, and perhaps unlimited surge in global population. In the second part what seems to be underway is a steady transition toward a global population of perhaps 9 billion.

Rapid growth began in the nineteenth century and, according to cautious assumptions, will continue until the second half of the twenty-first century. The effects of altered behavior in reproduction and health take a long time to play out because humans live so long. Even an instantaneous curtailment of fertility to replacement level, about 2.1 births per woman in countries where mortality is low, would not stop population growth until people born in the 1970s, 1980s, and 1990s have completed their reproductive years.

Nor did the population growth of the twentieth century occur chiefly in areas best equipped to handle it. In the nineteenth century and the first half of the twentieth, rich countries grew faster than poor countries. In the second half of the twentieth century the reverse was true. Furthermore, areas with vast quantities of arable land did not necessarily grow faster than areas with scarce agricultural resources. By 1993, Egypt, with 3 percent of its land arable, counted 563 peo-

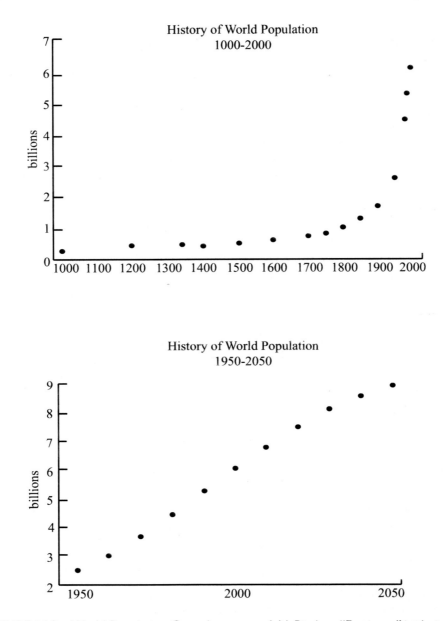

FIGURE 14.2   World Population Growth. SOURCES: J. N. Biraben, "Essai sur l'évolution du nombre des hommes," *Population* 34 (1979), 13–25; Massimo Livi Bacci, A *Concise History of World Population* (Cambridge, Mass.: Blackwell, 1992), p. 31; and United Nations, Population Division, *Long-range World Population Projections: Two Centuries of Population Growth, 1950–2150,* Population Studies No. 125 (New York: UN Department of International Economic and Social Affairs, 1992), p. 14.

ple per 1,000 hectares, and Kuwait, with 8 percent arable, counted 1,024 people per 1,000 hectares. Yet Uruguay, with 85 percent arable land, counted only 180 people per 1,000 hectares. No particular pattern of economic resources or economic prospects drove population growth.

Historically world religions often promoted population growth: "Be fruitful, and multiply, and replenish the earth," God said to Adam and Eve, as recorded in the book of Genesis. But people consistently refused to heed that advice. They were more attracted to such views as those of Han Fei-Tzu, who warned around 2500 B.P. (500 B.C.E.) about the costs of having too many children. Instead of the maximum number of children that each fertile couple might reproduce, a dozen or more, actual fertility across the ages barely exceeded mortality. Consider the global population estimated for 1750: 771 million. The actual number of births that year totaled about 25 million, but it could have totaled more than 46 million. Women elected to begin reproducing later than age fifteen or so, when they were biologically capable, and they elected to stop reproducing before they were unable to do so, in their upper thirties rather than in their mid-forties. They elected to space births further apart. And many individual women also elected not to reproduce.

At the moment when rapid population growth began, around 1800, a curious transformation occurred in ideas. Earlier thinkers, such as the theologian Johann Peter Süssmilch, had urged population growth, promising that it would produce stronger nation-states while also satisfying religious dictates. As growth began, but before anyone had a good factual grasp of population levels or trends, more pessimistic forecasts emerged. Thomas Malthus warned in 1798: "The power of population is so superior to the power of the earth to produce subsistence for man, that premature death must in some shape or other visit the human race." Unrestrained population growth would certainly lead to disaster. Malthus theorized a system in which crises in mortality, rather than human choices about fertility, ultimately controlled population growth. Many people who heard the Lutheran pastor Süssmilch preach or who read his books must have rejected his advice about having more children; at any rate, as the opinions of theorists shifted toward Malthus's view, so in an uncanny way did popular practice also shift. Whereas in earlier times people had held their fertility at a level very close to mortality, thereby preventing rapid population growth, in Malthus's day people elected not to do that. Mortality began to decline in the late eighteenth century in Western Europe, but there and elsewhere people kept fertility at its traditional levels. They still did not reproduce as rapidly as they might have, but for several decades they kept reproducing at a rate that ensured population growth.

For a long time demographers theorized that people did not immediately notice that mortality had declined. That may be true, but it seems unlikely. What seems likelier is that, in the nineteenth century, people wanted the larger families that followed from the widening gap between fertility and mortality. That was not a baby boom, but it was a new form of behavior.

Through the nineteenth century and into the twentieth most theorists remained Malthusian. As they learned more about the actual size of population and its growth rate, they expressed graver misgivings. This anxiety reached a peak during the 1960s, at the moment when the growth rate itself also peaked, in a small book, entitled *The Limits of Growth,* published by a group of observers who styled themselves the Club of Rome. Led by the economist and industrial manager Aurelio Peccei, this self-selected group adopted as its thesis the idea of limits to growth: Within a century, they held, the earth's potential to support further population growth and pollution, to provide food, and to tolerate resource depletion would be exhausted. The problem, the most intense element of which was overpopulation, was urgent. The club adopted the hope that a dramatic shift could be taken toward something called sustainable growth. Collaborative action

FIGURE 14.1
Greenpeace activists. Members of the
Greenpeace organization await arrest
while chained to an "apple hut" on Seal
Island in the Beaufort Sea north of
Alaska, April 2000, in protest against oil
exploitation and potential environmental
degradation in the Arctic region. (Photo
courtesy of Greenpeace)

among countries across the world would be needed to address these problems and to adopt the
radical new policies for which the club called.

Rather than producing new policy initiatives, the Club of Rome sparked two global debates.
One debate pitted people who feared explosive population growth, such as Paul Ehrlich, against
those who feared the unfettered consumption of scarce resources by rich populations, such as
Germaine Greer.

In an influential book entitled *The Population Bomb* (1968), Paul Ehrlich argued that the problem was too many people. He wrote: "I came to understand [the population problem] emotion-
ally one stinking hot night in Delhi [as] my wife and daughter and I were returning to our hotel
in an ancient taxi." He went on: "The streets seemed alive with people. People eating, people
washing, people sleeping. People visiting, arguing and screaming. People thrusting their hands
through the taxi window begging. People defecating and urinating."

Greer, an Australian expatriate living at the time in India, countered with disgust in *Sex and
Destiny: The Politics of Human Fertility* (1984): "In order to feel in his bowels the reality of overpopulation, Ehrlich had to go to India; others feel it more strongly when they come across dis-
carded aluminum beer cans in the wilderness." To Greer the problem was that Ehrlich and his
compatriots were too rich; they used too large a share of the globe's resources.

In the second great debate, proponents of the idea of sustainable population growth encountered such thinkers as the economists Julian Simon and Esther Boserup, who argued that population growth is a cause of economic growth rather than a threat to it. Simon observed that economic growth in the developed states of Western Europe and North America had coincided with
population growth, and that those nations had found a way dramatically to increase per capita

wealth and income even while the populations grew. Close scrutiny of rates of population growth and per capita output showed that the relationship changes over time. In the 1960s and 1970s, many studies that compared countries to one another indicated that there was no statistical association. In the 1980s population growth tended to reduce economic growth in poor countries, but it sometimes seemed to drive economic growth to higher levels in rich countries.

The Club of Rome, the Worldwatch Institute, Greenpeace, and other groups warning about limits to growth discounted the power of human ingenuity, failing to consider such things as the ongoing evolution of energy resources from animal power and wind to coal, oil, nuclear energy, and solar energy. Simon, Boserup, and their allies in turn overlooked the more numerous countries where population growth had not stimulated economic growth, investing their hopes in a future replete with solutions to ever more intractable problems of growing food, controlling pollution, and finding new resources. If the Club of Rome members were often alarmists, their critics were often Pollyannas.

The crises that Malthusians foresaw appeared only in a muted form in the second half of the twentieth century, but the idea of a grave and threatening future did not disappear. How did humankind cope with explosive population growth?

Family Planning and Lower Fertility

In the long span of human history people have controlled fertility more successfully than mortality. Up to the eighteenth century, as we have seen, people across the globe elected to reproduce far below their capacity, in that way forestalling the kind of catastrophes that Malthus forecast. The modern experience of the Hutterites, a small religious community living in the Dakotas and Canada, suggests that women might bear an average of as many as twelve children each. That example does not give us a realistic gauge of potential fertility throughout human history, however, because that average was achieved by women with good diets and good health, most of whom married soon after menarche and survived through their childbearing years. But it does provide us with an idea of the upper limit of natural fertility. No historical population has approached that limit. In early modern Europe, to date the most closely studied historical population, women bore an average of four to five children, of whom up to half died before reaching adulthood. In Mali in the late 1980s, women on average bore 7.14 children, of whom 4.32 had survived at the moment of the survey. High infant and child mortality rates can encourage people to have more children in order to be surer that the number they want to have will survive.

For some years after World War II fertility increased nearly everywhere, although in the industrial countries the baby boom was short-lived, collapsing in the 1950s or 1960s. At that moment new means of family limitation began to be introduced to supplement traditional methods such as condoms, withdrawal before ejaculation, and abstinence. The pill, the IUD, injectable contraceptives, and other technological aids to birth control made it possible to limit family size without giving up sexual pleasure. The new methods had surprisingly little effect on reproduction. Some Western observers claimed that youths increased their sexual activity in the 1960s, having intercourse earlier, more often, and with more partners, because they had been freed from the risk of pregnancy. But illegitimacy continued to increase, suggesting that attitudes about sexual activity had changed independently of these new contraceptives: The change had begun earlier and was not much affected by the putative sexual revolution.

The new contraceptives offered an easy way to limit family size, but parents wanted more, not fewer, children, especially in farm villages, where most of the globe's people lived. People wanted large families because such families conveyed more status and because parents felt a moral responsibility to enlarge the family and the clan. They wanted children for the help they would provide on farms, and for the support more children could give their parents in old age. That is, people often saw a direct connection between large families and economic advantage, rather than disadvantage. At the global level large populations and population growth seemed to auger poverty. But at the individual level in poor countries they paid dividends. Furthermore, the views of men and women often differed—the male wanting a larger family, the female uncertain or opposed, but the male ultimately deciding the issue. By 1990, 57 percent of global couples including women at reproductive ages practiced contraception, almost all by modern methods. Social experiments, among them one in Matlab, a rural Bangladeshi district of some seventy villages, showed the attractiveness of modern contraceptive methods, but they also showed that people would not necessarily use them to reduce fertility. In Matlab people used contraceptives to space their children rather than to reduce the number of them. Since this kind of spacing has often preceded reductions in the number of births, it was still a hopeful sign.

In the period 1960–1990 a sense of urgency motivated the effort to reduce fertility in regions where birth rates were high. Thus campaigns intended to provide people with information about and access to the IUD, the pill, male sterilization, condoms, and other family planning means were sometimes accompanied by pressure to adopt these things. One country embarked on a sustained program of compulsory family planning. In 1979, alarmed by the rapid growth of the three decades since Mao's revolution, Chinese authorities introduced the one-child policy. Urban families would be allowed only a single child, and rural families only two or three children, on pain of losing privileges, including housing allowances and permits to move around. Although many couples resisted, the one-child policy sharply reduced China's growth rate. Chinese leaders expected compulsory family planning to make economic growth easier, but instead it created serious problems—disaffection from ruling authorities, a deficit of females in a society that preferred sons to daughters, and a misshapen population pyramid—without bringing the expected advantages.

China's program was not taken up as a model for population policy elsewhere, even in countries where growth seemed equally alarming. More commonplace in Asia and Africa was a program of social development that people created for themselves in the 1980s and 1990s. In preceding decades national leaders across the world defined growth and progress in terms of more economic activity and income. In the 1980s and 1990s there arose from the families and households in many nations far apart from one another a contrary idea, which is that progress should be defined by improvements in the quality of life. These improvements were taken to be those that reduce infant and child mortality and maternal deaths in childbirth and that add schooling and literacy. People who favored social development wanted to have fewer children so that they could invest more in their children's education and health care. Thus the idea of social development, which arose as a solution for everyday problems, favored family limitation. It also favored the greater authority of women in making decisions about how family resources should be spent and the number of children a couple would try to have.

During the 1990s fertility declined in almost every country. In rich countries it fell far below the replacement level, to as few as 1.2 children per woman of reproductive age (compared to the 2.1 children required for a stable population). In poor countries it fell from levels as high as 8 children per woman toward 2. Experts recast downward their projections of future population, estimating an ultimate future population not of 12 billion, which many theorists had projected around 1990, but of 9 billion. Commentators continued to warn about hazards ahead, especially in the world's capacity to feed or to provide economic opportunities to so many people. But the catastrophe forecast by the Club of Rome in the 1960s had not come to pass. People had moved slowly to reduce their fertility, but they had made the necessary moves. Suddenly commentators worried about future depopulation in countries with low reproduction rates as much as they did about continued explosive population growth.

Living to Be Old

Survivorship began to rise around 1800, with the first signs emerging in northwestern Europe: the Nordic lands, Britain, and France. There are three especially useful patterns to notice in the health transition. First, there was an epidemiologic transition. The leading diseases causing death moved through stages, shifting from infectious diseases, communicated from person to person, such as smallpox and tuberculosis, to degenerative organ diseases, such as heart disease and cancer. Second, different age groups benefited at different times. In the nineteenth century in Europe the main beneficiaries were people aged between 1 and 65. Infant mortality dropped sharply in the early twentieth century. People aged 65 to 79 died at declining rates first in the 1960s, and people at higher ages first in the 1980s. In each case the pattern emerged in countries on the leading edge, but it was followed in other countries. By the end of the twentieth century death rates were declining at all ages in most countries, even where those rates were already low. Third, the health transition began in northwestern Europe but soon expanded into other areas. By 1900 the remainder of Europe, Japan, the United States and Canada, Australia and New Zealand, and some countries in Latin America (Mexico, Costa Rica, and Paraguay) shared rising life expectancy. By 1950 the health transition was underway in nearly the entire world. The principal complexity in this scheme is that the shift from infectious to degenerative diseases, which occurred in sequence among countries that initiated the health transition in the nineteenth century, occurred simultaneously in many countries that initiated this transition in the twentieth century. Thus Chile in the 1980s, an example emphasized by a World Bank study, had to contend at once with the mostly communicable diseases of childhood and the mostly degenerative diseases of adulthood, without being able to specialize in the orientation of its health services.

So momentous an achievement, one accomplished mostly by human intervention, might have taken the form of industrial modernization, which was led first by cotton textiles and then by heavy industry. Even among the pioneer countries, however, the means and methods of the health transition differed from country to country. All countries shared a certain set of options: Reforms and improvements in public health, medicine, income, nutrition, behavior, and education made it possible to reduce death rates so much and so rapidly that the trend stood out as unique in the scheme of human experience. Nevertheless two or more countries rarely elected to do just the same thing at the same time, or to repeat steps in the sequence followed by predecessors. The health transition was an exuberant exercise in national individuality.

Still, countries that came later to it compressed the time involved, indicating that they had learned useful things from the experience of predecessors. Across its long transition, Sweden, one of the pioneers, added life expectancy at a pace of less than a quarter of a year of survival time

PICTURE 14.2
Public water fountain, Lome, Togo. Many cities in developing countries are unable to provide essential services for growing populations. Here people gather around a water fountain in the Togolese capital. (Photo courtesy of the United Nations/B. Wolff)

per year of calendar time. Many countries, among them Japan between 1947 and 1980, China during the 1950s, the Soviet Union between 1945 and 1965, most of Latin America from 1930 to 1960, and Nigeria from 1963 to 1980, added to life expectancy at a rate of between 0.7 to 1 year per year of calendar time.

Vaccination constituted one of the most important elements in the health transition. Smallpox vaccination, introduced in 1796, replaced an older technique, inoculation, by injecting a variant form of the disease, cowpox, to deceive the immune system. Edward Jenner, who devised small-pox vaccination, imagined the possibility of eradicating one of the leading causes of death. That dream was realized in 1978, when the last person with smallpox was isolated and his contacts vaccinated or revaccinated. In the end this disease was conquered by a combination of medical and public health measures: mass vaccination plus the active surveillance of people at risk of contracting the disease and the isolation of infected patients. Every country ultimately deployed smallpox vaccination, but at different times and, most important, in different ways, giving differ-ent amounts of weight to those three measures.

The main elements of the health transition began more prosaically, even before germ theory had been worked out, when people began to recognize that important diseases were communi-cated from person to person by water, especially water contaminated by feces from people with disease. To protect against the hazards of waterborne disease, British health engineers devised an elaborate scheme for filtering and purifying the water delivered to households in order to prevent human contact with urine and feces. The main elements were piped water, household toilets in place of outhouses, plus water and sewage treatment. Those measures, enormously expensive and imaginable only for countries undergoing economic growth, protected people against cholera, typhoid fever, and many other diarrheal diseases. In this case, however, the health transi-tion remains incomplete. At the end of the twentieth century about half the world's households still lacked access to clean piped water, and still more lacked the fully enclosed systems of waste disposal associated with toilets. Waterborne diseases remained a leading cause of death even though they had been pushed into retreat.

At the beginning of the health transition neither countries nor social classes differed much from one another in life expectancy. During the nineteenth century differentiation appeared, with rich countries and individuals gaining a decided advantage. That development led to the

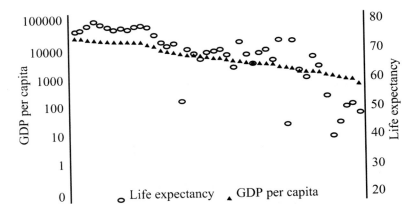

FIGURE 14.3   Life Expectancy and Income in 44 Countries. SOURCE:
United Nations, *World Population Prospects: The 1998 Revision* (New York:
UN Department of International Economic and Social Affairs, 1998), vol.
1, 2–3.

idea that higher income, or perhaps a higher level of economic development, helped push death rates downward. A comparison of life expectancy between rich and poor countries at the end of the twentieth century, shown in Figure 14.3, suggests that this relationship, for the most part, still holds. Richer countries and richer households certainly have more options in deciding how to protect themselves against disease and in seeking treatment. There are no rich countries with low levels of life expectancy; however, there are many poor countries with life expectancy levels matching those of rich lands. Thus income seems to make the achievement of life expectancy at birth above 70 years easier, but poverty does not prevent such an achievement. For countries and individuals, poverty remained the leading factor behind premature death throughout the twentieth century.

Before the health transition began and in its early stages, in many countries poor nutrition contributed to mortality hazards. Some people did not have enough to eat, and some people ate diets lacking one or more of the elements later found to be essential to good nutrition and a healthy immune system. Food science, which took shape in the late nineteenth century, did not quickly discover consistent recommendations about diet. Initially urging more protein intake, nutritionists later favored diets adequate rather than abundant in calories, balanced in nutrients, and led by fruits and vegetables. Such advice assumes that people can make the choices that nutritionists urge, which was rarely the case before the refrigeration of food and is still rarely possible among people who are poor. At the end of the twentieth century many people living in poor countries and often also poor people living in rich countries suffered from undernutrition. Meanwhile people in rich countries and often also rich people in poor countries suffered from overeating, especially from the contributions that obesity and fatty diets make to heart and circulatory diseases.

Changes in human behavior also helped survival rates to rise. The idea that disease arises from environmental filth persuaded people to cleanse their environments and to ventilate living quarters. Germ theory persuaded people to cleanse their bodies much more often than they had, to wash their hands after using the bathroom, to clean food preparation surfaces, to vacuum dust, and to avoid spitting. (Both dust and spit were suspected of harboring tuberculosis bacteria.) Probably the most important behavioral innovations focused on the child. Parents, who previously had been loving and caring but not informed in detail about how to care for children, were urged, beginning in the early twentieth century, to invest in the next generation. Children would be educated, when sick they would be taken to the doctor, and they would receive not just a fair share but preferential treatment in food. Child-centered parenting helped reduce infant mortality, which had remained high until about 1900, and it helped continue the reduction of child mortality in pioneer countries and to initiate it in other countries. As in nutrition, however, it proved to be one thing to identify the characteristics of child care optimal for good health, and another thing for poor people to implement those ideas. Countries with scarce resources often decided to invest their scarce resources in village and neighborhood clinics that could provide prenatal care and advice, vaccination against common diseases, and treatment for other maladies.

Last among these tactics of the health transition comes education. For a long time, from the mid-nineteenth century until the 1970s, political leaders and parents alike promoted education because they hoped it would improve the economic opportunities available to children. Social scientists doing research in developing countries discovered in the 1970s and 1980s that education had quite another effect. The parents who had more schooling, especially the mothers, were able to provide better care for their children and to obtain more assistance from outsiders, such as the nurses or doctor at a clinic. The schooled parents knew more, they possessed more authority and prestige, and they negotiated more effectively in the household, the village or neighborhood, and the wider sphere. Although many people in such villages had been disappointed by false expectations about the benefits of education, such as hopes of a wider range of economic opportunities, it did bring about this unexpected result: Education, it turned out, helped reduce risks to survival. By the end of the twentieth century some authorities argued that the most effective thing that could be done to continue the health transition, and to speed its pace in poor countries, was to provide more schooling for the children growing up to be parents.

Most accounts of the health transition narrate the achievements of pioneer countries. There is even more to be learned from examining the experience of latecomers, especially those struggling against poverty. China telescoped its reduction of mortality as dramatically as any country. In 1947, at the time of the Maoist revolution, life expectancy probably did not surpass 30 years; by 1992 it had reached 68 years. Most impressively, China doubled its life expectancy while remaining one of the poorer countries of the world. Its strategy is revealing. Chinese authorities set out in the 1950s to elevate life expectancy by democratizing access to health care, training many more doctors, albeit only for a few months, expanding public health reforms, educating the entire population, and engaging everyone in something called the Patriot Health Campaign. Many government initiatives also hindered the Chinese health transition. The Great Famine of 1959, a by-product of forced collectivization, may have caused as many as 30 million deaths, and the Cultural Revolution disrupted the training of nurses and doctors and the provision of health services.

Two major reverses threatened the health transition. First and most important in its scale, the appearance of Acquired Immunodeficiency Syndrome (AIDS) around 1980 introduced a new infectious disease with uncommon traits, among them a nearly universal fatality rate. AIDS, caused by a virus, acts by disabling the immune system, making its victims more susceptible to other diseases as well as debilitating them on its own account. By 2000, more than 50 million people worldwide had contracted this disease, which is most often spread by sexual contact. More than

16 million of them had died, leaving more than 34 million people with the disease. In the West, AIDS was most typically a disease of homosexual males and intravenous drug users who shared needles. In Africa, South Asia, and Haiti, however, it began and remained a disease of heterosexual males and females, mostly under age 25. Although medications had been found to slow the replication of the virus responsible for this disease, few of the some 34 million sufferers could afford those drugs.

The second major reverse for the health transition developed in the Soviet Union and Soviet bloc countries in the 1980s. Economic deterioration in the 1980s undercut funding for housing, food, and medical care, and the collapse of the Soviet system in 1991 aggravated these things. Men bore the heaviest emotional costs, and they may also have confronted the economic deterioration more directly. Although life expectancy among females leveled off, that among males plunged, led by rising death rates for older men. AIDS proved that the modern health system was not secure against the continuing human drama of exposure to new diseases. Declining survivorship among males in the Soviet Union and much of Eastern Europe showed that the complex system developed to protect people against health risks could falter or even collapse. Future gains in life expectancy—indeed, maintaining its existing level—could not be taken for granted.

Implications and Consequences of Rapid Population Growth

A global population in disequilibrium, either growing or declining, means that relationships of scale are changing. Table 14.1 shows the grand pattern of these changes over the past 1,000 years among major global regions. Asia has always counted a majority of the world's population; the important thing to notice lies in the decline of Asia and Africa between 1750 and 1900, and the rise of Europe and the Americas in the same period. Then, in the second half of the twentieth century, Asia and Africa reasserted themselves in terms of population size. Future growth rates seemed likely to continue this pattern into the twenty-first century, diminishing the significance of Europe and North America, measured in this way, and elevating that of Africa, Asia, and Latin America.

The most important implications of these shifts in population geography involve how they affect the allocation of power among nations and peoples. How should they be represented, for example, in international organizations such as the United Nations and its agencies or in such nongovernmental organizations (NGOs) as the Red Cross and Oxfam? The rising importance of such organizations during the second half of the twentieth century made this question more urgent. The UN solved the problem by granting one vote to each member country in its General Assembly and by setting up special councils with executive authority. Thus the Security Council is led by the major military powers. That response limited China and India, which together account for about a third of the world's people, to a much more limited role than the one indicated by their populations. Meanwhile NGOs tended to be governed either by councils composed of national representatives or by appointed groups. Any steps toward a democratization of influence in international agencies and NGOs alike would elevate the importance of the world's largest countries, indicated in Table 14.2 for 1950 and 2000, and diminish that of most of the military powers, especially France, Britain, and Russia.

TABLE 14.1   Regional Distribution of Population (in percentages)

Year	Africa	The Americas	Asia	Europe and Russia
1000	15	7	60	17
1500	19	9	53	18
1750	13	2	65	19
1900	8	10	55	26
1950	9	13	55	23
1997	12	14	59	15

Source: J.N. Biraben, "Essai sur l'évolution du nombre des hommes," *Population* 34 (1979), 16; and United Nations, *Human Development Report, 1999* (New York: UN, 1999), pp.197-200.

TABLE 14.2   Population of the Thirteen Largest Countries in 1950, 2000, and Projected to 2050 (in millions)

Country	1950	1998	2050
China	555	1256	1478
India	358	982	1529
United States	158	274	349
Russian Federation	102	147	121
Japan	84	126	105
Indonesia	80	206	312
Germany	68	82	73
Brazil	54	166	244
United Kingdom	51	59	57
Bangladesh	42	125	212
Pakistan	40	148	345
Nigeria	31	106	244
Ethiopia	18	63	169

Source: www.popin.org/pop1998/5.htm.

How should countries be ranked? The answer implicit in most of the information we receive, based on maps, stresses geographical extent. Another answer reports aggregate income. And a third based on population shows that rankings vary quite substantially according to the measure used. There is no simple answer to questions about the comparative importance of nations. In any case, conventional maps, which show countries by their land areas, often misrepresent the relative importance of a country. Table 14.3 makes this point by reporting the ten largest countries considered not only by land area but also by population and aggregate income, two other possible measures of importance.

In the twentieth century people also moved about more freely, crossing political frontiers and oceans in rising numbers for the sake of resettlement and tourism. At no point in the past had so many people known so much about other cultures, either through direct travel experiences or

TABLE 14.3   The Ten Most Important Countries by Different Rankings

Rank	Country	Land Area (thousands of sq. km.)	Country	Population (1997, in millions)	Country	Aggregate Income (1997 GNP in billions of US dollars)
1	Russian Federation	16,889	China	1,227	U.S.	7,690
2	China	9,326	India	961	Japan	4,772
3	Canada	9,221	U.S.	268	Germany	2,320
4	U.S.	9,159	Indonesia	200	France	1,526
5	Brazil	8,457	Brazil	164	U.K.	1,220
6	Australia	7,682	Russian Federation	147	Italy	1,155
7	India	2,973	Pakistan	137	China	1,055
8	Argentina	2,737	Japan	126	Brazil	773
9	Kazakhstan	2,671	Bangladesh	124	Canada	584
10	Algeria	2,382	Nigeria	118	Spain	570

Source: World Bank, *World Development Report*, 1998/99 (New York: Oxford University Press, 1999), pp. 190–191.

through the reports of foreign correspondents. Although not direct effects of population growth, migration and travel were nevertheless significant demographic issues. The idea that ethnic groups have homelands persists, however, despite much evidence to the contrary. Humans have made a habit of moving about, a habit modified but not eliminated by the advent of settled agriculture some 10,000 years ago. Over the intervening centuries people have repeatedly been pushed to migrate by economic hardship, overcrowding, and military force. They have been pulled to other places by the appeal of those places, and sometimes by deceitful stories about that appeal. And they have been forced to leave their homelands by war or by enslavement. Some ethnic groups and multiethnic nations appear to have developed migrating cultures. So commonplace has migration been for so long that few if any countries can claim to have homogeneous populations or even a lengthy history of population homogeneity.

Europeans have been the most avid emigrants: Some 61 million people left Europe in the period 1800–1960, of whom 41 million settled in the United States. Take, for example, the Portuguese, persistent migrants, albeit in small numbers. In the early centuries of the modern era they immigrated to South America, especially Brazil; Asia, especially Goa and the East Indies; and Africa, especially Morocco and the islands off the northwest coast. In the twentieth century still more Portuguese emigrants searching to improve their lot have settled in the same regions, plus Mozambique and Angola, Macao, Spain and France, the United States (from New England to Hawaii), and Canada. The movement has been mostly one way, a pattern in which the Portuguese resemble Irish, Dutch, Chinese, and Japanese migrants.

Italy provides an example of migration in another pattern. In the latter decades of the nineteenth century Italians immigrated in unusually large numbers to South America, especially Argentina, and to North America. In the first decade of the twentieth century nearly 11 percent of the entire Italian population immigrated to other countries, mostly to the United States. Since then Italians have continued to immigrate, although in smaller numbers, and they have added some new destinations, including Australia. But Italy has shifted position from an exporter to an importer of people. By the early 1990s, there were twenty-five countries that each had 10,000 or more nationals living in Italy. Bangladeshis, for example, were drawn to Italy by the opportunity to make a better living. The immigrants, mostly young men, became street vendors, employees in the underground economy, and restaurant workers. These occupations allowed them to make about five times the average per capita income of Bangladeshis at home; many had left their families behind but remitted some of those earnings to them by mail. Italians have continued to immigrate overseas, especially those from the south, while northern cities draw most of Italy's emigrants from abroad.

Some migrations constitute diasporas, or forced dispersions, the classic example being the Babylonian exile of the Jews from Palestine, which resulted in the formation of colonies of people who maintained an ethnic and religious identity. The term is also used more broadly to identify people who preserve or cultivate some features of ethnic or cultural identity with homeland groups while living elsewhere. The twentieth century is noteworthy for the degree to which people identified their interests with those of others from their homeland. They often retained influential memories of life in their native lands as well. At the end of the twentieth century tens of millions of people of African origin lived in the Americas, mostly owing to forced migration and the slave trade; on a similar scale people of European origin lived in the Americas and Australia and New Zealand, and many people of Asian origin lived in Africa, the Pacific Islands, and the Americas.

Migration is often temporary. Transportation improvements, which made travel faster and cheaper, made it possible for migrants to move by road, rail, or air across vast stretches of the globe: from Turkey into Germany; from Pakistan, Bangladesh, Egypt, and Sudan to Kuwait, Saudi Arabia, and elsewhere in the Middle East; from north and west Africa into Italy; from China to North America; from Brazil to Japan. Often these moves were initiated to find work. Even though they were paid low wages, migrant workers managed nevertheless to send a total of more than $30 billion to their families at home in 1988.

In the colonial era, gifted students were often sent abroad for university study, sometimes to return, as Ho Chi Minh and Jomo Kenyatta did, and sometimes to remain. In the postcolonial era this flow of human capital continued, chiefly to the benefit of the United States, Canada, and Britain. People with unusually high levels of education or particular talents migrated from Brazil, Argentina, West Africa, South Asia and China, and Eastern Europe and Russia to continue their education or improve their economic opportunities in other countries.

In some other respects, too, migration changed in character during the twentieth century, increasing in scale and becoming more variegated. The movement of Europeans to the Americas and Australia, which dwarfed other migrations in the nineteenth century, gave way to migrations from nearly every part of the world to nearly every other part. Reasons for migrating became more varied, and migrants became more mobile. In the postwar era, Western European countries recruited guestworkers for manufacturing and service jobs too numerous and too unattractive for their home populations. Women became the leaders of some migratory movements, whereas in the past the first wave of migrants along any route had been mostly men. And migrants learned new ways to outwit barriers to entry to the countries where they wished to go. Hence migration intensified as a political issue, pitting opponents against the migrants: For example, Indians decried the arrival of Sri Lankans, North Americans resisted Latinos, and Germans objected to Poles. Although some opponents, German skinheads, for example, terrorized migrants to try to drive them out, they were overwhelmed and outwitted by the migrants. Fostered by economic and population growth, and by education, international travel and tourism exploded in the last decades of the twentieth century. In the process people created for themselves an additional definition of well-being, consisting of familiarity with the cities, cuisines, major buildings, art, and other artifacts of world cultures.

In a more direct way rapid population growth pushed the age structure of world demographics first in one direction and then in another. Populations where fertility and mortality are balanced have stable age structures, typically ones that look like a pyramid where the base counts infants and children and the peak counts the oldest people. Up to about 1960, declining death rates for infants and children and the lag of the fertility transition meant that the number of children in population statistics was rising faster than the number of adults; in other words, the world population, on average, was growing younger. After about 1960 in the developed countries, and after about 1990 in developing countries, fertility declined and people survived longer.

In some important ways the twentieth century was the age of the young. They were numerous because of high fertility and low mortality, and world cultures reflected their influence. It was, for survival prospects, a good time to be born. Continuing survivorship patterns mean, however, that the twenty-first century will be the century of the old. The estimated median age of the world population in 1970 had fallen to just under 22 years; by 2050 it is expected to rise to 33 years. Older people can expect death rates to continue to decline at ages above 65; the number of centenarians will grow. The twenty-first century will be abundantly supplied with wisdom and maturity, and also with the health problems of the old, which are often protracted and intractable. For older people in countries unable, because of their poverty, to provide pensions, the twenty-first century may also be a century of poverty.

Population growth on the scale observed between 1800 and 2000 could not easily have occurred without a major change in residence patterns across the globe—that is, without the dramatic shift from rural to urban areas. Modern urbanization began in the mid-nineteenth century in Europe, where cities first began to grow more rapidly than the overall population. In the nineteenth century many cities became great industrial centers, and in the twentieth they developed into unrivaled centers of trade, retailing, education, the arts, and other services. Cities seemed to be dynamic, offering jobs when none were to be had in agricultural regions, and this image drew many migrants, most often young men and women starting out in life. Perhaps the greatest factor behind urban growth was rapid gains in the productivity of farm labor, which sharply reduced the number of people who needed to work in agriculture. In places where labor remained largely a matter of using human and animal resources rather than machines, such as in China, urbanization lagged. In 1950, 11 percent of China's population lived in cities, and in 1995 still only 30 percent, well behind the global average of 45 percent. Indian census authorities counted 557,138 villages in the 1980s: Many of India's cities were large and growing rapidly, but the average Indian was a villager.

Cairo's growth illustrates the trend of rapid expansion in the cities of Africa, Asia, and Latin America in the twentieth century. In the 1897 census, Egypt counted 9.6 million people, of whom 905,000, or 9.4 percent, lived in Cairo. By the 1947 census, Egypt's population numbered 19 million, and Cairo's 2.8 million, but still fewer than 15 percent of Egyptians lived in Cairo. Since then, however, Cairo's share of the national population has risen to more than 22 percent even while Egypt has grown to a population of 59 million (1995). Much of that growth occurred

PICTURE 14.3
Urban slums in Popoyan, Colombia. With inadequate housing in many cities in developing countries, many people have to live in flimsy shelters in shanty towns with no amenities. (Reprinted from *Colombia: Special Programs for the Alleviation of Poverty* [Washington, D.C.: World Bank])

because villagers moved into new urban communities attached to Cairo, such as Manshiet Nasser, a hillside settlement formed on what had been public land.

Considering crowded settlements such as Manshiet Nasser, and Cairo's primitive housing and facilities for providing clean water and sewage disposal, the city can be described as overcrowded. But in another sense it and many of the world's capital cities are underpopulated. Around 1976 Cairo counted 20.4 percent of Egypt's population, but 40 percent of its government investment, 55 percent of its university places, and 40 and 43 percent, respectively, of its private- and public-sector jobs. Given those distributions, it is apparent why so many people moved into cities, especially provincial and national capitals, in the second half of the twentieth century.

In 1950 about 29 percent of the globe's people lived in cities; large cities and urbanization were both chiefly restricted to industrialized countries. During the second half of the twentieth century most of the remainder of the world joined the trend toward urbanization. The United Nations projected that more than 61 percent would live in cities in 2025. In 1950, New York, London, Tokyo, Paris, and Moscow were the world's largest cities. By 2010 the largest are expected to be Tokyo, São Paulo, Bombay, Shanghai, and Lagos. The turnover between these two lists is a sign of how far urbanization has expanded its reach.

Urbanization reduced some problems but aggravated others. In 1850, in its earliest stages, cities were much less healthy places to live than were rural villages. By 1950 this problem had disappeared because cities attracted investment in public health improvements and health facilities, and because the urban populations were richer and more highly educated than rural dwellers. But city growth often outpaced job opportunities, water and sanitary facilities, and housing, leaving the city a bifurcated place where the prosperous lived a much more sheltered and favored life than the poor. Many of the latter lived in overcrowded settlements such as Manshiet Nasser. In the first half of the twentieth century most cities built their infrastructures as fast as, even faster than, their populations grew. That was no longer generally true in the second half of the century. Mexico City outran its fresh water sources, having to pump water as much as 1,000 meters uphill from reservoirs as distant as 100 kilometers. Los Angeles drew water from northern California and from the Colorado River. Alexandria tried to accommodate the waste of 4 million people with sewage facilities built for no more than 1 million.

Population growth outstripped the capacity, or willingness, of societies to build housing, especially housing for the poor. The rich lands, nowhere more dramatically than in Hong Kong, Singapore, and the Netherlands, reduced the problem of providing living quarters to so many people by building upward, housing people in high-rise buildings. Poor countries and poor people could rarely afford such a step, with the result that the especially rapid urban growth in poor countries between 1950 and 2000 led to many more being quartered in makeshift dwellings without running water, indoor toilets, heat or air conditioning, or other amenities. Urban authorities occasionally cleared slums, but they seldom managed to replace them with affordable housing. Thus new slums appeared, and more people packed themselves in. In Mumbai, a city under intensive housing pressure, nearly 40 percent of the population lived in slums in the 1970s; the typical housing unit was a single room accommodating more than five people.

Rapid and ongoing population growth brought many challenges in its train. But it did not bring the catastrophic famines that so many observers had predicted in the 1950s and 1960s. The principal population catastrophes of the twentieth century were made by people rather than by nature. The inexorable conflict between population growth and the growth of food and other resources that Malthus had identified never developed.

Two kinds of activity stand out for their cruel effects upon survival. First, war was brutalized, extending its effects to civilian populations while spreading the reach of each weapon. In the 1860s men fought chiefly with muzzle-loading weapons that, although exceedingly deadly, could be fired no more often than once every few minutes and were accurate only at short distances. By World War II it was no longer necessary to march through Georgia, as William T. Sherman had with federal troops in 1864, to destroy the homes and livelihoods of civilian populations, nor even to allow civilians themselves to escape, as Sherman had done. An enemy could bomb at a distance, via rockets or long-range aircraft, killing civilians while also destroying their homes and livelihoods. World War II claimed more than 50 million lives, over and above the mortality that would be projected without war. Civilians became leading targets after 1945, suffering the most from hostilities and conflicts such as ethnic cleansing in Rwanda and Bosnia, the Western embargo on Iraq after the Persian Gulf War, and guerrilla activities in Latin America.

Second, the great socialist experiment, which forcibly collectivized land, was resisted in every case, even at the cost of starvation. In the Soviet Union in the late 1920s, in China in 1959–1961, and elsewhere where collectivization was imposed, the peasants and farmers whose land was taken from them refused to plant, tend, or harvest crops. Rather than redistributing output more evenly, collectivization produced famines larger in scale and effect than any known in the past. Other authoritarian policies of socialist governments, such as Stalin's program of forced grain procurement, also provoked famine. About 5.5 million people died in Ukraine during 1931–1934.

Malnutrition and famine emerged as serious threats in the 1970s and 1980s, most notably in the Sahel, the band stretching across Africa south of the Sahara. One of the most agonizing television images of those years was the picture of a child whose malnutrition was so severe that the child's stomach was distended. Drought, a natural disaster, and three effects of rapid population growth—deforestation, soil exhaustion, and overgrazing—combined to reduce food supplies to dangerously low levels, causing widespread malnutrition. People fled areas where food was in shortest supply. James Waller, who worked in the Sudan for the International Rescue Committee, related the story of a relief camp near the Sudanese town of El Fau and the people who sought help there in *Fau: Portrait of an Ethiopian Famine* (1990). He told of Ngistie Abraha, her husband,

PICTURE 14.4   Ethiopian refugees, 1984. In the early 1980s, the world became accustomed to pictures of famine victims in the Sahel and Horn areas of Africa as droughts and related environmental degradation plagued the region. (Photo courtesy of the United Nations/John Isaacs)

and daughter, who were driven from Gwaro, Ethiopia, by hunger. Walking and riding, they found the Fau camp, along with 40,000 other refugees. But hundreds of people died en route, and tens of thousands who did not flee their homes starved. Rain returned to Ethiopia in 1986. When the Sahel drought eased, tens of millions of people still faced an uncertain future of access to food.

In the twentieth century, global food production increased ahead of population growth, but food production did not increase at this pace in every global region, leading to a profound and dismaying irony. During the century in which agronomists learned the most about how to augment food output using chemical fertilizers, plant and animal hybrids, and mechanized farming, famine was no less a threat, and perhaps even a greater threat, than it had been in the past. In Malthus's perspective, famines seemed likeliest to occur where population growth was the fastest. In the event, however, that pattern did not hold. Many areas where growth was rapid did not experience famines, and many areas where growth was moderate did. Reflecting upon the Bengal famine of 1943, Amartya Sen suggested another explanation. Famines occur when people lack entitlements, that is, when they lack the resources they need to buy food. Sen observed in Bengal in 1943 and in other cases, too, a lack of proportion between the small scale of food shortage and the large scale of food unavailability. People starved because they could not afford food rather than because food was absent.

Global famine did not occur, but rapid population growth did demand every measure of human ingenuity in increasing food output and improving distribution. Humans responded with the Green Revolution, with massive improvements in famine surveillance and in the mobilization of relief supplies, and with the creation and expansion of international agencies charged with famine relief. Regional famines still occurred, and none of these innovations quite matched the demand for food with its supply.

Conclusion

Across the twentieth century families grew smaller, but many villages grew into towns, towns into cities, and cities into megalopolises. People limited the number of their children in order to invest more into each of them, signaling across the world that they shared a vision of better times ahead for their children to enjoy. Many hazards to survival were brought under control, to the point that, by 2000, the average child born anywhere on the globe could be expected to live nearly 70 years. To have discovered how to accommodate so many more people, to house, feed, and employ them, and moreover, to give them the prospect of living to old age was the singular achievement of the twentieth century.

15

Nations at Risk

The experience of nations with well-being is exceedingly brief. Nearly all, throughout all history, have been very poor.

John Kenneth Galbraith,
The Affluent Society
(1958)

We have no choice but to open and to compete in the world market to survive and prosper.

Richard Hu,
Minister of Finance,
Singapore (1997)

THE EFFERVESCENT GROWTH OF WEALTH IN THE NINETEENTH AND twentieth centuries had unexpected consequences. In this chapter we explore three of those developments—antagonism between rich and poor nations, globalization, and economic restructuring and information technology—and the risks they posed for nations and for individuals. The widening gap between rich and poor countries put them at odds with one another in new ways. No longer was it chiefly territorial ambition or national pride that provoked antagonism between nations; with the differentiation of rich from poor emerged the prospect of conflict, rhetorical and actual, about the unequal division of wealth and opportunity. The differentiation itself arose in the period 1600–1900 from the active engagement of a few countries in trade and manufacturing in ways that allowed them to control the mechanisms that set prices for raw materials, manufactured goods, and labor. Two factors contributed to this development. One was colonization (see Chapters 3 and 7). The other was a style of economic activity emphasizing not agriculture but manufacturing and trade, which arose especially in the nineteenth century with the Industrial Revolution. By 1950 the world was divided between rich and poor nations, and for many years thereafter there was little movement from the large group of poor nations into the small group of rich ones.

This gap put nations at risk; so did the revival of globalization. The economic interdependence of nations—which is only one form of globalization, albeit a leading one—arose in the period from 1870 to 1914, waned between 1914 and 1945, and then exploded. Globalization put both weak and strong economic systems into a dangerous position by fashioning highly competitive global markets. At the epicenter of these markets stood the prices charged and paid by the most efficient firms operating anywhere. Local and national markets where firms could not match the terms set on global markets found themselves at a disadvantage. They could respond only by trying to close themselves off from global trade, by finding ways to compete, or by failing. The whole business exerted enormous downward pressure on the price of raw materials, on the wages of manual workers, and sometimes also on the costs of such familiar manufactured goods as televisions and computers.

The third factor to challenge nations consisted of a fundamental shift in the nature of economic activity. That activity had been based on agriculture, manufactures, and trade, all of which underwent technological revolutions in the nineteenth century. The service sector, of which trade is part, had been growing throughout the nineteenth century and into the twentieth. After World War II, however, it grew faster than manufacturing and began to reformulate itself. To the traditional activities of retail sales, public service, education, communications, entertainment, insurance, and banking were added quite new ones. Those consisted of information creation and management assisted by electronic computers and by direct communication links between consumers and suppliers. In addition to the familiar services performed by merchants, teachers, lawyers, and doctors, which added value by the expertise that each group brought to its activities, there emerged forms of service able to create wealth, or to lose it, in impersonal ways: In one day early in the year 2000 the leading U.S. stock market, the New York Stock Exchange, added half a trillion dollars to the national wealth by bidding stock prices upward. On another day a single firm, Microsoft, lost $78 billion in equity value in one day's trading of its stock. Economic restructuring put nations at risk by creating economies so vast and so volatile that even the strongest governments could not control them.

Rich and Poor Nations

When is a society well off? The conventional answer, the one given by materialism and capitalism, is based on a measure of income and wealth. During the twentieth century, income increased in nearly every country, but a few countries became rich to an unprecedented degree. Table 15.1 gives a capsule history of the distribution of wealth among countries. The countries that were rich in 1960, mostly in Europe plus the United States, Canada, Australia, and New Zealand, became much richer by 1995. In the 1980s a few Asian countries joined the rich lands, or moved toward them, but most of the world's countries remained poor. Even though the average per capita GDP across the globe had risen by 1995 to more than $3,000, distribution of the wealth had become more uneven. By UN estimates, the richest nation in 1995 was the United States, with a per capita GDP of $26,977, fifty-nine times greater that the per capita GDP of $455 in the poorest country, Ethiopia.

Neither the size of the difference in the 1950s nor its growth thereafter went unnoticed. In the newly formed United Nations, representatives from Mexico, India, Chile, and Syria argued that the inequitable distribution of wealth among nations threatened world peace and social tranquillity and undermined the political goals of the UN. They called for a Marshall Plan for the poor nations of the globe: Rich nations should provide aid to poor, just as the United States was helping Europe rebuild after World War II. The call was heard. Whereas private investment abroad had become commonplace, often in association with the exploitation of colonies, publicly financed aid and loans had been unusual. In the second half of the twentieth century, UN agencies such as the World Bank, aid agencies, and private banks supplied loans and subsidies. Individual countries also provided aid; for example the United States formed the Agency for International Development to give assistance. In 1993, not an atypical year, twenty-one countries, led by Japan, the United States, and Germany, furnished a total package of government assistance to poor countries of $56 billion. Nevertheless, at a total of less than $15 for each person living in poor countries, the aid was not large enough to make a major difference.

Why did the rich countries become richer, and why did most of the poor countries remain poor? Two answers emerged in the 1950s and were restated thereafter up to the 1990s. Poor countries argued that they were trapped in a position of dependence within a world economic system that would not allow them to become rich. Nonaligned nations meeting in 1973 in Algeria put the argument this way:

Imperialism not only hampers the economic and social progress of developing countries but also adopts an aggressive attitude toward those who oppose its plans, trying to impose upon them political, social, and economic structures which encourage alien domination, dependence, and neo-colonialism. . . . This situation accounts for the considerable disparities between the industrialized countries and the underdeveloped world. . . . The developing countries in general are

TABLE 15.1   Trends in GDP Per Capita, 1960–1995 (in 1987 US $)

| GDP per capita | Numbers of Countries | |
	1960	1995
$20,000+	0	7
15,000-19,999	1	7
10,000-14,999	1	9
5,000-9,999	18	8
2,500-4,999	8	15
1,000-2,499	20	33
<1,000	65	66
Totals	113	145
Global Average	$1,951	$3,417

Source: United Nations, *Human Development Report 1998* (New York: Oxford University Press, 1998), pp. 140-142.

still subject directly or indirectly to imperialist exploitation . . . as is illustrated by the manifold and increasingly pervasive activities of transnational and monopolistic commercial, financial, and industrial companies.

Raul Prebisch, secretary general of the UN Economic Commission for Latin America in 1949, formulated a theory of dependency. Poor nations are dependent because the rich nations monopolize the processing of raw materials into finished products. Poor nations, usually former colonies, produce raw materials—foods, minerals, textiles, and many others—which are undervalued on international markets in terms of the labor and skill that went into their production, compared to processed goods. Neocolonialism, a perpetuation of the economic terms of colonialism even after independence, keeps the playing fields of international trade tilted in favor of rich countries, which set price and wage levels.

Rich countries, too, sought to explain poverty, arguing that the now-rich lands were once poor and had grown out of poverty by shedding habits of mind and institutions that made growth difficult. They modernized, meaning not so much that they built modern industrial facilities as that they built modern social and legal systems. First, in place of class and caste systems, the rich countries claimed to have built societies open to merit. In the new system people won jobs not because of whom they knew but because of what they knew. Second, the rich countries narrowed disparities in individual wealth and income. Between the rich and poor extremes of the two-tier economic system of the past they created a middle class that enjoyed the fruits of economic growth. Third, rich countries established systems of law that protected the powerless from the powerful, safeguarded property rights, and nullified such religious roadblocks to growth as the prohibition against charging interest on loans and investments common to Christian and Islamic societies. Economic growth occurred not just because people wanted to be rich, this theory goes, but because they adopted new attitudes.

In the heyday of modernization theory, the 1950s and 1960s, many people in rich and poor countries remained optimistic about prospects for growth. Economic development experts, believing that the key to a country becoming rich was to build modern industry, set out to force the development of manufacturing plants, hydroelectric facilities, transportation infrastructures, and other elements of a modern industrial economy in poor countries. Some of those experts pointed to the path that Western nations had followed in becoming rich. Others pointed to the Soviet Union's success at transforming itself from a poor to a middle-income country between 1925 and 1970, and especially to Stalin's program of a command economy favoring industry. Either model suggested that Mexico, India, Brazil, and Egypt, four countries where the most aggressive efforts were underway, could be transformed by manufacturing facilities that would stimulate growth across the economy.

Under the influence of such hopes, buoyed in the 1960s and 1970s by temporarily high prices for raw materials, many poor nations borrowed huge sums from Western banks to invest in transportation, industrial equipment, dams for irrigation and electricity, and other things. They anticipated that these investments could be turned into profitable enterprises in a few years, that raw material prices would remain favorable, and that they would easily pay back the loans. In Brazil, for example, government strategy sought rapid growth through foreign borrowing and expected export earnings to pay interest on the debt. During the boom years, 1968–1974, Brazil's foreign debt rose to $13 billion and then jumped upwards, to $73 billion, in 1982. At that time it was the largest debt owed by a single country. Brazil had to borrow money just to pay the interest, a disastrous position. The government's expectations had not panned out. In the 1980s, when the sum of debts owed by countries surpassed $1 trillion, many could no longer pay interest on their debts much less redeem them. International collaboration averted a debt crisis that might have caused the collapse of the lending banks in Germany, the United States, and Japan. The plan involved rescheduling repayments. The principal effect of this fiasco was to undermine confidence in the idea that countries could become rich by borrowing to build up their industrial sectors. Hopes that the entire world could become rich were dampened.

If there were many stories of failure, there were also stories of brilliant success, the most impressive of them provided by Japan's economic miracle. In the era before World War II, Japan had modernized much of its economy but had not become a rich land. After the war Japan devised a strategy that took maximum advantage of international trade. Poor in most raw materials, Japan imported those and used its skilled and educated workforce to transform itself from a nation known for cheap products of poor quality into one known for competitive products of excellent quality. Close collaboration of big business and government, directed by the Ministry for International Trade and Industry, played a central role in Japan's strategy. Moreover, Japan learned to export more than it imported and to use the proceeds to modernize its industrial and transportation networks—building the famous bullet trains, for example. Japan pioneered in the development of robots to perform simple repetitive steps in manufacturing. The Asian tigers—Taiwan, South Korea, Hong Kong, and Singapore—and other countries in that region paid close attention to Japan's strategy and set out to mimic its central elements. By the 1990s, Japan, in competition not just with such older industrial powers as the United States and Germany but also with Asian rivals that had the advantage of lower labor costs, began a protracted recession. It remained one of the richest countries in the world, but it no longer stunned the world by its rapid growth.

These five Asian lands showed not just that countries could make the jump from poor to rich but also that alternatives to the Western strategy of modernization could produce equal or better results. Across the globe in the 1980s other countries studied what was underway in Japan and the Asian tigers, searching for policies and programs they could adopt for themselves. Whereas in 1950, the West—Europe, North America, plus Australia and New Zealand—made up a single pole of global wealth, by 2000 there were two poles, one Western and the other East Asian.

Two jolts in the 1970s further challenged the optimistic notion that every nation could become rich. First, the poor nations that controlled production of a number of strategic raw materials and popular foodstuffs—oil, bauxite, and coffee, for example—formed cartels. By controlling production and sales, they hoped to charge enough for their raw materials to acquire the resources needed to build modern economies. In the rich nations people suddenly waited in line to buy gasoline at sharply higher prices and rationed their coffee. This first jolt showed that the international pricing system need not remain stacked in favor of the rich countries. Such primary goods as oil and coffee could be made much more costly. Within a few years, however, the prices the cartels charged for their crude oil and coffee beans dropped while the prices that consumers in the rich countries paid for gasoline and coffee remained high. The windfall profits of cartelization were transferred from the raw material–producing nations to the business middlemen who processed and marketed oil and coffee.

In the second jolt, prices and unemployment rose together in most of the rich countries, a combination called "stagflation." Confidence in economic theory and in economics as a discipline weakened because theorists had consistently argued that inflation and high unemployment would never coincide. More important, the working people who made up the bottom half of the middle class started becoming poorer rather than richer. The middle class in developed countries ceased to grow and began to shrink, and the gap between the richest and the poorest members of society, which for many decades had narrowed, began to grow. All these developments—failure of foreign investment to spark economic growth in poor countries, Japan's pioneer development of a non-Western model of growth, stagflation, and the shrinkage of the middle class in rich countries—diminished confidence that informed people understood perfectly how economic systems worked and could manage them.

Meanwhile a new theory about economic development was emerging, one that blended values of capitalism and socialism but was distinctive in the way that it redefined well-being. "Social development theory" portrayed well-being as a function of the quality of life rather than the level of income. People who live long lives and enjoy ready access to education, health clinics, adequate housing, and affordably priced food and clothing can be well-off without being rich. Many characteristics of social development theory were stated first in the Nordic lands, the Netherlands, and Belgium in the 1950s and 1960s as those countries restructured the social purposes of government after World War II. They intentionally raised taxes and expanded the public sector in order to build more schools, provide national health care, and pay pensions to the disabled and the elderly. Those were also rich countries, so that their citizens enjoyed both a high standard of living and well-financed social services.

A more significant example of social development theory, described briefly in Chapter 14, appeared in the behavior of ordinary people living in poor countries who managed to find ways to improve the quality of their lives even though they remained poor. They lived out the principles of social development theory, creating well-being through health and longevity, literacy and education, shared decisionmaking between women and men, and a more equitable distribution of resources. Social development allowed people in Sri Lanka, Costa Rica and a growing number of Latin American countries, the Indian state of Kerala, and elsewhere to achieve levels of life expectancy, infant and maternal health, literacy, and popular engagement in public affairs equal or superior to those in the rich lands.

In the 1990s yet another novel economic model came about with the appearance of middle-income countries. In the previous decades the most promising news for world income had come

TABLE 15.2   Energy Use, CO_2 Emissions, and GDP Per Capita in Sixteen
Countries, 1996–1997

	CO_2 Emissions Per Capita (in metric tons)	Commercial Energy Use Per Capita (in Kg)	GDP Per Capita
United States	19.7	8,051	$29,010
Japan	9.3	4,058	24,070
Sweden	6.2	5,944	19,790
Germany	10.5	4,267	21,260
Rep. of Korea	9.0	3,576	13,590
Argentina	3.7	1,673	10,300
Costa Rica	1.4	657	6,650
Mexico	3.7	1,525	8,370
Saudi Arabia	14.2	4,753	10,120
Russian Federation	10.7	4,169	4,370
Brazil	1.7	1,012	6,480
China	2.8	902	3,130
India	4.2	476	1,670
Indonesia	1.1	672	3,490
Nigeria	0.7	722	920
Ethiopia	not available	284	510

Source: United Nations, *Human Development Report*, 1999 (New York: Oxford
University Press, 1999), pp. 134–137, 201–208.

from the achievements of the Asian tigers. During the 1990s, when recession slowed economic growth in Asia, the most promising news came from the rising number of countries that fell into the middle of the economic spectrum. During the 1980s and early 1990s, the average annual growth rate surpassed 5 percent in Cyprus, Thailand, Malaysia, Pakistan, India, Indonesia, China, Oman, Botswana, Swaziland, Uganda, Western Samoa, and several other formerly poor countries. In every region of the globe some countries were finding ways to promote rapid economic growth. In 1975, 29 countries reported levels of per capita income surpassing $5,000, including 19 surpassing $10,000. By the end of the 1990s those numbers had risen to 59 and 25 countries, respectively (in constant dollars). Even though disparities in income among countries continued to rise, more and more countries found ways to break out of the ranks of poor countries, creating a new category of middle-income countries.

Rich countries defined themselves not just by the material comforts their citizens enjoyed and their high levels of schooling but also by a greater consumption of natural resources. Table 15.2 shows levels of CO_2 emission, output measured by energy use, and GDP per capita in the 1990s among 16 countries selected to represent high-, middle-, and low-income countries. Differentials in energy use and CO_2 emissions between the top and bottom of the ranking surpassed even those in income. Could the whole world consume natural resources at the heady pace at which these things were consumed in rich countries? Could the globe support 6 billion rich people? What would a gallon of gasoline cost if everyone had an automobile and a share in gross domestic product equal to the U.S. average?

Both the social development model and the example set by middle-income countries suggested alternative paths to well-being. According to social development theory, everyone could be rich if they shared the social characteristics of longevity, education, and an equitable distribution of resources. According to experience in many countries that achieved middle-income status, people could be rich enough without having to consume natural resources at the rate those things were used in the most profligate rich countries. Thus the clash between rich and poor lands deepened and became more complex between 1950 and 2000. What started as a debate about the unequal distribution of wealth among countries and the unfair advantage that rich countries retained in setting prices became a debate about how to measure well-being and how to use natural resources. At the century's end the poverty of many nations and many people remained one of the greatest challenges facing the world community. World Health Organization officials identified extreme poverty as the leading cause of early death across the world. The poorest people—women, children, the elderly, and the disabled—were those least able to fend for themselves; the poorest nations were those with the scarcest resources, the most limited savings, and the lowest levels of literacy and schooling. All of these factors made it nearly impossible for them to find an independent path out of poverty. The problem of global poverty deepened between 1950 and 2000.

Globalization

During the second half of the twentieth century goods and services, knowledge and technology, foods and cooking styles, music and recordings, clothing and styles of dress, and many other tangible and intangible things crossed international boundaries in sharply rising volume. Some of the effects of globalization seem to have been unequivocally positive: People traveled more and learned much more about the ways of life and habits of thought of people in other lands. Some effects were mixed: Cultural styles crossed borders, giving people a wider choice of food, music, reading matter, and other things but also threatening to crowd out indigenous forms of these things. Some effects were negative: Transnational (or multinational) firms pursued sales and profits regardless of the costs of their actions for individuals. Most unsettling of all, some of the effects of globalization could not be assessed: Markets for labor and many goods became global, putting people into competition with one another at great distances and in a completely impersonal way. Workers who had made refrigerators for General Electric in a plant in Bloomington, Indiana, found themselves in competition with workers in Tijuana who could assemble the same refrigerators for lower wages, and the jobs moved to Mexico. In rich and poor countries alike people expressed growing anxiety about how globalization in this form would play out. Would it make goods and services cheaper? Would it also drive down wages and salaries? Would everyone eventually share in the benefits or drawbacks of globalization? Sometimes the global competition resulted in tragic consequences for families. For example, the former workers at White Furniture Company in Mebane, North Carolina, experienced the sadness of losing their jobs and having to retrain for new ones. Bill Bamberger and Cathy Davidson captured this experience in photographs in *Closing: The Life and Death of an American Factory* (1998).

This reorientation toward things outside local and national experience has a long history. None of the forms evident between 1950 and 2000 were new; what was new was a staggeringly greater scale. Global exports jumped from $375.8 billion in 1950 to $3.8 trillion in 1992, both sums expressed in constant dollars. Per person in the global community, exports rose from $149 to $696, a nearly five-fold rise, and people regularly consumed goods and services produced or created in another country. Countries poor in capital resources, which includes most countries, sought loans and aid abroad and by the 1980s also promoted foreign direct investment from the United States, Japan, and Germany. A few countries, notably China, Mexico, Indonesia, Brazil, and Argentina, attracted heavy investing, but the largest sums continued to flow into countries already rich. In 1993 the United States drew $440.9 billion, compared to China's $55.5 billion and Indonesia's $44.1 billion. In theory foreign direct investment would enable developing countries to catch up by sponsoring rates of economic growth higher than those in rich countries after a waiting period during which those investments were put to use. In practice, however, a few countries made large strides in catching up, but most continued to fall further behind.

Whereas Marx had faulted capitalism as an economic system that served as a tool of national interests, and for its single-minded pursuit of profit, late-twentieth-century critics took the argument a step further. The disabling fault of capitalism, argued international affairs specialist Ozay Mehmet, is the entry price. By the 1970s, Mehmet maintained, the capital-rich countries were still able to grow, but the capital-poor countries were no longer able to do so. The established industrial countries found globalization a challenge, but one they could surmount. Three countries alone—the United States, Japan, and Germany—accounted for 60 percent of the global sum of manufacturing output in 1994. For industrializing countries, each much smaller in scale, the problems were greater, and for countries with little industrial might the problems were still greater. In terms of allowing the rest of the world to become rich, at least by capitalist means, capitalism had succeeded too well. The rich countries were too rich.

Many governments sought to stimulate economic growth by increasing exports and replacing imported goods with goods made at home. Figure 15.1 shows the share of merchandise exports in total GDP in 1992 in 35 countries: The proportion ranges from a low of 1.7 percent in India to a high of 71 percent in Belgium. Many countries, especially members of the European Union, depended on exports for a significant share of their economic activity; for them international trade was not an option but a necessity. Moreover, transnational firms, wanting to expand, aggressively sought foreign markets. Savings moved across frontiers on an unprecedented scale, where they were invested initially in government bonds and real estate and then, by the 1980s, increasingly in equities (i.e., company stocks). International borrowing in 1976 totaled $95.6 billion; by 1993 it reached $818.6 billion. The number, scale, and significance of transnational firms soared.

In the old scheme of things national governments tried to regulate imports and exports, the movement of capital, wages, working conditions, and other matters by adopting laws that governed the activities of national firms. Governments also tried to bend the activities of individual firms to national objectives, using tax advantages, loans, and other inducements to persuade national firms to follow the lead set by government policy. Thus Japan used its Ministry of International Trade and Industry to induce national firms to buy Japanese goods and services whenever possible while augmenting exports. Some international agencies, especially the International Monetary Fund (the IMF, formed in 1947 to promote monetary cooperation) and the World Bank (formed in 1944 to promote economic development, especially in poor countries), and some other economic bodies and treaties, such as the European Union (EU) and the North American Free Trade Agreement (NAFTA), had the capacity to influence elements of economic globalization. But they could not control it. Indeed the most important element of globalization consisted of an escape from national regulation. A company that could not do something it wished to do in one country could, to an increasing degree, move part of its operations into another country. Some lands attracted companies by offering few or no regulations on banking, working conditions, wages, and other things. Meanwhile a few companies grew so large that their

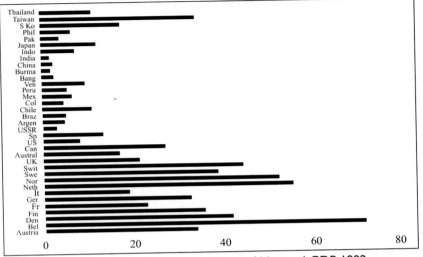

FIGURE 15.1   Export of Goods As a Share of National GDP, 1992.
SOURCE: Angus Maddison, *Monitoring the World Economy, 1820–1992*
(Paris: Development Centre of the Organisation for Economic Co-operation
and Development, 1995), pp. 180–92 and 236–37.

annual sales surpassed the GDP of even sizable countries. By 1995 the sales of six companies (Mitsubishi, Mitsui, Itochu, General Motors, Sumitomo, and Marubeni) exceeded the GDP of Denmark, at $146.1 billion. Exxon's sales surpassed the GDP of Finland, and Wal-Mart's topped Poland. Could nations adequately control firms doing transactions on such a scale?

Globalization put companies in competition with one another, leading to swift changes in the distribution of manufacturing. In 1960 U.S. automakers produced 6.7 million units, 51 percent of global output; British makers made 1.3 million units, 10 percent of the total; and Japanese makers produced 0.2 million units, 1 percent of the world total. By 1989 Japan's share of the world output of 35.5 million cars had risen to 26 percent, the U.S. share had fallen to 19 percent, and the British share to 4 percent. In just two decades the center of auto manufacturing moved to Japan. Then Japan began to lose market share; by 1995 South Korea and Brazil together accounted for 9 percent of world output. These swift changes showed the capacity of global trade to elevate or dash hopes even in an industry requiring vast investments in engineering, factories, parts making, distribution, and repair facilities.

For individuals the most anxiety-ridden elements of globalization came in the form of the integration of markets for skilled and unskilled labor. (Markets not integrated set their own prices and wages, which may be quite different; in integrated markets, prices and wages in one place compete with those in other places.) In the case of unskilled labor, manufacturing migrated toward lower-wage countries. Many U.S. manufacturers relocated to Mexico, Indonesia, and Vietnam; Japanese firms moved to Malaysia and Thailand; and some German and Japanese firms moved to low-wage areas in the United States. Moreover, manufacturers that kept plants at home often imported foreign labor, as Sweden's Volvo plants did. In contrast, for skilled workers migration was a more characteristic response to changing economic opportunities. The United States kept increasing its quotas for the six-year visas offered foreign workers with special skills, especially in high-tech industries. Well-educated and talented youth from many developing countries sought graduate and postgraduate degrees in the United States, Japan, Germany, and Australia. To some degree countries competed to attract physicians, engineers, scientists, and computer experts, offering higher wages than skilled people could earn at home. With the development of the Internet, many of those jobs could be performed without leaving home and without earning much higher wages. Thus the integration of labor markets successfully sought to economize on wages, putting workers at a disadvantage.

The international community adopted policies promoting free trade in the years after World War II, employing the General Agreement on Tariffs and Trade (GATT) and, from the mid-1990s, its successor, the World Trade Organization (WTO), as councils where countries could negotiate trade agreements. The creation of regional free-trade associations in Europe and North America furthered this trend, as did the preference for unregulated markets among capitalist economic theorists. Open markets and open economies—meaning those not limited by national boundaries—promised to create new wealth on a vast scale, perhaps even to solve the problem of poverty.

Poorer countries often competed to attract manufacturers only to find that, once in place, the same firms that had moved there in search of lower wages could move yet again to pursue still lower wages or a more flexible regulatory environment. In national markets, labor unions had provided workers with a way to bargain for better wages in the era of national firms. No analogous organizations appeared in the 1980s or 1990s to give international labor power against the transnational firm migrating in search of lower wage costs or looser regulations. The UN, NAFTA, and other organizations adopted policies concerning wages and working conditions but failed to enforce them; only the EU managed to set and enforce common policies on wages and working conditions among member states. For more than a century income disparities had narrowed, but now the gap began to widen again. Henry Ford, who wanted in the 1920s to build a car that his workers could afford, understood the profitability of wide demand. His successors—who were sometimes entrepreneurs of singular talent, such as Bill Gates of Microsoft, but who more often were business managers answerable to stockholders—did not always grasp Ford's insight. Thus globalization increased the variety of goods and services available to consumers while holding down or diminishing cost, but in the 1980s and 1990s it also undermined the capacity of wage earners to buy those goods and services.

Economic globalization's most daunting effect lay, however, in the emergence of transnational firms as actors on the world stage, which was set for a competition between democracy and capitalism. Democracy, which insists on individual political equality and the equality of opportunity, gained ground as a political system in the second half of the twentieth century. More countries selected democracy as a form of government, from India at its independence in 1947 to the successor countries to the Soviet Union. Some one-party democracies gave way to multiparty systems. Democratic forces often decided whether countries would adopt policies recommended by the World Bank or the IMF. Capitalism, which insists on the economic inequality of individuals as an essential stimulative element, also gained ground, defeating communism and overcoming stagflation. More countries selected capitalism as an economic system, and many large firms successfully made the transition from national to transnational operations. Globalization offered capitalism a way to escape national controls, leaving markets in charge of deciding winners and losers. Democracy and capitalism laid out these lines of battle in the 1990s, in which political theory stood at odds with economic theory.

In the global economy people consumed products from other lands, and some of the more complex goods they bought and used were made from parts manufactured in many lands. Mexi-

PICTURE 15.1   Fast-food restaurants in San José, Costa Rica. Signs of globalization are easy to find. Directly across the street from the Museo de Oro Precolumbiano (Museum of Pre-Colombian Gold) in San José, Costa Rica, Taco Bell and Burger King restaurants compete for business. Just down the street are a Pizza Hut and a McDonald's. (Photo courtesy of Todd Richardson)

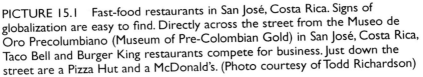

can plants along the U.S. border specialized in assembling clothing, television sets, and other products using parts made in the United States and Asia. U.S. automakers tried to declare the homemade portion of parts in their cars, as distinct from parts produced in Canada, Japan, and elsewhere. Any traveler abroad increasingly found familiar stores and products. A westerner visiting Suva, the capital of Fiji in the South Pacific, could have noticed a McDonald's, Levi jeans, fans made in Taiwan, cinemas playing Indian movies, restaurants featuring Malaysian cuisine, an Irish bar drawing Guinness on draft, a Wesleyan church, a mosque, Western doctors and dentists, ayurvedic practitioners of traditional Hindu medicine, and many other examples of a global market in goods, art, religion, and popular culture. To some observers the intrusion of goods and cultural artifacts from other lands, and especially the intrusion of Western goods and artifacts into non-Western countries, amounted to cultural imperialism. No longer able to control other lands as colonies, Western lands were trying to control them through food, drink, clothing, music, language, and other elements of popular use, said the critics. In some countries, other observers rejoined with the argument that eating a Malaysian dish or a hamburger from McDonald's did not weaken simultaneous attachments to the local culture.

It would be a mistake to concentrate only on economic globalization, important as it has been. Other forms of globalization also gained power during the second half of the nineteenth century, and some of those types placed nations at risk in new or more intense ways during the twentieth century. One of the most potent of these noneconomic forms of globalization concerned the microbial unification of the world, a process in which disease-causing pathogens migrated wherever

PICTURE 15.2
Soft drink
advertisement. Another
sign of globalization can
be seen in this ad, which
appeared in 1989 on a
main road in Brazzaville,
Republic of Congo. It
suggests that the
product is associated
with good times and is
the mark of a
thoroughly modern
middle-class nuclear
family. (Photo courtesy
of Phyllis Martin)

climate and other local conditions would permit them to survive. Three diseases, malaria, tuberculosis, and AIDS, posed especially dire threats to global health. Malaria, which up to about 1960 had been receding across the globe, began to expand once again, most devastatingly in countries where the strain of malaria was the deadliest and the effects therefore the greatest. The mosquitoes that transmit malaria from person to person had been countered by expanding tillage, by natural methods of mosquito control, and by the chemical pesticide DDT. DDT had to be taken out of use because it damaged other insects, birds, and mammals. Meanwhile, health researchers failed to find a vaccine, and mosquitoes developed resistance to insecticides. Another debilitating disease, tuberculosis, caused 2.5 million or more deaths each year in the 1990s, mostly among children. Drug-resistant strains of the bacteria threatened to reintroduce tuberculosis as a cause of death in rich countries. And AIDS, a viral disease communicated chiefly by sexual contact, infected rising numbers of people, most widely in central and southern Africa. All three diseases, and in the case of malaria the disease and its vector, spread more quickly and more easily as a result of travel and migration. Globalization therefore helped to spread medical and public health remedies to disease but also assisted pathogens in finding more victims.

Economic Restructuring and the Information Revolution

In a nutshell, the economic restructuring of the period from about 1980 to 2000 maintained the importance of producing primary materials, such as food, textile crops, and minerals, and of processing those materials into industrial and consumer goods. It elevated the importance of retail and wholesale trade in local and international markets. And it added new income and wealth on a vast scale in the acquisition, exchange, analysis, and interpretation of information. Three developments contributed to the rise of businesses based on information technology. First, computers, software, and Internet-related activities sharply expanded productivity in many occupations. Writers could save time making manuscripts because word-processing software simplified editorial tasks and publishing. Accountants could make many more computations with perfect accuracy by employing spreadsheet software. Marketing specialists could build databases that made their customers and suppliers more accessible, and scientists and social scientists could build huge databases to be analyzed with statistical software. Virtually no job involving the manipulation of words or numbers failed to become easier and faster to do. Software programs also piloted planes and spaceships and directed the repetitive work of industrial robots. No one had planned that information technology would have such an effect on productivity, but by the 1990s it was the most dynamic sector of enterprise. In the United States, while manufacturing jobs flowed abroad, to the automakers of Japan and the clothiers of Mexico, Malaysia, and Vietnam, information technology turned the 1990s into the most prosperous decade in national history.

Second, computers, software, and allied goods and services created a new range of products that had the particular benefit not of freeing time for leisure, as much earlier technological improvement had done, but of enhancing productivity. These new products paid more dividends down the line than, say, kitchen equipment, adding machines, or typewriters. Information technology stood on a par with the steam engine, the harnessing of electricity, and the internal combustion engine in energizing economic activity.

Third, information technology made money hand over fist for the people who created it, turning its most successful entrepreneurs into the richest people the world had ever known. Never before had so much equity wealth—meaning wealth consisting of the investing public's appraisal of the value of stock companies—been created; never before had the equity value of companies grown so quickly. No longer were the people earning the highest salaries sports heroes, movie celebrities, and CEOs of manufacturing companies; in the 1990s they were the young men and women who founded Internet companies and created software.

Those developments in turn fed the emergence of information and knowledge as central elements of national well-being. From one perspective, the scale of this transformation is apparent in a vast increase in the volume of information available for people to consult, learn, and apply. The Library of Congress, the largest storehouse of printed information in the world, held 9 million volumes in 1950, 19 million in 1980, and 26 million in 2000. Meanwhile, formally published material in books and magazines had been complemented by material housed on the Internet. In 2000 some estimates suggested that the Internet contained more than a billion web pages, each of them one or many conventional book pages in length. Nearly 9 million companies had registered web addresses. Internet retailers recorded each transaction so that they could greet a returning customer with some shopping suggestions calculated to appeal to his or her tastes.

Personal computers and the Internet swiftly transformed the individual's capacity to acquire and create information, but the process was uneven across lands. In 2000, the United States, Canada, and Europe accounted for 79 percent of an estimated 250 million people online, although together they claimed only 12 percent of global population. Thus the remaining 88 percent of the world's people shared only 21 percent of Internet users. In the United States about 43 percent of people had access to the Internet, as did 20 percent or more in Germany, the Netherlands, and the Nordic lands. But in Spain only 5 percent had access, in Portugal only 2 percent, and in most countries outside the West fewer than 2 percent. Many countries were held back by the unavailability of telephone lines—Cambodia counted less than one telephone per 100 people—as well as the expense of technical equipment.

This distribution, roughly similar to the distribution of spending on research and development, gave North America and Europe a huge advantage in developing the technology, software,

PICTURE 15.3   Computers, 1959. A view of the new Computing Center at Indiana University in 1959 showing the data processing machines available at the time. (Photo courtesy of the Indiana University Archives)

and commercial opportunities of the Internet. The lands that lagged behind could look forward to avoiding the mistakes and errors the leaders made, and thus to catching up faster than the leading countries had moved ahead. But to the end of the twentieth century the leaders maintained a decisive advantage. They benefited most from such innovations as fiberoptic transmission, which allowed information to be transmitted in ever-expanding volume and at ever-diminishing cost. Some observers feared that the leading countries were too far ahead ever to be caught. Thus the information revolution threatened to aggravate inequalities among nations.

Information technology affected people's lives in other ways, too. Grocery stores induced their customers to carry "shopping cards" consisting of a bar code that identified the holder and allowed the store to track that person's purchases. Medical researchers used insurance records to collect information about how individual patients responded to specific therapies, hoping thereby both to test the efficacy of medications and procedures and to follow the patient's health history.

The new information technology revolution was, at one and the same time, a great democratizer and a great autocrat. On one hand, it gave people ways to evade the information control practiced by religious institutions, some governments, and the media companies that owned newspapers, magazines, radio stations, and television outlets. In China, the student democracy movement used the Internet to communicate; in Egypt, Islamic revolutionaries used the Internet to avoid government censorship; and in the United States, both ultraradical and ultraconservative groups attracted new members and communicated among themselves along this new route. Every mode of speech and every point of view could be heard. Yet only people with access to the Internet could communicate in this way.

Bill Joy, chief scientist at Sun Microsystems, discerned another danger: Information technology threatened an Orwellian future in a new form. In George Orwell's *1984,* an efficient authori-

PICTURE 15.4   Computers, 1995. By 1995, access to and use of computers were integral parts of the educational experience of most U.S. students. But such opportunities to explore the "information highway" were not available for most students around the world. (Photo courtesy of the Indiana University Archives)

tarian bureaucracy controlled thought and the imagination. In his essay for *Wired* magazine, "Why the Future Doesn't Need Us" (2000), Joy sketched out a picture of a world of the future where individual freedoms are handed over to machines. The new technology, especially hypothetical forms combining traditional components with biological material to produce, say, programmable robots using brain cells, promised to do wonderful things. But it also threatened to build machines utterly without conscience and able, moreover, to replicate themselves. In Joy's view such machines would be superior to people, and therefore people would be able to alter the terms of evolution by introducing nonliving entities better adapted to survival than humans. For a solution Joy suggested that well-informed authorities should decide which avenues of biotechnology should not be explored, in effect closing off the wellspring of curiosity.

Other observers greeted information technology much more eagerly, imagining a present and a future in which even the simplest tasks of daily life could be performed by machines. In the rich countries most householders already owned both televisions and remote control devices, which allowed them to change channels without rising from their chairs. Would the future hold an unbounded selection of video entertainment and education: sporting events, movies, all the television shows ever made, music, interviews, even lectures?

Many earlier innovations, such as the steam engine and the internal combustion engine, required scores of years to show the full scale of their effect; communications and computer technology produced results more quickly. Devised in the 1940s, first for single functions, commercial computers appeared in the 1950s. Miniaturized versions were introduced in the 1960s, portable computers by 1980, and equipment inexpensive enough for middle-class households to buy in the 1980s. By the 1990s, interactive use of computers allowed people, via the Internet, to hold conversations with counterparts around the world, opening to someone sitting at home many of the advantages that travel offers in encountering unfamiliar ideas and outlooks.

The grandest information project of the twentieth century, begun in 1990, combined information technology and microbiology to map the entire human genome, thereby capturing the staggering volume of information embedded in the DNA code in the nucleus of each cell. Concurrent projects mapped the genome of fruit flies and nematodes, long important laboratory specimens, and other life forms. These maps would form the basic library necessary to study the roles played by individual genes and the interactions of groups of genes in the appearance and mechanics of the body, disease, and aging. They showed that some genetic material is common to different life forms, and that the same material may play different roles in different organisms. Certain gene mutations lead to cancer, and preliminary work suggested that the identification of those genes could lead to ways of combatting uncontrolled cell divisions. Observers predicted that physicians eventually would be able to anticipate disease in individual patients by conducting genetic tests and even to forecast responses to particular therapies. Pharmaceutical makers would be able to design drugs for specific functions on the model of the AIDS drugs that successfully interfere with the way the HIV virus replicates itself. It would become possible to design therapies for each individual person's genotype, even to select a diet of optimal benefit. Nearly everyone involved in genetic research predicted that the new information would make it possible to construct better medications for diseases already treatable and to find treatments for many diseases that are still mysteries. The boldest and most optimistic among them predicted that people might, by 2050, live to be 150 and also suffer much less from disease and disability.

Behind this dramatic explosion of scientific and technical information lay an equally profound change in popular access to information through education. The history of gains in literacy and schooling was, in the long period before 1950, marked by excruciatingly slow progress. England, one of the most closely studied lands, moved from a literacy of about 10 percent in 1500 to one of about half the adult population in 1750, and on to universal literacy by about 1900. That process was telescoped in time in most of the world, where literacy levels remained low in 1950. Tanzania's literacy rate jumped from 17 percent in 1968 to 63 percent in 1975, Nicaragua's from less than 50 percent in 1979 to 87 percent by 1983, and Mozambique's from 10 percent in 1975, when the country gained independence, to 94 percent in 1991. Among developing countries as a whole, adult literacy rose from about 43 percent in 1970 to 61 percent in 1993. In Saudi Arabia it jumped from 9 to 61 percent, in Iran from 29 to 66 percent, in Papua New Guinea from 32 to 71 percent, and in the Central African Republic from 16 to 56 percent. Developing countries expanded the number of schools and trained more teachers, allowing more children to attend school; many countries also underwrote adult schools for people who had not had an opportunity to learn to read and write as children. By the end of the 1990s, 65 countries could boast that adult literacy surpassed 90 percent of their populations. Considering people 15 and older, and therefore looking backward to earlier attainment, the average schooling of people in developing countries rose from 2.1 years in 1960 to 4.4 years in 1990. Among developed countries the average rose from 7 to 9 years.

In 1950 in most of the world people were differentiated from one another chiefly by the wealth, status, and opportunities inherited from their parents. By 2000, another marker had been added based on educational attainment. In this marker, years of schooling and enrollment in particular disciplines were what mattered. In every country, income distributed itself in a hierarchy ordered by education, with people having little or no schooling earning the most meager wages and attaining the lowest life expectancies and those having the most schooling earning the

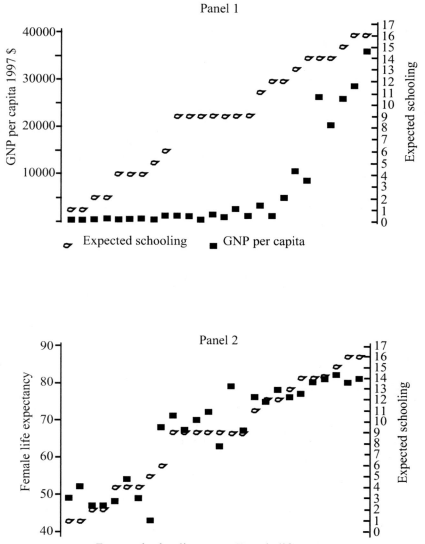

FIGURE 15.2   Income, Education, and Life Expectancy in 26 Countries.
SOURCE: World Bank, *World Development Report 1998/99: Knowledge for Development* (Washington: Oxford University Press, 1999), pp. 190–193 and 200–201.

highest wages and attaining the highest survival rates. Figure 15.2 explores these relationships in 26 countries. In the first panel, which compares years of education and GNP per capita, it is apparent that countries that schooled children for 16 years have much higher levels of GNP per capita than do countries with fewer years of schooling, but the relationship is not especially close. The second panel, which compares education and life expectancy, shows a much closer relationship between each pair of country markers. Evidently the impressive rise in literacy and schooling during the second half of the twentieth century has been more closely associated with improvements in the quality of life than in income. Whereas the status hierarchy of 1950 seemed to bar progress for most people, schooling opened a potential path for nearly everyone to escape poverty and to improve the quality of their lives. Moreover, education could be offered even to adults who had missed out, giving them a chance to update their skills and expand their intellectual horizons.

Information technology stressed immediate availability and impact, but rising levels of literacy and education were for the long term. The effects of the latter would play out over the remaining lifetimes of the people who benefited, laying the foundations for continued improvements in quality of life into the twenty-first century. Even though they lagged in income and life expectancy, most developing countries could expect the investments they made in education between 1950 and 2000 to pay off in many ways, including better child survival rates.

Meanwhile, many developed countries also pushed ahead in pursuing educational goals. By 2000, the United States, Germany, the Czech Republic, and Norway counted 80 percent or more of their populations aged 25–64 as high-school graduates, versus fewer than 20 percent in most developing countries. The United States, Canada, and northwestern Europe led also in the number of people earning advanced degrees. Thus even though most developing countries had telescoped the process of raising literacy to a few decades or even a few years instead of several centuries, the developed countries had upped the ante by emphasizing postgraduate studies. Information technology also seemed to aggravate differences among nations rather than to ameliorate them. Moreover, globalization simplified the ease with which schooled and talented people could migrate to the most attractive and lucrative opportunities.

These accomplishments and the anxieties they created existed also in individual countries. India had one of the lowest literacy rates across the globe and had the largest absolute number of people unable to read or write. It also emerged during the 1990s, however, as a major contributor to information technology, creating and exporting software and contributing to advanced science and social science. Within countries and between countries information technology threatened to aggravate divisions within society while also making those divisions more difficult to overcome. English became the leading language of the Internet, with perhaps 80 percent of websites in that language. Yet fewer than 10 percent of the world's population speaks English. Overall, information technology was much more readily available to richer and better educated young adult males speaking English than to other groups.

Information technology also gave rise to new challenges in relations among nations and business firms as people began to pose questions about rights to and ownership of knowledge. The questions multiplied much more rapidly than the answers. Individual firms tried to patent DNA information, for example, on the basis of having discovered the knowledge first. Observers worried that weak international laws governing intellectual rights would dampen innovation and that tight regulations would choke future growth by giving too much power and wealth to a few firms and countries.

Conclusion

For nations the second half of the twentieth century did more to build bridges than any earlier period while also erecting higher walls separating one nation from another in attributes. Thus the United Nations and its agencies, regional economic and political agreements such as the European Union and NAFTA, and many other forms of international collaboration and adjudication created the means for nations to speak their mind to one another, to negotiate, and to plan. At the same time the wealth of rich countries and the divide separating them from most world nations grew. Globalization offered countries with greater investment potential, larger and stronger transnational firms, and earlier involvement the opportunity to jump further ahead, and all of the rich countries took advantage of these opportunities. Advances in information technology, which appeared somewhat later, added to the advantages rich countries claimed, and to their capacity to compound their head start by investing more in research and development, educating more people at higher levels, and exploiting such advantages of wealth as plentiful telephone lines.

For individuals, too, the second half of the twentieth century was a time of division and differentiation. People living in rich countries maintained and enlarged their lead over people living in poor countries in income, housing, and the conditions of material life. Although people living in poor countries did much catching up in literacy and life expectancy, two important elements in the quality of life, their counterparts in rich countries upped the ante, setting the requirement not as literacy but advanced education, not just survival but good health. The migrations of people associated with globalization and information technology reduced divisions among nations, bridging cultural divides. Those same migrations aggravated divisions among people by exaggerating the differences based on income, education, access to English, even age. In 2000 the economic prospects of a well-educated young male living in Silicon Valley, California, were better than those of young people almost anywhere else in the world.

Conclusion: Century's End

· ·

HOW CAN WE DRAW A LINE AND CONCLUDE A CENTURY? WE MAY celebrate as the hands of the clock reach midnight and hang a fresh calendar, but it is not that easy to discern the beginnings or ends of deep-seated processes of historical change. In the Introduction to this book, we noted that our goal was to write a thematic history of the twentieth century that focused on significant human experiences. Such experiences hardly begin and end at the turn of centuries, or if they do it is coincidental.

Human experience itself has caused us to write a history of a long twentieth century that started around 1880 when capitalism, conviction, and technology powered a new imperialist expansion into most world regions. It was a time when older notions of democracy inspired by the French Revolution and newer Marxist socialist ideas were fusing in the revolutionary arsenal of radically minded and oppressed peoples. And it was a period when competition among European nation-states was gathering steam in a process that led to World War I, a colossal tragedy that left a permanent dent in the idea of progress.

As the century closed, some later twentieth-century experiences were still working themselves out and continuing into the twenty-first century. Social inequities of class and gender were in many regions as stark and volatile as they had been earlier in the century, although in a few areas some advances had been made. Gaps between haves and have-nots within and between countries found expression in religious and secular terms and were mobilized around fundamentalist and ethnic ideologies. Pressures on key world resources such as water, food, and oil were increasing, as were new ways to deal with them. While some thinkers subscribed to chaos theory or catastrophe theory as principles underlying historical change, others remained confident that human ingenuity would carry global society through the twenty-first century. Science in the twentieth century had proven to be double-edged: It offered solutions to many of the dilemmas of human life but also presented new dangers, even the potential destruction of humanity itself. Although the world wars that had killed millions before 1945 were avoided in the second half of the century, nuclear arsenals were not fully dismantled; indeed, new states joined the "nuclear club" in the 1990s. At the same time, guerrilla warfare and terrorism had emerged as the tools of the weak, faced as they were with the overweening economic dominance and military strength of Great Powers who constituted the enemy. Yet, peace movements and organizations had also proliferated in the twentieth century. At all levels, local and international, private and public, individual and corporate, people worked to diffuse tension and to resolve conflict peacefully. Such contradictions growing out of twentieth-century experience continued at the heart of global relations in the last decade of the century. Commentators talked of a new world order and of a new world disorder, of human rights crises and of the ever wider acceptance of bold documents defending such rights issued by the United Nations and other international organizations. It was in this contradictory vein that the old century gave way to the new.

Specific years are in retrospect turning points in history, and readers can reflect on some that have been highlighted in the pages of this book. Even from the short vantage point of a decade or so later, 1989 could be appreciated as an important year in global interactions. Events in the Communist world affected much of the world's population, and certainly those who lived in Europe. In the Soviet Union, the heroic dreams of prosperity that had grown out of the victory of Communist forces over the armies of the Third Reich and the subsequent enlargement of Soviet dominance in Eastern Europe were clouded by the 1970s through economic decline, environmental decay, and a stagnant bureaucracy. In 1985, Mikhail Gorbachev became general secretary of the Communist Party and in attempting to reform communism introduced new policies of *perestroika* (economic reform) and *glasnost* (openness). His willingness to let Eastern Europeans work out their own futures so that Soviet resources could be concentrated at home was an opportunity quickly seized by people doubly outraged by foreign domination and economic stagnation under communism. Throughout Eastern Europe, demonstrations reached a crescendo as the months of 1989 rolled by. Barbed wire fences and policies that had blocked the flow of goods and people were torn down, and new governments committed to change came to power in Poland, Hungary, East Germany, Bulgaria, Czechoslovakia, and Romania. In October 1989, peaceful demonstrations in the East German city of Leipzig grew to huge proportions across the country. The East German government, cognizant of the changes going on in other East European countries and overwhelmed by popular sentiment for change, decided to open the nation's borders and end the division of Germany. Hundreds of thousands of people took to the streets and joyously assisted in tearing down the Berlin Wall and the rest of the 830-mile barrier that had separated the two Germanys for twenty-eight years. In an Act of the Congress of the People's Deputies, the Soviet Union was formally dissolved in December 1991. The breakup of the Soviet Union was complete, and republics stretching from the Baltic to central Asia gained their independence.

Relatively peacefully, therefore, the stand-off between the two superpowers and their allies had come to an end. There remained under Communist rule a few hard-line governments—for example, North Korea, Cuba, and most important, China. But even that large nation started to experiment with a range of novel interactions with the capitalist world, although at home mass demonstrations against corruption and for political openness that broke out in Beijing and other cities were violently crushed in June 1989. Although Chinese struggles for democracy continued to find their way blocked in the 1990s, the same was not true elsewhere. Democracy was very much in the vogue and in the 1990s countries in Latin America, Asia, and Africa overthrew dictators and held elections, sometimes supervised by teams of UN observers. Although there had not yet been time to ascertain in 2000 whether this trend might continue in the long term, it did seem that a new world order dominated by capitalism and democracy (not always compatible forces) might be emerging. The threat of war that had dominated the Cold War period (c. 1945–1991) and had produced such chillingly described policies as "mutually assured destruction" (MAD) seemed less of a threat as far as the world powers were concerned.

Yet, had a new world order truly emerged or had the removal of two camps only created doubt, confusion, and a vacuum to be filled by smaller nations and groups who had the potential to inject confusion into world affairs? A 1999 article in the *New York Times* entitled "Who's in Charge?" talked of a new world disorder: "In the last year of the century, the newer, saner world order confidently anticipated when Communism collapsed a decade ago is nowhere to be seen," the writer claimed. He went on to note the retreat of the United States from engagement in global cooperative strategies, the economic and social turmoil in Russia, the overstretched resources of United Nations and privately funded aid agencies, and the civil wars that raged on every continent outside the conventions written for conflicts between states. Some developments, such as the cooperation of the fifteen-member European Union—an unthinkable alliance only five decades previously—seemed to offer a new regional order; however, another commentator for the *New York Times* wrote: "These days not much depends on major powers. There are new actors on the world stage." And it was, of course, likely that these new actors, especially those who had been historically under Western imperialism and neocolonial domination, would have their own visions of order and disorder.

Another phrase increasingly popular in international discourse at century's end was "globalization," particularly when applied to the economic interdependence of nations and to cultural flows between people in disparate parts of the globe. In Chapter 15, we carefully analyzed the ramifications of economic globalization, quoting the statement from a 1973 meeting of non-aligned nations that "the increasingly pervasive activities of transnational and monopolistic commercial, financial, and industrial companies" constituted imperialist exploitation. Thus, the forms of relations that developed in the second half of the century were not new but greater in scale. By the last decade of the century multinational corporations, with their huge transnational power, were a threat to democracies, since globalization allowed them to respond to market forces and escape national controls. In rich and poor countries alike, people expressed anxiety about how economic globalization would play itself out. The most anxiety-ridden elements of globalization for workers came in the integration of job markets for skilled and unskilled labor, which allowed firms to relocate to other countries and take advantage of the most profitable arrangements. The different yet interconnected roles of powerful corporations and nation-states is something still being worked out and represents another continuing theme overlapping into the twenty-first century.

Cultural flows were also an essential part of increasing globalization. Although often characterized as Americanization or westernization, these flows were by no means a one-way street. From Hong Kong martial arts films making box-office hits in the West to the spread of Japanese video games and the proliferation of karaoke bars, global interactions were evident especially in popular culture. That the world became smaller may be an obvious comment but it was a critical reality nevertheless. Transportation systems carried travelers across the world in hours, capitalism allowed the easy flow of material goods, and the media could transmit popular culture, recorded or instantaneous. Madonna and Ricky Martin could be viewed on Indian MTV, Kentucky Fried Chicken was on sale near Beijing's Tiananmen Square (some of the student hunger strikers of 1989 went there to break their fast), and supermarket shoppers bought imported plastic Christmas trees in Congo and Venezuela. Soccer, which had started its life as a schoolboys' game in nineteenth-century England, was made known by teachers, soldiers, missionaries, and amateur enthusiasts around the colonial world. It was a cheap and popular street game played by boys in urban slums and by national teams in celebration of old and new identities. The game became localized as well as internationalized with different meanings, styles, and preparations. By 1998 soccer had established itself as the world's most popular sport and over a billion and a half of humanity tuned in on television to the watch the World Cup. Like economic globalization, the flow of culture was not just a twentieth-century phenomenon, but colonialism, capitalism, and technology speeded up its transmission in the late century.

Anxieties about the loss of regional distinctiveness and the homogenization of world culture were circulating by century's end. Were MTV, Macintosh, and McDonald's pressing societies into one commercially homogeneous global network? Would the rise of Starbucks, Nike, and Disney mean that all individual distinctiveness would be lost? Although this may be the larger perception, the micro-view seemed to suggest that local trends were just as important, at least in the 1990s. Some analysts even referred to "glocalization," the simultaneous strengthening of global and local trends.

Historians of the British and French Empires, who once wrote of the hegemonic power of the cultural forms introduced by colonial rulers, sensed a similar interplay between the local and the international in an earlier period and backed away from older certainties. Imperial power was seen as much more uneven and much less certain than previously thought. The ability of people to appropriate imported cultural forms—sports, clothing, music, food, or even religious belief— and to use them as building blocks in shaping their own dynamic cultural visions has been well documented. Appreciating something in its local context appeared as important in understanding global processes as study of the workings of world capitalism. In the 1990s, some researchers took a look at the spread of McDonald's, surely an icon of globalization. In the United States, McDonald's may be considered a fast-food family restaurant but in other parts of the world, such as East Asia, it is often a place for upwardly mobile couples to go on a date or for junior executives to gather for a fancy lunch. All over the world multinational corporations have to localize products and their marketing and management strategies. By the time Big Macs reach the other side of the world, they may have taken on any number of local meanings. They may be made of tofu or seafood and they may be viewed as a snack instead of a meal. Through a wide range of cultural artifacts such differential consumption can create diversity in the face of what appears to be homogenization.

Although we could describe emerging themes in world history as the twentieth century drew to a close, it is too early to draw conclusions about many of them. It is possible, however, to discuss trends as a means of looking to the future. This exercise can be useful even if answers will be cautious and appropriately subject to debate. Is greater democratization here to stay? Will those who construct their world narrowly, for example, religious fundamentalists, withdraw even more into tightly framed cultures in the face of globalization forces? Will women receive equality of opportunity with men? Will the gap between rich and poor grow less? Will nations develop the will to work multilaterally for the development of a more peaceful world?

Thus, the chapters in this book do not represent parts of a puzzle that can be neatly fitted together to arrive at definitive solutions. Rather they are a collage of human experiences made from overlapping pieces and woven together by themes of crises, revolution, and change—to which we might add at century's end continuity, for there remained many open-ended questions. Together the pieces constitute a twentieth-century image of turmoil, even darkness and confusion, yet there are bright dashes of creativity, achievement, and optimism. Some of the pieces are worn and faded with time, others have worked their way into the picture more recently. Their significance will only become clearer in the emerging character of the twenty-first century.

*   *   *

The chapters and above conclusion of this book were written before the shocking and tragic events of September 11, 2001, when terrorists flew commercial aircraft into the twin towers of the World Trade Center in New York and into the Pentagon in Washington, D.C. The horrific acts, which seemed unimaginable except in Hollywood fantasies, were beamed over televisions across the world. People now could not escape the implications and realities of living in a "global village." Americans who had felt protected by two oceans no longer felt safe at home, a sense accentuated by bioterrorist attacks that followed soon after the explosions in the two major cities.

The last clearly defined segment of the long twentieth century, the Cold War era (1945–1991) had ended relatively quietly on the world stage with the fall of the Berlin Wall and the demise of the Soviet Union. An uncertain and indeterminate period had followed. We must leave it for future historians to say with the passage of time if the twentieth century came to an end in 2001. Yet, for those of us who have lived through recent events, it seems that the world has been dramatically propelled into the twenty-first century. Many familiar features of the landscape, from the structure of diplomatic alliances to the meaning of skyscrapers, seem suddenly altered. At the same time, however, the problems at the heart of this book are as relevant as ever, for they provide the context out of which contemporary actions emerge. Issues of "peace" and "war"—including their basic meaning—now loom as large as ever. Understanding the various forms that "fundamentalism" can take is of paramount importance. The consequences of the patterning of world relations through old and new imperialism carry added import. Topics such as disparities between wealthy and impoverished nations, the uses of science, population, the environment, and hunger remain of pressing concern. The working out of more equitable gender relations remains an area of high tension. Whether or not this new era will be yet another of revolutions remains to be seen, as do many other things, including the ways that the epochal events of September 11 may change interpretations of modernity and progress. The tragedies have made it painfully evident that we need a greater and deeper knowledge about the world beyond national boundaries. Wherever we have arrived at this point in time, a clear understanding of what happened in the twentieth century seems essential as we try to navigate the uncertainties of the present.

Suggested Readings
and Other Resources

Chapter 1

Achebe, Chinua. 1996. *Things Fall Apart.* Portsmouth, N.H.: Heinemann. A powerful novel detailing the devastating impact of British rule on the Igbo peoples in Nigeria.

Applebey, Joyce, Lynn Hunt, and Margaret Jacob. 1994. *Telling the Truth About History.* New York: W. W. Norton. A very readable account of changes in the way historians view their discipline and practice their craft in the twentieth century.

Forster, E. M. 1924. *A Passage to India.* Reprint, San Diego: Harcourt, Brace, 1984. A novel about the mutual incomprehensibility that overlay the interactions of the Europeans and Indians under British rule.

Freud, Sigmund. 1989. *Civilization and Its Discontents.* New York: W. W. Norton. A representative work by an intellectual in the early twentieth century assessing the impact of modernity on European culture.

Hobsbawm, E. J. 1987. *The Age of Empire, 1875–1914.* London: Weidenfeld and Nicolson. One of the best accounts of the material basis of European imperialism.

Said, Edward. 1992. *Culture and Imperialism.* New York: Knopf. The author argues that the West created a picture of the backward Orient in order to legitimize its own modernity and progressiveness.

Weber, Eugene. 1986. *France: Fin de siècle.* Cambridge, Mass.: Belknap Press. Explores the tensions in French society as a result of the discontinuous and uneven spread of modernization.

Films and Videos

Cabaret (Bob Fosse, 1972). Set in Weimar Germany, this movie portrays the decadence of the interwar years.

Enthusiasm (Dziga Vertov, 1931). A tale celebrating the factory and the proletariat that focuses on coal workers in the Don basin.

Gandhi (Richard Attenborough, 1982). A rather hagiographical account of the Indian national leader who led his nation to freedom using nonviolent means of struggle. The film is a dramatization of his life from his years as a lawyer in South Africa to his role in the independence struggle against British colonial rule and his assassination.

Howard's End (James Ivory, 1982). A tale about love, class struggle, and hypocrisy among the upper classes in Edwardian England.

Modern Times (Charlie Chaplin, 1936). A satire on the human condition in the factory age of assembly lines.

Reds (Warren Beatty, 1981). The dramatic adventures of the American Communists John Reed and Louise Bryant in the Soviet Union during the Russian Revolution of 1917.

Chapter 2

Anderson, Benedict. 1983. *Imagined Communities: Reflections on the Origins and Spread of Nationalism.* London: Verso. An analysis of how our patriotism and perceptions of the nation are learned and shaped through life experiences. On a national scale these are sometimes developed through the power of the state.

Cohen, William B., ed. 1980. *European Empire Building.* Saint Louis: Forum Press. On the causes of the "new" imperialism, with chapters representing the points of view of different scholars.

Conklin, Alice L., and Ian Christopher Fletcher, eds. 1999. *European Imperialism, 1830–1930: Climax and Contradiction.* Boston: Houghton Mifflin Company. Good introduction and extracts from primary sources on various aspects of imperialism.

Hobsbawm, Eric, and Terence Ranger, eds. 1983. *The Invention of Tradition.* Cambridge, U.K.: Cambridge University Press. Various chapters, including one on colonial Africa and another on imperial India, show how both imperial rulers and imperial subjects invented and appropriated "traditions" for empowerment in the new colonial society.

LaFeber, Walter. 1984. *Inevitable Revolutions: The United States in Central America.* New York: W. W. Norton. Demonstrates U.S. economic and military intervention in Central America with case studies from the history of different countries.

Ngugi, wa Thiong'o. 1965. *The River Between.* Portsmouth, N.H.: Heinemann, 1965. A striking novel by East Africa's foremost writer showing various responses of Gikuyu villagers to the arrival of European missionaries, settlers, their ideas, and demands.

Strobel, Margaret. 1994. *Women in the Second British Empire.* Bloomington: Indiana University Press. A discussion of gender in colonial society, looking at the lives of both indigenous and foreign women and their relations to the men in their lives and work.

Films and Videos

Africa (Home Vision, 1984). Written and presented by the historian Basil Davidson. Programs 5 and 6, "The Bible and the Gun" and "This Magnificent African Cake," are particularly useful for the background and impact of imperial expansion.

Black and White in Colour (Jean-Jacques Arnaud, 1976). This amusing and satirical film made in West Africa depicts colonial relations in two imaginary African villages, one on the French side of the border and the other on the German side. The absurdity of national and colonial identities is depicted when the Europeans discover that World War I has broken out in Europe. Won the Academy Award for Best Foreign Film.

Black Man's Land (David Koff and Antony Kowarth, 1986). A three-part documentary ("White Man's County," "Mau Mau," and "Kenyatta") on colonialism, nationalism, and independence in Kenya through the diaries, reports, and photographs of contemporaries; especially good on the African perspective. Part one deals with the conquest period and the early African nationalist movement.

The Last Emperor (Bernardo Bertolucci, 1987). This lavish and epic film recreates the life of the last emperor of the Qing Dynasty who was deposed as a boy and reinstated by the Japanese as a puppet ruler in Manchukuo. It includes several key scenes filmed inside Beijing's Forbidden City. Major events from the Chinese Revolution are portrayed and discussed.

Out of Africa (Sydney Pollack, 1986). A romanticized but convincing view of life in colonial Kenya through the diaries of a white settler, Isak Dinesen, in the early century; a good film to critique on its portrayal of colonial relations. Glorious footage of East African scenery.

Passage to India (David Lean, 1985). Based on E. M. Forster's celebrated novel about colonial relations in India, the story focuses on the fate of an Indian doctor who is perceived to have crossed permissible social boundaries in his relations with white women.

Chapter 3

Cameron, Rondo. 1997. *A Concise Economic History of the World*, 3rd ed. New York: Oxford University Press. Provides a broad context, focusing chiefly on the modern era and the West.

Davies, R. W. 1998. *Soviet Economic Development from Lenin to Khrushchev*. Cambridge, U.K.: Cambridge University Press. Surveys the Soviet economy and differing interpretations of its performance.

Feuerwerker, Albert. 1995. *The Chinese Economy, 1870–1949*. Ann Arbor: University of Michigan Center for Chinese Studies. An accessible survey of a national economy in this period.

Headrick, Daniel R. 1988. *The Tentacles of Progress: Technology Transfer in the Age of Imperialism, 1850–1940*. New York: Oxford University Press. Describes the division of labor between colonies, which produced primary goods, and colonizers, who used technology and processed the primary goods.

Kemp, Tom. 1983. *Industrialization in the Non-Western World*. London: Longman. Discusses industrialization in the West as well as in Japan, India, China, Brazil, and Nigeria.

Mokyr, Joel. 1990. *The Lever of Riches: Technological Creativity and Economic Progress*. New York: Oxford University Press. A sparkling history of technological innovation.

Orlove, Benjamin, ed. 1997. *The Allure of the Foreign: Imported Goods in Postcolonial Latin America*. Ann Arbor: University of Michigan Press. Argues that internal social factors influenced the demand for European and U.S. goods in Latin America.

Pacey, Arnold. 1990. *Technology in World Civilization: A Thousand-Year History*. Cambridge, Mass.: MIT Press. Especially useful as an introduction to railroads and weapons.

Films and Videos

Andrew Carnegie (PBS Video, 1997). A two-hour video on Andrew Carnegie, the self-made industrialist and philanthropist.

Business and Industrial Growth (Films for the Humanities and Sciences, 1999). In two parts, 31 and 40 minutes, respectively. Part 1, "From Boom to Bust," deals with the early-twentieth-century United States, and Part 2, "Riding the Cycles," with the period from Roosevelt's New Deal to the 1990s. Films for the Humanities and Sciences also has a five-part series on the Industrial Revolution in Britain, of which Parts 3 and 4, 20 minutes each, are most closely re-

lated to the material treated here. Additional videos produced by this company can be identified via the website www.films.com.

Thomas Hart Benton (PBS Video, 1996). A 90-minute video showing the painter, his work, and
the human energy required in the Industrial Revolution.

Music

Guthrie, Woodie. This folk music singer and composer captured the trials and troubles of working-class life in the United States in the early century. His works are available in several collections, including one on the Vanguard label.

Websites

http://users.erols.com/mwhite28/20centry.htm. This website presents Matthew White's *Historical
Atlas of the Twentieth Century*, providing much useful economic geography in the form of de-
tailed maps.

Chapter 4

Almond, Mark. 1996. *Revolution: 500 Years of Struggle for Change.* London: Di Agostini Editions.
A richly illustrated survey of the upheavals of the last half-millennium.

Azuela, Mariano. 1915. *The Underdogs: A Novel of the Mexican Revolution.* Reprint, New York:
Signet, 1986. A fictional tale of Mexican revolutionaries and bandits and the fragile alliances
formed and broken between different insurgents. The writer well conveys the liveliness and
violence of the times.

Bergère, Marie-Claire. 1998. *Sun Yat-sen.* Stanford: Stanford University Press. An excellent biography of the Chinese revolutionary leader by one of France's leading China specialists.

Hunt, Lynn. 1996. *The French Revolution and Human Rights: A Brief Documentary History.* New
York: Bedford Books. A prominent historian of the French Revolution introduces and places
into context documents on freedom and equality from 1789 to 1799 that inspired many and
provoked debate for two centuries.

Knight, Alan. 1986. *The Mexican Revolution: Porfirians, Liberals, and Peasants.* Reprint, Lincoln,
Nebr.: University of Nebraska, 1990. An important study of the events of the first two decades
of the twentieth century in Mexico.

Rius. 1976. *Marx for Beginners: Philosophy, Economic Doctrine, Historical Materialism,* edited by
Tom Engelhardt. Reprint, New York: Pantheon, 1989. A humorous but factually accurate introduction to some basic ideas associated with Marxism, conveyed through comic strips.

Films and Videos

Danton (Andrzej Wadja, 1982). A leading Polish filmmaker's depiction of the intrigues that break
out between revolutionary leaders and the process through which these leaders become de-
tached and alienated from the masses they claim to represent. The film is set in France in the

1790s but has much to say about the dynamics of many revolutionary settings in the early twentieth century.

1900 (Bernardo Bertolucci, 1976). A beautifully filmed epic that well conveys the degree to which revolution was in the air at the turn of the century in Europe.

Viva Zapata (Elia Kazan, 1953). This film, starring Marlon Brando and Anthony Quinn, makes for powerful viewing. It recounts the life and loves of a leader of the Mexican Revolution. The screenplay was by the noted American novelist John Steinbeck.

Chapter 5

Cammett, John. 1967. *Antonio Gramsci and the Origins of Italian Communism.* Stanford: Stanford University Press. Major study of an Italian Communist activist and theorist.

Close, David, and Carl Bridge, eds. 1985. *Revolution: A History of the Idea.* Totowa, N.J.: Barnes and Noble Books. A wide-ranging reader that contains works on many times and places by social scientists and historians. It pays particularly close attention to socialist revolutions.

De Fronzo, James. 1996. *Revolutions and Revolutionary Movements,* 2nd ed. Boulder: Westview Press. Contains many good case studies of twentieth-century revolutions.

Fraser, Ronald. 1979. *Blood of Spain: An Oral History of the Spanish Civil War.* New York: Pantheon. Firsthand accounts of the Spanish Civil War by participants and observers from varied ideological backgrounds.

Orwell, George. 1938. *Homage to Catalonia.* Reprint, New York: Harcourt Brace, 1987. A powerful eye-witness account of revolution and civil war in Spain in the 1930s.

Preston, Paul, and Ann L. Mackenzie, eds. 1996. *The Republic Besieged: Civil War in Spain, 1936–1939.* Edinburgh: Edinburgh University Press. Contains a great deal of information on how events unfolded in the battle between left- and right-wing groups in Spain.

Reed, John. 1960. *Ten Days That Shook the World.* Reprint, New York: Penguin, 1977. A classic account of the Russian Revolution.

Skocpol, Tkocpol. 1979. *States and Social Revolutions: A Comparative Analysis of France, Russia, and China.* Cambridge, U.K.: Cambridge University Press. Influential work by a social theorist who sees similar patterns in the French, Russian, and Chinese Revolutions (1789, 1917, and the period 1911–1949, respectively).

Trotsky, Leon. 1932. *History of the Russian Revolution,* translated by Max Eastman. Reprint, New York: Pathfinder, 1980. Important study by one of the key players in the event.

Films and Videos

Battleship Potempkin (Sergei Eisenstein, 1925). A gripping account of the 1905 Russian Revolution. It is epic filmmaking at its best even if some liberties were taken in portraying historical events.

The Good Fight: The Abraham Lincoln Brigade in the Spanish Civil War (Noel Bucker, Mary Dore, and Sam Sills, 1984). Retells the story of Americans who fought against the dictator Francisco Franco in the Spanish Civil War.

October (Sergei Eisenstein, 1928). The most famous cinematic reconstruction of the Bolshevik Revolution. Some of the scenes were filmed where the events in question actually took place in 1917. The film contains powerful footage and was path-breaking in the methods the director used.

Chapter 6

Adam, Peter. 1992. *Art of the Third Reich*. New York: H. N. Abrams. An illustrated survey of the arts under the Nazis.

Arendt, Hannah. 1963. *Eichmann in Jerusalem*. New York: Viking. Details the career and petty motivations of a German bureaucrat who presided over the Final Solution in Europe.

Browning, Christopher. 1992. *Ordinary Men: Reserve Police Battalion 101 and the Final Solution in Poland*. New York: HarperCollins. Analyzes the training and military experiences that converted "ordinary" German men into killers under the Nazi regime.

Grazia, Victoria de. 1981. *The Culture of Consent: The Mass Organization of Leisure in Fascist Italy*. Cambridge, U.K.: Cambridge University Press. Examines the attempts of the regime to create a national political culture based on ideological consensus.

Hilberg, Raul. 1961. *The Destruction of European Jews*. Chicago: Quadrangle Books. A balanced and concise overview of the Holocaust and the policies leading up to it.

Kershaw, Ian. 1987. *The "Hitler Myth." Image and Reality in the Third Reich*. Oxford: Oxford University Press. Analyzes the creation and dissemination of the various images of Hitler crafted for popular consumption by the Nazi regime.

Koonz, Claudia. 1987. *Mothers in the Fatherland, the Family, and Nazi Politics*. New York: St. Martin's Press, 1987. A persuasive account of why reactionary Nazi policies and feminist ideology appealed to German women.

Peukert, Detlev. 1987. *Inside Germany: Conformity, Opposition, and Racism in Everyday Life*. New Haven, Conn.: Yale University Press. Demystifies Nazism and shows how it affected everyday life in German communities.

Films and Videos

Lucie Aubrac (Claude Berri, 1997). A true story about a female resistance fighter who plots to secure the freedom of her imprisoned Jewish husband.

My Name is Ivan (Andrei Tarkovsky, 1962). The brutal reality of the German attack on Russia as seen through the eyes of a young boy.

Saving Private Ryan (Steven Spielberg, 1998). A visually stunning production of the Normandy Beach landings that ended World War II.

Shoah (Claude Lanzmann, 1985). This film, nine and a half hours long, presents a set of interviews with Holocaust survivors and SS men.

Sophie's Choice (Alan J. Pakula, 1982). The experiences of a Polish Catholic mother in Auschwitz and her efforts to save her children.

Triumph of the Will (Leni Riefenstahl, 1934). A propaganda film made about the 1934 Nuremberg Rally that showcases the emotional appeal of Nazism.

Chapter 7

Birmingham, David. 1995. *The Decolonization of Africa.* London: University College Press. A readable and concise account mainly of the personalities and political developments of the decolonization years.

_____. 1992. *Frontline Nationalism in Angola and Mozambique.* Trenton, N.J.: African World Press. An analysis that sorts out the complexities of the wars of liberation in southern Africa, especially as they related to apartheid in South Africa.

Chamberlain, M. E. 1985. *Decolonization: The Fall of the European Empires.* Oxford: Blackwell. A useful overview of the European context for the decolonization process.

Emecheta, Buchi. 1979. *The Joys of Motherhood.* New York: Braziller. A wonderful novel about life in colonial Lagos from the point of view of an Igbo woman. Written by one of Africa's foremost feminist writers.

Nehru, Jawaharal. 1959. *The Discovery of India.* Garden City, N.Y.: Doubleday. An autobiographical account of life under British colonialism written by a leader of the nationalist struggle and India's first prime minister.

Ngugi, wa Thiong'o. 1967. *A Grain of Wheat.* Portsmouth, N.H.: Heinemann. An account of life in late colonial Kenya and the ramifications of the armed struggle against white settler rule. Written by Kenya's most celebrated novelist.

Nkrumah, Kwame. 1957. *Ghana: The Autobiography of Kwame Nkrumah.* London: Thomas Nelson. The autobiography of Ghana's first president, covering his childhood, his education in the United States, the formation of Ghana's earliest political parties, and the triumphs and problems of the early postcolonial years.

Olson, James, and Randy Roberts. 1991. *Where the Dominoes Fall: America and Vietnam, 1945–1990.* New York: St. Martins. An informative and balanced analysis of the origins, course, and aftermath of the Vietnam War.

Films and Videos

Africa (Home Vision, 1984). Written and presented by the historian Basil Davidson. Programs 7 and 8, "Decolonization" and "The Colonial Legacy," are particularly useful for their analysis of the late colonial and early independence period.

Battle for Algiers (Gillo Pontecorvo, 1965). A powerful film about the Algerian war of liberation, made from the point of view of guerrilla fighters in the capital.

Empire of the Sun (Steven Spielberg, 1987). A popular film adapted from a book about the Japanese invasion of Shanghai and life in a prison camp during World War II from the perspective of a British schoolboy.

Platoon (Oliver Stone, 1986). One of the most gripping and realistic Hollywood films on the Vietnam War.

Sambizanga (Sara Maldoro, 1972). A powerful film about popular resistance to the Portuguese in Angola, including the 1961 storming of the Luanda prison.

Chapter 8

Bianco, Lucien. 1971. *Origins of the Chinese Revolution,* translated from the French by Muriel Bell. Stanford: Stanford University Press. This overview of the Chinese upheavals of the 1910s–1940s is accessible and interesting. Written by a leading French Sinologist, the book pays particularly close attention to the actions of peasants.

Gao, Mobo. 1999. *Gao Village: A Portrait of Rural Life in Modern China.* Honolulu: University of Hawaii Press. Part memoir and part sociological analysis, this book traces patterns of village life during the dramatic events that transformed China during the decades following World War II.

Gould, Jeffrey L. 1997. *To Lead as Equals: Rural Protest and Political Consciousness in Chinandega, Nicaragua, 1912–1979.* Chapel Hill: University of North Carolina Press. Using a combination of oral testimonies and archival documents, this study reconstructs the roles that villagers played in a Central American revolution.

Hobsbawm, Eric. 1963. *Primitive Rebels.* New York: Praeger. A classic study of insurgency by one of the premier European historians of modern times. The book is particularly good at bringing out the ideological aspects of peasant movements.

Moore, Barrington. 1966. *Social Origins of Dictatorship and Democracy.* Boston: Beacon Press. A seminal study of comparative history by a leading social theorist who is particularly good at tracing the varied political roles of villagers in different systems.

Scott, James. 1990. *Domination and the Arts of Resistance: The Hidden Transcripts.* New Haven, Conn.: Yale University Press. By a leading ethnographer and political scientist known for his work on Southeast Asian peasantries and the dynamics of popular revolt.

Shanin, Teodore, ed. 1971. *Peasants and Peasant Societies.* New York: Penguin. A reader compiled by a scholar of Russian peasants that brings together important works on villagers by everyone from novelists to revolutionary leaders.

Wolf, Eric. 1966. *Peasants.* New York: Prentice Hall. A major anthropologist's introduction to the topic. This is a wide-ranging study and particularly valuable for its discussion of the role of peasants in political upheavals in Latin America and Asia.

Films and Videos

One Village in China: A Trilogy (Carma Hinton and Richard Gordon, 1987). A trio of short documentaries set in the same Chinese village, Long Bow. The directors make extensive use of interviews from the 1980s that were conducted with peasants who talk about their past and present experiences.

Yellow Earth (Chen Kaige, 1984). A film set in North China in the 1930s that evokes patterns of village life and the repression of women while also telling the story of a revolutionary cadre who seeks to mobilize support for the Communist revolution.

Chapter 9

Ali, Tariq, and Susan Watkins, eds. 1998. *1968: Marching in the Streets.* New York: The Free Press. A month by month, country by country account of the year, filled with compelling excerpts from protest documents and effective photographs and other illustrations.

Fink, Carole, et al., eds. *1968: The World Transformed.* Washington, D.C.: German Historical Institute. A truly global collection of essays. The titles of the first two reflect the scope of the book: "Tet and Prague" and "From Chicago to Beijing."

Gitlin, Todd. 1987. *The Sixties: Years of Hope, Days of Rage.* New York: Bantam Books. Part memoir, part history of activism in the United States up to and after 1968, this book is written by a leading figure in the radical group Students for a Democratic Society.

Kastiaficas, George. 1987. *The Imagination of the New Left: A Global Analysis of 1968.* Boston: Southend Press. A wide-ranging survey of protest ideologies during the 1960s, which pays particular attention to the interplay between socialism and new forms of radical thought.

1968. A special issue of *Media Studies Journal* published in Fall 1998. This collection, while largely focusing on the role of the press in the events of the time, includes discussion and powerful photos on everything from Prague Spring to the Mexico City massacre.

Passerini, Luisa. 1996. *Autobiography of a Generation: Italy, 1968.* Hanover, N.H.: Wesleyan University Press. A look at the upheavals of the 1960s in Italy that draws heavily on oral histories collected from roughly sixty activists and former activists.

Wolfe, Tom. 1968. *The Electric Kool-Aid Acid Test.* New York: Farrar, Strauss, and Giroux. A book of reportage by one of America's leading journalists highlighting the complex interactions between the political radicalism and counterculture movements of the 1960s. It includes descriptions of antiwar rallies and of some of the most influential American poets, novelists, and musicians of the period.

Films and Videos

Berkeley in the Sixties (Mark Kitchell, 1990). This documentary, which combines archival footage and interviews with former participants in student protests, brings to life campus events from the early 1960s (demonstrations linked to the Civil Rights Movement and the Free Speech Movement) and the late 1960s (antiwar marches). It draws attention to fissures within the student movements as well as to tensions between students and the administration and law enforcement agencies.

If (Lindsay Anderson, 1968). This film details the radicalization of a British teenager in the 1960s. It shows him being influenced by counterculture lifestyles in London, and then rebelling, when back in school, against the repressive rules and regulations he encounters there.

Antonio-das-Mortes (Glauber Rocha, 1968). This film by a leading Brazilian director tells the tale of a hired killer who decides to side with a group of Latin American peasants against their brutal landlords. It glorifies the actions of Ché Guevara–like insurgents in their struggles against oppression.

Chapter 10

Abu-Rabi, Ibrahim M. 1996. *Intellectual Origins of Islamic Resurgence in the Modern Arab World.* Albany, N.Y.: State University of New York Press. Presents the ideas of a few influential Islamic thinkers of the twentieth century.

Armstrong, Karen. 1993. *A History of God: The 4000-Year Quest of Judaism, Christianity, and Islam.* New York: Knopf. An immensely readable history of the changing ideas of monotheism in the three religions.

Esposito, John L. 1991. *Islam: The Straight Path.* Oxford: Oxford University Press. A very accessible guide to Islamic history, culture, and politics.

Faksh, Mahmud A. 1997. *The Future of Islam in the Middle East.* Westport, Conn.: Praeger. A good survey of the theories and practices of Islamic fundamentalist movements.

Keddie, Nikki R. 1995. *Iran and the Muslim World: Resistance and Revolution.* New York: New York University Press. Using Shiism as a prism, this book analyzes the reasons why Iran has undergone so many revolutions in the twentieth century.

Lewis, Bernard. 1993. *Islam and the West.* Oxford: Oxford University Press. A collection of incisive essays on various aspects of the culture clash between Islam and the secular West.

Voll, John Obert. 1994. *Islam: Continuity and Change in the Modern World.* Syracuse: Syracuse University Press. A comprehensive essay that analyzes the influence of Islam in developing countries from the eighteenth century to the present.

Yazbeck, Yvonne. 1997. *Islam, Gender, and Social Change.* New York: Oxford University Press. Studies the impact of Islamic fundamentalism on women in Muslim communities from North Africa to Southeast Asia.

Films and Videos

Destiny (Youssef Chahine, 1997). After the disciple of a twelfth-century philosopher is burned at the stake for heresy, his son is caught in the battle between philosophy students and the religious fundamentalists who object to their ideas.

Honey and Ashes (Nadia Fares, 1996). Features three young women in contemporary North African Islamic society who are caught between the demands of tradition and the freedom of modernity.

Lawrence of Arabia (David Lean, 1961). Story of T. E. Lawrence, a British officer, and his involvement with the Arab struggle for independence against Turkey during World War I.

Rape of Innocence (Yves Boisset, 1974). Deals with racism against Arab immigrants in modern France.

Taste of Cherry (Abbas Kiarostami, 1997). Set in contemporary Iran, this video features a middle-aged man who is contemplating suicide and looking for somebody to bury him.

White Balloon (Jafar Panahi, 1995). A seven-year-old child's quest to find a goldfish turns into a wry commentary on contemporary Tehran.

Chapter 11

Ahmed, Leila. 1992. *Women and Gender in Islam: Historical Roots of a Modern Debate.* New Haven, Conn.: Yale University Press. A scholarly but readable survey of the Islamic ideals of gender and women, focusing primarily on Egypt.

Brittain, Vera. 1933. *The Testament of Youth.* New York: Macmillan. An unsentimental coming-of-age memoir of a British woman who leaves her studies to pursue nursing at the front during World War I.

De Beauvoir, Simone. 1957. *The Second Sex.* New York: Knopf. A foundational text for the modern feminist movement tracing the construction of woman as a category in Western society.

Markandaya, Kamala. 1954. *Nectar in a Sieve.* New York: J. Day Company. Narrates the life of a peasant woman in India as she fights against poverty, disease, and hunger in order to survive.

Mernissi, Fatima. 1990. *Beyond the Veil: Male-Female Dynamics in Modern Muslim Society.* Bloomington: Indiana University Press. Mernissi argues that Islamic fundamentalism is in part a backlash against changes in women's roles and public perceptions of them in the modern age.

Nupur, Chaudhuri, and Margaret Stroebel, eds. 1992. *Western Women and Imperialism: Complicity and Resistance.* Bloomington: Indiana University Press. Details the careers of individual white women in the colonies.

Smith, Bonnie. 1989. *Changing Lives: Women in European History Since 1700.* Lexington, Mass.: D.C. Heath. As the title implies, this book is an excellent survey of European women's history in the modern age.

Wood, Elizabeth. 1997. *The Baba and the Comrade: Gender and Politics in Revolutionary Russia.* Bloomington: Indiana University Press. Details the efforts of the Soviet government to draw women into the public sphere while battling traditional misogynistic culture among the reformers and the targeted audience.

Films and Videos

Fried Green Tomatoes (Jon Avnet, 1991). Set in the American South, the film shows how women can remake themselves and their public identities.

Home and the World (Satyajit Ray, 1984). Details the adventures of an upper-class Indian housewife at the turn of the century who is encouraged by her "modern" husband to venture outside the home and dabble in nationalist politics.

Not Without My Daughter (Brian Gilbert, 1990). The story of an American woman caught with her daughter in the middle of the Iranian Revolution.

Raise the Red Lantern (Zhang Yimou, 1991). The story of a twenty-year-old college student who becomes the fourth wife of a wealthy aristocrat in prerevolutionary China.

Rebro Adama (*Adam's Rib*, Russian) (Vyacheslav Kritofovich, 1992). Shows three generations of Soviet women who use different strategies to cope with the social and economic system.

Rosa Luxemburg (Margarethe von Trotta, 1985). This biography features Luxemburg's tempestuous life as a political radical and feminist.

Chapter 12

Alonso, Harriet Hyman. 1993. *Peace as a Women's Issue: A History of the United States Movement for World Peace and Women's Rights.* Syracuse: Syracuse University Press. An excellent overview of the connection between women's issues and peace, from the nineteenth-century abolitionist movement to peace encampments in the late twentieth century.

Boulding, Kenneth. 1978. *Stable Peace.* Austin: University of Texas. One of several books by a Quaker economist on the potential for a more peaceful world.

Faley, Joseph, and Richard Armstrong, eds. *A Peace Reader: Essential Readings on Justice, Non-Violence and World Order.* 1987. Mahwah, N.J.: Paulist Press. Readings from religious and secular thinkers and authorities on peace.

Hogan, Michael J., ed. 1996. *Hiroshima in History and Memory.* Cambridge, U.K.: Cambridge University Press. Different authors discuss how the dropping of the first atomic bomb is remembered in Japan and the United States.

Keegan, John. *The Face of Battle.* 1974. London: Penguin. A classic work by a leading scholar on the history of war. Includes a chapter on the battle of the Somme.

Remarque, Erich Maria. 1928. *All Quiet on the Western Front.* Reprint, New York: Fawcett, 1982. By a German writer, this powerful novel recounts the experiences of a group of young men in the trench warfare of the western front in World War I and their return home.

Whittaker, David J. 1995. *United Nations in Action.* New York: M. E. Sharpe. A useful account of the history and work of the United Nations with sections on structure, peacekeeping, nuclear questions, human rights, new nations, and new initiatives.

Winter, Jay. 1995. *Sites of Memory, Sites of Mourning: The Great War in European Cultural History.* Cambridge, U.K.: Cambridge University Press. A leading cultural historian of World War I discusses how war is celebrated and remembered through the burial of the dead in cemeteries scattered throughout the regions of the western front.

Films and Videos

All Quiet on the Western Front (Lewis Middleton, 1930). The all-time great war movie based on the novel by Erich Maria Remarque tells the story of a group of German recruits during World War I.

Breaker Morant (Bruce Beresford, 1980). Three Australian lieutenants are put on trial for shooting Boer prisoners during the South African Anglo-Boer War (1899–1902). The film reveals the ambiguities and complexities of war.

The Great War and the Shaping of the Twentieth Century (BBC/PBS, 1996). An eight-part documentary series on World War I.

Mrs. Miniver (William Wyler, 1942). The tranquillity of an English middle-class family and their village community is rudely shattered by World War II, but they display fortitude and patriotism to survive the ordeal.

Paths of Glory (Stanley Kubrick, 1957). A powerful antiwar film that takes place in France in 1916.

Platoon (Oliver Stone, 1986). A young recruit experiences jungle warfare in the Vietnam War and struggles to find himself.

The Thin Red Line (Terence Malick and John Toll, 1998). This story follows the efforts of a U.S. platoon to capture the Japanese-controlled island of Guadalcanal through the individual stories of the platoon members.

Chapter 13

Bailey, Janet. 1995. *The Good Servant.* New York: Simon and Schuster. Relates how the scientists of Los Alamos saw the bomb and their own part in the Cold War.

Conway, Gordon. 1997. *The Doubly Green Revolution: Food for All in the Twenty-First Century.* Ithaca, N.Y.: Penguin. Anticipates food needs in the twenty-first century.

Hersey, John. 1946. *Hiroshima.* New York: Knopf. Explores the experiences of five survivors.

Ibuse, Masuji. 1969. *Black Rain.* Tokyo: Kodansha International. Gives a moving fictional account of atomic destruction based on interviews with survivors of Hiroshima and Nagasaki.

Imperato, Pascal James. 1975. *A Wind in Africa.* St. Louis: W. H. Green. Relates the author's experiences in Mali in 1966–1971, illuminating Cold War motives and the relations between outsiders and locals in the global smallpox eradication campaign.

Kanda, Mikio. 1989. *Widows of Hiroshima.* New York: St. Martin's. Relates the stories of nineteen widows living in an agricultural village near Hiroshima whose husbands, serving in work crews, died in the blast. These are sad lives saddened further by the bomb.

Leaf, Murray J. 1984. *Song of Hope: The Green Revolution in a Panjab Village.* New Brunswick: Rutgers University Press. Tells an interesting story, though his account also includes some arcane arguments with other anthropologists.

Ryan, Frank. 1993. *The Forgotten Plague: How the Battle Against Tuberculosis was Won—and Lost.* Boston: Little, Brown. This author, a physician, tells a good story while relating the modern history of tuberculosis.

Snow, C. P. 1980. *The Physicists.* London: Little, Brown. The British novelist, who knew Einstein, Rutherford, Bohr, and other nuclear physicists, completed this personal history of the first fifty years of particle physics just before his death in 1980.

Wainwright, Milton. 1990. *Miracle Cure: The Story of Penicillin and the Golden Age of Antibiotics.* Oxford: Blackwell. A fascinating account with many anecdotes about the people involved in the history of antibiotics.

Films and Videos

The China Syndrome (James Bridges, 1979). This film works out a theme based on the dangers of nuclear energy.

Madame Curie (Mervyn LeRoy, 1943). A celebration of early research in radiation.

On the Beach (Stanley Kramer, 1959). Explores the effects of fallout, positing the elimination of human life across the globe as the consequence of a nuclear war.

The Story of Louis Pasteur (William Dieterle, 1936). An example of the heroic image of this scientist as he was portrayed in popular culture.

The Third Man (Carol Reed, 1950). A story exploring the harmful effects of the diluted and adulterated antibiotics often employed in black-market medicine in the mid-1940s, when antibiotics were difficult to obtain.

Chapter 14

Ambler, Eric. 1959. *Passage of Arms.* London: Heinemann. A novel discussing the Chinese diaspora in Southeast Asia.

Bertrand, Jane T., and Judith E. Brown. 1992. "Family Planning Success in Two Cities in Zaire." World Bank Working Paper Series 1042. Explains how family planning occurs and how it is evaluated.

Caldwell, John C., and Pat Caldwell. 1990. "High Fertility in Sub-Saharan Africa." *Scientific American,* May. Discusses why Africans want to have many children.

Castles, Stephen, and Mark J. Miller. 1998. *The Age of Migrations: International Population Movements in the Modern World.* New York: Guildford Press. A study that clarifies the very complex picture of migration in the twentieth century.

Gillis, John, Louise Tilly, and David Levine, eds. 1992. *The European Experience of Declining Fertility, 1850–1970.* Cambridge, Mass.: Blackwell. Tries to explain why and how Europeans began to reduce family size.

Riley, James C. 2001. *Rising Life Expectancy: A Global History.* Cambridge, U.K.: Cambridge University Press. Explains how life expectancy has increased so much and in so many countries.

Tien, H. Yuan, Zhang Tianlu, Ping Yu, Li Jingneng, and Liang Zhongtang. 1992. "China's Demographic Dilemmas," *Population Bulletin* 47, no. 1. Addresses population problems in the most populous country.

United Nations. 1991. *The World's Women, 1970–1990: Trends and Statistics.* Social Statistics and Indicators, Series K, no. 8. New York: UN. A good source to build a picture of social development.

Waller, James. 1990. *Fau: Portrait of an Ethiopian Famine.* Jefferson, N.C.: McFarland. An example of how people experience famine.

Films and Videos

"The Africans" (Ali Al'Amin Mazrui, 1986). The second in a series entitled *A Legacy of Lifestyles,* this 60-minute video explores what constitutes a family in Sub-Saharan African cultures.

Bread and Chocolate (Franco Brusati, 1973). This feature film deals with Italian concerns about emigration.

China's Only Child (Time-Life Video, 1984). This 60-minute documentary shows how authorities enforced the one-child policy.

Lessons from Kerala (Media Guild, 1992). This series includes a 24-minute segment entitled "Women and Public Action" that shows women leading in social development in one of the poorest states in India.

Maragoli (Sandra Nichols Productions, 1976). This 58-minute documentary reflects discussions among villagers in Western Kenya in the mid-1970s about social and economic aspects of the population problem.

"Marrying" (Misha Scorer, 1984). In the *Heart of the Dragon* series, this 57-minute program explores how China's one-child policy affects marriage.

Websites

www.freedomsnest.com. This site presents quotations by numerous thinkers on various subjects, including Julian Simon.

www.iiasa.ac.at/research/LUC/chinafood/index.html. This site explores the issue of whether China can add to food output fast enough to keep up with population growth.

www.pbs.org/kqed/population_bomb. This site is a useful resource for exploring Paul Ehrlich's views.

Posters

The International Human Suffering Index. 1992. Washington, D.C.: Population Crisis Committee. This poster is updated every five years.

Chapter 15

Bradshaw, York, and Michael Wallace. 1996. *Global Inequalities.* Thousand Oaks, Calif: Pine Forge Press. Introduces the main problems and debates surrounding this issue.

Franke, Richard W. 1993. *Life Is a Little Better: Redistribution As a Development Strategy in Nadur Village, Kerala.* Boulder: Westview. Relates the practical effects of social development.

Hellman, Judith Adler. 1994. *Mexican Lives.* New York: New Press. Through narratives about the experience of a cross section of individuals, Hellman explores the effects of the integration of the Mexican economy into the global economy.

Longworth, Richard C. 1999. *Global Squeeze: The Coming Crisis for First World Nations.* Chicago: Contemporary Books. An accessible guide to economic globalization and its hazards for rich countries.

Mehmet, Ozay. 1995. *Westernizing the Third World: The Eurocentricity of Economic Development Theories.* New York: Routledge. This author argues that globalization has favored the rich countries.

Sen, Amartya. 1999. *Development as Freedom.* New York: Knopf. A study redefining the end of economic growth from income and wealth to freedom. The author also exposes the ideas of social development.

Thomas, Frederic C. 1997. *Calcutta Poor: Elegies on a City Above Pretense.* Armonk, N.Y.: M. E. Sharpe. An explanation of how the residents of one city have dealt with poverty.

Websites

www.econ/lse.ac.uk/~dquah/tweirl).html. Professor Danny Quah discusses information technology and its implications.

Conclusion

Drakulic, Slavenka. 1999. *Café Europa: Life after Communism.* New York: Penguin. A collection of provocative short essays and pieces of reportage by a feminist journalist from Croatia. It captures poignantly and sometimes amusingly the varied changes that have occurred in Central and East Europe since 1989.

Jowitt, Ken. 1993. *New World Disorder: The Leninist Extinction.* Berkeley: University of California Press. A thoughtful assessment of the reasons for the fall of the Soviet Empire and the impact its collapse had on the world at large.

O'Meara, Patrick et al. eds. 2000. *Globalization and the Challenges of the New Century.* Bloomington: Indian University Press. A wide-ranging collection of essays by scholars in varied disciplines as well as prominent journalists and policy-makers.

Wasserstrom, Jeffrey N., Lynn Hunt and Marilyn B. Young, eds. 2001. *Human Rights and Revolutions*. Lanham, Maryland: Rowman and Littlefield. A series of case studies that move through time from the 1600s to the 1990s and across space from Western Europe to the Islamic World to China and Vietnam.

Watson, James L. ed. 1998. *Golden Arches East: McDonald's in East Asia*. Stanford: Stanford University Press. Looks at the widely varied meanings that a single fast food franchise can have as it interacts with the specific local cultures of different cities, including in this case Seoul, Tokyo, and Beijing.

Websites

www.ssrc.org. The "After September 11" section of this home site of the Social Science Research Organization contains a series of short essays by leading social scientists and historians, all of whom grapple with ways that academic approaches can help us make sense of the horrific events of 2001.

Index